Microsoft Windows® 2000 Server

Todd Brown
Chris Miller
Bryan Porter
Keith Powell

SAMS

Unleashed

Microsoft Windows® 2000 Server Unleashed

Copyright© 2000 by Sams Publishing

All rights reserved. No part of this book shall be reproduced, stored in a retrieval system, or transmitted by any means, electronic, mechanical, photocopying, recording, or otherwise, without written permission from the publisher. No patent liability is assumed with respect to the use of the information contained herein. Although every precaution has been taken in the preparation of this book, the publisher and authors assume no responsibility for errors or omissions. Neither is any liability assumed for damages resulting from the use of the information contained herein.

International Standard Book Number: 0-672-31739-7

Library of Congress Catalog Card Number: 99-63535

Printed in the United States of America

First Printing: February 2000

02 01 00   4 3 2 1

Trademarks

All terms mentioned in this book that are known to be trademarks or service marks have been appropriately capitalized. Sams Publishing cannot attest to the accuracy of this information. Use of a term in this book should not be regarded as affecting the validity of any trademark or service mark.

Warning and Disclaimer

Every effort has been made to make this book as complete and as accurate as possible, but no warranty or fitness is implied. The information provided is on an "as is" basis. The authors and the publisher shall have neither liability nor responsibility to any person or entity with respect to any loss or damages arising from the information contained in this book.

ASSOCIATE PUBLISHER
Michael Stephens

ACQUISITIONS EDITOR
Don Roche

DEVELOPMENT EDITOR
Clint McCarty

MANAGING EDITOR
Charlotte Clapp

PROJECT EDITOR
Carol Bowers

COPY EDITOR
Bart Reed

INDEXER
Joy Dean Lee

PROOFREADERS
Candice Hightower
Gene Redding

TECHNICAL EDITORS
Dave Bixler
Ted Daley
Jason Genser
Brett Jungels

TEAM COORDINATOR
Pamalee Nelson

INTERIOR DESIGN
Gary Adair

COVER DESIGN
Aren Howell

COPY WRITER
Eric Borgert

PRODUCTION
Eric S. Miller

Contents at a Glance

Introduction   1

PART I Overview   3
1   Windows 2000 Introduction   5

PART II Windows 2000 Operating System Environment   19
2   Architecture   21
3   Installation Considerations   39
4   File Systems   71
5   Networking Brief   127
6   Printing   149
7   The Registry   179
8   TCP/IP Networking   195

PART III Active Directory and Account Management   229
9   Directory and Access Concepts Brief   231
10   Active Directory Design   263
11   User Account Creation and Management   277
12   Intellimirror and User Control   305

PART IV Network Services   329
13   Network Browsing   331
14   Remote Access (RAS)   355
15   Multi-Protocol Environments   405
16   Client Workstation Considerations   421

PART V Connectivity   449
17   NetWare Connectivity   451
18   UNIX Host to Windows 2000 Server Connectivity   471
19   SNA Connectivity with BackOffice   489

Part VI Internet Applications, Communications, and Tools   499

20 Internet Information Server   **501**

21 Other Internet Services for Windows 2000   **549**

22 Virtual Private Networks   **569**

Part VII Server Administration   587

23 Server Management   **589**

24 Optimizing Performance Tuning   **605**

25 Server Backup Utilities   **669**

26 Recovering from a Disaster   **707**

Part VIII Appendixes   725

A Troubleshooting / Error List   **727**

B IP Address Decimal to Binary Table   **741**

Index   755

Contents

Introduction   1

PART I   Overview   3

1   Windows 2000 Introduction   5
A Network Operating System 6
    An Operating System 6
    Windows 2000 and your Network 7
    Network Security 8
    Performance Monitoring 8
The Product Family 9
    Common Features 9
    Windows 2000 Advanced Server 16
    Windows 2000 Datacenter 17
Summary 18

PART II   Windows 2000 Operating System Environment   19

2   Architecture   21
The Subsystem and Kernel Architecture 22
    User Mode and Kernel Mode 23
    The Hardware Abstraction Layer 24
    The Kernel 25
    The Windows 2000 Executive 26
    Subsystems: A Closer Look 28
    The Win32 Subsystem 30
    The POSIX Subsystem 32
    The OS/2 Subsystem 33
Memory Model and Management 34
    The Memory Model 34
    Memory Management 37
Summary 38

3   Installation Considerations   39
System Requirements 40
Hardware Compatibility List 41
Installation Overview 42
The Installation Process 45
    Booting Windows 2000 45
    Upgrade Information 50
    Configuring Windows 2000 50

	Network Configuration	55
	Licensing Options	58
	Scenario 1: Per-Server Licensing	59
	Scenario 2: Per-Client Licensing	59
	Automated Installation	61
	Installing the Recovery Console	62
	The BOOT.INI File	65
	The Emergency Repair Disk	66
	Migration from Preexisting Systems	66
	Advanced Hardware Notes	67
	Interrupts	67
	EIDE Devices	68
	Windows Update	68
	Busses and Devices	69
	Summary	69
4	**File Systems**	**71**
	Hardware Considerations	72
	Hard Disk Technology	73
	Hard Disk Controllers	75
	Principles of SCSI	77
	Advanced Controller Technology	78
	Hard Disk Partitions	81
	System Startup	81
	Basic Disks	83
	Dynamic Disks	84
	Basic and Dynamic Disks	84
	Using the Disk Management Application	86
	Starting Disk Management	87
	Disk Properties	87
	Volume or Partition Properties	88
	Partition and Volume Management	93
	Working with Dynamic Disks	96
	Setting Up Disk Quotas	96
	File System Formats	99
	The FAT File System	100
	NTFS	101
	Working with Formats	109
	Recommendations	110
	Working with Volumes	111
	Working with Simple Volumes	111
	Spanned Volumes	112
	Mirrored Volumes	112

Contents

	Striped Volumes	114
	RAID-5 Volumes	115
	A Few Notes on Windows 2000 Volumes	115
	Working with Network Shares	116
	Sharing Directories	116
	Connecting to Shared Directories	120
	DFS: The Distributed File System	121
	DFS Concepts	122
	Setting Up DFS	122
	Using DFS	123
	Remote Storage Server	123
	Remote Storage Concepts	124
	Setting Up Remote Storage	124
	Removable Storage Management	124
	Summary	126

5 Networking Brief — 127

- Microsoft Networking Concepts 128
  - Workgroups and Domains 128
  - Active Directory 138
  - Network Services Setup 140
- Networks (Your LAN or WAN) Versus Networks (Segmentation) 140
  - Switched Segmentation (Collision Domain Segments) 142
  - Routed Segmentation 144
- RRAS 145
  - Remote Dial-In 145
  - Multiprotocol Routing 146
- Summary 147

6 Printing — 149

- Printing Concepts 150
  - Printers 150
  - Fonts 152
  - Print Drivers 152
  - Communicating with Printers 153
  - The Life of a Print Job 155
- Creating Print Queues 155
- Using Print Manager 159
- Managing Print Queues 164
  - The Forms Tab 164
  - The Ports Tab 165
  - The Drivers Tab 166
  - The Advanced Tab 167

Troubleshooting 168
    Diagnosing Client-to-Server Printing
      Communications Problems 168
    Diagnosing Print Quality Problems 176
    Know Your Printer's Limitations 176
    Know Your Printer's Specifications 176
    Know Your Driver Versions 177
    Matching Everything Up 177
Summary 178

7 The Registry   179

What Is the Registry? 180
The Structure of the Registry 181
    The `Classes` Hive 181
    The `Users` Hive 182
    The `Local Machine` Hive 183
    The `Current Configuration` Hive 185
How the Registry Is Used by Applications 185
Using the Registry Editor 187
    When to Use Registry Editing Tools 187
    How to Use REGEDIT 188
    Finding Registry Changes Using REGEDIT 191
    How to Use REGEDT32 191
Using the Last Known Good Configuration 193
Summary 193

8 TCP/IP Networking   195

TCP/IP Concepts Brief 196
    IP Addressing 196
Microsoft TCP/IP 205
    Introduction to Microsoft TCP/IP 205
    Installing 205
    Routing 207
    Dynamic Host Configuration Protocol (DHCP) 208
    Windows Internet Name Service 217
    Dynamic Domain Name Server (DDNS) 220
    Migrating from WINS to DNS 226
    Multiple Address Assignment for One Card 226
    IP Security 227
Summary 227

Part III Active Directory and Account Management 229

9 Directory and Access Concepts Brief 231

Security Concept 232
- Kerberos 232
- NTLM 237
- ACL 239

Active Directory Control 239
- Workgroups and Domains 239

Active Directory/Domain Objects 251

Which Comes First: The Users or the Groups? 252
- Creating Objects 253

Controlling User Access to Resources 257
- File Share Permissions 257
- Printer Permissions 260

Summary 261

10 Active Directory Design 263

Sites and Replication 264
- Sites 265
- Replication 266
- Site Creation 267

Design Standards 269
- Political 270
- Geographic 271
- Mixed Environment 272

Organizational Units 272

Dynamic DNS 273
- How Dynamic Update Works 274
- Secure Dynamic Update 276

Summary 276

11 User Account Creation and Management 277

User Accounts 278
- Predefined or Built-in Users 278
- Naming and Password Conventions 280
- User Creation 282
- User Environment Needs 287

Hard Drive Space 298

Groups 300
- Group Scope 300
- Creating a New Group 302
- Predefined (Default) Groups 302

Summary 304

12 Intellimirror and User Control 305

Nuts and Bolts of Intellimirror 306
Control Concepts 307
    Profiles 308
    Policies: A General Introduction 311
Managing Group Policies 315
    Creating and Assigning 315
    Policy Modification 319
    Group Policy Administrators 319
Windows Installer 320
    WinInstaller 321
    Delivery of the Package 324
Remote Installation Services 325
Summary 327

PART IV Network Services 329

13 Network Browsing 331

Understanding Network Browsing Concepts 332
    Browser Server Roles 334
    Browser Election Criteria 336
    Election Process 337
Browsing Operations 340
    Browser Announcements 342
    Master Browser 343
    Browse List 344
    Multiple Domain and WAN Considerations 344
    Browsing Failures 349
    Configuring a Windows 2000 Server to Never Be a Browser 350
    Active Directory–Based Browsing Considerations 352
Summary 354

14 Remote Access (RAS) 355

Understanding the RRAS Service 356
Protocol Support 357
    Transmission Control Protocol/Internet Protocol (TCP/IP) 357
    AppleTalk 358
    NWLink IPX/SPX/NetBIOS Compatible Transport 358
    NetBIOS Extended User Interface (NetBEUI) 359
Remote Access Security 359
Installing the RRAS Tools 361
    Remote Access Server Configurations 362
    Advanced Remote Access Server Configurations 369

Routing Configurations 389
Protocol Support 399
Modem Considerations 400
WAN Support 400
Authentication 401
Troubleshooting RAS 402
Summary 403

15 Multiprotocol Environments — 405

Supported Protocols in Windows 2000 406
    Installing New Protocol 406
    Load Them All! 408
    Connection Style 409
    TCP/IP 409
    IPX/SPX 411
    AppleTalk 414
    NetBEUI 416
Routing and Remote Access Services 417
    PPP 418
    RIP 418
    Troubleshooting 419
Summary 420

16 Client Workstation Considerations — 421

Client Services Brief 422
Specific Client Operating System Considerations 429
    Novell NetWare Clients 430
    DOS, OS/2, Windows 3.x and Windows for Workgroups 436
    Macintosh 440
    UNIX Connectivity 444
Summary 447

PART V Connectivity 449

17 NetWare Connectivity — 451

Conceptual Differences 452
    Security 452
    Active Directory Versus NetWare Directory Services 453
    File Shares 455
    Printing 456
Connectivity to NetWare 457
    Gateway Service for NetWare 458
    File and Print Services for NetWare 463

		Directory Service Migration Tool	463
		NDS for NT (by Novell)	469
		Summary	470
18	**UNIX Host to Windows 2000 Server Connectivity**		**471**
		Conceptual Differences Between Windows 2000 Server and UNIX-Style Operating Systems	472
		User Accounts	472
		Security	473
		Directory Services	474
		Different Flavors of UNIX	475
		Simple TCP/IP Tools	476
		Telnet	477
		FTP	479
		The Lesser-Known Utilities	482
		Application Connectivity	484
		XWindows and Windows 2000	484
		Connecting to NFS	485
		About Samba	486
		Printing in a UNIX World	487
		The Future: Microsoft and UNIX	488
		Summary	488
19	**SNA Connectivity with BackOffice**		**489**
		Host Computing Brief	490
		SNA Server Concepts	491
		Manageable Secure Connectivity	493
		Routing and Distributing Connections	493
		SNA Connectivity Options	495
		LU Configuration	496
		Summary	497
PART VI	**Internet Applications, Communications, and Tools**		**499**
20	**Internet Information Server (IIS)**		**501**
		Internet Information Server Concepts	502
		Before You Begin with IIS	503
		System Requirements	503
		Internet Connectivity	505
		Installing IIS	507
		Administering and Configuring IIS	511
		Common IIS Controls	511
		Administering the FTP Site	534
		Advanced Web Site Administration	535
		Administering the Gopher Site	538

		Administering the Telnet Service 539
		Advanced Security Concepts 539
		Summary 547
21	**Other Internet Services for Windows 2000**	**549**
		Access Security and Speed with Proxy Server 550
		Acquisition and Caching 550
		Access Control 551
		Network Security: Firewall 553
		Logging of Traffic 554
		Exchange Email Server 556
		Robust General Email 556
		Public Folders 557
		Directory Structure 559
		Internet Access and Reception 559
		FrontPage 564
		Creating Web Sites, Not Just Web Pages 565
		Server Extensions 567
		Summary 567
22	**Virtual Private Networks**	**569**
		Making the Internet Your Own WAN 570
		What Is a Virtual Private Network? 571
		Security and Encryption 572
		Tunnel Servers 573
		VPN Tunnel Servers and Firewalls 574
		Filtering Traffic with a Tunnel Server 575
		Microsoft Windows 2000 VPN 576
		IPSec 577
		Layer 2 Tunneling Protocol 577
		Synchronous and Asynchronous Keys 578
		L2TP and IPSec 579
		Setting Up a Basic VPN in Windows 2000 579
		Setting Up a Tunnel Server VPN with Windows 2000 582
		RRAS Enhancements 585
		Summary 586

PART VII Server Administration   587

23	**Server Management**	**589**
		Microsoft Management Console (MMC) 590
		Server Management Utilities 593
		Event Viewer 594
		System Information 599
		Device Manager 600

	SNMP	603
	Summary	604
24	**Optimizing Performance and Tuning**	**605**
	Windows 2000 Support Tools	606
	Automatic Optimization	611
	Avoiding Fragmentation	611
	Multiprocessing	615
	Prioritizing Processes and Threads	616
	Caching Disk Requests	629
	Stripe Sets and Virtual Memory Pagefiles	630
	Striped Volumes	630
	Optimizing Virtual Memory Pages	636
	Performance-Monitoring Utility	641
	Objects and Object Counters	644
	Creating a Chart	649
	Interpreting Charts	652
	Reports and Logs	655
	Summary	667
25	**Server Backup Utilities**	**669**
	Windows 2000 Backup Utility	670
	Windows 2000 Server Backup Operator Permissions	672
	Backing Up Windows 2000	673
	Attended Operations	690
	Unattended Operations	691
	Command-Line Backup	693
	Restoring a Backup	694
	Authoritative Restore	701
	Restoring Encrypted Files	702
	Supported Backup Drive Devices	703
	Recovery Console	703
	Emergency Repair Disk	704
	Third-Party Backup Tools	705
	Summary	705
26	**Recovering from a Disaster**	**707**
	Have a Plan, Work the Plan	708
	Documentation and Events	709
	Disaster Staff	710
	Physical Considerations	710
	Data Recovery	712
	Backup Operations	712
	Time-tested Backup Plans	715

Hardware Fail-Over Options 718
    Hardware-Controlled RAID 719
    Clustered Servers 719
Disaster-Recovery Planning Software and Sites 722
    Binomial's Phoenix 3.0 722
    CDI Vaults Company 723
    Business Protections Services'
      Business Protector for Windows 723
Summary 724

PART VIII   Appendixes   725

A   Troubleshooting/Error List   727

Service Packs 728
STOP Errors 728
    Steps for Kernel Mode STOP Screens 728
    STOP Error Solutions 731
Summary 739

B   IP Address Decimal to Binary Table   741

Subnet Mask Answer Sheet 750

Index   755

About the Authors

Todd C. Brown is a Field Systems Engineer with Bell Industries in Indianapolis. He has been involved in operating system support and PC networking for 14 years. His primary activity is designing, implementing, and troubleshooting networks and operating systems for clients throughout Indiana. In the time that Todd has worked with operating systems, he has had extensive experience with Windows NT (MCSE), NetWare (Master CNE), Macintosh OS, and OS/2. With these operating systems and his experience, he has developed networking strategies for thousands of companies.

As an author and technical editor, Todd has been part of the Macmillan Computer Publishing family since 1992. He began as a technical editor and has worked on titles that range from operating systems to networking basics and the Internet. Todd's experience in the field and his ability to convey his ideas on paper have lead to several authoring opportunities.

Chris Miller has been working with Windows NT 3.1 since its initial release. He endured the trials and tribulations of Windows NT Advanced Server 3.1, NetBEUI, and the joys of setting up printers through DLC back before Microsoft discovered the Internet. Now he spends his time as a Database Administrator for Microsoft SQL Server, responsible for maintaining performance on several Windows NT boxes so they can provide data to Web sites. He is a graduate of the University of Missouri-Rolla. He lives in Kansas City, Missouri, with his wife, Jennifer, and their two dogs, Peekaboo and Dogbert.

Keith Powell has over 11 years of experience in the technology industry and is presently employed as a manager for KPMG Consulting in Chicago. As a Microsoft Certified Systems Engineer, he devotes the majority of his time in the Microsoft Windows and BackOffice arenas for clients, focusing on e-commerce architecture, strategies, security, and development. He works with clients in the planning and implementation of Microsoft BackOffice suite components, including the various Windows 2000 versions as well as all versions of Windows NT. His 14-year history with the Windows environment includes extensive experience with all the 16- and 32-bit Microsoft operating systems. Keith is available via the Internet at `kpowell@kpmg.com`.

Dedication

Todd Brown:

To my wife, DaRhonda, who is my friend, my lover, my support team, my fan club, and the mother of my children.

To my mother, who taught me that there are few problems that can't be helped by laughter. Nothing matters more than being happy, so just do it.

Acknowledgments

Todd Brown thanks:

Writing about an operating system that is new to the world can be pretty tedious, because there is very little solid information on the subject. Oh, there is a great deal of hype, but little solid information. So I needed to depend on a lot of people to cover my backside while I worked.

As usual, my wife DaRhonda is the first to thank. She kind of plays goalie around me while I work on these projects and keeps the problems out of my way. There are things that go on in my world that I don't even realize until I step away from the computer. By then she has already handled them. She makes it possible for me to do the extra work.

I would like to thank the great people at Sams Publishing for the opportunity to work on this project: Don Roche, who was my champion at Sams and who kept the faith, and Clint McCarty, who has kept me between the margins and put up with me in a few spoiled author moments. I hope I work with them all again soon.

As is tradition for me, I'd like to thank my grandfather (William O. Newton), who said, "I am not the smartest man in the world, but I know where the books are." No more profound words have ever been spoken to me. Here's one more, Grandpa...

Chris Miller thanks:

I would like to thank my wife, Jennifer. It really wouldn't be worth the effort without her in my life. I would also like to thank Darrin Canter, one of my co-workers, for the suggestion to use VMWare to capture setup screen shots. I'd also like to thank all of the people I work with at GeoAccess for making my day job a whole lot of fun and paying me to do the kinds of things that I like to do.

Keith Powell thanks:

The Acquisitions Editor, Don Roche, for his patience and confidence in my ability to complete this work. Additional thanks goes to Clint McCarty for his excellent contributions as the Development Editor. I would also like to thank those persons who have helped me thus far through life, especially those in the following areas:

To Jack Langowski and Jerome McEvoy, who continue to push me toward new technologies that further my technical skills;

To Michael Durr, the greatest friend and attorney one could ever hope to have;

To Vannessa Tomlinson, someone who constantly lifts my sprits and encourages me to continue to write books;

And to Jerry Blaesing, who reminds me that there is still much to learn in the many facets of life.

Tell Us What You Think!

As the reader of this book, *you* are our most important critic and commentator. We value your opinion and want to know what we're doing right, what we could do better, what areas you'd like to see us publish in, and any other words of wisdom you're willing to pass our way.

As an Associate Publisher for Sams, I welcome your comments. You can fax, email, or write me directly to let me know what you did or didn't like about this book—as well as what we can do to make our books stronger.

Please note that I cannot help you with technical problems related to the topic of this book and that, due to the high volume of mail I receive, I might not be able to reply to every message.

When you write, please be sure to include this book's title and author, as well as your name and phone or fax number. I will carefully review your comments and share them with the author and editors who worked on the book.

Fax: 317-581-4770

Email: `Michael.Stephens@macmillanusa.com`

Mail: Michael Stephens
Associate Publisher
Sams
201 West 103rd Street
Indianapolis, IN 46290 USA

Introduction

With the Windows 2000 operating system, Microsoft moves into a portion of the networking environment that the world has been waiting for. Microsoft finally delivers a hierarchical directory system. Not only a Directory service, but a standards based (X.500) and respectable service that was worth the wait.

Because this operating system is so closely tied to that new directory, it's important that a solid text be written to get you started right. "Windows 2000 Server Unleashed" is just such a book.

This book, like the other books in the Unleashed series, is a solid reference for the working administrator; this book will follow you to work. It's full of the "how-to" information as well as the "why" information. You need to understand the reasons for what's being done, and this book delivers that information.

A great deal of coverage is given to the new technologies found in the management and comfort of the user base known as *Intellimirror*. The Intellimirror feature set in Windows 2000 has introduced to the operating system the addition of a new layer of control and delivery for the user. Intellimirror is not single application but rather a technology set that allows the administrator to control almost every aspect of the user experience. This text explains in detail how to better understand and how to implement the technologies found in Intellimirror.

We begin by providing you with a basic understanding of the building blocks that make up Windows networking.

An understanding of the TCP/IP protocol is no longer an option when administering a Microsoft Windows network. With Windows 2000 there are services that require a deep understanding of TCP/IP addressing and relationships. Services like DNS, DHCP, and WINS are no longer options, but an integral part of the operating system. An in depth coverage has been given to TCP/IP and the other protocols that can be used with Windows 2000 (IPX, AppleTalk, NetBEUI, etc).

An extensive coverage of Windows security (including Kerberos, the new addition to Windows authentication). Windows 2000 makes a great paradigm shift from a severely ridiculed security scheme to a global standard in security that can be trusted on the public network. Without a strong understanding of Kerberos and public/private key encryption schemes the average administrator could quickly become lost in this more complex structure. Windows 2000 Server Unleashed provides a good understanding of these technologies and relates these complex topics to your world.

Policy and profile control is now a part of a directory system that can help you pinpoint users and groups without using a separate application. The directory tools explained here are used to access almost every object in the operating system. The tools for creating these profiles and an explanation of why you should create them can be found here.

Applications are now delivered and modified for the users and workstations from within this directory system. Even operating system upgrades and installs are monitored and controlled by the Intellimirror technologies. The use of and planning of application distribution in the enterprise is outlined in detail in this book. Microsoft has packaged a version of the Veritas WinInstaller product and the use of this package to send packaged installs is covered in full. The directory is now ready for the Enterprise.

Becoming a Directory System Architect is not going to happen through experiencing the user interface. There are many factors that go into developing a usable and efficient directory, as well as many pits to fall into. This book explains the placement and division of directory objects, including where to break domains, when you should create a new domain or an organizational unit, how to configure traffic flow across WANs, and how to create trusts and when they're needed in the new system.

The Windows 2000 Server Unleashed team has followed the Window 2000 project since its introduction two years ago. They have a unique perspective on the product and its NT parentage. This team was made up of Field Systems Engineers, Developers, and Administrators who are experienced in the problems and solutions that you will be involved in. They have been exposed to this product and its early stages for the last two years. This experience and real world knowledge make this title an excellent resource.

Overview

PART
I

IN THIS PART

1 Windows 2000 Introduction   5

Windows 2000 Introduction

CHAPTER 1

IN THIS CHAPTER

- A Network Operating System 6
- The Product Family 9

Windows 2000 is the newest version of Microsoft's Windows NT operating system. It includes a lot of new technology. This chapter introduces the Windows 2000 product family and talks briefly about the entire product, including what's new and improved as well as some new ways to accomplish regular tasks.

This chapter will discuss the following main points:

- A Network Operating System
- The Product Family
    - Common Features
    - Windows 2000 Professional
    - Windows 2000 Server
    - Windows 2000 Advanced Server
    - Windows 2000 Datacenter Server

Windows 2000 is the future of Microsoft's operating system lineup; it contains the workstation version in Windows 2000 Professional as well as the super-high-end version Windows 2000 Datacenter Server.

A Network Operating System

So, what's a network operating system? It's an operating system for a network. Basically, a network operating system should have the ability to coordinate and allocate resources across a network. Let's break it down a bit more and talk about what an operating system is and then look at why Windows 2000 is a network operating system. In order to have an effective network operating system, there has to be effective security and performance monitoring.

An Operating System

The classical computer science definition of an operating system is very narrow and basically defines the primary tasks of an operating system: resource allocation and access. *Resource allocation* means that an operating system has to be the sole resource-allocation mechanism of a system, providing each client with the resources it requests—memory, disk storage, and processor time, for example. The operating system is responsible for working with multiple processes and making sure that the hardware is as efficiently used as possible. A full discussion of how Windows 2000, the operating system, works is found in Chapter 2, "Architecture," where topics such as memory allocation, the process model, and hardware access are covered.

Microsoft's definition of an operating system starts with the computer science definition and adds on several hundred megabytes of user interface as well as a Web browser, text editors, authentication systems, directory services, Internet services, and Solitaire. Many of these features are mere window dressing, put there to distract the unwary or to please some pointy-hair boss somewhere. The rest of the features are what makes Windows 2000 a network operating system—they're what connects Windows 2000 to the outside world.

Windows 2000 and Your Network

A network operating system has a few features above and beyond a standard single-computer operating system. It has to be able to work with other computers and cooperatively handle resource allocation and job sharing. The basic example of this is file storage. Windows 2000 needs to function as an allocator of disk resources, allowing programs to read and write data. A more complex example of this is security services; Windows 2000 has to be able to verify that a user is allowed to save a file where requested.

That type of cooperation between computers is what makes up a network operating system. One of the keys that Windows 2000 uses to achieve this status is its cross-platform access. Windows 2000 can interact with several other vendors' systems to share files and printers as well as other network resources. Windows 2000 Professional can interact with NetWare servers and authenticate with NDS, and the Server products can interact with NDS by acting as gateways between NetWare servers and clients that won't authenticate with NetWare. For more information on NetWare connectivity, see Chapter 17, "NetWare Connectivity."

UNIX is the most prevalent server operating system on the Internet. It provides a high level of reliability and performance that's untouched by any other system available. Because Microsoft wants Windows 2000 to be the operating system for the Internet, it only makes sense that it should include tools for connecting to UNIX via FTP, Telnet, SMTP, and HTTP. There are additional third-party tools that even allow access to XWindows and NFS. Chapter 18, "UNIX Host to Windows 2000 Server Connectivity," has all the details.

One of the most interesting features of Windows NT 4.0 was the addition of the Terminal Server Edition. This feature has been carried forward into Windows 2000 Advanced Server and Windows 2000 Datacenter Server. This feature allows clients to connect to Windows 2000 as if they were sitting in front of the server's console. The client that's used is very lightweight, so it can run on older hardware and provide access to very fast servers. In addition, there are new clients so that even handheld PCs can join in the fun and connect to servers.

Network Security

Without network security, the data that flows on a network is completely open and available to anyone. The resources that are available on servers are wide open, giving everyone from the janitor to the CEO equal access. Although this may be a cracker's dream, it's a system administrator's nightmare. Network security implies a lot of different things. From the operating system perspective, it includes user authentication and access verification.

User authentication involves making sure the users are who they say they are. Windows 2000 provides a few different ways of performing this operation. The traditional user ID/password combination is time tested, but it only works as well as the users' brains, which are notoriously unreliable. Windows 2000 implements a smart card security system that requires the user to place a plastic card into a card reader, which more easily verifies that the user is actually there. Possibly the ultimate new authentication scheme is the biometric security system, which analyzes fingerprints or handprints or checks facial patterns or other similar features. At least with a biometric system, nobody will be able to pass around a smart card or write a password on a sticky note placed thoughtlessly on the monitor.

Access verification is another sticky problem of network security. How can you keep track of which users have access to what files, and how do you keep those files secure? That's all covered in Chapter 4, "File Systems."

So how does Windows 2000 address the concerns of verifying users and allowing them to access resources? The major new change in Windows 2000 is the introduction of the Active Directory. Active Directory is a combination of a phone book and a sentry. When a user logs in, the Active Directory handles the problems of user authentication, and it does so in such a way as to not transmit the password over the network, which would be a security problem. Active Directory uses a special security system developed at MIT called *Kerberos*. This system provides a way for the Active Directory to verify that you are who you say you are, without you telling the Active Directory anything that you know. In addition, the Active Directory has a very sophisticated replication scheme, which allows it to distribute data far and wide across an enterprise, which, in turn, allows users to log on anywhere and be authenticated quickly and reliably.

Performance Monitoring

One of the jobs of a network operating system is to measure what's happening on the network as well as on the individual computers on the network in order to know how best to increase the capacity of the system and to help pinpoint problem areas. Windows 2000 comes with several tools to help you monitor performance and find errors.

The Windows 2000 System Performance Monitor replaces the old Performance Monitor application with a Microsoft Management Console (MMC) plug-in component. The System Performance Monitor charts all the statistics from the operating system for easy analysis. A full description can be found in Chapter 26, "Recovering from a Disaster."

Another important part of performance monitoring is seeing what's on the network. Windows 2000 ships with a product called *Network Monitor*, which can view all incoming and outgoing packets from the local machine. The Systems Management Server comes with a more advanced version of the product that allows all network packets to be displayed. Other hardware and software solutions allow similar operations.

The Product Family

In order to better market Windows 2000 Server, Microsoft has divided the product into three different packages, each with different capabilities and roles in a network. Each of these products has the same set of core features, which are basically part of the operating system. Windows 2000 Advanced Server adds some features and expands some capacities, whereas Windows 2000 Datacenter Server adds even more capacities.

Common Features

All the Windows 2000 Server products implement certain core functions. These functions can be broken down into the following areas:

- Server management
- Active Directory
- Security
- Storage and file systems
- Networking and communications
- Application services
- Symmetric Multiprocessing (SMP) support
- User interface
- Backup

Let's take a brief look at each of these common features.

Server Management

Server management in Windows NT 4.0 involved several different applications: User Manager, Server Manager, Printer Manager, Disk Administrator, and so on. In Windows 2000, there's a new shell called the *Microsoft Management Console* (or MMC), and each of the aforementioned applications has been replaced by a plug-in to the MMC. This allows for a lot of consolidation and customization to the MMC. For example, you can open the Computer Management MMC snap-in by going to Start, Settings, Control Panel, choosing Administrative Tools, and starting Computer Management. MMC console starts up, as shown in Figure 1.1. The Computer Management snap-in contains nearly all the other snap-ins in one convenient location, including user management, disk management, and starting and stopping services.

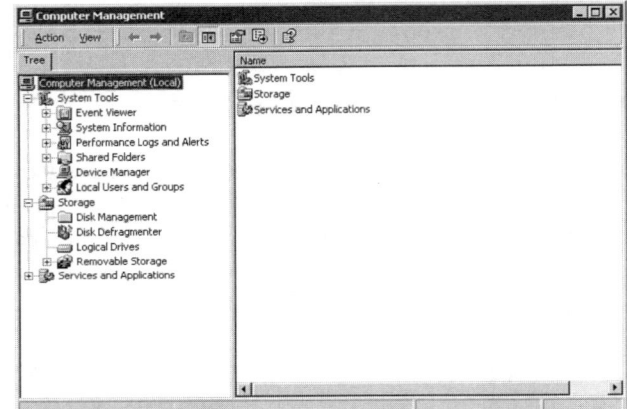

Figure 1.1
The Microsoft Management Console, or MMC, provides the administrative interface for Windows 2000.

Let's look at the MMC a little closer. It consists of two window panes. On the left side is a tree view of the snap-in, and the right side is where the actual data is, and it's where you'll normally work. For example, click the symbol next to Storage and then click Disk Management. Now, the right side of the window will show the tools for performing disk partitioning.

Another great tool for managing servers is Web-Based Enterprise Management (WBEM). This tool allows any Windows 2000 server running the Internet Information Server service to be administered from any Web browser.

Active Directory

The Active Directory system is probably the most important of all of the new features in Windows 2000. It integrates all the user account and group data together into a decentralized database. In addition, Active Directory integrates with Microsoft Exchange Server. This can help eliminate the duplication of effort between managing email distribution lists and security groups, which tend to have a lot of overlap.

Windows NT uses a master domain replication model, which means one server performs all the tasks of replicating user security data to all the servers in the network that can handle logons. With Active Directory, there's no master controller; all servers are equally capable of storing changes and making changes. This allows the system to be more scalable because one server doesn't have to serve as a central point for distributing changes. It also allows for more fault tolerance and easier configuration changes because any server can be a domain controller, and any domain controller can revert back to being a simple server.

The Active Directory system was created to compete with the Novell Directory Service (NDS). Both are X.500-based standards, and both use the Lightweight Directory Access Protocol (LDAP) to use their respective directories. Of course, the two directories aren't very compatible, because that would make all our lives way to easy. To make up for that, Microsoft has included tools that allow NDS to be migrated into Active Directory. See Chapter 17, "NetWare Connectivity," for details.

The Active Directory uses the X.500 directory standard, which lays out what types of information are stored and how the information is accessed. The information is stored hierarchically in structures called *trees*. Multiple trees make up a *forest*. By combining trees of directories together, the entire Active Directory system becomes extremely scalable because it can work with very large organizations while still being efficient in smaller organizations.

Active Directory is so important, and so new, that there's an entire part of this book dedicated to designing and implementing it (Part III, "Active Directory and Account Management," which includes Chapters 9 through 12). Chapter 9, "Directory and Access Concepts Brief," covers the basics of security and domain structures. Chapter 10, "Active Directory Design," covers the design and configuration of Active Directory. Chapter 11, "User Account Creation and Management," covers the creation and management of user accounts, and Chapter 12, "Intellimirror and User Control," covers the user-management tools.

Security Features

One thing the technical media is always critical of with any Microsoft product is the lack of built-in security, as well as how the small amount of security that is present can be circumvented. There's at least one program available that can grab encrypted passwords on the network and decrypt them. In addition, there are numerous other encryption and data privacy issues that can be resolved with a good encryption foundation.

Windows 2000 fixes a lot of the security problems that were present in earlier versions of Windows. With the proper network settings, Windows 2000 will not send encrypted passwords over the network but will instead use Kerberos authentication, which uses a challenge-response system that doesn't require a password to be sent to the server.

Kerberos Security

Kerberos is a security system that's designed for use over insecure communications media, such as a wide area network (the Internet) or even a local area network where data security is at a premium.

What traditionally happens when a user is authenticated on a network is that the user types in a user name and a password, which are then transmitted to a server. The server checks the user name and password against a list. More sophisticated systems, such as Windows NT, still transmit the password, but they encrypt the password first. Either way, the password is sent across the network to a server. Even if the password is encrypted, there's still a good chance that some enterprising programmer could capture the network packets containing the user name and password and use them, either by decrypting them or by submitting the old packets to a server for authentication later.

If you're doubting the decryption of the passwords, go check out www.l0pht.com (that's a zero in the name—lima-zero-papa-hotel-tango). This site has a program called L0phtCrack that watches the network, captures packets that contain passwords, and then decrypts the passwords using both a dictionary attack (checks to see whether the password is in the dictionary) and a brute-force attack. It's very speedy, and it can decrypt most passwords in a couple hours.

So, if all the passwords can be decrypted anyway, how can a network be secured? It boils down to this problem: The workstation has to prove to the server that it knows the password without having to send the password across the network. How does that happen? Basically, the workstation uses the password as the key to a mathematical function. Then, the server sends a question across the network to the workstation. The workstation uses the mathematical function it generated with the password and the question posed by the server and then transmits the resulting number back to the server. There's a lot more detail to it than that (How do passwords get changed? How does the server authenticate that the response comes back from the right workstation?), but that's the general idea. For more information, there's a great nontechnical, easy-to-understand story that explains the whole thing at the following URL:

```
http://web.mit.edu/kerberos/www/dialogue.html
```

In addition, Windows 2000 implements public key encryption for both the purposes of encrypting and validating data. In public key encryption, two pieces of information are required to decrypt a message—a public key and a private key. The public key is published and generally available to anyone. The private key is kept private and hidden.

When a user wants to send a message to another user and only wants that other user to be able to read the message, he or she will encrypt the message with the receiver's public key. If the user wants to assure the recipient that the message was not tampered with, the message can be encrypted with the sender's private key. The decryption would then require the sender's public key, which would validate that the message was from the sender, as well as the receiver's private key, to decrypt the message. Therefore, public key encryption ensures that a message is safe from eavesdropping as well as safe from tampering.

Another new feature is the Encrypted File System. A file or directory can be encrypted and from then on can only be accessed by the user who encrypted it. EFS is only available on partitions formatted with the NTFS file system and works the same as the compression features of NTFS. More on the EFS can be found in Chapter 4, "File Systems."

Windows 2000 implements interfaces for smart card readers. These allow a new level of security, because they prevent authorization from users who just know a password. A smart card along with a password provides a very high level of security, because if the password is figured out, the person trying to break in still has to have the smart card, and if the smart card is stolen, the intruder still has to know the right password. Smart cards have built-in safeguards that render them tamperproof and very difficult to copy. A smart card infrastructure is built into Windows 2000, and setup varies depending on the vendor of the card-reading device.

Another new feature is IPSEC, the Internet Protocol Security system. IP is the underlying protocol for both TCP and UDP. IPSEC provides end-to-end encryption and content verification for network packets. More information on IPSEC can be found in Chapter 24, "Optimizing Performance Tuning."

Storage and File System Support

Windows 2000 provides several key features to provide easy access to storage media. The Remote Storage Server system allows archive media such as backup tapes and optical disks to be accessed as if they were online by accessing a share point. The system will automatically load the correct file from an archive source.

In addition, Windows 2000 has improved support for tape libraries and robotic tape changers. The Removable Storage Management system catalogs and tracks cartridges and tapes, allowing them to be easily found later. This works in concert with the Remote Storage Server as well as the new and improved backup program.

At long last, Windows 2000 introduces a unique and integrated disk quota system. Disk quotas allow users and groups to be assigned disk space, with different warnings and restrictions placed on users who use too much disk space. Systems such as this have been around a long time for both UNIX and Novell NetWare and are just now being added in to Windows 2000.

The Distributed File System allows important and frequently accessed files to be distributed across a network while providing users with a single access mechanism for the files. In other words, a file can be stored on several different servers across the network, but the users all access the file by the same name and access the file closest to them.

All this is covered in a lot of depth in Chapter 4, which goes into depth about building and maintaining high-performance file systems and how to implement features such as Remote Storage Server.

Networking and Communications

What would a server be without the capability to communicate with workstations? A doorstop. Fortunately, Windows 2000 Server implements the usual gaggle of protocols that make it unique among operating systems. Of course, there's the wide protocol support, including support for TCP/IP, IPX/SPX, and even the infamous NetBEUI. In addition, because all the protocols are implemented as installable components, some third-party and infrequently-used protocols can be easily used with Windows 2000.

Windows 2000 also includes multiprotocol routing. If multiple network devices are installed on a server, it can act as a router between the different devices, moving data between one network and another.

Another greatly enhanced feature is Remote Access Services (RAS). This has been enhanced to include Virtual Private Networking (VPN) functionality. RAS adds the capability to Windows 2000 Server of receiving connections from outside sources, such as modems, ISDN adapters, and even just standard Internet connections, and make the computers on the other side of those connections act as if they were connected locally (but a bit slower due to bandwidth constraints). VPN adds the capability to connect from a point on the Internet into a Windows 2000 Server machine and to participate on the network the same way as if the computer were sitting on the local network. VPN also encrypts packets that are sent on the Internet to enhance security.

Windows 2000 includes support for Asynchronous Transfer Mode (ATM) adapters. This isn't a bank machine—it's a high-speed packet switched data network that provides for multiple types of information on the same network.

The Windows 2000 network infrastructure also adds support for Quality of Service features. These features allow certain network addresses and certain types of packets to be granted a higher priority than other types of communication. In other words, the actual work going on in the company can now take precedence over the streaming video and music that's coming in from the Internet.

More information on networking can be found in Chapter 8, "TCP/IP Networking," and in Part IV, "Network Services," which includes Chapters 13 through 16. Chapter 13, "Network Browsing," covers the troublesome topic of network browsing. Chapter 14 "Remote Access (RAS)," includes information on Routing and Remote Access Services (RRAS). Chapter 15, "Multiprotocol Environments," covers working with multiprotocol environments, and Chapter 16, "Client Workstation Considerations," covers how client workstations interact with servers.

Application Services

Windows 2000 provides some features that help applications be more intelligent and provide data more quickly. The Windows Scripting Host (WSH) is a service that runs different scripting languages, such as VBScript and JavaScript, to provide services to clients. The scripts can be run remotely so that the server can do work for the client workstations. In addition, the Indexing Service provides a central location for searching across large disks for documents with specific information in them. The Indexing Service watches all the files on the server, keeps track of what's in the files, and organizes that information to make it easy for a user to figure out where the May budgets are, for example.

In addition, Windows 2000 provides the widely used Win32 API, with all the appropriate extensions, so all the Win32 applications that have been written can be used with Windows 2000 without modification. Most important for the Windows 2000 Server user is that all the current BackOffice programs and other server-side applications work well, including SQL Server and Exchange. As a matter of fact, Windows 2000 features a very high level of Exchange integration by enabling you to make Windows 2000 user groups into Exchange distribution lists, and vice versa.

Symmetric Multiprocessing (SMP)

The entire Windows 2000 product line, from Windows 2000 Professional to Windows 2000 Datacenter, provides support for multiple processors. Windows 2000 Professional supports two processors for advanced workstations. Windows 2000 Server supports up to four processors, whereas Windows 2000 Advanced Server supports eight. Windows 2000 Datacenter's extent of SMP support hasn't been formally announced at this time, but it's expected to be in the 16 to 32 range.

What does SMP do? Well, it doesn't make everything run faster. Instead, it requires programs built to take advantage of multiple processors to use all the processors. However, the outstanding feature of SMP is that a program that can run on multiple processors doesn't need to know how many processors there are, and it will even work on machines with only one processor. Therefore, the programs don't need to be rewritten, and in most cases the same version of a program will run on machines with one or more processors without having to be recompiled.

Windows 95/98 Ease of Use

The new graphical user interface is based on the technology in Internet Explorer 5 and is consistent on every version of Windows 2000. It includes features associated with Windows 95/98, using the desktop metaphor with a Start menu. It also has features that aren't included in Windows 95/98, such as menus that fade in and out as well as a mouse cursor that has a shadow, depending on the graphics hardware in the server.

Windows 2000 also doesn't need to be rebooted as often as prior versions of Windows NT. In Windows NT 4.0, even the smallest change to some settings requires a reboot, and you can forget about adding hardware on-the-fly. Windows 2000 reduces the number of reboots and introduces native support for Plug-and-Play technologies, ranging from PCMCIA and USB, all the way to Hot-Plug PCI slots.

Backup and Data Recovery

Windows 2000 implements an all-new data backup and recovery program, with the underlying services actually usable now. Of course, it includes the basic functionality that you'd expect, such as high performance, the ability to interface with tape changers, and the ability to perform full, incremental, and differential backups. The improvements include the new Windows 2000 Removable Storage Management system, which essentially provides support for tape changers and tape catalogs.

Those are the features that all the Windows 2000 Server products share, and they're the features included in the Windows 2000 Server product. Windows 2000 Advanced Server and Windows 2000 Datacenter Server provide even more functionality.

Windows 2000 Advanced Server

Windows 2000 Advanced Server includes some features that are necessary for large applications or servers to be used to their full potential. Windows 2000 Advanced Server includes enhanced application failover clustering. *Clustering* allows an application to be set up on two servers and to be running on one server. If the server that's running the application fails, due to a hardware failure, an operating system problem, or an application failure, the other server will take over and resume processing.

> **Note**
>
> Here's an historical note: The *Advanced Server* name was originally applied to Windows NT 3.1 Advanced Server, which was the server version of Windows NT 3.1. The workstation version of Windows NT 3.1 was simply called *Windows NT 3.1*. Most of the people who have worked with Windows NT since those days are glad to see the Advanced Server name come back, almost as much as they hate the name *Windows 2000*.

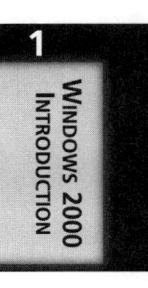

In addition, Windows 2000 Advanced Server provides load balancing at both the network layer and the component layer. This means it can run multiple network interface cards and balance the load between the network cards. By using the Microsoft Transaction Server technology, it can also use multiple servers to balance the processing load for multiple components.

Hardware Scalability

Windows 2000 Advanced Server supports up to eight processors using hardware that supports symmetric multiprocessing (SMP). In addition, Windows 2000 Advanced Server can use up to 4GB of physical RAM, and applications that support the capability can address 3GB of application memory.

Windows Terminal Services

Windows Terminal Services, included with the Advanced Server version of Windows 2000, allows several different "thin" clients to attach to a server and get a screen that looks just like the server console screen. Many of these thin devices, sometimes called *Windows terminals*, are diskless stations that have a keyboard, a mouse, a monitor, and a network connection. All the actual computing happens on a centrally located server. There are a variety of thin clients, such as the aforementioned Windows terminals and machines running Windows CE. Even normal PCs can take advantage of the computing power available on a server.

Windows 2000 Datacenter

Windows 2000 Datacenter is the high-end version of Windows 2000 Server. It includes all the features of Windows 2000 Advanced Server but increases the number of supported processors to 32. In addition, Windows 2000 Datacenter provides advanced clustering, which goes beyond just failover into the realm of actual load balancing. Windows 2000 Datacenter will be released after the Windows 2000 Server and Advanced Server products are released.

Summary

The Windows 2000 operating system is designed to be scalable and network oriented. It has a large set of core features that are present in all the products. The Advanced Server and Datacenter versions have features that make them extremely useful in large enterprises hosting large applications. In the next few chapters we'll start to look at the Windows 2000 architecture, the operating system architecture and the network architecture that make Windows 2000 powerful.

Windows 2000 Operating System Environment

PART II

IN THIS PART

2 Architecture *21*

3 Installation Considerations *39*

4 File Systems *71*

5 Networking Brief *127*

6 Printing *149*

7 The Registry *179*

8 TCP/IP Networking *195*

Architecture

IN THIS CHAPTER

- The Subsystem and Kernel Architecture 22
- Memory Model and Management 34

There are certain tasks any operating system has to do. It has to allocate memory resources, control access to drivers, and handle switching which programs are currently running and which are waiting. Windows 2000 is no different. The process works the same on all the different types of Windows 2000, so this chapter is a generic look at how the operating system works, independent of the services overhead and largely independent of the hardware underfoot. The architecture of the operating system can be broken up into pieces to make it easier to study:

- The subsystem and kernel architecture
- Executive services
- A closer look at subsystems
- Memory model and management

Let's get started with a look at the subsystem and kernel architecture, the core of Windows 2000.

The Subsystem and Kernel Architecture

In its infancy, in the days when the operating system was still called "Windows NT 3.1," there were several operating systems vying for desktop dominance. Windows NT was the newcomer, with its rivals for competition being OS/2 and UNIX. In addition, Microsoft knew the market for 32-bit Windows applications would grow slowly at first. As a result, Windows NT was originally designed to run several compartments, or *subsystems*, that allowed it to run programs from different operating systems. Windows NT allows programs using these subsystems to simultaneously coexist and share resources such as CPU time, disk drives, and video hardware, but in such a way that any one program's bad behavior wouldn't adversely affect any other programs.

The subsystems were written such that if any program were to run amok and destroy the integrity of its host subsystem, it wouldn't take down the operating system, nor would it effect the other subsystems.

In order for all these subsystems to operate independently, there has to be one central resource allocation mechanism, or *kernel*, and a lot of other systems that work together to provide basic services. First of all, the processor has to be able to prevent user applications from overwriting memory that belongs to the kernel and the other services by implementing a User mode and Kernel mode. Then, in order to prevent the kernel and executive services from causing problems with the hardware, and to make it easier to move from one processor architecture to another, all the hardware interaction has to be done through the Hardware Abstraction Layer (HAL). Then the kernel has to be able to schedule processes, and the various executive services have to be able to create those processes, manage memory, and enforce security controls. Then, on top of all that architecture, the subsystems have the services they need to supply to applications as well as the application programming interfaces they need in order to interact with the user. See Figure 2.1 for a diagram of what the upcoming sections will cover.

FIGURE 2.1
The basic architecture of Windows 2000. Each layer below the User Application layer will be discussed in depth in upcoming sections.

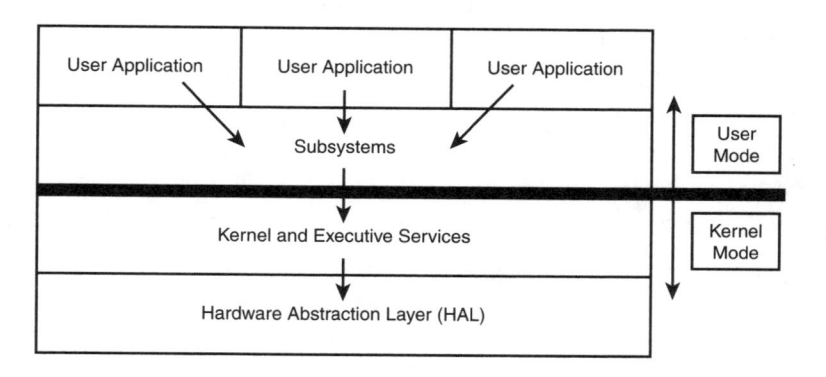

```
User Application    User Application    User Application
                                                              User
              Subsystems                                      Mode
―――――――――――――――――――――――――――――――――――――――――――――――
         Kernel and Executive Services                        Kernel
                                                              Mode
         Hardware Abstraction Layer (HAL)
```

User Mode and Kernel Mode

Windows 2000 uses two different processor modes to execute. One mode, called *Kernel mode*, runs the executive services. The other mode, called *User mode*, runs user programs. Kernel mode services are protected by the processor, and User mode services are protected by the operating system. This is done by preventing any program operating in User mode from writing to the memory used by any program running in Kernel mode. The processor prevents programs running in Kernel mode from writing data into the space where programs are stored, and it also causes a Kernel mode exception, which Windows 2000 translates to a "Blue Screen of Death" (BSOD). A BSOD is a blue screen (hence the name) full of text that helps the support staff at Microsoft figure out what's wrong with your computer. Usually a BSOD is caused by a faulty driver of some type that's trying to write data where it shouldn't be writing.

> **Note**
>
> If the Kernel mode is so much more reliable, why doesn't everything run in Kernel mode? It requires so much engineering and testing to put something into Kernel mode that the new releases would be even later than they are. A comedian once asked, "Why isn't the whole airplane made out of the same stuff as the black box?" If the airplane was made out of the same stuff, it would be too heavy to fly. Different question, same answer. If everything ran in Kernel mode, programs would have to be so big to handle all of the possible exceptions that they'd never be released. Therefore, we have to deal with programs that can possibly crash, but (hopefully) usually don't.

With Windows 2000, as much of the operating system as possible runs in User mode, thus reducing the amount of extremely critical code in the kernel in an attempt to keep it manageable. The difference between a User-mode program crashing and a Kernel-mode program crashing is that a User-mode program will write an event into the event log and all the rest of the programs on the server will be fine. If a Kernel-mode program has a problem, the server halts with a BSOD. Take a look back at Figure 2.1. The components below the heavy dark line are running in Kernel mode, whereas the components above the line are running in User mode.

Starting with Windows NT 4.0, parts of the Win32 subsystem, specifically the User and GDI parts, run in Kernel mode. This has been a slightly controversial decision, which will be discussed more in the Win32 subsystem section later in this chapter.

User-mode programs running on the system communicate with the kernel using specific application programming interfaces (APIs). These APIs are used to define a stable method of communication between the various programs running and the operating system.

The rest of Kernel mode is generally divided into three parts. The Hardware Abstraction Layer (HAL), which provides a consistent interface to hardware, the kernel, which runs the whole show, and the NT Executive Services, which handle low-level operations such as security, task scheduling, and memory.

The Hardware Abstraction Layer

Windows 2000 is portable, which means that with some amount of effort, it can be made to run on different types of hardware. Windows NT used to be available on Alpha, MIPS and PowerPC, but there weren't enough people buying it to justify the expense of producing it.

Windows 2000 is portable because it's almost entirely written in C++, and C++ compilers are among the first things written for new processors. The parts that aren't written in C++ are written in assembler native to the machine that's being ported to, and these parts are all shoved into something called the *Hardware Abstraction Layer*.

The HAL is the only part of the operating system that interacts directly with the hardware. It does so by providing a fixed interface to the kernel above it and masking over the irregularities of the hardware below it. Therefore, the kernel doesn't need to know about the hardware peculiarities, so it doesn't need to be modified as much when it's ported from one hardware architecture to another.

The HAL presents the kernel with an abstract view of the hardware so that the kernel doesn't need to be rewritten in order to use a different processor. The kernel just needs to know how to access one type of processor, and that's the type that the HAL provides to it. The HAL deals with taking requests from the kernel and turning them into instructions that the processor in the machine can understand.

The HAL also provides the base level of support for symmetric multiprocessing (SMP). It knows how to use the processors and simply presents the kernel with multiple processors if multiple processors are present. Whenever a machine is upgraded from a single processor to multiple processors, the HAL must be replaced. On most systems, especially server systems, a program disk is included with the server that will install a hardware manufacturer–supplied HAL to enable SMP support.

One other important note: The HAL is the only part of the system that communicates directly with the hardware, and the kernel is the only part of the system that communicates directly with the HAL. This reduces destructive contention for hardware and increases security because rogue applications have to get past both the kernel and the HAL in order to cause problems with the hardware.

The Kernel

The *kernel* is the central part of the operating system from an architecture perspective. Windows 2000 uses a *microkernel design*, which means the kernel provides a very minimum level of functionality and relies on other services to add to that functionality. The kernel is primarily responsible for figuring out what's going to run next on the processor.

When a program is run, it has a process associated with it, and the process has at least one thread associated with it. A *process* is a memory space and at least one thread. The *thread* is what actually gets executed—it's the "program" part of the application, and the process is the program plus all the data associated with the program. The difference between a process and a thread is that a thread is given processor time by the operating system, while a process isn't. Threads are allocated execution time by the operating system, not processes.

The kernel deals with three types of tasks. First of all, it schedules thread execution. Each thread gets a priority assignment that ranges from 0 to 31. The kernel picks the thread with the highest priority that needs to run and allows that thread to run on a processor for a given amount of time. At the end of that time period, the kernel looks at the thread list again and picks one thread per processor to run based on priority.

Another task the kernel has to deal with is *interrupt handling*. When a device, for example, a hard disk, is asked to read data, the request is sent to the hard disk; the hard disk retrieves the data and then notifies the kernel by causing an interrupt signal to be sent to a processor. When an interrupt occurs, the kernel automatically preempts whatever process is running on a given processor and handles the interrupt; then it returns control to the process that was preempted.

The third type of task the system has to deal with is a *kernel exception*. If something happens and a program running in Kernel mode causes a protection fault or any other type of fault, the kernel tries to handle the fault. In some cases, the kernel can deal with the fault without any problems. In many cases, the kernel cannot handle the fault, and then it's BSOD time.

The Windows 2000 Executive

An operating system has to perform a number of different duties in order to provide a good environment for applications. The Windows 2000 microkernel design dictates that the kernel just handle basic services such as task switching. Because Windows 2000 has a microkernel design, all the rest of the important services required are still run—they're just run outside of the kernel. Most of these get dumped on the Windows 2000 Executive, which comprises a large set of different services that handle different distinct tasks.

The Windows 2000 Executive runs completely in Kernel mode. It has full access to the kernel and full access to I/O devices. Most user applications don't directly use any part of the Executive; they instead rely on a subsystem, such as the Win32 subsystem, which in turn calls the Executive for services. Figure 2.2 shows the different components of the Windows 2000 Executive.

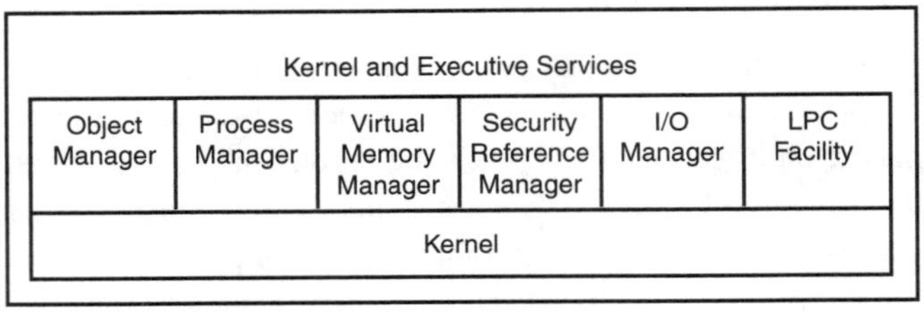

FIGURE 2.2
The different parts of the Windows 2000 Executive that work together to provide the basic operating system services.

Kernel and Executive Services					
Object Manager	Process Manager	Virtual Memory Manager	Security Reference Manager	I/O Manager	LPC Facility
Kernel					

The Executive handles a variety of different services:

- Object Manager
- Process Manager
- Virtual Memory Manager
- Security Reference Manager
- I/O Manager
- The local procedure call facility

The following sections detail what each of these services does.

Object Manager

The Object Manager is very critical; it's used to create, manage, and delete objects used by the system. The Object Manager receives a request for a resource, such as a serial port, and it returns a handle to the serial port. The handle includes a method for accessing an object as well as security information that determines how the object can be accessed.

The Object Manager also hands out other types of handles, such as handles to devices (serial and parallel ports, for example), in order to prevent contention for the devices.

The Object Manager communicates extensively with the Security Reference Manager (SRM), discussed later. The SRM creates the security information that's attached to a handle before the handle is given back to the calling program.

In addition to that, the Object Manager watches for orphaned objects. If a program accesses a serial port and then the program crashes, the Object Manager is responsible for finding the handle and closing it to recover the resources used.

Process Manager

The Process Manager is an intermediary between the user and the Object Manager, and its primary job is to create and manage processes. The Process Manager is responsible for receiving requests to create processes, calling the Object Manager to create the processes and their threads, and then keeping the list of processes available.

Virtual Memory Manager

When a process is created, it receives a 4GB address space to use (this address space starts at 0 and goes to 4GB). For Windows 2000 Professional and Windows 2000 Server, the memory is allocated with 2GB for user space and 2GB for the system. Windows 2000 Advanced Server allocates 3GB of user space and 1GB for the system. This is how Windows 2000 supports memory protection: A program can't address any memory outside its own memory space.

When an application requests a read from memory, the Virtual Memory Manager (VMM) is what actually handles the mechanics of retrieving the data. The VMM maintains a table in order to keep track of what parts of a process's memory space are actually in physical memory and which parts are not. When a process needs to read some of its memory, the VMM checks to see whether the data is actually in physical memory; if it's not, the VMM handles fetching the data from disk. The final section in this chapter, "Memory Model and Management," goes into more detail on the topic of the VMM and memory allocation.

Security Reference Manager

The Security Reference Manager (SRM) is the basis for security in Windows 2000. When a user logs on, the logon process generates a security token for the user. Whenever the user requests access to an object, the Object Manager asks the SRM to examine the token and determine what level of access the user should have. Then the Object Manager returns the handle to the object, with the level of access as part of the handle.

I/O Manager

The I/O Manager deals with all the device I/O that the system needs. The I/O Manager provides services to both device drivers and applications so that the device drivers don't need to know about how the applications will be using them, and the applications don't need to know how to use the devices.

For example, the I/O Manager relates all hard disk drives and high-capacity removable media down to SCSI devices. Therefore, when a manufacturer needs to make a certain device work with Windows 2000, it needs to write a driver that the I/O Manager can treat like a SCSI device, which is a very standardized interface. Also, the manufacturer needs to translate those calls into whatever the piece of hardware will understand. An application only needs to know to ask its subsystem for a disk read, and the subsystem asks the I/O Manager for a disk read. The application and the subsystem don't need to know how to read data from the disk—they only have to know what to read from the disk.

Local Procedure Call Facility

Windows 2000 is a client/server system. What happens when the client and server processes are running on the same machine? One method is to use the remote procedure call (RPC) facility, which has a fairly large amount of overhead. However, Windows 2000 has the local procedure call (LPC) facility, which allows it to use the same interfaces as RPC but with far less overhead. By using this type of interface, the system can provide faster response without changing the interface.

Subsystems: A Closer Look

A *subsystem* can be thought of as an environment that interfaces with the kernel and applications to allow programs to run by providing the services and APIs they expect, while at the same time using the APIs to call the kernel and ask it politely for the needed resources. Basically, a subsystem is a translator that sits between a group of applications and the kernel.

> ### What's an API
>
> An API is an *application programming interface*. Still in the dark? Well, an API is what allows a program to talk to the outside world. For example, a program that needs to perform encryption can use the CryptoAPI from Microsoft, which has a standard set of functions that perform encryption. The program itself doesn't need to know how to perform encryption; instead, it can rely on the API to handle the encryption.
>
> An API is a set of functions used by programmers to define how programs interact. By using an API, the vendor of the interface (Microsoft, in this case) can change the inner workings of the CryptoAPI, and as long as the interface doesn't change, the developer and the programs will be none the wiser. If Microsoft creates some fancy new encryption doodad, it can implement this feature into CryptoAPI, and programs can use it without needing changes.
>
> The important concept here is *interface consistency*. For example, toasters have a consistent interface. Any toaster will have one or more bread input ports, an activation lever, and a toast darkness selector. Some toasters may be more elaborate and have a device that watches the bread and determines when it's toasted to perfection. Some toasters may have extra-wide input ports. However, they're all the same basic toaster, and the user doesn't have to guess about how to use one.
>
> An API works the same way. A programmer can write for one specific version of an API, but if a newer one comes along with additional bells and whistles, the programmer can still put in the old input (bread) and get the same output (toast). With the new version of the API, a new program can use the same interface to put in a new type of input (bagels) and get out a new type of output (toasted bagels).
>
> Now that you're hungry, you may as well go enjoy some nice toast. The book will be here when you get back.

A subsystem runs a whole herd of programs and handles their access to the kernel, which means all of a program's hardware access goes through the subsystem. Therefore, for a program to play a sound, it has to tell the subsystem to play a sound. The subsystem tells the kernel to play the sound, the kernel tells the HAL to play the sound, the HAL manipulates the hardware into playing the sound, and then the sound gets played.

There are two types of subsystems. The Win32 subsystem is in a class by itself; all other subsystems are basically translators between whatever subsystem they emulate and Win32. For example, the POSIX subsystem takes the POSIX API and maps it over to the Win32 API.

So, what does a subsystem look like? Well, each Windows 2000 system has executables that are the subsystems. Once such is called `CSRSS.EXE`. This is the client/server resources subsystem, better known as the *Win32 subsystem*.

The Win32 Subsystem

The Win32 subsystem is the subsystem most often used, and it's the only critical subsystem. Originally, the Win32 subsystem was just another subsystem. Because all the user functions in the operating system use Win32, portions of the Win32 subsystem actually run in Kernel mode as part of the Windows 2000 Executive. These portions are the User and GDI pieces, which control the user interface and graphical display, respectively. Therefore, if the Win32 subsystem crashes, the entire operating system will crash.

> **Note**
>
> Of course, in Windows NT 3.51, if the Win32 subsystem crashed, the operating system would generate a blue screen even though the User and GDI portions were not part of the kernel. It was set up so that if the kernel didn't have an active user interface, the kernel would generate a blue screen. Because the entire user interface relies on User and GDI, if either of these crashes, the OS crashes. Therefore, moving these parts of the subsystem into the Executive isn't as big a deal as it seems. The move occurred because there's a performance penalty during every switch between User and Kernel mode. Reducing these context switches improved performance of Win32 applications significantly.

Of course, this doesn't mean that applications run in Kernel mode—just parts of the subsystem. Therefore, the subsystem and the operating system as a whole are secure against rogue applications. The operating system detects the protection fault and stops the rogue application before it causes damage.

The Win32 API covers all the operations necessary for a Windows application to run. This includes everything from reading and writing to files to using DirectX. The Win32 API is a very complex API, and it includes a lot of functionality. All new Windows development is done using Win32. See Figure 2.3 for an overview of this subsystem layer.

The Win32 subsystem also contains the MS-DOS and 16-bit Windows (Windows 3.1 and Windows 3.11) subsystems. Because Windows 3.1 isn't really an operating system (it's actually a layer of graphical interfaces on top of MS-DOS), the system had to be able to run MS-DOS applications first.

FIGURE 2.3
The subsystem layer of the Windows 2000 architecture shows how all the subsystems interact with the Win32 subsystem, which is the only subsystem that directly interacts with the Executive.

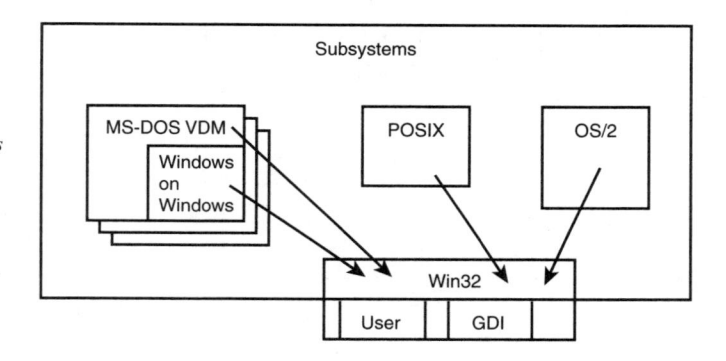

MS-DOS applications are run inside a program called the NT Virtual DOS Machine (NTVDM). Even though the OS is called Windows 2000 now, there's still an NTVDM. The NTVDM runs all DOS applications by emulating the MS-DOS 5.0 environment. Each DOS application runs in its own NTVDM as well as in its own memory space. These NTVDMs can be started up and used until there's no system memory available. The NTVDM supplies a full network redirector as well as mouse and CD-ROM support for applications, and it still provides enough free memory (620KB) to run MS-DOS applications very nicely.

Now that there's a way to run DOS applications, all that's left is to be able to run Windows 3.1 applications. That's accomplished using a system called Windows on Windows (WOW). WOW interfaces the 16-bit architecture of Windows 3.1 to the 32-bit architecture of the Win32 subsystem by translating calls for services using a process called *thunking*. Thunking is a method for translating 32-bit data values into 16-bit data values (and vice versa), without losing any data. The actual mechanics of thunking depend on what data is being passed. All the calls to User, GDI, and Kernel libraries in the Win16 API are converted to appropriate calls in the Win32 API. See Figure 2.4 for a further explanation.

Programs running in WOW are all run in the same instance of WOWEXEC (the program that handles the Win16-to-Win32 system calls). This is done both to reduce overhead (each one of the WOWEXEC instances uses some memory) and to allow the individual Win16 programs to perform the OLE and cut-and-paste operations they need to do in order to operate properly.

Windows 3.1 implements multitasking using a technique called "cooperative multitasking". The operating system assumes that each program will be nice and occasionally give the processor up so the next program can execute. Of course, every programmer thinks their program is the most important thing in the world, and should never give up the processor, so Windows 3.1 had a lot of performance problems. The system Windows

2000 uses, "preemptive multitasking" sets up the operating system to allocate CPU time, and the operating system will preempt any running program whenever it's allotted amount of CPU time is done.

FIGURE 2.4
The different parts of the Windows on Windows (WOW) system and how they interact with the Win32 subsystem.

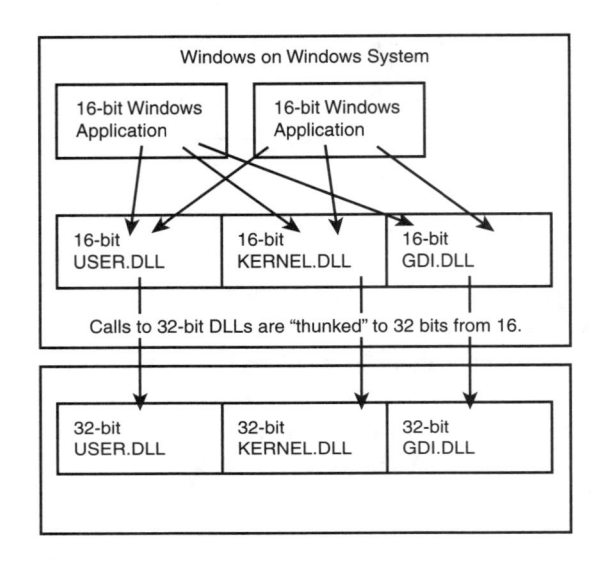

```
                    Windows on Windows System
        ┌──────────────────────┬──────────────────────┐
        │  16-bit Windows      │  16-bit Windows      │
        │  Application         │  Application         │
        └──────────────────────┴──────────────────────┘

        ┌────────────┬──────────────┬────────────┐
        │  16-bit    │  16-bit      │  16-bit    │
        │  USER.DLL  │  KERNEL.DLL  │  GDI.DLL   │
        └────────────┴──────────────┴────────────┘

        Calls to 32-bit DLLs are "thunked" to 32 bits from 16.

        ┌────────────┬──────────────┬────────────┐
        │  32-bit    │  32-bit      │  32-bit    │
        │  USER.DLL  │  KERNEL.DLL  │  GDI.DLL   │
        └────────────┴──────────────┴────────────┘
```

The Windows 2000 thread scheduler does some unique things to enable Win32 applications to run properly. Remember that all threads are preemptively multitasked. In WOWEXEC, the only thread that can run is the one that was running the last time. In other words, for each instance of WOWEXEC, only one thread can be active at a time, and that thread must voluntarily give up the processor before another 16-bit Windows program can execute any instructions. In other words, a 16-bit Windows application that does not yield the processor will prevent other 16-bit programs from running. This policy was implemented because many Win16 applications make incorrect assumptions about how they're executing in relation with the rest of the operating system and the other Windows 3.1 applications in order to pass data back and forth; if the operating system schedules the applications differently than real Windows 3.1, some application compatibility will be lost.

The POSIX Subsystem

According to Microsoft, the POSIX subsystem was created so users could run UNIX applications under Windows NT. POSIX is a standard that specifies different operating system services and API calls that have to be available for applications. POSIX, by the way, stands for *Portable Operating System Interface*. Nobody knows where the *X* came from.

There are different levels of POSIX compliance, and Windows 2000 only supports the very base level, called *POSIX.1*. This level specifies a very minimum set of services and requires support for case-sensitive filenames, hard links, and the ability to keep users from accessing files in a specific way (called *traverse checking*). Traverse checking specifies that in order for a user to have access to a given file, the user must have access to the entire directory path for the file. In other words, for the user to have access to the file `D:\Data\Documents\Foo.doc`, that user would have to have read access to the root directory on drive `D:`, read access to the *Data* directory, read access to the `Documents` directory, and read access to the file `Foo.doc`. Normally, a user in Windows 2000 has a special user right called *Bypass Traverse Checking* turned on, which means the user doesn't need access to any directories above a given file if he or she has access to the file.

For a long time, specifically during the design phases of Windows NT, POSIX compliance was a requirement for any operating system purchased by the U.S. federal government. Some cynics might point out that the only reason Microsoft put POSIX compliance into Windows NT was because of the U.S. government's buying rules. These cynics would probably be right.

POSIX.1 is a low-enough level of compliance that it's almost useless. Two systems that are POSIX.1 compliant don't have to use the same binary file format, so they can't necessarily run the same programs. The system is loose enough at the POSIX.1 level that porting applications from one OS to another is still very painful. As a matter of fact, the POSIX.1 standard doesn't specify any network interface, so programs written for the POSIX subsystem will have no network access.

The POSIX subsystem works by translating the C language calls into Win32 subsystem calls. Therefore, the POSIX subsystem is dependent on the Win32 subsystem, and the POSIX subsystem can't do anything the Win32 subsystem can't do. In addition, the overhead for translating these calls makes POSIX applications run slower than similar Win32-only programs. Again, cynics might say that this is yet another reason to just port programs to Win32 natively and ignore UNIX and POSIX altogether.

The OS/2 Subsystem

When Windows NT was first designed, Microsoft considered it to be the replacement for OS/2. Microsoft figured out that the Windows interface was a lot more popular than the OS/2 Presentation Manager, so it decided to make the new operating system use a Windows interface, renaming the product to Windows, New Technology (or Windows NT).

The little history lesson aside, the OS/2 subsystem is a very limited subsystem that was created specifically to run OS/2 1.*x* Character-mode applications. It cannot run graphical applications, and it cannot run any OS/2 2.*x* or higher programs. The OS/2 subsystem, like the POSIX subsystem, relies on the Win32 API. Essentially, it converts OS/2 API calls to Win32 calls, but it only includes the core OS/2 1.*x* API set along with some basic LAN Manager networking calls to give the programs network access, thus making the system one step ahead of the POSIX subsystem, which has no network support.

Memory Model and Management

One of the major tasks of any operating system is allocating and monitoring memory. Determining how memory will be allocated to different processes and how the processes will access the memory is part of the memory model of the operating system. Figuring out how to handle physical memory, including swapping pages to disk, is part of memory management.

The Memory Model

Windows 2000 uses a process and task model to describe how processing gets done. A *process* is an object that owns a memory allocation and a set of tasks. A *task* is a unit of execution (that is, it's what the kernel executes).

In Windows 2000, each process is given a memory space that it can address from `0x00000000` to `0xFFFFFFFF`, which is 4GB of memory in a flat address space. This is how Windows 2000 achieves memory protection.

So, what's the big deal about protected memory? Imagine an operating system, such as Windows 3.1, with a shared memory space, which means that all the programs run in one piece of memory. Imagine that a programmer creates a program that stores data in memory and retrieves the data back from memory and displays it. This particular program is a text editor, and it works by reading an entire file into memory and then displaying the file (probably the worst way to do this, but it's how `NOTEPAD.EXE` works). When a program needs memory, it asks the operating system for memory, and the operating system either hands back a pointer to the memory or it says "I don't have any memory to give you." So, if the programmer requests 2KB of memory and the file is actually 3KB, the file gets read and the program keeps reading the file, stuffing its contents into memory. When the program hits the 2KB barrier, it keeps on going. It's like putting 30 pounds of fertilizer into a 20 pound bag: The other 10 pounds have to go somewhere. For fertilizer, the other 10 pounds goes all over the floor. In the case of memory, however, the 1KB of data just continues to write into consecutive memory spaces until it's all done.

When the memory overflows its usual boundaries, there are only two options. The data either goes into memory the operating system hasn't allocated yet or it goes into another program's memory. Because there's no memory protection, the operating system doesn't know about the problem. Meanwhile, the program adjacent to the text editor in memory just got it's code overwritten by a bunch of data, and the next time it tries to run, it will crash. As Murphy's law predicts, the worst thing that can possibly get overwritten is the operating system, so that's what usually happens.

This is all pretty much taken for granted now, but way back then (late 80s and early 90s) this was a big deal for a PC-based operating system. The only PC-oriented operating system that featured memory protection was OS/2, and it wasn't very well liked by the population in general.

When an application attempts to write into memory that doesn't belong to it, the resulting condition is a *protection fault*. One such type is the *General Protection Fault*, which is the most common type in Windows operating systems. It occurs when an application accesses, by reading or writing, a piece of memory that it isn't allowed to.

Why do protection faults cause programs to halt? Well, one other option would be to prevent the memory from being written to and to continue executing the program. Let's say a user is using this alternative operating system and is typing a document into a text editor, and the text editor starts writing data where it shouldn't. The operating system ignores the writings, because they're invalid, and the user types along oblivious to the problem for the next few hours. Then the user tries to save the text to a file, but the file isn't in memory. Rather than losing a little data, the user has just lost an afternoon's worth of work. Therefore, this is not a good solution because it results in data loss.

Why can't the operating system simply notify the program that it's doing something wrong? Well, programs aren't set up to work that way, but even if they were, a program has to have some serious problems to cause a protection fault, usually badly written code. If a program is written badly enough to be causing a protection fault, is it going to accept and deal with a message from the operating system to mend it's wicked ways? It will most likely ignore the message altogether, and either the program locks up because the operating system isn't allowing it to run or the protection faults are ignored altogether, in which case there's a loss of data. This is not a good solution either. Therefore, Windows 2000 will crash a program rather than risking continued data loss.

One way of making sure that programs don't overrun their data spaces and corrupt other images in memory is to prevent them from addressing the other programs' spaces at all. If the program only knows addresses from 0 to 4GB, and all of that space belongs to the program, then it can't possibly overwrite another piece of data. This is how Windows 2000 manages memory: Every process gets its own 4GB of virtual memory space, and it can do anything it wants in that space. Check out Figure 2.5 for a diagram of how this works.

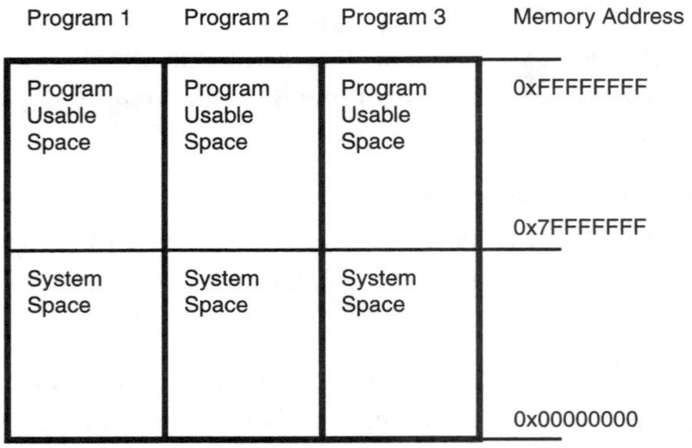

FIGURE 2.5
The virtual memory model. Each application has it's own memory space and doesn't even know about any other applications' memory spaces.

	Program 1	Program 2	Program 3	Memory Address
	Program Usable Space	Program Usable Space	Program Usable Space	0xFFFFFFFF
				0x7FFFFFFF
	System Space	System Space	System Space	
				0x00000000

Processes still have to ask the operating system for memory before they can use it, even though they have a full 4GB of address space. The reasoning behind this is simple: The memory manager has to know how much memory a process is using in order to know whether there's enough system memory for the program to run and so that the Virtual Memory Manager (VMM) knows how to address the memory.

There's another limit on processes. The 4GB of addressable memory is not all usable. Some of the memory space is only available for the system's use, and the rest is usable by the program. In Windows 2000 Professional and Windows 2000 Server, the breakup is 2GB each for system and application. In Windows 2000 Advanced Server and Windows 2000 Datacenter, the line moves to 3GB for the application and 1GB for the system. To enable this change, edit the file `BOOT.INI` on the system partition and add `/3GB` to the entry that will boot. For example, take a look at the following `BOOT.INI`. The entries in the `[operating systems]` section show the `/3GB` switch added to the Windows 2000 startup:

```
[boot loader]
timeout=30
default=multi(0)disk(0)rdisk(0)partition(2)\WINNT
[operating systems]
multi(0)disk(0)rdisk(0)partition(2)\WINNT=
     "Windows 2000 Advanced Server" /3GB
multi(0)disk(0)rdisk(0)partition(2)\WINNT=
     "Windows 2000 Advanced Server [VGA mode]" /basevideo /sos
```

In a real BOOT.INI, the lines don't break at the equal sign, they continue on. Due to publishing limitations, the lines were broken up.

In addition, in order for an application to use the new memory model, the operating system needs to know the application is able to use the memory. Therefore, a flag in the header of the EXE file called `IMAGE_FILE_LARGE_ADDRESS_AWARE` has to be turned on (set to 1). On the Windows 2000 Advanced Server CD in the Support folder, you'll find a program called IMAGECFG.EXE that will set this flag on an executable. For example, to change the file ACCRECV.EXE to use the larger memory model, the following command would be used:

Imagecfg -1 ACCRECV.EXE

This can be reversed by issuing an `imagecfg -0` command.

Memory Management

The Virtual Memory Manager (VMM) is charged with handling memory allocation, paging, and translating an application's request for a certain block of memory into a read for a block of physical memory.

We need to cover some key points before getting into memory management. Windows 2000 tries to make use of every bit of memory in the system, leaving a small amount available for program startup. If there aren't any applications using the memory, most of the memory in the system is used as disk cache by the operating system. As more memory is required, the VMM always keeps a certain amount of memory available for disk cache. If a computer is running as a file server, there isn't any way to tell Windows 2000 to use the memory for disk cache—it already does that.

Next, there's physical memory (chips inside the computer) and virtual memory (which is actually on the hard disk). Memory is divided into chunks called *pages*. A page is 4KB of memory, and it's the unit the VMM uses to push memory around. A page exists in at least one of three places: physical memory, the paging file, or on a list waiting to get paged out (called the *wait list*).

The VMM has to keep track of all the virtual memory allocated to a process and the status of that memory as well as whether it's actually in physical memory or has been paged to disk. The VMM also keeps track of whether an individual page contains code or data. The VMM knows the difference between code (executable programs loaded into memory) and data (information used by code). Code is read-only; data is read-write. This helps the VMM know when a program has "gone nuts" and started writing into memory it shouldn't. The VMM handles all the memory read and write requests, so it knows when a program has attempted to write into read-only data, and it prevents those types of situations.

The VMM also keeps track of the physical memory in the computer: which pages have been allocated, which process the pages belong to, and when the pages were last used (read or written to).

When the VMM receives a request to read a piece of data for a certain program from a certain memory location, the VMM consults a table that contains a list of all the pages that belong to the given program and a status bit that determines whether the page is in physical memory. If the information is in physical memory, the VMM hands the requested data back to the subsystem directly. If the information is not in physical memory, the VMM checks the wait list to see if the page is available there; then it will attempt to load the page from disk.

When the VMM cannot find the page available in memory, the resulting condition is a page fault. There are two types of page faults. A *hard page fault* is what happens when the VMM needs to find a page and it isn't in physical memory or the wait list. A *soft page fault* is what happens when the VMM needs to find a page in memory and the page doesn't exist in physical memory but does exist in the wait list. The VMM then restores the page back to physical memory without having to read it off the disk.

When the VMM needs to allocate memory, either as new memory for a program or to read a page from disk, it checks a table that contains the list of free pages. It then allocates the necessary number of pages of memory. When the system falls below a set threshold of free memory, the VMM will start a process to determine which pages get paged out. Remember how the VMM tracks when pages in physical memory get used? Well, that information is used to determine which pages get to stay in physical memory and which ones get flushed to disk.

The VMM decides which pages get put on the wait list based on the last time they were used. It uses an LRU (least recently used) algorithm to decide which pages get sent to disk. Pages that haven't been used in a while get sent to disk, whereas frequently used pages stay in memory.

To monitor this activity, a whole bunch of performance monitor flags are available. For detailed instructions about how to use the System Performance Monitor application, see Chapter 24, "Optimizing Performance Tuning" which covers performance monitoring.

Summary

Windows 2000 is a preemptively tasked microkernel operating system with memory protection, virtual memory, and several different mechanisms for running different types of programs. A preemptively tasked operating system allocates processor time to each process, and preempts the application when that time has elapsed. Memory protection makes the operating system more reliable since programs cannot change each other's data. Virtual memory allows the physical memory in a machine to be used by the data that is accessed the most, with the data that isn't accessed often being placed on disk. Windows 2000 supports different subsystems that enable it to run programs from OS/2 and POSIX.

CHAPTER 3

Installation Considerations

IN THIS CHAPTER

- System Requirements   *40*
- Hardware Compatibility List   *41*
- Installation Overview   *42*
- The Installation Process   *45*
- Automated Installation   *61*
- Installing the Recovery Console   *62*
- The BOOT.INI File   *65*
- The Emergency Repair Disk   *66*
- Migration from Preexisting Systems   *66*
- Advanced Hardware Notes   *67*

Looking back over Windows NT's past, nearly every review has mentioned its easy and well designed installation procedure. Windows 2000 is expected to get the same glowing reviews because the installation procedure is now even better. The key to a successful installation is still, however, adhering religiously to the Hardware Compatibility List.

This chapter will discuss the following aspects of installation:

- System requirements
- Hardware Compatibility List
- Installation options
- Licensing options
- Automated installation
- Installing the Recovery Console
- The `BOOT.INI` file
- The Emergency Repair Disk
- Migration
- Advanced hardware notes

Let's get started.

System Requirements

Windows 2000 does more than Windows NT 4.0, so it only makes sense that the hardware requirements are higher. Here are the base Windows 2000 requirements for Intel systems:

- At least one Pentium 166MHz or higher processor. Multiple processors are supported. Pentium II, Pentium III, and Xeon processors are included. Equivalent processors such as Cyrix and AMD processors are included.
- 64MB of RAM minimum, 128MB recommended. 8GB maximum for Advanced Server and 4GB for Server.
- A hard disk with a lot of available disk space. How much is a lot? Well, 850MB for the installation, plus 2MB for each 1MB of memory in the system. For example, if the system has 128MB of RAM, it would need 1,106MB (850MB + 128MB * 2). If this is a network installation instead of a CD-ROM installation, allow an additional 200MB for the temporary install files. If this is an upgrade to an existing Domain Controller and Active Directory is being implemented at the same time, allow a lot more disk space because the upgrade process uses up to 10 times as much space as the user accounts database.

- A VGA or better resolution monitor.
- A keyboard.
- A mouse or other pointing device is optional, but you won't get much done without one.
- For a CD-ROM installation, a CD-ROM drive, preferably at least 12× speed, and a 3.5-inch disk drive, unless the system can boot CD-ROMs.
- For network installations, a network card that's on the Hardware Compatibility List, and there has to be a copy of Windows 2000 on a server somewhere to install from.

Except where noted, these are minimum settings.

> **The Author's Setup**
>
> The installation on my desktop is Windows 2000 Advanced Server on a Pentium II at 233MHz, 96MB of RAM, an 8.4GB EIDE hard disk, a 52× ATAPI CD-ROM, two 9.1GB Ultra2 Wide SCSI drives, an Nvidia RIVA 128 AGP video card, and a Permedia 2 PCI video card, with full dual-monitor support.
>
> Dual-monitor support is new for Windows 2000. If you're considering implementing it, read the Hardware Compatibility List very carefully before purchasing hardware. Some motherboards require some odd settings in order to support two video cards. Be sure to check with your motherboard's manufacturer.
>
> The 9.1GB SCSI drives were installed to do the research on Chapter, 4, "File Systems." They're outrageously fast for an overgrown workstation and are definite overkill for writing. The CD-ROM is a Kenwood 52× TrueX CD-ROM; it makes installations go very quickly.

Hardware Compatibility List

Possibly the most important piece of documentation that involves Windows 2000 is the Hardware Compatibility List (HCL). This is the list of all the hardware on which Windows 2000 is supported. This is the list of systems, network cards, disk controllers, printers, and other devices that are supported by Windows 2000. The list of devices is kept online by Microsoft at http://www.microsoft.com/hwtest/hcl/.

> **Note**
>
> Microsoft has a very bad habit of publishing URLs and then changing the location of the content. About half the URLs in the SQL Server 7.0 Help files don't work, for example, because Microsoft changed the URL scheme. If the article you're looking for doesn't show up, try using the Search feature of Microsoft's Web site.

The Hardware Compatibility List represents a list of all the hardware that Microsoft has tested and validated to work with Windows 2000. Usually, the manufacturer of the hardware has provided the driver to Microsoft, who then tests the hardware and updates the compatibility list. However, to cover the expenses of this, Microsoft charges the hardware vendor a nominal fee, for which the vendor gets its name in the HCL if it passes. Over the years, some vendors have elected not to pay Microsoft and just provide the necessary drivers with their hardware. This involves some risk on the part of the user, because Microsoft support can easily claim that the problem is not Windows 2000 but rather a bad driver. To avoid this kind of problem, only get hardware on the HCL.

Installation Overview

The installation process has to accomplish certain things. It has to ensure that Windows 2000 system files are copied to the system partition, and then it has to configure Windows 2000 to work with the hardware on the machine. Next, the installation has to configure Windows 2000 to participate on the network (it wouldn't be much of a server if it wasn't on a network). This section provides an overview of the installation process.

First, the system has to boot Windows 2000. This is either done by booting from a CD-ROM, which immediately boots Windows 2000, or by running the WINNT32.EXE program from Windows NT or Windows 9x, or by running WINNT.EXE from a command line. Either way, the program will set up the hard disk to boot Windows 2000.

When starting Windows 2000 setup using the WINNT32.EXE or WINNT.EXE program, you can use command line switches to make setup an easier task. Here are the switches used with WINNT.EXE:

- /s:[sourcepath]. The path to the source of the Windows 2000 files, such as d:\i386. This can also be a network path, such as \\intrepid\install\i386. If this isn't specified, the setup program will prompt you for the location.
- /t:[temppath]. The path that temporary files will be placed on. These are the files required to boot Windows 2000. If this isn't specified, the setup program will try to find a drive to put the files onto.

- `/u:[answer file]`. The name of the "answer file." See the upcoming section on automated setup for details.
- `/udf:id[,UDF File]`. The ID number used to get unique information from the UDF file. The UDF file is the *uniqueness database file*, and it's used by automated setup for all the questions that require unique answers. See the upcoming section on automated setup for details.
- `/r:[folder]`. The path to a directory to be installed by the setup program. The directory will continue to exist after setup completes. This is normally used to install the special drivers to the hard disk of the computer being installed after setup in order to make changing or adding drivers easier.
- `/rx:[folder]`. The path to a folder that will be installed by setup but removed after setup completes.
- `/e:[command]`. Specifies a command to be run when the GUI part of setup completes.
- `/a`. Specifies that the Accessibility options should be turned on when setup completes.

Because the `WINNT.EXE` program is designed to run from within a booted command prompt or MS-DOS, it will have different options than `WINNT32.EXE`, which is designed to run from within a command prompt started from Windows 95, Windows 98, Windows NT, or Windows 2000. The `WINNT32.EXE` program takes the following command-line parameters:

- `/s:[sourcepath]`. The path to Windows 2000 source files, such as `d:\i386`.
- `/tempdrive:[Drive Letter]`. The drive to use for temporary files.
- `/unattend`. If this switch is present on the command line, setup will run a fully unattended setup. This will bypass the display of the End User License Agreement (EULA). It shouldn't be used by OEMs who are installing Windows 2000 for resale. OEM's, or Original Equipment Manufacturers, are computer manufacturers who install Microsoft operating systems before shipping the computers to the user. It should be used by corporations who are installing Windows 2000 for use inside the company.
- `/unattend[id]:[answer_file]`. This switch specifies the UDF ID for the setup and the path to the answer file. See the upcoming section on automated setup for details.
- `/copydir:[folder]`. This switch creates a folder inside the Windows 2000 directory that will stay around after setup completes. It's similar to the `/r` switch of `WINNT.EXE`.

- /copysource:[folder_name]. This switch creates a folder similar to the /copydir switch, but it will remove the folder when setup is complete.
- /cmd:[command_line]. A full command line to be run after the GUI mode of setup is complete.
- /debug[level]:[filename]. The level of debugging information that should be kept and the file the debugging information should be written to.
- /udf:id[,UDB File]. The ID number in the UDF file that should be used for this machine. See the upcoming section on automated setup for details.
- /syspart:[drive letter]. When this switch is specified, setup will copy the files necessary to a hard disk partition, mark the partition active so it will boot, and then stop setup. The hard disk can then be removed and put into another machine, where setup will resume. This switch will only run from Windows NT or Windows 2000; it's not available from Windows 9x. It must be used with the /Tempdrive switch.
- /checkupgradeonly. This switch causes setup to not install anything; instead, it just checks to make sure the machine can be upgraded from its current operating system. For a Windows 9x machine, there will be a report called Upgrade.TXT in the Windows directory. For Windows NT machines, there will be a winnt32.log file in the Windows NT folder (usually \winnt).
- /cmdcons:. Installs the Recovery Console. This is only used after Windows 2000 is successfully installed.
- /m:[folder]. If this switch is present, Windows 2000 will replace the Windows 2000 installation with the files in the specified folder.
- /makelocalsource. This will copy the installation directory to the hard drive of the machine being installed to make it easier to add and remove components later.
- /noreboot. This switch will cause setup to not automatically reboot at the end of copying files so that other commands can be executed.

After Windows 2000 boots, it will determine whether this is an upgrade or a new installation. For new installations, the setup program will guide you through creating disk partitions and formatting at least a system partition for use with Windows 2000. For upgrades, the system must use the same system partition as the system being upgraded.

Windows 2000 setup will then begin copying files to the system partition, and after it's done, the system will restart.

When the system boots again, it will start Windows 2000 in a graphical mode and will then ask you a series of questions to help get Windows 2000 configured properly. These are questions about licensing, installation paths, and so on. During this phase, Windows 2000 performs device discovery, which will take a long time (up to 15 minutes).

After discovering and configuring the devices, Windows 2000 will ask a few more questions about setting up the network. There aren't any questions about joining a domain or being a Domain Controller; all Windows 2000 servers are installed as standalone servers, and after the installation, you can change the setup to a Domain Controller. This is a vast improvement over Windows NT, where the decision gets made once and the only way to change from a standalone server to a domain controller was through reinstallation of the system.

After installation, the system is ready to be configured for domain membership, if necessary, and the system will allow other services to be configured or installed.

That's a brief road map of what's coming up in the next section. Now let's take an in-depth look at the entire installation process.

The Installation Process

The installation process involves booting Windows 2000, configuring Windows 2000, and then configuring Windows 2000 network access.

Booting Windows 2000

Windows 2000 can install from either a CD-ROM or from disk. For CD-ROM installations, the best course to take is to put the CD-ROM in the drive and reboot. The CD-ROM will boot Windows 2000, and the installation process will begin.

For installs from disk, whether it's a local disk or a remote disk, run `WINNT32.EXE` from Windows 95, Windows 98, or Windows NT or run `WINNT.EXE` from a command prompt. This will make a copy of the files that are normally booted from CD-ROM onto the system; then the system will reboot and begin installation at the same point as if the CD-ROM had been booted in the first place. One key thing to remember about setting up from disk is that the system partition must exist before Windows 2000 can be installed. Basically, the WINNT program copies all of the files to disk, and these files can't be removed during installation, so the system can't repartition the disks during setup if the setup was started using WINNT.

The Windows 2000 boot process has to figure out what kind of disk media are available to install from. Basically, it has to scan the machine and find all the IDE and SCSI adapters in the system. If the adapter in the machine was available when Windows 2000 shipped, there won't be any problem, and the system will detect the SCSI adapter and start up. Otherwise, you may need a disk from the hardware vendor to load the adapter drivers during the load process. At the very beginning of the boot process, there's a point where the system will prompt you to hit F6 to install a third-party adapter. If the adapter won't install from the Windows 2000 installation media, this option *must* be used to set up the drivers necessary to complete the boot process.

If Windows 2000 cannot boot, the installation will terminate with an `INACCESSIBLE_BOOT_DEVICE` message. This message occurs when Windows 2000 is unable to boot from the partition that it set up to boot from. This should only occur when the adapter for that disk isn't available or if there was some user intervention that made the setup partition unusable.

The first screen in the boot process where user intervention is requested is shown in Figure 3.1, which shows three different options. The first option is to set up Windows 2000, which is the option you'll probably want. The second option is to repair an existing installation, which is done by pressing the R key. This option is used to repair installations and is described fully in the later section on the Emergency Repair Disk. The final option listed is to abort setup, which is accomplished by pressing the F3 key.

FIGURE 3.1
This is the first screen where Windows 2000 setup forces you to make a decision. Press the Enter key to continue with setup.

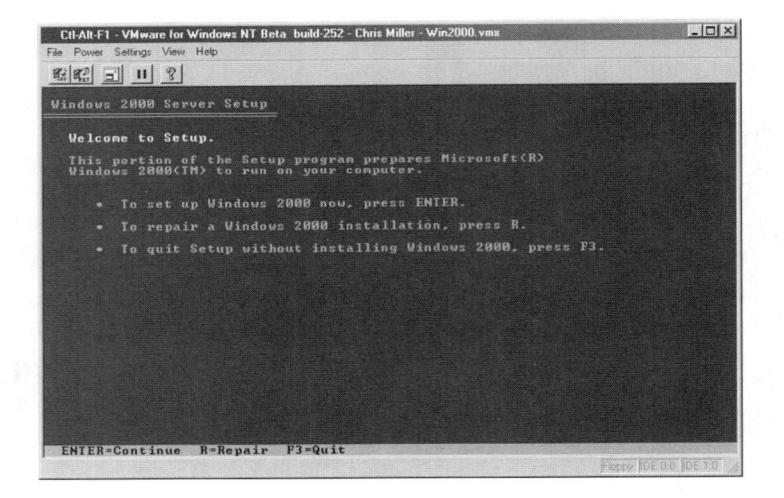

The setup program then checks to see which disks are available for installing Windows 2000. First, it checks to see whether there are any formatted partitions available, and it will ask you to confirm its findings if it cannot find any partitions on the disk. If there are disks available, the setup program will check to see whether there's a system partition and whether the system partition has an operating system on it. Next, the system will check to see whether the existing operating system can be upgraded. If there's already an operating system, you'll be asked whether the installation should be a new installation or an upgrade from the previous version.

At this point you'll be required to agree to a license agreement. Press the Page Down key to get to the bottom and then press the F8 key to accept the license agreement. You should read the EULA at least once, but it gets old reading it every time you install the operating system.

For new installations, there will be an added step of setting up a disk partition on which to install Windows 2000. This is done with the screen shown in Figure 3.2. On this screen, the C key will create a new partition. To delete a partition, use the arrow keys to highlight the partition and press the D key. Windows 2000 setup has a system that allows the entire disk to be partitioned. Be warned, however, if the installation is occurring from disk or from a network drive, the partition that contains the temporary Windows 2000 setup files shouldn't be deleted. Otherwise, setup will fail.

FIGURE 3.2
The setup program needs to know where to install the operating system. In this case, there's only one disk, so press the C key to create a partition.

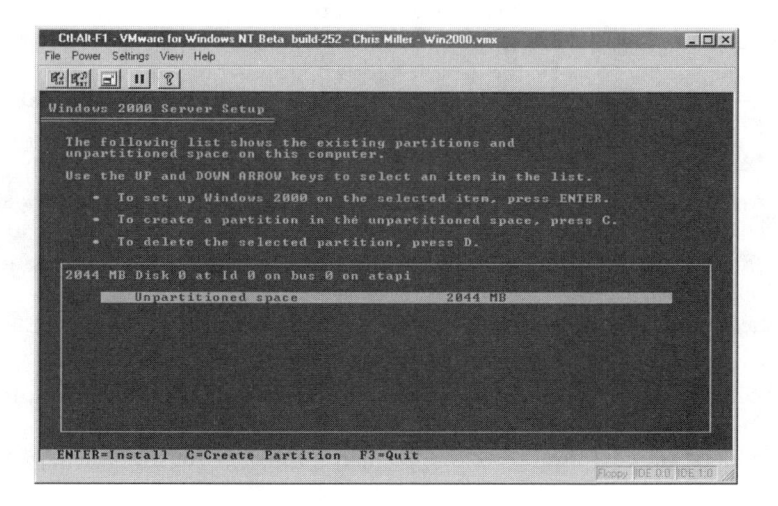

Disk Partition Layouts for Installation

There is some amount of controversy about which file systems and disk layouts are best when installing Windows 2000. Mostly, this controversy stems from the inability to boot an operating system that can access partitions formatted with the NTFS file system. There are two schools of thought on this: boot FAT and boot NTFS. If you don't know what FAT and NTFS are, go read the file systems section in Chapter 4, "File Systems."

continues

> The folks in the "boot FAT" camp have a lot of compelling reasons on their side. First of all, there are a lot of different disk utilities available to diagnose and repair FAT partitions but very few available for NTFS. In addition, it's nice to be able to boot from a floppy disk and replace files that are in use, because when Windows 2000 is running, some files can't be overwritten. Also, because the system partition is very rarely written to, there isn't a lot of need for the additional overhead of transaction logging that's associated with the NTFS file system, so using FAT actually increases performance.
>
> The folks in the "boot NTFS" camp thinks that the boot partition should be formatted with NTFS so it can be secured using NTFS file permissions. Also, they claim the fact that NTFS isn't reachable during a floppy drive boot is an important security feature, because it keeps people from walking up to the server, booting the server with a floppy, and walking away with information.
>
> The common solution to this dilemma has been to use FAT on boot partitions on servers that are physically secure and to use NTFS on servers that don't have the same level of security. If the server is physically secure, that means only trusted people are able to boot the system off a floppy, which would allow all the features of booting from a FAT partition. If the server is not physically secure, NTFS should be booted to prevent users from booting the machine and accessing files.
>
> Another way to approach this problem is to use NTFS always but install the Recovery Console, which will be discussed a little later in this chapter. Active Directory services require the boot partition to be NTFS, so this whole question may be moot if the server is a Domain Controller for a Windows 2000 Active Directory.

After you choose the system partition, Windows 2000 will prepare the system partition for the next phase of setup. Usually, this involves removing parts of the old operating system for an upgrade installation and then installing the new system files into the Windows 2000 directory, which still defaults to C:\WINNT. The File Copy screen is shown in Figure 3.3. After the system finishes copying files, it will reboot and the configuration phase will begin.

Installation Considerations
CHAPTER 3

FIGURE 3.3
The File Copy screen appears when the system is copying to disk the files necessary to run Windows 2000.

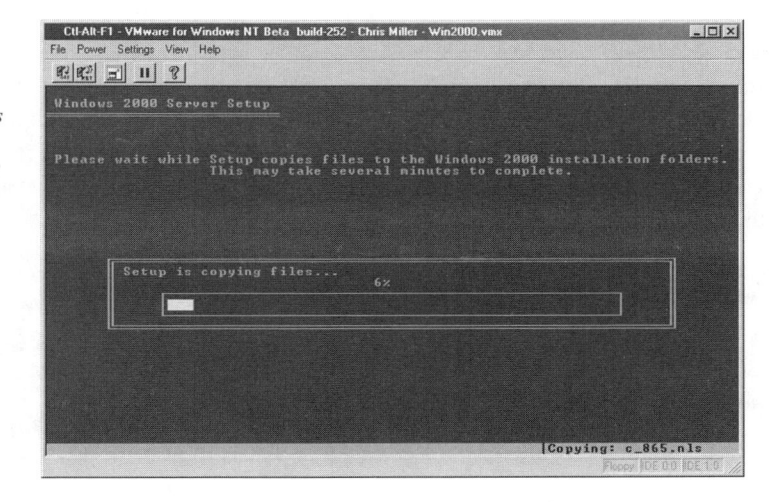

How Are You Taking These Pictures?

During the text-based portion of setup, there's no way to run any programs, much less the sophisticated screen-capture programs required to take pictures for this book. So, where are the installation screenshots coming from?

A company called VMWare makes a product called *VMWare for Windows NT*. It's a virtual machine product that allows an operating system to run a full simulation of another computer, complete with BIOS, network card, operating system, sound, and graphics. It's a very cool product and can be used to run Linux, Windows NT, Windows 9*x*, or Windows 2000 in a window on a system running Windows NT, Windows 2000, or Linux. It creates a file on disk to simulate the hard disk for the virtual machine and provides network access by bridging over from the virtual machine to the system.

Using VMWare is a little slower than running natively, but my system performed flawlessly even without the full hardware requirements for VMWare met. This is a very good product that provides an interesting alternative to dual-booting.

These screenshots were taken with a beta version of the VMWare product. You can visit VMWare at `http://www.vmware.com`.

Upgrade Information

During an upgrade installation of Windows 2000, the system will remove most of the Windows NT installation, at least with respect to system files, and will then replace the system files as part of the Windows 2000 installation. The upgrade will preserve user and system settings and will preserve application registration, so there's no need to reinstall applications after an upgrade.

Drivers and driver configuration is not preserved during an upgrade. For example, if there's support for a certain sound card in Windows NT 4.0, and Windows 2000 doesn't support that sound card, the sound card isn't going to work in Windows 2000 because Windows 2000 cannot use drivers from Windows NT 4.0. Same concept applies to upgrades from Windows 98.

In addition, there are some file location changes between new installations of Windows 2000 and upgrades. In Windows NT 4.0, user profile information was stored in `C:\WINNT\PROFILES`. Now, the same information is stored in `C:\Documents and Settings`. If the system is installed from an upgrade, however, Windows 2000 will not move the files; instead, it will just continue to use the `C:\WINNT\PROFILES` path.

Configuring Windows 2000

After Windows 2000 setup finishes the text-mode file-copy process, it will reboot the system and the configuration phase will begin. The system will boot into Windows 2000, as shown in Figure 3.4, and then the process of configuring the system will begin by starting the Windows 2000 Setup Wizard.

FIGURE 3.4
Windows 2000 booting into GUI mode for the first time.

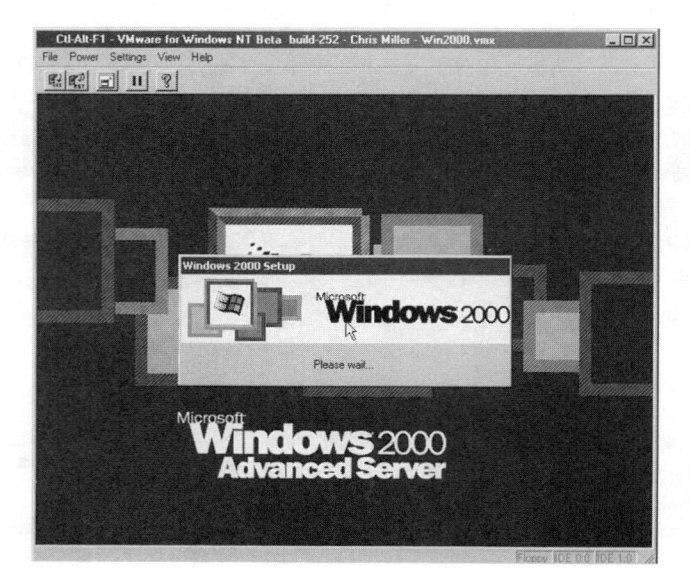

Then, Windows 2000 begins looking for devices. If all the devices in the system are on the Windows 2000 HCL, there's nothing to worry about—the system will probe the system and locate all the hardware it can and will then configure the drivers for the hardware. This process takes a long time (15 minutes to a half hour in some cases). The screen will flash several times as the system probes to find out what kind of video hardware is present. The system will stop a few times as it queries the serial ports, which have long time-out intervals. Go grab some coffee, sit back, relax, and watch the pretty blinking lights for a while.

If the system hangs for an unreasonable amount of time with no disk activity, the mouse won't move, and the keyboard isn't responding, you should wait for at least 15 minutes before doing anything. Certain devices are probed that take a long time to respond and for the setup program to configure properly. If the installation is on a laptop, make sure the floppy drive is plugged in, because it's possible that the system is waiting for a response from the floppy drive before proceeding.

Next, setup asks you where you live and what kind of keyboard you have. The system defaults to the standards for U.S. English; to change them, click the Customize buttons shown in Figure 3.5.

FIGURE 3.5

The internationalization interface for the setup program. To change languages or keyboards, click one of the Customize buttons.

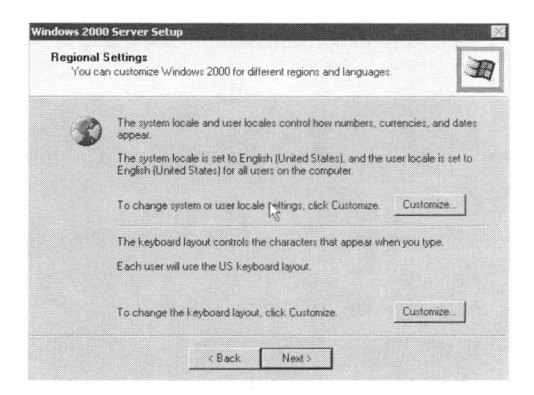

The next setup screen asks some questions about ownership and licensing. The ownership question asks who you are and what business the software should be registered to. The next screen asks about licensing, which is covered in the section titled "Licensing Options," later in this chapter. If you're not sure about which licensing option to choose, go with the default, because the default is Per Server, and it can be upgraded to Per Seat. However, if you choose Per Seat, you can never go back to Per Server.

Next, the computer name and administrator password have to be entered into the window shown in Figure 3.6. The default computer name will be a combination of the name entered in the ownership screen and a randomly generated number. This is done because all the computer names have to be unique on a network, and by going with a randomly generated number, the chances of two machines having the same name are reduced. Pick out a computer name for the server that's descriptive and unique. The administrator password is the password for the local administrator's account. It should be a secure password that's easy to remember.

FIGURE 3.6
The Computer Name and Administrator Password dialog box requires a unique computer name to be entered.

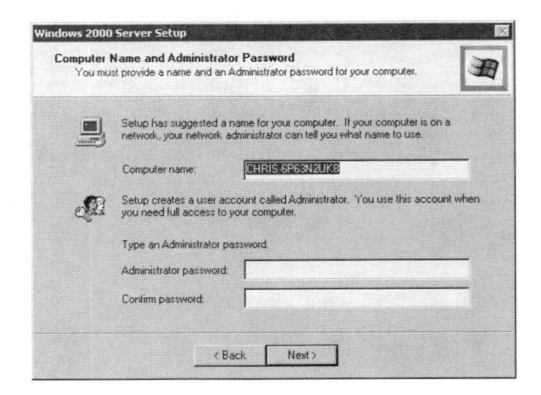

Finally, there are some optional components. The components are broken down into the following categories:

- *Accessories and Utilities*. This includes most of the user interface utilities and goodies. The Accessibility Wizard utility helps folks with disabilities to use the computer by providing various services.
- *Accessories*. This category is actually part of the Accessories and Utilities category. It includes the following accessories:
    - *Calculator*. A simple calculator program that's useful for calculating anything from simple addition to network masks.
    - *Character Map*. Allows the keyboard map to be changed to allow different characters to be assigned to different keys.
    - *Desktop Wallpaper*. Desktop Wallpaper is a collection of background bitmaps for display on the desktop.
    - *Document Templates*. Templates for use in WordPad.
    - *Mouse Pointers*. A package that includes various animated mouse pointers. Access the mouse pointers through Control Panel, Mouse and check out the Pointers tab.
    - *Object Packager*. Creates and imbeds linked documents in various system applications. Very rarely used.

- *Paint*. A very simple paint program. Normally used for simple screenshots (Press Ctrl+PrintScrn and then paste into PaintBrush).
- *Screen Savers*. OpenGL and standard screen savers.
- *WordPad*. A simple but very handy word-processing program.
- *Communications*. This item contains three components:
    - *Chat*. A network-based chat program that allows two parties to type messages back and forth to each other. Requires the NetDDE service on both machines.
    - *HyperTerminal*. The very poor replacement for Windows Terminal. HyperTerminal controls modems and dial-up using a very bad user interface that makes it difficult to use for direct terminal communications, which is the main uses for HyperTerminal anyway.
    - *Phone Dialer*. If the machine has a modem in it, you can put phone numbers into the phone dialer and have it dial for you. (For the chronically lazy only.)
- *Games*. Includes four classic Windows games: FreeCell, MineSweeper, Space Cadet Pinball, and Solitaire.
- *Multimedia*. CD-ROM and sound card programs, including sound schemes, volume control, and a CD player application.
- *Certificate Services*. These two components, Certificate Services CA and Certificate Services Web Enrollment Support, are used to support public certificates for encryption and user verification.
- *Cluster Services*. Available only in the Advanced Server version. This option will install all the programs to set up and enable Windows 2000 clustering.
- *Indexing Service*. This is a service that can maintain the locations of all the filenames and file properties across a server to speed the process of searching for files.
- *Internet information Services (IIS)*. Allows Windows 2000 to provide standard Internet services, based on which subcomponents are installed.
    - *Common Files*. Required if any of the other IIS options is chosen.
    - *Documentation*. Documentation for all the services (in HTML format for easy reading).
    - *File Transfer Protocol (FTP) Server*. Implements the standard FTP protocol, which allows client machines to send and receive files from the server.
    - *FrontPage 2000 Server Extensions*. Extensions that are required in order for the IIS Server to publish webs made with FrontPage 2000.
    - *Internet Information Services Snap-In*. The IIS Snap-In allows IIS to be managed from within the MMC (Microsoft Management Console).

- *Internet Services Manager*. This allows all of the Internet services to be managed using HTML. Only works if the WWW Publishing Service is running.
- *NNTP Service*. Allows the server to operate as a network news transfer server.
- *SMTP Service*. Allows the server to provide SMTP services, which is the Internet-standard mail system. This allows mailboxes and forwarding routes to be set up on the system.
- *Visual InterDev RAD Remote Deployment Support*. Allows Visual InterDev to remotely deploy applications (components and ASP pages) to the server.
- *World Wide Web Server*. Allows the server to serve HTML pages, and process and serve ASP.

- *Management and Monitoring Tools*. These are tools used to manage Windows 2000 and monitor the network interface on a Windows 2000 server.
  - *Connection Manager Components*. This manages virtual private networking phone books and connections.
  - *Network Monitor Tools*. This is Microsoft's protocol analysis tool, otherwise known as a *packet sniffer*. These tools need to be installed along with the Network Monitor Agent in Network Setup.
  - *Simple Network Management Protocol (SNMP)*. The protocol used for remotely monitoring equipment and servers over the Internet.

- *Message Queuing Services*. The Microsoft Message Queue (MMQ) is only available on Windows 2000 Advanced Server, and it's a high-reliability, end-to-end component, message-transfer service used by some programs to communicate across a network.

- *Networking Services*. The files and systems necessary to have network access.
  - *COM Internet Services Proxy*. Allows COM objects to communicate using the HTTP protocol, enabling them to pass through many proxy servers and firewalls successfully.
  - *Directory Service Migration Tool*. The tool used to migrate from Novell's Directory Services to Microsoft's Active Directory. Requires and installs Gateway Services for NetWare.
  - *Domain Name System (DNS)*. The Internet-standard naming system, now required for Active Directory. DNS translates from a network name (such as www.microsoft.com) to an IP address (such as 207.46.130.50).
  - *Dynamic Host Configuration Protocol (DHCP)*. The protocol used to grant IP addresses to workstations on a network.

- *Internet Authentication Services.* Allows the authentication of incoming VPN (virtual private networking) and dial-up networking connections via RADIUS.
- *QoS Admission Control Service.* Monitors and meters incoming network traffic, allowing high-priority packets to receive higher levels of service.
- *Simple TCP/IP Services.* Includes simple services such as Quote of the Day (fortune), Character Generator, Daytime, Discard, and Echo.
- *Site Server ILS Services.* Monitors and maintains user information.
- *Windows Internet Name Services (WINS).* A deprecated protocol. Replaced by the vastly superior and more standard DNS.
- *Other Network File and Print Services.* Contains components such as File and Print Services for Macintosh as well as Print Services for UNIX.
- *Remote Installation Service.* Allows Windows 2000 Professional to be installed onto machines that have remote boot–enabled network hardware.
- *Remote Storage.* Used to install less-frequently-used files on magnetic tape or other removable media. See Chapter 4 for more information.
- *Script Debugger.* Allows scripts written in VBScript and JScript to be debugged.
- *Terminal Services and Terminal Services Licensing.* This is only available in Advanced Server installations.

Those are a lot of different components. Any components that aren't installed during setup can be added later using Control Panel, Add Remove Software, Windows Setup. Most of the time, for a server, most of the accessories, except for WordPad and Calculator, are turned off. Other services are only installed if needed and can even cause problems if they're installed when they aren't needed (DHCP, for example).

Network Configuration

The next step in the setup process is network configuration. The new default settings for Windows 2000 are TCP/IP Only, File and Print Sharing for Microsoft Networks, and the Microsoft Networks Client. TCP/IP is configured using DHCP by default. If these settings will work in your environment, use the Typical Settings option. Otherwise, you'll have to go through the Custom Settings path.

The Custom Settings path starts with all the typical settings stuff installed, and it allows components to be added or removed as necessary using the dialog box shown in Figure 3.7.

FIGURE 3.7
This is how network settings are established during setup. Click the Install button to add components.

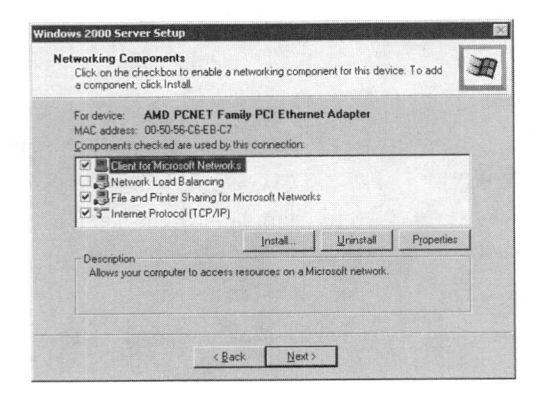

To add components, click the Install button. This will bring up a list of component types. There are three component types: Client, Service, and Protocol. A *client* is a component that allows a logged-on user to connect to another machine. A *service* is a resource to be installed on the local machine that other computers can access over the network. A *protocol* is the how the machines will access services on this computer, and how this computer's client will talk to other computer's services. An example of a client is the Client for Microsoft Networks, which allows the local machine to connect to other Windows servers. An example of a service is File and Print Services for Microsoft Networks, which allows other computers to access the local machine as a file server. An example of a protocol is TCP/IP, which allow servers to talk to clients.

Click the type of component to add and then click the Add button. Then choose the component from the list and click OK. Some components require other components (for example, the Client Service for NetWare requires the NWLink protocol). In that case, the setup program will install all the dependencies to make the selected component work.

To configure an existing component, choose the component from the list and click the Properties button. For the Internet Protocol (TCP/IP) component, the component can either be configured automatically via DHCP or manually. There are three required settings for TCP/IP setup: IP Address, Subnet Mask, and Default Gateway. The IP address has to be unique on that network, and it has to be numeric. An example of an IP address is 10.1.1.3. The subnet mask identifies which part of the IP address is used to identify the network and which part is used to identify the particular computer. A subnet mask of 255.0.0.0 means that the first part of the address is used to identify the network, and the rest is used to identify the individual computer. All the subnet masks on a network must be identical. For more information on subnet masks, see Chapter 8, "TCP/IP Networking." The default gateway is an IP address in the local subnet of a device that knows how to get to other subnets. This is the IP address of the local router.

Now, this may seem like a lot of stuff to keep straight, and it's really a management nightmare. Therefore, Microsoft also implemented a standard called *DHCP*, the Dynamic Host Configuration Protocol, which allows computers to get their network information from a server on the network that's configured to get this information. Choosing the Obtain IP Address Automatically option will force the system to use DHCP for network configuration.

In addition, the network probably has at least one DNS server. A DNS server is used to take an IP address (10.1.1.3) and turn it into a nice friendly name (intrepid). The DNS server address can be entered manually or acquired via DHCP. If the network is using Active Directory services, then you'll need to have a DNS server.

Other TCP/IP related services can be installed at this time. For more information about how to install these services or how these services are configured see Chapter 8.

> **Note**
>
> During setup, install the minimum amount of network protocols and services necessary to get the server online and communicating with other servers. This will reduce the number of things that have to be examined if there's a problem with installation. Simplifying troubleshooting is a very worthy cause. Protocols and services can always be added after installation. See Chapter 15, "Multiprotocol Environments," for more details on installing protocols.

In addition, some other protocols can be installed at the time of setup. The AppleTalk protocol is used to communicate with Apple computers, including the Macintosh. The DLC protocol is normally used to connect to old print server devices, such as older versions of the HP JetDirect. The NetBEUI protocol is an old protocol that's (hopefully) dying out as the primary LAN Manager protocol. The Network Monitor Driver protocol is used by the Microsoft Network Monitor to watch packets go by on the network.

Last but not least, the NWLink protocol, which is Microsoft's implementation of IPX/SPX is also included. This protocol is used to communicate with Novell NetWare servers. Each of these protocols are discussed in more depth in Chapter 15.

By default, the system installs the TCP/IP protocol, which is helpfully noted as the Internet Protocol. Then the File and Printer Sharing for Microsoft Networks service is added, and the Client for Microsoft Networks provides access to other Windows 2000 and Windows NT servers available on the network.

Also, optional services and client software can be installed. There are two additional services that can be installed. The first is the QoS Packet Scheduler, which works with routers to communicate Quality of Services information. The SAP Agent, another service, is also used in conjunction with Novell NetWare and is useful for communicating server information.

When all the network information is selected, click Next, and the system will prompt you for the role of this computer in the grand scheme of the entire network. A server can be a standalone server, or it can be part of a domain. If the server is not on a network, or if there's no domain, choose the No option; otherwise, choose the Yes option. At any rate, put the name of the workgroup or domain in the box at the bottom of the dialog box, which is shown in Figure 3.8.

FIGURE 3.8
This dialog allows you to choose whether or not the computer will be participating in a domain, and to pick the domain it will use.

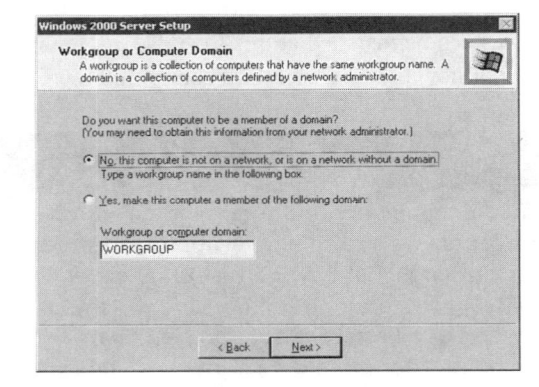

When network configuration is complete, Windows 2000 will set up the rest of the operating system. Mainly, this involves installing components into the Registry and removing temporary files. If the system partition was formatted with NTFS, the installation program will set the permissions on the system files so that administrators have access to what they need while securing the system files.

Licensing Options

Microsoft has to get paid for all of this, and the way it measures its payment is by keeping track of the number of users on a server. Licensing is a very complex topic, and it requires a very good understanding of not only the legal language of licensing but also which license your organization is using to buy Windows 2000 services with. Also, just to make things more confusing, Microsoft has been known to completely revamp its licensing structures to make them simpler. When Microsoft says it's making licensing simpler, though, it's a lot like the U.S. government simplifying the tax code: The forms get longer, and most people end up paying more.

There are two sides to the licensing story for Windows 2000 Server. The Server license is a license that allows you to install and use Windows 2000 Server on one computer. A client license allows you to access Windows 2000 Server from one computer on the network.

One of the key things to remember is that a Windows 2000 Server license can be considered a File and Print license. That means if the server is being used to store files or host printers, each client that accesses the server must have a client license, and each server must have a server license. If the server is being used for SQL Server or Exchange Server and isn't being used for File and Print services, Windows 2000 Server client licenses aren't required, but a Windows 2000 Server license and a SQL Server or Exchange Server server license is required along with SQL Server or Exchange Server client licenses.

In other words, for an Exchange Server that's hosting mailboxes, the required licenses would include a Windows 2000 Server license, an Exchange Server server license, and one Exchange Server client license for each client that will be accessing Exchange Server.

If a machine is being used as a File and Print server, a Windows 2000 Server license is required, plus one client access license for each client.

There are two types of client licenses. A *per-seat* license means that each client computer needs one license, and it can access as many servers as it wants. A *per-server* license means that each server needs as many client licenses as there will be simultaneous client connections. Microsoft really pushes everyone to use the per-seat licensing because it's easier to administer for the system administrators and has a lot more flexibility because each client is licensed and can then access all the servers it wants. The per-server license is a lot more complicated because it requires the administrator to actually pay attention to how many clients are currently attached to a server. Per-seat and per-server licenses cost the same amount of money, and a server configured to use per-server licensing can be switched to per-seat licensing once, and the change cannot be undone. Therefore, once the server is licensed as "per seat," it has to stay that way.

The next sections present a couple scenarios to help explain the difference between the per-server and per-client licensing.

Scenario 1: Per-Server Licensing

The XYZ company runs a service center, and each employee has his or her own computer. The service center has one server and 60 employees. Only a third of the computers are in use at any given time. This company can buy 20 per-server licenses for the server or 60 per-client licenses.

Scenario 2: Per-Client Licensing

The XYZ company expands the service center's computing capacity by ordering four additional servers to store files on and to host printers. At that point, it can either continue to buy per-server licenses and purchase an additional 60 licenses (for a total of 80 licenses), or it can purchase an additional 40 licenses and then convert all its licenses to per-seat licenses. Converting to per-seat licenses allows each client to connect to as many servers as it wants, so it's more economical to convert to per-seat licensing.

Licensing is controlled in the License Manager application, which is launched in Control Panel. During installation, you have to choose per-seat or per-server licensing. If you choose per-server licensing, you must enter the number of client licenses that have been purchased for that server. If you choose per-seat licensing, you must use the License Manager application to set up the number of licenses purchased. The License Manager will automatically share licensing information with other servers in the domain when the server is in per-seat licensing mode. Warning messages are logged to the Windows 2000 Event Log whenever the number of licenses are exceeded.

To add licenses, go to Control Panel and open the "Licensing" application. Figure 3.9 shows the application. In the figure, the server is set up with per-server licensing for five licenses. To convert to per-seat licensing, choose the Per Seat option. To view the licensing for other products installed on the server, click the down arrow to view the list of installed licensable products.

FIGURE 3.9
The License Manager application. To add licenses, click Add. To convert to per-seat licensing, click Per Seat.

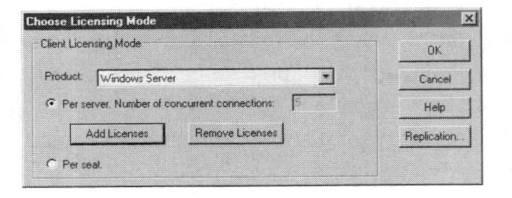

To add licenses, click the Add button and choose the number of licenses purchased. Licenses can also be removed by clicking the Remove Licenses button.

This application works great for handling licenses of Windows 2000 Server, but it doesn't work as well for dealing with other licenses. In addition, there's also a need to see what licenses are on other machines and convert to per-seat licensing for all applications. To perform these operations, you'll need the License Manager application. To start the License Manager, go to Start, Programs, Administrative Tools, Licensing. The licensing application will start up on the Purchase History tab, showing all the license purchases that have been made. To view all the licensable products, click Products View and see the list. By default, the only products listed are Windows Server and Microsoft BackOffice. A BackOffice license is a client license for any of the BackOffice products (Windows 2000, SQL Server, Exchange Server, Systems Management Server, and SNA Server).

> **Note**
>
> Certain BackOffice products, such as SMS, require per-seat licensing and are not compatible with per-server licensing.

To view the number of per-seat licenses and which users are using those licenses, click the Clients (Per Seat) tab. This will show all the users who have ever used a product, and which products they've used. When a user leaves the company, he or she can be removed from this screen and his or her license will go back into the pool for another new user.

Per-seat licensing also doesn't prevent access to applications. Instead, it allows the applications to be used but puts recurring messages into the Windows 2000 Event Log.

Automated Installation

Microsoft has supplied tools for automating the setup process to make deployments to a large number of machines more efficient. This process involves creating two separate files: an answer file, which contains answers to all the questions that are asked by Setup, and a uniqueness database file (UDF), which will override the answers in the answer file with specific settings for a given machine, such as the computer name.

Microsoft supplies a file called UNATTEND.TXT that provides a baseline for the unattended setup installation. The file is a basic INI file format, with section names in brackets, followed by a list of value names and values. Any line starting with a semicolon is a comment. An example section is shown here:

```
[GuiUnattended]
; Sets the Timezone to the Pacific Northwest
; Sets the Admin Password to NULL
; Turn AutoLogon ON and login once
TimeZone = "004"
AdminPassword = *
AutoLogon = Yes
AutoLogonCount = 1
```

The section is called `GuiUnattended`, and the next three lines are comments because they start with semicolons. Finally, there are four values in the section, and the first one is called `TimeZone` and has a value of `"004"`.

There's a full set of options available on Microsoft's Web site in the support section, which has changed URLs so often that putting a URL in this book would be silly. Just go to www.microsoft.com and click the Support icon.

Installing the Recovery Console

The Recovery Console is a Windows 2000 boot option that will start a command line that will have access to all the NTFS shares on the system and will enable some very important operations, such as replacing files and changing boot options. This is very helpful when a server has stopped booting because of a driver problem or when a file needs to be replaced that's in use when Windows 2000 is running.

To install the Recovery Console, first complete the Windows 2000 installation. Then, from a Windows 2000 command line, go to the directory that contains the Windows 2000 setup program and type in this:

`Winnt32 /cmdcons`

The dialog box shown in Figure 3.10 will appear and guide you through the setup process, as shown in Figure 3.11. When completed, the dialog box shown in Figure 3.12 will appear and setup will be complete. To start the Recovery Console, choose the Recovery Console option from the boot selection menu when starting the computer.

FIGURE 3.10
The Recovery Console setup confirmation dialog box allows you to abort the installation of the recovery console.

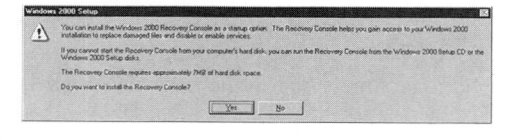

FIGURE 3.11
During Recovery Console setup, the setup program needs to copy about 7MB of files to the local hard disk.

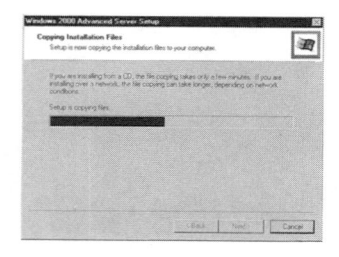

FIGURE 3.12
When the Recovery Console is successfully installed, this dialog box will be displayed.

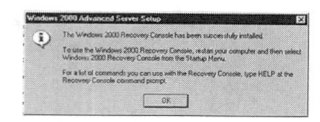

Installation Considerations

CHAPTER 3

To use the Recovery Console, restart Windows 2000 and choose Microsoft Windows 2000 Recovery Console, as shown in Figure 3.13. This will start the Recovery Console program. If the Recovery Console option isn't installed, you can also boot from the CD-ROM and choose the Repair option, and then choose C to start the recovery console.

FIGURE 3.13
The boot selection menu from Windows 2000. To start the Recovery Console, choose the Recovery Console option.

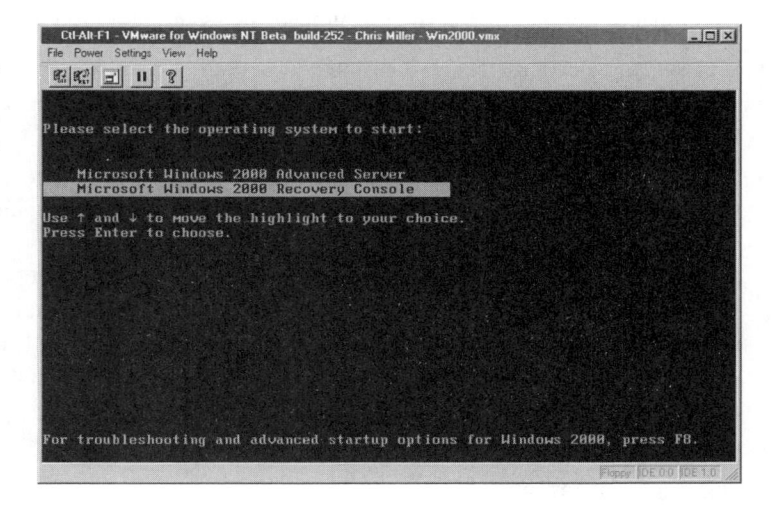

The Recovery Console allows third-party SCSI or RAID devices to be installed by pressing the F6 key during startup. A series of dots will go across the screen, similar to a normal Windows 2000 boot, but usually with a lot more dots. Then, the Recovery Console will ask you which Windows 2000 installation to log on to, as shown in Figure 3.14.

FIGURE 3.14
The Recovery Console is asking which installed copy of Windows 2000 it should retrieve logon information from.

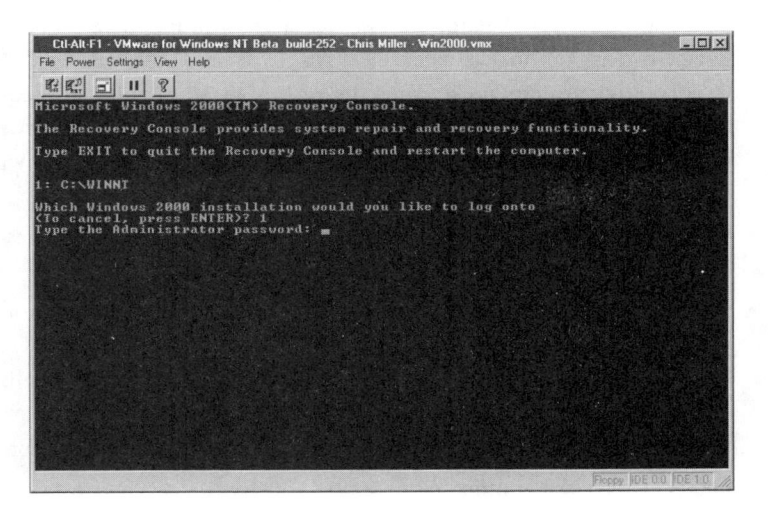

The recovery console uses most of the command shell commands that are common to the normal command shell. To view a list of commands, type in **help**. To view help for a specific command, type **help <cmd>**; for example, `help fixmbr` would provide help on the `FIXMBR` command.

Several commands not part of a normal command shell warrant a little more investigation:

- `LISTSVC`. Creates a list of services and shows their current startup state, whether the service is enabled or not. These are the service names that can be used by the `ENABLE` and `DISABLE` commands (covered next).

- `DISABLE` *and* `ENABLE`. Enable or disable system services. They take the format `ENABLE <servicename>, [start type]`. The `<servicename>` parameter is the name of the service to start or stop. The `[start type]` parameter is the type of startup for the service. If the start type is left off, the `ENABLE` or `DISABLE` command will print the current start type. If a particular service or driver is preventing the system from starting, disabling the driver will prevent the service from starting and causing the problem in the first place. If a critical service accidentally gets disabled, it can be reenabled here. Here are the valid start types:

  SERVICE_DISABLED

  SERVICE_BOOT_START

  SERVICE_SYSTEM_START

  SERVICE_AUTO_START

  SERVICE_DEMAND_START

  `SERVICE_DISABLED` is fairly self-explanatory. Setting a service to `SERVICE_BOOT_START` is for drivers that are part of the system boot process, such as device drivers for boot devices. `SERVICE_SYSTEM_START` will start the driver after the operating system has finished the early stages of the boot process. `SERVICE_AUTO_START` sets the service to automatic startup, and it will start with the rest of the services. `SERVICE_DEMAND_START` will start the service when a service that relies on it starts.

- `FIXBOOT`. This command will automatically regenerate the boot sector on the specified drive. It's called as `FIXBOOT C:` to fix the C: drive.

- `FIXMBR`. The `FIXMBR` command takes one parameter, which is optional, and is the name of the device that needs a new MBR. An MBR is a *master boot record*, which is a piece of data on the first hard disk in the system that tells the computer where to start loading the program that will boot the computer. `FIXMBR` will check the master boot record, and if it is corrupt, it will you prompt before replacing it.

- `LOGON`. This is the command that automatically runs at the start of the Recovery Console session and detects the installed Windows 2000 systems. It allows you to choose one to log on to.

- **MAP.** Shows the currently mapped drives—that is, it shows which drives are available for use in the Recovery Console. These are local drives, such as IDE, SCSI, CD-ROM and floppy drives, not network drives. Network drives are not available from the Recovery Console.
- **EXIT.** Quits the Recovery Console and reboots the system.

The Recovery Console will help fix most problems that prevent Windows 2000 from booting. It can enable and disable services as well s copy files from the distribution CD-ROM. The only thing it can't fix is a corrupt Registry. That requires some help from the Emergency Repair Disk, which is discussed in Chapter 26, "Recovering from a Disaster."

The `BOOT.INI` File

The `BOOT.INI` file is what tells Windows 2000 what operating systems are where and how it should start. This file is contained in the root directory of the system partition and is usually marked as Read-only, Hidden, and System, so it won't show up unless you've set Explorer to view these types of files. It has two main sections. The Boot Loader section tells Windows 2000 how long to wait before using the default operating system, and the Operating Systems section tells Windows 2000 which operating systems are on the local system.

The Operating Systems section contains one line for each operating system available. There are two formats used by the lines in this file. Windows 2000 and Windows NT use a format similar to the following:

```
multi(0)disk(0)rdisk(0)partition(1)\WINNT="Microsoft Windows 2000 Advanced Server" /fastdetect
```

This means that the operating system is stored on the primary IDE channel (`multi(0)` means primary IDE, where `scsi(0)` would mean the first SCSI channel and `multi(1)` would mean the secondary IDE channel) on the first disk (`disk(0)`) on the first primary partition (`rdisk(0)`) and on the second logical disk (`partition(1)`). The boot menu will read "Microsoft Windows 2000 Advanced Server" and will use the `/fastdetect` switch to start.

The second type of entry found in `BOOT.INI` is for any other operating system besides Windows NT or Windows 2000. It takes the following form:

```
C:\CMDCONS\BOOTSECT.DAT="Microsoft Windows 2000 Recovery Console" /cmdcons
```

This is for the Windows 2000 Recovery Console, but entries for Windows 98 or even Linux would share the same format. The part to the left of the equal sign is the path to the boot sector file for the operating system. For Windows 9*x*, it's usually called `BOOTSECT.DOS`, and for Linux, it's whatever you decided to name the boot sector when you copied it to a file. The part to the right of the equal sign is the text that will appear in the Boot Selection menu. Any options that follow the text are passed to the system on startup.

The Emergency Repair Disk

The Emergency Repair Disk, or *ERD*, is an actual floppy disk that contains a backup of the system settings and is used to recover a Windows 2000 system that has a Registry problem. To create an Emergency Repair Disk, use the Windows 2000 backup program (Start, Programs, Accessories, System Tools, Backup) and choose Tools, Create an Emergency Repair Disk from the menu. An Emergency Repair Disk requires a 1.44MB 3.5-inch floppy disk. Put the disk in the drive and let the system create the Emergency Repair Disk.

The Emergency Repair Disk will have to be re-created every time system settings change. Specifically, whenever the drive partition scheme on the server changes, whenever a service pack is applied, and before and after any hardware is added to the system.

To use the ERD, boot Windows 2000 from the CD-ROM or from the setup boot floppies and choose "R" when prompted to repair Windows 2000. Windows 2000 will prompt you for the ERD.

Migration from Preexisting Systems

Many of the installations of Windows 2000 Server will be from existing installations of Windows NT Server. There are some special cases that need to be taken into account when planning a migration from different versions of Windows NT, as well as when migrating from a NetWare platform.

Which version of Windows 2000 to purchase depends on what the system is being upgraded from. The following table explains what versions of Windows NT can be upgraded to which versions of Windows 2000:

If you bought...	*You can upgrade from...*
Windows 2000 Advanced Server upgrade	Windows NT 4.0 Enterprise Edition
Windows 2000 Advanced Server full product	Windows NT 3.51 Server Windows NT 4.0 Server Windows NT 4.0 Terminal Server Windows NT 4.0 Enterprise Edition
Windows 2000 Server upgrade	Windows NT 3.51 Server Windows NT 4.0 Server
Windows 2000 Server full product	Windows 3.51 Server Windows 4.0 Server

Windows NT Server has three different roles that a server could play in the mission of network validation. There's one Primary Domain Controller in each domain and zero or more Backup Domain Controllers in each domain. A server can also be a standalone server, which means it doesn't participate in authenticating network logons but may be part of the domain. These are also called *member servers* if they're part of a domain but are not Domain Controllers.

Windows 2000 supports a multiple-master replication scheme for Active Directory. That means there's no need to have a Primary Domain Controller/Backup Domain Controller system—there are only Domain Controllers. There are still "member servers" that don't participate in validating logons but are still part of the domain.

When upgrading from Windows NT Server to Windows 2000 Server, the setup program allows the following options for upgrading:

Role in Windows NT Domain	Role in Windows 2000 Domain
Primary Domain Controller	Domain Controller
Backup Domain Controller	Domain Controller or member server
Member Server	Domain Controller or member server

Except for the case where only one Domain Controller exists, a Domain Controller can be converted to a member server without rebuilding the server. Conversely, a member server can always be upgraded to a Domain Controller.

The system partition on a Domain Controller must be NTFS, and the upgrade process will enforce this. If the system partition (the drive containing the \winnt folder) isn't already NTFS, it will be upgraded to NTFS during setup.

For more information about how Active Directory works, see Chapter 9, "Directory and Access Concepts Brief."

Advanced Hardware Notes

A lot of complexities are involved in setting up hardware on servers. PC hardware is notoriously difficult to configure, but many new technologies such as PCI, USB, and IEEE 1394 (FireWire) are fixing many of the outstanding issues with installing and configuring devices. This section covers some miscellaneous topics that may help you deal with hardware problems.

Interrupts

Every device that interacts with the CPU is assigned an interrupt request line (IRQ). This is a signaling line that's used to tell the CPU that the device needs attention; it's how the device interrupts whatever the CPU is doing so the CPU will pay attention to the device.

There are 16 different interrupts in normal PC hardware, numbered from 0 to 15. In the old days, every device had to have it's own interrupt; however, with the advent of the PCI bus and interrupt-sharing devices, devices are now able to share interrupts, which makes systems more expandable. Here's a list of the standard interrupts and what they're used for:

- *Interrupt 0.* System timer. This interrupt drives things like the clock and the system scheduler.
- *Interrupt 1.* Keyboard. Every keypress causes a keyboard interrupt.
- *Interrupt 2.* System BOARD. Interface to low-level system devices.
- *Interrupt 3.* Serial ports COM2 and COM4 normally use this interrupt.
- *Interrupt 4.* Serial ports COM1 and COM3 normally use this interrupt.
- *Interrupt 5.* Parallel port LPT1 or not assigned.
- *Interrupt 6.* Floppy disk drive.
- *Interrupt 7.* Available.
- *Interrupt 8.* Real-time clock.
- *Interrupt 9.* Available (sometimes shared by PCI Bus).
- *Interrupt 10.* Available.
- *Interrupt 11.* Available.
- *Interrupt 12.* Available.
- *Interrupt 13.* Numeric data processor (the floating-point processor).
- *Interrupt 14.* Primary IDE controller.
- *Interrupt 15.* Secondary IDE controller.

EIDE Devices

EIDE (Extended Integrated Drive Electronics) devices are devices such as disk drives, tape drives, and CD-ROM drives that plug into the EIDE bus. There are normally two EIDE channels on a computer: One is the primary and the other is the secondary. Each channel can have two devices attached to it: One is called the *slave device* and the other is called a *master device*. When a machine doesn't boot after a new device is added to the EIDE bus, chances are the master/slave jumpers are not connected properly.

Windows Update

The Windows Update site (http://windowsupdate.microsoft.com) provides the latest certified drivers for different hardware devices in addition to patches and service packs for Windows 2000. Windows Update has a feature called *Critical Update Notification* that watches the Windows Update site and will inform you when there's a critical update for the system, such as a security patch.

Busses and Devices

There are several different methods of connecting devices to a PC. The most common in a server is the PCI bus, which is a full Plug and Play bus that detects hardware and automatically prompts Windows 2000 to attempt configuration of the hardware. There's a new version of the PCI bus that actually allows devices to be removed while the server is running after the device has been powered down. Check your server documentation carefully before attempting to use this feature.

USB, or *Universal Serial Bus*, is a 12Mbps bus that's used to connect low-bandwidth devices to a computer, such as pointing devices, keyboards, modems, and removable storage (floppy drives, ZIP drives, and ORB drives, for example). It's a Plug and Play bus that allows you to add and remove devices without powering down the system.

Apple Computer has published a standard that has been accepted by the IEEE as "IEEE 1394." This system, also called *FireWire*, is a high-bandwidth connection that can be used to connect all manner of devices to a system. It's also "hot pluggable," so you can add and remove devices from a FireWire channel without shutting down the system.

For laptops, the standard is still the venerable PCMCIA device, which is a credit card–sized slot usually used for network adapters and modems. The new PC Card implementation offers higher throughput for 100MB networking.

Summary

This chapter has covered the basic setup and configuration of Windows 2000 Server. We started with basic system requirements and covered the entire setup process, including the optional components and network setup. Then we took a look at some of the side issues surrounding setup, such as licensing, the Recovery Console, the Emergency Repair Disk, and advanced hardware topics.

CHAPTER 4

File Systems

IN THIS CHAPTER

- Hardware Considerations *72*
- Hard Disk Partitions *81*
- Using the Disk Management Application *86*
- File System Formats *99*
- Working with Volumes *111*
- Working with Network Shares *116*
- DFS: The Distributed File System *121*
- Remote Storage Server *123*
- Removable Storage Management *124*

There are a huge number of Windows 2000 Server machines that are deployed as simple file servers, with their sole purpose through their useful lives being the storing and retrieving of files. There are also a huge number of Windows 2000 Server machines that will be deployed as Web servers that will be responsible for retrieving files and formatting them for display. There will also be a huge number of Windows 2000 Server machines that are deployed as database servers, with the task of reading data from disk in a structured manner, performing fairly complex tasks, and writing the information back to disk. All these servers, and just about any other use a Windows 2000 server will be put to, revolve around the storage subsystem in Windows 2000.

This chapter covers the storage subsystem—from the hardware level, to the software level, to the network level. It provides a lot of vital information that will have a direct impact on the performance and integrity of any Windows 2000 Server.

Here's what's going to be covered in this chapter:

- Hardware considerations
- Hard disk partitions
- Using the disk management application
- File system formats
- Working with volumes
- Working with network shares
- The Distributed File System (DFS)
- Remote storage servers
- Removable storage management

This chapter starts out talking about hardware, covering the different types of disk technology and discussing interfaces and data transfer rates. It goes on to talk about disk partitions and then discusses the tool used to make disk partitions.

Hardware Considerations

Looking back, it's amazing how far storage technology has come, and it's going to be fun to see where disk subsystems are going. This section covers the basics of hard disk technology and terminology and then covers the standard methods used to control and communicate with disk devices. Then, we'll take a look at some of the newer technologies that sit on top of the controller architecture, such as RAID and Fibre Channel.

Hard Disk Technology

A hard disk, even back in the old days of the IBM Winchester disk packs, has always had the same basic components. There's a spindle, which is the axis of rotation for a series of one or more flat platters. These platters rotate at anywhere from 3,600 RPM to 10,000 RPM for the new modern technology. Floating above these platters are the drive heads, which are capable of reading magnetic fluctuations on the platters and changing the magnetic field on the disk to read and write data. These disk heads are mounted on arms that move back and forth across the disks all at once.

A disk is measured in three dimensions: *sectors*, which are lines radiating outward from the center of the disk (there is a fixed number of sectors on the disk, all the way out); *tracks*, which are the circles going around the disk; and *heads*, which is the number of usable surfaces on the platters. Keep in mind that some of the platters are used on both sides. Data is stored on a sector-per-track basis, with a fixed number of bytes being stored on each track in each sector. See Figure 4.1 for a diagram of how all this really works.

FIGURE 4.1
This diagram shows a representation of a disk with four sectors and three tracks.

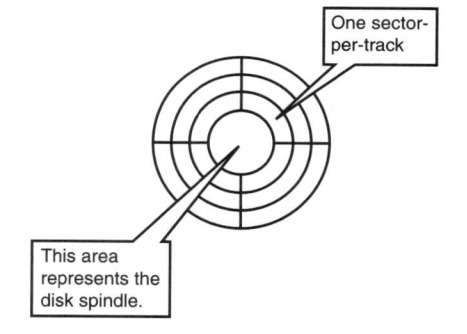

One sector-per-track

This area represents the disk spindle.

Given these two moving parts—heads and platters—a hard disk has two speed limitations. One of them is *seek time*, which is the average amount of time it takes for the head to move between two tracks. The other is the *rotational latency*, which is how long it takes, on average, for the platter to spin around to the area with the desired data on it. Therefore, there are two ways to make hard drives find data faster: spin the platters faster and move the heads faster.

Here are a couple of other interesting facts about hard drives. A drive takes a finite amount of time to go from its "powered down" state to its "powered up" state. During this time period, the drive pulls the maximum amount of current from the power supply. Therefore, if a system has multiple hard disks, it'd be much easier on the power supply if the disks spun up one at a time, which is how most drive arrays work. If you're building a server from parts, you may want to ensure that the disks spin up this way in order to prevent inconsistencies during the power-up process. Another interesting fact is that the heads of a disk drive are floating above the platters such that there's no room to spare at all. Nothing gets between a disk head and a platter but air (and there's not much room for air). Opening a hard disk is an easy way to ensure complete data loss and unreliability from the equipment because dust and other contamination will get into the drive, causing a head crash. A *head crash* is what happens when the drive head comes in contact with the platter, either because of a manufacturing defect, normal wear, or debris between the head and the platter. Besides the inevitable data loss that results, it also makes an absolutely horrendous squealing noise. Hard disks are fragile and should be treated carefully to help prolong their life.

Hard Disk Geometry

Okay. What I said about sectors and tracks really used to be true. And as far as the computer is concerned, it *is* true. However, the disk drive manufacturers know a little about geometry, and there are some funny numbers going on here that are totally irrelevant to Windows 2000 but which might be interesting to geometry and hardware geeks.

If you think about the sector-per-track length, which is what determines the data capacity of a hard disk, and you really look at what a sector is, you'll notice that there's a lot of wasted space out around the rim of the platter. On a platter that's 3 inches across, with the first track three-quarters of an inch from the center (assuming 16 sectors per track), the first track's sector length would be 0.29 inches:

```
Circumference = 2 * pi * Radius
              = 2 * pi * 3/4 inches
                about 4.7 inches
```

Because there are 16 sectors on a track, the length of a sector per track at three-quarters of an inch from the spindle is about 0.29 inches. The length of a sector per track at the outer rim of the disk (3 inches) would be about 1.17 inches. Therefore, a lot of disk media is being wasted.

The way the disk manufacturers avoid this problem is by making the entire addressing scheme virtual. The computer addresses a sector-track-head address, the hard drive's electronics take those measurements and convert them to where the data really is, and all of the sector-per-track lengths are more or less equal. That's why you'll see an 8GB hard disk that's 1 inch tall and configured with 16 heads. How do they fit 8 platters in 1 inch? They don't. There aren't really 16 heads at all; the drive figures out where the data really is and sends the right bits back.

Anyone working in the computer industry knows that computers are relatively fragile items. What makes them fragile is running hard disks. Avoid moving computers that have running hard disks. When a computer is turned off, the hard disk has a capacitor in it that discharges and pulls the heads to a part of the disk called the *landing zone*, where there's no data written. That way, if the disk gets banged on while the machine is off, there's less chance of a failure.

That's all there is to know about hard disks from a conceptual standpoint. Hard disks are high-speed storage and retrieval mechanisms—nothing more, and nothing magic.

Hard Disk Controllers

Most of the performance improvement in hard drives comes from the technology used to control the drives, combined with the disk drive's onboard electronics. Therefore, disk-controlling technology is as important, if not more important, than the drives themselves.

Several standards of hard disk controllers are around today, but the two principal standards are IDE and SCSI. The IDE (Integrated Development Environment) standard is less expensive but comparable to most SCSI standards. Also, it doesn't provide much expandability. The SCSI (small computer standard interface) name covers a whole pile of disorganized, badly named standards that cover the plethora of truly high-performance hardware available now.

Principles of IDE

The IDE standard is based on a fairly simple idea: Make the drive do the work. Each drive has an integrated controller board that handles all the complex tasks, such as mapping cylinder/head/sector addresses to actual addresses on the disk, retrieving data, and caching. A newer version of IDE, called *ATAPI* (AT Attachment Packet Interface), allows a wider variety of devices to be controlled, such as CD-ROMs, tape drives, and removable media (such as zip disks). Because the bulk of the complex processing is actually done by the drive itself, the controllers are comparatively simple and are usually integrated onto motherboards.

The primary limitation to today's ATAPI technology is expandability. Without jumping over some fairly high technical hurdles, a normal ATAPI setup can handle two devices per channel, with a maximum of two channels, for a total of four devices. This isn't enough storage space for a "serious" server. However, most serious servers have IDE controllers in them to handle the CD-ROM drive, and it's handy to have on a server in order to deal with shared zip disk drives.

Here's how the IDE standard works: There are two channels on a computer—the primary channel and the secondary channel. Each of these channels can support a master device and a slave device. The boot disk must be on the master device on the primary partition. If there's only one device on the channel, it must be the master device.

Most workstations have only two ATAPI devices, a hard disk and a CD-ROM, so the master device on the primary channel is the hard disk, and the master device on the secondary channel is the CD-ROM. There's no requirement to have a slave disk on a channel, but if there's a single disk, it's always a master disk.

> **Controller Channels**
>
> Both ATAPI and SCSI controllers have the concept of a *channel*. A channel is a group of devices that are all connected to the controller using the same cable. So, for an ATAPI channel, there are two devices: one master and one slave. For a SCSI channel, there can be at least seven, and up to 16, devices. A single ATAPI controller can work with two channels, whereas a SCSI controller can usually handle at least two, and up to four, channels.
>
> Copies from one channel to another are significantly faster than copies between devices on the same channel. This is true of any disk subsystem, and here's why: A channel has a fixed bit rate, so if there are two devices on the channel, and you're copying from one device to another, data has to go from the source device to the controller and then back down the same channel to the target device. Therefore, if the total bandwidth of the channel is 20Mbps, the effective bandwidth of this transaction is 10Mbps. If there are two channels involved, the reads will happen at 20Mbps and the writes will happen at 20Mbps, so the copy should happen twice as fast.
>
> Think of a channel as an individual queue. Commands that need to go to devices on the channel will queue up on the channel and are sent by the controller in the order received. If there are multiple channels, then there are two queues. Therefore, theoretically, devices can receive data twice as fast.
>
> It's important to keep two things in mind with channels. First, don't split a RAID array across channels. A RAID array is a way to store data on several disks for redundancy and performance. We'll talk more about RAID later in this section. Best case, it doesn't add anything to performance because RAID controllers are not built that way. Worst case, it has caused data loss before. The second thing to keep in mind is to work with channels so that devices that frequently need to talk to each other are on different channels. For example, putting a CD-ROM and a hard disk on separate channels will speed installation of software, because software installation is largely a copy from CD-ROM to hard disk. For a database, putting the data on one channel and the transaction log on another channel is often very helpful.

Setting a disk up as a master or slave disk is usually a simple matter of moving a jumper from one set of pins to another. Disk manufacturers are usually pretty good about putting the pin configurations on the sticker on top of the drive itself, but sometimes it's necessary to go find a manual or go onto the Internet and find a reference guide.

IDE and ATAPI drives are great for users of very small servers and workstations, who can usually deal with the lack of disk expandability, don't need outrageously fast disk systems, and don't have a lot of money to spend on the latest, greatest SCSI-only disk drives. IDE drives are cheap, reliable, and quick enough for most tasks. EIDE, the Extended IDE standard, includes some new technologies that provide higher levels of throughput. It uses all of the same concepts (master and slave drives) as IDE.

Principles of SCSI

SCSI is the architecture of choice for large disk subsystems. Any medium-to-huge server is going to use some form of SCSI to access disk drives and tape drives. SCSI has a lot going for it: a huge number of vendors, high performance, low processor overhead, and expandability. It's also at least 15 percent more expensive than comparable IDE hardware with the same capacity. On a server, though, people are willing to spend more money to get the marginal performance benefit and, more importantly, the ability to chain up to 16 devices together, depending on which SCSI standard is used.

There is a whole bunch of different kinds of SCSI—the standard has evolved a lot since its inception. Table 4.1 shows the different SCSI standards, their maximum bus speeds, and the maximum number of devices they support.

TABLE 4.1 SCSI Standards

Name	Speed	Devices	Cable Length	Cable Pins
SCSI-1	5Mbps	8	6 meters	25
Fast SCSI	10Mbps	8	3 meters	50
Fast Wide SCSI	20Mbps	16	3 meters	68
Ultra SCSI	20Mbps	8	1.5 meters	68
Wide Ultra SCSI	40Mbps	16	12 meters	80
Ultra2 SCSI	40Mbps	8	12 meters	80
Wide Ultra2 SCSI	80Mbps	16	12 meters	80
Ultra3 SCSI	160Mbps	16	12 meters	80

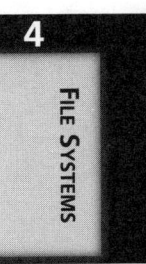

A computer that uses SCSI for interacting with drives must have a SCSI controller (or *host adapter*). The host adapter counts as one of the devices on the SCSI channel, so if the table says that 8 devices are allowed, that's one adapter plus 7 disks, for example. A SCSI host adapter does a lot more than any IDE controller; it will actually queue up commands for different devices and issue the commands on-the-fly. This means that SCSI uses a lot less CPU resources to transfer data around, which is a very big deal on busy servers. Another note on the table: most vendors use the term "ultra wide" instead of "wide ultra." They're the same thing.

> **Note**
>
> What about SCSI-3? Well, the SCSI-3 standard is actually a set of standards that includes all of what is called "SCSI" today. Fast Wide SCSI is the same as Fast Wide SCSI-3. Essentially, everything that's SCSI is now actually SCSI-3. This is why a Wide Ultra2 SCSI controller is much faster than a Fast Wide SCSI-2 controller.

Each device on a SCSI channel has to have a SCSI ID. This number is unique on the channel. For most systems, there are three jumpers that control the SCSI ID, and they're usually documented on the drive. If they aren't, go find the manual or check the manufacturer's Web site.

Advanced Controller Technology

As mentioned in the section on hard disks, the performance of a single disk drive is limited by the rotational latency and the average seek time. Well, it wasn't long before people started figuring out that if there were more drives, each drive would have less overall data to search. In addition to that, a bunch of initiatives were underway to make PCs, and specifically PC-based servers, more reliable, and the key to making the hardware more reliable was making the hard disks more reliable and better able to deal with problems.

Therefore, these researchers all got together and figured out that if they took a bunch of cheap hard disks and strung them together, performance would improve. They started with just two disks, and the disks had the same information on them—they were exact duplicates. When a bunch of requests came to the controller for these two disks, the controller would direct the requests such that both disks were used, which provided some performance benefits. Also, if one of the two disks crashed, you could still run off of just one, with a performance penalty, until the broken disk could be replaced. This is called *disk mirroring*.

This was all well and good, but it was wasting a lot of space. There's twice as much raw capacity on two disks, but the researchers were allowed to use only one disk. So they figured out that they could actually just put the data on a whole bunch of disks, but put chunks of data on each disk; that way, they'd be able to access data much more quickly than on a single large disk of the same size. It wasn't as fast as the disk-mirroring method, but it was still pretty quick. Basically, a large file would be broken up into fixed-size chunks, and each chunk alternated through the series of drives, so parts of the file were on each drive. This is called *disk striping*.

Then someone figured out that this was probably not a good solution from a reliability standpoint. If one of those drives in the disk stripe set crashed, all the data would be lost. Then, the researchers started storing *parity information*, which is redundant data, so they could do the disk striping and, in the event of a disk crash, they would be able to reconstruct the contents of the disk that crashed based on the parity information.

> ### So What's Parity, Anyway?
>
> *Parity* is a basic method for checking data consistency. Well, it started out that way until somebody figured out how to use parity to actually fix broken data. Here's how it works. Let's say there's a single character of information, eight bits long, that looks something like this:
>
> 0010 1010
>
> So, we'll build a parity bit for this. There are two types of parity: even and odd. For even parity, if there is an even number of ones, the parity bit is set to 0, and if there is an odd number of ones, the parity is set to 1. For odd parity, if there is an even number of ones, the parity bit is set to 1, and if there is an odd number of ones, the parity bit is set to 0. Here, we'll use only even parity, for the sake of clarity.
>
> The parity bit for the sample binary number would be 1, because there are three 1's in the data (0010 1010). What happens is that if the data is transmitted or just read out of memory, the computer figures out what the parity bit should be, compares it to the actual parity bit, and decides whether the data is corrupt. The computer doesn't know which bit is bad, it just knows that one of them is bad.
>
> So, how can parity be used to determine whether data is corrupt? It's actually pretty simple. It has to be done in groups of eight bytes, though. Compute the parity on each number (such as 0010 1010) and then compute the parity on each column, as shown here:
>
> | | *Data* | *Parity* |
> |--------|-----------|----------|
> | Byte 1 | 0010 1010 | 1 |
> | Byte 2 | 1101 1010 | 1 |
> | Byte 3 | 1111 0000 | 0 |
> | Byte 4 | 0011 0011 | 0 |
> | Byte 5 | 0101 0101 | 0 |
> | Byte 6 | 0101 1010 | 1 |
> | Byte 7 | 1100 0011 | 0 |
> | Parity | 1111 0111 | |
>
> *continues*

> If any single bit flips, there are two parity bits available. Therefore, if the fourth bit in byte 3 changes to 0, the computer could figure out that byte 3 changed, because the row parity is off, and that column 3 changed, because the column parity is off. The system can then deduce that the bit should have been a 1. This method will also figure out more than one error on a set of eight bytes, as long as no more than two bytes fail in any row or column. Actual disk-striping routines use something based on this that's more complex, and it can actually reconstruct entire lost sets of bytes.

By storing external parity on a single drive, the researcher found that the entire thing worked great. It had the advantages of spreading the data across drives, like slower spindle delays, and of redundant data, like mirroring, but without wasting nearly as much space as mirroring. This is called *disk striping with parity*.

Then, somebody figured out that the parity could be striped instead of all stored on one drive. This would speed up data searches if a drive crashes as well as provide some other small improvements. This is called *disk striping with striped parity*.

Next, a small group of disk drive manufacturers went totally over the top and figured out it would be even faster and more bulletproof if the stripes were actually mirrored. This is called *mirrored disk striping with parity*.

Then, a group of engineers figured out that there's a ton of money to be made if disk controllers could use standard SCSI disks and implement all this striping and mirroring technology. Then they designed hardware with fault tolerance so the disks could be added and removed without taking any of the other disks offline—thus, hot-pluggable RAID was born.

RAID, or *Redundant Array of Inexpensive Disks*, was started in a research lab. The researchers wanted to see if they could use a bunch of cheap disk drives instead of buying new, higher-capacity drives. They could, they did, and now every major server has some type of RAID system either built in or available as an option. Here are the different levels of RAID:

- *RAID Level 0*. Disk striping, no parity
- *RAID Level 1*. Disk mirroring
- *RAID Level 4*. Disk striping with parity
- *RAID Level 5*. Disk striping with striped parity
- *RAID Level 10*. Mirrored disk striping with striped parity

These RAID systems provide a very high level of availability and fault tolerance along with very high performance. These cards used battery-enhanced data caching to cache disk writes without losing them in the event of a power failure. Most new RAID systems allow more disks to be added without any downtime and without reformatting any existing disks. RAID is the enabling technology on high-availability, high-performance servers.

Another controller technology that's been getting a lot of attention lately is called *Fibre Channel*. Fibre Channel is a high-speed data channel that can be used to connect RAID arrays together. Most Fibre Channel cards connect a main server chassis to an external storage chassis, which is loaded with SCSI disks. The Fibre Channel controller directly addresses these disks and handles all the duties of a high-performance RAID controller. Fibre Channel provides more throughput than existing SCSI (100 Mbps), except for the SCSI Ultra3 standard, which at the time of this writing has no hardware available and exists only as a standard.

Both of these mechanisms use the standard SCSI drives, and they basically sit on top of SCSI drives, accessing the drives and performing caching and queuing for each drive. Windows 2000 sees stripe sets (or arrays) of disks set up with these controllers as a single physical disk, and Windows 2000 doesn't even know there is anything special about the disks.

Hard Disk Partitions

Now that we've established what a hard disk is, it's time to look at how data is stored on disk. This section contains a discussion of hard disk partitions, and the next session contains a discussion of how disks are formatted.

Disk partitions are ways of breaking up a large physical disk into sections. Often, there's just one large partition on a physical disk, but sometimes there are several partitions and volumes to help better organize and secure data. In addition, partitions play a large role in how system startup works because the "first" disk drive contains the master boot record (MBR), which is a small program always located on a specific spot on the disk that's used by the system BIOS to start the computer.

The first thing we'll look at in this section is how system bootup works, as well as why it's relevant to hard disk partitions. Then we'll look at the Windows 2000 partitioning schemas: basic disk and dynamic disk. We'll also look at how to upgrade from basic to dynamic.

System Startup

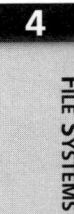

Ever wonder how a computer boots? Here's a fairly brief overview that covers the Intel boot process. Basically, when the system is turned on, the CPU begins reading from the BIOS and executing instructions found there. The BIOS program runs the system through the Power-On Self Test (POST) routines, which will usually handle initializing the video, counting up all the memory, enumerating all the installed PCI devices, and enumerating all the fixed disks installed. Then the system picks a disk to start up from.

If the system is configured to boot from a floppy first, it will attempt to start from the floppy drive if there's a floppy in the system. If the system can boot from a CD-ROM, it will attempt to do so if there's a bootable CD in the CD-ROM drive. If the system has any IDE hard disks, the system will attempt to start from the active partition on the master disk on the primary disk channel. If the system uses SCSI disks, the system will attempt to start from the active partition on the disk with a SCSI ID of 0 on the first SCSI channel.

If all these options fail, the system will return an error. Most systems will return a "Missing Operating System" message or something similar. Others will return "Missing ROM BIOS," which means the system attempted to boot from a ROM chip and failed.

When one of the hard disk boot options succeeds, the BIOS will read the master boot record of the disk partition in question and begin running the program found there. On a Windows 2000 system, the MBR contains the little program that pulls up the Operating System Selection menu. On a Windows 98 system, the MBR is a program that displays "Starting Windows 98..." and gives the user about three seconds to hit one of the function keys to access a boot menu. For other operating systems such as Linux, a system such as LILO is generally used to perform the same operation as the Operating System Selection menu in Windows 2000.

At any rate, the program in (MBR) the MBR serves only one purpose: To start an operating system. For Windows 2000, the Operating System Selector will either start Windows 2000 by running the program specified in the BOOT.INI file, which is discussed in Chapter 3, "Installation Considerations," or by running the stored image of another operating system's MBR. When Windows 2000 is installed, if there's an existing MBR, Windows 2000 replaces the existing MBR with its own and then writes the old MBR to a file called BOOTSECT.DOS. Then it writes an option in the BOOT.INI file to boot the old operating system by loading the file BOOTSECT.DOS as if it were an MBR.

So, where does all this lead? Basically, the Windows 2000 boot loader has to have an active partition on the "first" hard disk, which is either the master disk on the primary IDE channel or the disk with SCSI ID of 0 on the first SCSI channel. That active partition contains a master boot record, which is used to boot the computer. The active partition's MBR can start an operating system on any primary partition on the "first" hard disk. So, what's a primary partition? It's a type of partition found on a basic disk.

Basic Disks

A *basic disk* is a disk that uses the old standard primary partition, extended partition, and logical drive schema to define how disk space is used. There can be up to four partitions on a basic disk. A *primary partition* is a partition that cannot be subdivided and may contain an operating system. A single basic disk can hold up to four partitions total, and only one of those partitions can be an extended partition. Therefore, there could be three primary partitions and one extended partition, one primary partition and one extended partition, or just one primary partition or just one extended partition. An extended partition can be further broken up into logical drives.

> **Note**
>
> The "How To" for creating partitions and removing partitions and partition types can be found in the section titled "Using the Disk Management Application," later in this chapter.

All these partitions provide a fixed amount of space that's available for use within the partitions. In other words, a partition is defined by the amount of space it uses, and the size of a partition isn't easy to change. Usually, changing the size of a partition involves deleting the partition and rebuilding it bigger and, because a partition must be contiguous on disk, that usually means deleting all the partitions on the disk, which is not a trivial thing to do. If you create a whole bunch of small partitions on a logical drive, it can be very inconvenient if one partition runs out of space. That's why there are volume management and disk quotas, which provide an alternative to the use of disk partitioning schemes for controlling the use of disk space. So don't break up a big partition just to keep users from going out of control with their disk space usage; use quotas instead. Disk quotas and quota management get their own section later in this chapter.

Then what good is partitioning a disk if there are better tools for controlling the use of space? Most of the reasons for partitioning a disk are now restricted to dynamic disks, but partitioning also creates some interesting options for troubleshooting and operating system recovery, as covered in Chapter 3. Also, if a computer is going to be used with several different operating systems, associating a primary partition with each operating system is the mechanism used to boot multiple operating systems. We covered that in the preceding section on system startup.

What about extending partitions and stripe sets? Well, in Windows 2000, those features are available only on dynamic disks.

Dynamic Disks

All of the cool stuff that Windows 2000 can do with disk management requires the use of dynamic disks. Although any extended volumes, stripe sets, and mirrored volumes that were created in Windows NT 4.0 will be upgraded as dynamic disks, creating new extended volumes, stripe sets, and mirrored volumes will require all the disks involved to be dynamic disks.

Dynamic disks are not accessible from any operating system other than Windows 2000. Setting up dynamic disks on the "first" disk means that Windows 2000 is the only operating system that will run on that machine.

When a disk is first noticed by Windows 2000, either when Windows 2000 is installed or when the new disk is installed, Windows 2000 uses the disk as a basic disk. Converting the disk to a dynamic disk requires an upgrade process, which is covered in the next section.

The essential difference between a basic disk and a dynamic disk is that a basic disk has partitions, whereas a dynamic disk has volumes. This may seem trivial, but in Windows 2000, wherever the term *volume* is used, it will be in reference to a dynamic disk and, whenever the term *partition* is used, it's in reference to a basic disk.

The major features of dynamic disks, such as mirror sets, stripe sets, and volume sets, will be covered in a later section. For now, let's look at comparing and contrasting the basic and dynamic volumes and how to perform an upgrade.

Basic and Dynamic Disks

A *basic disk* is a "normal" disk partition and can be accessed directly by any operating system, including Windows 2000. So if a machine is used with multiple operating systems, such as Windows 2000 and Windows 98, then only the basic disks will be usable by Windows 98. Basic disks use the standard schema of primary partitions and extended partitions with logical drives. Whenever changes are made to a basic disk, the system must be restarted before the changes can take effect. Basic disks are accessible from other operating systems, such as Windows 98, if the system has both operating systems available.

> **Note**
>
> Just because a partition is available to different operating systems doesn't mean the file system format is accessible across both operating systems. Partitions formatted with NTFS are still unavailable to Windows 98, even if the NTFS partition is on a basic disk. FAT32 partitions on basic disks are available to both Windows 98 and Windows 2000.

A *dynamic disk* allows changes to the disk layout on-the-fly, without rebooting. That means that adding space through extending a volume or working with mirror sets is supported on dynamic disks.

The dynamic disk and basic disk properties apply to whatever Windows 2000 sees as a physical disk—whether it's just one disk or a disk array with a hardware RAID controller, Windows 2000 sees all the space as one disk. The entire disk has to be upgraded to a dynamic volume. Dynamic volumes are not available on portable computers due to limitations with the suspend/hibernate features and the interactions these features have with the disks and the file system.

Upgrading from a basic disk to a dynamic disk is virtually a one-way process. After an upgrade to a dynamic disk, the disk cannot be turned back into a basic disk without completely removing all of the disk partitions, thus losing all the data on those partitions. Although it's possible to go back to a basic disk, the process is quite painful.

To upgrade from a basic disk to a dynamic disk, follow these steps:

1. Be absolutely certain that this is something that needs to be done.
2. Check again and make sure this is something you want to do. It's very hard to go back to a basic partition afterward.
3. Remove all other operating systems from the disk that's to be upgraded. They won't be accessible after the upgrade, so remove them now.
4. Make a good backup of the entire system.
5. Open the Disk Management application by going to Control Panel, Administrative Tools, Computer Management, Storage, Disk Management, as shown in Figure 4.2. For more information about how the Disk Management application works, check out the next section, "Using the Disk Management Application."
6. Right-click the disk to upgrade and choose Upgrade to Dynamic Disk. If it doesn't work, try right-clicking the disk (for example, Disk 0) instead of the partition (for example, C:). If there are multiple partitions on a disk, then the disk area has to be right-clicked; otherwise, the partition area can be right-clicked.
7. Choose the disks to upgrade from the Upgrade to Dynamic Disk window, shown in Figure 4.3. Click the OK button.

After the upgrade, nothing really obvious changes except that none of the partitions on the dynamic disk are available from any other operating system except Windows 2000.

FIGURE 4.2
The Disk Management tool, started from within the Computer Management tool.

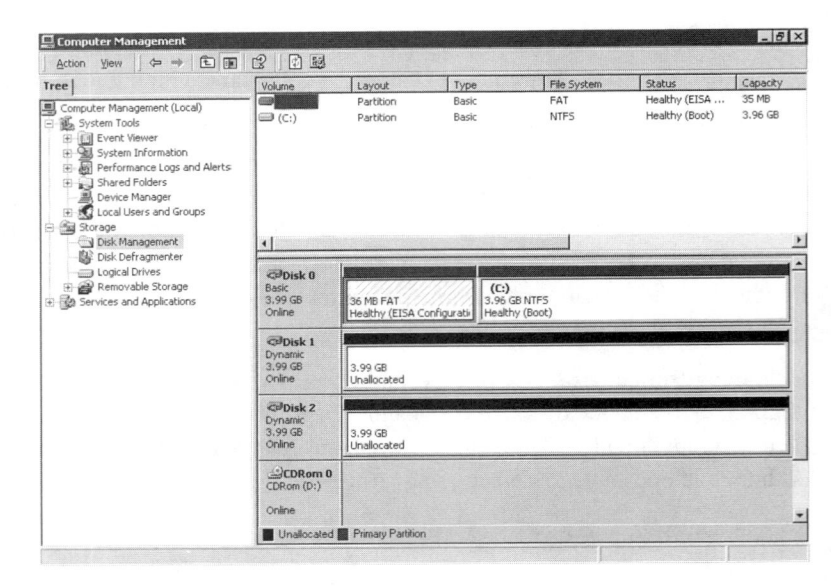

FIGURE 4.3
Getting ready to upgrade Disk 0 to a dynamic disk. All that's left to do is check the box next to Disk 0 and click OK.

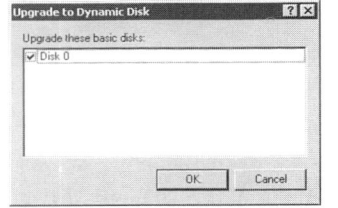

Using the Disk Management Application

The Disk Management application replaces the Windows NT 4.0 Disk Administrator program. It's the primary method used to manage disks, partitions, and volumes. That covers a lot of territory. Here's an overview of what we'll cover about the Disk Management tool:

- Starting Disk Management
- Creating and deleting partitions
- Extending volumes
- Changing drive letters
- Using drives without drive letters

The Disk Management application also handles making stripe sets, but that will be covered in the section on stripe sets. For now, let's just take a look at how to start the Disk Management application.

Starting Disk Management

The Disk Management application is a Microsoft Management Console (MMC) snap-in, so the application is actually contained in the file `diskmgmt.msc`, located in the `%SYSTEMROOT%\system32` directory. There are a few different ways to start the application. One way is to open the Computer Management MMC snap-in and go to the Storage item and choose Disk Management. The Computer Management snap-in is started by going to Control Panel, Administrative Tools and double-clicking the Computer Management icon.

The faster way to start it is to go to Start, Run and type **DISKMGMT.MSC**. This will start the snap-in without the extra screen space required by the Computer Management snap-in. Typing the name of the snap-in file into the Start, Run dialog box can start any snap-in.

The Disk Management tool is shown back in Figure 4.2. Take a minute and look over the interface. The top part of the window shows the drive letters, partitions, and volumes available on the local system (in this case, there's just a few drive letters). Notice that the CD-ROM drive is included in the list. This is done to make changing the drive letters allocated to the CD-ROM possible and to show the drive letters that are currently in use.

The bottom half of the window shows the partitions that are defined in the top half of the window but relates them to the actual physical disks they're part of. The hard disks in a system are numbered, starting at Disk 0. Each disk shows the partitions that were created on that disk, the size of the partitions, and the type of file system that each partition is formatted with.

Disk Properties

To examine the properties of a given disk, right-click the disk and choose Properties. The Properties window for a disk, shown in Figure 4.4, displays all the information about that disk:

- *Disk Type*. Basic or dynamic.
- *Status*. Online or offline. This is used for removable media products such as the Iomega Jaz drive or the Castlewood ORB drive.
- *Total Capacity*. The total disk capacity, including partitioned and unpartitioned space.
- *Unpartitioned Space*. How much of the disk isn't a part of any partition. This shouldn't be confused with "Free Space," which is space that's part of a partition but not used yet.

- *Device Type.* This defines the adapter type used to access the disk, and it will define the SCSI ID or Master/Slave status. Port:0 defines the channel number in use, and a value of 0 is the primary channel. The LUN:0 value is the Logical Unit Number, which will be populated with the SCSI ID for a SCSI drive or will be equal to 1 for the slave drive in an IDE chain.
- *Hardware Vendor.* The vendor of the hardware, and usually the model number, which is helpful for ordering spare parts and expanding capacity.
- *Adapter Name.* The name of the adapter used to access this disk, which can be cross-referenced with Device Manager to assist in troubleshooting.
- *Volumes.* A list of all the volumes or partitions contained on the disk.

Figure 4.4
The properties for a dynamic disk, Disk 1, which is a SCSI disk with a SCSI ID of 1.

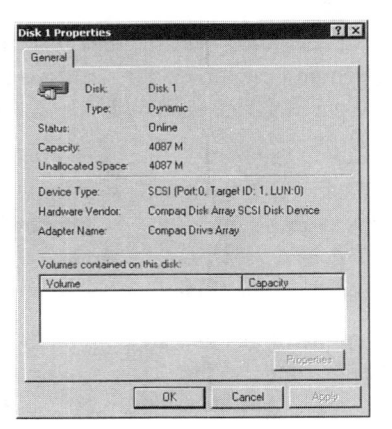

Volume or Partition Properties

In addition to displaying the properties of a given disk, Disk Management can also display the properties for a given volume or partition. The same screen can also be accessed by right-clicking the drive letter in Explorer and choosing Properties. The Properties window for a disk has a lot of options spread out over eight different tabs, as shown in Figure 4.5.

The General Tab

As shown in Figure 4.5, this tab displays general information about the disk, such as the total capacity, the used and free space, and a pie chart that shows what percentage of the space is free and what percentage is in use.

This page also allows the volume label to be set. A *volume label* is a way to define the contents of a disk by attaching a freeform text label to it. Basically, it's a comment field used to describe the disk, and the most common usage of a disk label is to label the system disk (to make administration a little easier).

FIGURE 4.5
The properties of a partition. Notice the number of tabs. This picture shows just the General tab.

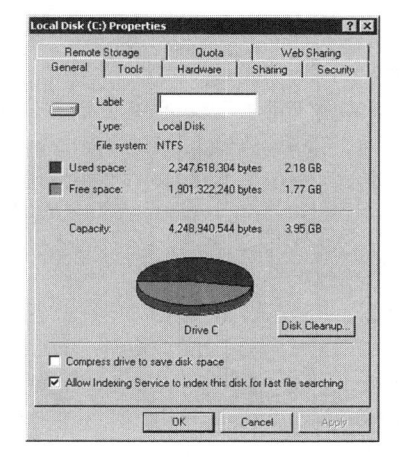

The Disk Cleanup button runs the Disk Cleanup application, which can be used to recover disk space. The Disk Cleanup application performs some very useful tasks, as shown in Figure 4.6. First of all, it offers to delete any temporary downloaded program files, which includes ActiveX controls and Java applets. It also offers to clear the Internet Explorer cache, empty the Recycle Bin, compress files that haven't been used for awhile, and clean up the files used by the Content Index system. By default, only the Downloaded Program Files and Temporary Internet Files options are turned on. For each option, the View Files option will display a preview of the affected files.

FIGURE 4.6
The Disk Cleanup application is used to remove unused and temporary files from the disk.

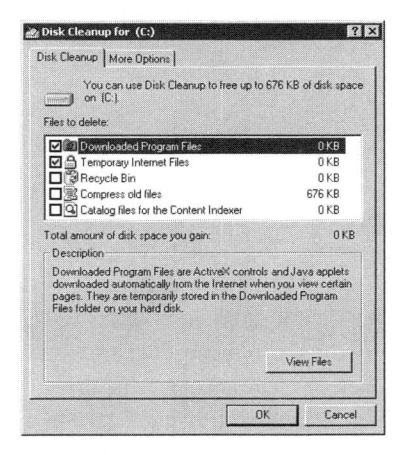

The Compress Drive to Save Disk Space option will be available on any drive that uses NTFS. This will apply NTFS compression to the entire disk drive, and any new files created on the drive will be compressed. This is useful when a file server has a lot of extra processing time and contains a lot of document files that compress well, such as Microsoft Word and PowerPoint files.

Finally, the Allow Indexing Service to Index This Disk option will make the Microsoft index service run periodically and create indexes, which can be used later to search for files on disk. For large volumes this can be handy because it will index all the header information in Microsoft Office documents, making documents that relate to a given topic easier to find.

The Tools Tab

The Tools tab, shown in Figure 4.7, has shortcuts for three often-used disk tools. The error-checking application, called Check Disk, will check a drive for errors and can fix a lot of errors in drive structures. The Backup option starts the backup system, which is described fully in Chapter 25, "Server Backup Utilities." The Defragmentation tool will run the Defrag program, which will help reduce disk fragmentation.

FIGURE 4.7
The Tools tab is a quick way to start disk defragmentation, error checking, and backups.

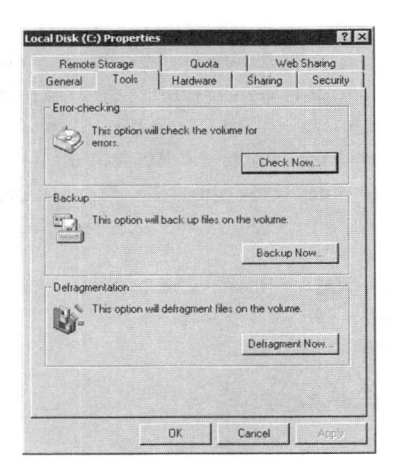

Disk fragmentation is a normal occurrence on disks that have read and write operations done on them. The operating system divides the available space on disk into clusters. When it's time to write a file to disk, the operating system writes the file one cluster at a time. Sometimes, all the clusters for a particular file can't be stored next to each other, so the file is fragmented and stored on different places all over the drive. This makes saving files faster; however, over time, excessive fragmentation can cause performance problems because, in order to load a file, the operating system has to search all over the disk to get all the parts of the file. The defragmentation process essentially rewrites all the fragmented files so they're all contiguous on the disk.

The Hardware Tab

The Hardware tab enumerates all the drives on the system, showing each device's name, model number, and status. From the Hardware tab, the Device Manager's Property tab for any disk device is just one click away, so drivers can be updated and troubleshooting can occur just by hitting the Properties button.

The Sharing Tab

If the entire drive is to be shared out, an entry must appear on the Sharing tab. This tab allows users to access the entire drive via a network share. All disk drives (but not CD-ROM drives) are shared out via a hidden share that corresponds to their drive letters, followed by a dollar sign (C$ for drive C:, for example). These default shares allow administrators to access a drive directly, and they cannot be removed.

Of course, the drive can be reshared with a new name, even a nonhidden name. This is done by clicking the New Share button and filling in the simple dialog box shown in Figure 4.8.

FIGURE 4.8
The Sharing tab allows a disk or folder to be shared out to users on the network.

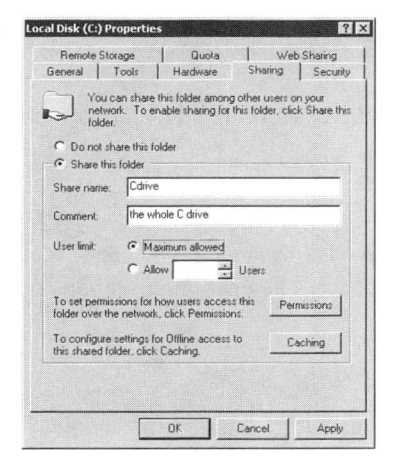

To change the properties of an existing share, choose which share to change by selecting it from the Share Name drop-down box. Then the comment, user limit, permissions, and caching for the folder can be changed. The comment for a folder is just a simple comment that will appear next to the folder name when the user is browsing the server. The user limit is the maximum number of users that can be simultaneously connected to the share. This is helpful in limited-bandwidth situations.

To change the permissions for a share, click the Permissions button. The permissions for the administrative shares, such as C$, cannot be changed, but if a new share is created, the permissions for that share can be changed. The administrative shares all default to permissions for the Administrators local group only and can't be changed. If a new share is created, it will default to full permissions for the group Everyone. To change the permissions, add users using the Add and Remove buttons to choose the users who should have permissions; then choose each user and set his or her permissions in the Permissions window at the bottom of the dialog box, which is shown in Figure 4.9.

FIGURE 4.9
This Permissions box is used to assign which users have access to a share. This particular setting provides full control to all users.

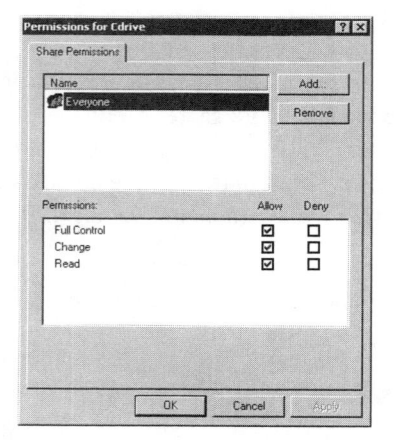

For more information, see the section titled "Working with Network Shares," later in this chapter.

The Security Tab

The Security tab appears only if the drive is formatted with NTFS. It allows the user to set up the file security across an entire drive. The upcoming section on file system formats will go into how the security is set.

The Quota Tab

The disk quota system allows the administrator to control the amount of disk space used by any user or group of users. There's an entire section devoted to the quota system later in this chapter.

The Web Sharing Tab

Although it probably won't see a lot of use on a disk-wide basis, the Web Sharing tab allows an entire disk to be shared out to the Internet, either via the default Web site or by a whole new Web site. This tab will appear only if the Internet Information Server is up and running. For more information, see Chapter 22, "Virtual Private Networks."

Now that the basic interface has been covered, it's time to look at how to create, modify, and remove disk partitions and volumes.

Partition and Volume Management

In addition to providing pretty pictures about drive status and making minor changes to drive sharing, the Disk Management tool can also be used to add, change, and remove partitions from disks.

"Removing a partition" may sound nice and innocent, but this is yet another way to completely destroy data. Don't go messing around with the partitioning tools unless there's a good backup of the entire system, even if the changes aren't supposed to effect data. Bad things happen, and messing around with partitions is generally just asking for trouble.

Creating a New Partition

Creating a new partition requires an available area in the Disk Management tool that has a status of Unallocated or Free Space. Space that's unallocated is space on a disk that's not already part of another partition, whereas free space is part of an extended partition that hasn't been turned into logical drives yet. To create a partition, right-click in the Unallocated or Free Space area and choose Create Partition. The Create Partition Wizard will start up. The first question the wizard will ask, as shown in Figure 4.10, is what type of partition to create: Primary, Extended, or Logical Drive. If an area marked Unallocated was right-clicked, the Logical Drive option won't be available. If an area marked Free Space was right-clicked, the Logical Drive option will be the only option available.

FIGURE 4.10
The Create Partition Wizard is asking what type of partition to create. A primary partition is chosen here.

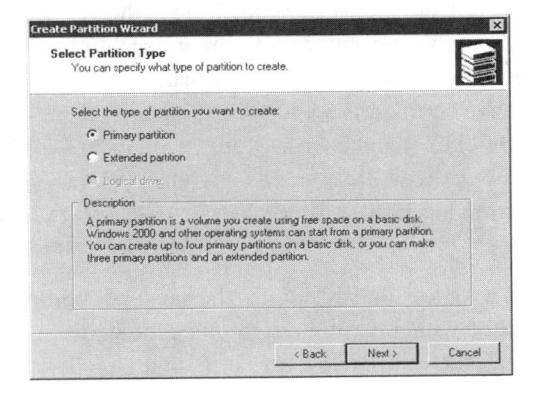

Next, specify the amount of space to use for this new partition. The minimum size for a partition is shown and will change, depending on the size of the disk and other factors. The default setting is to use the entire chunk of unallocated space.

The final page of the wizard is the summary page, shown in Figure 4.11, which is presented before any changes actually take place. There's still a chance to use the Back button and make changes, or you can click Finish to commit the changes.

FIGURE 4.11
The summary page for the Create Partition Wizard provides a last look at the action about to happen. Clicking Finish will commit the changes.

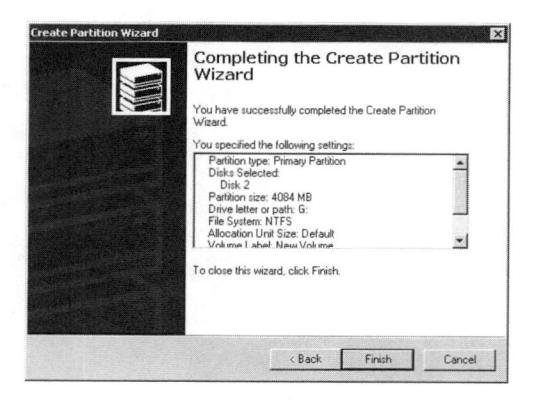

Clicking the Finish button completely commits the change. In other words, it's automatically saved and written to disk, and the new partition is immediately ready for Wizard formatting.

Changing Partitions

There are two major types of changes that can be made to a partition. The partition can be made active, and the partition's drive letter can be changed.

Making a partition active makes the BIOS in the computer look to that partition as the partition to start from. In other words, the *active partition* is the partition that the system will use to boot. There can only be one active partition on an entire system, and it must be on Disk 0, the first disk in the system. If the chosen partition isn't bootable, the system won't boot until the active partition is set to something a bit more reasonable. To make a partition active, right-click it and choose Mark Partition Active. If the partition is already marked as active, the option will be grayed out. Only primary partitions can be marked as active, so the option to set the partition as active doesn't even appear on an extended partition.

Changing the drive letter is a lot less drastic but has the same possibilities for data loss. To change the letter associated with a partition, right-click the partition and choose Change Drive Letter or Path. The Edit Drive Letter or Path dialog box will appear, as shown in Figure 4.12. This dialog box allows the drive letter to be changed and allows for a path to be added so that the drive can be accessed as if it were a directory on another path. This is similar to the UNIX idea of a "mount" command. The drive can actually be mounted to several different locations in different file systems.

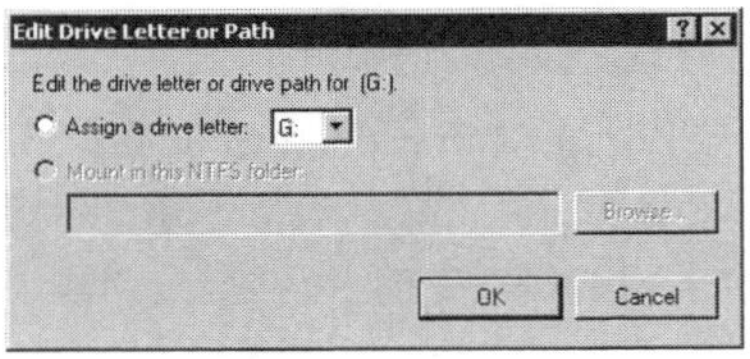

FIGURE 4.12
This is how drive letters get changed. Be careful, this may cause problems with applications!

> **Note**
>
> Before you get to thinking that this whole "mount a drive into a directory" idea is a great new Microsoft innovation, you might want to know that UNIX has been doing this since it started in the early 1970s, and Microsoft is just now catching up. The whole concept is almost as innovative as a white sock.

Don't change a drive letter if any of the following conditions exist:

- You shouldn't change a drive letter if there are *any* applications installed on the partition. Most applications store the location of their executables and modules in the Registry, and these changes won't be cascaded to the Registry if the drive letter changes.
- You shouldn't change a drive letter if there are services on the machine that rely on data to be on the drive. For example, if there are SQL Server databases on drive D: and the drive letter changes to E:, then the databases will be marked as suspect (corrupt) when SQL Server is restarted.
- You shouldn't change a drive letter if there isn't a better reason than making the drive letters contiguous.

When a drive letter is changed, any directories that are shared out will continue to be shared out correctly, and all user rights/permissions will be carried along correctly.

Deleting Partitions

Deleting a partition is exactly as harmful as it sounds. Once a partition is completely deleted, the partition is gone. The data the partition contained will be gone. This data is lost, irrecoverable, irretrievable, and just plain gone.

In order to delete a logical partition, first remove all logical drives from that partition and then remove the extended partition. This is a safety feature; it makes sure the user understands exactly what's about to happen before the data is removed.

To delete a partition, simply right-click the partition to remove and choose either Delete Partition or Delete Logical Drive, as appropriate. There will be one message box that asks for confirmation, and then the partition will be removed.

Working with Dynamic Disks

Dynamic disks provide a couple of other options that need to be covered but that also require some additional background work. Upcoming sections in this chapter cover working with some of these features. The first section, "Working with Volumes," covers how to extend volume sets, and the second, "Striped Volumes," covers how to use RAID (covered previously) using Windows 2000.

Setting Up Disk Quotas

For a long time, Microsoft has included all the security hooks in its operating system to support disk quotas, and there are several third-party applications that implement all those hooks and others within the file system to enforce disk quotas. With Windows 2000, Microsoft finally implemented disk quotas into the operating system. It's about time.

Disk quotas is a feature of the file system that allows the administrator to set limits to the amount of space a user can have to store files. It doesn't pre-reserve data space for the user, so it's a very flexible way of managing storage. Disk quotas have been around for a long time in other operating systems, but they're just now fully implemented in Windows 2000.

Quotas are set up on a partition-by-partition basis (or per logical drive), which is another argument for having large partitions and drives. Because partitions aren't reservations for a user, it's fairly common to over-reserve space on a server, because (hopefully) not all users will use all the space they have.

The dialog box for setting up quotas is shown in Figure 4.13. To get to this dialog box, right-click the appropriate partition and choose Properties from the pop-up menu; then click the Quota tab. This dialog box controls all the options for disk quotas on the selected partition. Quotas are available only on the NTFS file system; they are not available on other file systems. The next section covers file system types.

FIGURE 4.13
The Quota tab enables disk quotas for the volume.

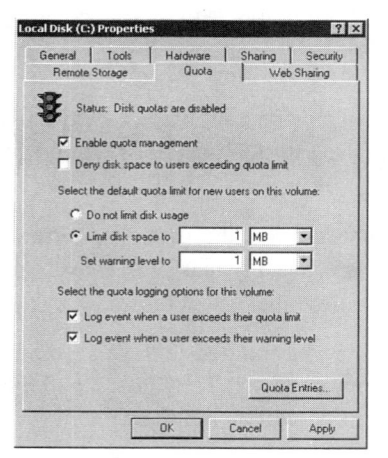

To enable quotas, click the Enable Quota Management check box. This will activate the rest of the dialog box, which has almost everything on it disabled until the check box is enabled. To impose hard limits on disk space usage, check the Deny Disk Space to Users Exceeding Quota Limit check box. Choose the disk space limit by clicking the Limit Disk Space To option button and then choose the hard limit level and the warning level. The warning level will display messages to the user when his or her quota has been exceeded. The hard limit level will display harsher messages or prevent users from exceeding the limit, depending on whether the hard limit or soft limit options are chosen. If the check box for Deny Disk Space is not turned on, the entire quota process will simply account for disk space by individual users without really providing any type of enforcement of policy.

Disk Quotas and Philosophy

There are a couple of philosophical issues that need to be discussed before any quota policy is implemented. They're philosophical because they don't really have right-and-wrong answers, and they'll require some guesswork combined with logic to get good answers.

Basically, there are two ways to approach disk quotas: soft limits and hard limits. It's possible to turn on quota management such that a user can exceed his or her quota, and that information will simply be available to the administrator. The other approach is to set quotas so that a user cannot exceed his or her quota and will be unable to save any work until he or she first removes some things from the disk. The first method can be thought of as a soft limit; the second would be a hard limit.

By imposing a hard limit, there's a fair chance that applications may not realize that they've run out of space, or the user may not realize it in his or her rush to shut down the machine before leaving. In that case, the user may just ignore the dialog boxes, shut the machine down, and go home. Expect an angry phone call the next morning.

By using the soft limit approach, users will not get any warning messages, and they'll have no real incentive to clear off some disk space. This is a much safer approach, but it's also a lot more difficult to enforce.

Now, weigh the costs of the two. A hard limit will probably cause more help desk calls and more anger from the client base. A soft limit will cause the help desk to have to call users and tell them to clear up some space, because chances are they won't do it themselves.

One more point to consider: Are disk quotas really a good idea in the first place? Weigh the costs and benefits. Adding more disk space is getting less and less expensive, whereas the cost of support personnel is getting more and more expensive. Add in the bad feelings generated when users hit the quota limit and then evaluate all of these factors into your situation and environment. There aren't really any easy answers.

If you need a remedial course in metric prefixes, Table 4.2 shows what all the units in the drop-down box translate to.

TABLE 4.2 Metric Prefixes

Abbreviation	Units	Size (Bytes)
KB	Kilobytes	1,024
MB	Megabytes	1,048,576
GB	Gigabytes	1,073,741,824
TB	Terabytes	1,099,511,627,776
PB	Petabytes	1,125,899,906,842,624
EB	Exabytes	1,152,921,504,606,846,976

You may have known the first three or four of those items, but did you know the last two? This is Microsoft's way of trying to plan ahead for new storage media.

The two event-logging options determine when entries will be made into the Windows 2000 Event Log. When the first option is checked, the warnings are only logged when the user exceeds his or her quota level. When the second option is checked, events are logged when the user exceeds his or her warning level. Usually, either the first box is checked or both boxes are checked.

The Quota Entries screen shows all the quotas that apply to different users on the current partition. A sample one is shown in Figure 4.14. It will show a list of all the users with files on the system and how much space they have used. You can change individual users' quotas using this screen by double-clicking the user and then setting the quota in the Quota Settings dialog box, shown previously in Figure 4.13.

FIGURE 4.14
The Quota Entries dialog box shows the disk quotas for each user, as applied to this particular partition.

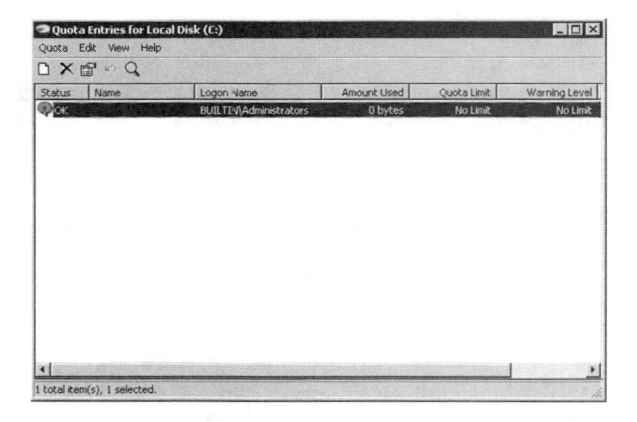

> **Note**
>
> Quotas cannot be set on members of the Administrators group. Administrators can use as much disk space as they want.

To remove a quota for a particular user, turn it off by double-clicking the user in the Quota Entries window and choosing Do Not Limit Disk Usage in the Quota Settings dialog box. To find and reassign or delete the files that belong to a user, find the user's name in the Quota Entries dialog box and select Quota, Delete Quota Entry.

Because quota settings have to be saved for each partition and because doing that is a pain on a bunch of servers, the quota settings can be exported and imported. After setting up quotas on a partition, choose Quota/Export from the menu and save the quota settings. Then use Quota/Import later to import the quota settings.

File System Formats

Once the partitions are built, they have to be formatted before they can be used to hold data. If a disk was compared to a road map, *partitioning* would be laying out the boundaries of the map, and *formatting* would be the map grid. Formatting a disk allows the operating system to keep track of the data on the disk and store items such as security information outside the user's ability to tamper with them.

The main chore of a file system is to provide the lower levels of the operating system with the interior map of how the disk is laid out. A file system has to keep track of all the files on the disk and know what parts of the disk are in use at all times as well as how a file is linked together on disk in order to retrieve the whole file.

There are three major file system types that every administrator will run into. The *raw* file system is a totally unformatted file system and is simply raw disk space. This isn't used very often, but some versions of Microsoft's SQL Server product can actually write data into the raw partitions on a disk, even though that type of thing is very rare. The only real use for raw data space is to format it to another file system.

The two real file system types that will be used are FAT and NTFS. The FAT file system is very old and doesn't have many features beyond the capability to store files. An improved version of FAT, called FAT32, adds the capability to address more disk space, but it doesn't add anything else. NTFS is a transaction-based file system with full security and compression built in. It's very technologically advanced but also very sound and reliable.

This section will take an in-depth look at the two file systems, including how the file systems work and the utilities used to manage them.

The FAT File System

The FAT (file allocation table) file system is the original file system used by MS-DOS. It uses a table stored on disk that keeps track of where files and directories are located on the disk. The FAT file system stores two copies of this data on disk at the very beginning of the disk. In theory, both copies of the file allocation table are kept in sync at all times, but sometimes they fall out of sync and have to be checked and resynchronized.

In order to be able to write data efficiently, a file system uses chunks of data, usually called *clusters*. In the FAT file system, a cluster is always 2,048 bytes, or 2KB. A cluster represents the smallest amount of disk space that the file system can allocate. In other words, a file that has 500 bytes in it will take up a full 2KB of storage, and a file that's 2,047 bytes will take up 2KB of storage, but a file that's 2,049 bytes will take up 4KB of storage.

> **Note**
>
> This note applies more to workstations than servers, but it's still good for illustrating the effect of cluster size. The 2KB cluster size is usually not that wasteful, on average, unless there's an application installed that uses hundreds of small files. One example of such an application is a C++ development environment, which will have literally hundreds of small files and can take up significantly more room than the sum of its file sizes.

When a file is written to disk, it gets written into the next two available spots on disk, which might not be next to each other. For example, if a program is accessing a data file that's stored on two clusters, and it adds a third cluster because it needs to store more data, the file system may give it a cluster that's nowhere near the existing clusters. It's faster to allocate one cluster and write the data than it is to allocate three new clusters and copy them somewhere else so they'll all sit next to each other on disk.

How does the file system keep track of these transactions? They're stored in the file allocation table, which keeps track of all the clusters, whether or not they're used. If they are used, it keeps track of the next cluster for each file. In other words, the whole thing is a big linked list (for the computer science geeks). When a program needs to access a certain part of a file, it makes a request to the operating system, and the operating system calculates which cluster the particular parts are in and follows the linked list down to that cluster and then reads the data and hands it back to the program.

This sounds like a long process, but it really isn't as bad as it seems. These algorithms are fairly standard, and they've been incredibly well optimized because they're very important. When a change needs to be made, the new cluster is allocated, and both copies of the file allocation table are updated. When a file is deleted, the entire chain of clusters is marked as available.

There are some inherent limits to this technology. It tends to be more susceptible to power failures or similar problems because of its reliance on the file allocation table being updated. This is yet another reason to always shut down the machine instead of just turning it off, because an orderly shutdown will make sure everything is written to disk before the machine is powered down.

The FAT file system has some definite limitations when it comes to the amount of disk space it can manage. The FAT file system can be used only on partitions smaller than 4GB, and a file cannot be any larger than 2GB. It uses a 2KB cluster size, so even the smallest file will take at least 2KB on disk. The FAT32 file system supports volumes between 512MB and 2TB (terabytes), but Windows 2000 will format a FAT32 partition to only 32GB.

FAT and FAT32 are accessible from Windows 95, Windows 98, and Windows 2000, as long as the partitions are on basic disks, not dynamic disks. Remember, the only operating system that can access a dynamic disk is Windows 2000. Also, this applies only to dual-boot systems that can be started with either Windows 2000 or another operating system. Any of these partition types can be accessed over the network from any client software, regardless of operating system version.

So, why would anyone use the FAT file system instead of FAT32? One major reason is that versions of Windows 95 prior to the so-called "OSR-2 release" cannot access FAT32. The other reason is that FAT32 doesn't fit on a floppy, so all floppy disks are formatted with FAT. This goes for most of the "enhanced floppy" disks, such as the LS120 SuperDrive and zip. These are all formatted with the FAT file system.

The other major advantage of FAT32 is the smaller cluster size. FAT32 uses a 512-byte cluster by default, so it can store smaller files much more efficiently.

With all the capabilities of FAT32 for dealing with larger volumes, it still has the major disadvantages of dealing with a file allocation table scheme and not being transaction based. It also doesn't support file-level security. So, what is this transaction-based file system thing, and how does file system security work? Let's take a look at NTFS.

NTFS

NTFS, the NT File System, is the file system everyone is supposed to use with Windows 2000. There are certain big advantages to using NTFS as well as certain drawbacks. The big advantages are that NTFS uses a transaction-based file system and that it supports file-level security. The drawbacks include the fact that nothing but Windows 2000 is supposed to read NTFS and that NTFS has a certain amount of disk space and processor overhead above and beyond the FAT file systems. First, we'll check out what "transactional file system" means; then we'll look at the file-level security offered by Windows 2000.

Transactional File Systems

A transactional file system is a way of storing data on a disk that relies on tracking changes to the file system in a particular way. A nontransactional file system, such as the FAT file system, writes data to disk like this:

- It finds empty clusters.
- It writes data to empty clusters.
- It writes two copies of the changes to the file allocation tables.

Now, what happens if the disk loses power between the second and third steps? The information is written to disk but, because the file allocation table isn't aware of the new clusters added to the file, the information won't be accessible. In addition, if the system is stopped during the third step, one of the tables may be updated and the other not. What's more, one of the file allocation tables could be left in an inconsistent state, where part was written and part was not.

To prevent this, a transactional file system does something like this:

- It finds empty clusters.
- It writes into the journal the intention to use the empty clusters and write data into them.
- It writes the data to the clusters.
- It updates the journal to show the data was completely written.

If power is turned off at any point during any step, the file system can recover when it's started back up by reading the journal and "rolling back" any changes that were not marked as completed by the last step. In other words, the file system will assume that any transaction that did not complete the last step was interrupted by the power loss, the clusters used will be deallocated, and the file will return to the state it was in before the transaction.

This sounds like a complicated system, but it's got two very important things going for it. First of all, it's very fault tolerant. This is basically how database management systems handle transactions; it's a complete, verified model, and it has held up well for a long time. The advantage of this more-complex system is that, because it's used by databases, it has been very carefully scrutinized and optimized to perform very well. The difference in performance is almost negligible.

The concept of a transaction-based (or journaling) file system is not at all unique to NTFS. It's been around in high-end UNIX systems for a long time, and there are new journaling file systems that are in testing for Linux and other free operating systems.

The journal used by NTFS is self-managing, so it easily deals with removing completed transactions from the log so the log won't consume much disk space. There isn't really a concept of a transaction log backup like there is in a database system, but each file is kept with a modified date anyway, so it's easier to just back up the files that changed since the last backup. Transaction log backups are done by many database systems as a way of performing point-in-time recovery.

File System Security

In any file system on a networked machine, it's nice to be able to restrict access to certain files to certain users. Windows 2000 allows this type of administration only on NTFS partitions. There are two unique concepts involved with any file security system: permissions and users. *Permissions* are the controls to how users can interact with files. *Users* are entities that need to interact with files.

NTFS supports several different permissions and then groups these permissions in a way to make them easier to use. Here's a list of the types of interaction that NTFS can either allow or deny:

- *Traverse Folder/Execute File*. If the permission is set on a folder, it allows the user to go through the folder to get to a subfolder. For more information on traversing folders and traverse checking, go back to Chapter 2, "Architecture," in the section on the POSIX subsystem. If the permission is applied to a file, it allows the user to execute the file. The user can execute the file without being able to read the file.
- *List Folder/Read Data*. If applied to a folder, this will allow the user to read a list of all the files and subfolders in the folder. If applied to a file, this will allow the user to read the file.
- *Create Folders/Append Data*. If this is applied to a folder, it allows new folders to be created within the folder. If it's applied to a file, the user can append data to the end of a file without being able to add any data into the middle of the file.
- *Delete*. Allows the user to delete the specific object that the delete permission is set on. If the delete permission is set on a file, the user is allowed to delete that one file. If the delete permission is set on a subfolder, the user can delete the subfolder, but only when the subfolder is empty.
- *Delete Subfolders and Files*. Allows the user to delete all files and subfolders of a given folder, without granting the access to read or write to the files and without giving the user access to know what's in the subfolders being deleted.

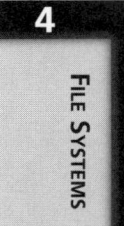

- *Create Files/Write Data*. If applied to a folder, this allows the user to create files in that folder. If applied to a file, it allows the user the ability to change the contents of the file.
- *Read Permissions*. Allows the user to read the permissions set on the object, whether it's a file or a folder.
- *Change Permissions*. Allows the user to change the permissions on the file or folder.
- *Read Attributes*. Allows the user the ability to see what attributes are set on the file, such as read-only and hidden. This applies to the standard NTFS file attributes.
- *Write Attributes*. Allows the user to change the attributes set on a file, such as read-only and hidden. This applies to the standard NTFS file attributes.
- *Read Extended Attributes*. Allows the user to read application-defined extended attributes in a file. These attributes include the properties of a Microsoft Word document (author, language, comments, summary, and so on), for example. These are commonly used by the indexing service to help files be found more quickly.
- *Write Extended Attributes*. Allows the user to write extended attributes to files.
- *Take Ownership*. Allows the user to take ownership of a given file.
- *Synchronize*. Allows the user to synchronize the file or folder to his or her local workstation.

That's a pretty complex system of rights. As a matter of fact, it's a lot more complex that most administrators want to deal with in most cases. Those rights are called *special permissions*, and there's a set of rights called *Permissions* that's simply a group of the special permissions most commonly used together (see Table 4.3).

TABLE 4.3 Special Permissions and Permissions Matrix

Special Permissions	Full Control	Modify	Read and Execute	Read	Write
Traverse Folder/ Execute File	X	X	X		
List Folder/ Read Data	X	X	X	X	
Read Attributes	X	X			
Read Extended Attributes	X	X	X	X	
Create Files/ Write Data	X	X			X

Special Permissions	Full Control	Modify	Read and Execute	Read	Write
Create Folders/ Append Data	X	X			X
Write Attributes	X	X			X
Write Extended Attributes	X	X			X
Delete Subfolders and Files	X				
Delete	X	X			
Read Permissions	X	X	X	X	X
Change Permissions	X				
Take Ownership	X				
Synchronize	X	X	X	X	X

Most of the time, only two of these types of permission are used: Full Control and Read and Execute. Usually either a user needs to be able to completely control a file or he just needs to read data from the file. The rest of the permissions shown are more restrictive but really aren't seen too often.

Now that you have an understanding of permissions, we need to discuss users. There are three types of users that are important here: the special user (called *CREATOR OWNER*), an individual user, and a group. A *CREATOR OWNER* user is the owner of an object, an object being either a file or a directory. A CREATOR OWNER user has full control of the object and cannot be assigned anything less than full control of the object. Ownership of a file is an important concept for NTFS. The owner of a file can always do anything with a file, including give it away to another user. To transfer ownership, the CREATOR OWNER must grant the user the "take ownership" permission; then the person who wants the file has to actually take ownership of the file.

> **Note**
>
> Windows 2000, unlike most other operating systems, doesn't allow the administrator full control of all files automatically. This is actually a nice security feature. However, the administrator can get access to any file by taking ownership of it. An administrator can always take ownership of any file. However, because ownership can never be given back, the administrator then owns the file until a user comes back and takes ownership from the administrator.

Three things affect a user's ability to access an object: the allow permissions of the user, the allow permissions of the group, and the denied rights of either the user or the group. If a given user account has access to a file, the permissions of the user account will be used. If a given user has no permissions (either allowed or denied) to a file, the user will be able to access the file if there's a group that the user is a member of that has user permissions. If either the user or a group is denied a specific permission to a file, the user will be denied that permission to the file.

If the user is a member of two groups and has no access rights of his or her own, the user will be granted the least restrictive set of rights to the file. In other words, if the user `cmiller` is a member of the group `DatabaseAdmins`, which has read and write access to a file, and a member of the group `ExchangeAdmins`, which has only read access to a file, the user `cmiller` would have read and write permissions.

It goes like this:

Current Permission	Action by Windows 2000
The user or group is denied.	The user is denied.
The user has rights.	User rights are used.
The group has rights; the user has none.	Group rights are used.

Permissions also have something called *inheritance*. This feature allows a new subdirectory to take on the properties of its parent directory and allows each file to take on the properties of the folder in which it's created. This is handy because it allows permissions to be set at the top of a tree, and it controls the spread of the permissions to new objects without the administrator having to modify the permissions manually when new objects are created. Therefore, a new file that's created in a folder that anyone in the Accounting group can use will also be usable by everyone in the Accounting group, and it will have the same permissions as the accounting folder. Inheritance can be shut off for certain directories if it's desirable to do so.

Inheritance will only affect files that are created after the permissions are set. To modify the permissions on any objects below a certain folder, the permissions have to be reset all the way down the tree of folders.

Setting file permissions is fairly easy. There is a nice user interface that can be used to set permissions. Right-click the object and choose Properties from the pop-up menu. Then click the Security tab, which is shown in Figure 4.15. This window shows a list of names at the top and the list of permissions at the bottom. The names are all the users and groups that have assigned permissions to the file. The Permissions box shows what permissions the individual user has. Select a user from the list at the top of the screen, and the list at the bottom of the screen will change to reflect the permissions the user has. The check boxes can have three possible states: checked, unchecked, and gray. A checked box in the Allow column shows that the selected user has that particular permission on the object. A checked box in the Deny column means the user will be denied the rights to the file.

FIGURE 4.15
The Security tab allows the file permissions for individual users to be set.

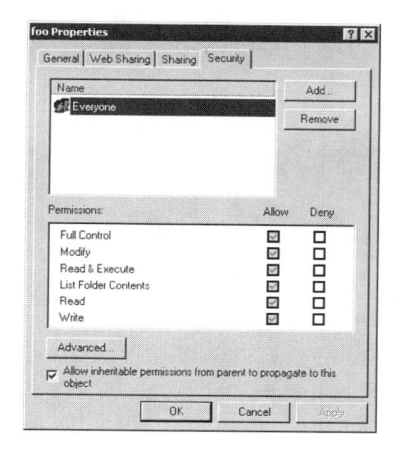

If the Permissions box is gray, the permissions were inherited from the parent object. To change permissions that are gray, either turn off the check box at the bottom of the screen that's labeled Allow Inheritable Permissions from Parent to Propagate to This Object or change the permissions on the parent object. Also, if the grayed box is the Allow check box, clicking the Deny check box will deny access even though the Allow check box is turned on and gray.

When setting the permissions on a folder, sometimes you'll need to reset all the permissions on the existing child objects. Remember that setting the Allow Inheritable Permissions... check box will only affect new files and will not do anything to existing files. In order to set the subfolders and other files of a directory, you have to click the Advanced button from the Properties window to open the Access Control Settings dialog box, shown in Figure 4.16. This shows all the permissions currently in effect for the object, and it allows those permissions to be changed. Clicking the View/Edit button will allow the special properties for the folder to be set. Turning on the Reset Permissions on All Child Objects and Enable Propagation of Inheritable Permissions check box will go through all the subfolders and files from the current folder and copy the permissions shown in the Permission Entries box.

> **Note**
>
> Recursively resetting permissions on a directory that contains thousands of objects will take a while. This shouldn't affect users except for the increased disk and processor activity.

FIGURE 4.16
The advanced properties allow subfolders and included files to be reset to the current object's settings.

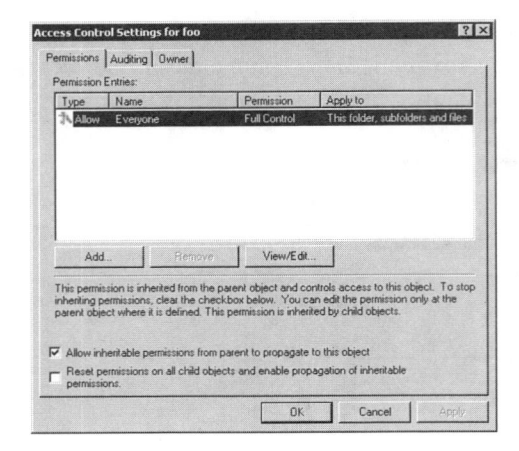

The Owner tab of the Access Control Settings window allows the ownership of the file to be changed. Ownership can only be taken; it can never be given away. To give someone ownership of a file, grant the "take ownership" permission; then that user has to go to the Access Control Settings window and actually take ownership of the file.

> **"This Is Nuts! How Do I Do This in Real Life?"**
>
> Well, there's a lot to setting file permissions, and it takes some thought and insight in order to really understand how it all works. This section covers all the mechanics of how file permissions work and how to use them.
>
> Most networks have three types of file security situations: user home directories, group directories, and public spaces. User home directories are always set up with the user in full control and all objects inheriting permissions from the top-level folder. The user will automatically own all the objects in that folder, because he or she will be creating the objects in the first place.
>
> Group directories are similar to user directories. These contain all the files used by specific groups inside of the company, such as an Accounting folder to hold all the inventory information. That folder should be granted Full Control permissions to the Accounting group and no permissions to anyone else. That will secure the accounting data.
>
> Some networks use a wide-open directory for users to exchange files back and forth. This type of general space should have the group Everyone with Full Control. There are, of course, certain policies and other restrictions that should be placed on the folder so it doesn't grow uncontrollably. This is probably a good place to use disk quotas.

File security is something that's important to experiment with. The first step is to create a partition that's formatted with NTFS. Then create folders in the partition and experiment on the folders, first by turning off their Allow Inheritable Permissions check box and then by manipulating files and logging on as different users. Next, experiment with the different file permissions and see how they work.

Working with Formats

FAT and FAT32 disk formats can be upgraded to NTFS. Once a disk is converted to NTFS, it can't be reduced back to FAT or FAT32. NTFS requires at least 5MB of disk space of overhead, which it uses to store the journal and security information.

To format a partition, open Disk Management, right-click the partition, and choose Format. This will bring up the Format dialog box, as shown in Figure 4.17. Type in a volume label and then choose the disk format to use and the allocation unit size. The *allocation unit size* is the smallest amount of disk space that can be allocated. Larger volumes require larger allocation units. Usually, choosing the default is best; the system will choose the smallest allocation unit that will work in the size volume being formatted. A "quick format" simply erases all the allocation information from the disk without actually initializing the whole disk. It's a lot faster for large volumes.

FIGURE 4.17
Choose which format type to use and then click OK to start formatting.

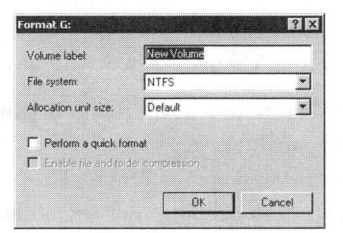

To convert a partition from one of the FAT file systems to NTFS, open a command shell by going to Start, Run and typing **cmd**. Then use the `convert` command. For example, to convert the volume C: to NTFS, use this command:

```
convert c: /fs:ntfs
```

If the drive is being used, if the drive is the system disk, or if the drive has the pagefile on it, the conversion won't happen until the system is rebooted. Otherwise, the conversion will begin immediately.

Another way to format a disk is to use the `format` command from the command line. Here's how to format a disk using the FAT32 file system:

```
Format d: /fs:fat32
```

Recommendations

There are ongoing debates on how to partition and format disk space for use on servers. This section reflects my opinions, but I'll try to give counterpoints where possible.

I always make boot partitions and the system partition with the FAT file system. I also usually make them about 2GB. I do this for several reasons, which can all be traced back to one simple fact: Any FAT partition can be accessed using an MS-DOS boot disk. If the primary partition has a problem, I can use any number of disk utilities from either Microsoft (ScanDisk) or Norton Disk Doctor to scan and possibly repair any damage to the disk. In addition, if I need to install some DLLs manually and Windows 2000 won't let go of them, I can boot the server using a boot disk and handle it.

The counterpoint to this would be that if I can go up to my server and boot it using a boot disk, so can anyone else. My argument to that is that, if a bad guy can get to my server and put a boot disk in it, the server wasn't secured anyway, and I deserve what I get. In addition, there are a number of utilities out there that will read NTFS volumes from a boot disk, either by booting Linux or by booting MS-DOS and using some utilities.

If the server is properly configured, there won't be any significant traffic writing to the boot disk, because there won't be any paging and there won't be any user data stored on the volume. Therefore, keeping the file allocation tables healthy and in sync won't be a problem, because it's pretty rare that something changes on the disk anyway.

Volumes that store data are always NTFS. The power-down reliability of NTFS with the journaling file system, the security, and the small cluster sizes (even for fairly large disks) all combine to make NTFS perfect for large data volumes. The NTFS security system also allows a lot of flexibility with respect to keeping files secure but easily accessible to the right people.

The SQL Server machines I run use a 2GB FAT system partition, which is mirrored, a 2GB pagefile partition, which is not mirrored, and a 2GB utility partition opposite the pagefile. Then I use a separate SCSI channel with mirrored 4.3GB drives to hold the `tempdb` database, which is used as a scratchpad for SQL Server. I also have a huge Fibre Channel array with RAID-5 to store data.

On my dual-boot workstation at home, I use a 2GB FAT system partition and a 2GB ext2 partition for Linux. The rest of the disk is formatted with FAT32, because it's accessible from both Linux and Windows 2000.

These are just suggestions. The important thing is to come up with a scheme that allows for easy repairs and high performance for your systems.

Working with Volumes

Volume is the term used to describe partitions that are used on a dynamic disk. This section covers how to use volumes, how to create stripe sets and, in general, how to work with the special features in dynamic disks. Windows 2000 supports the following types of volumes:

- *Simple volumes*. Similar to the primary partition on a basic disk
- *Spanned volumes*. Volumes that extend over more than one disk
- *Mirrored volumes*. Two disks that contain the exact same information to provide fault tolerance
- *Striped volumes*. Three or more disks that can be treated as a single volume, with the data distributed evenly across the disks
- *RAID-5 volumes*. Three or more disks with data distributed across the disks and parity information stored evenly across the disks

Let's start with a look at simple volumes.

Working with Simple Volumes

A *simple volume* is a volume created on a single dynamic disk. It can take up the entire disk or just a portion of the disk. Figure 4.18 shows a display from Disk Management with some simple volumes and some unallocated space on Disk 1. The figure shows that Disk 1 is 3.99GB, online, and dynamic. The volumes G: and H: are simple volumes created on the disk, and there's some space left on the disk.

FIGURE 4.18
The Disk Management tool, displaying how some simple volumes are represented onscreen.

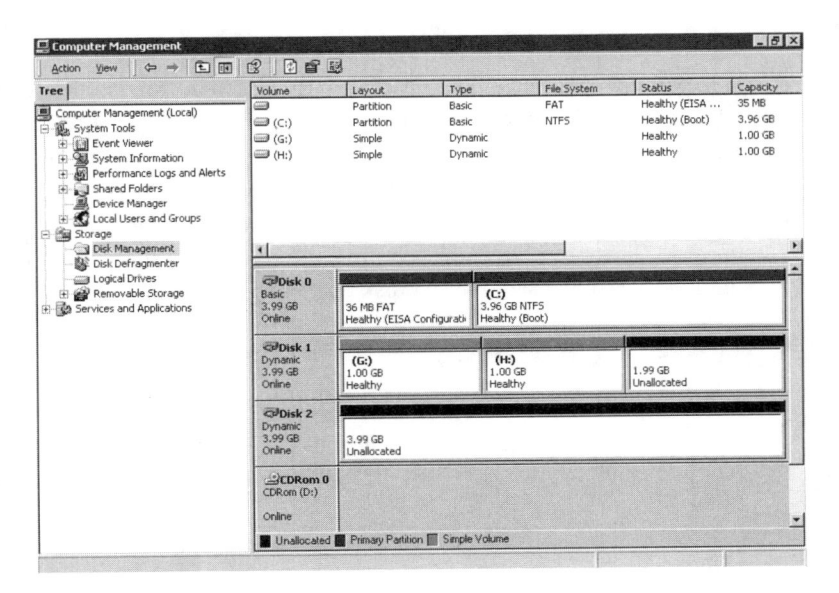

Simple volumes are created by right-clicking the unallocated space on a dynamic disk and choosing Create Volume. The Create Volume Wizard asks what type of volume to create, which disks to create it on, and how to format the new volume.

Right-clicking the volume and choosing Delete Volume will delete simple volumes. This will destroy all the data on the volume, so be careful. In addition, right-clicking a volume allows the drive letter or path to be changed and will also allow the drive to be reformatted.

Spanned Volumes

When a small server runs out of disk space, it's easy to add another disk. But it might be more difficult to use that disk. It would be nice if the volume that contained all the user files could just be extended onto the new disk. Well, that's what spanned volumes allow. Basically, they extend a volume from one disk to another without needing a new drive letter created; they simply add the space onto the existing volume. This is very handy on small servers that start with a limited amount of disk space but need to grow a little to accommodate the growing needs of users. Extending the volume simply adds space to the volume, and it's much easier than trying to split the data across separate drive letters.

> **Note**
>
> A little note about spanning disks: If a volume is spanned across two disks, and one of the disks goes bad, the entire volume will be unavailable and must be restored from backup. By having two disks involved in a volume, the chance of a hardware failure causing data loss is doubled. Consider using mirroring or RAID-5 before using spanned volumes on important servers.

To span a volume, you must have an NTFS partition to expand and some empty space to expand onto. Then, in Disk Management, choose the NTFS partition and then right-click it and choose Extend Volume. The Extend Volume Wizard will start. Click Next and then choose the volumes to extend the partition onto, using the dialog box shown in Figure 4.19. Individual disks can be added by selecting them from the window on the left and clicking Add. Then, by selecting each disk from the list on the right, you can change the amount of space to be used on each disk by typing the new amount into the Size box.

Mirrored Volumes

A *mirrored volume* is a volume that contains duplicated data across two disks. Both disks involved in a mirrored volume contain the exact same data, and when data is written to the volume, it's automatically written to both disks.

FIGURE 4.19
The Disk Management tool is being used here to expand a volume into some empty space.

Mirrored volumes allow for fairly high performance on reads but slower performance on writes. Reads go faster because each disk can be reading something different at the same time. Writes are slower because they have to happen to both disks at the same time.

To create a mirrored volume, first create a simple volume and then right-click it and choose Add Mirror. A dialog box, shown in Figure 4.20, will pop up and ask which physical disk to mirror onto. Choose one disk and click Add Mirror. The mirroring process will start.

FIGURE 4.20
The dialog box used to mirror a disk. Choose the disk to mirror the partition onto and then click Add Mirror; then the mirroring process will begin.

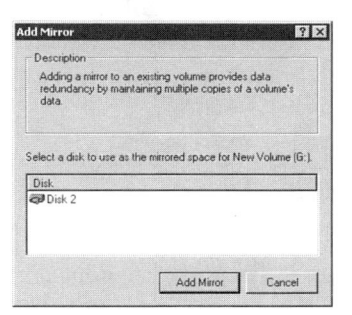

After the mirror is created, the volume will be accessed with one drive letter or through one part of the path if the drives are mounted onto an NTFS partition.

If one of the disks in a mirrored volume fails, there are some steps to take to get the mirrored volume back to fault tolerance. First, it might be a good idea to try just reactivating the disk after powering the system down. If the errors don't happen consistently, it may just be that the drive's logic has a problem that can be cleared out by rebooting. Take a moment to inspect the cabling to the drive and make sure neither the data nor the power cables have wiggled loose. On a SCSI chain, be sure the terminator is firmly seated on both ends of the cable. After powering back up, open Disk Management again and then right-click the disk that failed and click Reactivate Disk. The status of the disk will change to Regenerating and then Healthy if the disk was able to reactivate successfully.

If the disk won't return to healthy status, it's time to install a new disk and rebuild the mirror relationship. This is done by first removing the mirror relationship between two volumes that are part of the set by right-clicking the healthy volume and choosing Remove Mirror. Then, right-click the healthy volume again and mirror the disk just like it was being mirrored the first time.

To remove one of the volumes from a mirrored volume, first right-click one of the volumes and choose Remove Mirror. The volume that was right-clicked will then revert to unallocated space, which can then be reused as a simple volume.

Striped Volumes

A *striped volume* is a volume whose data is spread across 2 to 32 disks. The disks are divided into blocks, and the blocks are spread across disks. For example, in a volume with three disks, the first block goes on the first disk, the second block goes on the second disk, the third block goes on the third disk, the fourth block goes on the first disk, and so on. This will distribute data across all the drives.

This is the highest-performance volume set offered by Windows 2000. For example, if a file is stored across three disks, in order to read the entire file into memory, the system will be able to read parts of the information from the three disks, and all the disks can search for their parts of the information at the same time. Ideally, this would be three times faster than if the document were only on one disk.

Striping provides absolutely no fault tolerance, so if one drive breaks, the entire volume will be gone. Striping should only be used with data that's fairly static or backed up very regularly (and outages for the replacement of hardware are not a concern).

To set up a striped volume, click some unused space on one of the drives to be placed into the striped volume. Then choose Create Volume. Choose Striped Volume and click Next. The dialog box shown in Figure 4.21 will appear. For each drive that should participate in the striped volume, click the drive in the left list and click the Add button. When complete, click the Next button. The next two screens ask for a drive letter and a path, just like creating a simple volume. Click Next after reaching the summary screen, and the system will begin creating the striped volume.

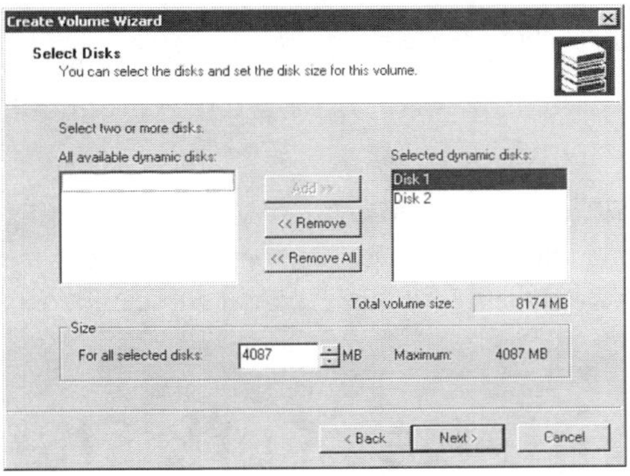

FIGURE 4.21
In this dialog box you choose which volumes will participate in a striped volume. Pick at least two but no more than 32 volumes.

RAID-5 Volumes

RAID-5 volumes take the concept of the striped volume and go one step further. In addition to storing the data itself, parity information is also stored in the stripe set, using the same methods discussed at the beginning of this chapter in the section "Advanced Controller Technology." RAID-5 is striping with striped parity, so the parity information is stored in blocks right next to the actual data.

To set up a RAID-5 volume, follow the same instructions as setting up a striped volume, but choose RAID-5 Volume instead of Striped Volume.

A Few Notes on Windows 2000 Volumes

Mirroring, striping, and RAID-5 volumes are great features of Windows 2000 and, depending on the choices you've made, they'll allow some great fault tolerance as well. However, they don't perform as well or add the great features that a good hardware-based RAID system will allow.

There's a lot of overhead involved in mirroring and striping. The processor has to compute where to put the various blocks and, with parity, the processor has to compute the parity pieces. The processor ends up doing a lot of I/O work that it can handle easily. There is a variety of hardware RAID systems, however, that offer the same capabilities that will offload all these computations from the CPU so that it can perform more interesting tasks.

In addition, hardware RAID systems can offer some neat advanced features, such as the capability to add storage or replace failed drives on-the-fly. Check the manufacturer's instructions carefully before trying either of these operations, but generally they're safe and easy and will cause no downtime.

Also, many hardware RAID systems provide features such as the capability to keep a *warm spare*, which is a drive that's sitting in the machine just waiting for another drive to fail. As soon as a failure occurs, the warm spare will take over for the failed drive and begin to regenerate parity information.

Basically, the Windows 2000 software RAID system is very interesting and provides a good feature set for someone who doesn't want to spend the money to buy hardware RAID. However, hardware RAID is a lot more efficient and can be more fault tolerant than software RAID.

Working with Network Shares

Many of the Windows 2000 Server installations will be performing the duties of a file server. A *file server* is a computer on a network that allows centralized, secure, and reliable access to files on a network. Windows 2000 Server uses the CIFS (Common Internet File System) protocol for sharing files. CIFS was previously known as *SMB* (Server Message Block) back before Microsoft knew about the Internet and started naming everything with the word *Internet* in it.

Windows 2000 uses a "network share" architecture to make files available to clients over the network. Any folder on a Windows 2000 computer can be shared out to the network, and permissions can be added to the share to govern both which users are allowed to access the share and how many users can access a share simultaneously.

Working with shares requires understanding two different pieces of software. First, the administrator has to share out a directory on the server, and then the user has to access the shared directory from a client workstation.

Sharing Directories

To share out a directory, use Explorer to go to the folder above the folder to be shared out. For example, to share out the folder D:\USERFILES go to D:\. Then right-click the folder to be shared out and choose Sharing. To share out a folder, click the Share This Folder option, shown in Figure 4.22. This will enable the rest of the dialog box. Then type in a name for the share. The share name doesn't have to be the same as the folder name, but that's the default value. The Comment field is optional but can describe the type of information being shared out. The User Limit field governs the number of simultaneous connections to the share, but it defaults to Maximum Allowed, which will allow as many connections as there are configured licenses.

FIGURE 4.22
The Sharing tab is used to make folders available to users across the network.

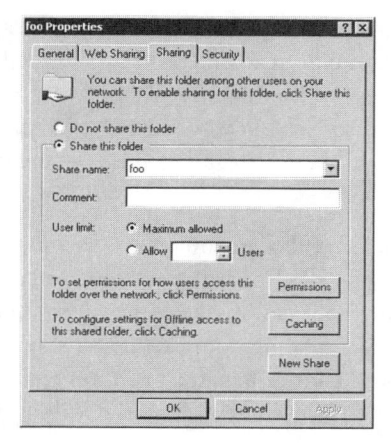

The Permissions button opens the Permissions dialog box, shown in Figure 4.23, which allows the permissions for the share to be assigned. If the folder is not on an NTFS volume, this will provide all the access control to the folder. Simply set up who should have access to all the files and folders in the shared folder and what types of access they should have. There are only three levels of access. Full Control access allows reads and writes to the files as well as the creation of subdirectories. Change allows only changes to existing files, and Read allows only reading of the files. These can be set on a per-user or per-group basis for each user or group listed in the Name box.

FIGURE 4.23
The list of the users who are allowed to access a share and how they can access the share.

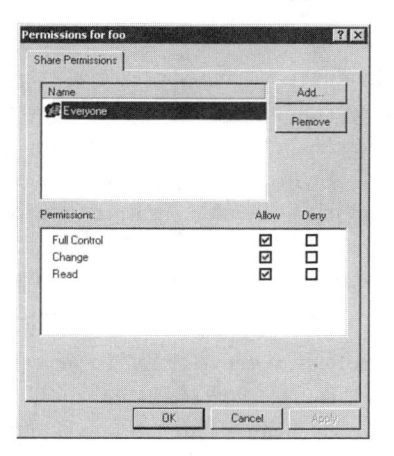

There are three levels of permissions (Full Control, Change, and Read) and three different options for each (Allow, Deny, and Neither). If Deny is checked, the particular action will be denied no matter what other options are chosen. For example, if Change is set to Allow, and Read is set to Deny, the files on the share will be write-only for that user. If

Full Control is set to Deny, both Read and Change will be set to Deny as well, because denying Full Control also denies the ability to read and write. To correctly set up read-only, the Read permission should be set to Allow and the Change permission should be set to Deny. Then, no matter what, the user will only be able to read that folder. In that case, even if a group that the user is part of has Change permission, the user will only be able to read.

If the shared folder is on an NTFS partition, the situation is a little more complex. In order to access a file that's shared out on an NTFS partition, the user has to be able to access the share and have access to the file. For the sake of simplicity, think of the share permissions and the NTFS permissions combining to make the most restrictive combination of permissions possible. Therefore, if a user has Read permissions to a share but Full Control of all the files on the folder and all its contents, the user will only be able to read files from the share.

Users and groups can be assigned access to a share, just like assigning access to a file. Click the Add button and then choose the users from the User Security dialog box. When you're done picking users and groups, click OK. The users will be added back to the Permissions dialog box.

The Caching button sets up the default caching of the folder. If the user chooses to cache that particular share, as the user reads and writes, the files will be copied and synchronized between the user's workstation and the server. This reduces network traffic but also allows the user to take files offsite, using a laptop or high-capacity media, and work on them elsewhere.

The Caching settings involve how individual users will cache local copies of documents or programs. Three cache settings are possible. The Manual Caching for Documents setting relies on the user selecting which documents will be cached and which won't. The Automatic Caching for Documents setting will cause every document to be cached locally as the document is accessed, and the Automatic Caching for Programs setting allows local copies of programs to be kept on the user's machine. In all cases, Windows 2000 monitors the user's local machine and copies data down in such a way as to overwrite older copies of programs or documents to make way for new documents.

After the folder is shared, it's immediately available to users. To stop sharing a folder, go back to the Sharing dialog box and click Do Not Share This Folder. Users will continue to be able to use files they have open on the share but will not be able to open new files and will not be able to reopen files after they disconnect.

To check out the current status of shares, open Computer Management and click Shared Folders. There are three items within the Shared Folders group: Shares, Sessions, and Open Files. The Shares item will display all the current shares on the local machine. There will be many shares that end with a dollar sign ($). These are hidden shares, and they aren't shown by a browser. Shares such as C$ are administrative shares; they're only available to administrators and are not displayed in the list of shares to network clients.

The Sessions object shows all the users currently connected to each share. It shows who is connected, how many files they have open, and how long they've been connected. A user can be disconnected by right-clicking the session and clicking Close Session. The user will lose contact with the server and may lose data, so don't do this unless it's really necessary. The Open Files object shows which files a networked user has open and whether he's reading the file, writing the file, or both. Right-click a file in this window and click Close File to close the user's access to that file.

> ### Sharing from the Command Prompt
>
> It's always a good idea to know how to perform operations from the command prompt as well as through the graphical user interface, for two reasons. First of all, if it can be done from the command prompt, it can be scripted into a batch file. Second, there are some low-bandwidth utilities such as Telnet and Remote Console (rconsole) that allow a text-only connection to a server. Telnet is covered in Chapter 19, "SNA Connectivity with BackOffice." These tools allow only a command prompt interface, and they work great over slow dial-up lines.
>
> - To share a directory from the command prompt, use the `net share` command. The `net share` command has five modes, depending on what arguments are passed.
> - Typing **net share** all by itself on the command line shows all the nonhidden shares available on the local server.
> - Typing **net share** *sharename* will show the share properties for the share called *sharename*. These include the name of each share, the local path to the folder being shared, the comment, the maximum number of users, and the current users of the share.
> - The third option is `net share` *sharename=drive:path*. This will share out the folder specified by *drive:path* as *sharename* to everyone, with no limit on connections. To specify a limit of users, use the `/users:50` command to make the limit 50 users (or substitute whatever number is appropriate).
> - The fourth option is the same as the third, but it doesn't specify the drive and path. This option is used to reset the properties of the path, such as changing the connection limit using the `/users` command.
> - The fifth option is to use `net share` *sharename* `/delete`. This will delete the share.

Connecting to Shared Directories

Now that the directories are shared, users will need to connect to them. This section provides a brief look at how clients connect to shares, because it's different, depending on which client software is being used.

To connect to a share, the user has to know the server name and the share name, which constitutes the UNC (universal naming convention) name of the share. UNC names are written as \\server\share. Therefore, for a server called Einstein and a share called Relative, the UNC path would be written as \\einstein\relative. Keep in mind that neither the server name nor the share name is case sensitive.

Users have two options when they want to view the data on the share. The user can map a drive letter to the share, and then the share becomes accessible as if it were a local disk. Otherwise, the user can just use the UNC path to name the share.

The easy way to map a network drive is to right-click the My Computer icon and choose Map Network Drive. This will display a dialog box, shown in Figure 4.24, that allows the UNC name of the share to be entered or, depending on the operating system, access to a Browse button that will allow the server and share to be selected from the Browse list. The only major option on that page that's consistent from client system to client system is the Reconnect at Logon box. If the user wants the drive mapping to persist the next time the user logs on, make sure this box is checked.

FIGURE 4.24
To map a network drive, either type in the UNC path to the share or use the Browse button.

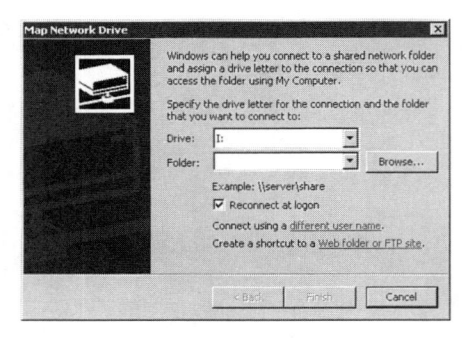

What actually happens when the user tries to connect to a share? Well, first the client sends the security token it received at login to the server, and the server checks to see whether that client is supposed to have access to the share. If so, the user is allowed to access the share.

If the token identification check fails, the system falls back to a username/password combination. Then, if that fails, the connection will fail. At this point, the next action depends on the operating system. On Windows 95 or Windows 98, the user will be denied access. On Windows NT or Windows 2000, the user will be prompted with a Connect As dialog box. At this point, the user can retry authentication with a different user account by putting in a username and password.

> ### Connecting with the Command Line
>
> Connecting with the command line requires using the `net use` command. The `net use` command has four different modes of operation. The first mode, which has no switches, displays all the connections the computer currently has. The second mode takes the form `net use <drive> <UNC path>` and maps a drive to a UNC path. The third method is used to connect to the user's home drive: `net use <drive> /HOME`. The fourth mode is `net use /persistent:[yes/no]`. This establishes whether drives will be reconnected at logon.
>
> In addition, to simply view a directory of a share, use the `dir` command with the full path, such as `dir\\intrepid\c$\winnt`. The full path to the share name has to be on the command line.

DFS: The Distributed File System

Wouldn't it be nice to have one big file system that spanned multiple servers? It would be great if that file system could automatically replicate data across the network so that when several users need a particular file, they could load it from a server that's near them.

The Distributed File System (DFS) is a feature in Windows 2000 that creates a server-spanning file system with automatic replication and locking to prevent change collision. It can distribute frequently used files across the network, allowing them to be accessed over higher-bandwidth short-haul connections, and keep less frequently used files in fewer locations, to save space. It can distribute data across the country for fault tolerance. If there's an earthquake and everything east of California falls into the Atlantic, the users in California will still be able to read all the data because it was distributed to their servers.

DFS has been a long time coming. Beta versions have been around for years but, until now, it was never really integrated into the operating system at this level. DFS provides distributed and consistent access to files so that users can access a file the same way every time. The user will always get the current file, and it will always be accessed the same way.

This section covers DFS, first by examining the general concepts upon which DFS is built and then by reviewing how to set up and administer DFS. Finally, it will look at how clients can use DFS to access files.

DFS Concepts

A distributed file system starts at the DFS root. This is the top of a hierarchical schema that's very similar to a normal folder-and-file directory system. A *DFS link* is the connection between a DFS root and a DFS shared folder. A DFS link masks the real location of the DFS shared folder from the user, so the actual data can be retrieved from any number of locations within a shared folder set. Shared folder sets can contain up to 32 replicas of a single shared folder.

DFS shared folder sets replicate data between shared folders according to an administrator-selected replication schedule. Here are the available replication schedules:

- *Automatic replication.* Automatic replication replicates changes on a timed basis to all the replicas within a set, the default cycle time being 15 minutes. Therefore, every 15 minutes, the File Replication Service checks all the replicas to ensure they're in sync. Automatic replication can only occur for files that are stored on an NTFS partition.

- *Manual replication.* Manual replication requires an administrator to start the replication process. When large files are stored within a DFS or if the files don't change very often, manual replication is probably a good idea.

In addition, the DFS root itself can be replicated. That way, if the other computer that holds the DFS root goes offline, the replica can take over requests.

There are two types of DFS roots. If a DFS root is hosted by a domain server that's participating in Active Directory, the DFS root is called *domain based*. A domain-based DFS root does not have a limitation on depth, and the DFS root functions as a DFS shared folder and can hold files. In addition, a domain-based DFS root is published to the Active Directory so that it's more accessible.

A standalone DFS root can be only one level deep (one DFS root pointing to one set of DFS shared folders). In addition, the DFS root itself cannot contain shared folders, so all the data must be on the other side of a DFS link.

Files stored in DFS are cached locally by each client that accesses the DFS tree. There's a configurable cache timeout that sets up how often the client will check to see if a new version of the file has been replicated.

Setting Up DFS

To start the DFS management tool, go to Control Panel, Administrative Tools and open the Distributed File System object. To begin using DFS, first create a DFS root by choosing Action, New DFS Root from the menu. The New DFS Root Wizard starts up and will ask several questions to set up the DFS root. First, choose whether to create a domain-based DFS root or a standalone DFS root from the dialog box shown in Figure 4.25.

Then click Next. On the next screen from the wizard, type in the name of the server that will host the DFS root and click Next. On the next screen, put in the name of the share and the server that will be hosting the DFS root; then click Next. Click Next again to reach the summary page and then click Next again to create the DFS root.

FIGURE 4.25
The New DFS Root Wizard steps you through the process of implementing DFS.

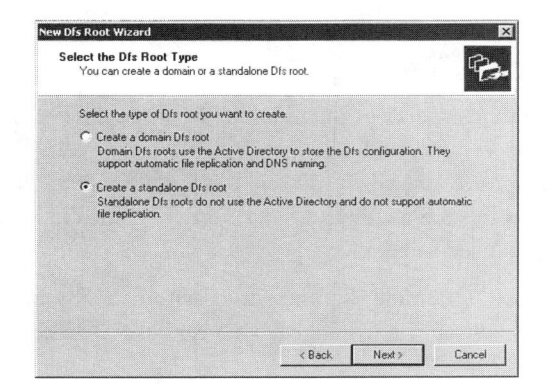

Using DFS

To connect to DFS from a DFS client, start DFS by going to Control Panel, Administrative Tools and opening the Distributed File System item. Then choose Action, Display an Existing DFS Root. You'll be asked to enter the name of a DFS root. There are three different ways to name a DFS root. For a domain-based DFS root, the form `\\<domain>\<root>` can be used, where `<domain>` is the fully qualified domain name for the domain (for example, `\\intrepid.com\dfsroot`). For standalone domains, the form `\\<server>\<root>` and `\\<server>\<shared folder>` are both valid. The DFS root can then be browsed from the DFS application.

Remote Storage Server

Remote Storage Server is a system that allows a piece of removable storage, such as a tape drive, CD-ROM drive, or optical disk drive, to be used as a normal drive over the network. It keeps an online catalog of all the files on different media and uses the Removable Storage Manager (RSM) to determine where the different media are and to get them loaded. RSM is discussed in the next section.

So what is this, really? It's a system that can provide automated retrieval of files from tape by users, provided that the requested tapes are online (either actually in a tape drive, accessible by a robotic changer) or requests can be queued up for operator intervention.

This is a system that will allow files that are old or rarely used to be archived to tape and extracted without administrator intervention. The concept is very old; mainframes have had the ability to automatically retrieve data from tape for a long time and have even had robotic tape changers for a long time. This system provides the same capability to access huge volumes of tape storage in a short amount of time. Tape storage is less expensive to purchase, expand, and manage than disk storage and, for files that are to be archived, the Remote Storage Server can provide some great benefits to users.

Remote Storage Concepts

Remote Storage uses a volume on disk as the interface between the user and the files on tape. Files are copied to the volume, and then the Remote Storage Server monitors the usage of the volume and removes the files from the file system that are less frequently used. The files are removed in such a way as to leave the filenames in place, but the actual data space used is reduced to zero.

When a user requests a file, the Remote Storage Server automatically figures out which tape the file is on and retrieves the file from tape. This can take awhile, so user education is pretty important.

Setting Up Remote Storage

First, install Remote Storage by going to Control Panel, Add/ Remove Programs and choosing Windows Components. From there, choose Remote Storage and let the Windows Components Wizard handle installing the software. After the installation is complete, wait until the system advises you that it needs to reboot.

After the reboot, go to Computer Management, Storage and open up the Remote Storage item.

Removable Storage Management

The Removable Storage Manager (RSM) is a system used to manage libraries of media, such as tape or optical disk libraries. It doesn't provide the disk-extension features that Remote Storage Server does; it just supplies applications such as Backup and Remote Storage Server with information on where data is located by keeping track of tapes and tape sets.

RSM uses two groupings to identify sets. A *library* is a piece of hardware that can read removable storage. An optical disk jukebox is an example of a library, and so is a tape changer. There are two types of libraries. A *robotic library* automatically changes media; a standalone drive library is a single-media device that requires a human operator to change media.

A *media pool* is a logical group of media used to group together individual tapes or disks. A media pool can only contain media (individual tapes) or other media pools. It is categorized as Unrecognized, Import, Free, and Application-Specific.

An Unrecognized media pool contains tapes that have not been initialized for use with RSM. Unrecognized media can be assigned to the Free pool, at which time the media will be initialized and available for use.

An Import media pool is a set of media that isn't recognized by the RSM on that computer but has been used by RSM somewhere else. Usually this will happen when media are moved from one machine to another or from one office to another. Media in the Import media pool can be moved either to the Free pool, where it will be overwritten, or to the Application-Specific pool, where it will be used.

A Free media pool is media that haven't been assigned to an application yet. In other words, media in this pool is free to be used.

The Application-Specific media pool contains media that are currently in use by an application, such as Backup. An application can control multiple media pools—for example, the Backup application can have a media pool for full backups and another for incremental backups.

Media pools are managed by the Computer Management application by opening the Storage, Removable Storage item. This item contains four objects: Media Pools, Physical Locations, Work Queue, and Operator Requests.

The Media Pools item is used to create and manage media pools. To create a new media pool, right-click Media Pools and choose Create Media Pool, which opens the Create a New Media Pool Properties dialog box, as shown in Figure 4.26. Fill in a name and description for the media pool and then define what the media pool will contain. A media pool can contain anything from floppy disks to DLT tapes, but they all have to be the same. In the Allocation/Deallocation Policy box, choose how media will be created and removed from the pool. Media can be manually added to the pool via a drag-and-drop mechanism after the pool is created or automatically allocated by the pool when the pool needs space. When a medium is no longer needed, it can be deallocated and returned to the Free media pool.

The Physical Locations item defines what physical devices are connected to the computer and helps set up which items are available for use by RSM.

The Work Queue item shows the requests that are currently being processed by RSM and their status. If a backup job is running, for example, the queue would show the status of the job and which tapes it was using.

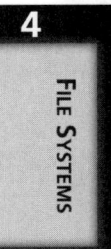

FIGURE 4.26
The Create a New Media Pool Properties dialog box allows a media pool to be defined.

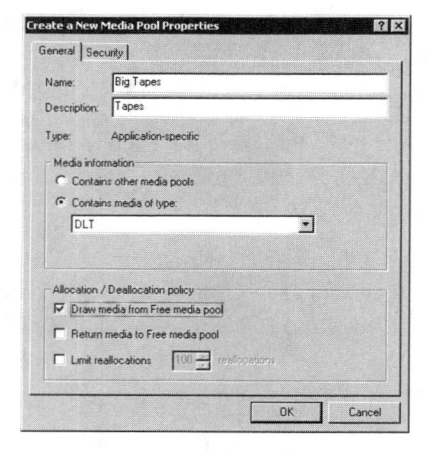

The Operator Requests item shows outstanding operator requests. An *operator request* is a request for the operator to change media in the drive, either by adding new tapes or returning existing tapes to be read.

Summary

This chapter has provided a look into the storage subsystems provided by Windows 2000. We started with the underlying hardware and standards, such as IDE and SCSI. Then, we examined disk partitioning and the Disk Administrator tool used to create disk partitions. We took a look at file systems, such as FAT, FAT32, and NTFS, and then covered sharing and security. Finally, the topics of the Distributed File System, Remote Storage Server, and Removable Storage Management were covered.

Windows 2000 implements a lot of new functionality for working with storage, such as dynamic disks and Removable Storage Management. These two new tools provide the administrator with a lot of flexibility for managing storage, providing the capability to make changes to disk layouts without interrupting users and providing access to offline storage more quickly.

CHAPTER 5

Networking Brief

IN THIS CHAPTER

- Microsoft Network Concepts *128*
- Networks (Your LAN or WAN) Versus Networks (Segmentation) *140*
- RRAS *145*

Microsoft Networking Concepts

If you came to this chapter for instructions on creating users or creating an Active Directory, you'll need to proceed on to Section III (Active Directory and Account Management). But if you need to catch your breath and gain some basic understanding of Microsoft networking and security, you have found the right launching pad.

This chapter is an introduction to the basic concepts of Microsoft networks and networking. A basic understanding of networking will allow you to make better decisions when forming a computing infrastructure. Throughout this book, mention will be made of various networking hardware and management items. This chapter is going to lay the groundwork for understanding these systems.

If you're going to manage a Windows 2000 network, it helps to understand the basic concepts of Microsoft networking. This is not to say that Microsoft strings together PCs with fishing line and hooks, or even that it does things so radically different that it's unrecognizable to the experienced networking engineer. However, Microsoft does have its own nuances. If you can understand those nuances, you have a head start.

Most of the peculiarities of Microsoft networking are not new. They have been around since the old Microsoft NetBIOS networks from the early and middle 1980s. However, if you haven't been involved with Windows NT, LAN Manger, or even LANtastic, you will gain some much-needed groundwork here.

A basic tenant of Microsoft Windows networking is the way Windows manages permissions to resources. The best way to describe this is to call it an "open to closed" system. This means that when a resource such as a network printer or file share is created, all the users have complete access. If the administrator of the system wants to control access to these shared resources, he or she must actively change the permissions for the resources.

In contrast to this, most network operating systems are "closed to open." Resources are created and no permissions to these resources are granted. By default, no one except the administrator has access to the resources.

Neither way of managing a system's permissions is right or wrong, but without being aware of this difference, a NetWare administrator, for example, could very easily leave the castle door wide open (not to mention the payroll spreadsheet).

Workgroups and Domains

Many features have been changed in Windows 2000, but workgroups and domains remain the basic building blocks of user account management. Workstations, users, and groups on a grassroots level are created, empowered, and managed through the use of these organizers. In order to understand the elaborate pieces involved in management of Active Directory, you must first understand these two forms of management.

Workgroups

The workgroup paradigm is used in peer-to-peer networking when the user population accessing the resources are around 5 to 10 users. This is due to the way workgroups maintain users and groups.

> **Networking Note**
>
> The term *peer-to-peer* evolves from the fact that no single machine in the network is considered the "server" or "client." All machines are both servers and clients. Therefore, they are *peers*.

Workgroups are a collection of Windows 2000, Windows 95/98, Windows NT, and/or Windows for Workgroup machines that appear within the same Network Neighborhood group. When users in the same workgroup attempt to use shared resources, they're presented with and allowed to attempt using the resources of those machines in their same workgroup. For that reason, it would be accurate to say that workgroups are an affiliation of machines, not users. Simply being allowed to see a resource does not mean you have access or even a valid username at that server.

In a workgroup, each server is responsible for maintaining a user and group list (see Figure 5.1). This list is not shared among the machines, and no permissions or users from a foreign list can access resources. For example, the fact that a user has been authenticated by Server A in Workgroup 1 does not allow that user to access a resource on Server B, even though Server B is in the same workgroup. In fact, the user account might not even exist on Server B.

The only exception to this fact would be if the same username and password were manually entered at each server, which is often the case. This would allow the user to enter his or her username and password one time. When the user attempts to access the other server, it would simply use the username and password already entered. This is convenient for the user, but now the administrator must maintain the same user list repeatedly for every machine.

In a peer-to-peer network environment, users are most likely looking to share only a very small number of resources. These networks popped up because small companies were buying very expensive resources such as the original Hewlett-Packard LaserJet printer. However, they could not afford to place them on everyone's desk. The solution was to connect the PCs and share the printer. When only a small number of PC files, shares, or printers are being shared, it's quite manageable for each user to maintain the trusted list of users.

FIGURE 5.1
User Manager inside of a workgroup.

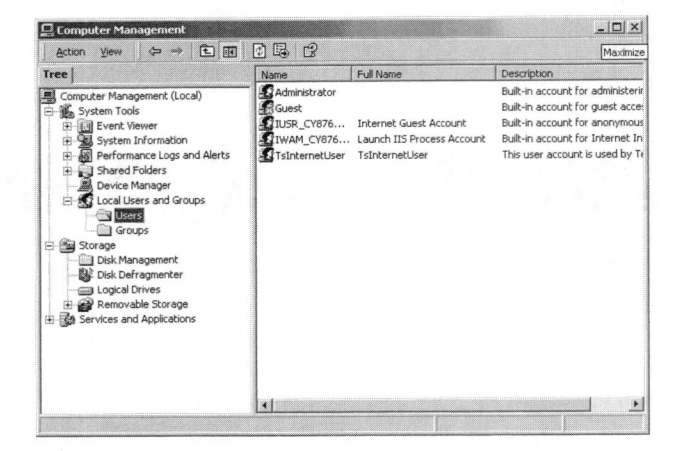

When a user in a small office attaches a new printer to his or her machine, the user can simply install the printer and share it (see Figure 5.2). Once the user shares it, all the machines in this workgroup can now see the computer and resource in their Network Neighborhood (see Figure 5.3). The user can then establish permissions to the resource for those users in his or her Machine User Manager listing.

FIGURE 5.2
The Sharing tab.

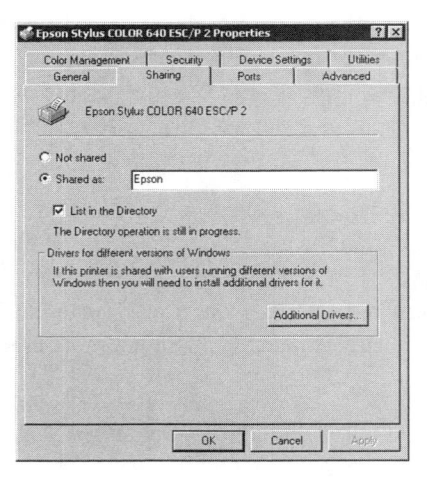

FIGURE 5.3
My Network Places, computer, and associated shares.

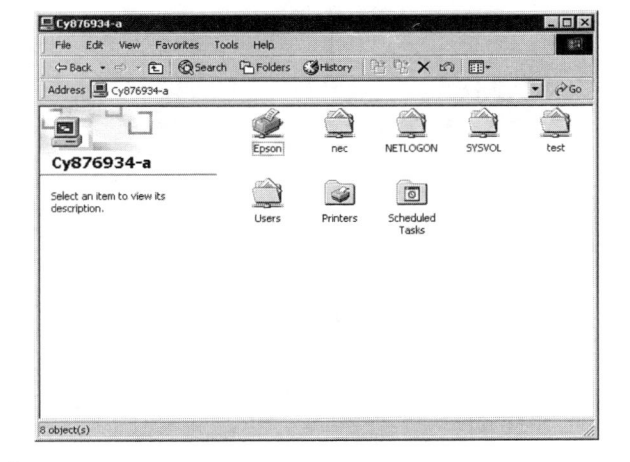

However, if the network begins to grow beyond 5 to 10 users or shares, the model collapses. The important point here is that the administrator must manage the users, groups, and permissions for each share at the server providing the shared resource. For example, the administrators of a 100-PC peer-to-peer network have to maintain 100 separate user lists, 100 different group configurations, and 100 different resource collections. All of this must be done by personally interfacing with 100 different servers.

This is where the domain model begins to make since.

Domains

Within Windows 2000, the domain model has become part of a much greater scheme called the *Active Directory*, but for the moment, we'll cover this smaller part. Before you start to use domains as a tool in this version, you must understand that they come as part of the Active Directory installation.

If the network being managed involves large numbers of resources and users, the domain model makes a better choice than workgroups. Domains are a collection of user accounts and groups of user accounts shared by multiple servers (see Figure 5.4). This allows these computers to be managed from a single location. It allows administrators to bring a great number of the administrative tasks to them instead of the reverse. It's far more attractive to large companies and campus settings.

When a domain is created, it should be given a name that's familiar to Internet surfers. The domain naming convention in Windows 2000 follows the domain naming convention used by the Internet.

FIGURE 5.4

The concept of a domain.

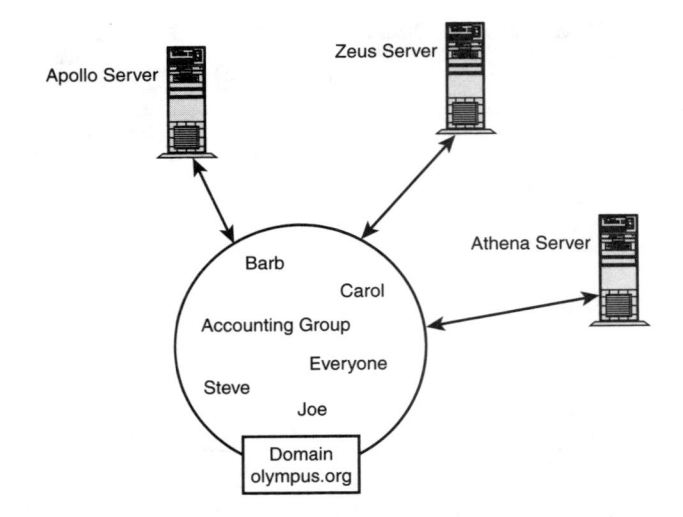

[Diagram showing Apollo Server, Zeus Server, and Athena Server connected to a domain circle labeled "Domain olympus.org" containing Barb, Carol, Accounting Group, Everyone, Steve, Joe]

The domain name is followed by an identifier (.com by default) that tells the type of organization that's using the domain name, thus producing names such as microsoft.com (Microsoft), whitehouse.gov (United States Presidential Home), bsu.edu (Ball State University). Here are the identifiers:

- .com for commercial
- .org for not-for-profit organizations
- .gov for the government
- .edu for educational organizations

Use of the DNS naming system allows Windows 2000 to use a global standard naming convention. It makes the location of Windows servers global as well, if the DNS server the domain is connected to is connected to the Internet and registered. Registering your domain name with the InterNIC is covered in the Chapters 8, "TCP/IP Networking," and 21, "Other Internet Services for Windows 2000," but it's important to realize where the naming convention comes from.

Domains have expanded to include the ability to interconnect through what are known as *trees* and *forests*.

Forests and Trees

A *domain tree* is a collection of domains that include domains and subordinate domains in a single DNS hierarchy. The root domain in a tree may have the DNS name (such as mcp.com or indiana.edu), but subsequent domains will expand on that convention. For example, you may have the domain bellind.com at the top of a tree that could contain sams.mcp.com and architecture.indiana.edu.

A *forest* is a collection of trees (well, of course it is). But it's not quite that simple. A forest is the connection of trees that do not share a contiguous DNS domain name. In the preceding example, you saw that everything in the bellind.com domain was one tree. If we then connect that tree to a tree containing all the domains of the mcp.com domain, we form a forest.

Although most companies will never grow to the size necessary to build trees or forests, it's becoming increasingly more common for companies to connect, merge, and become global. Domains, forests, and trees make this possible.

Organizational Units

Just as in physics there's macrophysics and microphysics, domains have both grown larger and become able to be divided into smaller pieces. Domains can now be divided into smaller units called organizational units (OUs). Those of you familiar with the NetWare NDS world will recognize these as the same division of the greater whole that has existed for years. If not, then here's the concept.

Domains are still the primary security borderlines and the point where control is based. But through the years, domains have been criticized because they're all inclusive. A domain administrator is all powerful, and there were few choices for making that more granular.

The administrator of a domain can create containers (OUs), create objects in those containers, and place different administrators in charge of those containers (see figure 5.5). All this can be done while at the same time maintaining control over the root of the domain. This gives a great deal more flexibility and growth to the domain model.

Through division of administration, the workload of a single administrator is lessened and the flexibility of the company information network is increased.

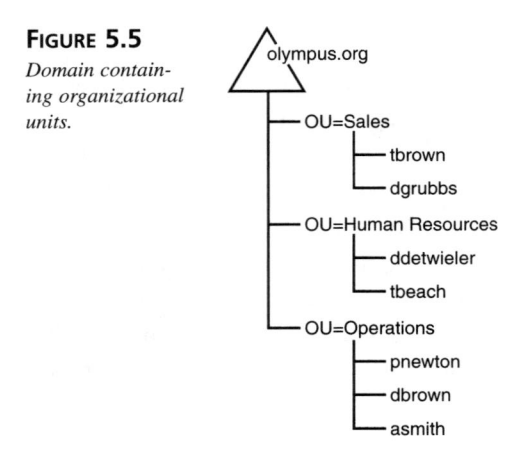

FIGURE 5.5
Domain containing organizational units.

```
olympus.org
   ├── OU=Sales
   │      ├── tbrown
   │      └── dgrubbs
   ├── OU=Human Resources
   │      ├── ddetwieler
   │      └── tbeach
   └── OU=Operations
          ├── pnewton
          ├── dbrown
          └── asmith
```

Domain Control

This is where the changes in Windows 2000 begin to become very obvious and appreciated. Domains have become far more flexible in both sizing and ability.

Domain control involves the management and passing of domain information among the servers that exist on the network. If a change must be made to a user or group definition, an authority must be established in order to make this system work. In order to allow for the growth of the system, a way must be found for allowing more than one machine to store and facilitate the use of these changes. Domain control allows this to happen.

Operations Masters

A Domain is created at the first server in the domain and that server is, for that moment, the operations master. This is important to know now because you must understand that domains are collections of information that require central control. This level of control can be moved to a different server at a later point, but during the life of a domain, in a strict domain environment, one machine will be responsible for recording various portions of change in the domain.

In Windows NT Server one machine controlled all changes for the entire Domain. In Windows 2000, domain control has been separated into individual tasks that can be spread across many different servers. These tasks include pieces that are either "one per domain" or "one per tree."

Here's a list of the one-per-tree items:

- *Schema master.* A schema master is the controller of all changes to the underlying information in the domain (known as the *schema*).

- *Domain naming master*. Controls the adding and subtracting of domains from the collection of domains (called a *forest*).

Here's a list of the one-per-domain items:

- *Relative ID master (RID master)*. Each domain contains one relative ID master. The job of this controller is the distribution of relative ID's to each of the Domain controllers.

  In order to differentiate between objects in a domain, each object is assigned a security ID (SID). A SID consists of a domain SID and a relative ID that's unique. Like a phone number consisting of your area code (domain ID) and your individual number (relative ID), the object can be identified by its domain and as a unique individual.

- *Primary domain controller (PDC) emulator*. To enable legacy Windows NT domain controllers to continue to participate in authentication, domains must have a PDC emulator. This allows the Backup Domain Controller to receive updates and continue operation through a migration.

- *Infrastructure master*. Every domain must have one infrastructure master in order to keep group references to users synchronized across domains. If a change is made to a user's group membership, the infrastructure master sends out the change.

Once an operations master is established, every machine that will participate in the domain must then register with the domain. By registering with the domain, the machine becomes a part of the resources offered by the domain. Any resources shared by the machine are controlled by the domain security. Restrictions placed on domain users and groups are enforced on the machines that have become part of the domain.

> **Standards**
>
> Windows 95/98 machines are not able to become part of a Windows 2000 or Windows NT domain. However, users can attach to the domain through these machines. This only impacts that amount of control that can be enforced on those machines.

Domain Controllers

Domain controllers (DCs) are established, like operations masters, when the first server is installed in the domain. These controllers are responsible for directory information, including users, groups, directory searches, and machine accounts. For the sake of fault tolerance and performance, it's good to have at least two DCs within your directory (see figure 5.6).

Figure 5.6
Server selection as a domain controller.

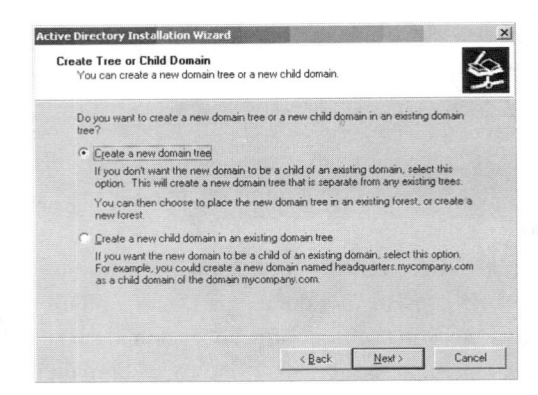

Once the first server is installed, other servers can be installed into the domain and promoted to participate in domain control. This machine is then part of a multimaster system domain. This is a great departure from the former (NT) single-master or primary domain controller role. In the multimaster model, no one controller stops the other from accepting domain object changes.

For example, in the Window NT world if the primary domain controller was down, no user could change his or her password. In a multimaster model, one domain controller accepts the change and replicates that change to the other domain controllers in the domain.

Trust Relationships

A *trust* is created between domains to allow users and groups from one domain to access resources from another domain. Windows 2000 has created two new forms of trust and has greatly advanced the trust concept.

Explicit Trusts (Classic Trusts)

Domains have traditionally been connected through what are known as *trust relationships* (and what are now called *explicit trusts*). An explicit trust is a one-way relationship that establishes a connection between one domain's resources and another domain's users and groups. Explicit trusts are so called because an administrator from each domain must explicitly create them.

If, for example, the administrator for Domain A creates a trust for Domain B, the administrator from Domain B must allow it. Then the users and groups of Domain B can be granted permission to resources in Domain A (see Figure 5.7). This is a one-way trust, and it's explicit.

FIGURE 5.7
A classic one-way trust.

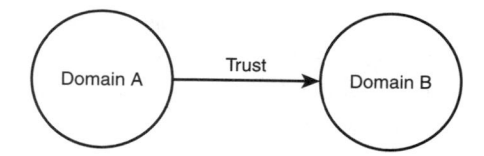

In order for the users and groups of Domain A to gain access to resources in Domain B, a separate trust must be established. This would involve Domain B trusting Domain A. With both trusts established, a "complete" trust is formed. Each trust must be formed separately and administrators in each domain must be involved.

You only need to add one more domain to this picture to understand how it can become a bit tough to maintain trust relationships (see figure 5.8). If a company with two domains were to purchase another company with a domain of its own and want to connect this domain in a complete trust to all the current domains, two connections (trusted and trusting) are needed for each new domain:

- Domain A must establish a trust with Domain B.
- Domain A must establish a trust with Domain C.
- Domain B must establish a trust with Domain A.
- Domain B must establish a trust with Domain C.
- Domain C must establish a trust with Domain A.
- Domain C must establish a trust with Domain B.

FIGURE 5.8
The beginnings of a large complete trust.

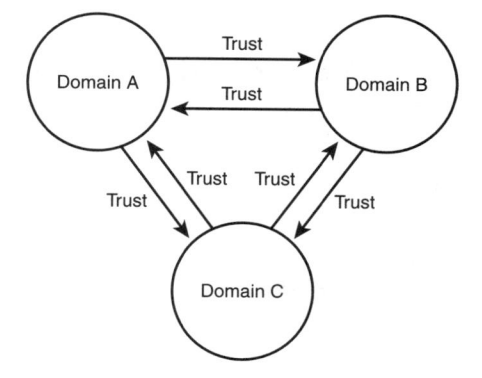

Simply establishing a trust from Domain A to Domain B and Domain B to Domain C does not establish trust from Domain A to Domain C. These classic trust relationships are not transitive from one to the other but are available in an Active Directory model.

To understand why the Windows 2000 operating system has been waited for with such enthusiasm, you need to understand that this is no longer the preferred method of connecting numerous domains. Imagine, if you will, connecting several domains together and the trust relationships that need to be established.

Intransitive Trusts

An *intransitive trust* is a trust formed between domains that are not part of the same tree or are not Windows 2000 domains. These trusts can be one-way or two-way trusts, but they cannot be transitive (see next section). Here are some examples:

- Windows 2000 domains connecting to Windows NT domains
- A Windows 2000 forest connecting to a Windows 2000 forest

Transitive Trusts

A *transitive trust* is not so much a creation of the administrator as it is a fact of domains being part of the same tree or trees that are part of the same forest. When subordinate domains are created within a tree, the two domains are, by virtue of this relationship, in a transitive trust. This trust is always a two-way trust and is not a choice that can be made or unmade.

You can create extra pathways to this form of trust called cross-linked trusts, but this is a performance issue. IT will be covered in more detail in Chapter 9, "Directory and Access Concepts Brief."

Active Directory

The single most awaited feature in the Windows network operating system has been a system that would allow users and resources to be managed in a hierarchical fashion. In other words, in the same way the files in a directory and records in a database are managed. Active Directory is the beginnings of that structure.

As can be seen in the forming of the explicit trust, it has become necessary in today's large enterprise-wide PC networks to produce a way of connecting users and resources. This method must be flexible enough to allow local administration but also allow for the transitive nature of the mobile employee or resource. It must allow for local managers to control their employees and employee information, but it must also allow the corporate IS department to control systems and policies on those systems.

Active Directory allows these things to occur by creating a structure that is multitiered, with relationships that transcend the boundaries of a particular container or domain (see Figure 5.9).

FIGURE 5.9
A hierarchy of domains, users, and machines.

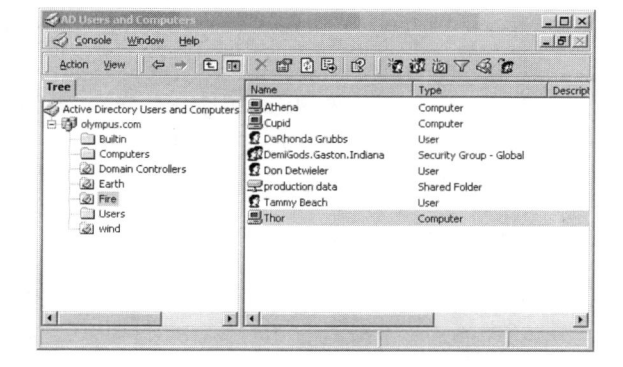

Directory Structure

In Active Directory, domains are part of a greater whole called a *directory tree*. Within the directory tree, any one piece can be linked to any other piece via the tree-like structure of the file system directory. The tree consists of container objects and leaf objects. A *leaf* is simply a user or resource that's to be contained and controlled. Obviously, *containers* are the items that contain leafs.

Container objects have already been covered in this chapter, but they haven't been called *container objects*. Domains and organizational units are examples of container objects.

User and resource objects become more powerful then simple accounts that can be granted the permission to access a share. The leaf object can now contain a number of items that previously required separate management. Leaf objects contain information fields and control fields that allow the directory to become an information store and control center for user activity and control.

A user object can contain the full name, email address, and phone number of that individual. It can contain information about how the user's Windows environment must look and feel when the user logs on to the network anywhere in the company. These utilities in the past required that the administrators store this information in multiple places and manage numerous different utilities to accomplish the same objectives.

No Master

In the classic domain model, the concept of a single master has never really disappeared. Recovery from a failure requires human intervention to put things right again. Active Directory is a multimaster system.

In this configuration, multiple copies of the directory are distributed across the network on several servers. When a change is made, the system that records the change then replicates the change across the directory. Changes are tracked at each controlling point by time and importance, thus allowing for smooth and efficient transfer of information.

This allows for better performance and fault tolerance, just as the BDC did in the classic domain model. However, it also allows for changes to be made to the directory from almost anywhere on the network as well as for those changes to take effect without dependency on any one system.

Directory-based network security and management is not new. Novell NetWare has been using it for most of the decade. However, it is a fresh new item for the Microsoft administrator.

Network Services Setup

Windows 2000 has many different layers that are not obvious on the surface. Among these layers are the services that control the utilities offered by your server. These services are no longer located in the same place in the Network Control Panel (if you're an old Windows NT veteran). They are found in a location that might be more familiar to a Windows 95/98 veteran. In windows 2000 services, protocols, and adapters are all listed under the properties for a particular connection. These items are all listed under the properties for My Network Places and by double clicking the individual connection.

Network services are the resource and application launchers that make it possible for users to log in, print, get an IP address, and perform many other tasks.

Networks (Your LAN or WAN) Versus Networks (Segmentation)

A big part of understanding how to deploy Windows 2000 and Active Directory involves understanding the network you're moving these resources across. You'll find, for example, that if you don't create domains, trees, or forests just right, you can bring the network to a screeching halt. The network infrastructure will ideally be built for maximum bandwidth. However, your job as the Windows 2000 administrator is to understand, as much as possible, what those systems are and how your system interacts with them.

Replication of domain information across expensive wide area network (WAN) lines can result in slow response to user requests. Therefore, it's important that you understand what a WAN is. If you're operating on what would be considered a large local area network (LAN), the decision to create a forest may be unnecessary. The terms *LAN* and *WAN* have now been joined by system area network (SAN), metropolitan area network

(MAN), and a plethora of other acronyms. For now, let's concentrate on the basic definitions:

- *Local area network (LAN).* A network that's completely contained in a building. LAN has also come to include high-speed campus networks staying at LAN speeds (2Kbps) or greater.
- *Wide area network (WAN).* Networks that cover a large enough area that they require special routing equipment and a phone company connection.
- *System area network (SAN).* A segment of the network that's dedicated to communications between servers and/or server components. A network created just for backing up the file servers would be a SAN.
- *Metropolitan area network (MAN).* A variation of a WAN that includes only systems in a single metropolitan area.
- *Network segment.* Systems identify each other on a network by the address of the machine and the networks address they're a part of. A *network segment* is the portion of the network that contains all the machines with the same network address.

> **Standards**
>
> The definition of a SAN is disputed by some to mean *storage area network*. According to Tandem Computers (now Compaq), the phrase was coined to mean a *system area network* involving any number of things, including a storage-based network.

Networks are built on the idea that you want to maintain the most possible throughput at all times. The amount of data you can pass through the network is referred to as the *bandwidth*. The goal is to maintain as much bandwidth as possible to every desktop, whether on a LAN or WAN.

One way of maintaining bandwidth is to control the flow of traffic by separating it into specific areas based on location and need. Ethernet is the prevalent topology for connecting PCs in a network today. Among these networks, it's very possible to separate machines to avoid excess traffic. This separation is called *segmentation*. This can be understood by taking a look at a couple of examples. For instance, users in the design department may be moving large graphics files across the network and slowing other users during the peak of the day. By putting the design department on a separate network segment, you cure this problem.

Similarly, users in New York may never access the server in Los Angeles, so it would be in your best interest to avoid cluttering up the Los Angeles network with New York user traffic. By creating the proper domain structure, you can completely eliminate this as an issue.

To understand segmentation, you must understand that there are two different actions referred to as *segmenting a network*. These are discussed in the following sections.

Switched Segmentation (Collision Domain Segments)

The first action is the separation of systems into different collision domains. When an Ethernet network is created systems communicate across that line in much the same way the humans communicate on a party line in the public phone system. All the systems are connected through either a continuous daisy chain or to a hub, as illustrated in Figure 5.10.

FIGURE 5.10
Ethernet connection styles.

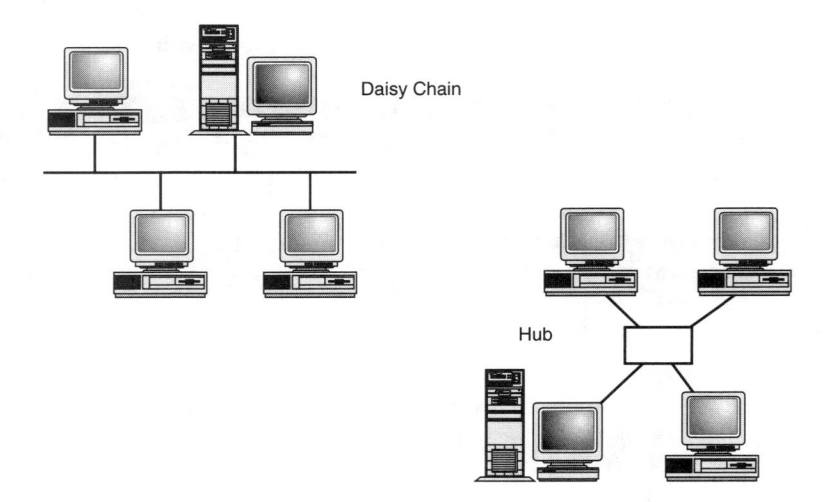

Daisy Chain

Hub

If a system attempts to communicate on the line, it first listens to find out whether another system is using the line. This is because only one system can use the line at a time. If the line is clear, the system begins to send a signal. If, at the same time, another system begins to send, a *collision* occurs. At that point, both systems wait a random period of time and attempt to send again. Because of this behavior, all the systems in a segment of Ethernet are said to be in the same collision domain.

Collisions are a natural part of Ethernet and are expected, but if they become too frequent, systems end up spending time waiting for the line to become free and not communicating. The solution is the same as for a phone line. Get the systems a dedicated line or at least make the party a bit smaller. The solution used to accomplish this is called *switching* or *bridging*.

> **Technical Note**
>
> The devices today that are called *switches* are a progression of the devices that used to be called *bridges*. Switches have gone beyond simply dividing a signal based on MAC address and have begun to do some routing.

The device that performs these tasks is called a *network switch*. When a system attempts to communicate with another PC and gains control of the line, it actually makes a broadcast call for that machine. It then waits for a response telling it where to find the specific hardware address of that machine, called the media access control (MAC) address. It then sends out a signal for that specific MAC address. This requires each machine to listen to those signals and determine whether the signals are for them. Again, like picking up the phone each time to listen and find out if a call is for you, it takes time.

If a separation can be made between groups of machines that would allow them to avoid some of these signals, a great deal of the clutter can be avoided. By separating the systems into groups or individuals that listen only to the items on their lines, you've created separate collision domains. Switches do just that.

A *switch* is a device that allows you to connect either individual machines or collections of machines on a hub to the switch, and each connection becomes a separate collision domain. These separate-but-connected sections of the network can be called *segments*. The switch listens to the systems that are connected to it and notes the MAC addresses of those machines (see figure 5.11). Then, when communications occur on the segments the switch is attached to, the switch notes each MAC address and points it to the proper segment.

FIGURE 5.11
Switched Ethernet allows for specific communications.

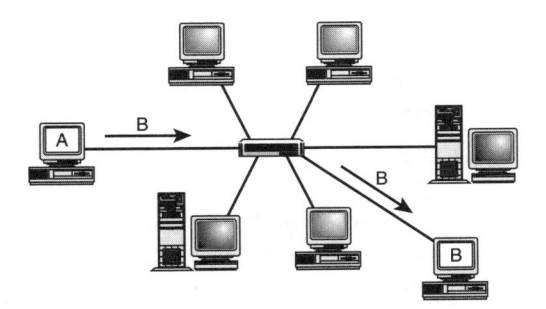

A single collision domain in Ethernet (10 or 100MB) should include no more then 35 active users. Now don't panic, remembering that there are hundreds of users attached to the hub at your office. The term *active user* means a machine putting a signal on the wire. Fifty users sitting at their desks while their screensavers run do not count as *active users*. Only you can determine how many active users you have at a given moment. However, to avoid bandwidth issues, you should keep those active users in groups of 35 or less.

Also keep in mind groups such as the design department group mentioned earlier. With these groups, you may want to consider putting them on a switch or switch port of their own.

Server connections to these groups should be direct to the switch. It's best if there's a direct path between users and the server resources. The idea is to avoid the server having to contend for the collision domain with user workstations. It could be a disaster if the server is giving poor performance because someone is downloading the latest version of an action game.

Routed Segmentation

Network communications are carried on in many different layers. You may hear these layers referred to as the *OSI Model* (Open Systems Interconnection Model). This frame of reference helps you understand why a segment discussed here is different than a collision domain. A visual helper for this model is in figure 5.12.

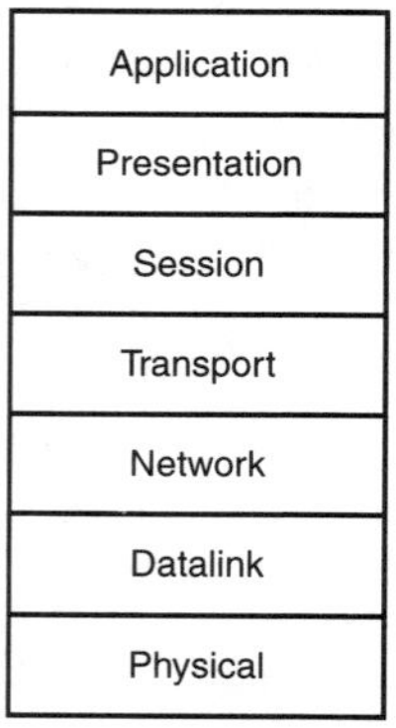

FIGURE 5.12
The OSI Model.

| Application |
| Presentation |
| Session |
| Transport |
| Network |
| Datalink |
| Physical |

This is not the place to take the OSI Model to task as a whole; instead, you should note that there are different points in the communications layers between systems in which decisions are made and traffic can be changed. These layers are the Network and Data link layers. These are the two layers involved in the initial communications after the physical connection has been made.

The Data Link layer is the layer used in a switching network. Among its duties is determining the MAC address of the machine.

The Network layer then determines the network address of the signal and whether it belongs to the system that has received it.

Routers are devices that separate traffic, much like switches, but instead of separating the traffic based of MAC addresses, routers separate traffic based on a knowledge of the network on which the systems are located (see the definition of *network segment at the beginning of the networking section of this chapter*).

Routers are often used for WAN traffic because the traffic flow from router to router is more specific. Routers are given or learn specific paths to given networks. Therefore, instead of broadcasting a call of a MAC address, a system first arrives at the proper network segment and then makes the request.

RRAS

Routing and Remote Access Services are services specifically created to allow for communications with remote systems. The original product was simply called RAS (Remote Access Services), and it was solely involved in communicating with users across a modem. The *Routing* addition to the service name has made Windows a more robust system for communicating over standard phone lines and the Internet.

Remote Dial-In

Remote users can make use of RRAS to connect to the office and use the systems there as if they were sitting at their PCs in the building. RRAS allows the user to use standard dial-up networking to connect to the server. From that point, the modem attached to the PC is the equivalent of a network card attached to the network in the office. The biggest difference is that the speed of a standard phone line is far slower then the network connection in the office (57.6Kbps versus 10,000Kbps). For that reason, users attaching through this method will want to run applications from their local workstations and retrieve data files from the network.

A good comparison to this form of connection is the Internet and the World Wide Web. When connecting to the Internet, you attach to the network and launch the Web Browser applications on your own system. The browser then attaches to the network and draws data from various hosts on the other side.

Multiprotocol Routing

In small companies and in many small routing applications, it can be prohibitive to purchase a separate router for routing traffic to a remote site or to a different in-house segment. It would be most convenient if you could simply put another network interface in the server and route traffic using the network operating system and the router.

In order to connect systems using Windows as a router, many changes needed to be made. Windows 2000 has made those changes, and it now makes a viable option for small network routing applications.

RRAS can route traffic from one network to the other through the server on IP and IPX networks. Third parties can add other protocols, but IP (the protocol used by the Internet) and IPX (the protocol used by many NetWare networks) are included.

On-Demand Routing

When you're attaching networks through standard telephone lines, it can be cost prohibitive to make that connection available 24 hours a day. Even a short distance call at one cent a minute would be $432.00 a month. For that reason, RRAS can be configured to make connection only when demand is there. If, for example, a user attempts to attach to a network resource at a network address on the other side of the dial-up WAN, the line would be activated. After a given time of inactivity, the line would then disconnect.

Virtual Private Network (VPN)

Because of the cost of installing dedicated lines between numerous locations, many companies are using the Internet and other public networks as their WAN connections. This creates a very affordable system of communications, but it opens a whole new can of worms. The Internet is the furthest thing from a secure network. It's comparable to using roadside billboards for interoffice communications. Someone else is going to see what you're producing.

One solution to this problem is to place the information in a safe package before you send it across the line. A Virtual Private Network (VPN) does just that. By using a protocol called the *Point-to-Point Tunneling Protocol* (PPTP), VPNs take the packets you're sending and package them in a private (encrypted) packet that can only be understood by the proper system on the other side of the public network. All that's required to create such a connection is a connection to the public network by both parties involved.

The appeal of this goes well beyond that of creating WANs that also include Internet access. However, the benefits include dial-up clients that now can attach to the network from anywhere they can attach to the Internet.

Summary

The concepts behind connecting up a computer network and making it communicate go far beyond actually connecting the wires and installing the operating system. If you've read this chapter, you have a better understanding of the technologies and relationships that will follow through the remainder of the book.

Small network systems of 5 to 10 users are most likely able to live in a workgroup environment. But once these groups get beyond that size, domains and Active Directory make administration more manageable.

Domains have been refitted to allow them to be more global with forests and trees and more granular with the advent of organizational units (OUs) and the information control in the objects themselves. Active Directory has delivered an enterprise-savvy Windows network operating system.

In order to allow your data to flow smoothly as well as to keep your directory planning from slowing down all your other plans, you can do many things at the network level. Networks can be divided into smaller collision domains. Also, network protocols can be routed to the proper segment of the greater network.

CHAPTER 6

Printing

IN THIS CHAPTER

- Printing Concepts   150
- Creating Print Queues   155
- Using Print Manager   159
- Managing Print Queues   164
- Troubleshooting   168

There's an old saying that goes something like this: Computers are simple, reliable, and easy to use compared to printers. One of the most obnoxious jobs any system administrator has to face is managing printers, and it doesn't matter if it's in Windows 2000, UNIX, or any other system. The interface between computer systems and printers has always been pretty bad, and printers have so many moving parts that they're a lot less reliable than even the cheapest workstation. Show me a truly paperless office and I'll show you another office that goes through a forest a day. This chapter's goal is to give you an understanding of the Windows 2000 print system so that you can more easily install, manage, and troubleshoot the printers on your network. Here's a quick view of what's in this chapter:

- Printing concepts
- Creating print queues
- Using Print Manager
- Managing print queues
- Troubleshooting

The sooner it gets started, the sooner this painful topic will be over. To start off, let's take a quick look at printing concepts.

Printing Concepts

Windows 2000 uses the same printer driver setup as Windows NT 4.0, and it integrates very well with the consumer versions of Windows (Windows 95 and Windows 98). Essentially, an application works together with the printer drivers to create a stream of printer commands that get sent to the printer. Then the printer has the task of deciphering the stuff sent by the printer driver and putting it on paper. To figure out how all this works, let's first take a look at how printers work. Next, we'll take a quick stroll through the land of fonts. Then we'll look at how print drivers work, and, finally, I'll offer some thoughts on communicating with printers. We'll also look at the life of a print job, from beginning to end, to see how all these parts fit together.

Printers

There are three types of printers. *Line printers*, which are very rare these days, print one line at a time. A line printer, such as a dot-matrix printer, is typically very slow, and the print quality is usually fairly poor by modern standards. A line printer takes about one line of text at a time into its memory and prints one line at a time. Some line printers can buffer a whole lot more text into memory, but the key is that they only work with one line of text at a time. Line printers are almost completely limited to text printing; their graphics quality being even worse than their already-poor text quality.

A *page printer*, such as a laser printer, a LED printer, and many inkjet printers, follows a different path. Rather than receiving a line of print at a time, the printer receives a whole page of text at a time and usually doesn't start printing until it receives the entire page. Page printers excel at printing graphics and text, and they even do both in color. Page printers are the standard in printing today. Many of the less-expensive inkjet printers are actually line printers, but they use advanced drivers to make them behave and perform like page printers. These new inkjet printers provide very sharp color and great quality output, but they tend to be a lot slower than laser printers.

One of the limitations of any page printer is the fact that it handles a fixed page size. Although this is great for printing on paper up to 11×17 inches, pages much larger than that usually require a plotter. A *plotter* is a device that can print very large output, up to several feet in width and length. Plotters are usually used in engineering and marketing applications. Engineers like to print out large-scale drawings, and marketing folks use them to print large signs.

Printers also use a variety of languages to communicate. The two common languages are HPGL, the Hewlett-Packard Graphics Language, and PostScript, which is from Adobe. Both of these languages describe how to lay out text and graphics on a page. The drivers essentially write little printer-control programs, which are then sent to the printer and executed. PostScript is the more complete of the two languages, providing a lot of functionality for handling geometric shapes and high-precision color. The PostScript language is generally found in most high-end printers, and it's also the preferred language for the Apple Macintosh. Therefore, output from a Mac tends to look best on a Postscript-enabled printer. Both page printers and plotters use some type of printing language for page layout.

Because page printers and plotters are executing programs, they require memory. The amount of memory in a printer directly impacts the amount of graphics and the number of fonts that a printer can handle. Older printers have 1 to 2MB of RAM, whereas newer printers have a lot more.

Here are a few logistical notes on printer mechanics. Most of them are common sense, but for people new to the world of system administration, these notes might be helpful. Printers require supplies such as toner, ink, developer cartridges, and paper. Keep at least two spares for each available and replace them when they go bad. The reasoning behind this is fairly obvious: Printers don't run out of toner unless something critical is being printed. If there's only one extra cartridge of toner available, it will be defective. Also, experiment with a printer to figure out what happens if it's turned off while printing. This will happen when a user accidentally prints something and believes that turning off the printer will fix the problem. Knowing where the paper will jam up when the printer is turned off will save you time.

Fonts

Fonts determine how text will look on a page and the typeface that will be used. A font will either be native to the printer or it will have to be downloaded. When a printer has a native font that means the font lives on the printer, either internally or as a font cartridge for the printer. When Windows 2000 sends a print job, it needs to know what fonts are already on the printer; that is, it needs to know which fonts are already available and which fonts will need to be sent to the printer.

Fonts come in two variations. A *fixed-width font* has letters that are all the same width. For example, a lowercase letter *l* would take up the same width as an uppercase letter *W*. Console fonts, and fonts used in applications where column width readability is important, usually use fixed-width fonts such as Courier. *Variable-width fonts*, on the other hand, look better and more natural, because that's how we tend to write. In this case, an uppercase *W* takes up more space than a lowercase *l*.

Fonts also have weight, angle, and an underline attribute. Font weight is either normal or bold, font angle is either normal or italic, and the underline attribute is either on or off.

There are two different ways to store fonts. *Raster fonts* are stored as pictures of the individual letters—usually several pictures of each letter in different sizes, weights, and angles. A raster font file, which usually has the extension .fon, is typically larger than a vector font file. *Vector fonts* have each character stored once, and they're stored in such a way to make scaling the font from very small to very large possible. Instead of including a picture of a letter, a vector font file stores how to make the letter, and making the letter bigger just means scaling the letter up to the appropriate size. Vector fonts will scale better and look considerably better at large sizes, but it takes more processing power to display and print vector fonts. For example, a vector font would store information on the capital letter *I* as having a top and bottom horizontal bar of length 2 and a middle part that's a centered vertical bar of length 4. To make a larger capital *I*, the vector font would simply multiply by a given factor. Therefore, the proportions will hold up and the letter will always look right.

When fonts are downloaded to a printer, they are downloaded from the machine that's actually doing the printing, not from the server. Therefore, installing extra fonts on a server won't help matters any, and it just introduces more complexity into the server setup process.

Print Drivers

Windows 2000, and all the other Windows operating systems, use a "minidriver" concept to build device drivers. Basically, the operating system provides applications with all the basics of how to interface with certain types of devices, and then it requires a driver to implement very specific features in order to perform those operations. Basically, it's a layered approach. An application only needs to know how to send data to the operating system's standard for a printer. The operating system only needs to know how to send data to a specific type of printer. The device driver only needs to know how to take the operating system instructions and data and make them print. The device driver doesn't need to know anything about the application being used, and the operating system doesn't need to know many specifics about how the printer itself works.

This system makes it fairly easy to deal with downloadable fonts, for example. The printer driver has to notify the system which fonts it has installed, and the operating system's idealized printer will figure out whether to use those fonts or download fonts to the printer for use. As a result, either the printer needs to be able to notify the operating system when a new set of fonts is installed, such as when a font cartridge is added, or the administrator needs to configure the driver so the driver knows which fonts the printer has. It depends on whether the printer can communicate the installed font list back to the driver, which depends on how old the printer is.

If Windows 2000 Server shares out a printer for use by other users on the network, it can also host drivers for those other users. For example, if both Windows 2000 Professional and Windows 95 clients are using a Windows 2000 Server machine, the administrator can install drivers for Windows 95 clients that will be downloaded when the Windows 95 client attaches to the network printer. That means the Windows 95 user will not be prompted to insert driver disks for the printer; instead, the drivers will just automatically be installed. Information on how to do this is presented in the "Creating Print Queues" section, later in this chapter. Every time a client workstation prints to a printer, it will version-check the print driver. Updating printer drivers on the server causes an upswing in server traffic, but this should be fairly spread out throughout the day.

Communicating with Printers

No matter what type of printers exist in an organization, computers have to be able to communicate with them. There are several different methods used to communicate with printers, including the use of parallel ports, serial ports, USB ports, direct file I/O, Windows 2000 network connections, TCP/IP printing ports, and LPR ports.

In the beginning there were parallel ports. The parallel port on a computer sends data out to the printer through a 25-pin parallel cable. This cable transmits all the bits of data in parallel and includes a synchronization signal, a ground, and a back channel so that the printer can communicate back to the computer. Parallel interfaces are not very fast by today's standards, running at 115Kbps, but they're fast enough to drive a printer for the most part. Parallel interfaces are pretty much the standard; it's difficult to find a printer without a parallel interface. Parallel printers use ports named LPT*n* (that is, LPT1, LPT2, and so on).

Serial printers use serial communication, up to about 56 or even 115Kbps. Unlike a parallel port, a serial port has to send one bit at a time instead of sending bits in parallel across several wires. A serial cable uses either a 9- or 25-pin connector, but usually only three or four of those pins are used. Serial printers can communicate bi-directionally; therefore, they can pass information back to the computer. Serial ports are usually named COM*n* (that is, COM1, COM2, and so on).

The Universal Serial Bus (USB) is a fairly new technology. USB has a lot of neat features going for it. It's bidirectional and, at a speedy 12Mbps, it's more than fast enough to handle printer communication. USB is also a Plug and Play technology, so when a printer gets plugged into a USB port, it notifies the operating system of its existence and the operating system will deal with setting up drivers and preparing the device for use.

Direct file I/O is very rarely used outside of testing different print operations. Essentially, printer output can be directed to a file, and the file can then be manually copied to a printer port. This can be handy for testing printer output as well as in the case where a user needs to print a file from a computer with no printers connected and no network connectivity. The user can print to a file, copy that file to a floppy disk, and then go to another computer and copy the file to the printer. Copying a file to a printer is not the same as printing a text file. To copy a file to a printer, go to a command prompt and literally copy the file:

```
Copy a:\file.prn lpt1:
```

This command copies the file `file.prn` to the printer connected to port LPT1. The advantage of using this procedure is that the computer connected to the printer doesn't need to have the application that created the printer file installed on it; instead, it only has to have access to the printer in question.

Windows 2000, Windows NT, and the 32-bit consumer versions of Windows all implement print sharing, which uses the same semantics as file sharing. A printer can be shared out, and then the printer can be accessed using a UNC name. For example, to access a printer called "lp" that's shared out on the machine "Kermit," use the name `\\kermit\lp`. The printer could even be mapped to a local port using the following command line:

```
Net use lpt1: \\kermit\lp
```

This will map the printer `\\kermit\lp` to the local device called LPT1. The `Copy` command shown previously could be rewritten as this:

```
Copy a:\file.prn \\kermit\lp
```

This would copy the file `file.prn` on drive `A:` to the printer lp on Kermit.

Print servers allow one or more printers to be plugged into parallel ports, and they have a network connection that makes the printers accessible via the LAN. They typically use a TCP/IP printing protocol to communicate with the print server, which then directs the incoming data to the correct printer. Newer, more advanced printers have this functionality built in, which allows very high throughput to the printer from individual workstations (or redirected through a server).

Windows 2000 provides LPR port monitoring to enable communications with printers connected to UNIX hosts. Setting up and working with printers via LPR is covered in Chapter 19, "SNA Connectivity with BackOffice."

The Life of a Print Job

A print job is created when a user chooses File, Print from an application. The application (for example, Microsoft Word) then figures out what needs to get printed and submits the print job to the operating system. The operating system checks to make sure it knows where the print job is going and checks with the printer driver to see what needs to get printed. The printer driver then assembles all this information and creates the actual stream of data that's sent to the printer.

The printer driver takes the stream of data and sends it to a queue. The queue takes the first job in line and sends it to the spooler. The spooler receives and stores print jobs and then hands them to the printer at a speed the printer can handle, and while it's sending data to the printer, the spooler allows the user to continue working. It can do this because all the "hard" work of rendering the page has been done, and the spooler is just communicating with the printer. When the spooler finishes sending the job to the printer, it deletes the print job and shuts down. It keeps a full copy of the print job until the printer finishes the job (in case the printer jams, gets turned off, or whatever). In that case, the spooler knows how far along the job was before it jammed and can resume from there.

Throughout this process, the spooler notifies the Print Manager of the status of the print job—how many bytes and pages have been sent to the printer and how many are left. During these updates, the spooler checks to see if the print job has been canceled or paused, and it takes appropriate actions if either of these events has occurred.

Creating Print Queues

In order for Windows 2000 to use a printer, a print queue must be created. A *print queue* is a structure that holds print jobs before they go to the printer. It's basically a way of making jobs wait in line to go to a spooler.

A print queue can send output to one or more printers. The entire group of printers must be identical or at least all use the same drivers. By adding more printers, you can process the jobs more quickly, and the occasional large job won't prevent all the one-page jobs from printing. As a logistical issue, it's a good idea if all the printers that share a single queue are located in the same place so users will know where to pick up their printouts. It's also a good idea to stock lots of supplies in this area, because if people are going to be doing that much printing, they'll go through toner like crazy.

In the section titled "The Life of a Print Job," there's really no differentiation made about which parts of the system exist on which computer. That's because all the jobs are handled the same way. The only difference is the location of the print queue. For local printers, the print queues are local. For a network printer, the queue is created on a server, and jobs are submitted over the network. A job is submitted to a queue and then spooled by the queue to the printer.

To create a print queue, go to Control Panel and double-click Printers or go to Start, Settings, Printers (there are probably a few dozen other ways to open the Printers window). Double-click the Add Printer item, and the Add Printer Wizard will start (see Figure 6.1). Click the Next button to continue.

FIGURE 6.1
This is the welcome screen to the Add Printer Wizard, which will guide you through the process of adding a new printer.

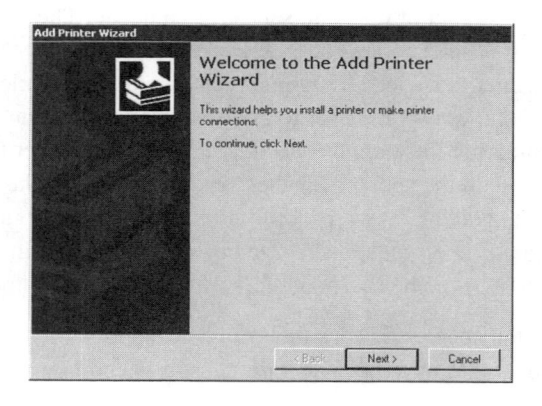

The next screen asks whether you want to install a local or network printer. This is misleading. A network printer will allow connections to another queue on another Windows 2000 computer. A local printer will connect to everything else, including networked print servers, UNIX LPR servers, and printers actually connected to serial, parallel, or USB ports on the local machine. Just remember that *network printer* in this instance means an existing Windows print queue, and *local printer* means anything that isn't an existing Windows print queue.

If you choose the Network Printer option, you have two options to consider. To print to a standard Windows 2000 print queue using Windows networking, either enter the name of the printer or click the Next button to browse for the printer. The other option is to print via the HTTP protocol. This requires a machine running IIS or Peer Web Services configured to allow print requests to come in via HTTP. This is convenient when there are firewalls or proxy servers between the local machine and the printer. This mechanism operates via the standard HTTP port 80, which is passed by most firewalls.

If you choose the Local Printer option and the printer is actually a local printer connected via a parallel, serial, or USB port, leave the Automatically Detect and Install My Plug and Play Printer check box selected. If the printer is connected via some other type of port, such as LPR or TCP/IP, turn the Plug and Play option off.

If the printer is automatically detected via Plug and Play, the queue will be created and drivers will be installed. If the printer isn't detected, choose the port that the printer is connected to or create a new port. The existing ports will be the normal list of parallel and serial ports, along with IR and the "FILE:" port, which will prompt you for a filename when printing and send the spooled output to the file.

To create a new port, select the Create a New Port option and then choose the port type. The following Port Type options are common, but the actual list is based on the options installed on the local machine:

- *Local port*. This option is used to create a new local port. This will just prompt for a port name.
- *Standard TCP/IP port*. This option is used to connect to print server devices, such as HP JetDirect ports. This option will start another wizard (the Add Standard TCP/IP Printer Port Wizard), which prompts for the IP address and port name of the printer.
- *LPR port*. This option is used to connect to UNIX servers and use printers connected to them. It will prompt for the name of the UNIX server and the name of the printer.

After creating the port, choose the type of printer that's connected to the port. If the printer doesn't show up on the list or if you have newer drivers on a disk or CD-ROM that came with the printer, click the Have Disk button and install those instead.

Once the drivers are installed, put in a name for the printer. This name is used to identify the printer, so if there are several printers of the same brand and model installed on the machine, you should name them something besides their brand and model.

The next step is deciding whether to share out the printer. Choose a name that the printer will be shared under, which has to be a unique name on the server. The next screen allows you to enter the printer location and a comment about the printer. The comment can include paper sizes, whether or not the printer supports color, and so on.

Next, choose whether to print a test page. For a server installation, it's usually a good idea just to make sure the printer actually works before people start using it. Finally, a summary page will appear, similar to the one shown in Figure 6.2. This page shows the share name, printer name, printer driver, and all the other details about the printer.

FIGURE 6.2
This is the status page shown by the Add Printer Wizard, summarizing the device that's about to be created.

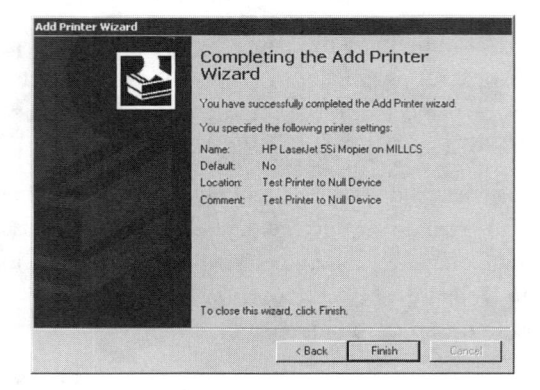

A Few Hints About Print Queues

For printers connected to print server devices, such as HP JetDirect boxes, it's a good idea to create a print queue for the device on a nearby Windows 2000 Server machine and share the printer out. Then have all the users connect to the Windows 2000 Server machine to print their data. That way, they can use the normal printer management tools on their workstations instead of having to install special software to manage the queues on the printer.

Be sure to give printers intuitive names. I used to work for a company that gave all the printers extremely cryptic names, which had nothing to do with either the location of the printer or the capabilities of the printer (for example, UKBLU3321). After much deciphering, I realized that the printer is in the United States (U), in the Kansas City office (K), has a blue square on it (BLU), and has an asset tag number of 3321. This is totally useless to a user trying to find a printer, especially when there are close to 800 printers in the Kansas City office. A better name would have been some combination of building number, the letters *BW* for "Black and White," and then a cube number that the printer is close to.

Always print test pages from servers. Always go get the test pages and make sure they're legible and correct. Otherwise, the next person to print to the printer will be someone who's a CEO, COO, CIO, or whatever, and he or she will wonder what kind of buffoon didn't realize the red toner was out on the brand new color printer that was just installed.

Using Print Manager

Print Manager is the tool used to manage documents inside of a print queue. Basically, this means it can view the items in a print queue, view the status of the jobs in the print queue, and, if the user has appropriate permissions, change the order of objects in the print queue and even remove jobs from the print queue.

Remember that a print queue is simply a list of print jobs waiting for service. Each of those jobs has certain properties that can be viewed, such as the originating application and the length of the job in pages. For someone assigned to the Print Operator role, the order of print jobs in the queue can be altered, and jobs can be removed from the queue altogether. A sample print queue is shown in Figure 6.3. Note that the queue is paused, and no jobs are leaving the queue.

FIGURE 6.3

This is a view of a print queue to a printer on the server MILLCS with one document, `ch6.rtf`, *waiting to be printed.*

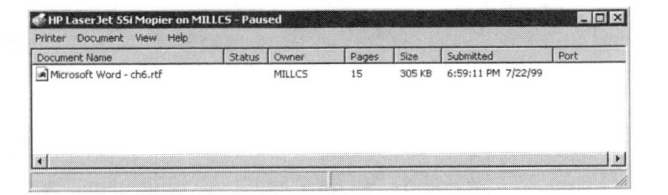

The Printer menu in Print Manager allows the user to make modifications to how the print queue is set up on the local machine. The Set as Default Printer option allows a printer to be chosen as the default printer, meaning that all applications will display that printer first in the list and that any toolbar print icons should automatically print to that printer. The Printing Preferences menu item allows you to choose various printer-specific settings, which usually include the orientation of the pages (portrait or landscape), the order in which the pages will be printed in, which paper tray to pull from, and the paper size to use. These options will vary from printer to printer, depending on the capabilities of the printer.

The next option, Pause Printing, will stop all print jobs in the queue without removing the jobs from the queue. This is handy if the printer is being replaced or if the printer is connected to a workstation and that workstation needs to have some processor time for a local user. The Cancel All Documents option will purge the print queue, stopping all currently printing jobs and deleting the rest of the jobs in the queue.

The Sharing option is the same setup option as when you set up the printer initially. It allows the printer to be used by other computers on the network, and the dialog boxes are the same as those used during the initial setup of the printer queue. This option is a shortcut to the Properties option, and it automatically brings up the Sharing tab (see Figure 6.4).

FIGURE 6.4
The Sharing tab of a printer's Properties dialog box.

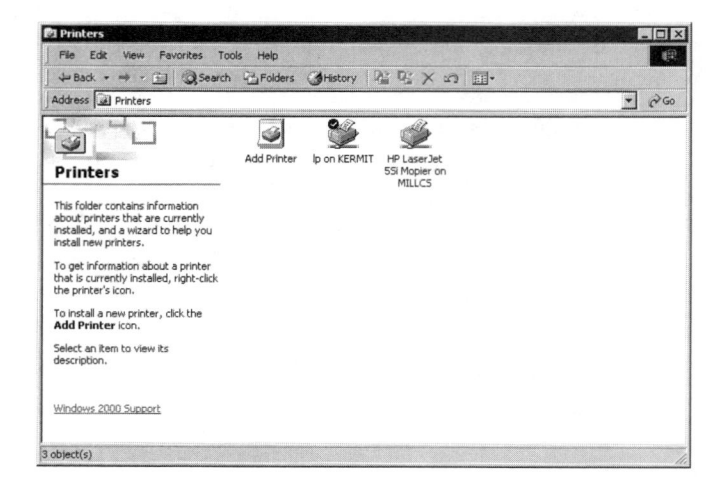

The Use Printer Offline option means the local machine will queue up the jobs to the printer and won't send the jobs to the printer until the local machine is back online. (This is good for wayward authors who are composing on their laptops and want to create a printout the next time they plug into a printer.)

The Properties option allows you to make adjustments to almost all the options for a given printer. The printer name, location, and comment data can be changed on the General tab, and the Print Test Page button will print a test page identical to the test page printed during the printer queue setup.

The Advanced tab, shown in Figure 6.5, sets a variety of interesting options. It allows the printer to have scheduled hours of operation. It defaults to Always Available but can be set so the printer is only used during a certain time every day. It also allows print jobs to be prioritized using the Priority box. This way, higher priority jobs will print first, and lower-priority jobs will print after all the high-priority jobs are finished.

The Advanced tab allows you to change the driver by either dropping down the list box or by clicking the New Driver button, which allows new drivers to be installed from a CD-ROM or from an Internet download. The Spool options determine how the print spooling will work. Normally, the spooler will begin printing a job immediately after the first page is spooled. If jobs get cancelled a lot, checking the Start Printing After Last Page Is Spooled option is a good idea. If the user wants to wait for the printer, the Print Directly to Printer option will basically disable the spooler and force the application to wait on the printer.

FIGURE 6.5
The Advanced tab of the printer's Properties pages. The default settings are shown here.

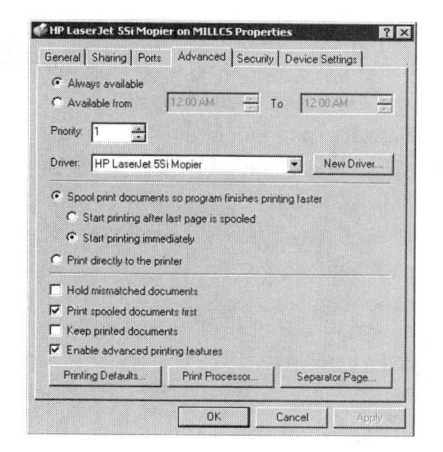

The final options on the Advanced tab involve spooler maintenance. The Hold Mismatched Documents option forces the spooler to not send print jobs to the printer that don't match the printer's settings. For example, if a print job is marked as requiring duplex printing (printing on both sides of a page) and the printer doesn't support duplex printing, the job will be held instead of printing as single sided. The Print Spooled Documents First option indicates that the printer will print jobs that have finished spooling first, even if they're at a lower priority than jobs that are still spooling. Remember that a print job can print before it finishes spooling. Therefore, if this option is turned on and there are two jobs in the print queue (one that has finished spooling and one that hasn't), the job that has finished spooling will print first, regardless of priority.

If the Keep Printed Documents option is checked, a print job won't be removed from the queue after it spools. This way, it can be reprinted as necessary. This is handy for printing multiple copies of several documents, because it allows the first copy to be proofed before committing the printer to a long run.

The Printing Defaults button pulls up the exact same window as the Properties menu option mentioned previously. The Print Processor button allows a different print processor to be chosen. A print processor is the component that takes the output from an application, compiles it, and sends it to the printer driver. The default print processor is called *WinPrint*, and it supports several different options for a default data type. Normally, the default data type isn't used; instead, the application chooses a data type (usually EMF) and sends it along. A safe format to choose for the default is RAW, which doesn't perform any compilation on the print job before sending it to the driver.

The Separator Page button allows a text file to be chosen to print as a page at the beginning of each print job to allow the print jobs to be divided up more easily when they all land in the same bin on the printer.

The Security tab, shown in Figure 6.6, specifies who can print to a given printer, who can make changes to the printer settings, and who can manage documents in print queues. By default, the Administrator and the Print Operators have full control over the printer, the Creator Owner of a print job has the ability to manage that one document in the queue, and Everyone can print. These options can be changed either by adding more users or by changing the options on the bottom half of the dialog box. Figure 6.6 shows an example where the administrators on the machine have rights to the printer, the group Everyone can create new jobs, Power Users can manage the print queue, and the CREATOR OWNER option allows users to manage their own print jobs.

FIGURE 6.6
The default security setup for a print queue.

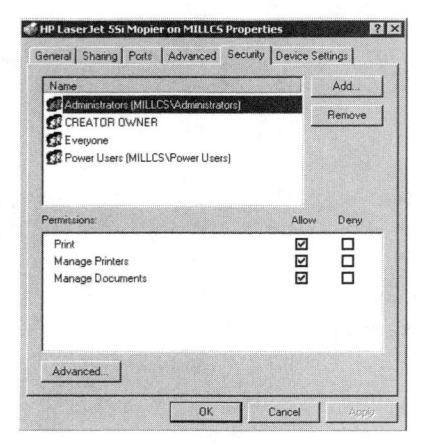

The Device Settings tab allows all the different device settings to be chosen. The device settings are very dependent on the type of printer that's being worked on, but they usually consist of items such as which paper tray contains what paper, which font cartridges are installed, and how fonts in the printer map to fonts on the computer.

The Document menu only contains four options, which are only available (not grayed out) if there are one or more documents in the queue (and at least one of those documents must be selected). The first and second options, Pause and Resume, will pause and resume printing for the selected jobs. The Restart option will start printing a job again, which is useful if there's a paper jam halfway through a job and a few pages are missing. The Cancel button cancels the selected print jobs, which will remove them from the queue.

> **Note**
>
> Another way to access the Document menu is to right-click a document in the queue. This brings up a menu for the selected document that's identical to the Document menu in the menu bar.

The Properties option brings up the dialog box shown in Figure 6.7, which shows all of the print properties for the selected jobs. The only items that can be changed on the Properties tab are on the General tab, and they involve changing the notification, priority, and scheduling of the print job. The Notify box will cause a message to be sent to the login listed in the box using a network send request. Print job priority starts at level 1 and can be escalated to level 99. Jobs with higher numbers have higher priority and will go first. The default is a priority of 1, so power users may decide to jump the lines and set their jobs way up there. Scheduling the job will delay printing of the job until a specified time, which is polite if the job is particularly large and the office printer is very busy.

FIGURE 6.7
The Properties page for a document that's in a queue. You can change the notification, schedule, and priority.

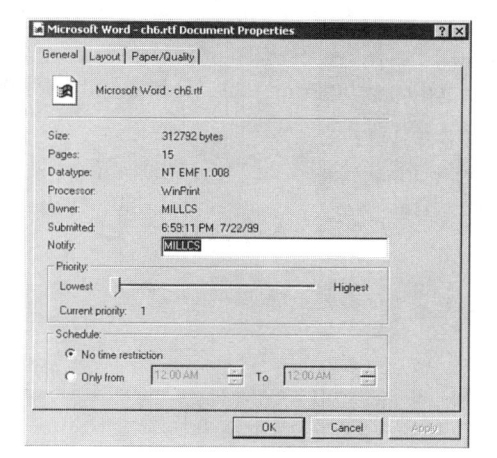

> **Note**
>
> Print notifications are sent using the network messenger service. This is similar to the old WinPopup service in Windows for Workgroups 3.11. Go to a command line and type **net send <machine> <message>**, where <machine> is a machine name and <message> is a message. For example, `net send millcs Hello` would send the machine named MILLCS a message. The message is displayed in a message box for the user. To disable messages on a given machine, stop the Messenger service in Control Panel, Computer Management, Services.

The other two tabs on the Properties option are Layout and Paper/Quality. The Layout tab is entirely read-only, and it displays the layout (portrait or landscape), the duplexing status, and the page order for the print job. The Advanced button brings up the same window as the Device Settings tab, mentioned previously, but without the ability to change anything. The Paper/Quality tab is also read-only, and it shows which paper source will be used and what type of paper will be used. The Advanced button on this tab does the same thing as the one on the Layout tab.

Another feature of Print Manager is that any of the column headings, such as Document Name, Status, and Owner can be clicked and the list of print jobs will be sorted by that column. Therefore, to see all the jobs for a specific user, it's easiest to click Owner and scroll down to that user. In addition, the columns can be reordered by dragging them and dropping them on a new location.

Managing Print Queues

There are two different methods for managing print queues. One is to use Print Manager to manage the print queue, and the other is to use the Print Server Properties set of tabs. The Print Manager, which is fully described in the section preceding this one, allows jobs within a queue to be managed by reordering them, changing their priority, stopping them, or removing them from the queue altogether.

The Print Server Properties pages are accessed by going to Control Panel, Printers and choosing File, Server Properties. There are four tabs on the dialog box: Forms, Ports, Drivers, and Advanced.

The Forms Tab

The Forms tab, shown in Figure 6.8, allows different forms to be selected. A *form* refers to the paper size. Windows 2000 comes with a specific range of form sizes that cover all the standard paper sizes and a bunch nobody has ever heard of. If there aren't enough forms listed or if it's necessary to custom name a paper size, a new form can be created on the Forms tab by checking the Create a New Form option. Enter the new form name, the dimensions of the paper (Width and Height), and the margins (Right, Left, Top, and Bottom) and click the Save Form button to save the new form.

FIGURE 6.8
The Forms tab of Print Server Properties page. It shows the available forms on a given print server and allows you to create new forms.

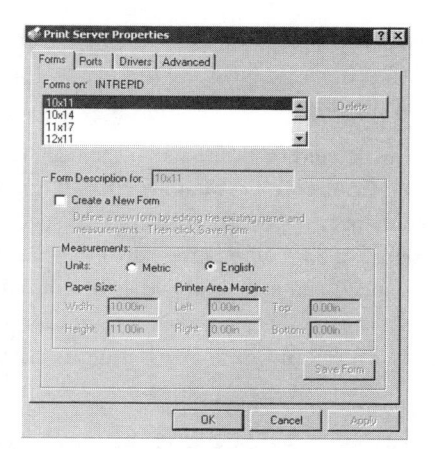

The Ports Tab

If there are a bunch of ports created on a machine that have no business being there, they can be deleted on this tab (see Figure 6.9). New ports can be created here also, but they'll usually be created as part of the Add Printer Wizard. To add a port, click the Add Port button; then the Printer Ports dialog box will appear. Choose a port type from the list. If the type required isn't in the list, click the New Port Type button. This button will prompt for a disk, CD-ROM, or file that will define the drivers for the new ports.

FIGURE 6.9
The Ports tab of the Print Server Properties page. It allows you to add ports as well as remove them.

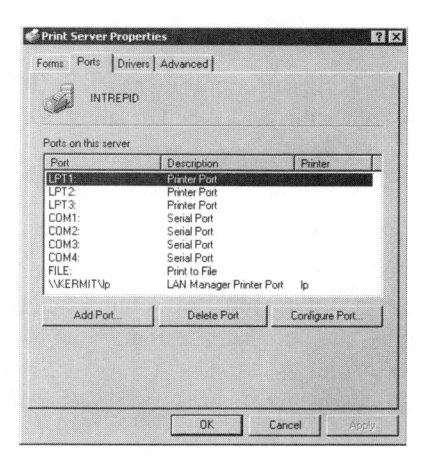

From that point on, a port type–specific set of dialog boxes will pop up to help you set up the new port. For the standard TCP/IP port, a wizard will pop up; for a local port, a box will prompt you for the name of the port.

To delete a port, choose the port to be deleted from the list and click the Delete Port button. For bonus points, guess what the Configure Port button does. It allows a port to be configured. For a parallel port, it specifies the port retry interval in seconds, which is how long the spooler will wait if there's a communications error before trying to send the job again. For a serial port, the data speed and settings have to be configured. For the "FILE:" port and any local port that's set up, there are no configuration settings, and Windows 2000 will just beep angrily if the Configure Port setting is clicked while these ports are selected.

> **Note**
>
> Microsoft tends to set any timeout to about 10 times the level it should be set to. The parallel port timeout value is set to 90 seconds. If the printer isn't responding within 10 seconds, chances are it's not there, so waiting the next 80 seconds is going to be frustrating. For problem printers, especially portable printers that might not be plugged in all the time, set the port timeout value lower so it won't take so long to time out.

The Drivers Tab

The Drivers tab, shown in Figure 6.10, is very useful; it manages the different print drivers on the machine. Specifically, it allows the drivers to be removed when they're no longer used. Drivers can be added here, too, but as with ports, drivers are usually added in the Add Printer Wizard.

The Drivers tab features four buttons. The Add button allows new drivers to be added to the system. This is handy for adding drivers for other operating systems or architectures, such as the Windows 98 drivers for a shared printer. The Remove button removes a printer driver. The Update button will search the local system for a new version of the selected driver and will update the driver on the fly. The Properties button displays every file associated with the selected print driver and allows the properties of each file to be displayed. This is a very handy feature for tracking down DLL version problems.

FIGURE 6.10

The Drivers tab of the Print Server Properties page. It shows the installed drivers on a given print server and allows you to add new drivers and remove existing ones.

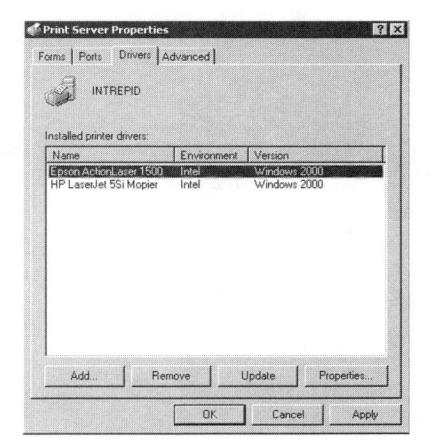

The Advanced Tab

The Advanced tab, shown in Figure 6.11, sets up some little-known and little-used options. The Spool Folder box shows the current location where print jobs will be spooled. The Log Spooler check boxes will log different levels of events to the Windows 2000 system event log, which can be accessed by going to Control Panel, Computer Administration, Event Viewer. Normally only the error events are logged, but the other options can be very handy to help track down spooling problems. The Beep on Errors of Remote Documents option is very helpful in a single-server shop, but this could be maddening in a huge data center. The Notify When Remote Documents Are Printed option sets up whether a queue will send back a notification to the user after a job has finished printing. The Notify Computer, Not User, When Remote Documents Are Printed option tells the queue to send the message to the computer that printed a job instead of the user who printed a job. This is handy for computers that submit batch print jobs and are all logged on with the same user account because it prevents all the machines from getting messages that are meant for just one machine. In Figure 6.11, notice the location of the print spool folder, which is used extensively in the troubleshooting part of the chapter.

FIGURE 6.11
The Advanced tab of the Print Server Properties page.

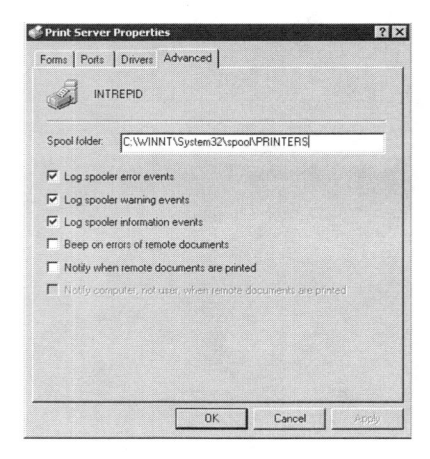

Troubleshooting

As mentioned in the introduction to this chapter, printers tend to be unreliable instruments at best, and at worst they seem to be out to destroy the reputations of every system administrator. Print systems are very complex and involve a lot of parts that come from a lot of different sources. Basically, it's a series of problems that no single vendor will ever take responsibility for causing.

There are two basic types of problems that occur when printing. Either the job doesn't get to the printer at all or the job arrives at the printer and doesn't print properly. First, we'll check out what to do when the job doesn't print at all; then we'll take a look at the steps to take when a job is printing out incorrectly.

Diagnosing Client-to-Server Printing Communications Problems

One method for troubleshooting printing problems on systems is to start at one end and work to the other, specifically starting at the client and working to the printer. Probably a better method is to start in the middle; that way half the job is already done. Check to see if the print job is in the middle of its flow; if it isn't, the problem is before the middle point. If the job makes it to the middle point, then it's somewhere after that in the process. For a print job, the middle of the process is reaching the print queue, so troubleshooting goes something like this:

1. Check the print queue.
2. Check the server. Specifically, check each of the following items to make sure they look right.

- Check server disk space
- Check server permissions
- Check the Event Viewer
- Check networking for network printers
- Check printer hardware

3. Check the client. Check each of the items in the following list to make sure the client isn't causing any problems.
   - Check client disk space
   - Check client login account
   - Check printer properties
   - Reload printer drivers

4. Test and diagnose other problems.

Check the Print Queue

Go to a computer on the network and check to see if the print queue is connected to that machine by going to Control Panel, Printers. Look through the list of printers. If the printer isn't connected, you can connect it using the Add Printer Wizard as described earlier. After the printer is installed, open Print Manager on the print queue by double-clicking the printer.

First, check to see if the queue is reporting any problems or if the printer is having some type of problem, such as a paper jam or low-toner problem. The availability and accuracy of these messages varies from print driver to print driver; some printers will report back that they're out of toner, others will just display a generic User Intervention Required status message. In either case, consult the front panel of the printer and the printer owner's manual for instructions on how to get the printer back online.

Then, see if any jobs from the user are in the print queue. If a lot of jobs are in the queue, click the Owner column heading, which will sort the queue by owner. If there are jobs that have reached the print queue from that user, the problem is somewhere on the server. If the jobs haven't reached the print queue, there's probably a difficulty with the client.

Tracking Server-Side Printing Problems

If there's a problem on the server side, the first thing to check is whether there's adequate disk space in the spooler's working directory for the print jobs. First, find out where the spooler's working directory is by opening up Control Panel, Printers and choosing File, Server Properties. Click the Advanced tab, shown previously in Figure 6.11, and take note of the Spool Folder line. This is where the spooler puts files that are waiting to be printed. To check for disk space, go to My Computer and click once on the name of the disk that has the spooler's directory on it. Depending on how the server is set up, there may be a nice pie graph showing the amount of available disk space; otherwise, the amount of space available will be shown in the status bar at the bottom of the window, as shown previously in Figure 6.11. The default path is `%SYSTEMROOT%\System32\Spool\Printers`.

> **Note**
>
> It's a good idea to limit the size of the partition containing the Windows 2000 operating system on the server (as discussed in Chapter 3, "Installation Considerations"). Because the spooler's working directory defaults to somewhere within this system partition, it's a good idea to either make the partition a bit bigger or move the spooler directory if there's going to be a lot of printing on the server.

If there's not enough disk space, either clear some space by carefully deleting unused files or move the spool directory to another disk. If the spool directory is changed, the spooler must be restarted. If the spool directory is on an NTFS partition, everyone who can print needs to have Change permission to that directory.

If there's enough disk space and the directory is on an NTFS partition, check to make sure the user has the Change permission on the directory. Users must have the Change permission in order for the printing system to write their jobs to the directory.

Next, check the Windows 2000 event log to see if there are any messages. The reason this wasn't done first, by the way, is because checking for disk space is quick and relatively painless, whereas digging through the event log can take a bit longer and is a bit of a chore. Open the Windows 2000 event log by going to Control Panel, Administrative Tools, Event Viewer. If this is done from the server, the Event Viewer will automatically display events on the server. Otherwise, right-click Event Viewer (Local) and choose Connect to Another Computer. Type the name of the server into the dialog box that comes up. The event viewer is shown in Figure 6.12.

The events that are relevant to printing problems will come from Spooler, Print, or maybe the LPDSVC source. The spooler will create events related to moving data from the print queue to the printer. Most print events will be related to printing from the server and won't be particularly relevant unless there's also a problem printing from the server itself. The LPDSVC event source is the LPD Service, and these are the types of events to look for if the client is running UNIX and printing to a Windows 2000 printer.

FIGURE 6.12

The Windows 2000 Event Viewer is used to track down a lot of different problems. Here, the events are sorted by source to help you find printer-related events.

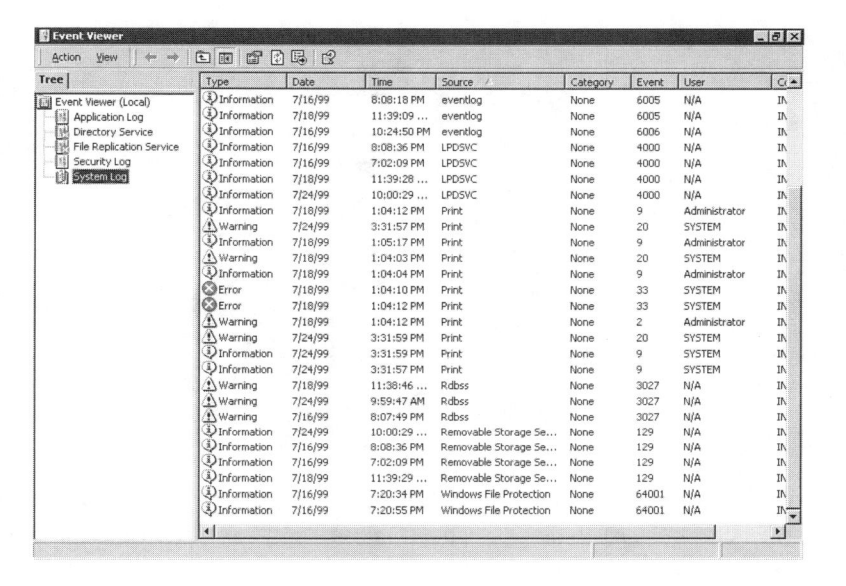

Typical events seen here are disk full events, permissions-related events, and printer communications errors. If there are no events, it might be a good idea to restart the spooler and move on. To do this, go to Control Panel, Services and double-click Print Spooler. Then click Stop and then Start.

If the printer is a TCP/IP printer, try to ping the printer's address. This can be done by going to the command line and typing `ping <address>`. To find the address, follow the instructions that came with the print server; most print servers have a diagnostic printout that will have the address on it. If the address does not respond to a ping, nobody is going to be able to print to the printer. The most likely cause of this problem is a bad TCP/IP address either on the print server or on the client workstation. If the client workstation can access other network resources, the problem is on the print server; otherwise, it's usually a problem on the client computer or in the network infrastructure (cables, hubs, switches, and routers) between the client and the rest of the network.

Next, check the status of the printer itself. This is done last simply because it'll probably involve getting out of your chair and moving. If the network tests show that the printer is reachable on the network or if the printer is a local printer, try printing a test page from another workstation or even from the server. To print a test page, go to Control Panel, Printers and choose the printer in question (or connect it with the Add Printer Wizard, if necessary). Then, right-click it and choose Properties. Next, click the Print Test Page button at the bottom of the form, as shown in Figure 6.13. If the test page prints correctly, all is well. If the test page doesn't work (and it's not working from anywhere on the network) and the jobs are piling up in the print queue, go check out the printer.

FIGURE 6.13
Click the Print Test Page button to print a test page. Test pages can be very helpful diagnostic tools.

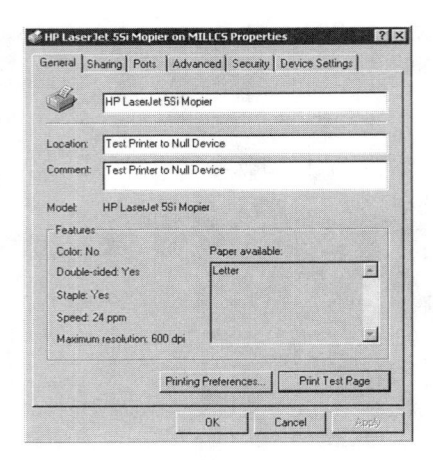

When checking the printer, first check any diagnostic messages on the printer console. Then check the easy things, such as making sure the printer isn't out of paper and that there isn't a paper jam in the printer. Then, check the cabling from the printer and make sure all the cables are plugged in and snug. Sometimes loose connections will make everything up the line think the printer is working, even if the printer can't receive any data. Therefore, always check the connections and then check them again.

At this point, all the server problems should be resolved. The server has adequate space and correct permissions in order to spool jobs to disk, the communications between the server and the printer have been verified using the `ping` command, and the printer is in good general working order with the level of paper and toner adequate for printing. After checking all these areas, a test page should be printed from the print server as a final check that everything on the server is in good working order. The spooler service has been restarted to ensure that it hasn't stopped processing. If all these things have been checked, the server part of the printing system is in good working order, and it's time to take a closer look at the client.

Tracking Client-Side Printing Problems

Client-side printing problems are fairly easy to diagnose. The key point to remember is to test baseline functionality first and then work upward. All these steps should be carried out on the client's workstation. First, make sure the user is logged in properly. Usually the fastest way to check this is to log the user off and then back on. The reason for this is because if the user changed his or her password on another machine while logged on at the current machine, the security tokens on the current machine aren't valid anymore and need to be replaced.

After logging off and logging back on, go to Control Panel, Printers. Double-click the printer in question and make sure that the user can see the jobs that go to the printer. This will help point out typos in the printer name that might not be obvious. Then look at the property page and verify the following settings:

- Check the Ports tab and make sure the printer is connected to the correct port on the server (for example, \\server\printer).
- On the Advanced tab, make sure Hold Mismatched Documents option isn't selected. This will prevent documents from printing if they require a printing service (such as duplexing) or a form size that isn't supported on the printer.
- Also on the Advanced tab, check the driver name and make sure it's valid for the type of printer connected to the port. If the driver doesn't match exactly with the printer model, reinstall the correct drivers.
- On the Security tab, make sure the user hasn't somehow revoked his or her access to print to the printer.
- On the General tab, click Print Test Page button and see if a test page comes out.

If, after checking all the settings, a test page appears, the problem should be solved, but always check to make sure the user can print from the application. Some graphics applications are very picky about printing certain ways, so you should ensure that the application causing the user problems is actually working. This should help prevent future angry phone calls.

If things still aren't working, check to make sure the local machine has plenty of disk space on its system partition. For Windows 2000 workstations, check the spool path, as outlined in the previous section, and make sure the drive that contains print jobs locally has plenty of space. If it doesn't, clean up the disk or move the spool path to another directory. On a Windows 9*x* system, open a command shell (Start, Run, "command") and then type **set**. Look for the line that reads "TEMP=" and make sure that the drive mentioned there has adequate space; then check out the folder and make sure it doesn't have a large number of files already in it. If there are a lot of files in the temp directory, reboot and then delete as many of the files as possible. The FAT file system has a limit to the number of directories that can exist in a single directory, and if this limit is reached, no new files can be created, so nothing can be printed. There will also be other weird things that happen (Microsoft's official term is *unpredictable results*), such as applications shutting down unexpectedly and the inability to save data from applications.

After checking the property pages and checking for disk space, there's usually only one thing remaining to do. Delete the print queue from the user's machine by going to Control Panel, Printers and then selecting the printer and hitting the Delete key. Then, re-create the printer. Make sure to load the print drivers either from the server or from another source that's known to work. After adding the new drivers, print a test page and everything should work fine.

None of That Worked! What Now?

If none of the aforementioned troubleshooting techniques worked, here are a few extra things to try. Basically, these techniques will completely circumvent all the print drivers and help isolate the problem even more. There are separate approaches to take depending on whether the printer is connected to a "real" local port, such as a parallel port, or a network port. To use either of these approaches, you'll need to get a couple of items together. For a non-PostScript printer, you'll need a text file. Any one- or two-page text file will work. If you need to make a text file, just open Notepad and type a couple pages of text. If the printer uses PostScript, you'll need to find a file that has PostScript commands in it. Your printer's software disks or CD-ROM should have something appropriate. Place the file (either text or PostScript) into a folder called C:\PRTEST.

Testing True Locally Connected Printers

If a printer is directly connected to a server via a parallel port and the printer won't print anything, here's one way to force it to print: Open a command prompt and copy the file directly to the printer port. For a file called TEST.TXT, use the following command:

```
Copy c:\prtest\test.txt lpt1:
```

This will send the job directly to the printer. For a PostScript file, just copy the file the same way. After the text file is sent, you may need to either use the Form Feed button on your printer (check the printer manual to see how to do this) or use the Copy Con LPT1: command. This command will copy from the console, which is the command shell that's open, to the port LPT1. Enter the command and type Ctrl+L and then press Enter. Then type Ctrl+Z. Ctrl+L, when on a line by itself, is a form feed command, and Ctrl+Z is the end-of-file marker. Basically, this forces the printer to eject a sheet of paper, which should contain the second page of the text file.

If this doesn't work, one of two things happened. First of all, you tried to send a text file to a PostScript printer. This won't work. The PostScript language uses a special command set, and if the right beginning and ending information isn't present, the file won't print and the printer will likely produce an error message. If it absolutely isn't a PostScript printer, either the printer is not working properly or the cabling between the computer and the printer is not right. You should then try different cables.

Testing TCP/IP Socket-Connected Printers

If a printer is connected to a TCP/IP socket-type local port, testing it can be a little tricky. The first thing to do is to get the Print Server device to send a test page to the printer. There are two basic types of print servers: internal and external. The *internal devices* are cards that reside inside individual printers, such as an HP JetDirect card inside of an HP LaserJet printer. Usually to get one of these devices to generate a status page, you have to use the internal setup menus of the printer. The *external devices* are black boxes with one or more parallel ports on them and usually only one button used to test the printer. These are marketed by HP, NetGear, and Intel as print servers. Read the documentation to determine how to get either type of these devices to print status pages.

After that status page is printed, make absolutely sure that the TCP/IP address is valid and reachable from the Windows 2000 Server machine that's hosting the print queue. This is done, as described earlier, using the `ping` command. In addition, the external print server devices usually support configuration via Telnet, so read Chapter 19 to learn to use Telnet. Then read the instructions with the print server to learn how to use the Telnet interface to the print server.

If the status page won't print, there's something wrong with the print server. Double-check all the setup information; then consider calling the manufacturer's support number. These devices tend to be very fussy to set up, but they run very well once they're configured properly. If the TCP/IP address isn't reachable from the server, read the TCP/IP chapter of this book to learn how TCP/IP and subnet masking work. Then reset the TCP/IP address. This is all covered in chapter 8, "TCP/IP Networking."

Testing Printers by Capturing Ports

If both of the previous tests don't work, there's probably something wrong with how Windows 2000 is connecting to the printer or there's still something wrong with the print drivers. Let's check out the printer connection next, since we've already discussed how to fix the bad driver problem.

Go to a command prompt. The easiest way to capture a printer is to invoke the `Net Use` command, like this:

```
Net use lpt1: \\server\printer
```

Of course, you'll need to substitute your server name and printer share name where appropriate. This also assumes that the local machine doesn't already have a printer on LPT1. If there is a printer on that port already, use another port, up to LPT4.

Next, follow the guidelines in the earlier section, "Testing True Locally Connected Printers," and copy a text file to the printer via the network share. By using the `Copy` command, the submitted print job will bypass all the printer drivers and print directly to the printer.

Diagnosing Print Quality Problems

Modern printers should consistently produce high-quality output that's legible, with the correct fonts and the proper grayscales or colors. Sometimes bad things happen to good printers, and sometimes Windows 2000 feeds them bad information. This section goes through how to figure out what information is correct and how to get more performance and quality from a printer. Here's how to realize the most from your printer:

- Know the printer's limitations
- Know your printer's specifications
- Know the driver version
- Match everything up

The first three items involve researching exactly what the printer is capable of delivering, from the pages per second to the resolution and color depth. The final item makes sure Windows 2000 realizes all these limitations and works within them to produce printed output.

Knowing Your Printer's Limitations

A printer has all sorts of limitations in terms of how fast it should perform, how many graphics it can produce, and the maximum number of colors or shades of gray it can produce. These are usually found in the printer's manual. Most manufacturers have online copies of their manuals that are searchable, which is very handy for locating the specifications for a given print device. Here are the key items to know:

- How fast should the printer print?
- How many colors can the printer produce?
- Which fonts are built into the printer?
- What is the exact model of the printer?

Most, if not all, of these pieces of information can be found in the manual or on the printer's status page (you'll have to read the manual in order to figure out how to print anyway).

Knowing Your Printer's Specifications

In many cases, companies will buy printers and add font cartridges and memory. In some cases, though, they'll remove memory and "dumb down" the printer in order to save money. Although this sounds shortsighted, when a company is buying a thousand printers, a couple hundred bucks per printer in options may actually be significant. So, beyond what the manual says, it's important to know exactly what's installed in the printer with respect to memory and font cartridges. Once again, a status page will probably do the trick, and some printers will actually print out a font sample set, with all the characters for every font installed in the printer.

Knowing Your Driver Versions

It's very important to know what driver versions are on the server that's handling a particular printer. As a matter of fact, you should know the versions and the file dates, because sometimes companies don't handle version numbers correctly, such as version 2.2 being newer than version 2.3. Check the manufacturer's Web site often for updated drivers and read the documentation for these new drivers carefully to see if they offer any enhancements to the existing drivers. Don't install new drivers unless they fix problems or offer substantial enhancements. When installing drivers, be sure to install the drivers for all the different operating systems and architectures that are supported and will be attaching to the server to print, including Windows 9*x*, the various incarnations of Windows NT that may access the printer, and Windows 2000. If the server drivers are current, the workstations that use the drivers should keep themselves up-to-date as well.

Matching Everything Up

After drawing all the information together, it's important to make sure Windows 2000 and the print server actually agree on which features are available and which ones are not. This is done on the Advanced Options page, which is shown in Figure 6.14. To view the Advanced Options page, go to Control Panel, Printers, choose the printer to modify, and then select File, Properties from the menu. On the General tab, click the Printing Preferences page, and on the Printing Preferences page, click the Advanced button.

FIGURE 6.14
The Advanced Options page enables you to match a printer up exactly with what Windows 2000 thinks it is.

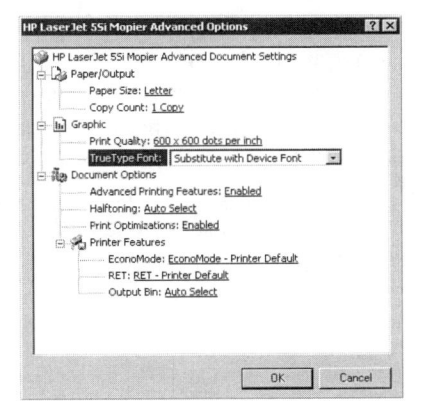

The Advanced Options screen displays all the printer options available. These will change from driver to driver and from printer to printer. Make sure the printer has accurately communicated the amount of installed memory to Windows 2000 and that the font mappings are correct. *Font mappings* are how the printer decides whether it has a given font installed. If a font in an application maps to a font on the printer, the font isn't downloaded because the built-in font will be used. This normally results in higher-quality printing that's also faster, because the font doesn't have to be downloaded. Other things to check include the graphics print quality and the color mappings. A sample Advanced Options screen for an HP LaserJet 5 SI Mopier is shown in Figure 6.15.

FIGURE 6.15
The Advanced properties page will differ from one model of printer to another; here's an example.

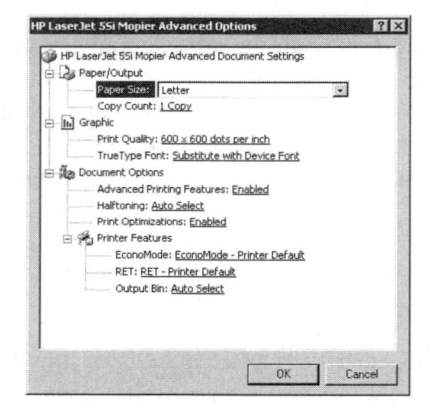

The printer will usually set most of these options correctly. However, especially on older printers, it's important to check these settings to make sure they're accurate.

Summary

Printing can be one of the biggest frustrations in the daily business of a system administrator because there are a lot of different components involved in the operation of printing. The client side has to have a link to the print queue, the server side has to have a link to the printer, there has to be enough disk space for spooling the intermediate files. The list of things that can go wrong is nearly endless. Printers rely on a lot of infrastructure, and if the infrastructure goes awry, printing is usually one of the first noticeable victims.

The Registry

CHAPTER 7

IN THIS CHAPTER

- What Is the Registry? *180*
- The Structure of the Registry *181*
- How the Registry Is Used by Applications *185*
- Using the Registry Editor *187*
- Using the Last Known Good Configuration *193*

For anyone familiar with any version of Windows NT, Windows 95, or Windows 98, the term *Registry* should conjure up pictures of the Registry Editor as well as many other things about the Registry. The Registry is a lot like a campfire. It's very useful, and anyone who camps a lot should know a lot about it. However, it's also dangerous, and serious problems will result if it's abused or neglected. One key thing to keep in mind: Screwing something up in the Registry is the fastest, easiest, and simplest way to totally break any Windows machine. This chapter will discuss safe methods for working with the Registry that will minimize the chance for problems.

This chapter will discuss the following topics:

- What the Registry is
- The structure of the Registry
- How the Registry is used by applications
- How to use the Registry editors
- How to use the Last Known Good configuration

Let's start by examining the role the Registry plays in the Windows 2000 architecture.

What Is the Registry?

The *Registry* is a large, hierarchical database that holds the persistent information needed by the operating system as well as any installed applications. The Registry exists in a set of files on disk in the directory %SYSTEMROOT%\system32\config called SECURITY, SYSTEM, SOFTWARE, and DEFAULT, as well as in another file in the %USERPROFILE% directory called NTUSER.DAT.

The Registry contains all the settings used by the operating system and by most applications. The operating system stores everything that makes the particular machine's setup different from other machines in the Registry, such as the TCP/IP address, the computer name, the installed printers, and so on. Any setting that can be made in Windows 2000 is set in the Registry.

The Registry is stored in a Microsoft-proprietary format. It cannot be edited with anything but a Registry Editor or by an application that makes the appropriate Win32 API calls. An application is allowed to access any Registry key that the user who started the application is allowed to access.

The Structure of the Registry

Without order, there is chaos. Microsoft has created standards for how information in the Registry should be structured and how to store data in the Registry. The Registry is secured using the same permissions that Windows 2000 uses to secure files. These permissions exist even if the system partition doesn't support file security.

The Registry is hierarchical, so it has to have a top. The Registry actually has four different tops, because it's actually four different databases (called *hives*). The four hives are `Classes`, `Users`, `Local Machine`, and `Current Configuration`. The Registry contains two types of items: keys and values. A *key* is like a folder in the file system but, instead of containing files, a key contains values. Every key has at least one value called (`Default`) and can contain many more values. Each hierarchy is divided a little differently, so let's take a look at each one.

The `Classes` Hive

The `Classes` hive, labeled `HKEY_CLASSES_ROOT`, is stored in the `SYSTEM` Registry file. This key stores the settings and registration for OLE or ActiveX (or whatever the name is this week of the Microsoft component architecture components). The hive is absolutely huge, even if there aren't any applications loaded.

Ever wonder how Windows knows how to start Microsoft Word when a file ending in `.doc` is double-clicked? The first several hundred keys in the `Classes` hive determine how to run programs for different extensions. They all start with a period, and the hives are always listed in alphabetical order, so they're easy to pick out. Each one of these keys has a default value that points to the class name to use (for `.doc`, the default value is `Word.Document.8`).

The next several hundred keys in the `Classes` hive include names of the installed classes on the machine and how to access them. Many of the installed classes have two different keys. The first one is a version-independent key, and the second is the version-dependent key. For example, there's a `Word.Document` key and a `Word.Document.8` key. The `Word.Document` key points to the `Word.Document.8` key, which in turn points to Microsoft Word.

Most of these classes have at least two keys beneath them—one called `CLSID` and one called `CurVer`. The `CLSID` key has a default value that corresponds to a globally unique identifier (or *GUID*) for the object. The `CurVer` key's default value is usually the name of the application's version; therefore, for `Word.Document`, the `CurVer` key contains `Word.Document.8`. A bit further down the list, a glance into the `Word.Document.8` key would show subkeys for the application, the location of the icon to use for the document in Explorer, and a key that explains to the operating system how to open one of these files when double-clicked. The Word.Document.8 key also contains the GUID for the class, which looks like this:

{00020906-0000-0000-C000-000000000046}

Every class has a unique identifier similar to this one. It's how the class is really identified.

The Users Hive

The Users hive, marked as HKEY_CURRENT_USER, contains the user-defined settings for all applications and for the operating system. The Users hive contains what's also called a *user's profile*, which encompasses all the settings from the desktop background image for how to place a window onscreen. Users tend to get antsy when these settings go awry, and for good reason—it takes a long time to set everything up "just right." In the Registry Editor, which is covered a little later in this chapter, there's also an entry for HKEY_CURRENT_USER. This entry is actually a link over to the HKEY_USERS hive, and it reflects the settings of the user currently logged on to the console.

The Users hive is broken down into two major sections: One is called .DEFAULT, which contains the default settings that a new user will get the first time he or she logs on to the system. The rest of the entries are GUIDs for all users, and they contain a profile for every user who has logged on to the machine.

When a user logs on, part of the logon process checks to see if the user has logged on to the machine before; if so, the HKEY_CURRENT_USER key is linked to the GUID for that user. If the user has not logged on before, a new entry with the GUID for the user is created, and then the contents of the .DEFAULT user are copied to the new user. If it's necessary to make changes for every user who is ever going to log on to a machine, making changes to the .DEFAULT user will make those changes for all new logins to the machine, but it will not make the same changes for existing users.

To remove a user profile from HKEY_USERS, right-click the My Computer icon on the desktop and choose Properties. Then click the User Profiles tab. This will show the user profiles that exist on the local machine. Delete profiles by clicking them and choosing Delete Profile. Certain profiles cannot be deleted. The currently logged-in user can't be deleted, and the administrator's profile can't be deleted.

For an individual user, the hive will contain a lot of different settings, depending on what's installed on the local machine. The Network item contains a key for all the drive letters that the user has connected that are reconnected at login. Each drive letter contains values that tell Windows 2000 how to reconnect the drive at login, such as the server name, the share name, and the network provider (such as Microsoft Windows Network for Windows 2000 or Windows NT server-connected drives or other entries for NetWare- or NFS-connected drives). Also, the username (in the format DOMAIN\USER) is stored so that the connection can be rebuilt.

Another interesting key is the Software key. The Software key contains data for all the applications stored on the machine, organized by the manufacturer of the software and by application. For example, the Adobe Acrobat software creates a key for Adobe and a subkey for Acrobat. There are numerous keys created below Acrobat, but beneath that level the organization is completely the responsibility of the software vendor (and ultimately the programmer).

The Local Machine Hive

The Local Machine hive contains user-independent information for the local machine. That means all the information that concerns startup and hardware interfaces, as well as information the software needs in order to run regardless of which user is logged on, is stored in the Local Machine part of the Registry.

The Hardware subkey contains information about the hardware detected on the local machine. An interesting key below Hardware is the DEVICEMAP key, which enumerates all the hardware on the machine, such as keyboards, parallel ports, serial ports, and SCSI adapters.

> **Note**
>
> Even if only IDE or ATAPI drives are connected to the local machine, the SCSI key will show up in the HKEY_LOCAL_MACHINE\Hardware key. The Windows 2000 driver model regards IDE drives the same as SCSI drives, which simplifies the driver model. This is a fairly normal way for modern operating systems to handle IDE devices—the SCSI standard is very mature and supports everything the IDE/ATAPI standard supports.

The Security key, located directly beneath HKEY_LOCAL_MACHINE, is restricted to operating system access only. It contains all the user account and security information, such as user account names, groups, encrypted passwords, and so on.

The Software key is very similar in organization to the Software key in HKEY_CURRENT_USER, which was described earlier. The Software key contains the information for applications on the local machine that doesn't change from user to user. For example, the path to the data files for the application or the registration information for the application is normally saved in this part of the Registry.

The `System` key is the most interesting key in `HKEY_LOCAL_MACHINE`. The `System` key contains all the Windows 2000 settings for the local machine. There are three keys that involve control settings: `CurrentControlSet`, `ControlSet001`, and `ControlSet002`. These three keys contain redundant sets of information on how the operating system is set up. The reasoning behind the extra copies is that if a piece of software makes settings in the Registry, the user can activate the previous good settings contained in one of the backup copies. See the last section in this chapter, "Using the Last Known Good Configuration," for information on how to use the Last Known Good settings.

The `CurrentControlSet` key contains several interesting subkeys. The first one, `Control`, contains all the hardware driver settings and network settings for the local machine. The `Class` hive contains a key for every device driver installed on the system, organized by GUID, and with information about the driver, including who made the driver, where the driver is located, and a "friendly name" for the driver.

The `ComputerName` key contains, of all things, the computer name. The `ActiveComputerName` key is the name of the computer now, and the `ComputerName` key is the name the computer will take upon rebooting.

The `hivelist` key contains a list of all the Registry hives and which files contain the hives. The information is in a format that uniquely identifies the location of the file, which looks like this:

`\Device\HarddiskVolume1\WINNT\System32\CONFIG\SOFTWARE`

This format uniquely identifies a file anywhere on the machine without using drive letters. That way, if the drive letters change, the operating system can still boot.

The `WOW` key contains information used by the Windows on Windows system. Windows on Windows is the system used to run 16-bit Windows applications under Windows 2000. It contains information about how to start the Windows on Windows system and, more importantly, the DLLs needed to run the software.

Another key under `CurrentControlSet` is `Services`, which controls how operating system services get started. Every key in the `Services` key contains certain values that help the `Services` subsystem start the various services. Most keys have a `DisplayName` value, which is how a service will show up in a list of services. The `ErrorControl` key determines what to do in the case of an error. In most cases, this is set to 1, which will cause an event to be registered and a dialog box to show up stating that a service failed to start. The `ImagePath` value is the path to the executable file. For services that are started from the `WINNT` path, the specified path is relative to the `%SYSTEMROOT%` variable. For services installed elsewhere, a drive letter and full path are allowed (with only 8.3 filenames), where the path `C:\Program Files` becomes `C:\PROGRA~1`.

The `Start` value determines how or if a service starts. In this list, several services are listed that clearly don't apply to the local machine, most of which are SCSI adapters. These keys will have a `Start` value of `0`. Services are started such that all the services with a value of `1` get started first, all the services with a value of `2` get started next, and so on. This allows device startups to be staggered, and it allows devices to start up so that dependencies get met.

Overall, the `HKEY_LOCAL_MACHINE` hive contains everything Windows 2000 needs to start successfully. A lot of troubleshooting and repair involves checking and making changes to this hive. Every device that gets installed makes changes to this hive, and understanding how the changes affect Windows 2000 is very important.

The Current Configuration Hive

The `Current Configuration` hive, displayed as `HKEY_CURRENT_CONFIG`, is used to contain transient information about the local machine configuration. This includes PCI setup information, the configuration information about PCMCIA, settings about the current video resolution, and so on. This information is discarded at system shutdown and will change as different applications are run.

How the Registry Is Used by Applications

Microsoft made the Registry available to applications so that applications could keep settings that were generic to the machine and those that were made by users independent of one another. That way, different users can make changes to the operating system settings, such as backgrounds and color schemes, without affecting other users. The user who likes his screen to be yellow on black won't affect another user who thinks traditional black on white is the way to go. Screen colors may seem on the trivial side, but how about users who make changes to the look and feel of applications, set up specific macros for certain keys, and so on? These types of changes enhance productivity and can be very important.

When an application installs itself, it makes changes to the various parts of the Registry that initialize the application. Most applications install their extensions into `HKEY_CLASSES` and then install basic user settings and window location information in `HKEY_CURRENT_USER`.

For services such as Microsoft SQL Server, information is saved all over the Registry. The client tools register their extensions, and the server components create entries in `HKEY_LOCAL_MACHINE/System/CurrentControlSet/Services` to control the service startup and `HKEY_LOCAL_MACHINE/Software/Microsoft/MSSQLServer` for the software itself. Once the service gets started by the information in the `Services` key, the application reads information from the `Software` key to complete its startup. This is fairly typical of service software.

Some applications still use INI files to store settings. An *INI file* is a text file stored on disk in plain text format, usually in the `WINNT` directory. Each file contains the settings for one application, and the format and usage of the INI file are completely up to the programmer.

When a user logs in to a Windows 2000 system, he or she can have programs start up automatically. There are several different ways to start applications at login, one of which is to put the applications' executable paths into a value in `HKEY_CURRENT_USER\Software\Microsoft\Windows\Run` or `RunOnce`. The user can also put apps into the Startup group in the Start menu. The most insidious method—and the one used most often by viruses that need automatic startup—is to put an entry into `WIN.INI` called `RUN`. This will run the program, and it can be very difficult to track down. To figure it out, simply open the `WIN.INI` file with Notepad. It can be found in the system directory, usually `C:\WINNT`.

The Registry database is a departure from the typical operating system. UNIX-style operating systems store machine setup data in text files in the `/etc` directory, and they store user settings in the user's home directory in text files. Why does Windows NT use the Registry, which requires special software for editing and maintenance, rather than using plain text files that can be edited with any text editor? There are a couple of interesting answers to this question. First, Windows 2000 uses a special character set called Unicode. Unicode characters take two bytes of storage each, and they can represent virtually any character in any language. Given that two bytes can hold 65,536 different values, that's a lot of characters. Because the Registry needs to hold foreign language strings, they should be stored as Unicode. Normal text editing tools can't edit Unicode data, whereas the Registry editing tools can.

The second reason for the Registry is that it provides a central location for all the system settings. It provides a single access mechanism for applications, which is a nice standard service for an operating system to provide.

For many programmers, this system is very offensive, and it represents a series of bad design decisions. As a result, many programs use something other than the Registry to store settings. One reason for this common feeling is that application installation becomes very complex. In order to install an application, a setup program has to be written that writes all the settings into the Registry rather than just copying a bunch of files and running the program.

In a corporate environment, if a program needs to be set up, customized, and distributed to several thousand users, great pains have to be taken to ensure that all the custom settings get carried along. Programs don't document what settings they use in the Registry, so it becomes very difficult to figure out what a program needs. A new type of utility program has been created simply to analyze the Registry and figure out what settings a particular program creates in order to build a setup program. Another whole industry exists on the consumer side to remove unused Registry settings for programs that have been removed but didn't clean up after themselves.

In addition, the Registry is a single point of failure. If one of the files that contain Registry information becomes corrupt, the operating system might not start. Therefore, if someone is playing a game and the part of the Registry that contains the game's settings gets messed up, the machine might not boot. On the other hand, if the game's settings were in their own file and these settings were corrupt, the game wouldn't function but the computer would start. Another objection to the Registry is that it becomes one more hurdle that needs to be jumped in order to port a piece of software to the Win32 platform. As a result, many of the recent multiplatform pieces of software don't use the Registry, or they use it to the minimum extent possible.

Using the Registry Editor

The Registry Editor is the tool used to view and make changes to the Registry. Because of the nature of these tools, as well as their importance to the Registry, no shortcuts exist in the Start menu for any Registry tools. Two Registry Editors ship with Windows 2000. One of them is called REGEDIT.EXE, a Windows 95–style Registry Editor with full search capabilities and a very nice interface. The other Registry Editor is called REGEDT32.EXE, the old, Windows NT 3.51–style editor.

When to Use Registry Editing Tools

It's been said before, but it definitely bears repeating: Be very, very careful in the Registry. Bad things can happen if values in the Registry are missing or set incorrectly. These bad things include but are not limited to failure to boot, services failing to start, hardware not working properly, damage to equipment (especially monitors), performance degradation, and career limitations. Don't mess up the Registry. It will not only cause you problems, but Microsoft support will laugh at you.

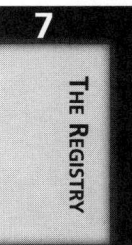

> **Warning**
>
> You probably know this already, but you should only use Registry tools when there's no other way to make a change to a value. Don't go into the Registry to change a setting such as the video resolution for monitor. Microsoft spent a lot of time building little Control Panel widgets for you to use to perform such tasks, and they've been extensively tested to work correctly. If there's any possible user interface for performing an operation, use that interface instead of using a Registry Editor. Using a Registry Editor to change system settings is like using a cheap knife to perform surgery. Just don't do it.

How to Use REGEDIT

The REGEDIT.EXE program is the Windows 95–style Registry editing program. It has a very nice user interface and a search mechanism to help you find Registry entries quickly. To start REGEDIT, go to Start, Run and type in **REGEDIT**. The Registry Editor, shown in Figure 7.1, will start up. Notice that the Registry is shown with a treeview-style tool. There's no read-only option for this editor, so be careful.

FIGURE 7.1

REGEDIT.EXE *is the more user-friendly Registry Editor. Shown here are the SCSI devices under the* HARDWARE *key.*

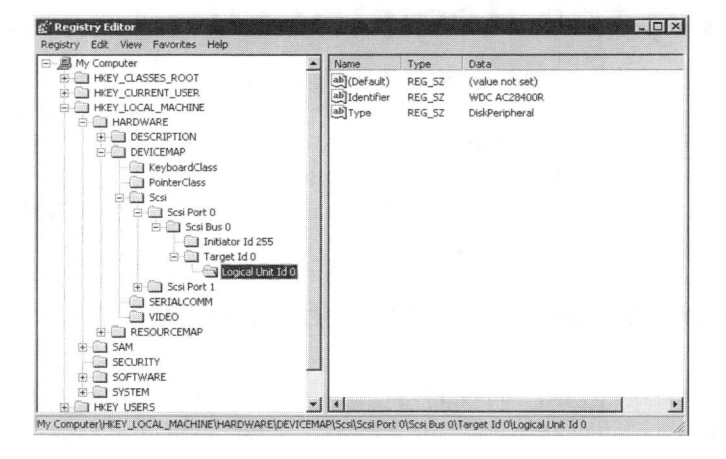

To browse the Registry, use the Outline control. If a key is shown with a plus sign next to it, the key has subkeys. Click the plus sign to expand the key, and the list of subkeys will be shown indented below it. To get rid of the expansion, click the minus sign, and the subkeys will contract back to one key. To view the values for a key, select the key and the values will be shown on the right side of the Registry Editor window. To search for a key, choose Find from the Edit menu and fill in the dialog box to search for a key. After the editor has found the first item corresponding to the search, choosing Edit, Find Next or pressing F3 will perform the Find operation a second time.

To delete a key, simply select it and press Delete. A confirmation prompt will appear. Be careful: Deleting the wrong entry may cause problems. Deleting a key will delete all subkeys and values attached to the key. This can seriously mess up Windows 2000 if extreme care isn't exercised.

To add a subkey, select the key to add to and choose Edit, New Key from the menu. The key will be added and named `New Key #1`. However, you can rename it. Name the key whatever you want. To change the name of any existing key, click the key and either choose Edit, Rename from the menu or press the F2 key. An example is shown in Figure 7.2.

FIGURE 7.2
To rename a Registry key, simply choose Edit, Rename from the menu and enter the new name. Here, the key `My Key` *is ready to be renamed.*

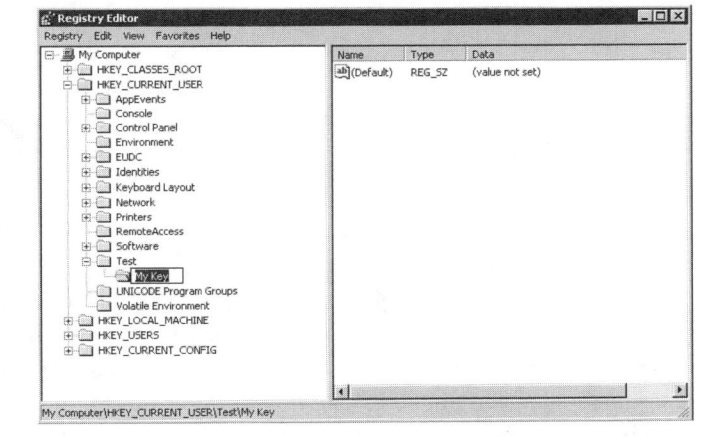

To add a value, click the key that the value should be added to and choose Edit, New and specify the type of value to be added. A string value can hold character strings, a binary value holds strings of numbers, and a `DWORD` value contains a double-word value (or a four-byte integer). By default, the name of the new value will be `New Value #1`, and it can be renamed by choosing Edit, Rename or by pressing F2. To set a value, double-click on the value. In most cases, `DWORD` values are used for `true` and `false`, where `1` is `true` and `0` is `false`. In this case, it doesn't matter if you're entering the value in hexadecimal or decimal. String values are entered by just typing in the string, but binary values must be entered in hexadecimal. String values are used to hold paths and other string information. Binary values hold binary data, usually encoded strings of some type. Figure 7.3 shows how to enter a new string value.

In addition, Registry keys can be exported to text files for use elsewhere. In the Registry Editor, choose the key to export and choose Registry, Export Registry File from the menu. A File dialog box will appear, and you'll have the option of either exporting the current key or exporting the entire Registry.

FIGURE 7.3
To add a Registry key, choose Edit, New, String Value from the menu and then rename and populate the key value. The value shown here has been renamed MyValue *and is being set in the dialog box.*

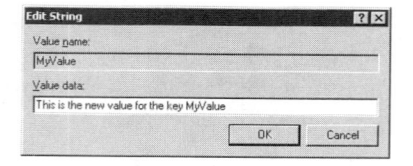

Registry file exporting is usually used when the same Registry entry needs to be made on several machines. First, make the Registry change on one machine; then export the key. To import the Registry file, either double-click it from Explorer or choose Registry, Import Registry File from the menu.

Registry files are set-format text files. They can be opened and understood with simple tools such as Notepad. Left-clicking a Registry file will show a context menu. Merge is the default action, but choosing Edit will open the Registry file in Notepad, which shows a list of keys and values. The keys are contained in brackets, and the values are beneath their respective keys in the format `"ValueName"="Value"`. When a Registry file is imported, it's actually merged into the Registry. If a key already exists and contains values, after a Registry file is merged, the key will still exist, and any existing values not in the Registry file are still present in the Registry after the merge. Therefore, if a Registry key called `MyApp` has two values, `Value1` and `Value2`, and the following Registry file is merged in

```
Windows Registry Editor Version 5.00

[HKEY_CURRENT_USER\Software\MyCompany\MyApp]
"Value3"="42"
```

the resulting `MyApp` Registry will contain `Value1`, `Value2`, and `Value3`. A Registry file cannot delete an existing Registry key or value—it can only add to existing keys and values and overwrite existing values with new data. This makes it a bit harder to mess up the Registry with a Registry export file.

Another nice feature of REGEDIT is that it can import Registry files from the command line. By using the /s command-line switch, REGEDIT can silently import Registry files, which imports Registry settings without any user input. This is useful for importing Registry files from a login script.

The REGEDIT program works very well for importing and exporting, but it does have a few problems. First of all, it can't handle security. All Registry keys can have security set on them according to the same scheme as NTFS security. The `REGEDIT.EXE` program does not have the capability to edit security on Registry keys, whereas the other Registry editing program, REGEDT32, does have this capability. Also, the data types available in REGEDIT are restricted to strings, double-words, and binary. REGEDT32 adds two additional data types, `REG_MULTI_SZ` and `REG_EXPAND_SZ`.

Finding Registry Changes Using REGEDIT

One of the most annoying things about the Registry is tracking the changes made to the Registry during the installation of new software. In order to successfully distribute software within a large corporation, you usually need to create customized installation programs that handle file placement, build the shortcuts on the Start menu, and then import the Registry changes. The REGEDIT program supplies some functions that allow these changes to be made a bit more easily. Prior to installing the application, perform a Registry export for the entire `HKEY_LOCAL_MACHINE` and `HKEY_CURRENT_USER` hives and then run the setup program. After setup is complete, reboot the machine, if necessary, and then export the same Registry hives again. Using the Windows 2000 command line, run the FC program to perform a file comparison:

```
FC UserPreInstall.reg UserPostInstall.reg > UserDiff.txt
```

This command will output the differences between the two Registry files to a file called `UserDiff.txt`. This file can then be read with Notepad and will contain a bunch of Registry settings that changed. Many of these settings, however, may not be relevant to the installation, so the output file needs to be examined carefully in order to determine which settings apply.

How to Use REGEDT32

The REGEDT32 program's interface is not nearly as nice as REGEDIT. It uses a separate window for each hive, so there are five windows open when REGEDT32 opens. To start REGEDT32, go to the Start menu, choose Run, and type in **REGEDT32**.

Browsing the Registry is similar to using REGEDIT. First, go to the window that contains the Registry hive in question and then scroll down the list. Keys are represented as file folders, and keys with subkeys are represented as files with plus signs in them, as shown in Figure 7.4.

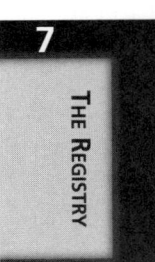

FIGURE 7.4
The Registry Editor shown here, REGEDT32, has a significantly different look and feel than REGEDIT.

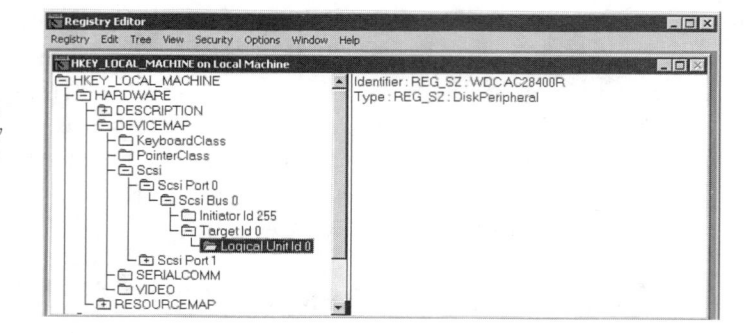

To add a key or value, choose Edit from the menu and then choose Add Key or Add Value. Add Key prompts for the name of the key to add, and Add Value prompts for the name of the key and the type. Next, choose the Registry value. REGEDT32 displays the data types differently than REGEDIT, as shown in Table 7.1.

TABLE 7.1 Registry Value Data Types

REGEDT32 Data Type	REGEDIT Type
REG_BINARY	Binary
REG_DWORD	Double-word
REG_SZ	String
REG_EXPAND_SZ	Not available
REG_MULTI_SZ	Not available

REG_MULTI_SZ allows multiple strings to be stored in one value, and REG_EXPAND_SZ is a normal string that can turn into a multistring value.

REGEDT32 is not nearly as capable as REGEDIT when it comes to importing and exporting values. The problem is that REGEDT32 doesn't have the capability to easily import files. To save a set of Registry keys, go to Registry/Save Subtree As and pick a filename. The file that's created is not a valid import file.

To change the security on a Registry key, select the key and choose Security, Permissions from the menu. The security dialog boxes are the same as those used for file security. There's also the capability to audit Registry access just like auditing file access. This allows Registry settings to be monitored; changes to the Registry can also be logged. These audit logs are kept in the Event Viewer's security log, just like the audit logs for a file. To turn on Registry auditing, choose Security, Auditing from the menu.

Using the Last Known Good Configuration

Despite all the warnings in this chapter and all the official warnings from Microsoft, sometimes people make changes to the Registry that will prevent Windows 2000 from starting up successfully. What happens next? Fortunately, the designers of Windows 2000 realized that this was a possibility and created a feature called *Last Known Good*.

During the boot process, Windows 2000 reads information it needs to run from within the `CurrentControlSet` portion of the Registry. When Windows 2000 is satisfied that it has booted properly, about the time the screen displays "Press Ctrl+Alt+Delete to log on," Windows 2000 relinks `ControlSet001` to `ControlSet002` and then copies the current settings over to `ControlSet001`. If the system cannot boot to the point where it rewrites the control sets, the user can reboot the machine and choose to boot from the Last Known Good configuration, which will read settings out of `ControlSet001` instead of `CurrentControlSet`, thus bypassing the bad entries in the Registry.

To access the Last Known Good configuration, reboot the machine, and at the operating system selection menu, press F8. This will allow you to select the Last Known Good configuration. This configuration will be the last configuration that worked prior to the last reboot. In other words, if the machine hasn't been rebooted in a very long time, the configuration settings may be very out of date, and many settings may be old, not just the one that prevented the machine from rebooting. Therefore, you might be wise to reboot prior to making changes to the local machine, such as installing new software or editing the Registry.

Summary

The Registry is critical to the performance of Windows 2000. Don't mess around in the Registry unless you know exactly what you're doing. The Registry allows programs to store startup information so that they'll start up the same way every time. Editing the Registry is done with either REGEDIT or REGEDT32, both of which allow Registry entries to be created, changed, or deleted.

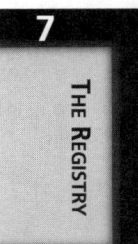

CHAPTER 8

TCP/IP Networking

IN THIS CHAPTER

- TCP/IP Concepts Brief *196*
- Microsoft TCP/IP *205*

The big winner in the protocol wars is currently TCP/IP. TCP/IP is not really a protocol but rather a suite of protocols that has been around since the 1960s and, oddly enough, is an open standard because it was created by the United States government for that other great freebie, the Internet.

Frankly, the TCP/IP protocol has become the *de facto* standard because of the Internet and because no one group owns it. Therefore, any vendors can use it, manipulate it, and create pieces of its standard.

TCP/IP Concepts Brief

The full name is *Transmission Control Protocol/Internet Protocol*, for those who are not familiar with it. This protocol suite is a combination of TCP and IP:

- TCP is a connection-based network protocol that allows systems to communicate without errors over any media.
- IP is the network-layer protocol that's responsible for delivering the packets created by TCP from one end of the network to the other.

These two protocols are the main players in the suite of protocols used to communicate among the many brands of hardware and operating systems. The protocol suite, itself, does not care about the hardware it's running on or the operating system that's hosting it. The job of the protocol suite is to provide the rules of communication once a physical connection has been established.

Like a human language TCP/IP first establishes that a medium exists to speak across; then it establishes a common language and begins to talk.

IP Addressing

The addressing scheme used by TCP/IP is simply called *IP Addressing*. It's a fairly straightforward addressing scheme. The administrator is involved in the configuration of all the addresses and the structure. If you understand the basic rules governing it, addressing becomes fairly simple to maneuver around in the scheme because you are in control of the setup.

The first thing to understand about an IP address is that it's a number consisting of four 8-bit numbers separated by periods (sometimes referred to as *four octets*). Octet means *eight* bits. Therefore, each octet in decimal format is written as a number from 0 to 255. This range is seen as 256 possible numbers because computers consider 0 to be a usable value.

Binary

If you do not understand how eight bits equates to a range from 0 to 255, you might not understand the basic concept of how computers compute. Everything computers do is done in a language called *binary*. Binary is simply a two-digit way of communicating numbers by presenting 1's and 0's (or something and the lack of something).

Decimal numbering is the standard form of human counting based on multiples of 10 (base 10) and most people understand it. As far as the computer is concerned the decimal value (standard number range) and the binary value are the same. Decimal numbering is only necessary for human understanding.

Here's a line of eight bits in binary:

00101100

In order to translate this number, you simply need to think of each row (running right to left) as a number double that of its neighbor, beginning with 1, like this:

128 64 32 16 8 4 2 1

To get the answer, take the numbers that correspond to a 0 and throw them out. Then take the numbers that correspond to a 1 and add them up, like this:

32 + 8 + 4 = 44

Let's look at some more possibilities:

- 00000001 = 1 = 1
- 10000000 = 128 = 128
- 10101010 = 128 + 32 + 8 + 2 = 170
- 01110111 = 64 + 32 + 16 + 4 + 2 + 1 = 119

That's binary. If you need some help remembering what an address translates to in 1's and 0's, you can look in Appendix B, "IP Address Decimal to Binary Table." It contains a complete listing of binary combinations along with the decimal and hexadecimal translations.

The Address

Now that you understand binary and the fact that an IP address is four octets separated by periods, what resulting address might look like this?

10000000.10101010.00000001.01110111

Keep this format in mind because it's not the normal look for an IP address. When you're attempting to calculate problems or find an ideal configuration, it's very useful.

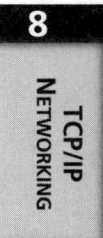

Address are normally expressed in decimal, so the same address would need to be entered into Windows 2000 as this:

128.170.1.119

Networks and Hosts

All machines in an IP network are called *hosts*. Servers, workstations, printers, and even your oven (if it attaches to an IP network) are considered hosts.

In order to locate a host, an IP address is divided into two distinct parts. These pieces allow the system to identify which system a packet has come from or needs to arrive at. Just as a telephone has an area code and a specific phone number, an IP address has a portion of the address that identifies the network were the system exists and a portion that identifies the given host.

These address portions are called the *network portion* and *host portion* of the address. In its simplest form, the address is divided at its periods, depending on the address class.

There are three primary classes of IP addresses: A, B, and C. The division is simple to remember by simply remembering what number position in the alphabet each letter is. From left to right, if the first octet is the network portion, the address is Class A. If the first two octets are the network portion of the address, the address is Class B. If the first three octets are the network portion of the address, the address is Class C. This might help explain the concept:

- Network.Host.Host.Host = Class A
- Network.Network.Host.Host = Class B
- Network.Network.Network.Host = Class C

To organize the available addresses and the separation of the classes the classes have been given specific ranges that they may operate in when attached to the Internet. This helps to determine the class of an address by simply looking at it.

- Class A networks will always begin with 0 in the first position.
- Class B networks will always begin with 10 in the first positions.
- Class B networks will always begin with 110 in the first positions.

This results in a range of possible addresses in each class.

- Class A 1.X.X.X – 126.X.X.X
- Class B 128.0.X.X – 191.255.X.X
- Class C 192.0.0.X – 223.255.255.X

> **Note**
>
> Note that 127.X.X.X is missing in the equation. This is because the number 127.0.0.1 has been reserved for the local machine testing and internal use. This address is also called LOCALHOST for that reason. In fact you can ping LOCALHOST for internal testing of the presents of the TCP/IP protocol.

Why would the network and host portions of the IP address be variable items? The answer is that some internetworks have need for more network segments and other internetworks have need for more host addresses. Consider these points:

- An Internet provider, for example, needs to be able to provide a great many host addresses. The numbers of user machines that dial into these systems require unique IP addresses for each host.
- A large company's WAN may have need for a greater number of network addresses. This would allow it more routed WAN connections but fewer hosts at each site.
- Network providers need a large number of both, and this is possible by creating subordinate pieces of the networks. This is covered in the section "Subnet Addressing."

The number of hosts and network addresses that a given class has can be determined by taking the number of addresses that exist on each side of the line dividing network from host. However, you must keep in mind that you cannot use 0 or 255 in the network portion of your addresses. You also cannot use all 0's or all 255's in your host portion. All 0's and all 255's have special meanings in IP. Therefore, you must subtract 2 from the number possible in each case:

- Class A has 126 possible network addresses and $256 \times 256 \times 256$ (or 16,777,214) possible host addresses.
- Class B has 16,384 possible network addresses and 256×256 (or 65,534) possible host addresses.
- Class C has 2,097,152 possible network addresses and 254 possible host addresses.

Subnet Mask

The portion of IP addressing that determines network versus host portions of an address is called the *subnet mask* (or simply the *mask*). The idea of the subnet mask is to mask those parts of the address that must be the network portion from those available as host addresses.

When you look at a mask in binary, you'll see that it contains 1's starting from left to right; all the portions of the address that are consumed by these 1's are not available to the host portion. Look at these simple examples of standard IP address classes and you'll start to get the idea:

Here are subnet masks for standard classes:

- Class A = 255.0.0.0 = 11111111.00000000.00000000.00000000
- Class B = 255.255.0.0 = 11111111.11111111.00000000.00000000
- Class C = 255.255.255.0 = 11111111.11111111.11111111.00000000

When the computer compares the address against the subnet mask, it uses the binary version to separate the network from the host by separating the 1's from the 0's. The part of the address that lines up with the 1's is for the network, and the part that lines with the 0's is for the host. It really isn't quite that simple, but that begins to give you the general idea. If you stay with the standard classes, it can be just that easy.

Subnet Addressing

Subnet masks can become more complicated than the standard examples just given. The examples given to this point have been in a perfect world that allows the system administrator to pick and choose the address range that he or she wants without regard for other networks or systems existing. What about the Internet? What about company subsidiaries that must take the IP address range that they're given and live within those boundaries.

These environments may cause you to split the subnet along less convenient lines. For example, you might have a subnet mask of 255.255.255.128 so that you can divide the Class C address that you were assigned into two networks. The same rules apply. This can be a bit more difficult to understand though if you allow yourself to make it more complex then it really is.

Here are two questions to keep in mind while splitting a subnet boundary:

- How many hosts will I need now and in the future?
- How many networks will I need now and in the future?

> **Note**
>
> The future is not always the best thing to have to guess at, but in this case, you should err on the side of excess. Once you've installed an IP scheme, you'll have a large undertaking on your hands if you have to *reinstall* it.

If you must split your network into nonstandard sections, you need to understand how to determine the number of networks and hosts addresses possible in that subnet.

Here is the way to get the number of possible hosts:

- Take the final digit (not 0) of the subnet mask and subtract it from 256 (the maximum number of allowed host addresses in an octet). Then multiply that number by 256 for every open octet (.0) remaining to the left. Then subtract 2.

    Here are examples:
    - Mask = 255.192.0.0
        256 − 192 = 64
        64 × 256 = 16,384 × 256 = 4194304
        4,194,304 − 2 = 4,194,304 possible hosts
    - Mask = 255.255.128.0
        256 − 128 = 128
        128 × 256 = 32768
        32768 − 2 = 32,766 possible hosts
    - Mask = 255.255.255.252
        256 − 252 = 4

        Rule says to multiply for each open octet (.0) there is none here. Drop the above result down.

        4 − 2 = 2 possible hosts
    - Mask = 255.___.___.___
        256 − ___ = 4
        ___ X 256(if needed)= ___ X 256(if needed) = ___ X 256(if needed) = ___
        ___ − 2 = ___ possible hosts

    (Look at the list I've provided in Appendix B).

> **Note**
>
> Remember that only the last octet that's not a zero effects the number of networks because it's the only one that will allow variation from what you were assigned.

Here are two ways to get the number of possible subnets:

- Take the binary position from the left (inverted position) double it and subtract 2. This will produce the number of networks.

    Example: 224 = 11100000 = 4 X 2 = 8 – 2 = 6 (the number of subnets
- The inverted position is just the opposite of the standard binary position:

    1 2 4 8 16 32 64 128

    Because 11111111 completely fills the mask and 0000000 leaves it open, they do not need calculation. 0000000 (0) allows only one network. 11111111 is not allowed.

The table below will help as a reference point in this calculation.

TABLE 8.1 Calculation Reference Table

Mask Number	Binary	Inverted Position Number	Number of Available Networks
192	11000000	2	2
224	11100000	4	6
240	11110000	8	14
248	11111000	16	30
252	11111100	32	62
254	11111110	64	126

You can create subnets with masks such as 255.255.184.0, but by the time you've found the true number of hosts and networks, I'll have written another book. This material is not covered here because it's highly unusual for such masks to exist and this is not a TCP/IP master-level book.

> **Note**
>
> The 10.X.X.X network range has been reserved for those creating private networks (those not being accessed by the Internet). This range is not being routed on the Internet and therefore makes a great choice for internal networks. It also allows for simple subneting because the entire range is available. It is as if the company is given a class A address.

IP Routing

If subnet masks are being calculated, there must be some need for routing on the network. IP hosts communicate with one another by either discovering each other on the same segment (see Chapter 5, "Networking Brief,") or by asking the default gateway (the router found in their IP settings) to forward the request to the proper network. (The process is a bit more complicated than this once you leave the host.)

> **Note**
>
> Routers in IP are sometimes called *gateways*, which is technically wrong. However, that's a fact of life you'll have to tolerate if you're going to manage Windows systems. When an IP host system ask for the default gateway address, it means the first router that your machine will go to when it cannot find a system on its own segment by broadcasting the request.

IP routers take the packets sent to them from host systems and forward the packets to the proper network or host. The router knows where the proper network is based on either having a direct connection to the network segment, by discovering the route through gathering information from other routers, or by the static installation of routes by the administrator (see Figure 8.1).

FIGURE 8.1
A packet finding it's way to the proper host.

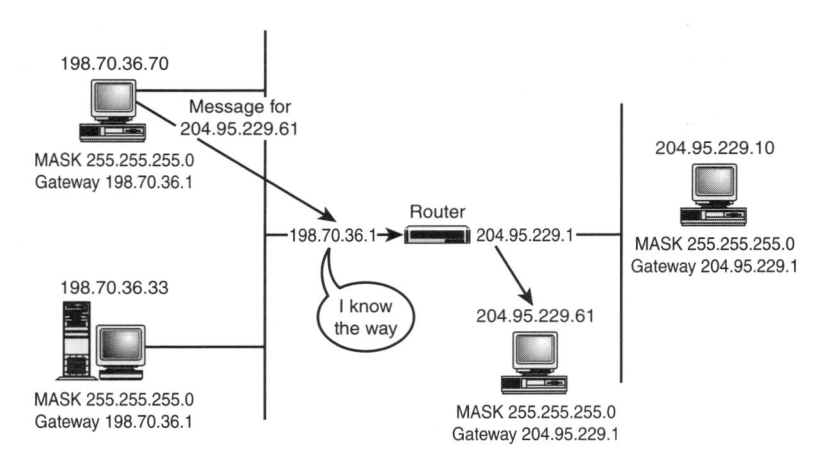

Every host on an IP network must have a router available to get to a network segment that it's not directly connected to. Routers that are not directly connected to a segment must also have another known router to make a connection to that segment. Each time a router makes a connection to a new network, it records the path that it took to get to that network segment (see Figure 8.2). As time progresses, routers build a more comprehensive list of routes and become more efficient. There are many different protocols that are used for this collection and use of routing information, but all accomplish the same general goal. The Internet is a very large example of this system.

FIGURE 8.2
A router finding its way to new routes and recording the paths.

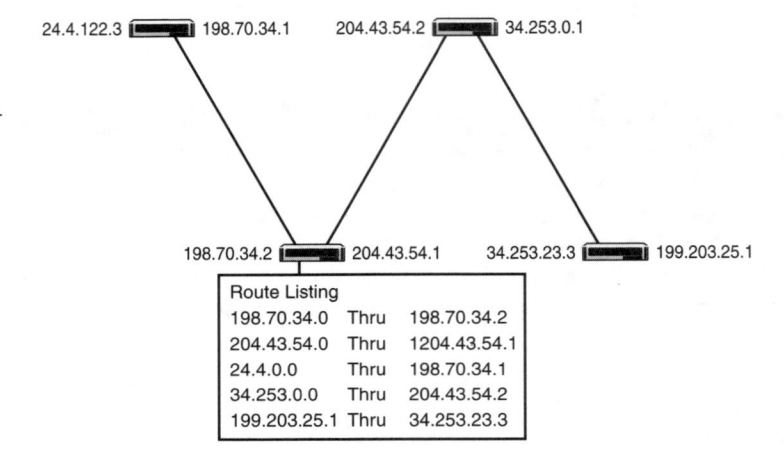

```
24.4.122.3 — 198.70.34.1     204.43.54.2 — 34.253.0.1
              \      /         \      /
               \    /           \    /
            198.70.34.2 — 204.43.54.1   34.253.23.3 — 199.203.25.1

            Route Listing
            198.70.34.0    Thru    198.70.34.2
            204.43.54.0    Thru    1204.43.54.1
            24.4.0.0       Thru    198.70.34.1
            34.253.0.0     Thru    204.43.54.2
            199.203.25.1   Thru    34.253.23.3
```

Service Ports

When TCP/IP is installed on any host, it listens for calls that come to it on different channels, called *ports*. A port is really nothing more than an open door that can receive a call to action. When a server wants to offer a service, it opens a port and makes the service available at the port number. A client application then makes a request at that port number and the communication begins.

An example of this would be the port used for most World Wide Web interaction—port 80. Port 80 is used by HTTP (Hypertext Transfer Protocol) to provide the Web service. When a client browser makes a call for a Web page, it makes the call to the HTTP address at port 80.

If a company wanted to present a private page, it could simply present HTTP at a different port number. Users wanting to attach to that page would then have to ask for the specific port in order to gain access to the page. That's fine because the port numbers are not set in stone. If Macmillan Publishing's HTTP protocol were being served at port 465, the user would need to type in the address as **http://www.mcp.com:465**.

These rules apply to all ports. Here are some common ports:

- 25 for SMTP (email)
- 21 for FTP (File Transfer Protocol)

- 80 for HTTP (Hypertext Transfer Protocol)
- 119 for NNTP (Network News Transfer Protocol)

The range of ports set aside for "well known" services is 0 to 1023.

Microsoft TCP/IP

Microsoft made a commitment to TCP/IP with the last version of Windows NT by making it the default protocol. With Windows 2000, Microsoft made that commitment even deeper by making the entire operating system depend on the protocol to function at its best.

If you've spent a great deal of time in the Windows NT and TCP/IP worlds, you'll find a great number of old friends in Windows 2000. If you had a large wish list for Windows TCP/IP, I think you'll find that quite a few of your dreams have come true.

Introduction to Microsoft TCP/IP

Microsoft networking depends heavily on the ability of a node on the network being able to find a resource. File servers, mail servers, printers, and even shared clients must make themselves available for other machines to see. This process is called *browsing*.

When you sit down at a Windows 2000 workstation, a Windows 95/98 workstation, or even a DOS client, if you query the network for servers, you're *browsing*. With Window 2000, you browse by opening My Network. The Windows NT and 95/98 item is called Network Neighborhood. In either case, you're seeing either a broadcasting of systems on your local segment or a list that has been provided to you.

Network browsing is not a native part of TCP/IP. Therefore, a network operating system that depends on browsing is going to have to provide this capability. Microsoft provides the system to perform browsing using a combination of tools ranging from WINS to Active Directory.

Installing

Unless you're purposefully trying to avoid placing TCP/IP on your server, you'll get TCP/IP as the default protocol during server installation. However, you can override the default. The question becomes, how do you install it if you did override the installation? Also, what services or options do you wish to apply to TCP/IP once its installed?

The process of installing TCP/IP is relatively easy. It's particularly easy if you're used to installing protocols and network services in the Windows 95/98 world. The interface is essentially the same simple interface.

Windows 2000 Operating System Environment
PART II

To install TCP/IP onto an existing network interface card (NIC), follow these instructions:

1. Open Network and Dial-up Connections by clicking Start, Settings and then clicking Network and Dial-up Connections.

2. Double-click the connection that you would like to install TCP/IP on, as shown in Figure 8.3.

FIGURE 8.3
The Network and Dial-up Connections screen.

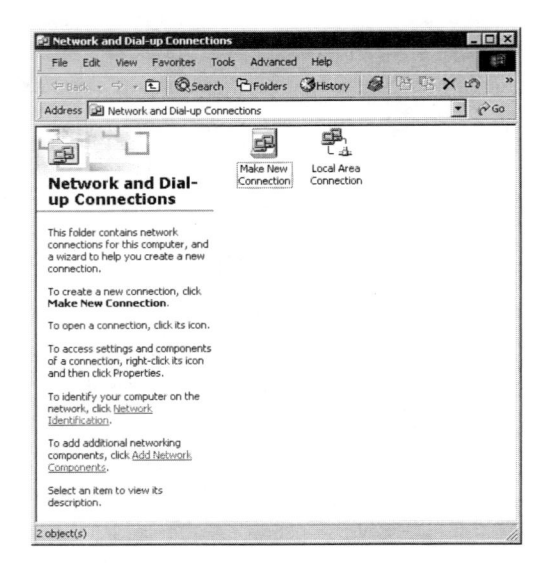

3. From the Select Network Component Type window, click the Protocol button (see Figure 8.4). Then click Add.

FIGURE 8.4
The Select Network Component Type window.

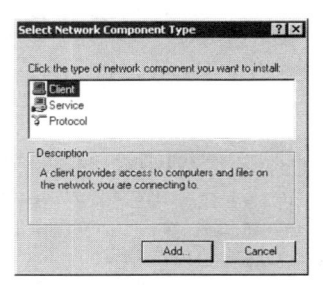

4. In the pop-up Select Network Protocol box that appears, choose Internet Protocol (TCP/IP) and then click OK.

Routing

Windows NT was always able to be a router, but not nearly to the extent that Windows 2000 can today. With the advent of RRAS (Routing and Remote Access Service), routing through Windows has become a viable option. It most likely will never be your first choice as a router for large implementations, but for small applications, it should work well.

As part of Windows TCP/IP installations, routing has always been a default part of the install. Windows 2000 Server has not changed that fact, but the placement of routing choices has changed. Because of the fact that RRAS now exist, the routing functions have found a separate home from the protocol and adapter configurations. This interface is the Routing and Remote Access Service (RRAS).

Windows 2000 Router

RRAS is installed when Windows is installed, but it's not activated. In order to activate it, you need to open the outing and Remote Access program (see Figure 8.5). You'll find the application in Start, Programs, Administrative Tools, Routing and Remote Access. Once it's open, follow these steps:

FIGURE 8.5
The Routing and Remote Access application.

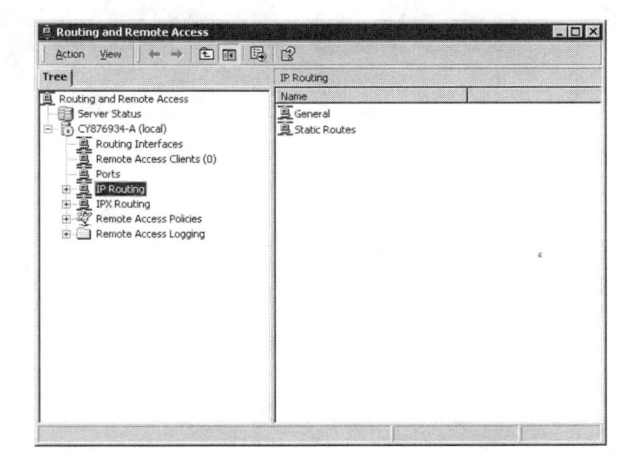

1. In the console tree, right-click Server Status and then click Add Server.
2. Open Add Server and click This Computer.
3. Click OK.
4. For the console tree, right-click the server added.

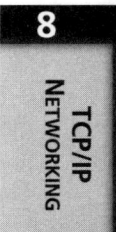

5. Click Configure and Enable Routing and Remote Access.
6. From the Routing and Remote Access Configuration Wizard, click either Enable Routing Only or Enable Routing and Remote Access to enable the Windows 2000 router.

Once you've finished with the wizard, you can start the router by right-clicking the server and choosing Start. The router is now started.

The RRAS service has many other uses. These options are included in detail in Chapter 14, "Remote Access (RAS)." However, one item that should be mentioned here is the Demand Dial Interface. Small companies that require either office-to-office connections or Internet connectivity will find this to be a viable solution. If connection between these offices can be handled by the bandwidth provided by a standard phone line demand dial can be used.

Demand dial is a setting in RRAS that allows a modem to dial to the opposite site when a request is made for a network address on the other side of the route. As an example; If a computer on network A needs an email server on network B then the RRAS server on network A, hearing the request, will dial the connection to network B.

> **Note**
> Keep in mind that dial-up connectivity is never a viable option for connecting to an application or large amounts of traffic. Internet connectivity usually involves minimal traffic.

Dynamic Host Configuration Protocol (DHCP)

A very difficult part of using the TCP/IP protocol is the fact that it requires every node participating on the network to have a unique address. Other protocols such as IPX/SPX will automatically assign a client an address upon startup, but IP addresses must be assigned. However, no one ever said that a human had to monitor this requirement.

Basic DHCP Protocol

The Dynamic Host Configuration Protocol gives TCP/IP networks the ability to assign client machines IP addresses on demand. The process works by having the operating system make a special type of broadcast on the wire exclaiming that a host needs an IP address. Any DNS server on the wire knows to respond with help.

The request that goes out is called a DHCP *discover packet*. The DHCP server hears this packet. The server then responds with an offer message. The client is then responsible for accepting the message and responding back that it will keep the offered address by making another request. Once the offer is confirmed, that client will then complete its IP information with the settings offered by the server.

Addresses are not commonly given to the client machine on a permanent basis. Generally, the address is given a lease time, meaning that the address will expire after a given period of time (called a *lease*). Each time a client is restarted, it checks with the server once again to be sure the lease it believes it has is still intact. If an acknowledgement is received or if no response is received, the client keeps the IP configuration. If no response is received, the client will begin looking for a new lease after 87.5 % of the lease time has expired.

More than simple IP address information is sent as part of these leases. IP communications depends on more than just the IP address and a DHCP server can be configured to send more than an address. Machines can receive IP addresses and the associated data as well as the following items:

- *Subnet Mask.* Specifies the subnet mask of the client subnet, as described in RFC 950, "Internet Standard Subnetting Procedure." The value for this option type is taken from the Subnet Mask field, as defined in a DHCP scope Properties dialog box in DHCP Manager.
- *Time Offset.* Specifies an offset value (in seconds) from the Universal Coordinated Time (UCT) that applies to the client's subnet. This value is configurable as a signed 32-bit integer. Positive offset values indicate a subnet location east of the zero meridian. Negative offset values indicate a subnet location west of the zero meridian.
- *Router.* Specifies a list of IP addresses for routers on the client's subnet. When more than one router is assigned, the client interprets and uses the addresses in the specified order.
- *Time Server.* Specifies a list of IP addresses for RFC 868 time servers that are available to the client. When more than one time server is assigned, the client interprets and uses the addresses in the specified order.
- *DNS Server.* Specifies a list of IP addresses for Domain Name System (DNS) name servers available to the client. When more than one server is assigned, the client interprets and uses the addresses in the specified order. DHCP client computers that are multihomed and obtain multiple DHCP leases can have only one DNS server list per host computer, not per adapter interface.
- *Host Name.* Specifies a host name for the client of up to 63 characters in length. (See RFC 1035 for possible character set restrictions.) In some cases, this name can also be fully qualified by appending the name value provided here with the

DNS domain name, as specified in the next option. For Windows clients, this option is not supported for use when configuring the client's host name, which is set in Computer Name in the Network Identification Properties dialog box on the client computer.

- *DNS Domain Name.* Specifies the domain name that the DHCP client should use when resolving host names using the DNS. For this option type, ASCII character text is used for the data value. The length of the value field depends on the number of characters used in the DNS domain name specified here. For example, if the domain name has 20 characters, the value field for this option should also be 20 octets in length.

- *IP Forwarding Enable/Disable.* Used to determine whether the DHCP client enables or disables forwarding of datagrams at the IP layer.

- *Nonlocal Source Routing Enable/Disable.* Used to determine whether the DHCP client enables or disables forwarding of datagrams at the IP layer, based on whether a received datagram is from a local or nonlocal source.

- *All Subnets Are Local.* Specifies whether the client assumes that all subnets of the client's internetwork use the same MTU as the local subnet on which the client is connected.

- *Broadcast Address.* Typically, this is the limited broadcast IP address (255.255.255.255), but it can be modified using legal values for broadcast addresses, as specified in section 3.2.1.3 of RFC 1122, "Requirements for Internet Hosts—Communication Layers."

- *Perform Router Discovery.* Specifies whether the client solicits routers using the router-discovery method in RFC 1256.

- *Router Solicitation Address.* Specifies the IP address to which the client submits router solicitation requests.

- *Static Route.* Specifies a list of static routes the client installs in its routing cache. Any multiple routes to the same destination are listed in descending order of priority. The default route of 0.0.0.0 is an illegal destination for a static route.

- *NIS Domain Name.* Specifies the Network Information Service (NIS) domain name as an ASCII string.

- *NIS Servers.* Lists the IP addresses in the order of preference for Network Information Service (NIS) servers available to the client.

- *NIS+ Domain Name.* Specifies the name of the client's Network Information Service Plus (NIS+) domain name as an ASCII string.

- *NIS+ Servers.* Lists the IP addresses in the order of preference for Network Information Service Plus (NIS+) servers available to the client.

- *WINS Server*. List the IP addresses for Windows Internet Naming Service (WINS) servers or NetBIOS name servers (NBNS).
- *NetBIOS Node Type*. Configures the client node type for NetBIOS over TCP/IP (NetBT) clients, as described in RFC 1001/1002. On multihomed computers, the node type is assigned for the computer, not to individual network adapters.
- *IP Address Lease Time*. This option type is used to negotiate and exchange lease-time information between DHCP clients and servers in two possible ways:
  - Can be used in a DHCP discovery or DHCP request message sent by a client to request a lease time for its IP address.
  - Can be used in a DHCP offer message reply sent by a server to specify a lease time the server can offer to the client.

Installation

First, you must realize that any machine that's a DHCP server must have a static IP address. A DHCP server cannot be a machine that received its address from a DHCP server. Installing DHCP server is done by following these steps:

1. Open the Control Panel screen by clicking Start, Settings, Control Panel.
2. Double-click Add/Remove Programs.
3. Choose Configure Windows and click Components.
4. Choose the Networking Options check box and then choose Details.
5. Choose Subcomponents of Networking Options, click the Microsoft DHCP Server check box, and then click OK.
6. Click Next, type the full path to the Windows 2000 distribution files (for example, `d:\i386`), and then click Continue. This will start the DHCP installation wizard.

After the DHCP wizard finishes, you'll need to restart the server in order to allow the service to activate.

Scope

The DHCP server will provide information to clients through the use of an information base called a *scope*. Before the server can answer the first discover packet, it must have ammunition to fire.

The scope provides the IP settings that the server provides to the DHCP clients. The scope is created for either all of the clients of the DHCP server (global) or individual segments. The settings in a scope include any item available for lease (see the list in the ealier section, "Basic DHCP Protocol").

The scope is administered from the DHCP console. This tool can be run either from the Administrative Tools menu under DHCP or from the MMC as a snap-in.

Creating a Scope

Once the DHCP console is open, perform the following steps to create a scope:

1. Select the DHCP server object in the console window (see Figure 8.6).

FIGURE 8.6
The DHCP console screen.

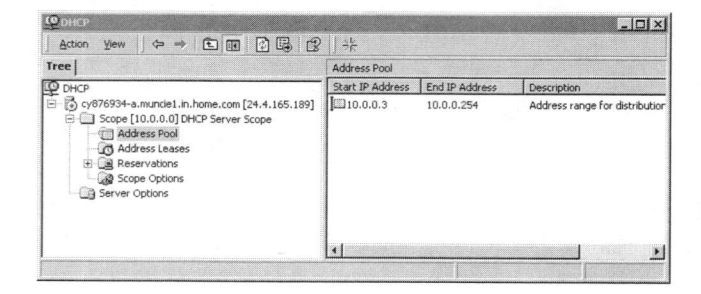

2. Click Action in the menu and select New, Scope. The Scope Wizard will appear.
3. Enter the name that you would like to use to identify the scope. Press Tab and enter a comment to help you remember the reasons for the scope. (These items will serve as identifiers for you at a later date.) Click Next.
4. Enter the beginning and ending IP addresses in the range that you would like assigned to your clients in the From and To fields, as shown in Figure 8.7. Press Tab.

FIGURE 8.7
The Address Range screen.

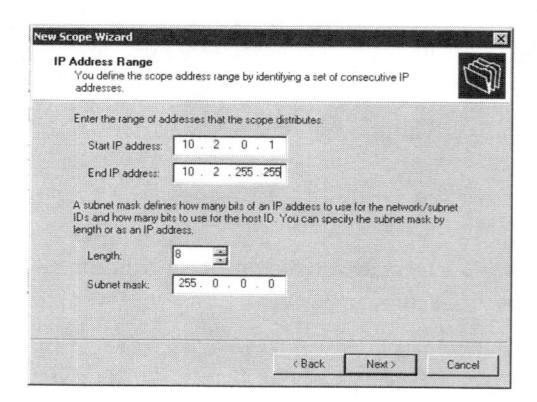

5. Now you can enter the length of the mask in bits (see the previous section on subnet masks), but it's probably easier to press Tab once again and enter the subnet mask manually. Click Next.

6. The Exclusions section allows you to keep certain addresses from being assigned in a large range (that is, to reserve certain addresses from being assigned). Enter the beginning and ending addresses in the fields supplied and click Add. To exclude only one address, type the address in the Start Address box and click Add. Click Next to proceed.

7. The Lease Duration screen, as shown in Figure 8.8, allows you to control the amount of time the client will be allowed to keep the address assigned. To change the default (eight days), either choose Unlimited or click the up and down arrows beside the desired value (days, hours, minutes). Click Next.

FIGURE 8.8
The Lease Duration options.

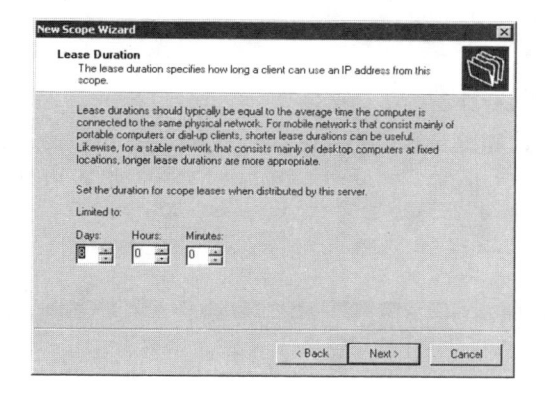

8. You'll now be asked if you want to proceed with setting the most common DHCP options. Choose Next to proceed and finish the install properly.

9. At the Gateways screen, type in the IP address of the gateways (router) that you want the clients to use. Then click Add. Add these in the order that you would like the system to search in. Click Next to move on.

10. The following screen allows for the setting of Domain Name Server information (see Figure 8.9). First insert the name of the client machine's home domain (for example, mcp.com) and then press Tab. Now enter the IP address of the first DNS server that you want the client machine to go to and then click Add. Repeat this until you have all the DNS servers you need listed. Click Next.

11. The WINS screen is very much like the DNS screen. Repeat the directions from the last step (replacing the WINS address for the DNS of the last step).

12. Finally, you're asked if you would like to activate the scope. If you choose No, you can activate the scope later. Make a choice and proceed to the final screen by pressing Next.

13. Finish by clicking Finish.

FIGURE 8.9
The DNS information screen.

Managing the Scope

Managing a scope that has already been created is as simple as opening the DHCP console screen and selecting the server and then scope that you want to manage. Once you select the DHCP server, you'll see the scope options unfold under the server, as shown in Figure 8.10.

FIGURE 8.10
The scope expanded.

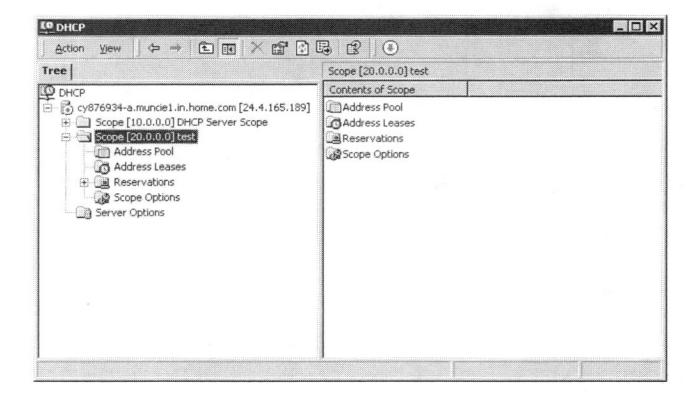

There are literally hundreds of different items that can be changed in your DHCP server. For the sake of giving some examples and pointing out the most common options, I'll provide instructions here. (See the following list options and take the appropriate actions.)

To make an address lease time change, follow these steps:

1. Right-click the DHCP server and choose Properties.
2. From the section Address Lease Duration for DHCP Clients, change the time to the new setting. Click OK.

To create another exclusion range, follow these steps:

1. Right-click Address Pool, New and then choose Exclusion Range.
2. Complete the From and To range and click Add.

To create a reservation, follow these steps:

1. Right-click Reservations and choose New, Reservation.
2. Type in the IP address that you would like reserved for a particular client and press Tab.
3. Type in the MAC address of the machine that you want the address reserved for, as shown in Figure 8.11. Press Tab.

FIGURE 8.11
The reservation screen.

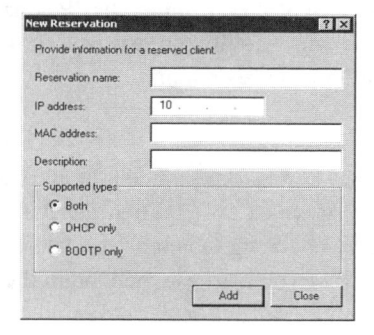

> **Note**
>
> To discover the MAC address of a particular machine, type **NET CONFIG WKSTA** at the command prompt of the Windows 2000 workstation. Then press Enter.

4. Enter a name and description of the workstation you're making the reservation for.

> **Note**
>
> Among the settings that are found in the DHCP server properties is *Dynamic DNS*. This will be covered in the "Dynamic Domain Name Server (DDNS)" section later in this chapter.

Other common scope options are changed or added under Scope Options, below the server in the DHCP console. By right-clicking Scope Options and choosing Configure

Options, you're presented with the list of possible scope options. Once an option is selected, a data entry point is opened for the more granular management of that section.

Superscopes

A *superscope* is a variation on DHCP scopes that allows for a progression in the use of scopes. A superscope allows you to group scopes in the same network. This allows several scopes to be activated or stopped from the same point. Where superscopes are not available or used, only a single DHCP scope can be active on the network at one time. If more than one scope is defined and activated on the DHCP server, only one scope is used to provide leases to clients. Creating a superscope allows you to extend or add scopes to a single network.

Superscopes are created by selecting the DHCP server in the DHCP console and right-clicking it. Choose New, Superscope. The wizard will then lead you through the simple task of adding scopes to the new superscope you're creating.

Enabling Clients

When a Windows 2000, Windows NT, or Windows 95/98 client is initially installed with the TCP/IP protocol, the default installation is as a DHCP client. DHCP Client is the option in Windows 2000 that's selected by choosing Obtain an IP Address Automatically, as shown in Figure 8.12. The other DHCP option is to use the Obtain the DNS Server Address Automatically selection.

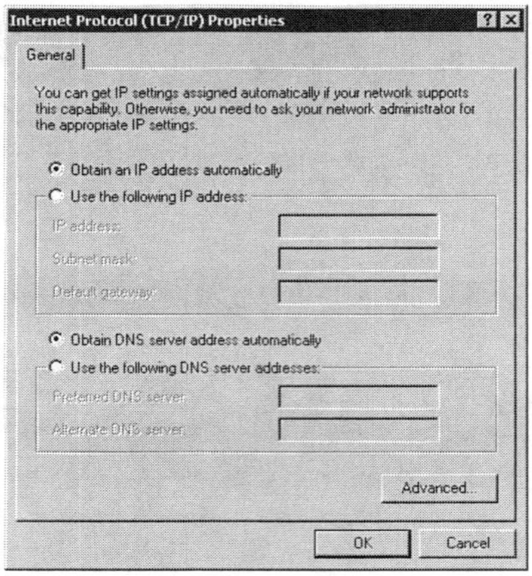

FIGURE 8.12
DHCP selection in the Internet Protocol properties page.

Windows Internet Name Service

The Windows Internet Naming Service (WINS) is the first Microsoft solution to the fact that TCP/IP does not include a way of facilitating network browsing. WINS creates a way for machines to keep the names and addresses of other machines in sync. WINS is changing and possibly might be on it's way out, but not just yet.

As mentioned earlier, *browsing* is the ability of networked machines to see one another when they search the network for resources. Windows depends on browsing to make the network work.

Because there's an entire chapter devoted to browsing (Chapter 13, "Network Browsing"), this topic won't be beaten to death here. Suffice it to say that you must find a way to present the network resources to the clients so that they can see the system in My Network Places, in Network Neighborhood, or even from a DOS NET command.

Naming Versus Browsing

When a computer is installed into a computer network, it's given a computer name. This name is also called a NetBIOS (Network Basic Input Output Service) name. This is the name presented to users as the opening point in My Network Places. It's the central point in network browsing.

This is not to be confused with the *domain name* of a machine. A machine's domain name is the name that's used within the Domain Name Servers (DNS) of the Internet and TCP/IP. Domains in TCP/IP can also be used to identify a particular host when the host name is added to the domain name. For example, the machine at IP address `10.1.23.44` might have the DNS record associated with the domains name `proxy.microsoft.com`. Therefore, "proxy" is the machines name in the domain.

These Netbios and Domain Host names can be associated, but in the long run, they have no real connection other than the ones that are created in Windows 2000 and NT to facilitate an easier use of the systems.

Architecture of Microsoft WINS 2000

The concept of WINS is to provide a single registration point for machines that must stay in contact with one another with NetBIOS naming.

The WINS service is installed on the server at the time of the initial install, but it can be installed later. Once installed, the service simply waits for other systems to be told of its existence, and it then retransmits the NetBIOS information that those systems report. You could say that WINS is a bit like a NetBIOS phonebook. It listens for new connections and registers their names and numbers (that is, the NetBIOS name and the IP address). It then provides that information to clients or other WINS servers.

Whenever a new system is attached to the TCP/IP network, it's given a WINS server address. Once the server starts TCP/IP, it reports to the WINS server that it exists, what its NetBIOS name is, and what its IP address is. After this, the machine keeps the WINS server apprised of any changes that occur in its IP address or NetBIOS name.

A single WINS server can only monitor one segment of the network at a given time. If the network includes more the one segment of TCP/IP, a WINS Agent or another WINS server communicating with the original WINS server must be installed in order to allow browsing to occur.

Now that the PCs have all registered with the WINS server, several benefits are realized:

- Broadcasts are minimized because machines have a direct source for NetBIOS information.
- The machine speed is marginally increased by no longer having to wait for random responses to requests.
- NetBIOS can now span network segments over TCP/IP.

Although Windows 2000 is able to function without WINS, it's not recommended by Microsoft that a Windows network attempt to run without WINS until all machines on the system are running Windows 2000. Therefore, this will take a while for large systems.

Replication and Persistent Connections

The WINS service increases its ability to perform well by allowing more than one WINS server to help in the process of maintaining the NetBIOS name list. Multiple WINS servers within the same network (LAN or WAN) can communicate with one another to form a sort of NetBIOS "answer web."

When one WINS server is made the replication partner of another, those servers record the NetBIOS changes of the systems registered with them but then share the information. By replicating the NetBIOS information that each recovers, both servers minimize their workloads. Many WINS servers may be connected, but they must be told of each other's existence.

In earlier versions of Windows NT, every time this connection was needed, a new connection between the servers had to be created and the process started from scratch. Windows 2000 has created what are known as *persistent connections*. With a persistent connection between replication partners, servers are able to maintain more timely and accurate information across the network. Persistent connections are configurable on a connection-by-connection basis.

Manual Tombstoning

When a record for a particular NetBIOS host is to be deleted in a WINS environment, this can be a difficult or at least time-consuming process. Because of the nature of the WINS database being a complete replication of all records, some deletions may never complete.

Use of the *manual tombstoning* feature marks a record for deletion so that the tombstone state for the record is replicated across all WINS servers, thus preventing an undeleted copy of the record on a different server database from being repropagated. In other words, a replication partner could actually bring a record back to life.

Autodiscovery of Partners

Previously, the installation of any replication partners in WINS required that any replication partners be manually introduced. However, WINS has been given the ability to automatically discover partners in Windows 2000. By listening to the wire for WINS announcements, WINS servers can now create lists of WINS servers. Any new WINS servers found on the network are automatically added to the partners' lists as a Push/Pull partner, meaning that they completely share information without human intervention.

This is a feature that can be turned off and on. It should be noted that this is not a feature that should be left on when more than three WINS servers exist on a single segment.

Installation

The WINS service can be installed during the initial setup of the server. However, if you need to install the service at a later time, you can install it by following these directions. To begin, go to Control Panel and double-click Add/Remove Programs, then follow these steps:

1. Choose Configure Windows and click Components.
2. Choose Networking Options and click Details.
3. In Subcomponents of Networking Options, choose Windows Internet Naming Service and click Next.
4. Give the path to your Windows 2000 installation files and click Continue.

LMHOSTS Files

When clients in the DNS environment cannot find a given host on the IP network, they're sometimes given a file called a *HOSTS file*. This file contains records of the IP addresses and corresponding IP addresses. When the system cannot be located, either by broadcast or by way of an authoritative DNS server, the client will check this list. NetBIOS-based searching can take the same approach by using a file called the *LMHOSTS file*.

The LMHOSTS file contains the NetBIOS names and corresponding IP addresses of systems that the client may need to attach to. If a connection to a WINS server is not possible or if the WINS server is not producing a response, the client machine can resolve the request itself.

A sample LMHOSTS file can be found in the `WINNT\SYSTEM32\DRIVERS\ETC` directory of your Windows 2000 or NT machine. In Windows 95/98, it's simply in the `Windows` directory.

Here's an example of what you'll find:

```
# 102.54.94.97      rhino         #PRE #DOM:networking  #net group's DC

# 102.54.94.102     "appname  \0x14"                    #special app server

# 102.54.94.123     popular       #PRE                  #source server

# 102.54.94.117     localsrv      #PRE                  #needed for the include
```

`#PRE` tells the operating system to load the information prior to the user interface. `#DOM:`*domain_name* tells the system that this system is part of the given domain. Everything beyond that point is a just a comment.

Dynamic Domain Name Server (DDNS)

The Domain Name Service (DNS) is used by systems running TCP/IP as their primary means of resolving a common name to an IP address. In other words, it takes a name better understood by humans (`www.domainname.com`) and translates it into an address better understood by computers (`10.33.54.91`). Computers do better with numbers, humans do better with names.

In much the same way that WINS translates NetBIOS names into IP addresses, DNS translates domain names into IP addresses. A DNS server is installed and client systems are told to ask that server for translation. The difference up to this point is that the process was one sided.

Unlike WINS, DNS in the classic sense is only a system that receives input to the list of names from other servers of its kind. A client that's started up with a brand new IP address and shiny new domain name is not known to the DNS server at all. This makes it very difficult to use this system for a complete record of the systems and shares. The system is static. If a human does not actively enter the names and translated addresses, he or she never enters the DNS world.

DNS Domains

The most basic unit of DNS is the DNS domain—so basic, in fact, that you probably think of them as one and the same. A DNS domain consists of the following parts.

- Top-level domain: .com (commercial), .edu (education), and .gov (government) These domains you find at the end of every domain request are represented by DNS servers that maintain a record of domains in each category.

- Second-level domain: microsoft. (of microsoft.com), Indiana. (of Indiana.edu), whitehouse. (of whitehouse.gov). These domains are the base name of the company, school, or government building that owns the domain name.

- Subdomains: Each additional level of the domain (www. of www.microsoft.com) is a subdomain. Subdomains are generally used to point to a specific machine within a domain.

A group called the InterNIC (www.internic.net) assigns domain names. This group assigns domain names to individuals and groups that apply and register those domains with the root-level servers. There is a small cost for registering, but once you've done so your company has exclusive rights to that name. A DNS server that's given responsibility for a top-level or secondary domain is said to be *authoritative* for that domain. The domain is now said to be a *fully qualified domain name* (FQDN).

DNS Records

There are several different types of DNS records. The record type helps DNS determine what type of service is being offered and/or requested. The following are examples of this:

- *"A" record (forward lookup)*. "A" records are the simplest form of DNS record because they're the record of a single host—a record that simply conveys that a particular domain name is equal to a particular IP address.

- *Reverse lookup record*. This type of record is used to do the opposite of an "A" record. It allows a system to take a known IP address and find the domain name of the host.

- *MX record (Mail Exchange)*. For each domain, an administrator can set a mail exchange record. This is the IP address that the DNS server will respond with if an email request is made to the domain. Email servers will ask for the MX record of a domain before sending email forward.

- *C-name record (canonical name)*. This is a domain name that will point you to another domain name. That domain name most likely will point to an IP address. For example, an administrator may want to have two domain names point to the same Web server. The administrator could create an "A" record of `kidsclothes.com.` to go to the IP address of the server (`123.43.64.100`). He could then create a C-name record called `babyclothes.com` to the "A" record for `kidsclothers.com`.

Dynamic Nature Evolves

The dynamic nature of DNS has come to light in Windows 2000, but I will caution you again that this is only available in a strictly Windows 2000 environment. Because Dynamic DNS counts on key features of DHCP 2000 and Active Directory, it's not possible currently to even make use of these features on Windows NT.

Dynamic registration of DNS records for Windows 2000 clients is done through the use of DHCP. By default, DHCP Server in Windows 2000 is set to enable the dynamic update of DNS client information. When a client machine receives an IP address from DHCP, the behavior is different depending on which version of Windows is being run.

Windows 2000 clients:

- The IP address request packet is sent.
- The DHCP server makes the offer and approves the lease.
- The DHCP client registers its own "A" record with the DNS server.
- The DHCP server registers the client's reverse lookup record with DNS.

It is important to see the same chain of events in the 95/98 world to recognize the advantage in the pure Windows 2000 world: Windows NT and 95/98 clients:

- The IP address request packet is sent.
- The DHCP server makes the offer and approves the lease.
- The DHCP server registers the client's "A" record with the DNS server.
- The DHCP server registers the client's reverse lookup record with DNS.

The important note here is that the Windows 2000 client registered with DNS on its own. The DHCP server did not need to intervene.

DNS Server Installation

To install DNS services, you, of course, have the option to install it during the installation of Windows 2000. The install process described here is to install DNS services after the installation of Windows 2000.

To install DNS, like DHCP or WINS, you need to be installing to a server with a static IP address. Clearly, you can't have your domain name server losing its lease on a DHCP-assigned address. To begin, go to the Control Panel and double-click Add/Remove Programs. Then follow these steps:

1. Choose Configure Windows and click Components.
2. Choose Networking Options and click Details.
3. In Subcomponents of Networking Options, choose Microsoft DNS and click Next.
4. Give the path to your Windows 2000 installation files and click Continue.

Boot File

The file that's referred to by DNS for the record of the domain at startup is called the *boot file*. The boot file specifies the location of the DNS configuration files and declares which domains the server is authoritative for.

To understand these files, you must have a great understanding of the concepts DNS and BIND. Luckily, the server is going to maintain the files for you. The important part of these files is that they're backed up and made available should you lose your DNS server.

Domain Database File

Every domain that the server is responsible for must be in the Domain Database file.

Cache file

This file contains host information that establishes basic DNS connectivity. It establishes the addresses for root name servers (such as .com and .edu).

Configuring DNS

Configuring DNS the first time can be either simple or scary. This is because when you open the DNS console for the first time, it's going to ask you to begin configuring, and a wizard will ask you many questions. If you know the answers, all will be well and you may be done sooner then you think. If you don't know the answers, that's the scary part. Be prepared before you get there. To configure the server follow these steps:

1. You'll be presented with the wizard screen shown in Figure 8.13. Click Next.

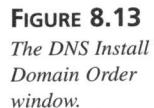

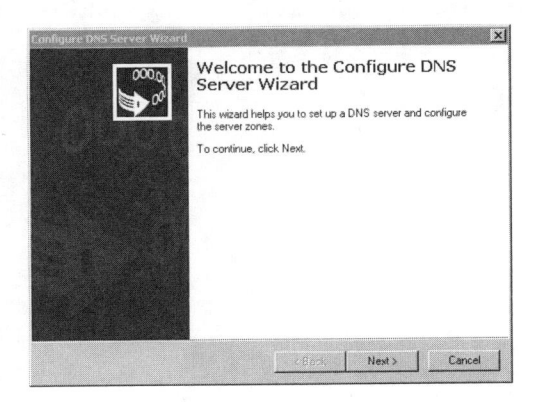

FIGURE 8.13
The DNS Install Domain Order window.

2. You're asked if the server you're installing to is the first server in the domain. If so, make that choice and click Next. If this is a secondary server, choose **Other DNS Servers Are Running on This Network** and type in the address of the primary DNS server.
3. Click Yes to add a forward lookup zone.
4. Select a zone type: Standard Primary or Standard Secondary. Click Next.
5. Type in your domain name. Click Next.
6. Create a new load file or import an old one. Click Next.
7. Choose Yes to add a reverse lookup zone. Click Next.
8. Choose a reverse lookup zone type: Standard Primary or Standard Secondary. Click Next.
9. Enter your reverse lookup name in the template presented. This is the same as the secondary domain name of your FQDN. Click Next.
10. Accept the filename for your zone reverse lookup. Click Next.
11. Click Finish.

You should take the time to record the results of the install for your records. These settings can often be a great help in troubleshooting.

Management

The management of DNS involves three main tasks after installing the initial server (see Figure 8.14):

- The addition or subtraction of zones
- The addition or subtraction of subordinate domains
- The addition or subtraction of new records

FIGURE 8.14
The DNS management console.

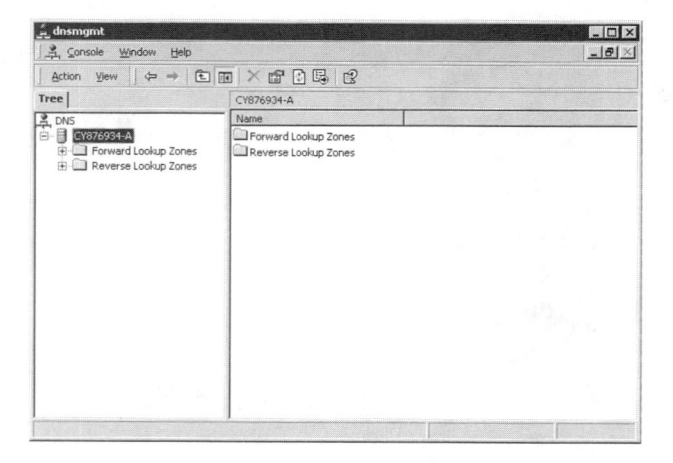

When the term *zone* is used with DNS server, it refers to the domains created as well as any subordinate domains created below them. This grouping is referred to as a *zone* because it's effectively one managed group but multiple domains.

When DNS is installed and opened for the first time, the first zone and domain are created as well as the reverse lookup for them. To create more zones, you simply need to right-click the server object from within the DNS console and choose Create New Zone. You're once again taken through the wizard that was presented the first time you opened the DNS console.

Creating a new domain is equally difficult. Once the DNS console has been opened, fully expand the zone you want to place the new domain in and right-click. Choose New, Domain. Once you enter the name, you're finished.

Creating new records is also done in the DNS console. Follow these steps:

1. Expand the server object and expand the zone object by clicking the plus signs beside them.
2. Right-click the domain object and choose New.
3. From the drop-down menu, select a record type and fill in the name to be given and the IP address.
4. For the best functionality, choose to create a PTR record by clicking the check box. This allows for the automatic creation of a reverse lookup record. Then click Add Host.

An MX record requires that you know which server you'll be sending email traffic to (See Figure 8.15).

FIGURE 8.15
A Mail Exchange record screen.

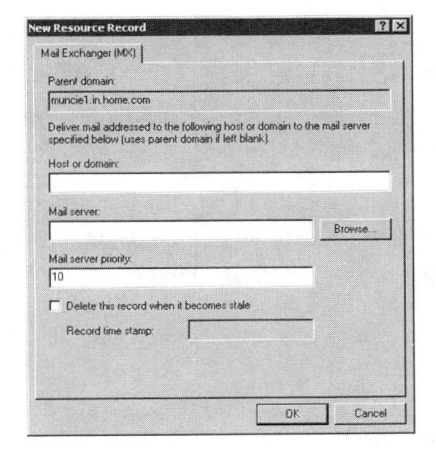

Migrating from WINS to DNS

Dynamic DNS can replace WINS and offers the benefits of reducing traffic and setting the system in an industry and Internet standard. However, be aware that removing the WINS service from networks and domains that still contain Windows NT, 95/98, 3.*x*, or DOS clients is not advisable. These systems are going to run better with WINS in place.

Before you begin removing WINS, be sure you feel comfortable that your DNS environment is strong and fully implemented. DNS and DHCP as a replacement for WINS is viable, but so is WINS. Removing a working WINS install for bandwidth sake could have you hiding in the castle while the villagers come with pick axes and torches.

Here are the steps to follow:

1. Remove the WINS client from each of the workstations by removing the entries for a primary and secondary WINS servers in TCP/IP Properties.

> **Note**
> Keep in mind that some users may be getting their IP information from the DHCP server.

2. Make sure all WINS server clients being removed are configured for DNS.
3. Begin removing WINS servers. Be sure to tombstone all the records owned by the WINS server being removed before removing it. Then make sure you have a replication of WINS before removing it. This allows the traffic involved in replicating those records to stop.

Multiple Address Assignment for One Card

Although it may seem odd at first blush, you can connect Windows 2000 Server to multiple IP addresses on one NIC. There's actually a very good reason for this.

One common use for this type of configuration is to provide two different versions of the same service. The server can then respond differently to the requestor based on the address that's asked for. A Web server, for example, could have one DNS entry pointing to the address of a public site and another for an internal site. The fact that each site has a different IP address registered does not mean that they must exist on different servers.

Multiple addresses are very simple to configure:

1. Open Network and Dial-up Connections by clicking Start, Settings, Network and Dial-up Connections.

2. Double-click the connection you want to add the IP address to (refer to Figure 8.3).
3. From the Local Area Connections window, click the Internet Protocol (TCP/IP) button and then click Properties.
4. In the pop-up Internet Protocol (TCP/IP) Properties box that appears, choose Advanced.
5. Once you're in the Advanced TCP/IP Settings window, simply click Add and enter the information for the new IP address.

IP Security

Part of the basic installation of TCP/IP is the addition of secure IP connections. This has become necessary again because of the growth of the Internet and because of the great knowledge of the user base. Ten years ago, an administrator would not have considered for a minute the idea that a common user could listen to his network wire and see a fellow user's password. Today, users can download network monitoring utilities for listening to the network from the Internet (even while sitting at their desks at work). Not only do they have access out, but that door swings two ways. Enter IP Security (IPSEC).

When used alone for interoperability scenarios, IPSEC performs Layer 3 tunneling, meaning the tunneled payload is a network-layer packet. The entire IP packet is encapsulated and secured for transfer by one of the IPSEC security protocols.

IPSEC is covered in great detail in Chapter 22, "Virtual Private Networks."

Summary

The TCP/IP protocol is probably the oldest protocol of the currently used standards. However, its direct rules and robust existence has made it a great choice for larger networks. By attaching its relatively young NOS to this protocol, Microsoft has made it possible to use this standard to build a robust and scalable network.

IP addressing provides a way of dividing your network along logical lines to allow for greater control. By dividing the network and host address, you allow the network to span the globe and still get back home.

Browsing in a TCP/IP world needed an industry standard way to accomplish what Microsoft was already doing with WINS. Active Directory, DNS, and DHCP have provided a solution that keeps both camps happy.

Active Directory and Account Management

PART
III

IN THIS PART

9 Directory and Access Concepts Brief *231*

10 Active Directory Design *263*

11 User Account Creation and Management *277*

12 Intellimirror and User Control *305*

CHAPTER 9

Directory and Access Concepts Brief

In This Chapter

- Security Concept *232*
- Active Directory Control *239*
- Active Directory/Domain Objects *251*
- Which Comes First: The Users or the Groups? *252*
- Controlling User Access to Resources *257*

Active Directory brings new considerations to the management of users but also to the controlling of resources. The directory system allows the administrator to become more granular in the control of the user environment and the presentation of resources.

Microsoft's use of the Active Directory is actually a move toward a standards-based tool that has been around for years. That standard is the X.500 directory structure. X.500 is an ISO (International Standard Organization) standard that defines how global directories should be formed. The hierarchical structure of Active Directory has many things in common with NetWare (version 4.X and higher) and many other directories because they all want to conform to a standard. This standard allows for interoperability and ease of learning. If you are a NetWare administrator, you will see some old friends in this chapter and many others throughout this book.

This chapter will repeat some of the information you learned in Chapter 5, "Networking Brief," but is meant to cover completely the actual creation of these separate components. Where previous sections have covered concepts, in this chapter we'll cover the "how to" and the "why."

Security Concept

When users attempt to attach to a resource, the domain that's responsible for the resource must first authenticate them. Authentication can be as simple as verifying that the users are who they say they are or as complex as passing those credentials through several servers or domains. In either case, there must be a protocol established for this authentication.

Authentication has changed in Windows 2000 by incorporating both NTLM (Windows NT LAN Manager), the legacy protocol, and the Kerberos security protocol. Both protocols are loaded at Windows 2000 startup to allow for the large number of Windows NT and 95/98 clients that exist. But given a pure 2000 environment, Kerberos is the sole security protocol needed. In this section, the two protocols will be covered and the relationship between them will be explored.

Kerberos

Microsoft has made a major change in the security protocol that's the default protocol used in Windows 2000. The Kerberos protocol has been chosen. Just like TCP/IP, Kerberos is not a new idea or a Microsoft innovation. However, it does give Windows a very secure base of operation in a standard that has been used in the host world for more than 10 years.

Kerberos is actually the name of three-headed dog that guarded the gates to the mythological Greek Hades (Cerberus). The name was given to the protocol because of the three-headed approach it takes to the maintenance of secure communications between systems. It was invented at M.I.T. as part a project called *Athena* in the 1980s. The barbs and arrows being shot at Microsoft over Windows NT security required a three-headed guard dog, and Kerberos was it.

Before starting any presentation of the Kerberos protocol and its place in Windows 2000, it's important to note that Microsoft only applies the protocol in pure Windows 2000 environments by default. This is not to say that no one else employs the protocol, but only that, by default, Windows 2000 only uses Kerberos when communicating with other Windows 2000 systems. Windows NT, Windows 95/98, Windows for Workgroups, and other NT clients are not able to access Windows 2000 using the protocol, but they can use the legacy NTLM (Windows NT LAN Manager) protocol to communicate.

> **Note**
>
> Because Kerberos is a standard public security protocol, Windows 2000 can be made a part of a Kerberos security system that's not controlled by Windows 2000. The system can be both a host and a client to non–Windows 2000 systems.

One would have to imagine that some consideration may be made for creating a Kerberos client for legacy operating systems.

The Communications Process

When two systems attempt to communicate in secret, they must establish a way of doing so before they can start. For example, if Todd would like to pass a secret note to DaRhonda, they both would have to agree on a way of scrambling and unscrambling the contents of the message before the message could be sent.

They could use a simple method that scrambles the message by substituting a number for each letter in the message, such as 1=a, 2=b, 3=c, and so on. When a message comes to DaRhonda, she could then apply the agreed-upon method and translate the message (20-15-4-4 12-15-22-5-19 4-1-18-8-15-14-4-1). This method is called an "encryption key" method because the key must be used or broken to translate. However, this form of message can easily be broken or intercepted.

In fact, the method they use must be one that they truly believe will be intercepted and that highly sophisticated forms of code breaking will be applied to. The Internet and other public networks have made it necessary to make our communications public a great deal of the time. For that reason, the encryption method must involve a very complex scheme.

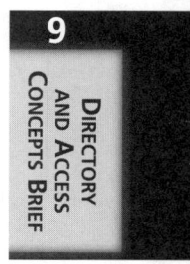

The first step in this process is simply to establish a way for the receiver to know that the message has come from the sender. This is called a *shared secret*.

Authentication could be established by agreeing on a password before communicating. Then the user would simply need to give the password before communicating. The problem with this method in the past has been that the signal could be intercepted and retransmitted (known as *spoofing*). It is called spoofing because the guilty party uses the intercepted network signal to pretend that he is now the original user. The interceptor simply records the original message and replays it at another time when he wants to pretend (spoof) that he is the original sender. It is a bit like recording someone giving the secret word at the door of the clubhouse and then replaying it later when you want to gain entry.

The way to avoid this is to combine the two solutions (encryption and passwords). The idea would be to encrypt the password. If the server understands the encryption, the password can be encrypted just like any other message. But even encrypted messages can be captured and re-sent as if they were originals. The receiver is simply looking at the result in this case. So, the interceptor would simply mirror the encrypted message that contains the password bit-by-bit. As in the preceding analogy, if you are replaying a recording of the password exactly as it was said, it will gain you entry.

> **Can You Intercept A Computer Message?**
>
> Messages between computers are not as easily intercepted as human conversation, but it is almost that simple. People who want to intercept these messages can make use of an application that is called a *packet sniffer* or *analyzer*. "Sniffer" is a slang term that refers to a very robust version of the general product.
>
> Analyzers allow the interceptor to capture computer network messages in the raw packet form (thus "packet" sniffer) from the network that the analyzer is connected to. Keep in mind that all of the computers on the network receive all of the packets sent across the network—even if they do not interact with it, they receive it. In its raw form, a packet can be as easy to read as a birthday card if it is not encrypted. Much of the content of the packet is in plain text. Windows 2000 even comes with a simple network analyzer called Network Monitor, which can be found in the Administrative Tools.

The next step in this process involves a way of making sure that the communications flow in a contiguous manner from the original sender and that the response that's returned is from the original destination. At this point, we begin to see the usefulness of Kerberos.

In Kerberos, this involves an *authenticator*. The authenticator portion of the message is a piece of information added to the message that will change with the progression of the messages. The two communicating systems must decide on a common authenticator, and it must be a variable that is known to both sides but changes with time. This can be a confusing concept. Time itself is an example. The time is never the same from one moment to another. But we can agree on the progression of time and what time it is at any given moment.

If I send you a message and attach the time to it, only I know what time it was sent. Kerberos normally uses the time that the message was sent as an authenticator. This avoids later retransmission of the same packets because when the transmission is decrypted, it will reveal that it has already been received. Time, plus another static client-specific piece of information (username, computer name, and so on), is the most common form of authenticator.

To continue the communication, the server sends a piece of the authenticator back with the return message. This confirms that the message came from the same server that the client sent the message to.

The communications might now look something like this:

- The client sends its password with an authenticator (the time and client username) to the server. Everything in the message is encrypted in the method only known to the client and server. Remember that the encryption is the "shared secret" mentioned at the beginning of this section.
- The server receives the message and decrypts it. It finds that the client's password matches the agreed-upon password and creates a return message to confirm communications can start. Included in the message is the time that the client sent it, which confirms that it's a valid response (see Figure 9.1).

FIGURE 9.1
Authentication and confirmation.

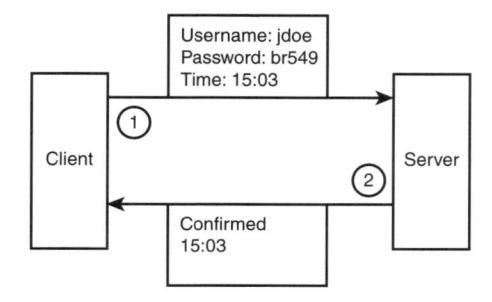

By sending the time back, the server is sending a piece of information that only a system with the proper encryption key (the client) would know. By continually changing the time in messages being sent, the client creates a way to prevent the capture and later use of the message for breaking into the system. This authenticator also allows the server a method of assuring the client that it's the proper responder.

The Key

Two heads have been put on our dog (Kerberos), but the third is the head that makes it unique. Many forms of communication use simple encryption keys, but the trick is in where the key is retrieved from.

It would be simple enough to give each system a key manually, but that would be incredibly time consuming. You could simply create a central location and tell all the machines to get their keys from there, but that would require that you get the key without encryption. Kerberos in Windows 2000 does create a central location for getting encryption keys. It's called the *Key Distribution Center* (KDC).

In Windows 2000 the KDC is also known as the Domain Controller. Domain Controllers (DCs) contain a complete information base of the objects included in the domain. Each object is given a unique initial encryption key called a *long-term key*. In this case the long-term key is the user's password. This means that the DC is uniquely positioned for governing transactions because it knows the passwords of each user. But how do the keys make connections to the client machines and servers without a security breach?

Distributing Keys

In the most simplistic fashion possible, what occurs during key distribution is what follows (see Figure 9.2 and the steps below). Be aware that there is difference between a *session key* and a *session ticket*.

FIGURE 9.2
The key creation and distribution process.

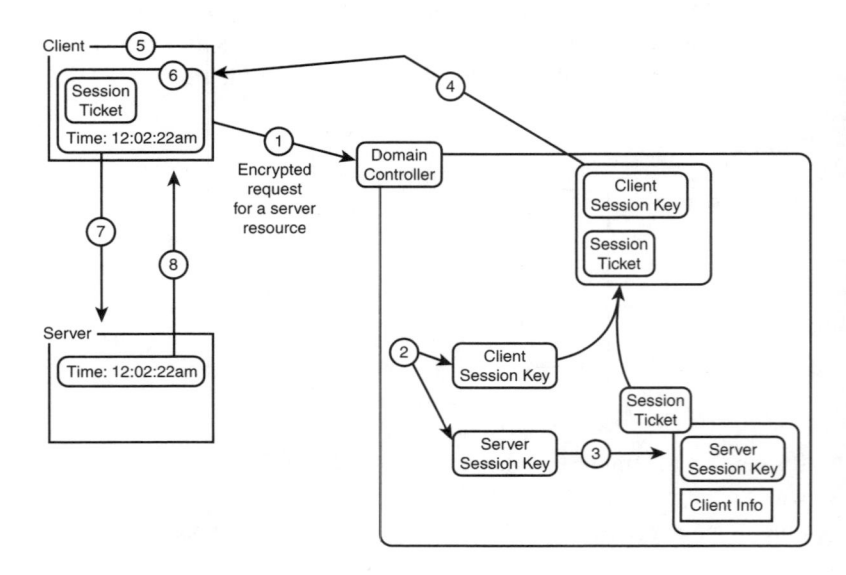

1. The client sends a request for a server resource to the Domain Controller. This request is encrypted in the client's long-term key.
2. This triggers the Domain Controller to create two unique keys called *session keys*—one for the server and one for the client machine.
3. The server's session key is packaged along with information about the client and encrypted with the server's long-term key. This package is called a *session ticket*.
4. The client's copy of the session key and the session ticket are encrypted with the client's long-term key and then sent to the client.
5. The client decrypts its portion of the session key. The session key contains the session ticket, but the client is unable to read the ticket because it is encrypted in the server's long-term key.
6. The client then packages the session ticket along with an authenticator (the time) and delivers that package to the server in order to start communications.
7. The server receives the session ticket and the authenticator, both of which are encrypted in the server's long-term key. The server then decrypts this package.
8. The server responds to the client with the client's authenticator.

This way of distributing keys allows both the server and the DC to simply deliver their information and not have to track the keys of users that have started communications with them throughout time. Because the key is maintained at the client and is for a particular session that the client wants to maintain, the server simply responds to the ticket. Tickets can be reused for their entire lifecycle (usually eight hours), so the DC does not have to constantly be involved in the process of issuing new session tickets.

Even the session ticket is received via the use of a special session ticket created when the client first attaches to the DC. Because the DC is still a server, the client must have a way to communicate within the Kerberos scheme. This session ticket is called a *ticket-granting ticket* (TGT).

NTLM

NTLM (Windows NT LAN Manager) may be unfamiliar even to those who have managed Windows NT before, but *NT Challenge Response* should be a familiar term.

The NTLM authentication process involves three pieces of initial information:

- The domain name
- The user's name
- The user's password

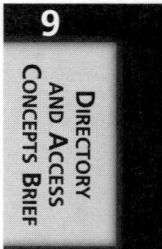

SID

The domain in this protocol is the authentication authority. In the domain is found the information about the users and the permissions that the users have. The information about the users is included in a package called a *security identifier* (SID). In the SID you'll find items such as the following:

- Passwords
- Group memberships
- Profile information

A SID is unique to the user account and will never be repeated for another user. Even if the user is deleted and re-created, the SID for that user will never be given to another user account. For this reason, when you delete a user in Windows NT, you'll be warned that the user will never be re-created exactly the same.

Requesting a Resource

The key element is that the user's password is never transmitted across the wire in clear text during authentication. This is both NTLM's strong point (for security) and its weakness. When a client application supplies a SID, that starts the following chain of events:

- The client NTLMSP (security provider) sends the domain, user, and machine information to the server NTLMSP.
- The server NTLMSP uses this information to generate a unique challenge sequence (of binary bits).
- The client NTLMSP receives this sequence and encrypts the sequence using the user's password as a key. This forms the response.
- The client NTLMSP sends the encrypted response to the server NTLMSP.
- The server NTLMSP calls the DC with the user ID, the challenge sequence, and the response sequence.
- The DC uses the password associated with the user ID to encrypt the challenge sequence and verify it against the response sequence, authenticating the user in the process.
- If successful, the authentication is completed, and the server NTLMSP will allow the communications.

An encrypted response is sent across the wire, but not the actual password. Because the server actually never receives the password, the server will have no way of using the password to access other resources that the user would have access to. Specifically, these may be network resources (files, databases, and so on) that the user is normally able to access. This is one weakness of NTLMSP that significantly reduces the possible tasks the server can perform on behalf of the client.

ACL

In order to establish an object's place in the security system, it's given a security descriptor containing the information needed to interact with users and groups. When a user attempts to access a shared object, the object checks the user's (ACL) SID against its access control list.

An *ACL* is a list of permissions associated with an object that identifies who has permissions at the object and what permissions each user or group has. The ACL is made up of a list of entries called the *Access Control Entries* (ACEs). An entry might say that Ben is allowed to read the file share and that the group Accounting is allowed to read and write to the share. This example constitutes two Access Control Entries in the ACL.

The ACEs are referred to as *Access Allowed* and *Access Denied* and contain an allowance or denial for specific permissions (read, write, and so on) and the user or group involved.

Therefore, you can think of an ACL as containing a list like an invitation list to an exclusive gathering. The user arrives at the door of the resource and is then told whether he has the permission he desires: "Yes, you can come in, but you can't eat."

Active Directory Control

Controlling resources and authenticating is, of course, going to depend on some sort of base of information. Kerberos and NTLM both require a common list of users, groups, and object information to work from. So far, you've learned that Active Directory is that information base. Now, let's look again at the individual pieces and how they're involved in the security scheme.

Workgroups and Domains

Domains and workgroups are the most basic building blocks of Windows 2000 security. The Domains model is the starter kit for Active Directory and enterprise security. The Workgroup model is really confined to the home or small office (SOHO) installation.

Once you arrive at a point of considering a hierarchical directory structure for managing users and resources, you've passed the point of using workgroups. However, I mentioned it again here as a stepping off point.

Workgroups

The Workgroup paradigm is used in peer-to-peer networking when the user population accessing the resources includes 5 to 10 users. This is because of the way that workgroups maintain users and groups.

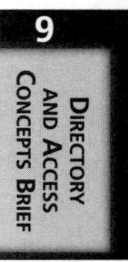

> **Note**
>
> The term *peer-to-peer* comes from the fact that no single machine in the network is considered the server or client. All machines are both servers and clients. Therefore, they are *peers*.

The Workgroup model, its creation, and its maintenance are discussed in full in Chapter 5. But for now, in the simplest terms, a workgroup is a collection of Windows (2000, 95/98, and/or NT) machines that share resources. These machines are connected to one another but are each responsible for maintaining their own security schemes and share points.

Once a machine is made a member of a workgroup, it's relatively easy to change the workgroup that it's a part of or to add the machine to a domain.

To change the workgroup membership of a machine or to add a machine to a domain, follow these steps:

- Right-click the My Computer icon and choose Properties. (This opens the System Properties control panel, which can also be accessed through Control Panel, System.)
- Choose the Network Identification tab and click Properties (see Figure 9.3).

FIGURE 9.3
The Network Identification tab.

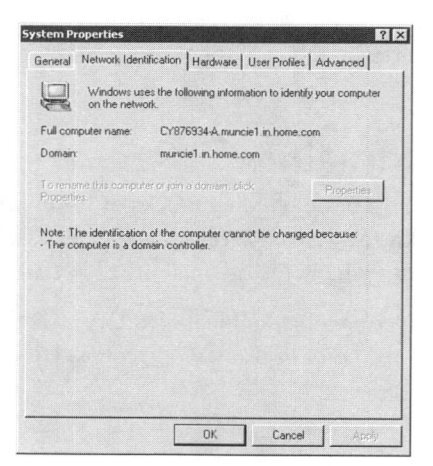

When a machine is added to a domain, you'll need to know the Domain Administrator password or have the machine's Domain account added to the domain by an administrator before starting this process.

Domains

Within Windows 2000, the Domain model has become part of a much greater scheme called the Active Directory but, for the moment, we'll cover this smaller part. Before you start to use domains as a tool in this version, you must understand that they come as part of the Active Directory installation.

If the network that's being managed involves large numbers of resources and users, then the Domain model is a better choice than Workgroups. A domain is a collection of user accounts and groups of user accounts shared by multiple servers (see Figure 9.4). This allows these computers to be managed from a single location. It allows administrators to bring a great number of the administrative tasks to them instead of the reverse. It's far more attractive to large companies and campus settings.

FIGURE 9.4
The concept of a domain.

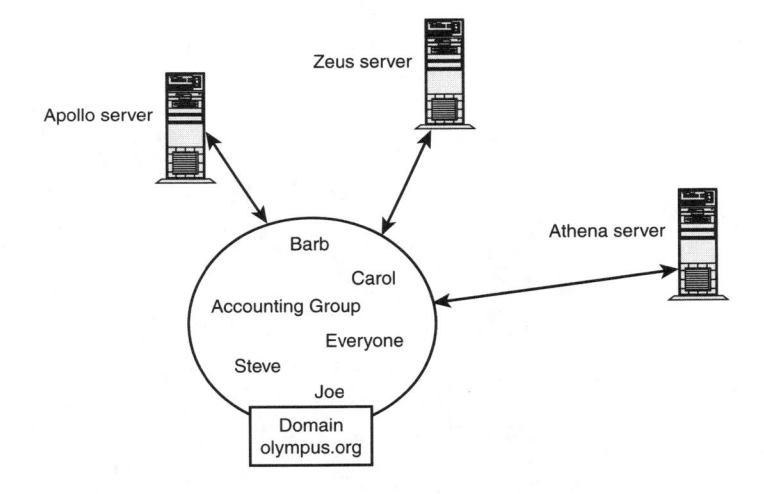

The domain is given a name that should be familiar to you if you've used the Internet. The domain naming convention in Windows 2000 follows the domain naming convention used by the Internet.

The name of the domain is followed by an identifier (.com by default) that tells the type of organization using the domain, producing names such as microsoft.com (Microsoft), whitehouse.gov (United States presidential home), and bsu.edu (Ball State University). Here's a list of identifiers:

- .com for commercial companies
- .org for not-for-profit organizations
- .gov for government agencies
- .edu for educational organizations

Use of the DNS naming system allows Windows 2000 to use a global standard naming convention. It makes the location of Windows servers global and the DNS server of the domain that is connected to the Internet registered. Registering your domain name with the InterNIC is covered in Chapters 8, "TCP/IP Networking," and 21, "Other Internet Services for Windows 2000," but it's important to realize where the naming convention comes from.

Domains are created when the installation of a server is started. The install will ask if you would like to make the machine a member of a domain. If no domain exists, then choosing to make a machine a member of a domain will start you down the trail of domain creation.

The install will complain that "an invalid domain was specified" and ask if you want to continue anyway. To create a new domain, simply choose Yes.

Once Windows 2000 starts for the first time, it will open with a screen attempting to clear up the domain situation (see Figure 9.5).

FIGURE 9.5
The opening screen in a new installation.

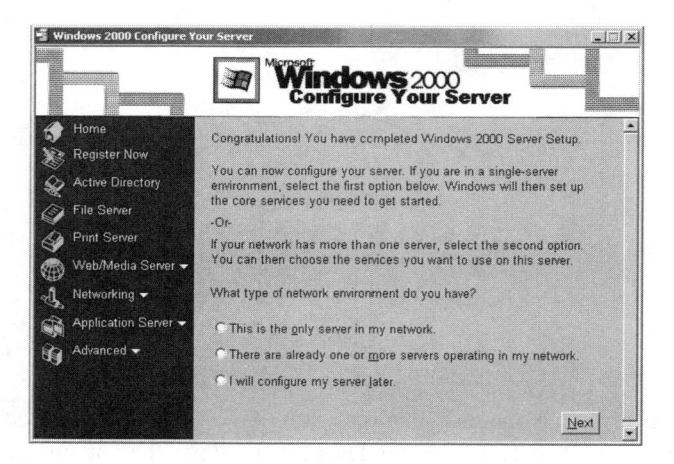

To continue the creation of a domain, follow these steps:

1. Choose This Is the Only Server in My Network. Click Next.
2. Read the information page, if needed, and then click Next.
3. Following the domain naming convention, add the name of your domain in the first open text box and press Tab.
4. If you've registered a domain name with the InterNIC, add the name (such as mcp.com, indiana.edu, and so on) to the second text box and press Tab again to see a preview of your domain name. If you haven't registered your domain, simply type **local** and then press Tab.

5. Observe the preview of your domain name properties, as shown in Figure 9.6, and then Choose Next, Next, and then Finish.

FIGURE 9.6
Domain properties and preview.

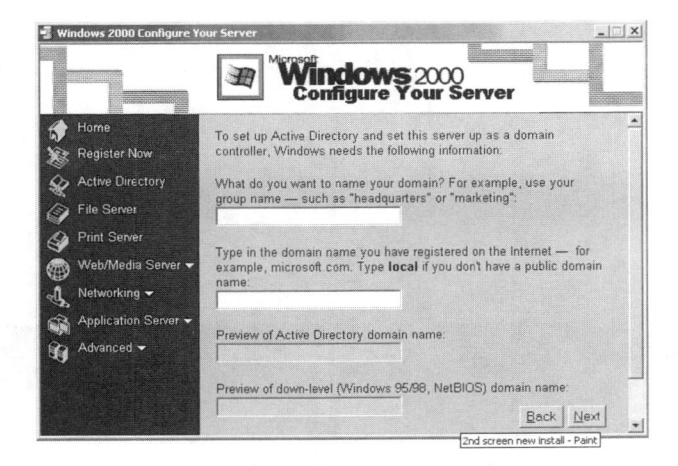

In previous versions of Windows, the domain choice was a permanent one. If a server was installed as a Domain Controller, it would be a Domain Controller until removed or reinstalled. This isn't true in Windows 2000. This is a very important point because it offers great flexibility. (Many Window NT administrators may have to read this twice because it's so powerful a change.)

Once a domain or workgroup choice has been made and the server is running, you're able to change that choice in many ways. The basic change is to create a DC where one wasn't before or to remove a DC from the role of Domain Control.

These processes are completed in the Active Directory Installation Wizard. To open the Active Directory Installation Wizard, click Start, Run and type **DCPROMO** and then click OK.

To Add a Domain Controller after installation, follow these steps:

1. Read the initial splash screen and make sure you have the right choice. Choose Next.
2. Select Domain Controller for New Domain and click Next.
3. Select Create a New Domain Tree and click Next.
4. Select Create a New Forest of Domain Trees and click Next.
5. Type in the domain name of the domain you're creating, including the top-level domain, if registered (for example, `bellind.com` and `bsu.edu`), in the text box and click Next (see Figure 9.7).

Active Directory and Account Management
Part III

FIGURE 9.7
Domain naming window.

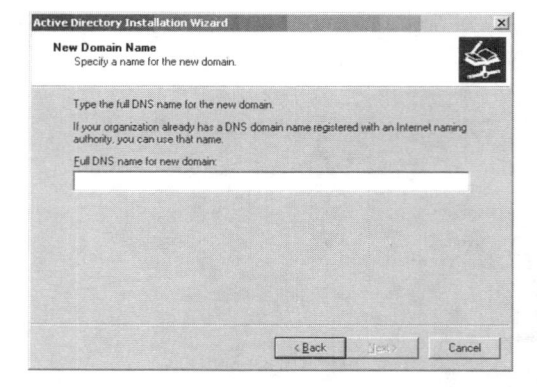

> **Note**
>
> This is a unique time in the creation of a domain. When using the wizard from the initial installation, you must use a three-level domain name (for example, `sams.mcp.com` and `CS.purdue.edu`). In the DCPROMO program, you're given an opportunity to create at the second level.

6. Type in the domain NetBIOS name in the text box and click Next.
7. The next two screens will ask about file placement. You can make changes here, but they're of no real value and can cause trouble finding files and troubleshooting them later. Make changes on each if you wish and then click Next.
8. If you're not running DNS Server on the server you're installing on, you'll be prompted to install it (see Figure 9.8). If you do not have a preferred DNS server, you should choose Yes and start the process now. If you have a DNS server for your domain already, you should choose No but check why this server is not seeing the current server for the domain. Choose Next.

FIGURE 9.8
DNS Server choices may appear.

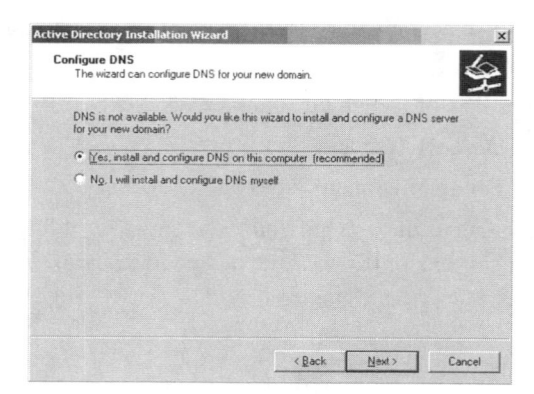

From this point forward, the choices may vary in many different ways, but they all depend on what's installed on your server prior to adding the DC. Following the wizards will answer most of your questions.

To remove a Domain Controller from a server, start the DCPROMO program as before and follow these steps:

1. Read the initial splash screen and make sure you have the right choice. Choose Next.
2. If this server is the last in the domain or the only server in the domain, check the box indicating that it is and choose Next (see Figure 9.9). This allows the operating system to remove the domain completely.

FIGURE 9.9
The domain "only server" removal screen.

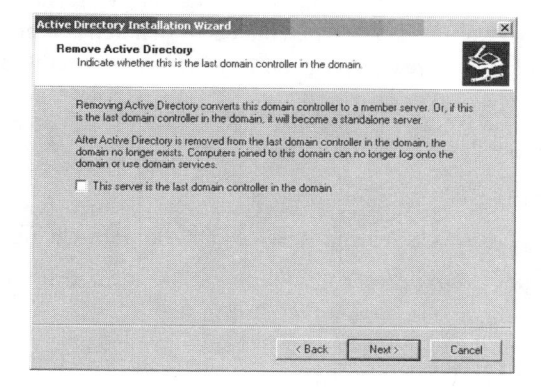

3. Enter the administrator username and password as well as the full domain name (auto-entered) and click Next.
4. Because the server will now be a standalone server, you'll need to enter and confirm the administrator password and click Next.
5. A summary of the choices made will appear; choosing Next will take you through the final removal of the machine from the domain. When done, click Finish.

Forests and Trees

A *domain tree* is a collection of domains that includes domains and subordinate domains in a single DNS hierarchy. The first domain in a tree may have the root of the DNS name (mcp.com or indiana.edu), but subsequent domains will expand on that convention. For example, you may have the domain bellind.com at the top of a tree that could contain sams.mcp.com and architecture.indiana.edu.

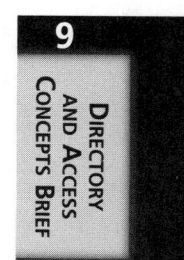

A *forest* is a collection of trees (well, of course it is), but it's not quite that simple. The distinction is that a forest is the connection of trees that do not share a contiguous DNS domain name. In the preceding example, you saw that everything in the bellind.com domain was one tree. If you would then connect that tree to a tree containing all the domains of the `mcp.com` domain, you would have formed a forest.

Although most companies never grow to the size necessary to build trees or forests, it's becoming increasingly more common for companies to connect, merge, and become global. Domains, forests, and trees make this possible.

Creating a tree is done from the moment the first domain is created. In fact, the steps include the option of creating a new tree or joining an existing tree. The third choice given during the install of a new domain is the choice of joining an existing tree or creating a new domain tree.

Forests, in the broad sense, are also created. However, to join two trees with diverse domain context names, a forest will need to be connected manually or created during the installation of trees. Simply put, forests are created by joining trees with different naming conventions.

To connect to forests, follow these steps:

1. Open Active Directory Sites and Services.
2. Right-click Active Directory Sites and Services and point to **Change Forest**.
3. In the Root Domain text box, enter the root domain of the forest. This is the root domain of the first domain tree created in the forest.

Organizational Units

Just as in physics there are macrophysics and microphysics, domains have both grown larger and become able to be divided into smaller pieces. Domains can now be divided into smaller units called Organizational Units (OUs). If you're from the NetWare NDS world, you'll recognize this as the same type of division of the greater whole that has existed for years.

Domains are still the primary security borderlines and the points where control is based. But through the years, domains have been criticized over the fact that they're "all inclusive." A domain administrator is all powerful, and there are few choices for making that more granular.

OUs allow the administrator of an entire domain to create containers, create objects in those containers, and place different administrators in charge of those containers (see Figure 9.10). All this is done while maintaining control of the root of the domain. This gives a great deal more flexibility and growth to the Domain model.

By allowing a division of administration, the workload of a single administrator is lessened and the flexibility of the company information network is increased.

FIGURE 9.10
Domain containing organizational units.

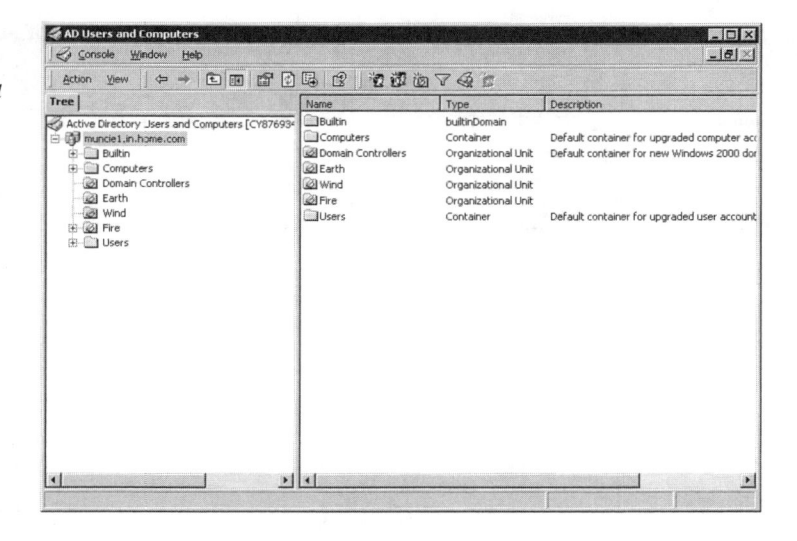

The creation of an OU is done within the Active Directory User and Computer console. Because the OU is a division of a domain, it's created within the domain. See the section "Creating Objects," later in this chapter.

Domain Control

This is where the changes in Windows 2000 begin to become very obvious and appreciated. Domains have become far more flexible in both sizing and capability. Because of these changes, administrators are able to grow domains into areas where they were restricted before.

Domain control involves the management and passing of domain information among the servers that exist on the network. If a change must be made to a user or group definition, an authority must be established in order to make this system work. In order to allow for growth of the system, a way must be found of allowing more than one machine to store and facilitate the use of these changes. Domain control allows this to happen.

Domain Controllers

Domain Controllers (DCs), like Operations Masters (seen in Chapter 5), are established when the first server is installed in the domain. These controllers are responsible for directory information, including users, groups, directory searches, and machine accounts. For the sake of fault tolerance and performance, it's good to have at least two DCs within a directory (see Figure 9.11).

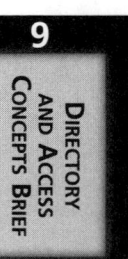

FIGURE 9.11

Server selection as a Domain Controller.

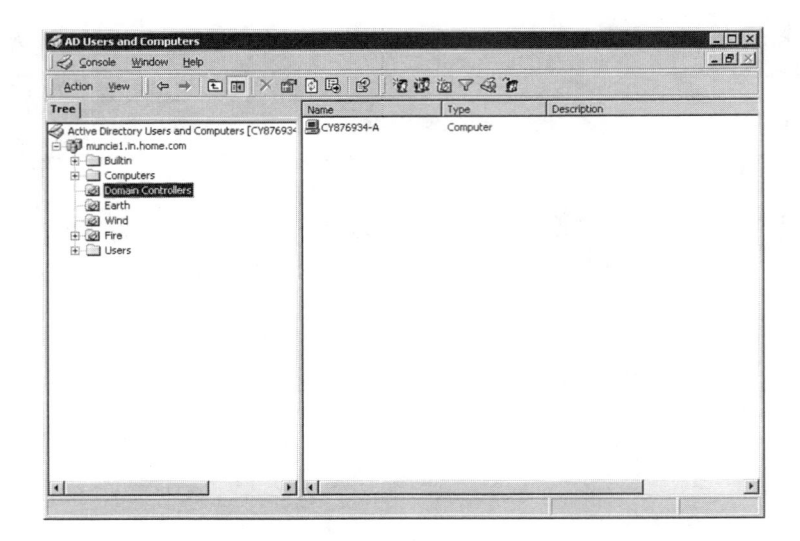

Once the first server is installed, other servers can be installed into the domain and promoted to participate in domain control. This machine is then part of a multimaster system domain. This is a great departure from the former (NT) single-master or Primary Domain Controller role. It's different because in the multimaster model, no one controller stops the others from accepting domain object changes.

For example, in the Windows NT world, if the Primary Domain Controller was down, no user could change his or her password. In a multimaster model, one Domain Controller accepts the change and replicates that change to the other Domain Controllers in the domain.

Trust Relationships

A *trust* is created between domains to allow users and groups from one domain to access resources from another domain. Windows 2000 has created two new forms of trust and has greatly advanced the trust concept.

Explicit Trusts (Classic Trusts)

Domains have traditionally been connected through what are known as *trust relationships* (now called *explicit trusts*). An explicit trust is a one-way relationship that establishes a connection between one domain's resources and another domain's users and groups. Explicit trusts are "explicit" because an administrator from each domain must explicitly create them.

If, for example, the administrator for Domain A creates a trust for Domain B and the administrator from Domain B allows it, the users and groups of Domain B can be granted permissions to resources in Domain A. This would be called a *one-way trust*, and it would be explicit.

If the administrators in both Domains A and B create trust of the opposite domain, this is referred to as a *two-way trust* or *complete trust*. In this case, users from either domain may be granted access to resources in either domain. In both cases the trust must be manually created and is considered explicit.

Classic trust relationships are covered in more detail in Chapter 5.

Intransitive Trusts

An *intransitive trust* is a trust formed between domains that are not part of the same tree or are not Windows 2000 domains. These trusts can be "one way" or "two way," but they cannot be transitive (see the next section).

Here are some examples:

- A Windows 2000 domain connecting to a Windows NT domain
- A Windows 2000 forest connecting to a Windows 2000 forest

Transitive Trusts

A *transitive trust* is not so much a creation of the administrator as it is a fact of domains being part of the same tree or trees that are part of the same forest. When subordinate domains are created within a tree, the two domains are by virtue of this relationship in a transitive trust. This trust is always two way and is not a choice that can be made or unmade.

Domain Mode

Domains in Windows 2000 are installed in what is called *mixed mode*, meaning that the domain will attempt to speak with Windows NT and Window 2000 domains. This is true because many domains that Windows 2000 will be installed into will be addressing both types of domains in trust relationships. At least initially, all upgrade environments will require this mode.

The opposite of mixed mode is *native mode*. In native mode, a domain is able to use all the new directory features of Windows 2000. Features such as nested groups require that native mode be running.

While in mixed mode, you're stopped from using some features of Windows 2000 due to backward compatibility. It's a bit like having to take your little brother with you to the mall. In order to move around, you must remember to keep things at his speed. Features such as nested groups and universal groups are not available to the old domains, so they're not available to you.

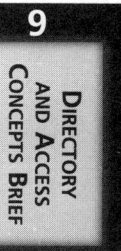

> **Note**
>
> Before changing modes, keep in mind that you cannot go back. The mode change is permanent. I can't be more adamant about this—there's no tougher predicament to be in than to be stuck in a spot you can't back out of.

Changing modes is very simple, but be careful. Here are the steps to follow:

1. Right-click the domain object and then click Properties.
2. Click the Change Mode button (see Figure 9.12).
3. Restart the Domain Controller.

FIGURE 9.12
The opening page for Domain Properties.

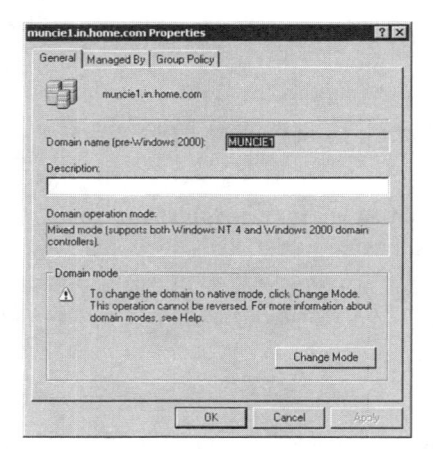

The next time you open Domain Properties, you're told that the domain is in native mode.

User Principle Name

When a user is attaching to the domain, he or she can use an assigned username and password and attach in a single domain environment just fine. But in a multidomain environment or through a remote connection, it may be necessary for that user to put in a more complete username entry in order to attach. In that case, the user might enter a full logon name that would include the domain name. This is very much like an SMTP email address (for example, `zeus@olympus.org`). Therefore, a user can be told to log in with his or her email address. However, this may not be as obvious as users might think.

For many good and justifiable reasons, some companies maintain several registered domain names to arrive at the same email server. For this reason, you may have some users who are in a domain whose email address does not match the domain the user object exists in.

For example, Pluto may be a member of the `olympus.org` domain. But for political or marketing reasons, he may prefer to receive mail at `hades.com`. Registering the MX records of both domains to arrive at the same place is perfectly fine and legal (see Chapter 8 for more information on MX records). Because both domain names are registered and arrive at the same domain, this causes no problem. But how does Pluto get to the `olympus.org` domain for logon?

The solution is a User Principle Name (UPN) that can be placed in the Active Directory domain properties. It allows the users in that domain to attach with numerous different `@DOMAIN_NAME` entries. When creating a user, you simply select the UPN that you want to be attached to the user's logon name. Then, when the user starts to log on, he or she can use the email name he or she is used to and still arrive at the domain you specified. I'm sure that Pluto would understand a little deception in his favor.

UPNs are set up in the Properties page of the domain from the Active Directory Domains and Trusts console. Simply right-click Active Directory Domains and Trusts and choose Properties. You'll see the entry point, as shown in Figure 9.13. See the section "Creating Objects," later in this chapter, for how to add the UPN to a user's account.

FIGURE 9.13
UPN suffix.

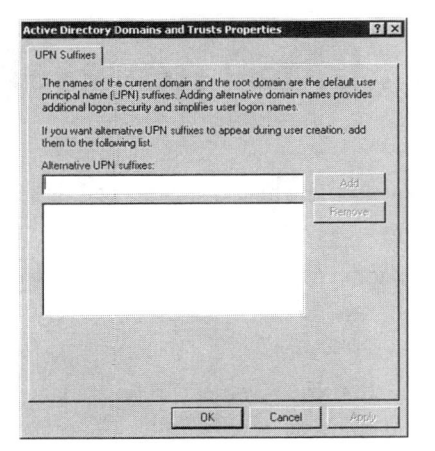

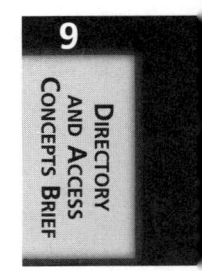

Active Directory/Domain Objects

Once a domain exists, it can be populated with the objects that are the reason for its existence. The creation of users, groups, and other objects is all done within the Active Directory Users and Computers console.

The objects that can be created include the following:

- *User*. The account name used to attach the domain. This is the base object that's granted permissions to resources and policies.
- *Computer*. The account created for control of computer objects.
- *Group*. A collection of user accounts and other groups that's used to manage user permissions and policies in mass to avoid having to make changes to each individual user.
- *Contact*. A management object created to allow the system to contact email accounts external to the system.
- *Organizational Unit (OU)*. An administrative division of a domain used to divide domain objects into usable and separately administrated portions.
- *Shared Folders*. An Active Directory object created from file shares so that the share can be managed as part of the directory.
- *Shared Printers*. An Active Directory object created from the printer shares of legacy Windows operating systems (Windows NT, 95/98, and WFW) so that the share can be managed as part of the directory.

A more complete description of the User and Group objects can be found in Chapter 11, "User Account Creation and Management."

Which Comes First: The Users or the Groups?

The creation of user and group accounts and which one is needed first is going to require us to spend some time on what the ramifications of each are.

User accounts are used to attach the domain. This is the base object that's granted permissions to resources and policies. It does not get a great deal more complex than that. Groups, on the other hand, can get complex.

Unlike in Windows NT, in Windows 2000 you can create groups that transcend domain boundaries as well as groups that can be nested within groups. This cannot be done in mixed mode, but in native mode these choices become possible.

Groups in Windows 2000 are separated into three categories:

- *Universal groups*. Groups with universal scope can have as their members any groups and accounts from any Windows 2000 domain in the domain tree or forest and can be granted permissions in any domain in the domain tree or forest. Universal groups are not allowed in mixed-mode domains.

- *Global groups*. Groups with global scope can have as their members any groups and accounts only from the domain in which the groups are defined and can be granted permissions in any domain in the domain tree or forest.
- *Domain local groups*. Groups with domain local scope can have as their members any groups and accounts from a Windows 2000 or Windows NT domain and can be used to grant permissions only within a domain.

Whether you create users or groups first greatly depends on your point of view from the start. The Microsoft point of view is that you should always create groups before assigning permission to a resource. Resources are less likely to be removed or changed than users are. What's more, users will almost always be added to the list of permitted users for a resource.

By creating groups that fill the job tasks and roles needed to complete network tasks and then assigning those groups the needed permissions, you have an easier security paradigm to follow. When a user needs a change in a job responsibility or a task list, it's easier to change his or her group membership than it is to have to find all the places he or she, as an individual, had permissions.

It can seem to be overkill to always create a group and then assign users, but once the network has grown, you'll find it works better. However, there will be exceptions.

There are two other distinctions that every Windows 2000 group can be placed into. Every group created will be either a security or distribution group. The distinction is that security groups are used for the application of permissions and security settings in the domain. A distribution group is very much like a contact object. It's more informational and can be used for email.

Creating Objects

Active Directory Users and Computers is a tool that functions very much like Windows Explorer, which Windows users have become so familiar with. Creating objects in Active Directory is much like creating new folders and/or empty files in Explorer. With a little common sense and the information in this chapter, you can probably even figure out where to start the creation process. This section will cover the process step by step.

To begin the creation process, open the Active Directory Users and Computers console either within the MMC or by itself from the Start, Administrative Tools menu.

Creating a New OU

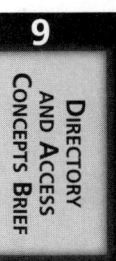

It may be necessary to delegate authority or management of users within a corporate structure, but it may not make sense from an IT standpoint to create a new domain. In that case it makes sense to create an Organizational Unit. An Organizational Unit (OU) is an administrative division of a domain. It is used to divide domain objects into usable and separately administrated portions.

To create an OU, follow these steps:

1. Open the domain you would like to contain the OU by clicking the plus sign beside the domain name.
2. Right-click the domain and choose New, Organizational Unit.
3. Type in the name of the OU you would like created and click OK (see Figure 9.14).

FIGURE 9.14
The Organizational Unit creation screen.

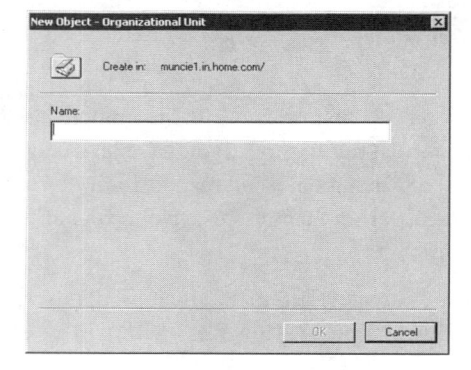

Creating Users

Again, user accounts are the basic object in the directory structure to attach to the domain. A user needs to be authenticated, and the user accounts make this possible. User is the account name used to attach the domain. This is the base object that's granted permissions to resources and policies.

To create a new user, follow these steps:

1. Right-click the domain or OU that you would like to create the user in. Choose New, User.
2. Type in the first name and then press Tab.
3. Type in the last name and then press Tab.
4. Type in the full name and then press Tab.
5. The user logon name is the actual account name used to attach to the domain (for example, `tbrown`, `user0129`, and so on). Type in the user logon name and then press Tab.
6. The choice you now arrive at is the Domain/UPN Suffix box. Select the domain name or UPN that has been selected for this user. Then press Tab.

7. If you want to have a different username for the user from the one used on legacy systems, you may change it in User Logon Name (pre-Windows 2000). If not, simply choose Next.
8. Type in the user password, press Tab, and then confirm the password.
9. Select the appropriate user options and then click Next.
10. Review the summary and click Finish.

Creating Groups

In order to allow administrators to affect more than one user at a time, the directory service uses groups. A group is a collection of user accounts and other groups that's used to manage user permissions and policies en masse to avoid having to make changes to each individual user.

To create a group, follow these steps:

1. Right-click the domain or OU that you would like to create the group in and choose New, Group.
2. Type in the group name and then press Tab.
3. If you have a domain name of more than 15 characters, you may have to type in a different domain name in the Group Name (pre-Windows 2000) area. Then press Tab.
4. Select a group type and choose OK.

Creating Computer Accounts

Computer is an account created for control of computer objects. Computer objects allow the administrator to control the behavior of any user who sits down and logs in to a particular computer. Even if the user is an administrator, there may be specific tasks that a computer is designated for, or there may be security reasons for not exposing certain parts of the network to this computer.

Follow these steps to create one:

1. Right-click the domain or OU that you would like to create the group in and choose New, Computer.
2. Type in the name of the computer that will attempt to attach to the domain.
3. Be sure to change the users or groups allowed access to the computer by clicking Change and selecting a group or user from the list.

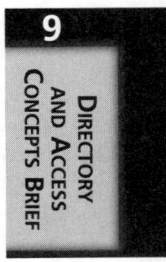

> **Note**
>
> Notice that the default is to allow only the members of Domain Admins access. This is new to Windows. It's a closed-to-open part of the system. Windows systems have traditionally been open-to-closed, meaning that resources are created and initially allow access to all users.

4. Click OK.

Creating a Shared Folder Object

Shared Folder objects allow the users and other directory objects to access server file shares by accessing the directory. Shared Folder is an Active Directory object created from file shares so that the share can be managed as part of the directory. This is different than looking in Network Neighborhood or My Network Places of the past. It is an advance that allows for the user to find resources even without being able to browse in the classic Microsoft sense.

To create one, follow these steps:

1. Right-click the domain or OU that you would like to create the group in and choose New, Shared Folder.
2. Type in the Active Directory object name that you would like the folder presented as. Then press Tab.
3. Type in the UNC address of the share and then press Tab.
4. Click OK.

Creating a Shared Printer Object

Just as Folder objects are the objects that make file shares available through the directory, Shared Printer objects make print shares available. Shared Printer is an Active Directory object created from the printer shares of legacy Windows operating systems (Windows NT, 95/98, and WFW) so that the share can be managed as part of the directory.

Follow these steps to create a Shared Printer object:

1. Right-click the domain or OU that you would like to create the group in and choose New, Printer.
2. Type in the Active Directory object name that you would like the printer presented as. Then press Tab.
3. Type in the UNC address of the share and then press Tab.
4. Click OK.

Controlling User Access to Resources

The user and group accounts that are to be assigned permissions to a resource are given permissions from the property pages of the resource. As in previous incarnations of Windows, you'll need to keep in mind that any share that has been created will be open and available to the group Everyone when the share is created (see Figure 9.15).

FIGURE 9.15
Initial permissions.

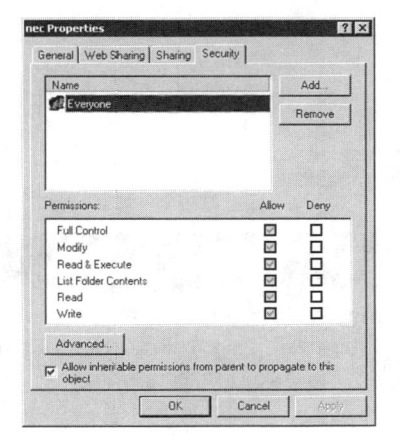

A share that has been created has a property page that's accessed by right-clicking the object and choosing Properties, just like every other Explorer object. This is the same for printer and file shares. However, this is the point where many administrators make a mistake in assigning permissions.

File Share Permissions

Two places in this property page allow permissions to be assigned. On the opening Sharing tab is a button called, innocently enough, Permissions (see Figure 9.16). This is a bit deceptive, because it's really a holdover item from the Workgroup model. It only controls permissions to the folder from the network. If a user can log in locally to the server, he or she is then using the permissions found in the Security tab.

It's best to move to the Security tab. Once you're at the Security tab, you can set permissions that are applicable to both local and network users. It's not necessary to change permissions in both places, because the Security tab permissions are applicable for both places. When you're accessing a resource from the network, if restrictions exist in one or both tabs, the most restrictive of both is applied. For example, if the Permissions button has Full access for the group Accounting and the Security tab has Deny, Accounting members are denied. By choosing to use the Security tab permissions, you have chosen to completely control the resource.

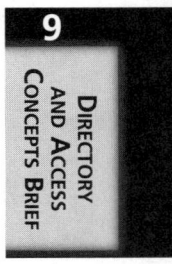

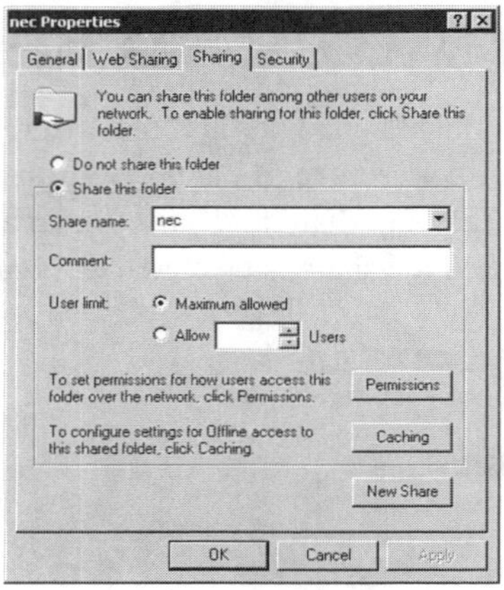

FIGURE 9.16
The Sharing tab.

> **Note**
>
> The Security tab will only apply when NTFS has been used to format the partition where the share has been established. It's not advisable that you share any portion of a FAT partition. FAT partitions are not secured at a local level.

By default, objects within a container inherit the permissions from that container when the objects are created. For example, when you create a `Programs` folder, all subfolders and files created within the `Programs` folder automatically inherit the permissions from that folder. Therefore, the `Programs` folder has explicit permissions, whereas all subfolders and files within it have inherited permissions.

Permissions to Active Directory objects have to do with the ability to access the objects and make changes to them once they exist or to create objects inside of other objects. All of this, of course, depends on the type of object.

The specific permissions that can be assigned to a folder are shown in Table 9.1.

TABLE 9.1 Folder Permissions

Permissions	Full Control	Modify	Read & Execute	List Folder Contents	Read	Write
Explore Folder/Execute File	x	x	x	x		
See Folder/Read Data	x	x	x	x	x	
See Attributes	x	x	x	x	x	
See Extended Attributes	x	x	x	x	x	
Create Files/Write to File	x	x				x
Create Folders/Append File	x	x				x
Write Attributes	x	x				x
Write Extended Attributes	x	x				x
Delete Subfolders and Files	x					
Delete	x	x				
Read Permissions	x	x	x	x	x	x
Change Permissions	x					
Take Ownership	x					
Synchronize	x	x	x	x	x	x

Here are the two types of permissions:

- *Explicit permissions*. Permissions given to a user or group in the properties of the specific object are considered "explicit."
- *Inherited permissions*. Permission is inherited if the user or group gains permission from the parent container of the object.

Before you can remove rights from a user to a particular object, you must first remove the check mark from Allow Inheritable Permissions to Propagate to This Object (see Figure 9.17). Once this is done, you can customize the permissions to your liking. You'll also notice that the Everyone group disappears from the list of permitted users.

To add/remove permissions, follow these steps:

1. Click Add.
2. Select a user or group and click Add and then OK.
3. With the user or group still selected, make the permission changes you would like by clicking the boxes beside the desired changes. Click OK.

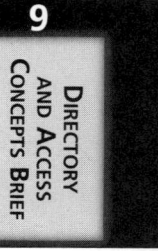

FIGURE 9.17
Inheritance removal.

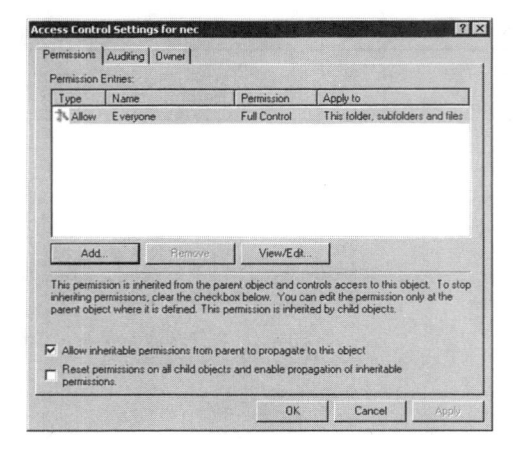

> **Tip**
>
> Keep in mind that you should always add the Enterprise Admins groups to the permission list with Full Control before exiting the screen. The group will still be able to change permissions later to gain access, but it will be a hassle to do so.

Printer Permissions

Printer security only involves the use of a Security tab. The security of a printer is not nearly as complex as the previous objects discussed.

Printer security usually involves the protection of an expensive resource. The new $12,000 color printer/copier doesn't need to be the personal coloring book of an executive's curious five-year-old (or even the executive, for that matter). Therefore, security allows you to choose who can print to the device, who is responsible for feeding and caring for it, and who can control the print jobs of others.

Printer permissions are broken into three categories:

- *Print.* The right to print to a printer share and to control your own documents
- *Manage Documents.* The Print permission plus the right to control the documents of others
- *Manage Printer.* The Manage Documents permission plus the ability to change printer properties as well as delete printer shares

Summary

This chapter has covered the security outer structure where objects are created and the security protocols that lock them down. Given the holes that existed in the Windows NT security and directory structure, many changes were needed. For most administrators, this chapter has covered the items on their wish lists.

Microsoft's switch from a proprietary security protocol to the standard implementation of Kerberos 5 has not only made it more secure but has also made it a standard that many companies can write to.

The domains, trees, and forest you learned about in Chapter 5 are fairly easy to create. This makes the creation of the outer structure of a directory easy as well. However, as you begin to create larger and larger directory trees, you'll find that there are many ways to paint yourself into a corner. Chapter 10, "Active Directory Design," will answer the questions that remain about the architecture of directory trees.

Active Directory Design

IN THIS CHAPTER

- Sites and Replication *264*
- Design Standards *269*
- Organizational Units *272*
- Dynamic DNS *273*

Knowing what Active Directory (AD) is and how to start a directory does not make you a good designer. In order to become a good directory designer, you need to ply some of the knowledge of networks you gained from Chapter 5, "Networking Brief," some of the directory information from Chapter 9, "Directory and Access Concepts Brief," and some good common sense. It's a bit like designing buildings. Just because you can buy a home design program doesn't mean that a contractor can build it without the walls falling in. Not only do architects need to understand how to make a building nice to look at—they must make the building capable of withstanding daily pressures.

Active Directories also have pressures that can be exacted upon them. LAN traffic can slow them down, WAN traffic can choke them off, and illogical placement of objects can make them near impossible to use. To become a Directory Architect (if you'll allow me that) you need to know where to shore up the wall, place a header, and reinforce the floor. In other words, you need to know where to divide the total directory listing, when to leave well enough alone, and how to please the political powers.

> **Tip**
>
> Humorous, but true. Be wary of leaving Active Directory designs hanging on walls. Executives and managers can mistake them for organizational charts and get "involved." As you'll soon learn, directory design based on political lines alone can be unmanageable and will seldom reach IT goals.

But not every directory is going to require an "architect." This chapter is of most value to those administrators who will be planning directories with more than one domain or at least multiple organizational units (OUs). Because the initial domain controller (DC) configuration has already been covered, we won't rehash it again here. Instead, a discussion of multiple DCs, OUs, forests, and trees will be the direction we head in.

Sites and Replication

The replication of domain information across the network is the primary reason for attempting to better design the directory. In order for users to be able to log on to the network and make use of the resources and security system put together for them, it's necessary that the domain information be available where they are. Therefore, if the user Brittney leaves the Denver office and sits down in the Indianapolis office, she still needs to be able to log on, access the drives containing her data, and interact with the directory resources.

Domain controllers in a single domain replicate information based on time. If a change is made in Denver to Brittney's password, the DC in Indianapolis should receive the update to her information and record that change. If the administrator in Indianapolis changes Brittney's password at the same time, the changes will be recorded and, *based on time*, the last change will be the change of record.

In order to understand how replication works, you need to understand two basic units of the network: sites and domains. Domains have already been covered in Chapter 5, "Networking Brief," and 9, "Directory and Access Concepts Brief." The piece that's necessary to understand for replication and directory design is that a domain is a logical division. In other words, a user could be using the same physical computer and IP address as another user but still considered in a different domain. They're physically in the same area but logically separate.

Sites

Sites involve a different type of separation. Systems in the same site are sites that, for all intents and purposes, share a physical structure. Although it's not necessary, it's easiest to think of them as systems in the same LAN. This is because a site is a collection of systems that should be within reach of one another through a network connected at a minimum of 1.5Mbps (T1), which is considered to be a fast WAN connection.

Sites can include numerous domains because the issue is one of physical or network location rather than logical location. Conversely, a domain can cross numerous sites. The question that is central to all the planning is the network speed between members of the site.

> **Note**
>
> Sites are often created based on the IP subnets that exist because IP subnets are most often in the same LAN and therefore in a network of system communicating at above 2Mbps. For this reason, two servers created in different subnets are often in separate sites.

DCs replicate directory changes with the DCs in their own site first. Replication to controllers outside the site is done on a less-frequent basis. The default site replication time is every 180 minutes.

When a client machine attaches to the network, it establishes what site it's in. When a client makes a request from the domain, the client directs those requests to domain controllers in its site. This avoids random traffic from crossing the entire WAN structure. It allows the client to have an Active Directory relationship that's as efficient as possible.

Sites make an important distinction between Microsoft's implementation of Directory Services and other forms (such as Novell's) because sites allow the domains, trees, and forests to remain independent of the replication process. Replication, therefore, means something separate.

Replication

DCs keep track of the changes that they've allowed to the directory and the times that those changes were made. On a schedule, the DCs will check to see whether other controllers in the directory have made changes to the directory, as well. If changes are found, the controller will ask for an update of the items that have been changed since the last time a change was received.

To stop repetitive writing of the same information, DCs use a property called *Originating Write*. By tracking which attributes are changed in an update and how many times the object's Originating Write property has been incremented, a DC knows what's current. A change that increments an Originating Write property indicates a change made to the object, as opposed to a change made by Active Directory when replicating updated directory information.

When the Denver domain controller is notified that an object in the Indianapolis directory has changed, it checks to see whether the change set the Originating Write property. If it's not set, no replication change is necessary for the Denver directory.

> **Tip**
>
> Active Directory DCs automatically checks for the most efficient way to establish replication with a site. You can manually add or configure connections and force replication over a particular connection, but the administrator should allow replication to be automatically optimized based on information provided to Active Directory sites and services.

Here are some site-optimization features:

- Occasional reevaluation of which connections are used and then the use of the most efficient path
- Selection of multiple routes to replicate changes, thus creating fault tolerance
- Replication of changed information only

Site Creation

Sites are very instrumental in the optimization of directory traffic, but this does not mean that sites are automatically created because of traffic needs. In fact, they are not. Sites are a function of the administrator trying to improve the performance of the directory and network. Sites are created in the Active Directory Sites and Services console (see Figure 10.1). An initial site is created along with the domain and directory. However, each subsequent site must be created and populated manually by an administrator.

FIGURE 10.1
Creating a site.

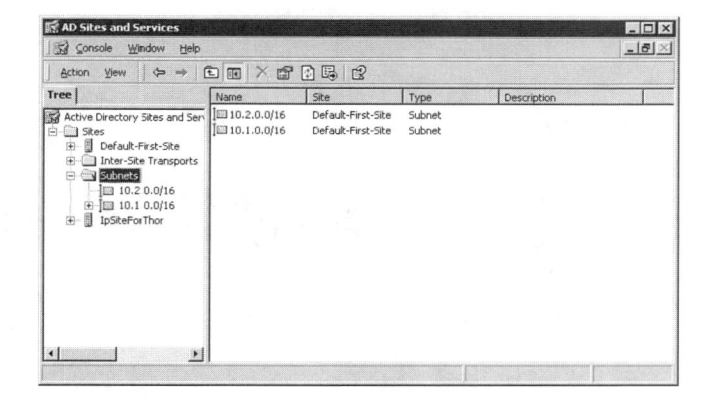

To create a new site, follow these steps:

1. Right-click the Sites folder and then click New Site.
2. Type the name of the new site.
3. Click a site link object and then click OK twice to acknowledge the message screen.
4. Right-click the Subnet folder and choose New Subnet.
5. Add the subnet address and mask and then click the site name to be associated with the subnet. Click OK (see Figure 10.2).
6. Move a domain controller from an existing site by right-clicking the server name, choosing Move, and then selecting the site you want. Click OK.

In the creation of a site link, you use what's called a *site link object*. This object doesn't just drop from the sky; it's created when the directory is created. DEFAULTIPSITELINK is created upon creation of the domain and directory, and it's given responsibly for the Default-First-Site-Name (this is the real name given to the first site created). To give the site link real purpose, you, of course, need more than one site.

FIGURE 10.2
Subnet creation.

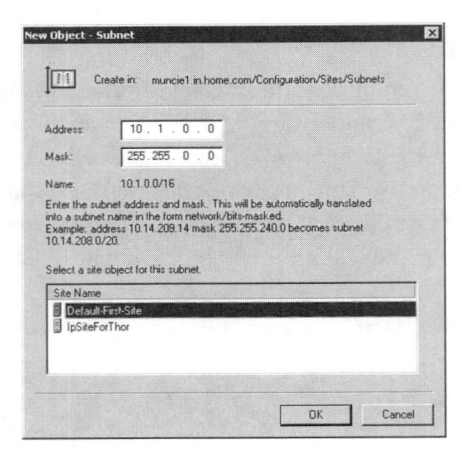

> **Tip**
>
> The fabulous names given to the initial site objects (Default-First-Site-Name and DEFAULTIPSITELINK) can be changed by right-clicking the object and choosing Rename.

If multiple communication methods exist between physical locations, multiple site links should be created to give fault tolerance to the process. In a scenario where a company has two WAN connections, there would be good reason for creating another site link to allow for the failure of one.

To govern the use of these links, the settings Cost and Replicate Every are attached to each site link. This allows the administrator to determine the link of choice (see Figure 10.3). The lower the cost of the site link, the more likely it is to be used. The Replicate Every option is used to control the frequency of the connection.

FIGURE 10.3
RedundantSiteLink Properties page.

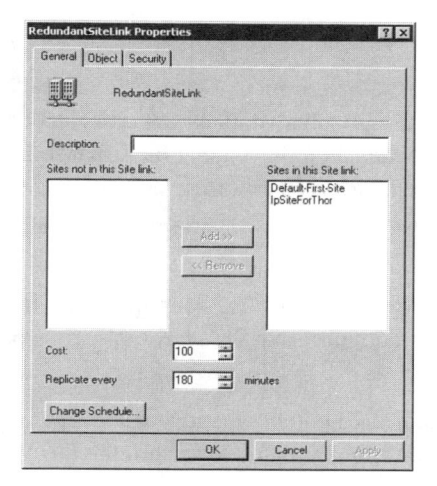

Design Standards

The actual design of the directory objects is a bit more open in the Active Directory world. However, there's still a great deal more planning that should go into the process of designing the structure of the tree.

Here are the two basic directory design considerations:

- *Political*. This involves making separations along departmental and political lines. In this case, you consider the departments or divisions that a company is made of as the place for the separation of domains, trees, and forests (for example, `Marketing.company.com`, `Operations.company.com`, and `Funding.company.com`).

- *Geographic*. This involves making separations along location lines. In this case, you consider the separation of buildings and land as the place for the separation of domains, trees, and forests (for example, `Paris.company.com`, `Asia.company.com`, and `NortheastUS.company.com`).

The use of political or geographic boundaries is not mutually exclusive in these forms; however, in order for you to learn the reasons for each, we'll restrict ourselves to the advantages and disadvantages of these basic forms. From that, you can decide whether it makes sense to have `vicepresidents.marketing.east.paris.company.com`, for example.

Political

The political model could be called the "departmental or divisional model" because it's really best for companies that are strongly divided along departmental or divisional lines. Many companies are so strongly divided along divisional lines that some employees might not even know that certain divisions are part of the same company. Things don't have to be that bad to employ this design (or parts of it), but the divisions must be fairly strong.

The reason is that this model lends itself to divisions that require self-maintenance of their own systems. If the process of administering the server or user population of another division's people is not being done, this is the model to use.

The concept is fairly simple. Domains are initially created to reflect the organizational chart, starting with the company name and moving down through the different divisions and then departments (see Figure 10.4).

FIGURE 10.4
A political plan.

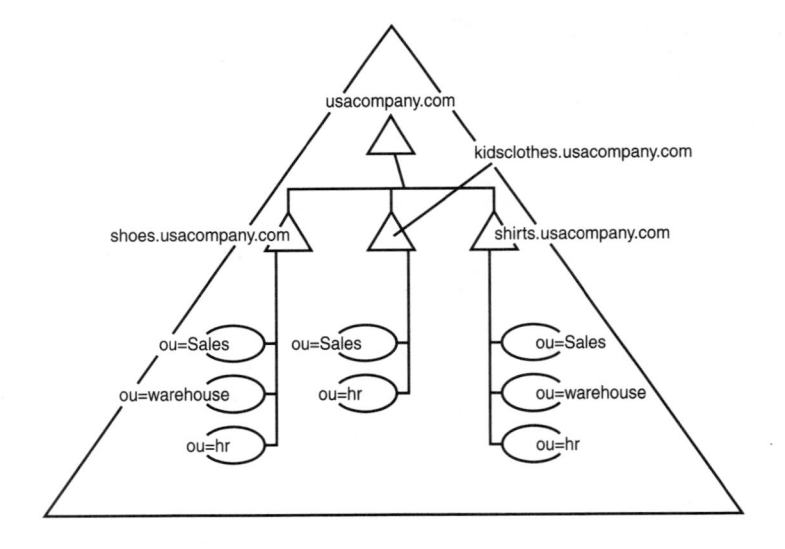

Through conformity to the divisional lines, it becomes very easy to separate IT costs and responsibility. It also becomes easier to get the boss to go along for the ride. There's less explanation of router and connectivity and more talk of who all are responsible and where they fit.

It's much easier in this model to create and maintain the DNS naming conventions. This is because the naming of the internal resources follows the naming plan that might be used to market the divisions themselves. It becomes very easy to tell what's meant by the `shoes.usacompany.com` domain.

The problems that can arise from this plan are the problems of company growth, merger, and division. For example, if the Kid's Clothing and Shirt divisions merge, having to move all the servers, users, printers, and possibly even organizational units to the new combined division can quickly become unwieldy and hard to manage.

Network efficiency is not improved by this plan. If all the divisions share the Human Resources department that is located in one building, then WAN traffic considerations are born. For that matter, the entire company could be contained in the same building, which can result in ridiculous confusion for users and administrators alike.

Geographic

Geographic design is truly meant for the company that covers geographically disparate areas. In other words, if your company has more then one site today or may expand to multiple sites in the future, you may want to employ a geographic design in planning your AD structure. If your company will always exist in the same building, chances are you're not going to be looking too deeply into the process of creating a large directory structure.

The concept of geographically designing your directory is based on the idea that directory division should be based on IT and network lines. In other words, if the network must be divided at a WAN line or into security divisions, a new container object should be created (see Figure 10.5).

FIGURE 10.5
Geographic design.

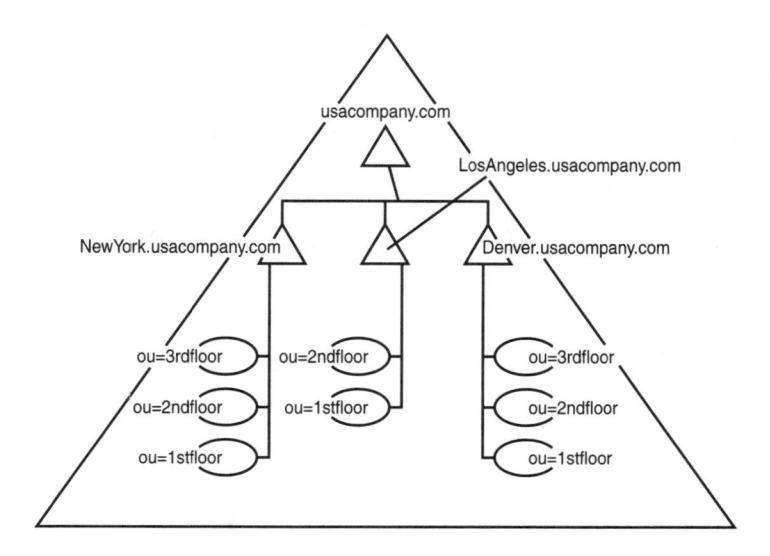

The geographic design allows the users and systems to be administered based on the locations in which they exist. This lends itself better to the paradigm used by network administrators or IT departments for managing users and resources. If Brian is a member of the Accounting department assigned to the Shoe department and is then given responsibility for the Shirt department as well, that does not affect the directory plan. If the Shoe and Shirt departments merge, only the movement or loss of employees affects the system.

Replication of the directory structure and any changes are also simplified because the site link divisions are fairly well cut on the same lines as the domain divisions.

The problem, of course, is that divisional politics can rear its ugly head. If the Kid's Clothing and Shoe divisions are at odds, the administrators of the network may have trouble getting appropriate approval on common resources. If the domains and OU's that contain these groups are intermingled then it becomes almost impossible to divide the users and groups.

Mixed Environment

Active Directory's design potential and limitations being what they are will most likely result in a "mixed environment." The mentioning of geographic and political designs is not to say that the environment cannot be split on less stringent lines. It may be more reasonable or manageable to split certain items along unplanned lines.

If, in the example earlier, the divisions share the Human Resources department, but that department must have locations in all the buildings, then a common dividing line has been found. In a strict geographic design, this departmental division would not allow for separate administration of this group. Due to the unique needs of a Human Resources department, it may be necessary to make the separation despite the master plan.

The key to the success of your design and your subsequent implementation of Active Directory will be a balance of political and geographic needs and good old common sense. Make the Active Directory structure work for you. Staying within a structure helps you better control the environment. However, when more work has to be done to stay within the structure than would be necessary by leaving it, such concerns need to be addressed as well.

Organizational Units

Organizational units are created primarily as dividers of responsibility and administration. They're not groups that are solely used to assign rights. Instead, OU's are used as a way of granting administrative territory.

For example, if the Human Resources department needs to create users in its own department and administer the permissions to the information in those user objects, an HR organizational unit should be created.

If the Order Entry group supervisor needs to be able to stop print jobs and disable the accounts of the users in his department, an OU would allow the administrator to assign these permissions.

To assign permissions to an organizational unit, follow these simple steps:

1. Open Active Directory Users and Computers.
2. Right-click the OU that you would like to add permissions to and choose Delegate Control.
3. Click Next to start the Delegate Control Wizard.
4. Click Add to select a user or group from anywhere in the domain (see Figure 10.6).
5. Click on a user you would like to add and then click the Add button (repeat this process until all the selections needed have been made). Click OK.
6. Click Next and select each of the tasks to delegate. Finally, click Next and then Finish.

FIGURE 10.6.
Assigning permissions to an organizational unit (in this case, a user).

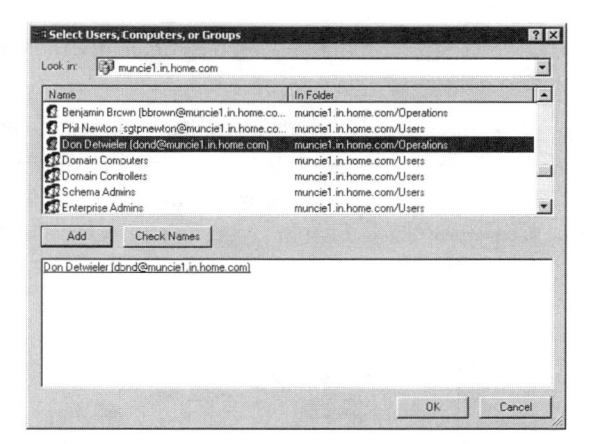

Dynamic DNS

Dynamic DNS enables DNS client computers to register and dynamically update their own A (address) resource records with a DNS server whenever changes occur. This reduces the need for manual administration of zone records, especially for clients that frequently move or change locations and use DHCP to obtain an IP address.

Windows 2000 provides client and server support for the use of dynamic updates, as described in RFC 2136 (http://www.ietf.org/rfc/rfc2136.txt). For DNS servers, the DNS service allows dynamic updating to be enabled or disabled on a per-zone basis, with each server configured to load either a standard primary or directory-integrated zone. By default, client computers running under any version of Windows 2000 dynamically update their A resource records in DNS when configured for TCP/IP.

By default, computers running Windows 2000 attempt to dynamically register both A (address) and PTR (pointer) resource records for all configured IP addresses used on the computer. When registering A and PTR records, most clients register an IP address based on the full computer name (the fully qualified domain name) created by appending the computer name to the DNS domain name for the computer, as configured in System Properties.

Dynamic updates can be sent for any of the following reasons or events:

- An IP address is added, removed, or modified in the TCP/IP properties configuration for any one of the installed network connections.
- An IP address lease changes or renews with the DHCP server or any one of the installed network connections (for example, when the computer is started or if the ipconfig /renew command is used).
- The ipconfig /registerdns command is used to manually force a refresh of the client name registration in DNS.

When one of the previous events triggers a dynamic update, the DHCP Client service—*not* the DNS Client service—sends updates. This is designed so that if a change to the IP address information occurs because of DHCP, corresponding updates in DNS are performed to synchronize name-to-address mappings for the computer. The DHCP Client service performs this function for all network connections used on the system, including connections not configured to use DHCP.

How Dynamic Update Works

For Windows 2000, dynamic updates are typically requested when either a DNS name or IP address changes on the computer. For example, suppose a client named "oldhost" is first configured in System Properties with the following names:

- Computer name: oldhost
- DNS name: example.microsoft.com
- Full computer name: oldhost.example.microsoft.com

In this example, no connection-specific DNS domain names are configured for the computer. Later, the computer is renamed "newhost," resulting in the following name changes on the system:

- Computer name: newhost
- DNS name: `example.microsoft.com`
- Full computer name: newhost.example.microsoft.com

Once the name change is applied in System Properties, the DHCP Client service performs the following sequence to update DNS:

- The client sends an SOA-type query for the DNS domain name of the computer.
- Windows 2000 determines the name of the zone to be updated (`example.microsoft.com`) based on the DNS domain name of the computer. It then sends an SOA-type query for the name of the zone.
- Server responds to the SOA-type query.

For standard primary zones, the primary server (owner) returned in the SOA query response is fixed and static. It always matches the exact DNS name as it appears in the SOA record stored with the zone. If, however, the zone being updated is directory integrated, any DNS server loading the zone can respond and dynamically insert its own name as the primary server (owner) of the zone in the SOA query response.

When the client attempts to contact the primary DNS server, it uses the name of the primary server returned in the SOA query response to again query, look up, and resolve that name to the IP address for the primary server. The client then attempts to contact the primary server. If the primary server is not available, the DHCP Client service can check whether the zone where the update is requested is a single-master or multimaster zone by determining if the zone is integrated with Active Directory.

If the zone is found to be integrated, the DHCP client queries again for Name Server resource records for the `example.microsoft.com` zone to locate another authoritative primary server that can process an update.

If a primary server can perform the update, the client sends the update and request, and the DNS server processes it. The contents of the update request include instructions to add A (and possibly PTR) resource records for `newhost.example.microsoft.com` and remove these same record types for `oldhost.example.microsoft.com`, the name that was previously registered.

The server also checks to ensure that updates are permitted for the client request. For standard primary zones, dynamic updates are not secured, so any client attempt to update succeeds. For Active Directory–integrated zones, updates are secured and performed using directory-based security settings.

Dynamic updates are sent or refreshed periodically. By default, Windows 2000 sends a refresh once every 12 hours. If the update results in no changes to zone data, the zone remains at its current version and no changes are written. Updates result in actual zone changes or increased zone transfer only if names or addresses actually change.

Note that names are not removed from DNS zones if they become inactive or are not updated within the refresh interval (12 hours). DNS does not use a mechanism to release or tombstone names, although DNS clients do attempt to delete or update old name records when a new name or address change is applied.

When the DHCP Client service registers A and PTR resource records for a Windows 2000 computer, it uses a default caching Time To Live (TTL) of 15 minutes for host records. This determines how long other DNS servers and clients cache a computer's records when they're included in a query response.

Secure Dynamic Update

For Windows 2000, DNS update security is available only for zones that are integrated into Active Directory. Once you directory-integrate a zone, Access Control List (ACL) editing features are available in the DNS snap-in so you can add or remove users or groups from the ACL for a specified zone or resource record.

By default, client computers running Windows 2000 attempt to use an unsecured dynamic update first. If an unsecured update fails, clients try to use a secure update. Also, clients use a default update policy that permits them to attempt to overwrite a previously registered resource record, unless they're specifically blocked by update security.

Summary

The concepts behind solid Active Directory design have much greater depth than the concepts involved in the creation of a simple reflection of the organizational chart of your enterprise. The greatest of these is the replication of information among domains and domain controllers.

Microsoft has taken the networking considerations out of the directory design as much as possible by creating the boundaries of sites. Sites allow the administrator to make directory traffic decisions based on network traffic design. If you've been exposed to other directory designs, you'll realize that this is not the case. Domain and container objects are often controlled by the fact that replication can only be split along container lines; this is not a requirement within Microsoft's implementation of Active Directory.

CHAPTER 11

User Account Creation and Management

IN THIS CHAPTER

- User Accounts *278*
- Hard Drive Space *298*
- Groups *300*

This chapter covers the process of creating, managing, and grouping user accounts. The nuts and bolts of user management includes simply getting the user base created and assigned to the groups that need to have access to resources.

Even though this chapter starts with the creation of users, don't let this influence the way you approach security. As mentioned in the previous chapter, it's better to first create the group for the resource and then assign the users. However, it's good to know what will inhabit the groups you create. Understand the animal, build the cage, get the animal.

User accounts are a great deal more powerful than they have been in the past, and Windows 2000 makes great leaps in this area. Think of this chapter as getting your wings in the management of user accounts. If you're already familiar with the creation of user accounts but instead are looking for insight into the creation and use of policies, you should move on to the next chapter.

User Accounts

The user account is where the rubber hits the road in the network operating system world. The user account is the key component used by people to attach to network resources, and it's the controlling point for every permission and policy. With Windows 2000, the weight that these accounts has grown immensely.

Before we begin creating these accounts, we have some ground rules and basic information to cover. The creation of groups and the addition of users to them is mentioned here, but this topic will be covered in depth later. If you're a novice administrator, it's probably best that you read this section before you create any accounts. This will help you avoid creating accounts that you then have to delete.

Predefined or Built-in Users

When Windows 2000 is installed, some user accounts are created immediately. These accounts are used by the system and by the initial users of the system in order to gain some access. Just like a new house that has an initial set of keys, these accounts can be changed or used. However, it makes good common sense to change these keys as soon as possible.

The accounts that exist depend on the services that are installed; however, on every server, the Guest and Administrator accounts will be created. These accounts are created to grant basic services. Opening the "Active Directory for Users and Groups" console and then opening 'Users' (see Figure 11.1) you can see the initial accounts.

FIGURE 11.1
A listing of default user and group accounts.

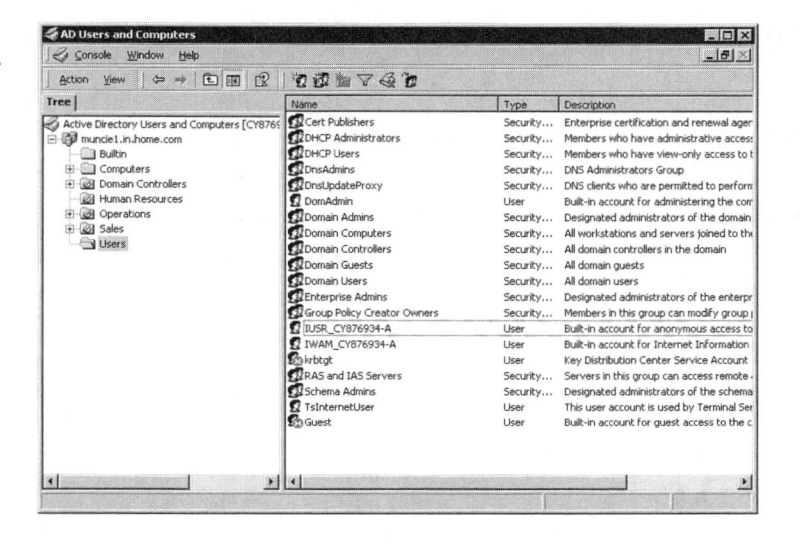

The Guest account is disabled upon installation, which is a wonderful state for it to remain in. The purpose of this account is to give visitors to your system access to public utilities such as printers or even common shares. The greatest value of the account is that it belongs to the Domain Users group; therefore, any common service offered to Domain Users or Everyone will be provided to the Guest account.

You should note that the Guest and Administrator accounts cannot be deleted. However, they can be renamed.

Among the first tasks you should perform is to rename the built-in accounts. Educated invaders of the system will attempt to log in using the built-in accounts. If they can gain access to an account name, they have half the battle won. If that account is the Administrator account, the war is over.

The Administrator account is created to allow for the initial login and the creation/start of services. Even if the server is not installed into a domain, the Administrator account will be created. The account will not be created in the domain each time a new server or DC is installed. When you're installing a new server into an existing domain, the system will ask for an administrator name and password in order to create the computer account in the domain.

Rename the Administrator account as soon as possible. If you're in a large corporate environment, you have no way of knowing who's watching or how long they may have been in the system before you rename the accounts.

The next step in this process is to create a second account that's a member of the Domain Admins and Administrator groups. By creating this account, a back door is in place in the event that something should render the Administrator account unusable. More often than not, the Administrator account has had the password changed to something that can't be remembered. This effectively locks the castle and throws the keys in the mote.

A good practice for system administrators to get into involves not logging in as the administrator account for your daily interaction with the domain. In other words, don't use an account that is all-powerful when you are working on a word processing document or spreadsheet. It is important to remember that when you are logged in as the administrator account or an equivalent account you are able to manipulate files without control. It can be like being Gulliver in the land of the Lilliputians. Something could get stepped on. Worse yet, if you walk away from the station and don't log out you have left the security system open.

All too often the owner or officers of a business have no idea what the administrator password is to the domain that contains their data. It makes sense to allow the owners or officers of the company have a record of these passwords in case of an employee leaving or being unavailable for any reason. This allows the officers to get back to their system.

Naming and Password Conventions

When creating user accounts, you should take the task seriously. Giving Robert Smith the user name "Bobby" and a password of "angela" (his wife's name) is no big deal in a small office setting. However, if you're installing 30 or more accounts, it begins to be a little tougher to come up with cute combinations. That's the least of your worries with the scenario just mentioned. Security in that environment is virtually broken when it's created.

Windows 2000 allows for the creation and use of any method desired for the naming of users and groups. However, it also allows for the control of the user's ability to use a certain password—passwords are case sensitive.

Here are several basic rules that, if followed, will make your system far more secure:

- Use passwords of at least eight characters, make them alphanumeric, and use capital letters when possible. This avoids the use of utilities that simply throw the dictionary at the server once a user name is discovered. By following this rule, you can increase the average time it takes to break a user's password from 1 hour to 4 days. Some examples are 492je429 and 7382jnne.

- Whenever possible, create and assign passwords to the users. This allows for tight control of what's used as a password. It does, however, create a paper trail of passwords that can be found.
- Set a password policy that causes users to be prompted to change their passwords every 30 to 90 days (see Figure 11.2).

FIGURE 11.2
The Password Policy page.

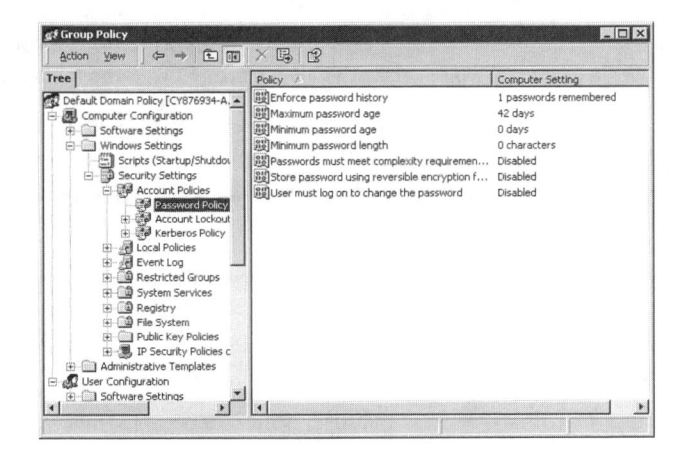

- Enforce the uniqueness of a password in the password policy. In other words, don't let a user use his or her cat's name as the password. Also, don't allow the user to switch between the name of his or her cat, dog, then cat again. The password should be unique over several iterations.

To enforce these password rules you will need to make changes to the Group Policies (specifically the Password Policy) for the users that you want to control. The Default Domain Policy would enforce the rule for all accounts by default. For more detailed information on Group Policies look to Chapter 12, "Intellimirror and User Control."

> **Tip**
>
> Keep in mind that for every blockage thrown in the way of the users, you'll receive more support calls. It can be a tough balance to strike when deciding whether you should be strict or you should make the policy more usable. The period of time when everyone's password expires can be your busiest time of the month.

User names are not nearly as worrisome as passwords. The toughest decision to make about user names is what convention to use and whether it makes sense for the company to have user names that map out to the users' real names in some way. There are two schools of thought on this.

The conventional thinking in today's Internet-influenced world is to give user names that are a variation on the users' actual given names. The reasoning is that it makes the identification of the users easier and makes it possible to incorporate the user names into other services—the user names can match the email names or SQL Server accounts.

The problem with this train of thought has already been mentioned. If a hacker knows that the user accounts in your company follow a convention of first initial then last name (Robert Newton = rnewton), he or she has half of what's needed to break into your system.

The opposite of this approach is to use user account numbers or alphanumeric names, similar to the passwords mentioned earlier. The thinking is the same as with passwords—the more complex and unnatural the user name and password, the less likely a hacker is to crack the combination.

The problem caused by this system is that users often don't remember the combinations themselves. This causes one of two problems to occur:

- Users begin to call for support more often because they either can't remember or mistype the combination.
- Users write down and sometimes post their user names and/or passwords. This is something that's seen and hated by many administrators.

> **Note**
>
> Keep in mind that the most common security breach to the corporate network is a user who logs into the system and then walks away from the system. Enforce the use of screen savers with password protection enabled to start after no more than 15 minutes of inactivity. This can also be enforced through the use of Group Policies.

User Creation

When you're creating users, the toughest part of the task is the decision of where to create them. You'll have to make that decision by reviewing the items you learned in the previous chapters. However, the basic decision is which container to put the user accounts in—domain or organizational unit?

Once these decisions have been made, you'll have several choices given to you during the creation process that you should record or already know before arriving at the creation screen (see Figure 11.3):

FIGURE 11.3
The user-creation screen.

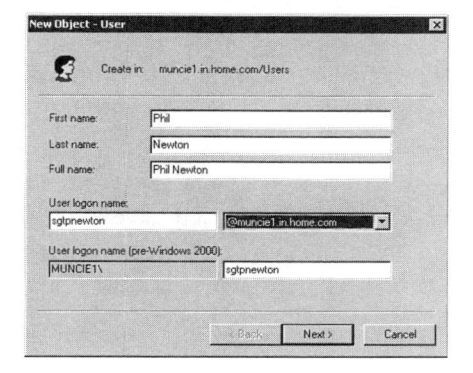

- *First Name.* The first name of the user.
- *Last Name.* The last name of the user.
- *Full Name.* This option will automatically be filled in as you add the first and last names. However, it can be edited for use as another field.
- *User Logon Name.* The name used at the logon interface.
- *User Logon Name (pre–Windows 2000).* If the user logon name that you choose is contains over 20 characters, this entry will automatically create a compatible account for legacy machines. It can be edited to make a more palatable name.

> **Note**
> Not all the name entries must be filled in. At least the First Name or Last Name entry must be filled in, and the User Logon Name entry must be filled in.

- *UPN Suffix.* If during the installation of the domain, UPN suffixes were created to give certain users unique domain log ins, this is the field that will allow the use of these UPN suffixes. (See Chapter 9, "Directory and Access Concepts Brief," for more detail on UPN suffixes.)
- *Password.* The password that this user will be asked for when he or she attempts to log on to the domain.

- *User Must Change Password at Next Logon.* This is a choice that will allow for the creation of an initial password that's only for the first logon. At that point, the user will be prompted to change his or her password.
- *User Cannot Change Password.* The user will not be allowed to change his or her password.
- *Password Never Expires.* If this choice is made, the password policies will be ignored. This is often a good choice for system accounts or for backup administrator accounts that are seldom used.
- *Account Is Disabled.* This renders the account unusable but does not delete it. If an account needs to be deleted, it's often best to just disable it for a short period of time. This allows the account to be reactivated (possibly even renamed) in case a need arises for a user with the same security requirements. (This is good for temp employees, interns, and even shaky resignations.)

Console Creation

Users are created in the Active Directory User and Computer console. If you're looking to create a large number of users, it may be best to refer to the following section, "Net User Batch Creation." However, if you have specific users to create and you need greater control, the console method is best.

To create a user, follow these steps:

1. Open the Active Directory User and Computer console and select the container object that you would like to contain the user object. This can be the user container for the domain or any organizational units that have been created.
2. Right-click the container object and select New, User.
3. Enter the user name data from the information defined previously and click Next.
4. Enter the password choices from the information defined previously and click Next.
5. Click Finished.

Net User Batch Creation

If your task is to create 100 users, the idea of using the console to create them one at time is a painful one. Luckily, there's an answer to this problem: Net User. The `net` command is a multipurpose command-line utility that allows for the fast and efficient use of network resources. The `net user` command combination allows for the display of information about, creation of, or deletion of user accounts.

The syntax for the command is as follows:

```
net user [username [password ¦ *] [options]] [/domain]
net user username {password ¦ *} /add [options] [/domain]
net user username [/delete] [/domain]
```

Each of the pieces of the command allow you to gain specific information or cause a desired effect. It's a bit like using the CD, RD, and MD commands in the modification of directories in the file structure. Here's a list of parameters that will cause different effects:

- *No parameters used.* Used without parameters, `net user` displays a list of the user accounts on the computer.
- *username.* Specifies the name of the user account to add, delete, modify, or view. The name of the user account can have as many as 20 characters.
- *password.* Assigns or changes a password for the user's account. A password must satisfy the minimum length set with the /minpwlen option of the `net accounts` command. It can have as many as 14 characters.
- **.* Produces a prompt for the password. The password is not displayed when you type it at a password prompt.
- */domain.* Performs the operation on the primary domain controller of the computer's primary domain. This parameter applies only to Windows 2000 Professional computers that are members of a Windows 2000 Server domain. By default, Windows 2000 Server computers perform operations on the primary domain controller.
- */add.* Adds a user account to the user accounts database.
- */delete.* Removes a user account from the user accounts database.

When the command indicates that it allows for options, it's looking for specific ways in which the data can be manipulated (for example, the option to add a comment to the newly created user account). To add one of these options, simply substitute the option for the *option* line in the syntax lines. Here's a list of the options:

- */active:{no ¦ yes}.* Enables or disables the user account. If the user account is not active, the user cannot access resources on the computer. The default is yes (active).
- */comment:"text".* Provides a descriptive comment about the user's account. This comment can contain as many as 48 characters. You must enclose the text in quotation marks.

- /countrycode:*nnn*. Uses the operating system's country/region codes to implement the specified language files for a user's help and error messages. A value of 0 signifies the default country/region code.

- /expires:{*date* | never}. Causes the user account to expire if *date* is set and does not ever set a time limit on the user account. Expiration dates can be in *mm/dd/yy*, *dd/mm/yy*, or *mmm,dd,yy* format, depending on the country/region code. Note that the account expires at the beginning of the date specified. Months can be numbers, spelled out, or abbreviated with three letters. Years can be two or four numbers. Use commas or slashes to separate parts of the date (no spaces allowed). If *yy* is omitted, the next occurrence of the date (according to your computer's date and time) is assumed.

- /fullname:"*name*". Specifies a user's full name rather than a user name. You must enclose the name in quotation marks.

- /homedir:*path*. Sets the path for the user's home directory. The path must exist.

- /passwordchg:{yes | no}. Specifies whether a user can change his or her password. The default is yes.

- /passwordreq:{yes | no}. Specifies whether a user account must have a password. The default is yes.

- /profilepath:[*path*]. Sets a path for the user's logon profile. This path points to a Registry profile.

- /scriptpath:*path*. Sets a path for the user's logon script. The *path* value cannot be an absolute path; *path* is relative to %*systemroot*%\System32\Repl\Import\Scripts.

- /times:{*times* | all}. Specifies the times the user is allowed to use the computer. The *times* value is expressed as *day*[-*day*][,*day*[-*day*]] ,*time*[-*time*] [,*time*[-*time*]], limited to one-hour time increments. Days can be spelled out or abbreviated (M, T, W, Th, F, Sa, and Su). Hours can be 12- or 24-hour notation. For 12-hour notation, use AM/PM, or A.M./P.M. The value all means a user can always log on. A null value (blank) means a user can never log on. Separate day and time with commas and units of day and time with semicolons (for example, M,4AM-5PM;T,1PM-3PM). Do not use spaces when designating times.

- /usercomment:"*text*". Specifies that an administrator can add or change the user comment for the account. You must enclose the text in quotation marks.

- /workstations:{*computername*[,...] | *}. Lists as many as eight workstations from which a user can log on to the network. Separate multiple entries in the list with commas. If /workstations has no list or if the list is *, the user can log on from any computer.

The best use of this command line in the creation of multiple users is to create one example of your desired account creation and replicate it in a batch file. It cannot be stressed enough how important it is that you experiment with this method a time or two before populating the batch file with a large group of users. Finding and cleaning up a hundred wrong user names can be nasty.

Here's an example of a batch file that could be used:

```
net user bnewton 23nre32 /add /comment:"Traveling Coordinator"
net user jschmo 12nrw53 /add /comment:"Traveling Builder"
net user snewton 2v2bt3 /add /comment:"Traveling Builder"
net user jmeyer hrn598 /add /comment:"Traveling Secretary"
```

This batch file would create users, their passwords, and comments the accounts. This is a small example, but you can see that an exported list of users from most any text source could be easily converted to an import for Windows 2000.

User Environment Needs

A great deal of the user experience on the network up to this point has been geared toward making the user unaware that the network even exists. With the advent of the Internet, users have become a little more tolerant of networks existing.

The concept of *user environment* refers to the way users interact with their PCs and the network. This has changed a great deal in the last two to three years. The meaning of *user environment* has grown from only providing and controlling access to resources to now involving the control of what the user sees (see Figure 11.4) as available.

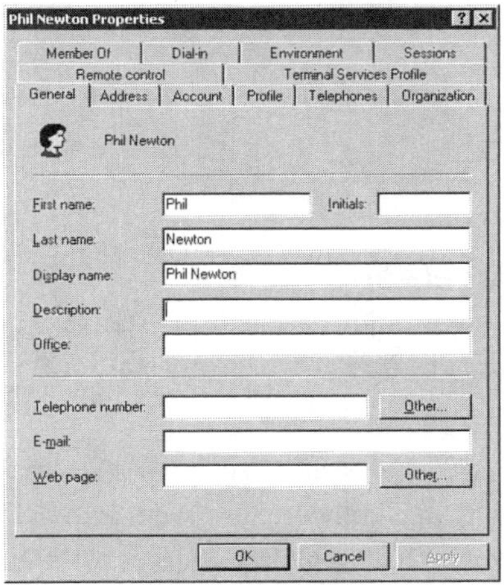

FIGURE 11.4
A user properties screen.

Controlling the OS Environment

The tools offered in the User Properties for Operating System Environment control include the user login scripts, login access, and time control.

Logon Scripts

The use of logon scripts in some operating systems can be difficult to learn and to use. In the Windows world, good old batch files have always been used (the command-line batch file has been around for about two decades). This interface has been used since the early beginnings of DOS and is still used in many other operating systems.

A *batch file* is a text file that contains command-line instructions to be carried out in succession. For example, if I want to run an application, echo a statement about the application, and then remove the result of the application all in one command, I might create a batch file.

Logon scripts are batch files used to set a user in an environment that make the network more usable. Users might be given a drive mapping through the batch file, have a printer port captured, or even have an application delivered.

In Windows 2000, some of these choices have expanded. The greatest difference is that scripts can now be assigned to container objects. In Windows NT, there's no concept of a *group logon script*. There's also a new member of the script family called a *logoff script*.

Scripts are executed in the following order, along with all other Windows 2000 user policy and profile data:

- Site
- Domain
- Organizational Unit
- Child organizational unit (etc.)
- User

Creation and Directory Placement

Scripts can be executed from any network file share, but the standard placement is the \WINNT\System32\Repl\Import\Scripts directory. The reason for this placement is the possible replication of these scripts.

Unless a specific path is mentioned, the clients of a Windows 2000 (or NT) server receive their login scripts from the DC that authenticates them into the network. Therefore, in a network that has several DCs, it makes since to maintain a current set of logon scripts on all the servers. Unless you want to copy the scripts to every server every time they're edited, it's necessary to set up file replication.

The only requirement for a script is that it be accessible from a share. Therefore, the file could be put in the \\mcp\scripts share and be picked equally as well.

As mentioned, a script is usually a batch (.bat) file. To give you some idea what a typical script might look like, here's a sample script:

```
***Beginning of script
echo off
cls
echo Welcome to the Macmillan server cluster.
echo The following resource mappings have been made.
net use f: /home
net use g: \\mcp\data
net use m: \\mcp\apps
net use lpt2 \\mcp\laser_3floor
echo Have a great day!
pause
```

This script would initially turn off the screen echo of commands. It would then clear the screen and welcome the user. It would also tell the user what environment variables were being made. Finally, it would tell the user to have a great day. The pause would force the user to see what was on the screen before moving on and wondering why everything sent to LPT2 is printing over on the Hewlett Packard 4MV.

A script is created in one of two places: the group policy object for a container or group, or the user object. This, of course, depends on which choice best applies.

First, here are some words of caution about where to create scripts. Creating scripts is a bit like granting permissions. It makes more sense to create group policy scripts whenever possible. Every action that can be taken against a group is easier to manage than trying to re-create the same action multiple times for numerous single users. Even actions needed for a single user should be handled in a group policy script whenever possible. Seldom do individual user needs remain individual for long.

To assign a group policy script, begin in the Active Directory Users and Computers console. Then follow these steps:

1. Right-click the container or group object that contains the group policy and choose Properties.
2. Choose the Group Policy tab and double-click the group policy to be modified. (If no group policy exists, it must be created before a script can be assigned. See Chapter 12 for creation instruction.)
3. Click the plus sign (+) beside User Configuration and then click Windows Settings.
4. Select Scripts (Logon/Logoff) and then double-click the Logon or Logoff icon and click Add.

5. In the Add a Script dialog box, set the options you want to use and then click OK:
   - *Script Name*. Type the path to the script or click Browse to search for the script file in the Netlogon share of the domain controller.
   - *Script Parameters*. Type any parameters you want to use as you would type them on the command line. For example, if your script included parameters called //logo (display banner) and //I (interactive mode), you would type the following:

     //logo //I

6. In the Logon or Logoff Properties page, specify any options you want to use:
   - *Logon Scripts For*. Lists all scripts currently assigned to the selected Group Policy object. If you assign multiple scripts, the scripts are processed according to the order in which you specify them. To move a script up in the list, click it and then click Up. To move it down, click Down.
   - *Add*. Opens the Add a Script dialog box, where you can specify any additional scripts to use.
   - *Edit*. Opens the Edit Script dialog box, where you can modify script information such as a name and parameters.
   - *Remove*. Removes the selected script from the Logon Scripts list.
   - *Show Files*. Used to view the script files stored in the selected Group Policy object.
7. Click OK.

To assign an individual user script, begin in the Active Directory Users and Computers console and then follow these steps:

1. Right-click the user object and choose Properties.
2. Choose the Profile tab.
3. Type the name and path (if not the default location on the DCs) of the login script file.
4. Click OK.

The net *Command*

An administrator who understands command-line directives and batch files is well ahead when it comes to understanding scripts. However, he or she might not understand the 'NET' commands. The NET command is mentioned here for the second time in this chapter because it controls far more than user creation and deletion. In fact, the NET command is used for network resources without the GUI interface and for that reason makes a good tool for scripts or any other batch process.

To use the net command, you simply need to type **net** and then follow it with the proper variable. The subject of creating users was covered a few sections back, but here are some command-line variables that can be valuable in a script.

The list below is a partial list of the variables that can be used along with the NET command to create an environment change or retrieve information. To use the variables simply type NET followed by the command. See the example below each variable to help with how to use it. The syntax would follow this pattern:

NET (variable) (parameter(s))

- USE. Connects a computer to or disconnects a computer from a shared resource or displays information about computer connections. The command also controls persistent net connections. Here are examples:
  ```
  net use [devicename ¦ *] [\\computername\sharename[\volume]] [password ¦
  *]] [/user:[domainname\]username] [[/delete] ¦ [/persistent:{yes ¦ no}]]
  net use devicename [/home[password ¦ *]] [/delete:{yes ¦ no}]
  net use [/persistent:{yes ¦ no}]
  ```
  Here's a list of some USE parameters:
  - *None*. Used without parameters, net use retrieves a list of network connections.
  - *devicename*. Assigns a name to connect to the resource or specifies the device to be disconnected. There are two kinds of device names: disk drives (D: through Z:) and printers (LPT1: through LPT3:). Type an asterisk instead of a specific device name to assign the next available device name.
  - \\servername. Specifies the name of the server and the shared resource. If *computername* contains blank characters, you must enclose the entire computer name from the double backslash (\\) to the end of the computer name in quotation marks (""). The computer name may be from 1 to 15 characters long.
  - \volume. Specifies a NetWare volume on the server. You must have Client Service for NetWare (Windows 2000 Professional) or Gateway Service for NetWare (Windows 2000 Server) installed and running to connect to NetWare servers.
  - *password*. Specifies the password needed to access the shared resource.
  - *. Produces a prompt for the password. The password is not displayed when you type it at the password prompt.
  - /user. Specifies a different user name with which the connection is made.
  - *domainname*. Specifies another domain. For example, net use d:\\server\share /user:admin\mariel connects the user identifier

"mariel" as if the connection were made from the admin domain. If `domainname` is omitted, the current logged on domain is used.

- *username*. Specifies the user name with which to log on.
- `/delete`. Cancels the specified network connection. If the user specifies the connection with an asterisk, all network connections are canceled.
- `/home`. Connects a user to the home directory.
- `/persistent`. Controls the use of persistent network connections. The default is the setting used last. Device free connections are not persistent.
- `Yes`. Saves all connections as they are made, and restores them at next logon.
- `No`. Does not save the connection being made or subsequent connections. Existing connections are restored at the next logon. Use the `/delete` switch to remove persistent connections.

- GROUP. Adds, displays, or modifies global groups on Windows 2000 Server domains. This command is available for use only on Windows 2000 Server domain controllers. Here are examples:
```
net group [groupname [/comment:"text"]] [/domain]
net group groupname {/add [/comment:"text"] ¦ /delete} [/domain]
net group groupname username[ ...] {/add ¦ /delete} [/domain]
```

- HELP. Provides a list of network commands and topics you can get help with. It also provides help with a specific command or topic. The available `net` commands are also listed in the Commands window of the Command Reference, under *N*. Click Windows 2000 Command Reference in the Related Topics list. Here are some examples:
```
net help [command]
net command {/help ¦ /?}
```

- SEND. Sends messages to other users, computers, or messaging names on the network. The Messenger service must be running to receive messages. Here's an example:
```
net send {name ¦ * ¦ /domain[:name] ¦ /users} message
```

- TIME. Synchronizes the computer's clock with that of another computer or domain. Used without the `/set` option, it displays the time for another computer or domain. Here's an example:
```
net time [\\computername ¦ /domain[:name]] [/set]
```

- USER. Covered previously in the "Net User Batch Creation" section.
- VIEW. Displays a list of domains, a list of computers, or the resources being shared by the specified computer. Here are examples:
```
net view [\\computername ¦ /domain[:domainname]]
net view /network:nw [\\computername]
```

Home Directory

A user's home directory is a bit like a base of operations for each user in the domain. It's not an absolute necessity, but it helps the user feel like he or she has a spot in the domain for his or her individual data.

The home directory of a user is determined by a setting in the Profile tab of the user object properties (see Figure 11.5). Before a home directory can be created, the shared directory where the home directory will be created must exist. The administrator must have access permissions to write to it, and the share must be available. Finally, a directory with the user's logon name should not exist.

FIGURE 11.5
The Profile tab of the user object.

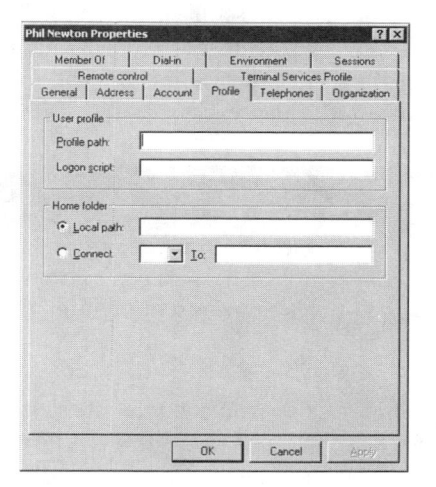

To assign a user home directory on a domain server, follow these steps from the Active Directory Users and Computers console:

1. Double-click the user object and choose the Profile tab.
2. Choose the Connect radio button.
3. Using the drop-down list, select a drive letter that will be available to the user when logged on. Press Tab.
4. Type in the UNC address of the directory that will be considered the user directory for this user and then click OK.

> **Note**
>
> The variable %USERNAME% can be used in the UNC for the creation of the home directory (\\servername\%username%). This allows you to create user templates that do not specify a user name but do create home directories when a new user is copied.

Profile and Profile Path

The profile of a particular user controls the behavior of the workstation operating system for that individual. A profile controls the software settings, background image, screen saver, manual drive mappings, and many other items. Each time a user of Windows 2000, NT, and even 95/98 (when configured) logs in to a new system, that system records the username and begins a profile for that user's preferences.

> **Tip**
>
> Profile settings can be overridden by policies that prohibit or promote certain behaviors (for example, you might want to assign users a custom Start menu.) These settings are complicated, and they're covered in Chapter 12.

A domain administrator can use profiles as a domain control tool as well as a desktop control tool at the local workstation. The concept is to create a profile that matches the environment that you want all users to be presented with and then make that profile roam with the users wherever they log on. For that reason this type of profile is called a "roaming" profile. Roaming profiles can even be made mandatory. This makes the profile unchangeable and maintains a consistent and enforceable profile. For more information on these profiles you should look to Chapter 12.

Logon Access and Account Options

Beyond the ability to control the environment that the user is placed in is the ability to control access to the domain. Through the use of the user object properties (refer to Figure 11.4), you can control user access and behavior, ranging from the times access is allowed to the specific computers that can be logged on to.

Logon Hours

Time restrictions are found on the Account tab under the Logon Hours button (see Figure 11.7). Once this button is click, you can select a group of hours by clicking and dragging and then choosing Logon Permitted or Logon Denied. Once the choice is made, the account will be denied or allowed on that basis.

FIGURE 11.7
The Logon Hours screen.

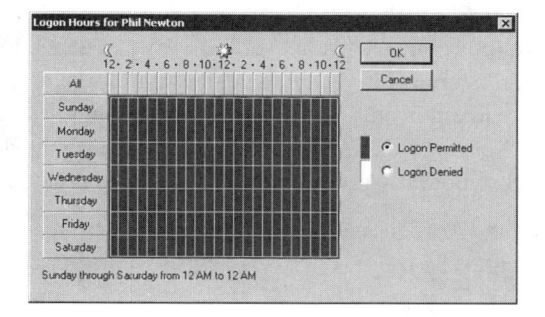

RAS Access

In order to control the dial-in access of the users on an individual basis, you can use the Dial-in tab (see Figure 11.8). This tab allows you to simply allow or stop dial-in access by clicking either the Allow Access or Deny Access radio button.

FIGURE 11.8
The Dial-in screen in User Properties.

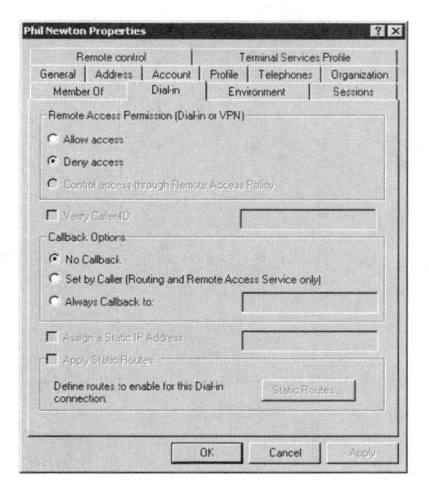

The other option available is a security feature called *callback*. The concept is that when users dial in for network access, the server will call them back in order to establish that they are who they say they are or that they're in a preapproved dial-in site.

The most secure of the options is to have the system always call back the account at a designated callback number. However, it is possible to allow the user to request a callback number. The idea behind this second choice is that the user has to know that the callback option is required. But the option also offers the flexibility of allowing a user to travel to your competitors and download your client list. That is self defeating.

Computer Restrictions

It's also possible to secure the computer that a user is allowed to attach to the domain through. If, for example, an intern is hired and he or she should stay at his or her PC, you can tell the domain that the intern is only allowed to log on through his or her PC. This is a "social butterfly" killer. Keeping in mind that the biggest threat to the domain is an unattended logged on workstation. It's very important to kill social butterflies.

This change is made from the Account tab in the User Properties screen by clicking the Log On To button (see Figure 11.9).

FIGURE 11.9
The "log on to" screen in User Properties.

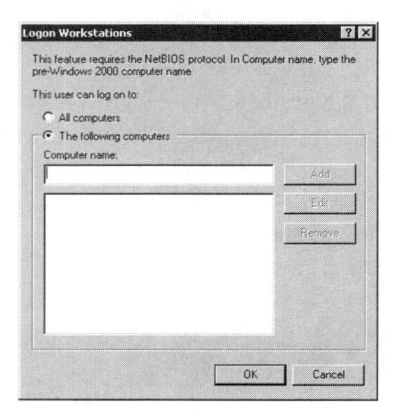

Once inside the option page, simply type in the name of the computer the user is allowed to log on to and click the Add button.

Account Options

Many features of the Account tab allow for the control of accounts that are in various states of being.

Under the Account Options section of this screen are options allowing or disallowing a great many things. The following list should help you to understand the options and why to use them:

- *User Must Change Password at Next Logon.* The user will be prompted for a new password the first time he or she logs on. The idea is to allow you to issue passwords on the first day of a roll out but to allow the user to control the password from that day forward. This increases the security to allow individual responsibility for those tasks done by a user within his or her account.

- *User Cannot Change Password.* If you are maintaining all passwords, this option must be set to prevent the users from setting there own passwords.
- *Password Never Expires.* This is the mark of a company with little need for security or of a lazy administrator. It does cut down on those password-change-request calls, though.
- *Save Password As Encrypted Clear Text.* This option is used for Macintosh clients who use the Apple client to log on. If Macintosh clients will be using the Chooser to log on, this option must be set to On.
- *Account Is Disabled.* This option is used to temporarily disable the account. When an account is to be deleted, this can be a better option in the short haul. For example, suppose your boss says to delete Ted's account because he's being dismissed. If, however, you see Ted leaving the boss's office smiling and shaking hands, you may have saved yourself some time by not having to re-create Ted's account. If, however, Ted is indeed let go, you can then go ahead and delete his account.
- *Smart Card Is Required for Interactive Logon.* Smart Cards allow the system to use a password that will be different each time a user logs in. This option allows the administrator to only allow this type of logon.
- *Account Is Trusted for Delegation.* This account is allowed to assign other accounts permissions within the directory.
- *Account Is Sensitive and Cannot Be Delegated.* This designates that the account can't be given a delegated portion of the directory. You might be asking, "Why not just not delegate the permission?" This option is present to help in a large environment to allow one administrator to alert another of an issue preventing the user from being allowed.
- *Use DES Encryption Types for This Account.* This option is for when you need to use the Data Encryption Standard (DES). DES supports multiple levels of encryption.
- *Do Not Require Kerberos Preauthentication.* Select this option if the account uses another implementation of Kerberos. Not all implementations or deployments of Kerberos use this feature. The Key Distribution Center (KDC) uses ticket-granting tickets (TGTs) for obtaining network authentication in a domain. The time in which the KDC issues a TGT is important to Kerberos. Windows 2000 uses other mechanisms to synchronize time, so using the Kerberos Preauthentication option works well.

The final option on the Account tab is simply an option for giving an account an expiration date. This option is meant for allowing the creation of temporary accounts. It's a good tool for accounts for temporary employees and interns who may be forgotten in the shuffle of administrative tasks.

The use of the tool is as simple as it appears. By simply choosing the End Of radio button and selecting a date, you can provide expiration date. At the end of that day, the user will no longer be able to log on to the system.

Hard Drive Space

The Windows NOS has for some time needed control of the rampant use of hard drive space by the user population. In Windows 2000, this has come to be. The control is implemented from a disk volume and is not a total user limit (as is the case with NetWare). However, it does offer much greater control.

To create a disk limit, you must first enable limits on the volume. To do this, you simple need to follow these steps from the server:

1. Right-click the hard drive icon and choose Properties.
2. Choose the Quota tab (see Figure 11.10).

FIGURE 11.10
The Quota tab in Disk Properties.

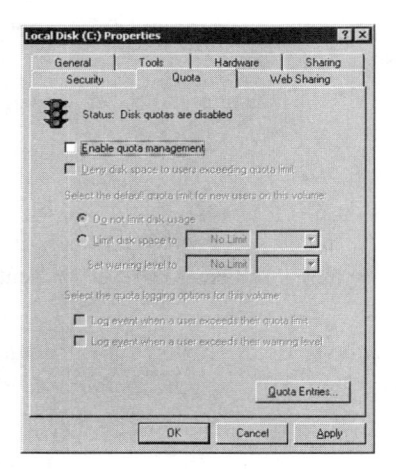

3. Choose the Enable Quota Management check box.
4. Click OK.

Once this is done, you can then begin setting up disk quotas.

This first screen has many settings that are available to you even before you begin to actually set disk limits. These are instructions to the system regarding how to handle the violation of limits if they occur:

- *Deny Disk Space to Users Exceeding Quota Limit.* This option stops users from writing to the disk if they exceed the limit allowed them. Although it may be inferred that the user would be stopped by you merely setting the limit, this is not the case. Setting a limit actually just gives a threshold for setting off a series of reactions, one of which is to stop a user from writing to a disk when the limit is exceeded.
- *Select the Default Quota Limit for New Users on This Volume.* The choices here allow you to be sure that users are given a limit in the event one is not set for them manually.
- *Select the Quota Logging Options for This Volume.* The options chosen here will allow you to be proactive about the fact that a user has exceeded the limit. It also allows you to warn users reaching the end of their disk space.

To create a new quota, begin by opening the Quota tab in Drive Properties. Then follow these steps:

1. Click the Quota Entries button.
2. Choose Quota, New Quota Entry from the menu bar.
3. From the Look In drop-down menu, choose the domain that contains the user or group that's to be limited.
4. Click the user or group entry and then click Add. Repeat this process until all the user/group objects desired are in the box below. Click OK.
5. From the Quota Entry screen now showing, select Limit Disk Space To and enter the "limit" and "warning" numbers (see Figure 11.11).
6. Click OK and close the Quota Entries console.

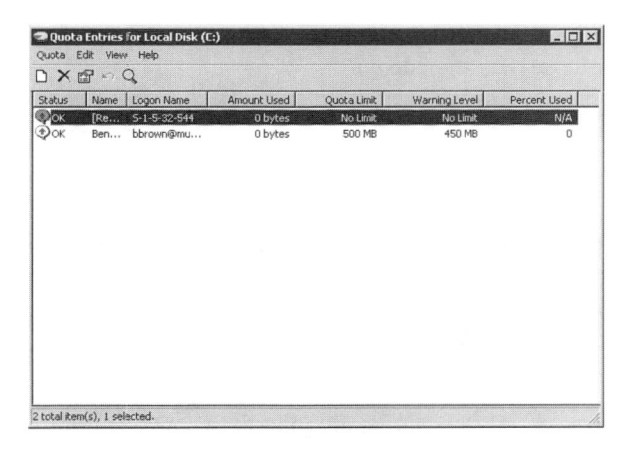

FIGURE 11.11
The quota entry screen.

Groups

Groups of users in Windows 2000 involve the grouping of user accounts for the purpose of controlling more than one user at a time. Like herding cattle, it gets a little tough to take them across the range one at a time. Putting users in groups should be your first inclination for how to manage users.

Group Scope

Group scope refers to the place in the Directory that the group is to be used and the membership the users may have. There are three basic group scopes: Domain Local, Global, and Universal.

The choice of group scope is going to be controlled by the mode of operation that the security system is currently in. If the domain controllers are in Mixed mode, only Domain Local and Global groups are available. This is because of the limitations of Windows NT to allow nesting of groups. In Native mode, all three choices will exist and groups will be able have member groups that have groups as members (nested groups).

Domain Local Groups

Domain Local groups are the Active Directory (Windows 2000) incarnation of the old Local Group from Windows NT. In fact, when Local Groups are migrated from Windows NT, they become Domain Local groups.

Domain Local groups are used to manage resources on the local domain. This is a bit different from the old Local Groups, but the concepts are a bit alike. A Domain Local group can have the following types of members:

- Global Groups
- Universal Groups (Native mode only)
- User accounts
- Other Domain Local Groups (Native mode only)
- Any mixture of allowed groups from this list (mode dependant)

The concept is to use Domain Local groups to contain the accounts and groups that will make use of a particular resource. If the group is created for the resource and the accounts are added to the group, it becomes very easy to add users to the resource and to know which users or groups have access to the resource by simply checking the resource's group.

If you need to add the entire Accounting group to those having permissions to attach to a drive share \\servername\accounting, it's easiest to create the group MATHSTUFF and assign the Accounting global group to the resource's group. If there are odd things happening to the share, it's simpler to check who had access and make changes.

Global Groups

A Global group is not the same in Windows 2000 and Windows NT. However, it is used in much the same way. A group with Global scope is a group that's used for the daily addition of users and other groups to groups for later assignment to resources.

The important words here are *users* and *daily*. What separates a Global group from a Universal group is that the Global group will not replicate across domain lines, nor can it have members from across domains. A global group can have the following types of members:

- Global Groups from their own domain (Native mode only)
- User accounts
- Any mixture of allowed groups from this list (mode dependant)

When Global group membership is changed or the permissions that are associated with a Global group are changed, they're only replicated inside the domain.

For that reason, it makes since to assign users to Global groups and then the Global groups to the Domain Local groups that control the resources. This is because the Global group will not replicate the domain information across the entire tree. The problem in Mixed mode is that you cannot assign global groups from other domains to the global groups that have been created to "herd" the entire collection of users.

Universal Groups

Groups of Universal scope are only available to be used once the domain has been changed to Native mode. Universal groups in their proper form can be thought of as the cross-domain glue for groups that must cross domains. It can be tempting to think of Universal Groups as 'magic' local groups that cross domain lines. Because they can have membership that includes:

- Global groups from any domain
- Groups with universal scope
- User accounts

The best idea though is to create these Universal groups, assign the Global groups to them, and finally assign the Universal groups to the Domain Local group in charge of the resource.

Group Model Breakdown

Local Domain administrators can add users to the global groups. Because these global groups are members of the universal groups that have permissions to the resource, the members have the permissions they need.

Cross-domain replication traffic only involves the names of the global groups that belong to the Universal groups. Because that membership change is very seldom needed, replication can be almost nonexistent. Intradomain replication traffic will occur, but that's limited to the population of the domain.

Domain Local groups allow the local administrator to be very aware of the groups and user accounts that have access to the resources. They also allow for removal and addition with much less trouble than attempting to find each group that has been assigned permissions.

Creating a New Group

To create a group, follow these steps:

1. Open Active Directory User and Computer and select the container object that you would like to contain the group object. This can be the user container for the domain or any organizational units that have been created.
2. Right-click the container object and select New, Group.
3. Enter the group name and press Tab.
4. Enter the group name for pre-Windows 2000 clients (if needed) and press Tab.
5. Enter the group scope type and press Tab.
6. Click OK.

Predefined (Default) Groups

Just like user accounts, the Windows 2000 operating system has predefined groups that are available when a computer and/or domain are created. These groups are created as a kind of public utility of group functions. The basic functions of the Domain are all a part of these groups.

Some of the groups are part of Windows 2000 in any form (workgroup or domain), and others are only created when a domain is created.

There are also groups known as *Implicit Groups* that are only available to the assigned permissions. They are not able to have memberships added and will not be seen in Active Directory Users and Groups. This is because they are created by the operating system for the operating systems use only. As you see the group descriptions it becomes more clear why the groups are needed.

Here's the list of these predefined groups:

- *Account Operators (Domain Only)*. Members can manipulate the user and group accounts within the local machine. This does not include domain users and groups.
- *Administrators (Domain and Local)*. Members are able to complete all tasks on the local machine. Members of this group on the domain controller are considered to be members of the group for all computers in the domain.
- *Backup Operators (Domain and Local)*. Members are allowed to back up and restore the files and folders of the system. They are also allowed to shut down the system.
- *Creator Owner (Implicit)*. The creator of an object (file, print job, folder, and so on) is automatically made a member of the CREATOR OWNER group for that object. This gives the user all permissions to the object.
- *Everyone (Implicit)*. A built-in and transparent group that includes all authenticated users on the system. The distinction between Users and Everyone is that Users implies domain membership, whereas Everyone includes local and/or domain users. Be careful to remember that this includes anonymous users over the IIS server.
- *Guests (Domain and Local)*. Members are allowed access to all the resources to which the groups Everyone and Users have access to.
- *Interactive (Implicit)*. Any user logged on to a system locally.
- *Network (Implicit)*. Any user logged in over the network. Be careful to remember that this includes anonymous users over the IIS server.
- *Print Operators (Domain Only)*. Members are allowed to control all printer functions, including print job control, sharing printers, deleting printers, and stopping/staring/deleting print jobs.
- *Replicator (Domain and Local)*. Members are allowed to create, delete, and manage directory replication jobs.
- *Server Operators (Domain Only)*. Members are effectively administrators minus the powers of account administrators. The server operators can control, create, and delete both file and print shares. They back up and restore files from the server, but they cannot grant permissions to perform any of these tasks.
- *Users (Domain and Local)*. This group is local to the machine on which it exists. Its members are any user account that's created on the machine and the domain group "Domain Users" if the machine is made a member of a domain.
- *Domain Admins (Domain Only)*. A Global group that's assigned to the Domain Local group "Administrators" of each machine in the domain. Members have all

the powers associated with that group and the ability to control everything in the domain, tree, and trusting forest.

- *Domain Computers (Domain Only)*. All computer accounts created in the domain are automatically assigned membership in this group. This is a utility group for making changes and assigning properties to all domain computer accounts.
- *Domain Controllers (Domain Only)*. All domain controllers created in the domain are automatically assigned membership in this group. This is a utility group for making changes and assigning properties to all domain controllers accounts.
- *Domain Guests (Domain Only)*. A Global group that's assigned to the Domain Local group "Guests" of each machine in the domain. The members have all the powers associated with that membership.
- *Domain Users (Domain Only)*. A Global group that's assigned to the Domain Local group "Users" of each machine in the domain. The members have all the powers associated with that membership.
- *Enterprise Admins (Domain Only)*. A Global group that's assigned to the Domain Local group "Administrators" of each machine in the domain. The members have all the powers associated with that group and the ability to control everything in the domain, tree, and trusting forest.
- *Group Policy Admins (Domain Only)*. Members have permission to edit and review group policies within the domain.
- *Schema Admins (Domain Only)*. Members are allowed to edit the information in the schema. That Active Directory schema can be used to store information and can also be edited to create more resources within the schema.
- *System (Implicit)*. Operations performed by the operating system.

Summary

The creation of users and groups can make for some tempting mistakes. You need to keep in mind that the rules of group creation and user addition are meant to make your life easier in the long run.

Try to always create the Domain Local group for the resource first and then add the Global groups to that group. Adding users to Global groups will give you the freedom to operate within the domain without having to chase the individual users to find out who has permissions to what resource.

Use Universal groups as a way of maintaining a cross-domain continuity and not a universal container for user and computer accounts. Universal groups help reduce traffic; they're not meant to be a panacea.

CHAPTER 12

Intellimirror and User Control

IN THIS CHAPTER

- Nuts and Bolts of Intellimirror   *306*
- Control Concepts   *307*
- Managing Group Policies   *315*
- Windows Installer   *320*
- Remote Installation Services   *325*

Controlling what the user is presented with when he or she sits down at the PC is one of the best ways to control the user. To this point in the process, the idea of controlling the user has been to create the user account and to control the environment by creating scripts and managing permissions. The next idea is more subtle from a user standpoint but can be more useful. This chapter will cover the use of policies, profiles, and direct software installation and maintenance to control the items that appear in front of the user everyday. All these items culminate in a group of technologies called *Intellimirror*.

Intellimirror might be thought of as the eventuality of ZAW (Zero Admin Windows). The idea behind ZAW and Intellimirror is leveraging of Windows networking tools to allow administrators to set up a less administration-intensive network. The difference between ZAW and Intellimirror is that the Intellimirror technologies are an integral part of the operating system. Intellimirror is not a Band-Aid slapped on the operating system to make it function. However, like ZAW, Intellimirror leverages tools that exist in the operating system.

Intellimirror is not a utility you can run or an application that's new in Windows 2000. ZAW actually includes an interface of its own. Intellimirror is more a technology direction that's taken by Windows 2000. When an administrator refers to Intellimirror technology, he or she is really referring to set of technologies that when put together allow for more powerful user management and convenience—that is, the "intelligent mirroring" of the user environment across workstations, LANs, and even WANs.

Nuts and Bolts of Intellimirror

Intellimirror is the culmination of four separate technology groups that you'll learn about throughout this chapter:

- *User Settings Management*. The use of policies has allowed the administrator to control the environment of the user and to leverage Active Directory to make these policies available across the network.

- *User Data Management*. By using the Active Directory controls of user profile settings, logon scripts, and group policies, the administrator can ensure that the user has a uniform storage structure. This platform also provides for the replication and backup of user data.

- *Software Installation and Maintenance*. By associating software installation with the power of the Active Directory, you can make sure that an application exists when the user attaches to the domain and that it's in proper working order.

Control Concepts

Controlling what appears to the user in his or her daily computing experience involves the purposes of both security and comfort.

From a security standpoint, the house on the block that's least likely to be broken into is the house that can't be seen. A good person that never sees the payroll folder on the server will most likely remain a good person. A hacker who can't see the My Network Places icon is less likely to look at the list of servers. If they can't see the front door, they're less likely to be tempted to break in.

The second most secure house on the block is the one that's very well lit. If the thief can't get in the house without everyone knowing, it becomes far less tempting. If users are given a specific look and feel, it becomes more obvious to them that they're in a location they shouldn't be in.

One example of this is a school system that has a different background and icons set for teachers' and administrators' logons than those maintained for students. If a teacher walks by a lab and sees a student with the background for a teacher on his screen (say, a bright blue background), that student is busted. The student is also less likely to spend a great deal of time in front of a screen that screams, "I'm breaking in."

For most users on the network, the idea of being exposed to an environment that allows them to destroy someone else's data or accidentally see confidential data is a nightmare. The computer scares them enough as it is. The idea is to place these users in an environment that contains only their tools and data. By putting users in an environment that allows them to make use of all the resources presented to them without the fear of accidents or retribution is perfect.

If you place a group of order-entry personnel in front of machines that only allow them to find products, place the orders, and communicate with their superiors, they're happy to use them. If you place those same employees in front of machines have a Web browser, Solitaire, and a spreadsheet program installed, then you shouldn't be upset when they surf, play cards, and calculate bills during slow times. Given the tools to waste time, humans waste time.

Windows 2000, like Windows NT before it, offers tools for controlling the user environment and make some of these choices more available and usable. These tools are user profiles and policies. The use of profiles and policies has grown to be a part of the Active Directory.

In Windows NT, it was necessary to create policies in a separate utility and place those policies in a central location to be picked up. They were also very difficult to coordinate with users and groups. As you'll see, policies have become much easier to incorporate, and profiles are no longer difficult.

Profiles

The use of profiles has existed since the beginning of Windows NT and Windows 95. The idea of a profile involves the individual behavior of the operating system based on the user who is logged in. When the first user logs on to Window 95, he or she is asked whether the system should keep his or her individual settings separate. The user is also asked for a password; then a profile is created. The profile keeps a record of the user's printer choices, application settings, desktop settings, and so on. When that user logs in again, he or she receives the same settings.

Windows 2000 continues this tradition. When a user logs on to a Windows 2000 computer, the user's settings are kept on the system in a profile. The profile that's initially created is present on the local computer. It contains the Start menu, the Desktop icons, the Programs menu, and all the individual application settings for the user. As an example, an administrator may notice that each time a new user logs on to the system, Internet Explorer will again create personal settings and ask how to attach to the Internet. This change is an attribute of the profile changing as the users change.

Users become very used to profiles over time. As a matter of fact, they begin to feel as if the computer is theirs based on the items controlled by the profile. A screen saver, a picture of the person's fishing trip, and the Favorites list in Internet Explorer all make it seem to the user as though the computer is his or her own. When that user sits at another desk, though, and none of those items are there, it becomes hard for him or her to use the system nearly as well.

There are two kinds of profiles in general—local and roaming—and many variations based on them. For now, though, let's just concentrate on the local and roaming profiles.

Local

A local profile is a profile that's presented by the local machine when the user logs in. Unless the administrator makes a special effort to create another type of profile, this is the only type of profile that will exist. The profile is called *local* because it exist on the local computer and it's created on a computer-by-computer basis. Therefore, the settings that have been made on one computer will not be found on another.

In Windows 2000, local profiles are stored in the `Documents and Settings\USERNAME` directory on the operating system drive (see Figure 12.1). By looking in this location, you can see and change the items in the Start menu and desktop.

FIGURE 12.1
Profiles in the Documents and Settings directory.

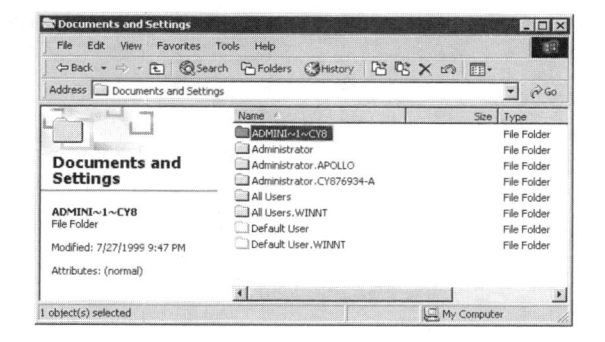

Noticed that there are profiles for All Users and All Users.WINNT. These profiles are for common profile items and allow the system to not have to reproduce common items over and over again.

> **Note**
>
> For Window NT administrators, note that the location of Local Profiles has changed. This is one the few changes in the profile scheme, but it could cause you a long night of looking. Some technical references for Windows 2000 were still listing the old location up until release.

Roaming

Roaming profiles are a way of making the profile settings available from any workstation the user attaches to. A roaming profile does not have to be created from a controlled account. It can be created from any account that has a profile listed in the My Computer, User Profiles tab. Therefore, if the travel district manager wants to see his desktop when ever he arrives at a new office, his profile can be copied directly from his machine.

The item that often gets lost in the shuffle of roaming profiles is that the resources to make a setting work must be available in the new location. For example, if the company logo is listed as the background of choice in the profile but it doesn't exist on the machine the user logs onto, the logo will not be the background. It's just that simple. If the network share that's used for mapping a drive is not available, the drive will not be mapped.

The rough part of the "missing resource" problem is when it causes an application to fail or misbehave. Roaming profiles work best in an environment with systems containing identical software. Identical hardware would be ideal but is not necessary.

If you are looking for more information on the creation of and use of roaming profiles look to Chapter 11, "User Account Creation and Management."

Mandatory

A roaming profile can be used by many different users to give a uniform presentation. This type of profile is generally set so that none of the users can make a permanent change to the profile. This is called a *mandatory profile*. In this scenario, users are not allowed to change their personal settings or they may change them only to find they have returned to the default when they log on again tomorrow.

Making profiles mandatory stops users from changing a shared profile to something that's not usable by the other users. The fact that John may want the Cattle Disease page as his home page does not mean that you want everyone exposed to a page about the effects of Mad Cow disease. The idea is to keep everything generic and palatable to the whole crew.

To make a roaming profile a mandatory profile is a very simple change. The process involves nothing more then renaming the NTUSER.DAT file in the profile directory to NTUSER.MAN. The file is found in different locations based on the way that you choose to implement the users profile settings. But the default location of the file is in the NETLOGON share of the DOMAIN controller. This can be done easily at the command prompt with the following command:

```
ren ntuser.dat ntuser.man
```

Press Enter. The next time the user logs in, the profile will be mandatory.

A mandatory profile can be created at the local level as well. The process is the same. However, this is not nearly as common.

Windows NT

Windows NT 4.0 profiles function in the same way as Windows 2000 profiles. You can create a Windows 2000 profile and share it to a common location and expect that NT and 2000 users will be able to share it.

Windows 95/98

Windows 95/98 roaming profiles are not compatible with Windows 2000 profiles and they're not stored in the same way. Here are some things you must do on the network in order to maintain roaming profiles for a Windows 95/98 system:

- Enable user profiles in 95/98. This setting is found in the Password Properties screen (see Figure 12.3).

FIGURE 12.2
The profile-enabling page in Windows 95.

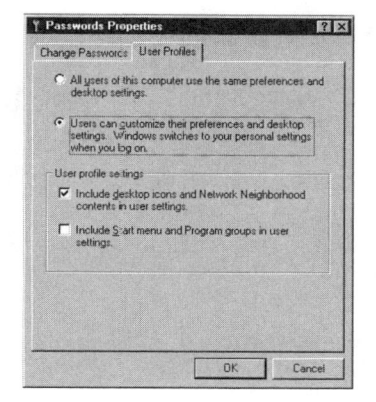

- Maintain user home directories for the users.
- Use a 32-bit network client (Microsoft Client for Microsoft Networks).
- Set Windows 95/98 to log in to the domain.

User profiles in Windows 95/98 are created in folders under the PROFILES directory in the Windows operating system directory (\Windows\Profiles). If profiles have been enabled, there will be a directory found here for every user who has logged in to the machine.

Unlike Windows 2000 and NT, Windows 9*x*'s process for creating a roaming profile does not involve a special copying process, but it does involve a specific folder and file location. Windows 9*x* requires that the profile be contained in the "home" directory of the user. For this reason, a user with a roaming profile must have a home directory.

A mandatory profile is also possible for these users, but again a home directory is required. To create a mandatory profile, simply create a roaming profile and rename the USER.DAT file as USER.MAN in every directory to which it's copied. For more information on this process see Chapter 11.

Policies: A General Introduction

A user or group policy takes control of the Windows 2000 Registry and controls the behavior of the operating system based on a selection of choices. The greatest difference between a policy and profile is the ability to choose from a menu of items those items that should be controlled and the ability to assign those changes to individuals or to groups.

A comparison that might help you understand a Windows 2000 policy is to think of a breaker switch. If every feature of the operating system were to have a switch on a master breaker box, that box would be comparable to policies. Policies allow an administrator to turn on a feature, turn it off, or to leave it unchanged. Just like the old breaker box, the Windows NT and Window 95/98 policies stay put until they are switched back.

In Figure 12.4, the policies for the user and the desktop can be seen. In the example, the administrator can turn off the ability to see the My Network Places icon on the desktop. It doesn't take a great imagination to understand the usefulness of hiding the resources that appear under this icon—it only takes a few days of being an administrator of a large network or a group of high school students.

FIGURE 12.3
Policy restriction examples.

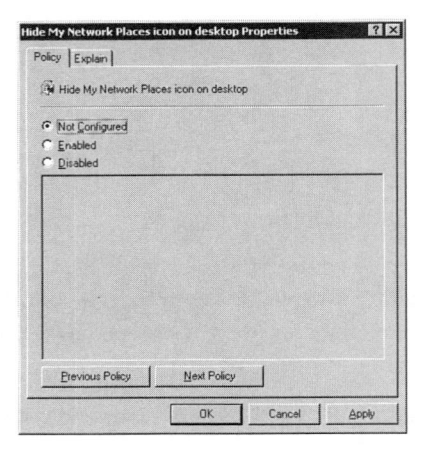

Windows 2000 policies are now group based on container objects. User groups are actually only used in group policies for security and filtering of the group policies (which will be seen later). The *group* in *group policies* is the container object Site, Domain, or Organizational Unit (OU). Just as login scripts are part of the group policy, the group policy is part of the container object.

Within each container object are created items called Group Policy Objects (GPOs). All group policy objects start out the same—as blank sheets that contain no changes for the Registry. The objects gain usefulness when they're edited to make changes to the Registry of the Windows 2000 PC the container comes in contact with. A container may have numerous group policy objects, and all of them are changed independent of the others. This can cause confusion and as you read on you will see how to avoid this.

Policies are enforced in a hierarchical and cumulative fashion based on the directory structure, meaning that the user will receive all the policies from each container that they are part of and that those policies will be enforced in the order of Site, Domain, Organizational Unit, and then any child organizational units the user may be a part of.

This is the order that has already been established for logon scripts. This is because logon scripts are part of the policy structure.

> **Note**
>
> If Windows NT policies still exist in the NETLOGON share (the NTCONFIG.POL file), those policies will be enforced before the Site, Domain, or OU polices. If the local computer that the user is logging in to happens to have local computer policies established, those policies will also supercede the Site, Domain, and OU (see *Windows 2000 Professional Unleashed*, Sams Publishing). Although it's unlikely that these scenarios would occur, it can help you when troubleshooting to know that you can have a modified policy-enforcement chain of NTCONFIG.POL, Local Computer Policy, Site, Domain, and OU.

Not only do policies have an enforcement order from container to container but also each container can have multiple group policies (see Figure 12.5). These policy objects are enforced based on the order you leave them in. By selecting the policy that should be enforced first and clicking the Up button, you can arrange the policies to be enacted in the proper order. In the "Creating and Assigning" section that follows you can see how this is done.

The important note here is that being first is not best in this process. If the Site policy contains a switch to set the background of all user computers to a picture of the company's three founding fathers, and the Organizational Unit policy sets the background to the three stooges, then the users will be seeing Moe, Larry, and Curly (not the founding fathers). This applies to any ordering of the policies, even within the container. For that reason, it makes more since to make the most valuable settings the last settings enforced.

This also brings some credence to the concept of creating a policy separate from the containers and adding the policy to the container. By separating the processes, you can create a uniform policy and then add it at the lower-level containers to ensure enforcement.

There are two basic types of policies:

- *User Configuration*. Settings that are specific to users in the container interfacing with any computer
- *Computer Configuration*. Settings that pertain to the computer logged in to, regardless of the user

FIGURE 12.4
Several group policies in a container.

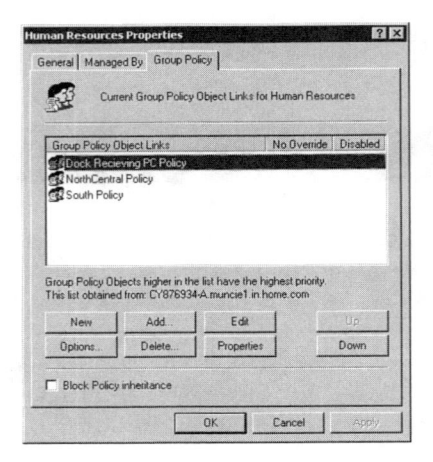

An example of the difference between these two types of policies would be the setting for Windows Settings, then Scripts. Both User Configuration and Computer Configuration portions of the policy have Scripts sections. Computers, however, do not have logon and logoff scripts because they do not log on and log off. They, instead, have startup and shutdown scripts. Computer Startup and Shutdown scripts are created so the domain can cause certain commands to occur on the systems in container at Startup and/or Shutdown. This might be particularly true in a site (see Chapter 10, "Active Directory Design").

Computer policies are also enforced synchronously, meaning that they are enforced before the user is given a chance to log on. This can be changed to asynchronous, but this is probably a greater hassle than it's worth. The collisions with other policies become hard to predict and hard to correct. Any policy that's preferred to enforce after logon should simply be assigned to the User Configuration portion of the policy. If the decision is made to make this change, the change is made in Group Policy console, *Policyname*, Computer Configuration, Administrative Templates, System, Group Policy.

Finally, policies are continually refreshed at the workstation to allow for periodic changes throughout the day and to correct user errors without administrator intervention. This refresh is done by default every one and a half hours. This refresh rate should be left alone if at all possible because it's going to require that the system communicate over the network, thus creating traffic. But the refresh is within the site and should not effect WAN traffic.

It can be useful to set the time shorter, though, if the user group is particularly likely to need a reset. If the decision is made to make this change, the change is made in Group Policy console, *Policyname*, Computer or User Configuration, Administrative Templates, System, Group Policy, Group Policy Interval for Users or Computers.

Managing Group Policies

The administration of group policy objects can be done from three different locations: the Group Policy snap-in (Microsoft Management Console - MMC), the Active Directory Users and Groups console, or the AD Sites and Services console. The reason for this is the intertwining of the Active Directory sites and containers and the group policies themselves. Many administrators will find it to be more intuitive to simply go with the container and to create and manage the policy in one place. However, others may find that it makes more sense to manage policy objects from the MMC to give a central location for policy management.

Although there's no right or wrong answer, it's good to keep in mind that each time the group policy is interfaced with, a group policy object will have to be referenced. It's conceivable that an MMC could be saved to contain all the group policies but that a container already exists in the form of the Active Directory Users and Groups console. By simply right-clicking a container object and choosing Properties, you'll be presented with the Group Policy tab.

> **Note**
>
> One possible answer to the issue of how to best arrive at the group policies is to create a Group Policy OU. Once the OU is created, simply create all group policies in that OU and add the policies to the other containers from that OU. Then, from this one OU, you can edit all the group policy changes.

Creating and Assigning

The creation of a group policy object (GPO) can only be done from within the properties of a container object. This might be another reason why it makes a great deal of sense to manage group policies from the Active Directory Users and Groups console or the AD Sites and Services console. This is because they must be a part of a site or container object from birth.

The creation of a GPO is a fairly simple process:

1. Open the Active Directory Users and Groups console or the AD Sites and Services console and find the site or container object that the GPO will be created in. Then right-click it.
2. Choose Properties.
3. Select the Group Policy tab and click New (see Figure 12.6).

FIGURE 12.5
New group policy object creation.

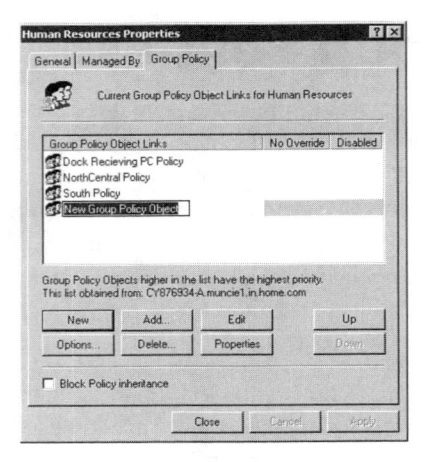

4. A blank policy object appears, with an area in which you can type its new name. Type in a descriptive name and press Enter.

The policy is now created and ready to be edited to include the desired Registry settings. If the group policy that's desired for the container has already been created for another container, that policy can be added to this container with only a slight revision of the directions. Follow these steps:

1. Open the Active Directory Users and Groups console or the AD Sites and Services console and find the site or container object that the GPO will be created in. Then right-click it.

2. Choose Properties and then click Add (see Figure 12.7).

FIGURE 12.6
Adding a group policy object from another container.

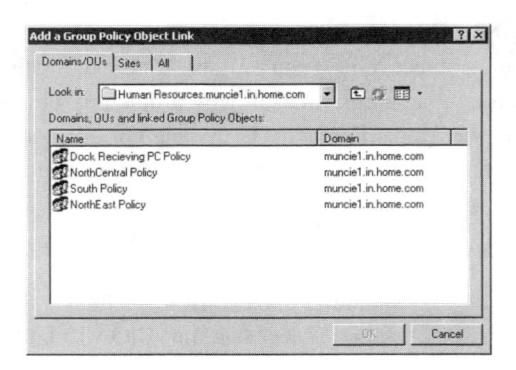

3. Using the Explorer interface, find the GPO that you would like to apply. Click the policy and then click OK.

Once a policy is added to a container object, the job of assigning behavior and control settings is now ready to be done.

Keep in mind that editing a GPO in one location makes changes to that GPO in all locations. This is not to say that a change in one GPO makes the same change in all GPOs. Remember that a GPO that has been used in several different container objects is still the same GPO in all the container object that it exists in. This is the reason for the possible creation of a group policy OU object. A group policy OU allows you to be more aware of the changes being made and their possible universal impact.

GPO editing is a very complex item to understand, but it's not a complex thing to do. Anyone can put paint on a canvas, but not everyone will have an end result that others would understand and enjoy.

First things first, though. You have to start by picking up a paint brush, and here is where the brushes are kept. Follow these steps to edit a group policy:

1. Open the Active Directory Users and Groups console or the AD Sites and Services console and find the site or container object that the GPO will be created in. Then right-click it.
2. Choose Properties.
3. Select the Group Policy tab and click Edit (see Figure 12.8).

FIGURE 12.7
The edit screen for a group policy object.

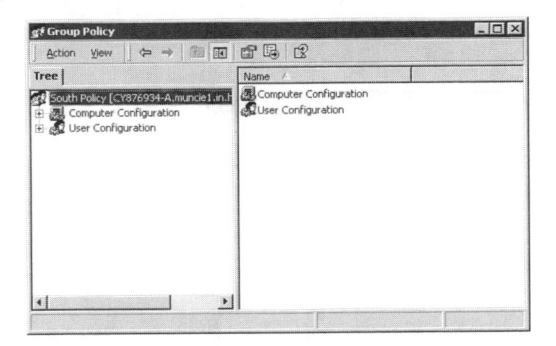

4. Using the Explorer interface, find the user or computer policy setting that you would like to modify.

Not only can you decide who has a GPO assigned to the group but you can also filter the way that a user or group makes use of the policy. Group policies are filtered in the same way that a file is assign security rights. Groups of users or even individual users can have changes made to a policy that allow them to receive special treatment in regards to what is enforced by the policy.

Some users or groups within a container may be best suited for existing in the container but not suited for one of the container's group policies. It then makes sense to filter that group from the scope of those affected by the policy—in just the same way that it might make sense for a user to be assigned to a group but specifically denied the permission to a specific folder or printer.

Here's how to filter the use of a GPO on the basis of a security group or user name:

1. Open the Active Directory Users and Groups console or the AD Sites and Services console.
2. Right-click the container object that contains the GPO to be edited and then choose Properties.
3. Choose the Group Policy tab.
4. Select the GPO and choose the Properties button. Select the Security tab (see Figure 12.9).
5. Click the Add button and select the group or user to be changed and then click Add.
6. Repeat the previous step until all the desired users and groups appear in the bottom portion of the screen. Click OK.
7. With the newly added name selected, modify the selections in the Permission pane to match the desired combination (see Table 12.1 for GPO permissions). Click OK and Close.

FIGURE 12.8
The group policy permissions page.

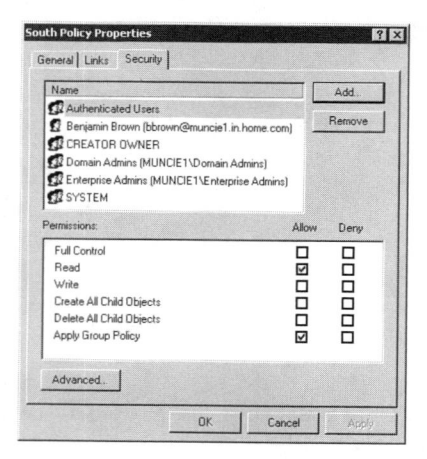

The permissions found on step seven above will specify the control you are implementing. The table below is a specific list of the permissions that can be granted:

TABLE 12.1 GPO Permissions

Permission	Use
Full Control	A user with this permission has been given the complete control equaled by being given all of the other permissions.
Read	Explicitly allow or deny the ability to read and use the GPO.
Write	Explicitly allow or deny permission to write changes to the policy.
Create All Child Objects	Explicitly allow or deny permission to create objects within the policy and edit those details.
Delete All Child Objects	Explicitly allow or deny permission to delete objects within the policy.
Apply Group Policy	Explicitly allow or deny permission to this group or user to use this policy. Without being a member of the GPO's container, the user or group is considered to be implicitly denied.

Policy Modification

Making modifications to a particular setting is the part of the GPO process that becomes much more complex. Each setting has its own interface based on the type of setting that it is. Some settings are the on/off type of switch described in the opening portion of this section. Other settings are very complex, giving you the ability to offer custom attributes to the operating system and custom control. Although the operating system is not "open" by any means, these controls offer companies the ability to put both custom controls and behaviors in place, just like the host systems of old.

Group Policy Administrators

Just as with any other portion of Active Directory, it's possible to allow users and groups other than the administrator to maintain and even create group policies. The control of group policies can range from creating and assigning policies to simply reading the policies.

The assignment of these permissions is done within the properties of the container itself or in the Security tab of the group policy. Depending on the approach, there are several different ways to assign permissions.

If the desired result is that the user only be able to edit existing group policies, the easiest way of creating those permissions is to make the user a member of a group that's delegated control over group policies in the Delegate Control Wizard. This wizard allows for the delegation of control over many parts of a container object. However, in the example that follows, only group policy control is given. Follow these steps:

1. In the Active Directory Users and Computers snap-in, right-click the Organizational Unit that you want to delegate and select Delegate Control.
2. In the Delegate Control Wizard, click Next to go past the introduction page.
3. Click Next. You'll be prompted for the names of the users and groups to which you want to delegate control.
4. Select a previously defined group (or user) and then click Next.
5. In the list of predefined tasks, select Manage Group Policy links and then click Next. Click Finish.

If the desired result is to make the user or group capable of creating group policy objects and to administer them, there are a couple of ways to accomplish this. The first is to just make them a member of the Group Policy Creator Owners group for the Domain. This method is the shotgun blast method.

To be more particular about the rights that are assigned, you can get very granular by using the property page for the group policy object (refer to Figure 12.9). By clicking Add and selecting a group, you can then add individual capabilities for the policy (refer Table 12.1 and the instructions for adding permissions).

By setting individual rights to the group policy, you maintain the most control over who has the right to create and manage objects in the group policy. However, this also creates a less predictable result. For example, if the idea of adding an administrator who can just open group policies for review sounds good, beware. A group that's given only the read permission to read a group policy cannot even open the group policy snap-in.

Windows Installer

Windows Installer is an application delivery and removal feature that allows you to maintain a consistent application landscape across the Domain. The concept behind Windows Installer has existed as part of various software products external to the Windows operating system for quite some time. Products such as Microsoft Systems Management Server (SMS) have allowed software delivery for several years. Windows 2000 delivers it within the operating system itself.

The idea is to use package files (.msi) that tell the system what software pieces should exist on the system. By comparing those packages to what does or does not exist, you can add or subtract on demand. This is all made possible by the fact that the operating system is controlled by a Registry that leaves a bread crumb trail for every application or operating system change that's made. By detecting these changes, a utility is able to search through the changes needed to maintain applications.

The basic system is enhanced by the fact that Windows Installer provides the management system to control the addition, subtraction, and modification of these applications. The applications can be housed at numerous file sites and through many different policies to provide a robust and fault-tolerant system.

There many possible applications for this tool that might not jump to mind, at first. Here are some very powerful uses:

- Restoring a corrupted application on a system that has become useless or completely restoring all applications on the system
- Performing mass upgrades to new versions of applications or application suites
- Preventing users from setting application variables that make their systems unusable
- Building new workstations by simply logging onto the domain
- Cleanly removing applications that have been removed from the company standards list
- Strictly enforcing software standards
- Control of the number of installs of a particular application for licensing reasons

Windows Installer actually is a combination of `WININSTALL`, the `MSIEXEC` program for package usage at the client, and Active Directory as a delivery mechanism.

WinInstaller

The first step in the process of software distribution is to create the application packages (`.msi` files) that will be delivered. The process of creating a package can seem laborious if done right, but it's well worth the hassle.

The great hassle is that it should be done on a PC that can at least temporarily be dedicated to the task of creating these packages. The reason for this dedication is because of the fact that packages will be delivered to many different machines and there will be many different application sets on those machines. It's best if the machine that the packages are created on contains no confusing information to be added to those machines.

The best bet for this dedicated machine is what Microsoft calls a "clean machine." A clean machine is a machine that contains only the necessary items to install and run the application:

- The Windows operating system (2000, NT, 95/98, or 3.x)
- The bare minimum drivers needed to run the hardware associated with the application

This PC would ideally have the application installed and be returned to a "clean" state every time a new package is created. It might be thought of as a whiteboard that's to be written on over and over again. If permanent changes are written to it, those changes may show up in the package that's delivered to the other users. Drive mappings, printer settings, or any software settings may affect the package.

> **Tip**
>
> Using a disk-imaging package such as Norton Ghost to return the "clean machine" to its original state can make the process much easier. If an image is created of the machine in its clean state and stored on CD-ROM, once a package is created, the machine can be immediately returned to it's original state. Otherwise, the time-consuming process of reinstalling the OS, drivers, and any patches will have to be done after each package is created.

Once the clean machine is installed and ready, the next step is to create "before" and "after" snapshots. Snapshots are created before and after the installation for the reasons covered in the opening of the section, mainly because the operating system of a target machine will be modified with the changes noted during the install by comparing these snapshots.

To enable your machine to create these snapshots you must first install the Veritas WinInstaller application. The process of installing this application is very simple. A limited version is included with the Windows 2000 Server CD. It is kept in the VALUEADD \MGMT\WINSTLE folder. To install simply double click the SWIADMLE.MSI file. Because it is a WinInstaller package itself, you have officially run your first WinInstaller installation.

To create a "before" snapshot, follow these steps:

1. Run the file DISCOZ.EXE (see figure 12.10) from Network Neighborhood or Windows Explorer or use the Start menu's Run command.

> **Note**
>
> Do not map a drive to the WinINSTALL share in order to perform the install. This mapping might show as part of the created package or cause a failure in the package.

FIGURE 12.9
The DISCOZ.EXE *screen.*

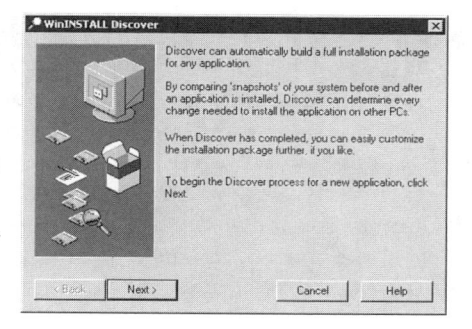

2. On the Overview screen, click Next.
3. Type the name of the application as you want it to appear. This type of entry is called an *application package name*. Create a meaningful name, using up to 40 characters.
4. Type the name of a Windows Installer file (without the extension) in which to store information about the installation. The path will be where you want to place files to the copy tree structure.
5. Select a button to indicate whether the application is designed to run for Windows 2000, Windows 3.*x*, Windows 95, or Windows NT.
6. Click Next to move to the next dialog box.
7. From the drop-down list box, click the drive where you want Discover to store its temporary work files. The Discover process, which "discovers" the changes on the system, will run much faster if this is a local drive. This drive should have a minimum of 250MB of space available. Discover will store the files in a temporary working directory (\\DISCOVER.wrk) and will delete them after the process is completed.
8. Click Next to move to the next dialog box.
9. Click at least one drive from the Available Drives list. You must choose one, but it's important to select only the drive(s) where actual application files will be installed.
10. The Windows directory will automatically be scanned for the WIN.INI and System.INI changes, even if it's not located on the selected drive.
11. Click Add or Add All.
12. Click Next to bring up the next dialog box.
13. Click the Files & Wildcard Entries button if you want to specify files or groups of files to exclude. Any files that you select in this way will go into the Directories & Files to Exclude list.

> **Note**
>
> The Discover utility uses exception files to determine what areas of the system configuration to exclude from a scan. These exception files are based on default exception files stored in the `WinINSTALL Administration Program` directory. The default 32-bit Registry exception file is named `Reg.xcp`, and the 16-bit file is named `Reg16.xcp`. The default exception file is named `Files.xcp`. The working exception files, `Reg.xcp` or `Reg16.xcp` and `xFiles.xcp` (where x is the name of each file system exception drive), are created during the Discover process and are stored in the Discover working directory.
>
> On this screen, you can exclude directories and/or files on any drive. Limiting scans in this manner can cut down on processing time. It's highly recommended that you use the default exclusions. In most cases, the defaults provide the most reliable scan of the computer. You cannot exclude the `Windows` directory or subdirectories under the `Windows` directory.

14. Click one or more directories from the All Directories list.
15. Click Add or Add All.
16. Click Next.

Now that the discover process has occurred and the application has been installed you will need to create an "after" snapshot. This allows the program to understand the changes that have taken place. To create an "after" snapshot, follow these steps:

1. From the reference PC on which you'll be creating the distribution package, run the `DISCOZ.EXE` program.
2. Click Next. Discover takes the after snapshot.

Once the packages are created, you can modify them. This is done through Package Editor. Package Editor allows you to edit items such as the INI files, the components, and the attributes of the applications to be installed.

This is not advisable unless you are very familiar with the application and the results of the feature change. It's best to make the desired changes on the clean machine and experiment there and then create the "after" snapshot.

Once the "after" snapshot is created, the package is available for distribution.

Delivery of the Package

MSI package delivery is facilitated through the use of Active Directory in the Windows 2000 world. Software delivery is part of both the User and Computer configurations in the Group Policy snap-in console. This makes is possible to distribute software based on Site, Domain, and Organizational Unit.

Before a package can be delivered, the client workstation must be able to interpret the package. This interpretation requires that the workstation be running the program MSIEXEC.EXE. The MSIEXEC.EXE program is a component of the Windows Installer. The MSIEXEC.EXE program uses a dynamic link library (MSI.DLL) to read the package files (.msi) and incorporate command–line options.

When Windows Installer is installed on a computer, the file-association capabilities of the operating system are modified to recognize the MSI file type. When a file having the MSI file extension is double–clicked, the operating system associates the MSI file with the Windows Installer and runs the MSIEXEC.EXE application. Because of this, packages can also be delivered through the use of logon scripts.

Delivering packages through the use the Active Directory is done within the properties of the group policy object (See Figure 12.11). Once the Group Policy snap-in is open for the selected GPO, follow these directions to add a software package:

1. Click the plus sign beside either the Computer Configuration or the User Configuration section, depending on the package you want to install.
2. Click the plus sign beside Software Settings and select Software Installation.
3. Right-click Software Settings and choose New, Package.

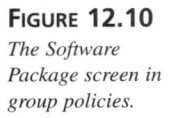

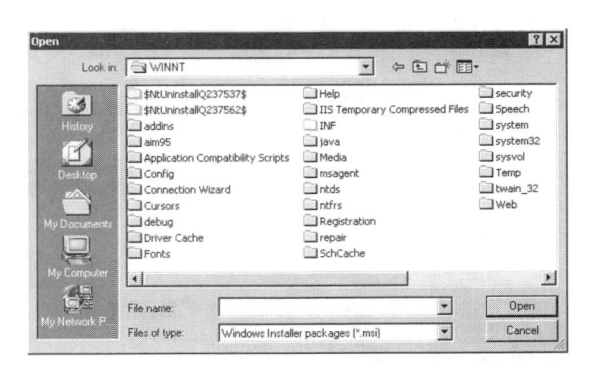

FIGURE 12.10
The Software Package screen in group policies.

4. Browse to find the MSI file that was created earlier and choose Open.

Remote Installation Services

The Remote Installation Service is a service that allows for the installation of the operating system on new PCs or on machines that the you would like to have the operating system reinstalled. This installation is done through the use of any client disk that will gain access to the domain.

To create a remote boot disk, use the `RBFG.EXE` utility that's installed with the Remote Installation Service. You can use the boot disk only with computers that contain supported PCI–based network adapters. To see the list of supported network adapters, start the `RBFG.EXE` utility and click the Adapter List option. Here are the steps to follow:

1. Click Start, Run.
2. Type the UNC path of the `RBFG.EXE` utility and then click OK. Here's an example:
   `\\server name\RemoteInstall\Admin\I386\RBFG.exe`.
3. Insert a formatted disk into the disk drive. Click the Destination Drive option and then click Create Disk.
4. Click Close when the disk is ready and then remove the disk from the disk drive.

The service is not installed by default. To install the Remote Installation Service, follow these steps:

1. Open Windows 2000 Configure Your Server (the Wizard you are initially presented with). Click Start, Programs, Administrative Tools, Configure Your Server.
2. Click Advanced and then click Optional Components.
3. In the Optional Components dialog box, click Start to begin the Windows Components Setup Wizard.
4. Choose Remote Installation Services from the list of available options and click Next to begin the installation process.

To access this process manually follow these steps:

1. Click Start and click Run.
2. Type **RISetup** and click OK to start the Remote Installation Service Setup Wizard (see Figure 12.12).

FIGURE 12.11
The Remote Installation Wizard.

3. In the Remote Installation Services Setup Wizard, you're prompted for the following information:

- *Remote Installation Services Drive and Directory*. Enter the drive and directory of where to install Remote Installation Services. The drive should be dedicated to the Remote Installation Services server and contain enough space to store as many client images as you plan on hosting with this server. The minimum should be a 4GB drive or partition.
- *Workstation Source Path*. Enter the location of the Windows 2000 Professional files. This can be the Windows 2000 Professional CD or the network share that contains the installation files.
- *Friendly Description and Help Text*. Enter the friendly description for the workstation installation. This description will be displayed to users/clients of this Remote Installation Services server. Help text is used to describe the operating system installation choice to users/clients of the Remote Installation Services.

Once the service is installed, it must be set to respond to client requests. By right-clicking the server in the Active Directory Users and Groups area and choosing Properties, you'll find the Remote Install tab. Within this tab are two choices that can be changed:

- *Respond to client computers requesting service*. If you select this option, Remote Installation Services are enabled and will respond to client computers requesting service. If you don't select this option, Remote Installation Services are paused and will not respond to clients requesting service.
- *Do not respond to unknown client computers*. This option controls whether this Remote Installation Services (RIS) server responds to unknown client computers requesting an RIS server. A client computer is considered known if there's an existing client computer account object (CAO) created within the Active Directory. You should preset client computers in the Active Directory prior to enabling this option.

If you select this option, the Remote Installation Services (RIS) server will not respond to unauthorized client computers. This option provides additional system security by eliminating the possibility of unauthorized access by unknown computers.

Summary

Some of greatest changes in the Windows NOS world have occurred in the land of user control. By incorporating the power of user policies into the Active Directory, Microsoft has made a powerful, but seldom used, tool hard to ignore.

Intellimirror, as a concept, delivers on the complete package of user control. The user's operating system and local applications can be delivered to a blank machine. The user's desktop and Start menu can be completely edited and locked down. Also, each portion of this control can be delegated to various members of the staff.

Network Services

PART IV

IN THIS PART

13 Network Browsing *331*

14 Remote Access (RAS) *355*

15 Multi-Protocol Environments *405*

16 Client Workstation Considerations *421*

CHAPTER 13

Network Browsing

IN THIS CHAPTER

- **Understanding Network Browsing Concepts** *332*
- **Browsing Operations** *340*

Understanding Network Browsing Concepts

Network browsing is a rather simple concept when it comes right down to it. Essentially, you perform this task when you want to see all the computing devices in your organization's LAN/WAN environment. Performing this task is easy to accomplish. Double-click the My Network Places icon found on the Windows 2000 Server desktop to reveal the My Network Places window, as shown in Figure 13.1.

FIGURE 13.1
My Network Places screen.

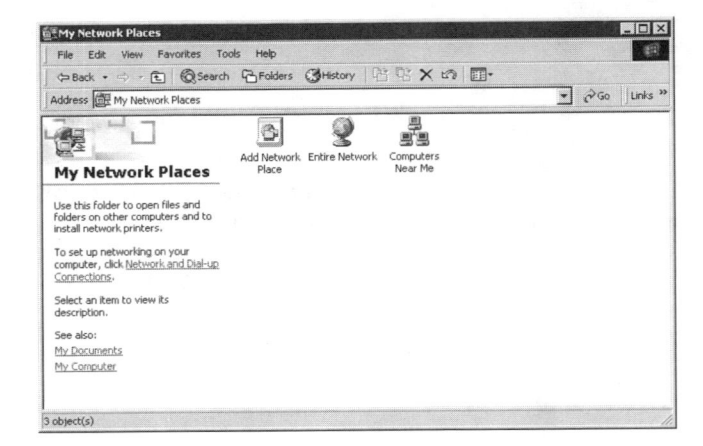

Within this window, you have a few options: to use one of the two icons to browse your local or wide area network (using the Computers Near Me or Entire Network icon, respectively) and to use Add Network Place, which is used to facilitate the connection between your Windows 2000 Server machine and shared folders, Web folders, and/or FTP sites within the realm of your computer's connectivity (including that of your own organization's networks as well as the Internet). All these terms and concepts are fully discussed and explained throughout the course of this chapter.

> **Note**
>
> Another quick way to check the browsing capability of your PC (assuming you're using a non-Windows 2000 machine) is to double-click the Network Neighborhood icon (on Windows 9x and Windows NT 4.0 systems) or the Network icon (found on Windows 3.11 and Windows NT 3.5x systems). This will display a listing of the various computing devices that may be available for use. Upon double-clicking a particular computer, assuming you have the proper permissions, you'll also be able to view the nonhidden shares available on any given computer shown in the browser listing.

Network browsing within the Windows 2000 Server environment has continued to evolve from its Windows NT origins. The Computer Browser service that's built into the Windows 2000 Server operating system can function much as it did under the Windows NT 4.0 Server environment. That is, it still supports the browsing of wide area networks (WANs) that use NetBIOS over TCP/IP, as well as the browsing of those domains that are still controlled by the older Windows NT 4.0 Server operating systems. Additionally, the use of both the Windows NT 4.0 Server WINS (Windows Internet Naming Service) as well as the WINS 2000 (Windows 2000 Server–based WINS) technologies are likewise supported.

As Microsoft moves its browsing capabilities forward with the advent of the Windows 2000 operating system, the browsing functionality is probably best accomplished via the publishing of computer information in the Active Directory via the use of *global catalogs* (refer to Chapter 10, "Active Directory Design," for more details on this facet of Windows 2000 Server). Essentially, though, a global catalog is nothing more than a Windows 2000 Service and data store that contains a replica of each object that already exists within the Active Directory throughout the forest of the organization, along with a few of its more regularly used attributes. What this means, then, is that when a user begins the browsing of a Windows 2000 Server network, his or her computer system will contact the Active Directory's global catalog (there's always at least one within every forest) and look up a particular computer name faster. Because a global catalog's attribute listing is smaller than the full Active Directory, its indexing is faster than if the user had attempted to retrieve computer information from the full Active Directory.

> **Note**
>
> Of course, although it's possible to have more than a single forest within an organization, it's very unlikely for a company to have more than one due to the inherent problems that will occur when a user tries to replicate objects and their attributes between multiple Windows 2000 forests.

Of course, not every organization will be using a forest or even the Active Directory technology along with its deployment of Windows 2000 servers. In those cases, there may be existing Windows NT 4.0 servers that are managing the network's browsing resources and capabilities via WINS (Windows Internet Naming Service) servers. Additionally, it may be that a Windows 2000 server that has just been deployed is actually the first Windows NT or Windows 2000 server system deployed at that organization, in which case there really isn't all that much to be browsed (in other words, if there's only one server present, it should not be too difficult to determine on which server the network's printing and file share resources are located).

By this point, you're probably wondering how all this works within the Windows 2000 Server environment. Therefore, without any further ado, let's continue on to an overview of the three primary browser subject matter areas:

- Browser server roles
- Browsing criteria
- Browser election process

Once you've gathered a basic knowledge of these three topics, it will become that much easier for you to understand how to configure and maintain an organization's browsing environment.

Browser Server Roles

As stated previously, the Computer Browser service runs on the Windows NT and Windows 2000 operating system environments, and is used by all Windows 3.11, Windows 9*x*, Windows NT, Windows Consumer (presently code-named *Millennium*), and Windows 2000 computers that operate on each TCP/IP subnet within an organization. The Computer Browser service helps to designate which of the computers on a particular subnet is designated as a "browser." It is important to remember that only the Windows 9*x* and later computers are able to store browse lists on their systems; a concept that will be touched upon in more detail in just a moment. To continue, it's the "browser" computer that keeps and updates the browse lists, which keep a synopsis of what computers, shared resources, and the like are available across the network.

In order to figure out which computer is the keeper of the browse list, you first need to understand all five different types of roles that a browser computer can play. There are several different types of browser roles available in Windows 2000 Server, ranked from the lowest-level browser to the highest-level browser:

- Non-browser
- Potential browser
- Backup browser
- Master browser
- Domain master browser

Keep in mind, though, that most computers on the organization's networks will not be a browser of any kind; rather, most computers will fall into the non-browser category. This is typical in corporate environments that have thousands of potential browser computers, as well as in a small business that has just a few computers. However, because many computers may also be available to the network as potential browsers, it's important to understand the differences between all these different browser roles. The information shown in Table 13.1 goes from the least capable of the browser list capabilities (the non-browser), all the way to the most powerful of the browsers (the domain master browser) found on the network.

TABLE 13.1 Browser Roles and Their Key Attributes

Browser Server Role	Browser Role Attribute(s)
Non-browser	Non-browsers do nothing when it comes to browser listings and their necessary maintenance.
	A non-browser can also be designated as never having the capability of becoming a potential browser, which means that it is safe from the burden of this additional networking overhead.
	The typical role attribute of a non-browser is to act as a client browser, which means it will request browser lists from the browser found within its own network subnet.
Potential browser	A potential browser can grow up to become a backup browser only if its subnet's master browser tells it to do so.
	Typically, a potential browser exists simply as a non-browser, which means it does nothing in the way of maintaining or storing browser listings.
Backup browser	A backup browser obtains its browser listing from the master browser found on its same network subnet mask. This browser listing covers only that single subnet, not the entire network.
	Upon the request of other Windows-based computers, the backup browser will dole out a copy of the listing to those computers.
Master browser	This role is very similar to that of the domain master browser, in that it builds and tends to the inventory of the available Novell NetWare, Windows NT, and Windows 2000 servers found within its network subnet (UNIX boxes do not normally appear within this catalogue listing).
	The master browser will also trade its inventory listing of servers with that of the domain master browser so that these two browser servers are best able to maintain an up-to-date listing for the rest of the network community to utilize.
	Another task of this role is to distribute copies of its network server inventory list to the backup browsers that exist within its same network subnet, in case of network problems (sort of an automatic redundancy for itself).
	The master browser can also inform potential browser computers that they are to become backup browsers, should the need arise.

continues

TABLE 13.1 continued

Browser Server Role	Browser Role Attribute(s)
Domain master browser	This role can only occur in domain environments (that is, at least one Windows 2000 Server machine must be a domain controller), and the default master browser will be that of the domain controller.
	This role acts as the master browser for the entire domain in which it operates, including all the various TCP/IP subnets that exist throughout the domain.

To move between the different roles, an event of some sort must first occur. This event might be the removal of the computer that was acting in a particular browser role, or it might stem from a hardware malfunction of one of the browser computers, and so forth. What actually causes the removal of a computer is irrelevant, because the focus here is what happens when a browser computer needs to be replaced. The automatically occurring replacement effort, known as a *browser election*, is discussed in more detail a little later on in this chapter. However, before we get to that, it's important that you first understand a bit more about the criteria used within the Windows networking environment to determine what each client computer requires to browse its local and wide area networks using these browser lists.

Browser Election Criteria

When browsing a network, a Windows-based client computer will most commonly use a Windows NT service known as WINS (Windows Internet Naming Service) or NetBIOS over TCP/IP (which, for some reason, is strangely abbreviated by Microsoft as NetBT). As we move forward into a pure or "native" Windows 2000 world (that is, all the servers and client computers use strictly a Windows 2000 operating system and the Windows 2000 Active Directory is also being used), the form of network name resolution will become that of Microsoft's DNS (Domain Name System). However, in today's mixed world of both Windows NT and Windows 2000 servers, coupled with Windows 9x, Windows 3.x, and MS-DOS client computers, the majority of the computers will be browsing LAN and WAN networks via WINS or NetBT.

When opening the Network Neighborhood icon (in Windows 9x or Windows NT 4.0) or using the My Network Places area from within Windows 2000 (both of these are found on the applicable operating system's desktop area), you're in effect beginning the browsing process for your organization's LAN or WAN. Your client PC will make a request to the computer that's acting as the master browser on the local subnet, which may or may not be an actual server computer (it's possible to have a Windows 9x computer filling the role of the keeper of the browser listing, which in this case would then be known as a *backup browser*). However, it's most likely there would be at least one Windows NT or Windows 2000 server on each subnet of your organization (this will make a bit more sense when you get to the election process, which is discussed next).

When browsing the network with the assistance of a browse listing, your computer is essentially attempting to resolve the nice-looking computer name you see in the Network Neighborhood or My Network Places window into the specific TCP/IP networking address that it needs in order to actually be able to "find" that target computer, either on the organization's series of networks or on the Internet. To help keep this topic a bit more simplistic, we will reserve this discussion to just locating computing devices on the LAN/WANs. For more information on locating devices across the Internet, refer to Chapter 8, "TCP/IP Networking," and look for the section on the Microsoft Windows 2000 Dynamic Domain Name System (DDNS). This process of finding a computer name and converting it over to a TCP/IP address (and vice-versa) is known as *name resolution*. There are two Windows NT 4.0 and Windows 2000 services that aid in this process: the Windows Internet Naming Service (WINS) and the Domain Naming Service (DNS).

> **Note**
>
> Actually, in Windows 2000 parlance, DNS becomes *DDNS* as it moves from a "static" addressing scheme to a "dynamic" one. However, because that discussion really falls outside of the scope of this chapter, you may want to refer to Chapter 8 for more details on DDNS.

WINS is used to map NetBIOS names over to TCP/IP addresses, whereas DNS has historically been used by Microsoft operating systems to resolve host names over to TCP/IP addresses. On smaller networks, such as those with just a single subnet mask, neither one of these server-based services is really necessary because simple NetBIOS over TCP/IP (NetBT) will typically suffice for locating and translating NetBIOS-based computer names to their appropriate TCP/IP addresses (that is, computer networks with less than 256 devices deployed on them). This information is important, because once you understand what's happening and why, it becomes a bit easier to grasp the many intricacies of network browsing and browser lists.

Election Process

The browser election process is a very important task that's automatically undertaken by Windows-based computers in a Windows NT/2000–hosted networking environment. The election process can also be manually manipulated in that network administrators can force a Windows 9*x*, Windows NT, and/or Windows 2000–based computer to not participate in the browser list maintenance and distribution process. The system administrator can designate any of these computer types to be seen as a non-browser by the rest of the network.

The election process is the method by which a new master browser computer is selected if it fits the criteria for role promotion. Elections for new master browsers only happen in one of three instances:

- If a computer somewhere on the subnet or WAN is unable to locate an existing master browser machine
- If a Windows NT/Windows 2000–preferred master browser suddenly becomes available (thereby forcing an "election" between it and the previously existing master browser)
- If a Windows NT primary domain controller or backup domain controller computer or a Windows 2000 domain controller is rebooted and starts up on the subnet or WAN

The process by which these elections occur is straightforward—they're based on the seniority of the role that the computer is already playing in the domain structure. Computers are ranked according to their stature in the Windows community. For example, in a mixed-mode Windows NT/Windows 2000 domain environment, the PDC emulator (primary domain controller emulator) will take precedence over all other computers for the maintenance of the browser lists. However, if this is an Active Directory–based deployment of Windows 2000, the global catalog server will be first in line to maintain the browser lists, with the domain controllers following a close second (note that in many smaller networks, the global catalog server and the domain controller will typically be the same physical computer). Likewise, if this were a native mode deployment of Windows 2000, there's no PDC emulator within the domain, just domain controllers.

Notwithstanding, the remainder of the browse listings is maintained in the following order (with the most important browser type at the top of the list and the least important at the bottom):

- The browser is presently acting as a backup browser.
- The `MaintainServerList` flag is set to Yes.
- The browser is presently acting as the master browser.
- The system is noted as being the preferred master (browser).
- The computer is a WINS server.
- The computer is a primary domain controller (Windows NT 4.0) or a domain controller (Windows 2000).

- The level of per-version criteria.
- The level of the election version.
- Windows 2000 Server/Windows NT Server.
- Windows 2000 Professional/Windows NT 4.0 Workstation.
- Windows 9*x* or Windows for Workgroups.
- Operating system type.

Unfortunately, winning a browser election is not as simple as being the most important browser type on the subnet or network. During a browser election, an election datagram packet is sent from the computer that initiated that particular browser election to the next PC in line for possible master browser status. Depending on the election criteria, one of the browsers involved in the sending or receiving of the election datagram will "win" the election based on the criteria. That criteria includes the following:

- If the browser that receives the election datagram ranks higher than that of the sending browser, that browser wins. Otherwise, the election process continues to the next election browser criteria. The level of the election criteria is a steady value that is not dependent or related to the actual version of the browser computer's operating system.
- If the election carries over to this next criteria level, an evaluation is performed between the receiving browser's election criteria and the sender's. If the receiving browser is higher, it wins; otherwise, the browser moves down to the next election criteria.
- This one is easy to understand. Simply stated, if the receiving browser's computer has been running longer than the sender's computer, the receiving system wins the browser election. Again, if it does not win, the election moves down to the final election criteria.
- If the browser election has not been decided by this juncture, the computer with the "lexically lowest name" wins the browser election. In plain English, this means that the system with the earliest appearing name (this includes alphanumeric characters of letters and numbers) in the alphabet wins the browser election. For example, a system with the computer name *Apple* would win out over one named *Microsoft* (because *A* comes earlier in the alphabet than the letter *M*).

Of course, even though this first "election" concludes with a winner, the process of actually promoting the winner to become the new master browser does not occur immediately. This is because once a browser computer has won, it enters a state known as the *running election state*. While in the running election state, that computer will repeatedly send out browser election datagrams to the other eligible computers within the domain.

Those other computers will respond based on varying delays (the delay is dependent on those computers' hierarchy within the domain), which will ultimately result in a final winner of the browser election. Once this occurs, the new master browser computer is promoted and begins the whole process anew whenever it, too, becomes challenged for the master browser position.

Browsing Operations

The operation of performing the browsing task consists of a few actions:

- Collecting browsing information
- Distributing browsing information
- Servicing client PC requests for browsing information

Windows 2000 uses the Computer Browser and the TCP/IP NetBIOS Helper Service services found within the Services function of the Computer Management tool, as shown in Figure 13.2, to permit the capabilities required to perform these three tasks.

FIGURE 13.2
Accessing the Windows 2000 Server services features.

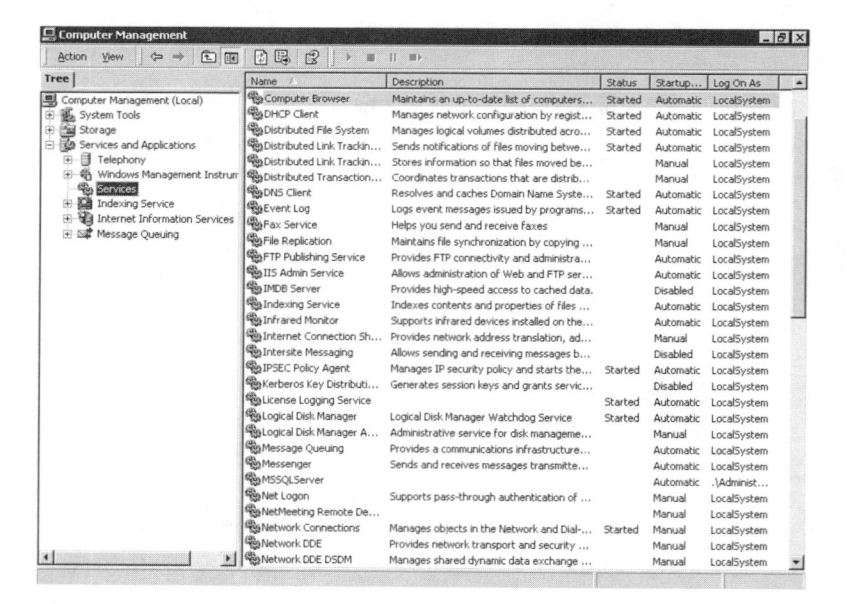

> **Note**
>
> In case you don't remember how to access the Computer Management tool, follow this very easy shortcut to managing your computer: First, right-click the My Computer icon found on the Windows 2000 Server desktop; then click the Manage menu option that appears on the small pop-up menu.

If either of these two services is not running on your Windows 2000 Server machine, click once on the service to select it and then click the "start" button (found at the top of the window; it looks like a "play" button on a tape player) to restart the service. Once these two services are running, you're assured of their capability to provide the browsing services required for your Windows 2000 computing environment.

Fundamentally, the browsing services between the old Windows NT 4.0 Server and the Windows 2000 Server environments remain similar, when viewed from a domain perspective. (How the organizational units configuration of Active Directory instead of a domain structure impacts browsing will be discussed in the final topic of this chapter.) Given that, the collection of browsing information works by the compilation of the various browse lists that the master browser for the subnet has gathered through broadcasts to their particular segment (subnet) of the network. The Windows 2000 servers use the Computer Browser and TCP/IP NetBIOS Helper Service services to perform this function, whereas Windows NT servers utilize their Server service.

These server services will use broadcasts of host announcement messages in the creation of the browsing lists. These browser announcement messages are gathered up by the master browser computer that's located on each subnet of the network (in a pure Windows 2000 Server environment, these messages will be TCP/IP based; if there are older Windows NT Server domain controllers present, the messages may be carried via the NetBEUI or IPX/SPX networking protocols). As the master browser receives the announcement messages, that browser computer will compare the computer name of the transmitting computer to its master browse listing. If the sending computer's name is not present, it's added to the master browsing list. Otherwise, if the transmitting computer's name is present, it's rejuvenated within the list if needed.

Once the browse list is complete, it must be disseminated out to all the backup browsers that exist on the subnet. Also, the master browser computer will also announce itself to all the computers on the local subnet so that each computer server and client will "know" who the master browser is and where it is located. If after a relatively short period of time (roughly 15 minutes) the master browser still has not sent out this periodic update, a backup browser will detect that the master Browser has somehow gone offline. At this point, a new browser election will be forced with the result being the creation of a new master browser computer.

The most important function of any browser computer, especially the master browser, is to service browser requests from the various client computers on the network. These requests appear in a variety of ways, including the initial request by a client computer as it first boots onto a particular subnet. Other requests may come in the form of computer name resolution for the backup browsers that are supposed to exist on that client computer's same subnet. The client computer is given a short listing of the backup browsers by the master browser when the client PC first starts up on the subnet.

Browser Announcements

Browser announcements is the technique by which the individual computers on the network help to maintain the accuracy of the browser listings that are created and maintained by the various browse masters (domain master browser, master browser, and backup browser) found across any Windows NT/2000 domain network environment. Master browser computers will receive these browser announcements on a periodic basis from many types of client computers, including the following:

- Windows NT 3.1 (Note that there was no "Workstation" designation with this first version of Windows NT)
- Windows NT 3.1 Advanced Server
- Windows for Workgroups 3.1 and 3.11
- Windows 95 (both the A and B versions)
- Windows 98 and Windows 98 Second Edition
- Windows Millennium (Consumer Windows)
- Windows NT Workstation 3.5, 3.51, and 4.0
- Windows NT Server 3.5, 3.51, and 4.0
- Windows 2000 Professional
- Windows 2000 Server, Advanced Server, and DataCenter
- LAN Manager–based systems

Pure Microsoft DOS–based client machines are incapable of making browser announcements, as well as those running the Windows 3.1 or 3.11 graphical user interface (this latter one is not the Windows for Workgroups version).

As you can see in Figure 13.3, the time frame for client machines to make these browser announcements is relatively short.

FIGURE 13.3
Browser announcement methods and timetable.

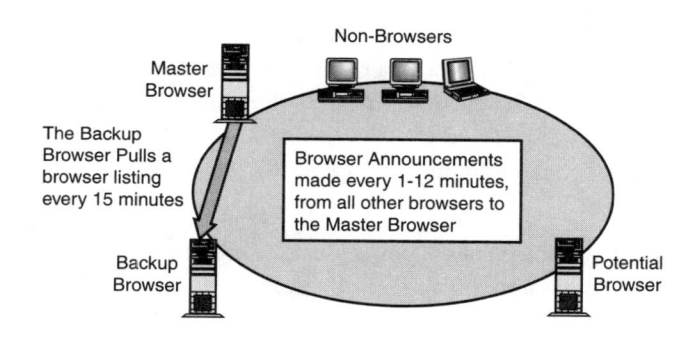

- Master Browser
- Non-Browsers
- The Backup Browser Pulls a browser listing every 15 minutes
- Browser Announcements made every 1-12 minutes, from all other browsers to the Master Browser
- Backup Browser
- Potential Browser

Additionally, the backup browsers will retrieve a copy of the new (or updated) browser listing every 15 minutes. The computers that are capable of being backup browsers are essentially the same as those that can make browser announcements, as shown in the following list:

- Windows NT 3.1. (Remember that there was no "Workstation" version in this first release of Windows NT.)
- Windows NT 3.1 Advanced Server.
- Windows for Workgroups 3.1 or 3.11.
- Windows 95 (both the A and B versions).
- Windows 98 and Windows 98 Second Edition.
- Windows Millennium (Consumer Windows).
- Windows NT Workstation 3.5, 3.51, and 4.0.
- Windows NT Server 3.5, 3.51, and 4.0.
- Windows 2000 Professional.
- Windows 2000 Server, Advanced Server, and DataCenter.

Master Browser

The master browser computer, as mentioned previously, is the browser computer that's responsible for gathering the information necessary to create the browse list for the domain. This browse listing will include the resolved computer names for all the servers that can be found in the master browser's particular workgroup or domain (provided that it doesn't span more than a single subnet) as well as a listing of the domains and networks on the organization's full network. Of course, this domain and network listing may not be able to "see" all the non-Microsoft domains/trees/workgroups such as those created by Novell NetWare servers, various UNIX servers, and so on. For a quick peek at your workgroup browser listing, open the My Network Places icon from the Windows 2000 desktop and then double-click the Computers Near Me icon to reveal such a list.

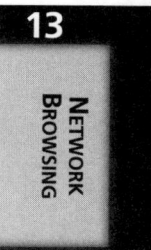

If a domain spans more than one subnet on the organization's network, the master browser is unable to maintain the browser listing for the entire domain. Instead, a new browse master type known as the *domain master browser* will be used as the overall controller of the browse listing. The domain master browser will coordinate the efforts of the master browsers that gather information for the creation and maintenance of each subnet's browser listing.

There are a few key attributes of the domain master browser of which you should be aware. First, the domain master browser will always be located on the primary domain controller emulator (PDC emulator) computer that exists for the entire Windows 2000 environment. The use of a PDC emulator assumes that you're operating in a mixed-mode network. Otherwise, if there are no Windows NT 3.51 or 4.0 servers in use on any of the subnets, you're really conducting business in a pure mode. This means that there's only Windows 2000 domain controllers found across the network and no PDC emulator is present. Again, we're assuming that Active Directory has not been deployed across the network, as well as Microsoft DNS (the DDNS version that comes with Windows 2000). If they have been deployed, refer to the section titled "Active Directory–Based Browsing Considerations" for more details.

Browse List

A *browse list* is simply the browser listing of the Windows NT/Windows 2000 domains and servers available on a given network. This listing is maintained by the Windows 2000 Server Computer Browser service, which functions on each of the various computer browser types (domain master browser, master browser, backup browser, and so on). The Computer Browser service's list is viewable by using the My Network Places feature (double-click its icon found on the Windows 2000 desktop), which sorts the browser listing into two parts: Computers Near Me and the Entire Network. Double-clicking the Entire Network icon will display all the computers, print devices, shared files and folders, and people found across the Windows 2000 network. Use of the Computers Near Me icon will permit you to view the browser listing for just those computers found on your local workgroup or domain.

Multiple Domain and WAN Considerations

You must take several things into consideration when your organization's networks span multiple subnets and domains. This topic becomes even more complex and convoluted when discussing where Microsoft DNS and Active Directory fall into the mix, so a portion of the topic is discussed in greater detail at the end of this chapter. To make things a bit easier, this section will take a closer look at just how browsing works across a wide area network (WAN) with TCP/IP as the network protocol in use, as well as how this all works when using NetBIOS over TCP/IP (NetBT) for the locating of domain controllers.

First up, you need to determine whether a technology known as the *Windows Internet Name Service* (WINS) should be utilized. In a pure Windows 2000 operating environment where all the servers are using Windows 2000 Server (or better) and all the client machines are functioning with the Windows 2000 Professional operating system, the NetBIOS over TCP/IP feature is not warranted. Of course, before you turn off NetBIOS, you need to perform a complete assessment of your network to be sure that there are no legacy Windows-based computers still out there (that is, those running any version of Windows 3.*x*, Windows 9*x*, Windows NT, or Windows Millennium). Remember that Windows 2000 is the first Windows-based operating system that's able to completely disregard NetBIOS over TCP/IP, so be certain before you start shutting down a technology that's regarded as vital to all the other legacy versions of Microsoft Windows.

The next step is that of figuring out whether all the client and server computers across your organization's networks can be configured to support the use of an alternative computer name–to–IP address resolution scheme, such as Microsoft DNS (actually this is the dynamic DNS version, which is now referred to as DDNS in the Windows 2000 world). Name resolution for Windows 2000 servers and clients will, by default, be configured to look towards DDNS for all name resolution. Additionally, all WINS clients that join an existing Windows 2000 domain will also, by default, point towards the Microsoft DDNS server for the resolution of computer names that either exceed 15 characters or have a period (.) in them. For those computer names that are less than 15 characters, these same WINS clients will first attempt a WINS server resolution method and then use DDNS, as a final resort, to obtain name resolution. Therefore, in short, to effectively perform browsing across the organization's WAN, assuming there's no deployment of either Active Directory or Microsoft DNS, a WINS server must be deployed to support browsing services.

Keep in mind, though, that if your small network spans multiple domains but not subnets, it's still possible to do without either the Windows 2000 WINS or DDNS servers installed. However, if the organization's network has more than 50 client machines, it really becomes a must to have either WINS or DDNS installed.

Once you've made the decision to go solely with a WINS deployment (assuming that neither the Active Directory nor Microsoft DNS technologies will be deployed), you have a few other topical areas to consider. When you configure the browsing of the organization's WANs using the WINS server service, you're essentially providing a means for NetBIOS name resolution to IP addresses. WINS does not provide host name resolution to IP addresses, which means that any of the UNIX client machines on your WAN will not be able to utilize this function (because DDNS is based on more open and non-Microsoft proprietary standards, it's able to "reach out" to non-Microsoft client machines for the purposes of network browsing). An alternative to this would be to deploy `Hosts` and `Lmhosts` files to non-Microsoft and Microsoft NetBIOS client computers, respectively. Of course, because both `Hosts` and `Lmhosts` files are static and must exist on each server/client machine, it's very cumbersome to update these types of files whenever a change is made to the network (in other words, it's virtually impossible to maintain such files across a WAN).

However, if the organization decides to deploy WINS servers (refer to Chapter 8 for more information on how to implement the WINS technology on your organization's networks), you'll immediately see a few ways to further the browsing process for a wide area network:

- Because WINS acts as sort of a replacement directory service for the resolution of NetBIOS names to IP addresses (and vice versa), making the domain master browser a WINS-enabled client will further enhance the browsing capabilities of a network because the domain master browser will automatically check with the WINS server four to five times per hour to obtain an updated domain server listing.
- Any WINS-enabled client computer—whether or not it's a browser—is able to check directly with a WINS server for changes to the NetBIOS name listings.
- WINS-enabled client computers become better equipped to "see" across subnets, because the name listings for all the domains that normally would be remote to them are stored on their local WINS server (and periodically replicated to the other WINS servers across the wide area network).

Perhaps if you view these WINS concepts in a graphical manner you'll more easily understand why WINS is so beneficial to the browsing process. For example, in Figure 13.4, you see four separate domains (this assumes that there's no Active Directory or Microsoft DNS in use), with one located in each city—Chicago, Boston, New York City, and Los Angeles—for a fictional company.

Each of these cities has its own Windows 2000 domain network. All are operating in a mixed-mode environment, with primary domain controller emulators handling the WINS server services for each one. Furthermore, we make the assumption that all the client computers within each domain are WINS aware. This way, everyone can gain the maximum benefit for browsing purposes. When the various primary domain controller emulators start on their respective networks, they will register their domain name with the preferred WINS server in each location.

Due to the WINS database replication process, each of the WINS servers that form the link between the various company sites (the two WINS servers that you see in the middle of the diagram) will gradually obtain all the computer names and IP addresses for the domains on both sides of the wide-area link. They, in turn, will then be able to share that information with the other WINS servers that exist within their routed network. This whole process is what best enables WAN browsing in a Windows 2000 mixed-mode environment.

FIGURE 13.4
Browsing a wide area network using WINS.

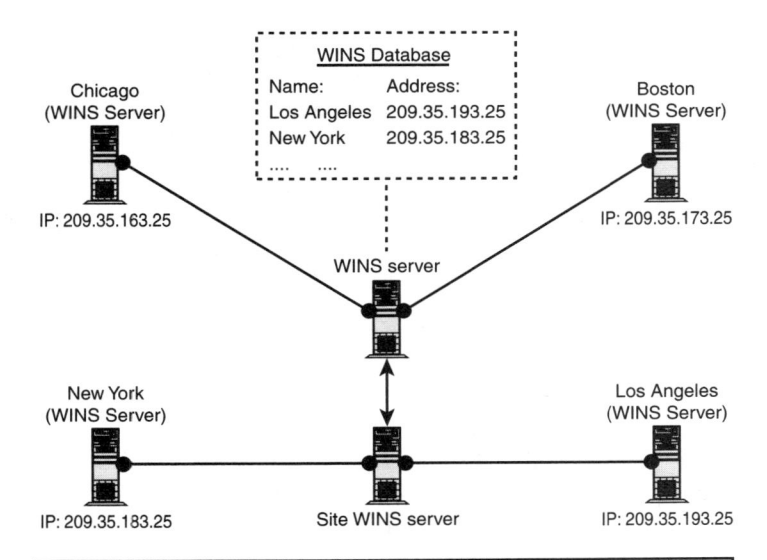

WINS Database
Name: Address:
Los Angeles 209.35.193.25
New York   209.35.183.25

Chicago (WINS Server) — IP: 209.35.163.25
Boston (WINS Server) — IP: 209.35.173.25
WINS server
New York (WINS Server) — IP: 209.35.183.25
Los Angeles (WINS Server) — IP: 209.35.193.25
Site WINS server

Assume that the WINS servers are located on the PDC Emulator (PDCE) for each domain, and that each PDCE is also the domain master browser for its domain.

Here are a few things to remember when you are working in a mixed-mode environment, when there's no Active Directory deployment:

- First, the operating system version of the domain master browsers that are not Windows 2000 Server computers cannot be less than version 3.5 (that is, no Windows NT 3.1 or Windows NT 3.1 Advanced Server machines can be deployed). This is due to the simple fact the all versions of Windows NT 3.1 cannot use the WINS technology (it wasn't invented yet).
- Next, all the client computers found throughout the workgroup must be WINS capable. In other words, they must all support the WINS networking service. Again, this is not a big deal in the Windows for Workgroups, Windows 9*x*, Windows NT (version 3.5 or later), and Windows 2000 client worlds, but be careful if you have a large number of Macintosh, UNIX, or DOS-based clients.
- Finally, be wary of the use of static domain names and IP addresses on non-Windows 2000 WINS servers, because they may result in stale records appearing in the WINS browsing lists in the event that a computer name or IP address is changed or deleted from the network.

The other manner in which a Windows 2000 or legacy Windows (Windows for Workgroups, Windows 9*x*, Windows NT) client can locate a domain controller is through a technique known as *using NetBIOS over TCP/IP* (NetBT). The locating of domain controllers is very important in the Windows 2000 networking world, because it's the domain controller box that controls access to the network. If a client machine cannot be authenticated to the network, it has no hopes of ever even beginning the browsing process. Because Windows 2000 domains are created and controlled using the Active Directory technology, the browsing process relies solely on DNS queries to resolve the names and locations of the Windows 2000 domain controllers. However, within Windows 2000 workgroups where there is no domain controller found, the authentication to the workgroup's resources (assuming that the client computers are controlled by a Windows 2000 Server machine in that workgroup) is dependent on the client computers finding the proper Windows 2000 server.

In the world of NetBT, this is done through the use of NetBIOS over TCP/IP name service broadcast messages that spread throughout the subnet and/or routed network using the UDP (User Datagram Protocol) port number 137. On a large number of routed networks, though, the use of UDP port 137 is blocked at the router level, because this is a common source of trouble that results in mass network broadcast traffic. However, if a routed network does not block this frame type, the network will appear as a single giant network segment to the browsing client. This makes the browsing of a small-to-medium-sized network possible without the use of either DNS or WINS servers (although the larger the network becomes, the slower the browsing process will also become).

Back on the more positive side, though, it's now possible to completely do away with both of the major browsing techniques—NetBIOS over TCP/IP as well as WINS servers—and move towards the Microsoft-designated future of the Domain Name System (DNS). DNS is an Internet and TCP/IP standard name resolution service that enables client computers to register and resolve computing device names. However, where Microsoft's Windows 2000 implementation of DNS varies from the past is in the fact that DNS will now dynamically update, store, and retrieve computer names and IP addresses. This new version is often referred to as the *Dynamic Domain Name System* (DDNS).

To completely eliminate the need for either NetBT or WINS implementations on your organization's Windows 2000 Server networks, your organization will need to perform a migration from all (if any) WINS servers to an exclusively Microsoft DNS environment. Additionally, the organization will need to disable any use of the NetBIOS-over-TCP/IP technology, which will then prevent any client computer from using NetBIOS-based name queries and UDP port 137 for any manner of name resolution. On a plus side, it has been estimated that nearly 80 percent of the Windows NT security problems in the past can be directly related to the unauthorized use of NetBIOS. Shutting this feature of Windows 2000 off will be a good thing for your organization from a security perspective. However, before your organization performs either of these two migratory steps, it would be prudent for you to completely assess the organization's servers and networks to be certain that there are no down-level (*legacy*) Windows clients that will require the services of either WINS or NetBT.

The Windows 2000 Server decommissioning process should proceed with the migration of all the WINS servers over to Microsoft DNS Windows 2000 servers. This process is started by the installation of the appropriate number of Microsoft DNS Windows 2000 servers, followed by the reconfiguration of all the client machines on the networks to use DNS and not WINS for their name resolution needs. Once this is complete, the decommissioning of the actual WINS servers themselves can commence, with the end result being the full deployment and use of DNS servers across the enterprise for browsing purposes.

Browsing Failures

There are several types of browser failures that can occur during the browsing process on a Windows 2000 Server network: the shutdown of a non-browser, the failure of a backup browser, the loss of a master browser, and the termination of the domain master browser. Take note that clustering browser failures can only occur on Windows 2000 Advanced Server machines and are therefore not covered within the scope of this book. In the event of a browser shutdown, the process works as follows:

- If the browser that's being shut down is a backup browser, it will notify the master browser through the browser announcement procedure. The backup browser accomplishes this notification process by modifying the browser announcement so that it does not include the Computer Browser or the TCP/IP NetBIOS Helper service in its listing of running server services.

- If the browser that's shutting down is the subnet's master browser and the shutdown process is graceful (that is, not a server crash), the master browser will force a new browser election to occur.

If the domain master browser, the master browser, a backup browser, or a non-browser is shutting down in a less-than-graceful way, the process becomes a bit uglier. These shutdowns are known as *browser failures* and are handled according to the type of browser that's failing or has failed.

In the event of a domain master browser failure, the task of creating a new domain master browser falls to the replacement of the Windows 2000 PDC emulator or the replacement of the new Windows 2000 domain controller (DC). Until the domain master browser is replaced, though, the master browsers for each subnet will continue to server just their subnet, leaving the My Network Places functionality a bit short on information. However, client computers will still be able to connect to computing devices on other subnets, provided they know the full Universal Naming Convention (UNC) name for each device's destination. For example, if the path of `\\servername\sharename\directory\filename` can be entered by the client computer (this is the full Windows 2000 name of a resource on a network), the destination will still be found.

In case of a master browser failure, one of the many backup browsers will be able to detect such a loss within a 15-minute time span. Once the loss of the master browser has been detected, the backup browser that discovered it missing will initiate the browser-election process to secure a new master browser.

If a backup browser should fail, it can take nearly an hour for its loss to be noticed and removed from the browser listing by the master browser. The loss of a backup browser is not of high importance, because the client computer that was requesting the browser list from that particular backup browser will now simply repeat the request to a different backup browser computer. If the client is unable to find a valid backup browser computer that's able to service its browser list request, the client computer will go up the line to the master browser. If it does not find a workable master browser, the browser-election process is started to find a new master browser.

In the event of a non-browser failure, there's very little impact on the whole browsing process. After a variable period of time—typically anywhere from 3 to 51 minutes—the Master Browser will remove the non-browser from the browser list. The reasoning for such a varied time period is due to the periodic browser announcement time frames for non-browsers as well as time delays between the updating of the browser list between the master browser and the backup browsers. Other than a slight increase in network traffic due to browser announcements from a non-browser failure, there's no noticeable impact on the browsing process.

Configuring a Windows 2000 Server to Never Be a Browser

To keep a Windows NT Server or Workstation computer and/or a Windows 2000 Professional, Server, Advanced Server, or DataCenter computer from participating as a browser is not too difficult a task. To do this, you'll need to first access the Registry Editor that comes with the Windows 2000 Server operating system. To do that, select Start, Run, and then type in one of the Registry Editor commands (`RegEdit.exe` or `RegEdt32.exe`). Then press the Enter key to start the Registry Editor. Performing these steps will result in the opening of the Registry Editor window. To make this as easy as possible, the example shown in Figure 13.5 relates to the older `RegEdit.exe` version of the Registry Editor.

FIGURE 13.5
Using the Windows 2000 Server Registry Editor.

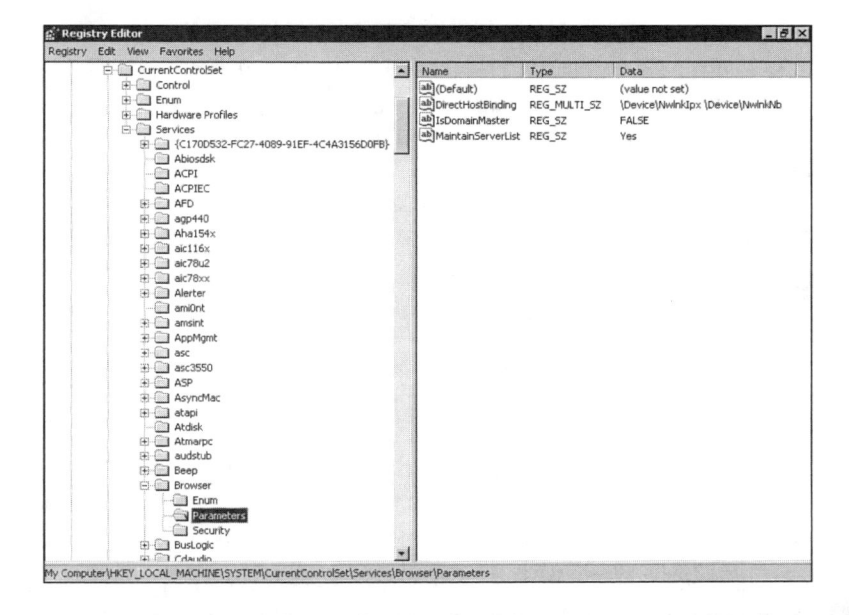

> **Note**
>
> Within Windows 2000 Server, there are still two different versions of the Registry Editor, just as there was with Windows NT Server 4.0. The command `RegEdit.exe` will start the older Registry Editor that you're probably very familiar with from your Windows NT days, which results in a single huge screen that you can scroll up and down to view, edit, or delete the contents of all five of the Registry hives.
>
> The `RegEdt32.exe` command starts up the fully 32-bit version of the Registry Editor, which displays all five Registry hives in a cascaded windows view consisting of a single Registry hive in each window. The nice thing about this version is that you can open the Windows 2000 Registry in a read-only mode, which helps to prevent accidental deletions (which can easily crash your entire system). The downside to this version is that Microsoft "forgot" to implement the full Find features and functions that you find in the older `RegEdit.exe` version of the Windows 2000 Registry Editor.

Once the Registry Editor window opens, scroll down to the `HKEY_LOCAL_MACHINE` `\System\CurrentControlSet\Services\Browser\Parameters` section and then click the `Parameters` folder to select it (as was done in the example). Once there, glance over to the `MaintainServerList` parameter name, where you'll see a `REG_SZ` type and probably a `Data` value of `Yes`. To hide this computer from the browser listing, you'll need to change this `Data` value to `No`. To do that, right-click the `MaintainServerList` parameter name, which will cause a small pop-up menu to appear. Select the top menu option, Modify, by clicking it. This will reveal the Edit String dialog box, as shown in Figure 13.6.

FIGURE 13.6
Modifying a Registry parameter.

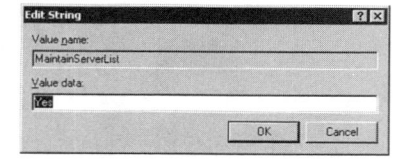

Type the value **No** into the Value Data box and then click the OK button to save your modification into the Registry. Note that there's no "undo" feature, so once you make a change to the Registry, it's permanent. It's advisable that you create a backup of the Registry prior to tampering with it, just in case something should go wrong.

An additional function that you might want to be aware of is the `IsDomainMaster` browsing parameter. If you alter this entry to `True`, this Windows 2000 Server machine will become a preferred master browser. This means that whenever you start this Windows 2000 Server machine onto any subnet of the network, it will automatically force a browser election. And, because it's a preferred master browser, it will most likely win that browser election because that designation takes priority over other computer systems during any browser-election process.

Active Directory–Based Browsing Considerations

The new Windows 2000 technology known as Active Directory changes just about everything that you know about how browsing works, is maintained, and is used within an organization's networking environment. Active Directory is a directory service that's loosely based on the X.500 directory service as well as LDAP (Lightweight Directory Access Protocol), and it serves as the basis for all serious networking efforts in the Windows 2000 computer systems world. Think of the Active Directory as nothing more than an information source that's used to store information about relevant objects. For example, your personal address book is a directory of sorts that stores information about close friends, their addresses, telephone numbers, email addresses, and the like. Your organization can use the Windows 2000 Active Directory directory service to store this type of information and more, as well as then being able to take advantage of the many benefits and tools with which Microsoft is surrounding the Active Directory technology.

Browsing the Windows 2000 Active Directory is much more complex to control and configure from the system administrator's perspective, but it's easier to do from the end user's standpoint. A partial reason for the increased complexity is the sheer number of servers that must be deployed to handle all the various functions of the Active Directory, of which only a small part is actually used in the browsing process. For example, an index is required for the enterprise directory of the Active Directory technology to function properly. This index, known as the *global catalog* (GC) for a Windows 2000 networking environment, consists of a partial replica of all the objects found within the Active Directory database. As you browse through the My Network Places functionality (this includes both the Computers Near Me and the Entire Network features) of Windows 2000, you'll actually be searching a part of the Active Directory. These searches (as well as domain logons) are based on the objects found within the global catalog.

The other major area of change when it comes to browsing is the whole concept of what a *domain* is. In the old Windows NT world, the domain was the heart of the network, and it stored all the logon information and controlled the user community as well as the resources found within the Windows NT network. In Windows 2000 Server, however, domains and domain controllers take on a completely new meaning. As you may recall from Chapter 1, "Introduction to Windows 2000," the concept of primary domain controllers and backup domain controllers are gone and have subsequently been replaced by just the nomenclature *domain controllers* (DCs). Of course, just to make things a bit more confusing, there's also a domain controller type known as a *PDC emulator* that's used by Windows 2000 servers that operate in a mixed-mode environment (that is, one with older Windows NT 4.0 backup domain controllers still in use). The PDC emulator only goes away when all the domain controllers on the organization's LANs/WANs have been migrated over to Windows 2000 domain controllers.

Therefore, to put it quite simply, think of the Windows 2000 domain as a single security boundary of the Windows 2000 networking environment and think of the Active Directory as being a conglomeration of one or more domains. Now, remember that a domain can be as small as a single computer (which obviously makes browsing easy on that level) but as large as one that spans multiple physical locations (refer to Figure 13.4 and imagine it as all four cities being glommed together as a single Windows 2000 Server domain). It is very possible for an Active Directory deployment to have many domains that are then connected to each other via trust relationships, which will then share many common resources, including the global catalog. A domain structure such as this is referred to as a *domain tree*, and, of course, many trees can all be connected together to form the domain's *forest*. Confused? Do not worry; this will eventually all click for you (refer back to Section III, "Active Directory and Account Management," for further details on how all this fits together if you have difficulty remembering what the differences are among all these terms).

Summary

You will want to keep yourself focused on the construction of your organization's networks where it relates to Windows 2000 browsing. The most important thing to remember when you are first configuring your Windows 2000 Server network is your design: Did you make it scalable enough so that you are using domains where you need domains and organizational units (OUs) where they are applicable? Along this same thought process, remember that browsing works much the same as global catalog object information replicates, so you will want to ensure that you have designed the organization's sites and site connectivity in the most efficient manner possible. This means that you should try to develop your Windows 2000 sites so that each client computer always logs onto a domain controller within the same site each time (having them bounce between sites for logon events is going to cost you just as much as having your users bounce from site to site for browsing information). Also, because Windows 2000 sites are supposed to consist of well-connected TCP/IP subnets, you will want to create sites that do not have any sites that span WAN connections (if they do span WANs, then browsing by client computers across those same WAN links will also likely result in slower browsing times).

Finally, remember that browsing is effectively controlled through client-based queries of the dynamic Microsoft Domain Name System, which resolves computer names to IP addresses, and vice versa. This formulates the core of the browsing system for Windows 2000 environments. If your organization's networks are well designed with sites that do not span WAN links and there are enough domain controllers and global catalogs to go around, then browsing within this new Active Directory style of networking should work just fine for your organization. To ensure effective browsing within your organization's Windows 2000-based networks, take the extra network design time to ensure the proper and sufficient placement of the browser servers. In the long run, you (and your organization's user community) will be glad you did.

Remote Access (RAS)

CHAPTER 14

IN THIS CHAPTER

- Understanding RRAS *356*
- Protocol Support *357*
- Remote Access Security *359*
- Installing the RRAS Tools *361*
- Authentication *401*
- Troubleshooting RAS *402*

Understanding the RRAS Service

Microsoft greatly updated and enhanced the Remote Access Server (RAS)/Dial-Up Networking (DUN) capabilities originally made available in its Windows NT 3.5x and 4.0 server versions with the new Windows 2000 Server operating system. In this updated Windows 2000 world, the terminology has changed ever so slightly, but the interface has been altered immensely. To access this technology you use the Administrative Tools menu option to start up the Routing and Remote Access (RRAS) tool set. This functionality not only gives you the ability to perform multiprotocol routing, remote access, and virtual private network (VPN), but makes it much easier to add, delete, control, and manage remote users than ever before. As you work through this chapter, you will begin to appreciate the many changes Microsoft has applied to its newest operating system, designed for the largest of organizations.

Table 14.1 lists the major new features of Windows 2000 Server Routing and Remote Access (RRAS).

TABLE 14.1 Notable RRAS Enhancements to Windows 2000

Windows 2000 Server Trait	Explanation
Integration with the Windows 2000 Active Directory Structure	Remote Access Server user attributes can be stored directly into the Active Directory's information bank, which makes browsing for information easier.
Microsoft CHAP 2.0	This next version of the Microsoft Challenge Handshake Authentication Protocol (CHAP) was designed specifically to make virtual private network (VPN) connections more secure than they have been in the past.
Extensible Authentication Protocol (EAP)	The purpose of EAP is to permit non-Microsoft vendors to create Windows 2000 RAS plug-ins for Point-to-Point Protocol (PPP) implementations. This comes in handy for organizations that want to deploy smart cards in their information technology (IT) structures.
Layer 2 Tunneling Protocol (L2TP)	The purpose of L2TP is to permit organizations to better deploy the new IP Security (IPSec) feature of Windows 2000, to provide a much greater level of routing and remote access security.
IP Multicast Support	Forwarding of IP multicast traffic between connected clients and the Internet or a corporate network is now possible. Additionally, Windows 2000 Server IP Multicast includes support of Internet Group Management Protocol (IGMP) version 2.

Protocol Support

The RRAS tools provided with Windows 2000 Server provide many new facets of routing remote access that were not available in the previous versions of Windows NT. For example, it is now possible to create a true virtual private network with Windows 2000 Server, whereas in the past you would have needed to use add-on tools and utilities (some of them created by third parties) to properly configure a secure VPN for use with Windows NT. System administrators who are already familiar with routing protocols and services such as Transmission Control Protocol/Internet Protocol (TCP/IP), Internetwork Packet Exchange (IPX), and AppleTalk are able to use Windows 2000 Server routing for precisely those services. Each protocol available is discussed to some degree in this section, so that you will better understand which protocol could and should be used in what circumstance.

Transmission Control Protocol/Internet Protocol (TCP/IP)

TCP/IP is the core networking protocol not only of Windows 2000 Server, but for the Internet as well. TCP/IP was not the original networking protocol of choice (Microsoft's NetBEUI was) for the Windows NT family way back in 1993 when Windows NT was first released, but it has come a long way since then. TCP/IP is actually a suite of protocols and is the default networking protocol installed into the Windows 2000 Server operating system.

The Windows 2000 Server capabilities of the TCP/IP protocol are extensive both for general local-area network (LAN)/wide-area network (WAN) networking and for the RRAS world. The fact that TCP/IP is probably the most routed protocol that can be secured through the use of IPSec makes it a very popular choice among systems professionals.

There are many pieces to the TCP/IP protocol suite—such as TCP, IP, and IGMP—and they are discussed in more detail in Chapter 8, "TCP/IP Networking." However, it may be helpful at this point to talk a bit more about IGMP, which is a Windows 2000 Server routing protocol that permits host computers on a network to join a multicast group. There are two pieces to the IGMP protocol:

- IGMP proxy, whose function is to separate multicast traffic from the Internet and direct it toward the IGMP router.
- IGMP router, whose function is to forward the multicast traffic to a client computer that is a confirmed member of the multicast group.

TCP/IP addresses can be resolved by one of two means within the Windows 2000 Server world: Microsoft Domain Name System (DNS) or the Windows Internet Name Service (WINS). RRAS supports both means, but the Microsoft Windows 2000 Server version of DNS is preferable because this new dynamic version of DNS makes the mapping of IP addresses to a computer name, especially within the Windows 2000 Active Directory structure, easier.

AppleTalk

AppleTalk is the networking protocol that you need to implement in order to support any Macintosh client computers that exist within your organization and require the use of resources located on a Windows 2000 server. This protocol must be installed on any Windows 2000 server on which Macintosh users want to store files or from which they want to retrieve or print files. To install this protocol, you use the Windows Optional Networking Components Wizard to configure your Windows 2000 server for file and/or print services use with Macintosh computers. (For a refresher on how to do this, refer to the section "Specific Client Operating System Considerations—Macintosh" in Chapter 16, "Client Workstation Considerations.") The AppleTalk protocol is one of the several protocols supported by RRAS as part of its multiprotocol functionality.

NWLink IPX/SPX/NetBIOS Compatible Transport

The NWLink Internetwork Packet Exchange/Sequenced Packet Exchange (IPX/SPX)/NetBIOS Compatible Transport is sometimes referred to by its shortened name, IPX/SPX, which essentially provides networking support for Windows NT, Windows 9x, and Windows 2000 users to access resources and information controlled by Novell NetWare computer systems. IPX is the piece that is used directly on the Novell networks and is a routable protocol just as is TCP/IP.

Windows 2000 Server provides Novell clients with many services, especially in the area of RRAS. When a RAS client running Windows 2000 wishes to access a NetWare server, then that client PC must be using a NetWare redirector, known as the Gateway Service for NetWare. The RAS can act as an IPX router, which can control the various types of network traffic that may traverse the distance between the RAS and the remote access client machine. These network traffic types include Routing Information Protocol (RIP), Service Advertising Protocol (SAP), and NetBIOS over IPX.

The RAS always automatically assigns the IPX network number to be used by IPX network remote access clients. This network number may come from a static pool of addresses or be dynamically assigned by the RAS administrator. Keep in mind that the NWLink IPX/SPX/NetBIOS Compatible Transport must be installed on the RAS in order for any connectivity to be provided to remote NetWare clients.

NetBIOS Extended User Interface (NetBEUI)

NetBEUI was included with the original version of Windows NT. It was designed for the peer-to-peer networking void that the original Windows NT server group was supposed to fill. NetBEUI is a very good and fast networking protocol for small LANs and private workgroups. The performance benefits remote users may achieve using NetBEUI as their Dial-Up Networking (DUN) protocol of choice should not be overlooked, but NetBEUI is really designed for point-to-point connectivity. That is, if you are a DUN client that is attempting to access or retrieve data from a single server or a small group of servers on the same LAN, then NetBEUI can be a good selection for you. However, because it is not a routable networking protocol, it obviously can only be used on bridged networks, not on routed networks. This issue is a giant downfall for NetBEUI in today's networked and internetworked worlds.

From an administrative standpoint, NetBEUI is also a great thing: There is very little management required other than the selection of a computer name, which must be 15 or fewer alphanumeric characters. This makes NetBEUI much easier to configure than TCP/IP, which requires a number of segments, subnets, and other settings.

NetBEUI is not all that great in a few major areas: It cannot be routed, which means no WAN access; it is not compatible with TCP/IP in that you cannot move packets of information directly from a NetBEUI-based LAN to the Internet; and it is not suitable for large numbers of computers. That is, if the network includes more than 50 computers and you use NetBEUI, the network traffic can become unbearable.

Remote Access Security

Windows 2000 Server supports L2TP, Microsoft Challenge Handshake Authentication Protocol (CHAP) 2.0, the Extensible Authentication Protocol (EAP), and the use of smart cards, with its implementation of the RRAS feature. Security for the RRAS implementation within the Windows 2000 Server operating system has increased greatly since the original RRAS deployment inside Windows NT Server version 4.0 (a Service Pack release). It is now possible to create a secure virtual private network by using just the software provided within Windows 2000 Server, without the assistance of any third-party tools or utilities (this does not include any physical smart cards or SecureID types of devices, though).

EAP is usefulfor groups that need to deploy smart cards throughout their organizations. You use the Edit Dial-In Profile section of the Remote Access Policy icon from within the Routing and Remote Access screen to modify these settings for your computer (refer to the sections "Installing RRAS Tools" and "Remote Access Server Configurations" in this chapter for more details on how to do this).

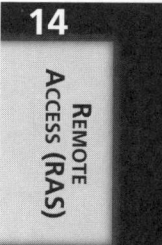

The Layer 2 Tunneling Protocol (L2TP) lets you deploy IPSec throughout your organization. L2TP then provides your organization with a much greater level of routing and remote access security. Keep in mind, though, that the Microsoft implementation of IPSec in Windows 2000 Server can negatively affect network performance by as much as 40 percent, so do not deploy IPSec across your organization's internal LANs or WANs unless there is a very good business reason to do so. Also, when using the L2TP as the basis of your VPN, make sure that you are using strong authentication whenever possible, with MS-CHAP version 2 deployed on the DUN clients; be sure you avoid using any type of LAN Manager authentication for any of your users—remote or local.

After you install RRAS, you should go back and configure in such a way that data and network encryption policies are also implemented and enforced. Additionally, you should turn on the various logging features so that you can properly monitor the use of RRAS within your organization and its complex arrays of networks and servers. Keep in mind that RAS will simply utilize the standard Windows 2000 Server user accounts that are available for use, so do not try to override the settings of one with the other and vice versa.

During a remote access connection, the remote client computer goes through a series of steps in order to connect and send and receive data from the RAS. Essentially, the remote access PC will contact the RAS through either an analog or a digital connection, either dial-up or via a leased line. When the initial connection is established, the RAS sends a challenge to the client, which responds with an encrypted answer to the server that includes the remote user's name, domain name, and password. The RAS then compares the remote machine's responses with the user accounts database or the Windows 2000 Active Directory structure, in order to determine the validity of the response. If the response was valid, the RAS then determines which remote access policies pertain to this user account and applies them accordingly. If any callbacks are required, the RAS initiates a callback to the client computer before finishing the connection negotiation process.

When the connection has been established by the RAS for the remote client, the remote user still has only the same rights that he or she would have if he or she were physically located next to the server instead of being many miles away. Also, the remote access client must still be authenticated in a separate step after logging on to the Windows 2000 server, in order to access any non-RAS resources or to even generate any network traffic on the organization's networks. The complete authentication and authorization processes can be completely encrypted by the Windows 2000 RAS. Additionally, it is important to ensure that all data/network traffic that is exposed to the outside world (such as when data is passing across the Internet) is kept private through the use of remote access policies and the encryption possibilities that are readily provided for with Windows 2000 Server.

Installing the RRAS Tools

Installation of the RRAS tools is quite easy. When you install Windows 2000 Server, the RRAS service is automatically installed as part of the normal Windows 2000 installation routine. Something that may not be readily apparent, though, is that the service installs itself in a disabled state, which means that you must first enable it and then configure it for use. That is actually the easy part, as long as you are able to access the Microsoft Management Console (MMC) configuration screen, which you do by using the Routing and Remote Access menu option.

In any event, to see if the Routing and Remote Access menu option is available for your use, click the Start button, then the Programs menu option, and then the Administrative Tools menu option. In the menu listing that appears next to the Administrative Tools menu option, scan down the list to a picture of a small computer that has two network-looking wires running into it (these wires are at both the top and the bottom of the icon) with the name Routing and Remote Access next to it.

Of course, if the menu option Routing and Remote Access does not appear on your screen, then you have a slight problem. This means that although the service has already been installed onto your server, you probably do not have administrative rights to use or configure this service. To have the appropriate rights, you must be logged on to Windows 2000 Server as a member of the Administrators group. If you do not possess this level of rights to the Windows 2000 Server that you are working with, then you need to contact your network administrator to obtain those rights before attempting any RRAS configurations.

After you are finished with the software part of the configuration process, you need to make sure that your Windows 2000 server meets the hardware requirements for supporting the RRAS tools. At a minimum, you need an analog telephone line such as an open fax line or a direct line (be sure you don't try to use one of your company's many voice telephones that connect through the main switchboard—that just is not going to work). On the high end, you might want to use some sort of digital line access such as an Integrated Services Digital Network (ISDN) or T1 data line through which to connect. Additionally, you need to have an available COM port (a multiport unit such as a Digi device works great here) and possibly a Network Driver Interface Specification (NDIS)–capable network adapter for better network connectivity. There are literally hundreds of different combinations of the hardware components that can be used with Windows 2000 Server, so it is best to use Microsoft's Windows 2000 Hardware Compatibility List (HCL) to determine whether your hardware installation is going to work correctly with the Windows 2000 Server operating system. You can find the HCL in several places:

- If you have a Microsoft TechNet subscription, you can find Windows 2000 HCL on one of the CDs.
- If you are a Microsoft Developer Network (MSDN) subscriber, you can find the HCL on your MSDN CD.
- If you have a modem and connectivity to the Internet, you can go to Microsoft's Web site (www.microsoft.com) and use the Search feature to find the Windows 2000 HCL.

Remote Access Server Configurations

To start the actual configuration process for the RRAS tools, click the Start button, the Programs menu option, the Administrative Tools menu option, and then the Routing and Remote Access menu selection to reveal the screen shown in Figure 14.1.

FIGURE 14.1
The Routing and Remote Access screen.

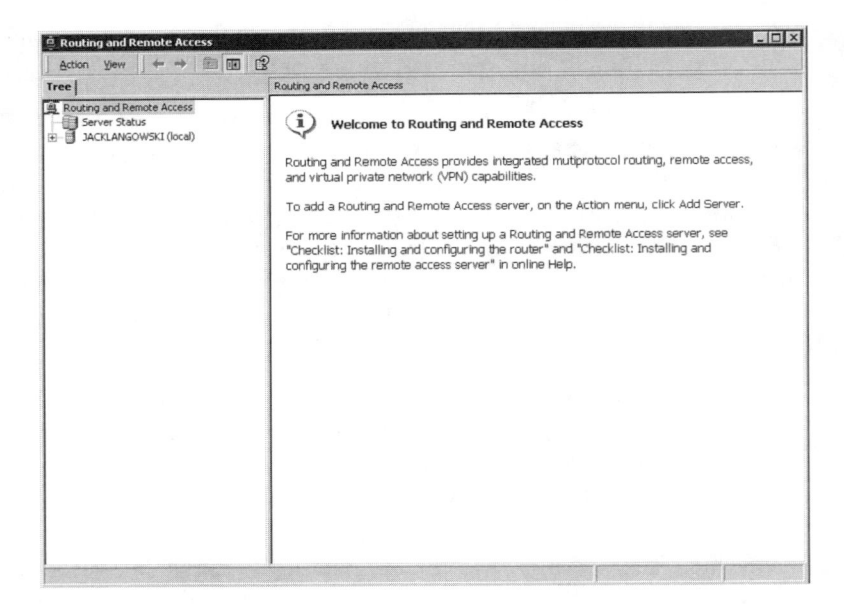

Remember that the Routing and Remote Access screen does more than just provide dial-up connectivity to your Windows 2000 server. It also provides multiprotocol software router connectivity in a virtual private network, LAN-to-LAN, LAN-to-WAN, and network address translation (NAT) routing manner. What this means is that you should first decide what type of connectivity you are attempting to configure, before actually performing the implementation of this technology. Otherwise, you might wind up with a jumble of nonsensical technology deployed in an insecure and perhaps needless manner. That is, avoid over-engineering any remote access solution, which leads many people to attempt using a VPN for a LAN-to-LAN solution when perhaps all they really needed was a simple WAN architecture. Remote access technologies typically are not as complicated as many people who lack true understanding believe them to be, so avoid the urge to unnecessarily complicate a technical solution with those items you do not truly understand.

Next, you need to re-examine the Routing and Remote Access screen shown in Figure 14.1. On the left side of this screen, you should see a tree-like diagram that has the Routing and Remote Access icon at the top of and at least two icons below it: One is labeled Server Status and the other is labeled with the computer name of your server (in Figure 14.1 the computer name is `JACKLANGOWSKI (local)`). The Computer Name icon will probably have a plus (+) symbol next to it, which means that it has more information located inside it. To figure out what secrets that icon has in store for you, click that plus symbol. This will probably reveal your computer's name with a red circular symbol on it. This means that the RRAS service for your computer is presently in a Stopped status. To confirm the status, click the Server Status icon just above the Computer Name icon, as shown in Figure 14.2.

FIGURE 14.2
Confirming your RRAS server status.

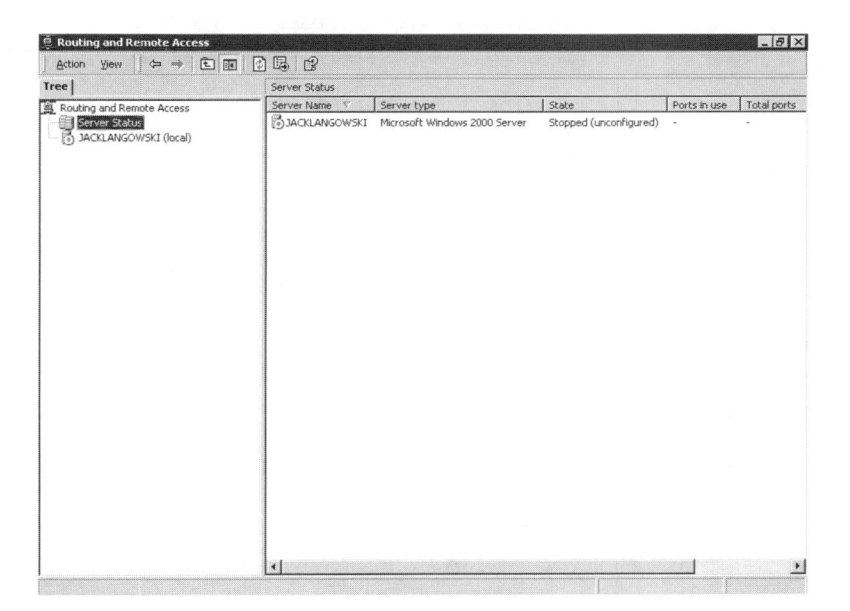

What you see in the right windowpane is a status of the computer names shown. For instance, in Figure 14.2 you see the computer named JACKLANGOWSKI that has a status of Stopped, which means that the RRAS service has not yet been started for that computer. If the computer were already started but not yet configured, there would be a small green circle on the computer's name in the left windowpane and the state Started (unconfigured) would be shown. To use the Windows 2000 Server configuration process for the RRAS service on the JACKLANGOWSKI computer, follow these simple steps:

1. Right-click the server's name (in either the right or left windowpane), and then click the Configure and Enable Routing and Remote Access menu option (the option at the top of this small menu). After you do this, the first screen of the Routing and Remote Access Configuration Wizard will appear.

2. The first screen of the wizard contains information that you should read closely so that you understand what you are about to do to your Windows 2000 server. To make this installation process a bit easier, we will step through it as if we are only going to configure the Windows 2000 server for remote access. After we have the remote access configuration in place, we will then configure the Windows 2000 server in a simple routing exercise. To continue with the Routing and Remote Access Configuration Wizard, click the Next button, and you will see the screen shown in Figure 14.3.

FIGURE 14.3
Enabling your server for remote access only.

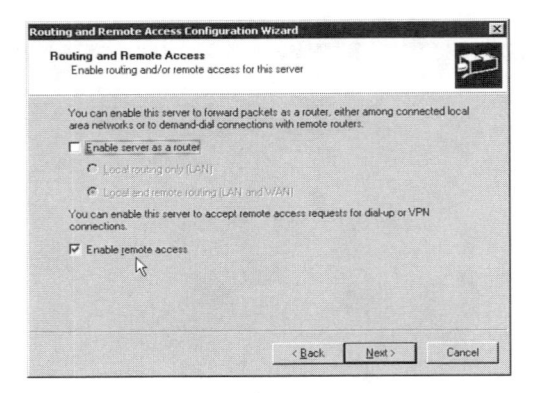

3. This screen of the Routing and Remote Access Configuration Wizard is where you determine what type of configuration is being conducted. On the top half of the screen is a check box that, if clicked on, enables the Windows 2000 server as a software router. At this point, leave this box unchecked. On the bottom half of the screen is another check box, which determines whether the server should permit remote computer systems to dial in to it for either VPN or dial-up connections. For this example, click the check box to place a check mark in it and enable that selection. To continue to the next step of the Routing and Remote Access Configuration Wizard, click the Next button, and you get the screen shown in Figure 14.4.

FIGURE 14.4
Choosing the dial-in or demand Iinterface.

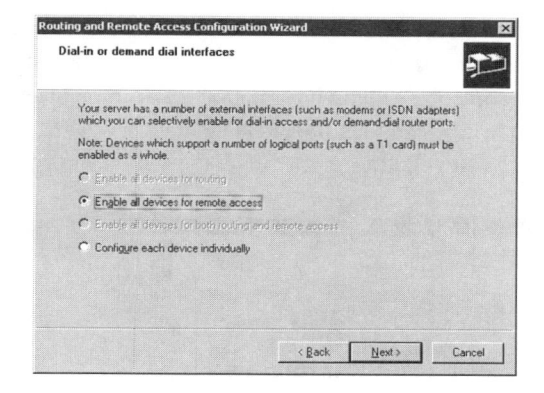

4. This screen is used to determine which modem interface is to be used in conjunction with the remote dial-in access. Your choices are simple: Either let the wizard configure all the available devices or select the bottom radio button (Configure Each Device Individually) to configure each device individually. As you can see, the other two radio button options, Enable All Devices for Routing and Enable All Devices for both Routing and Remote Access, are grayed out, which means that they are not available for you to select because on the previous wizard page you decided not to enable the software routing option. For this example, you have chosen the top choice, Enable All Devices for Remote Access. After you have made your selection, click the Next button, and you get the screen shown in Figure 14.5.

FIGURE 14.5
Selecting an authentication method.

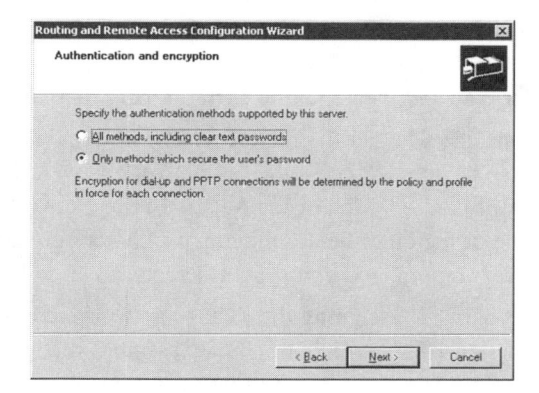

5. This screen is where you determine the authentication method for those remote access users. If all your dial-up users are Windows 9x or Windows 2000 users, then you should go with the bottom choice, Only Methods which secure the User's Password. Otherwise, if you have Macintosh, Windows 3.x, or UNIX-based users, you are probably stuck with the top choice, All Methods, including Clear Text

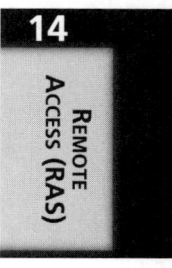

Passwords. The most obvious reason the top choice is not a good one is that it's a security risk to your organization. It is not too difficult for someone to use a network packet sniffer to read someone's logon information to glean that user's logon ID and password, perhaps so that he can then impersonate that user. After you have made your selection, click the Next button, and you get the screen shown in Figure 14.6.

FIGURE 14.6
Defining remote access rights for your systems.

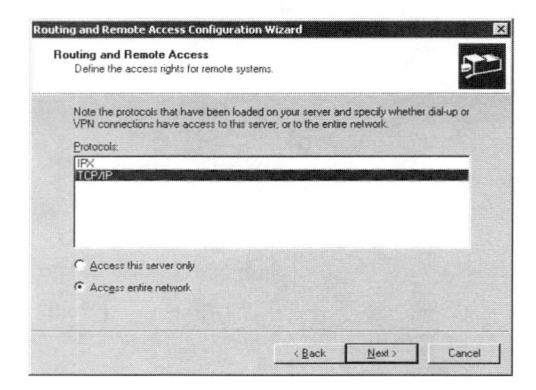

6. Use this screen to choose the networking protocol(s) you want to permit your remote users to utilize for their dial-up or VPN connections. Keep in mind that you will be presented with a list of only those protocols that are already installed in your Windows 2000 Server environment. This means that if you are expecting to be able to use NetBEUI, for instance, you should have already installed it before starting the Routing and Remote Access Configuration Wizard. In this example, we have selected only TCP/IP. However, you can choose more than one protocol by holding down the Ctrl key and then clicking each protocol that you want to install.

7. Finally, you need to decide whether the remote users who are going to be accessing this computer will also be able to access the full network as well. Click either the Access This Server Only radio button or the Access Entire Network radio button. (You must choose one or the other before moving on.) After you have made your selection, click the Next button, and you see the screen shown in Figure 14.7.

This wizard screen is used for assigning the TCP/IP network addresses to the incoming user connections. This screen, of course, assumes that you are using TCP/IP as at least one of the networking protocols for your Windows 2000 Server remote access. The top selection, Use DHCP, is used to dynamically assign TCP/IP addresses to the incoming client computers. DHCP stands for Dynamic Host Configuration Protocol; DHCP is discussed at great length in Chapter 8, "TCP/IP Networking." In this example, you have chosen to use DHCP for the automatic assignment of TCP/IP addresses to our remote users as they connect to our Windows 2000 server. However, the bottom selection, Use a Static Pool, is useful if you have a limited number of remote users or if you want to force remote users into a very specific TCP/IP address scheme that you might not use internally for either this Windows 2000 server or for the rest of the network. In any event, if you select the bottom choice, you are required to enter the TCP/IP address range and subnet mask numbers, which then automatically calculates both the static pool's range and the total number of IP addresses that the pool will contain. (I find this feature quite useful, especially when trying to determine an intermediate number of addresses for small to medium-size organizations.)

FIGURE 14.7
Selecting a DHCP-assigned or static TCP/IP address.

8. After you make your selection(s), click the Next button, and you see the screen shown in Figure 14.8. (If you do not have IPX/SPX installed, this File and Print Sharing Broadcast Packets window is not displayed, and you skip forward to the final screen of the wizard.)

FIGURE 14.8
Defining an IPX file and print sharing broadcast policy.

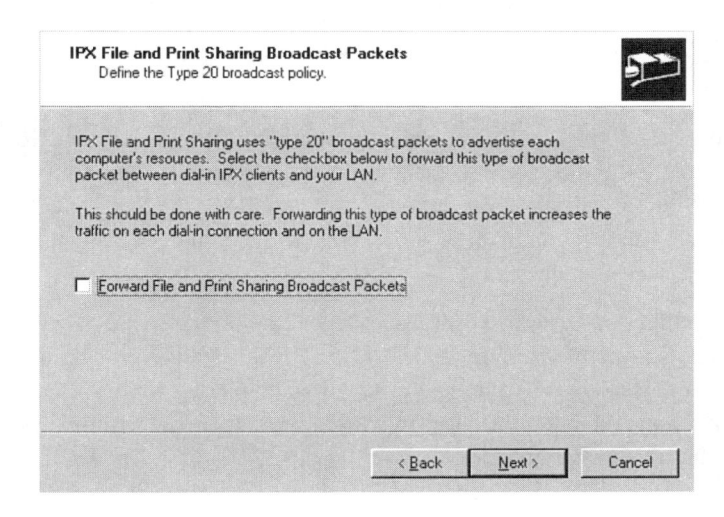

9. The purpose of the IPX File and Print Sharing Broadcast Packets window is for you to decide whether you want the Type 20 advertising broadcast packets to be broadcast across your network between your computer's IPX remote access clients and the LAN. Unless there is a good business reason to do this, you might want to stay away from this feature of Windows 2000 because it will have a negative impact on both your server and the remote clients' connectivity bandwidth. Using Type 20 broadcasting also means that you run the risk of additional network traffic that can cost the rest of your LAN's users in terms of their available bandwidth as well. To enable this feature, click the Forward File and Print Sharing Broadcast Packets check box. After you have made your decision, click the Next button to move on to the final screen of the wizard.

10. The final screen of the Routing and Remote Access Configuration Wizard process appears at this point. After you read the information presented on this screen, click the Finish button to complete this initial configuration process. After you click the Finish button, you are given a Routing and Remote Access dialog box, as shown in Figure 14.9.

> **Note**
>
> Keep in mind that this step merely closes out the wizard process, but you have not yet completed the configuration process for either the routing or the RAS section of Windows 2000 Server.

FIGURE 14.9
Deciding whether to start the RRAS service.

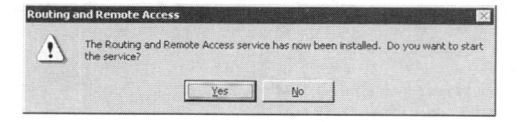

The Routing and Remote Access dialog box prompts you to start the RRAS. You probably want to click Yes because you cannot finalize the configuration process until you start RRAS. Therefore, click the Yes button, and you will see the Service Control pop-up window, which is an informational window that informs you to be patient while the system starts the service as requested.

There is nothing to do here except wait. Depending on the speed of your Windows 2000 server and its available memory and CPU cycles, this startup process may take anywhere from just a few seconds to a minute or more, so be patient while it starts. After the service starts, notice that there is an icon with a green up arrow within a white circle next to your computer's name.

This icon tells you that the RRAS service has started. You can also see in the right pane of this dialog box the total number of communications ports available, as well as how many of those ports are in use. In addition, the State column in this dialog box now shows the status Started.

Advanced Remote Access Server Configurations

As we move on to the more detailed portion of the configuration process, we will discuss some of the more popular options available within the RAS section of the RRAS service. Then we will go back and walk through the initial configuration process for the routing portion of the RRAS service, too. This should give you a better understanding of what it will take to support remote users with your Windows 2000 Server installation.

If you go back to the Routing and Remote Access MMC snap-in, you will see that your computer's RRAS service is up and running. By clicking once on the plus symbol next to the icon for your computer's name—in the example this is the icon next to the JACKLANGOWSKI (local) server—you see numerous new options and settings, as shown in Figure 14.10.

FIGURE 14.10
Viewing all the IPX and IP routing methods.

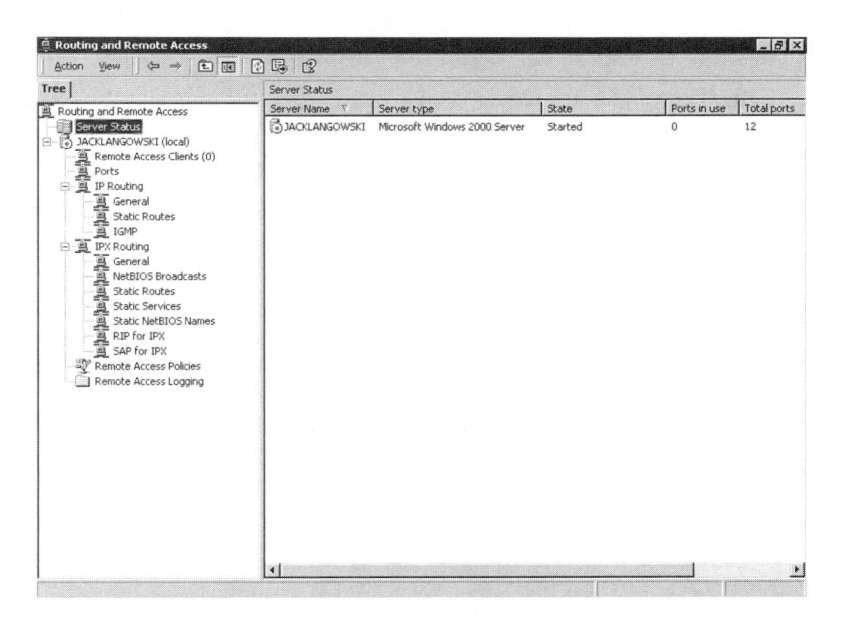

This window displays all the various connection methods that are possible within your server's implementation of RRAS, including both the IP and IPX routing mechanisms that we have not yet begun to configure for this sample server. For now, we will focus on the four sections of the left pane of this screen that pertain to the more detailed configuration of RAS for Windows 2000 Server:

- Remote Access Clients
- Ports
- Remote Access Policies
- Remote Access Logging

Remote Access Clients

The first piece that we will examine more closely is the Remote Access Clients section, which is found just under the computer name for our computer. In the example shown, JACKLANGOWSKI has zero clients connected to it.

> **Note**
>
> The number in the brackets next to the term Remote Access Clients denotes the number of remote access client computers that are presently connected to the Windows 2000 RAS. This number fluctuates over time, and in theory can go as high as 256, with the use of additional COM port hardware such as a Digi board device or other such hardware.

A system administrator would probably use this portion of the RRAS service to monitor those remote clients that are presently connected to a RAS. A very useful feature of RRAS is that you are able to monitor more than one RAS at a time by adding additional servers to this MMC snap-in screen. (This, of course, assumes that you have the proper administrative rights to look at other servers' Routing and Remote Access information.) To add another server, all you need to do is right-click the Routing and Remote Access icon at the very top of the tree structure to reveal a small pop-up menu. The top menu option, Add Server, is the option that you click to reveal the Add Server dialog box, which is shown in Figure 14.11.

FIGURE 14.11
The Add Server dialog box.

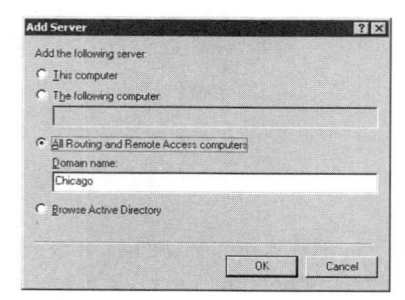

The options shown here except the bottom one are self-explanatory. The bottom option, Browse Active Directory, is used in conjunction with the All Routing and Remote Access Computers option, which provides the RAS administrator with the ability to search through his or her organization's Active Directory structure to find any available RRAS that can be monitored by that administrator. (Again, keep in mind that without the proper authorization, that RRAS administrator is not able to even view the available list, much less try to monitor a server.) The top option, This Computer, means your local RRAS Windows 2000 server. The other option, The Following Computer, gives you the ability to type in the Universal Naming Convention (UNC) for the computer that you want to monitor, assuming you know the full UNC for that Windows 2000 server computer. After you make your selection(s), click the OK button to return to the main Routing and Remote Access screen.

Ports

The next option that we will discuss is the Ports feature, whose general information is shown in Figure 14.12.

FIGURE 14.12
Available RRAS ports.

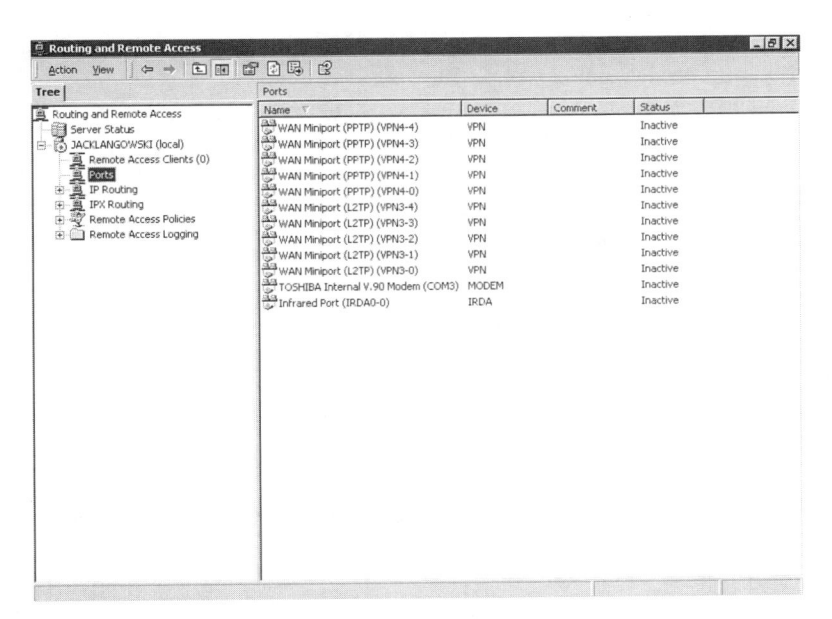

The purpose of the Ports option is obvious: It provides the RRAS administrator with a complete list of all the dial-up and WAN-based ports that are available for possible use for that particular RRAS. The ports shown with the device type VPN are the ports that can support the applicable encryption technologies necessary for the deployment of a VPN in the Windows 2000 Server RRAS world. For example, the first five WAN ports listed in Figure 14.12 (VPN4-4 through VPN4-0) are the ones that support the Point-to-Point Tunneling Protocol (PPTP) secured remote access method. The next five WAN ports listed (VPN3-4 through VPN3-0) support L2TP, which is another secured remote access method. (Additional details regarding both of these secured protocols can be found in the "Remote Access Security" and "Protocol Support" sections of this chapter.)

The second device from the bottom (MODEM) is the modem that is presently installed in the sample's Windows 2000 Server computer. The last device in the list (IRDA) is the infrared port device that is also presently installed in the sample's Windows 2000 Server computer. The bottom two devices are of the types that typically are not used for VPNs, though it is technically possible to use them for VPNs. The primary reason for not using devices such as these for an organization's VPN has more to do with bandwidth than any other single factor. An infrared port essentially provides up to 115Kbps of throughput, and a standard analog modem has trouble even mustering a mere 56Kbps of bandwidth. The bandwidth factor alone is usually enough to scare off any administrator considering a VPN type of solution to his or her remote access security problems.

If you right-click the Ports icon in the left windowpane and then click the Properties menu option that appears in the middle of the pop-up menu that you see, you see the Ports Properties dialog box, as shown in Figure 14.13.

FIGURE 14.13
Available RRAS devices.

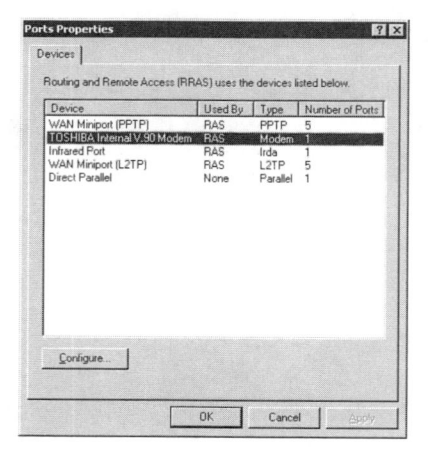

The primary purpose of the Ports Properties dialog box is to provide a summarized list of all the possible ports on the RRAS. The second function is to permit the RAS administrator a new way to configure and maintain the various remote access configurations and policies that an RRAS administrator can impose on the organization's remote access capabilities. For example, if you were to click TOSHIBA Internal V.90 Modem, as shown in Figure 14.13, and then click the Configure button near the bottom of the screen, you would be given access to the Configure Device dialog box, as shown in Figure 14.14.

FIGURE 14.14
Configuring a RAS device.

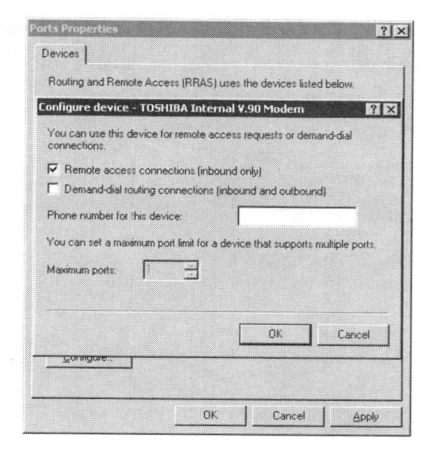

The Configure Device dialog box serves two main functions: to determine whether a specific device will act as a remote access device for inbound connections to this Windows 2000 server and/or whether it will support demand-dial routing connections for both inbound and outbound service. To enable either of these options, just click the appropriate check box. The box labeled Phone Number for This Device has quite a bit more meaning than you might think. You use this check box for Caller Station ID and with Bandwidth Allocation Protocol (BAP)–enabled connections. (For more information on the Caller Station ID, refer to the "Remote Access Security" section of this chapter, and for more details on BAP, refer to the "Protocol Support" section of this chapter.)

Remote Access Policies

Use the final option on this screen in conjunction with remote access devices that are able to support multiple ports, such as an ISDN or another WAN device. After you make your various selections, click the OK button to return to the Ports Properties window. To save all your changes and to return to the main Routing and Remote Access screen, click the OK button near the bottom of the Ports Properties window.

Next, click the Remote Access Policies icon near the bottom of the Routing and Remote Access tree in the left pane.

As soon as you click on the Remote Access Policies icon, you should see the columns in the right pane change to just two: Name and Order. The Name column provides a somewhat descriptive name of the remote access policy that has been installed on your RRAS computer, and the Order function is used when there is more than a single policy in effect. The Order function is important because it determines the precise order in which multiple remote access policies are utilized within your organization. Typically there is just a single remote access policy, Allow Access if Dial-in Permission Is Enabled, which is the default policy that is automatically implemented by Windows 2000 when the

RRAS service is initially installed onto your server computer. If you double-click on any policy, such as the one shown on your computer, you will be taken into the Properties screen for that particular remote access policy, as shown in Figure 14.15.

FIGURE 14.15
RAS policy settings properties dialog box.

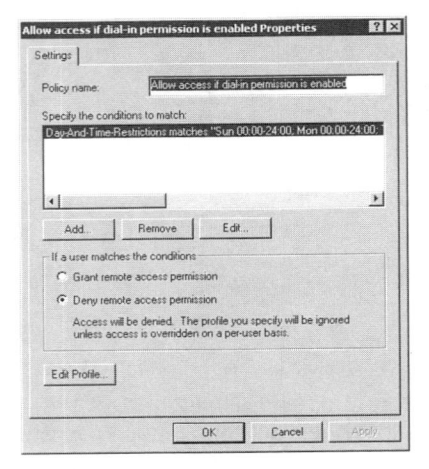

In the Policy Name box is a description of the remote access policy that you can alter at any time. The Specify the Conditions to Match box is used to specify under what networking conditions the remote access policy should take effect within your organization. The If a User Matches the Conditions area of the Properties screen is used to permit the remote access administrator the power to grant or deny remote access permission to the users who fall under the policy specified above. This permission is a global one that can only be overridden by user access that has been granted on a per-user basis. If you want to modify a remote access policy, just double-click on that specific policy from the main RRAS screen. After you do this, the Properties window for that policy appears. You need to click the Edit button to reveal the dialog box shown in Figure 14.16.

FIGURE 14.16
Setting time of day constraints.

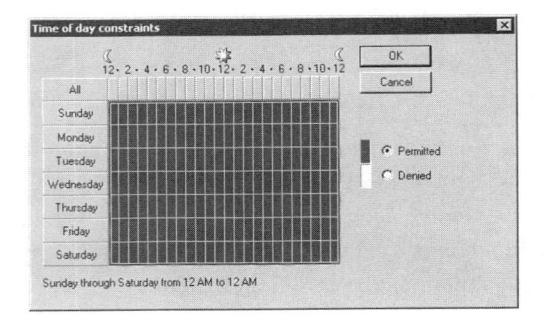

The Time of Day Constraints dialog box appears because the remote access policy that is being modified is specific to the day and time. To make a change, click on one or more of the time/day boxes that appear in the middle of this screen (use a mouse dragging movement to select more than one at a time). Then click either the Permitted or Denied radio button to change the permissions for the time/day box(es) you have highlighted. Then click the OK button to return to the Properties window.

In the Properties window, click the Edit Profile button that you see near the bottom left of the window. You do this so that you can further modify precisely the dial-in profile for this remote access policy. Next, you see the Edit Dial-in Profile dialog box shown in Figure 14.17.

FIGURE 14.17
Editing a dial-in profile to set configuration options for dial-in constraints.

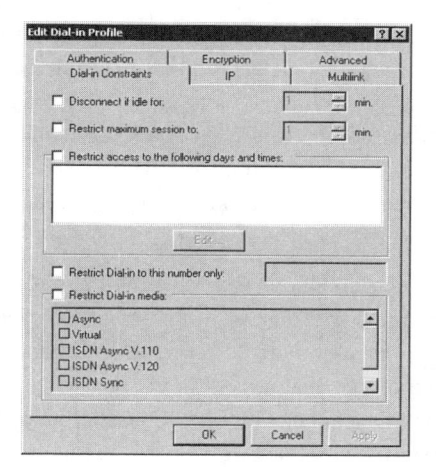

When the Edit Dial-in Profile dialog box appears, notice that it has six tabs:

- Dial-in Constraints
- IP
- Multilink
- Authentication
- Encryption
- Advanced

Dial-in Constraints

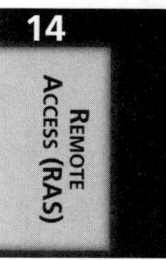

By default you will always start with the Dial-in Constraints tab, which is shown in Figure 14.17. One of the nice things about this new Windows 2000 feature is that you are now better equipped to deal with those remote users who tend to leave their remote sessions connected for long periods of time or like to walk away from their computers for lunch and still remain on the line. Those days are over for them because you are now able to disconnect users after a specified maximum period of time or if they have been idle for a set amount of time. You are also able to restrict the various times and days that someone can connect, by clicking the Restrict Access to the Following Times and Days check box to enable it. After you do that, click the Edit button that becomes available, so that you can select the times and days for this aspect of the policy to take effect. A Dial-in Hours pop-up box appears that looks similar to the Time of Day Constraints dialog box in Figure 14.22. Make the needed changes, and then click the OK button to accept those changes (click the Cancel button if you want to leave everything as you originally found it), which then returns you to the Dial-in Constraints tab.

The next option on this screen is the Restrict Dial-in to This Number Only check box. Selecting this feature makes it possible for you to enter a telephone number into the empty box to the right of that check box's label. This means that remote users must dial this specific telephone number in order to gain access to your Windows 2000 Server system. This is a handy feature if you are hoping to use the RAS service for administrative remote access to your Windows 2000 server, and not for a whole cadre of salespeople (limiting them to just a single number might seem like a nice payback, but reality tells you that you cannot or should not do that).

Next is the Restrict Dial-in Media section, where you can limit the dial-in methods to just those types that are selected in the box. To enable this type of restriction, you must first click the Restrict Dial-in Media check box to select it, which enables you to choose any of the connectivity restriction methods that appear in the box. Of the six methods shown here, probably the most popular manner in which to restrict your dial-in users is to force them to use a specific type of ISDN line.

You can use these options to eliminate the possibility that an unauthorized person can gain access to your Windows 2000 server and maybe even the rest of the network; not only would that person have to know the telephone access number and a user ID and password scheme, but he or she would need to have the precise type of remote access hardware to gain access to your systems, which is a very unlikely prospect.

IP

Next, click the IP tab to reveal the IP screen shown in Figure 14.18.

This tab's contents are split into two categories: the TCP/IP address assignment policy to be used and the routing and remote access IP packet filters that should apply during the remote users' connections. The IP Address Assignment Policy section is self-explanatory. You either let the Windows 2000 server define the policy via its own networking settings or you specify that either the client will request a specific IP address or the server must supply an IP address to each remote access client. To make your selection, simply click the appropriate radio button.

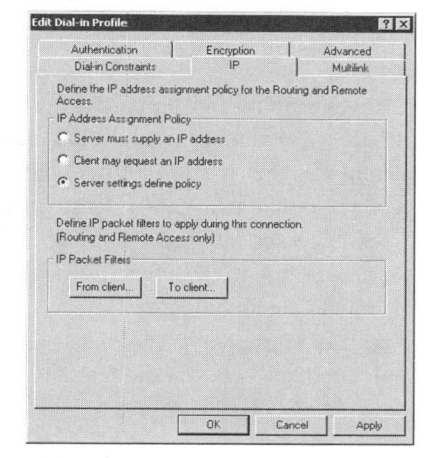

FIGURE 14.18
Defining IP address assignments.

The bottom section of this tab deals with the definition of the routing and remote access IP packet filters that will be applied during a remote user's connection to this specific Windows 2000 server. Although this is really a routing issue and less of a remote access issue, you may still want to examine this one a bit more closely. (For more information regarding this setting, refer to the "Protocol Support" section in this chapter.) After you have made any needed changes, click the Multilink tab to reveal the screen shown in Figure 14.19.

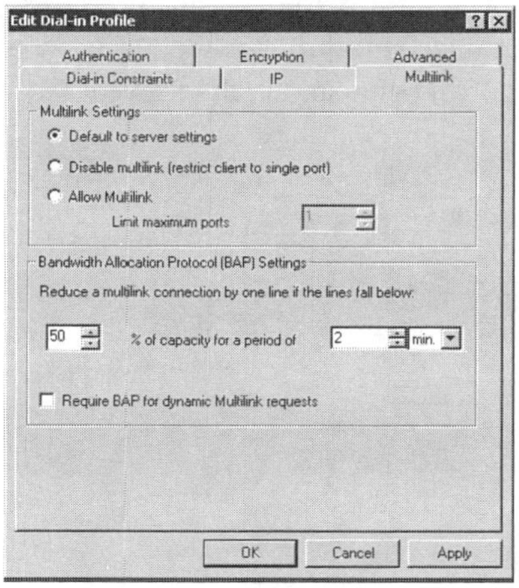

FIGURE 14.19
Configuring Multilink and BAP settings.

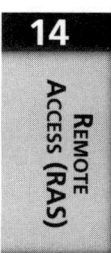

Multilink

The primary purpose of the Multilink tab is to provide remote users with possibly better bandwidth than they would otherwise have using just a single modem (be it an analog modem or a digital modem, such as ISDN). The gist of the Multilink technology is that you are able to bond two or more modems together to form a single remote access connectivity method. For example, if you were to take two V.90 56Kbps modems and multilink them, then your total bandwidth possible suddenly becomes roughly 112Kbps. (Keep in mind, though, that results vary according to the capability of the server-based modems to work well with the client's modem technologies.) The top half of the Multilink tab is designed to make this sort of arrangement possible—to provide the capability to share the bandwidth of multiple modems between the remote access clients and the Windows 2000 server.

The Multilink tab also helps you manage the quality of the Multilink process by using BAP. BAP is very useful in the Multilink world because it permits the number of modems linked together for a single connection to be added or subtracted as the bandwidth requirements demand. This on-the-fly changing of bandwidth availability for a particular remote user connection greatly enhances the Multilink experience and productivity for the remote user. To enable this RRAS feature, click on the up and down arrows next to the percentage window to set the percentage of capacity required to trigger the use of BAP. Use the up and down arrows next to the time amount window to set the amount of time (in either minutes or seconds) before BAP goes into effect. The bottom check box, Require BAP for Dynamic Multilink Requests, is used to specify whether BAP should be enabled for any additional Multilink connection sessions. After you have made any needed selections, click the Authentication tab to reveal the screen shown in Figure 14.20.

FIGURE 14.20
Choosing authentication options.

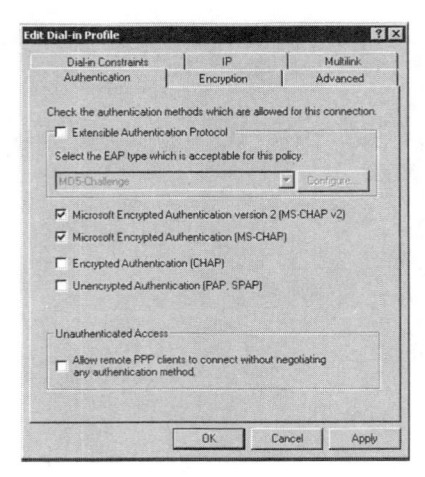

Authentication

The Authentication tab is where you set the authentication types for your RAS connections. Although most of the options presented on this tab deal directly with encryption, the ability to enable or disable encryption can only be set from the Encryption tab. Clicking once on the Extensible Authentication Protocol (EAP) check box enables that feature, which includes support for a wide range of authentication devices such as public key smart cards, one-time passwords, token cards, and the like. You need to enable the EAP feature in order to modify the EAP type drop-down list box that appears just below the EAP check box. The Configure button next to this drop-down list box become usable only if the EAP is able to modify the available options. For instance, the MD5-Challenge EAP has no configurable options, whereas a public key smart card usually does.

> **Note**
>
> The term MD5 itself is a term that does not really mean anything (though the letters MD refer to the terms message digest). MD5 was developed in 1994 as a one-way hash algorithm that takes any length of data and produces a 128-bit "fingerprint" for that data. This fingerprint is typically referred to as the message digest and cannot be reverse engineered. That means that it is computationally impossible for someone to determine the actual contents of your data based solely on its MD5 fingerprint. One very nice aspect of MD5 is that it does not contain any encryption, and so it can be exported without any worries of interference by the U.S. government.

The middle section of the Authentication tab permits the RAS administrator to enable or disable the various types of CHAP and SPAP/PAP (Shiva Password Authentication Protocol/Password Authentication Protocol) authentication methods, by checking their check boxes:

- Microsoft Encrypted Authentication Version 2 (MS-CHAP v2)
- Microsoft Encrypted Authentication (MS-CHAP)
- Encrypted Authentication (CHAP)
- Unencrypted Authentication (PAP, SPAP)

> **Note**
>
> Refer to the "Remote Access Security" section of this chapter to find more details on the differences between MS-CHAP, MS-CHAP version 2, PAP, and Shiva's SPAP. Keep in mind that the use of unencrypted authentication is not necessarily a bad thing, especially when you need to permit access to non-Microsoft clients such as Macintosh to access your Windows 2000 Server environment in a guest mode fashion.

You use the final option on this tab, Unauthenticated Access, when you need to permit any remote PPP client machine to access your Windows 2000 server without having to process an authentication routine. This is handy for guest or Macintosh client users, as well as for remote users whose originating telephone number is being used as the replacement authentication method (such as when you use the automatic number identification scheme known as ANI, or some other sort of Caller-ID identification scheme). After you have made all the appropriate selections in this tab, click the Encryption tab to reveal the screen shown in Figure 14.21.

FIGURE 14.21
Setting your encryption level.

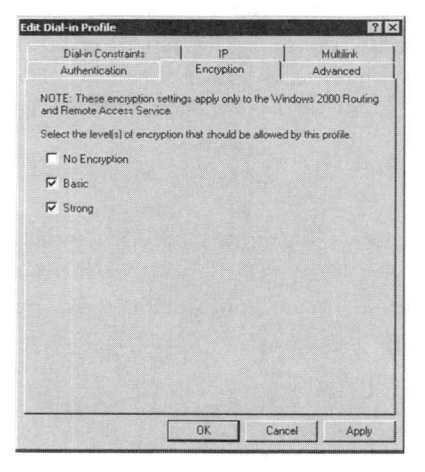

Encryption

The information and options on the Encryption tab are quite easy to understand and implement. In short, if you do not want to use any encryption levels with your RRAS clients, then click the top check box (No Encryption) to enable that feature. Enabling the middle check box, Basic, means that your organization is forcing its remote clients to adhere to a 40-bit encryption scheme that is usable not only domestically, but internationally as well. The bottom check box option, Strong, does just what you think it would:

It uses Microsoft's triple DES (Digital Encryption Standard, which is sometimes referred to as 3DES) encryption scheme, which means that two separate 56-bit keys are in use that will make your RAS services usable only within the United States, due to its high-security implementation (that is, you are not able to legally export this high-security encryption technology at this time). After you make any needed encryption selections, click the Advanced tab to reveal the screen shown in Figure 14.22.

FIGURE 14.22
Adding advanced options.

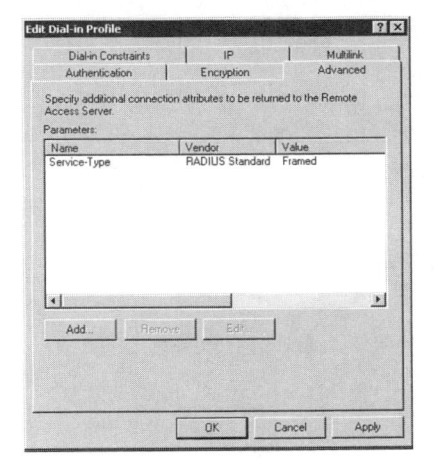

Advanced Options

On the Advanced tab you can configure your RRAS implementation to use additional connection attributes that must be returned to the RAS when remote users access it. This is part of the Remote Authentication Dial-In User Service (RADIUS) technology, which is an industry-accepted protocol based on Internet Requests for Comments (RFC) documents 2138 and 2139. The purpose of the RADIUS service is to provide authentication, authorization, and accounting services for DUN client computers. A RADIUS client may be an enduser's computer, but more likely it is a dial-up server that is being used by an Internet service provider (ISP) in conjunction with your organization's remote users. Four vendors are currently covered by Microsoft's Windows 2000 implementation: Ascend Communications; Cisco; the (Microsoft) RADIUS standards; and US Robotics. To add one of these RADIUS services, click the Add button to reveal the Add Attributes dialog box shown in Figure 14.23.

The Add Attributes dialog box is where you select the RADIUS attribute(s) that are required for your remote access networking needs. For example, in the example we have selected the Tunnel-Type attribute, which is a RADIUS standard vendor attribute type. After you have located the attribute that you want to use (you scroll up and down this pretty extensive list to find it), click the Add button to reveal the Multivalued Attribute Information dialog box, shown in Figure 14.24.

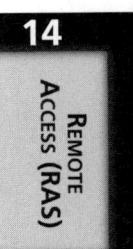

FIGURE 14.23
Choosing a RADIUS attribute.

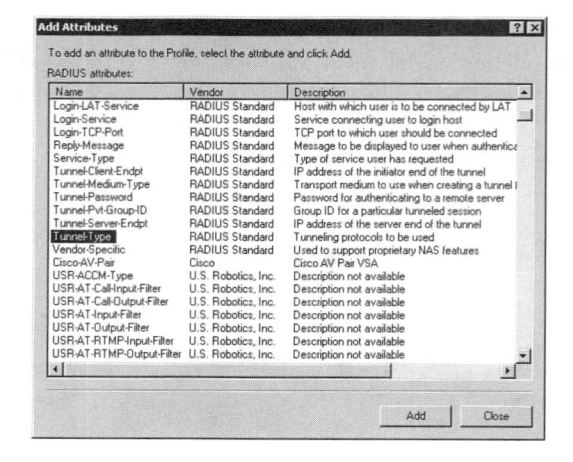

FIGURE 14.24
Using the Multivalued Attribute Information dialog box.

In the Multivalued Attribute Information dialog box, you finalize the configuration of the vendor and attribute information. To do this, click the Add button to reveal the Enumerable Attribute Information dialog box, which is shown in Figure 14.25.

At the bottom of this screen is a drop-down list box that contains the various enumerable attributes that are applicable to the multivalued attribute. For the example shown, L2TP is being selected. After you make your selection, click the OK button to return to the Multivalued Attribute Information dialog box, with your choice intact. From there you click the OK button to return to the Add Attributes screen. On that screen, click the Close button to return to the original Edit Dial-In Profile dialog box, with the Advanced tab displayed. From that screen, click the OK button to return to the general Routing and Remote Access screen.

FIGURE 14.25
Choosing an attribute value.

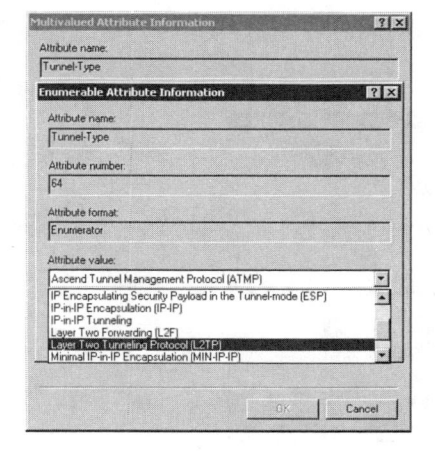

RAS Policies

Another aspect of RAS that you should be aware of is that countless numbers of remote access policies can be implemented via the Routing and Remote Access screen. To start the process for adding a new RAS Policy, right-click the Remote Access Policy icon near the bottom of the left pane. A small pop-up window appears, where you see the option New. Click this option to reveal the Remote Access Policy menu selection.

Next, you are taken to the starting point of the Add Remote Access Policy Wizard, as shown in Figure 14.26.

FIGURE 14.26
Entering a friendly name for your new RAS policy.

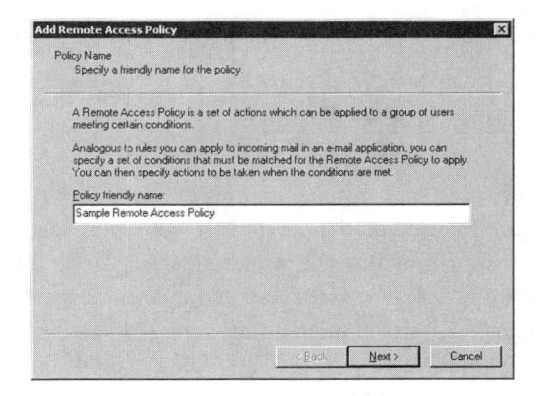

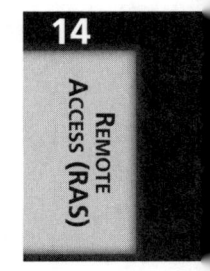

On this opening screen of the Add Remote Access Policy Wizard, you should type in a descriptive name of the new remote access policy that you are starting to create. You should make these names as descriptive as possible because when you have dozens of policies in place, it is difficult to sift through them in case of problems if the names are not clear. Click the Next button to proceed to the Select Attribute dialog box, as shown in Figure 14.27.

FIGURE 14.27
Choosing an attribute to add.

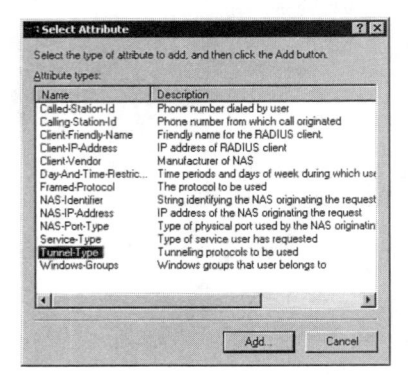

At this point, you need to choose the remote access policy attribute that you want to apply with this new policy. To select an attribute, click that attribute's name to highlight it, and then click the Add button to save your choice. This takes you to the attribute's details selection screen, shown in Figure 14.28.

FIGURE 14.28
Selecting a specific Tunnel-Type attribute.

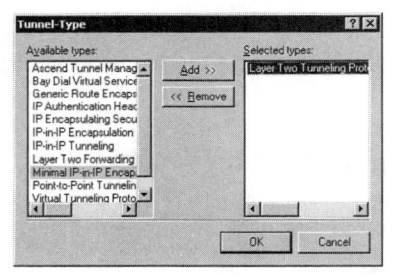

From the Tunnel-Type dialog box shown (note that this dialog box may vary, depending on what type of attribute you selected on the previous screen), you need to select the specific type of tunneling protocol policy that you want to restrict. To do this, click an option from the Available Types column on the left, and then click the Add button to move that option to the Selected Types column on the right (just as is shown in the sample in Figure 14.28). After you make your selection(s), click the OK button to proceed to the Add Remote Access Policy dialog box, with your newly selected attribute displayed, as shown in Figure 14.29.

FIGURE 14.29
Setting RAS policy conditions.

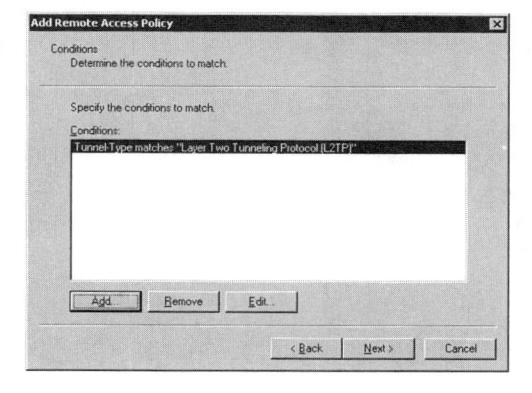

The process you have just walked through determines what conditions must be matched in order for this remote access policy to take effect. You may select as many conditions as you wish by clicking the Add button and repeating these last few steps. If you are satisfied with your selection(s), then click the Next button to proceed to the Permissions section of the wizard, as shown in Figure 14.30.

FIGURE 14.30
Determining whether to grant or deny RAS access.

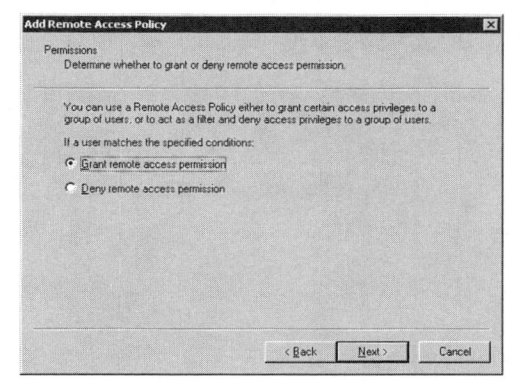

In this dialog box you determine whether you will be granting or denying the remote user access to your Windows 2000 server based on the conditions that you specified in the previous screen. You must choose one of the two radio button selections. Then, click the Next button to proceed to the User Profile section of the wizard, as shown in Figure 14.31.

FIGURE 14.31
Deciding whether to edit a user profile.

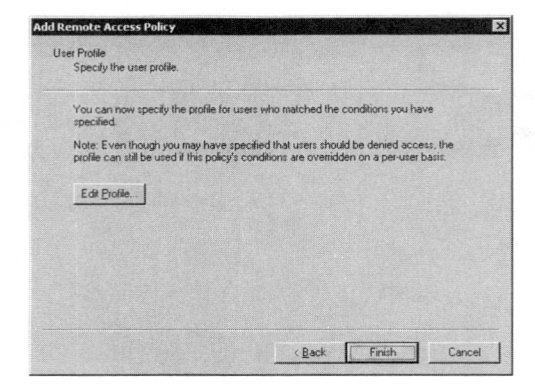

Now you need to determine whether to make this remote access policy selective. If you want this policy to apply to everyone, then do not make a selection here. Keep in mind, though, that the profile can still be overridden if this new remote access policy's conditions try to alter a higher authority's policy decisions. When you are satisfied with your decision, click the Finish button to complete the Add Remote Access Policy Wizard. You again see the Routing and Remote Access screen, with your newly defined policy displayed in the right pane, as shown in Figure 14.32.

FIGURE 14.32
Reviewing your newly created RAS policy.

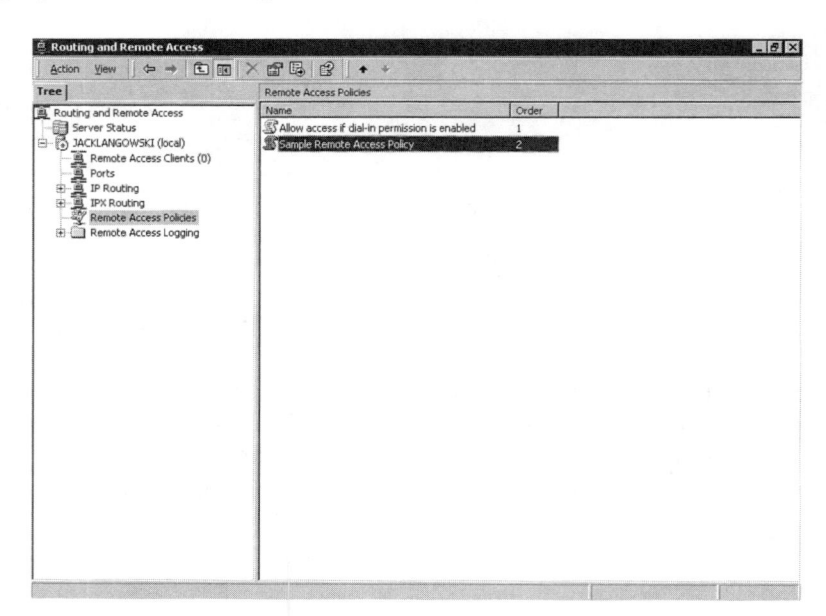

Remote access policies initially appear in the order in which they are created. To rearrange the sequence of the remote access policies shown in the Routing and Remote

Access screen, select the policy whose order you want to alter by right-clicking it, and then select the new order from the pop-up menu that appears.

The Move Up menu selection does what it sounds like: It moves the highlighted policy one position up, toward the top of the sequence. The Move Down option does just the opposite. If you want to delete a specific policy, click it to highlight it, and then use the Delete menu option from the pop-up menu. The Properties menu selection allows you to change any aspect of the remote access policy configuration that you performed during the initial wizard setup process.

Remote Access Logging

Next, click the Remote Access Logging icon at the bottom of the tree in the left pane. This opens the remote access log file and displays its contents in the right pane, as shown in Figure 14.33.

FIGURE 14.33
Reviewing Remote Access Logging.

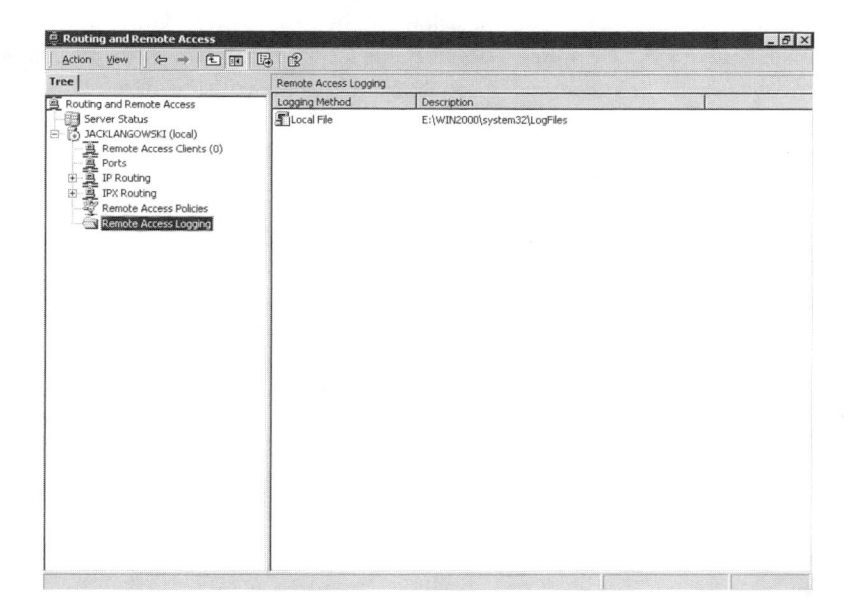

The right pane displays the logging method and a description of the logs, which is typically the location of the logging file. If you right-click one of the Logging Method/Description lines shown (in the example, there is just a single line), a menu with two options—Properties and Help—appears. Help will get you help with the Routing and Remote Access functions of Windows 2000 Server. Click the Properties option, which causes the Local File Properties dialog box to appear, as shown in Figure 14.34.

FIGURE 14.34
Setting local file properties for RAS logging.

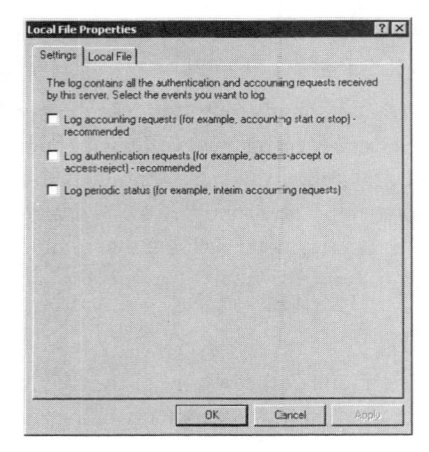

Figure 14.34 shows the three possible logging options for the Remote Access Server. To enable any of these options, click the check box that is next to the option you want to invoke. Then click the Local File tab to proceed to that screen, as shown in Figure 14.35.

FIGURE 14.35
Choosing log file options.

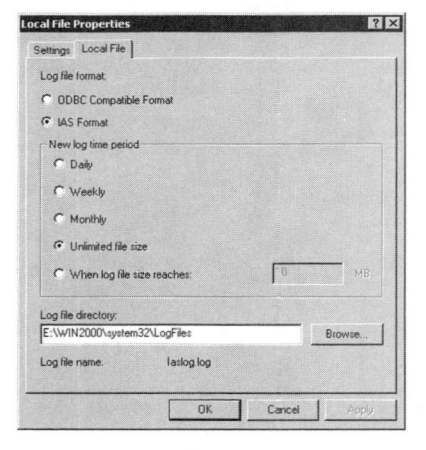

The Local File tab permits you as the RAS administrator to specify certain aspects of the logging functions, including the format of the logs, the time period covered by the log, where the log is kept, and the name of the log. One of the most important things to decide on this screen is whether the log should be stored in an Open Database Connectivity (ODBC)-compatible mode or in an Internet Authentication Service (IAS) format. The ODBC format permits the log to be stored in an ODBC-compliant database, whereas the IAS format is usually a text-based format that can then be read by other logging tools (including non-Microsoft ones). The available selections in both the New Log Time Period and the Log File format sections are pretty obvious, so we will not spend time discussing them here. After you have made your selections, click the OK button to save your changes and return to the main Routing and Remote Access screen.

Routing Configurations

To configure routing, first check to see if the Routing and Remote Access screen is already open on your Windows 2000 server. If it is not, click the Start button, the Programs menu option, the Administrative Tools menu option, and finally the Routing and Remote Access menu selection. This takes you directly to the main screen of the Routing and Remote Access administration screen, which is actually an MMC window.

Because we have already configured the Windows 2000 server as a Remote Access Server, you will already see your computer's name shown just under the Server Status icon in the tree in the left pane. The icons labeled with the term Routing in them are the start of the routing section. Part of the RAS configuration causes all the protocols already installed on your computer to appear as possible routing choices here. For example, notice that there may be entries for both IP Routing and IPX Routing. This would occur on those servers where both the TCP/IP suite and the NWLink IPX/SPX/NetBIOS Compatible Transport networking protocols were already installed on this server, before we performed the initial RRAS configurations in the previous section of this chapter.

If you want to manage more than one computer at a time, you can do this through the same Microsoft Management Console (MMC) window by right-clicking once on the Routing and Remote Access icon at the top of the tree. This causes a small pop-up window to appear.

In this menu you are given the option to add another server to your screen. Of course, you must have full administrative rights to that other computer, which also must already have the RRAS service running on it before you add it. To actually add a new server, click the Add Server menu option to reveal the window shown in Figure 14.36.

FIGURE 14.36
Adding another RRAS server to your MMC for remote administration.

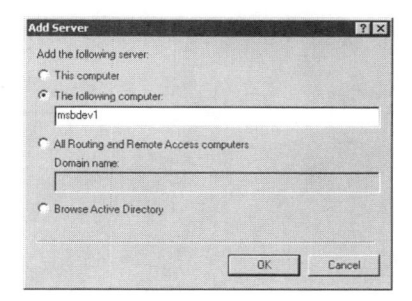

In the Add Server dialog box you have a few choices:

- **This Computer**—Select this option if you have not yet configured the Remote Access Server service.
- **The Following Computer**—Enter the computer name of the other system that you wish to manage, assuming that it exists via a high-speed LAN or WAN link (slow dial-up links to other computers just do not work with RRAS management tasks).
- **All Routing and Remote Access Computers**—Enter the domain name that contains all the Routing and Remote Access computers you want, and every one of them will automatically appear in your management list (this is much faster than the This Computer configuration route).
- **Browse Active Directory**—You should choose this option if the Active Directory technology has already been installed and configured for your environment, and you have the proper administrative rights to surf through the directory seeking RRAS information. Like the option The Following Computer, this one lets you surf through the Active Directory for a specific computer name and then install that computer only.

After you find the new computer you want to manage, click the OK button to confirm your selection. This returns you to the primary Routing and Remote Access screen, where you can see your new selection at the bottom of the tree in the left pane, as shown in Figure 14.37.

FIGURE 14.37
Viewing all RRAS servers available for administration.

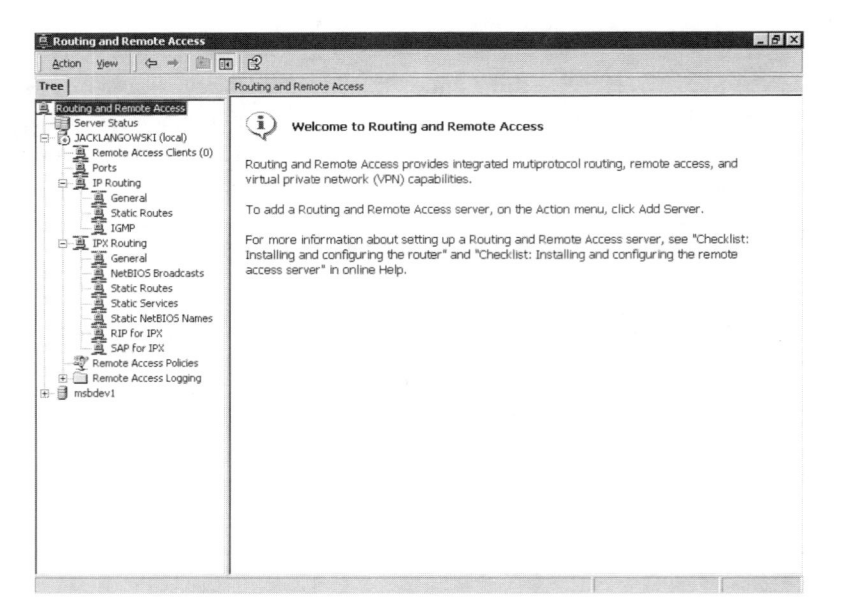

> **Note**
>
> To make this example easy to follow, we will stick to configuring just the local server for routing (the process is the same as that for a remote server, but the fact that we are already familiar with the local computer should make the examples easier to follow).

Click the General icon that appears just under the IP Routing icon in the tree, as shown in Figure 14.38.

FIGURE 14.38
Reviewing the general information shown for an IP routing scenario.

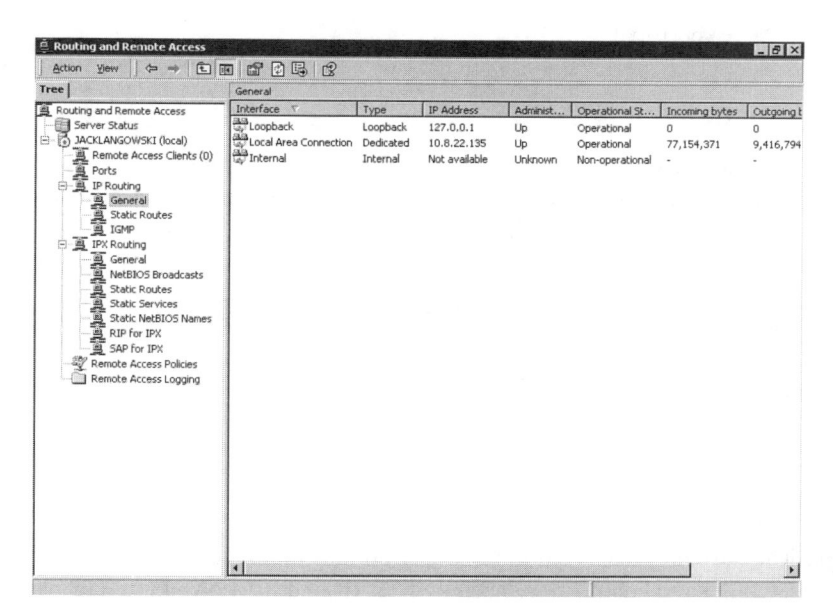

Immediately after clicking once on the General icon, you will see a few items appear in the right pane, under the first column (labeled Interface):

- Loopback
- Local Area Connection
- Internal

These items are the defined interfaces in your Windows 2000 server, which are available for routing configuration. Although it is possible to delete one or more of them, you might not want to if you are planning to use the routing capabilities of Windows 2000. To delete any of them, just right-click on that interface to select it and display the small pop-up menu from which you selected the Delete menu option.

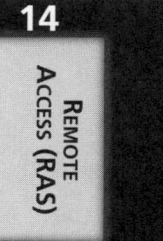

If you right-click the General icon again, a menu appears, with several selections on it:

- New Interface
- New Routing Protocol
- Show TCP/IP Information
- Show Multicast Forwarding Table
- Show Multicast Statistics
- View
- Refresh
- Export List
- Properties
- Help

Most of these options are self-explanatory, but a few of the screens that appear might need some explanation. For example, if you clicked the Show TCP/IP Information option, the screen shown in Figure 14.39 would appear.

FIGURE 14.39
Reviewing TCP/IP information settings for the JACKLANGOWSKI computer.

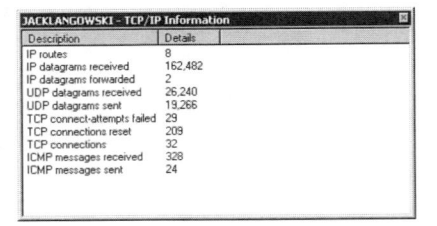

Description	Details
IP routes	8
IP datagrams received	162,482
IP datagrams forwarded	2
UDP datagrams received	26,240
UDP datagrams sent	19,266
TCP connect-attempts failed	29
TCP connections reset	209
TCP connections	32
ICMP messages received	328
ICMP messages sent	24

The attributes displayed in the Description column include information on the various TCP/IP suite components, such as TCP, IP, and ICMP. You use a display screen such as this one as a form of preventive medicine (you may notice a problem such as an increasing number of TCP connect attempts failing), or to help diagnose a routing problem that may be occurring with your Windows 2000 server.

If you use other options from this menu, such as Show Multicast Forwarding Table, you may see empty screens.

This occurs because the multicast routing has not yet been installed or configured for your Windows 2000 server. The lack of statistics is no cause for alarm, unless you think you have already configured your server for multicast routing. If this is the case, then your alarm is correct: You do have a problem.

If you select the Properties option, then you enter the General Properties window for IP routing on your server, which is where you begin the configuration process. The first screen you see shows the General tab, as in Figure 14.40.

FIGURE 14.40
Reviewing event logging options for IP routing.

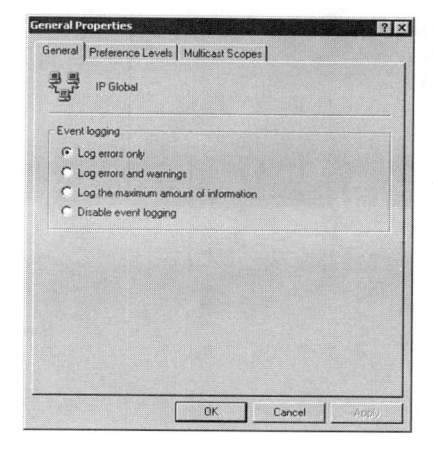

The purpose of the General tab is to set the various logging options for any IP routing you may be performing on your server. After you set the level of logging for the server in question, click the Preference Levels tab to proceed to the screen shown in Figure 14.41.

FIGURE 14.41
Setting preference levels.

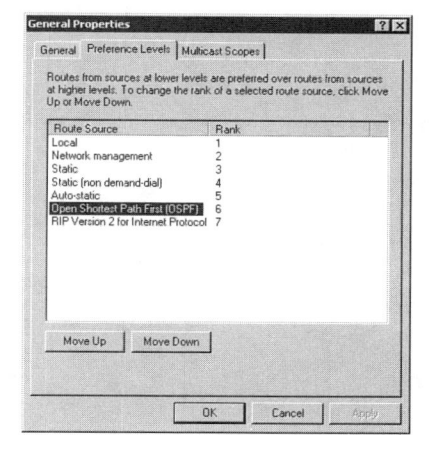

The Preference Levels tab is used to set the rankings of the various routes that are possible for your server. To change the level for a particular Route Source, click that item and then click either the Move Up button or the Move down button. This causes that particular route source to either increase or decrease a single level within the ranks. Click the Multicast Scopes tab to proceed to the screen shown in Figure 14.42.

FIGURE 14.42
Using the Multicast Scopes tab.

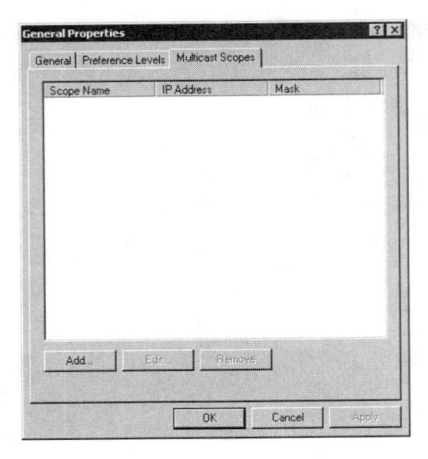

Presumably, the first time you enter this screen, its contents are empty. Therefore, to add multicast scopes to your IP routing configuration, click the Add button to reveal the Add Scoped Boundary dialog box, as shown in Figure 14.43.

FIGURE 14.43
Adding a scoped boundary.

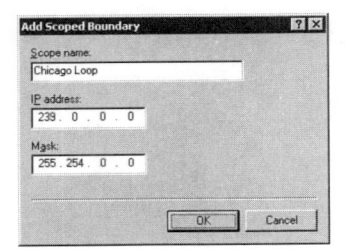

When the Add Scoped Boundary dialog box appears, you need to make three entries:

- Scope Name
- IP Address
- Mask

These entries are required for your boundary, which must include a valid boundary IP address and subnet mask for your computer's particular range of TCP/IP addresses (for example, do not try to use an address and a mask lower than the one shown, if your computer is to have a Class A IP address).

> **Note**
>
> If you do not understand how to properly create a range of TCP/IP addresses and the associated appropriate subnet masks, then you might not want to be messing around with this area of Windows 2000 Server. However, if you just want a nice refresher on the area of TCP/IP addressing within the Windows 2000 arena, then you might want to pick up a copy of the Microsoft Press book titled *Microsoft Windows 2000 TCP/IP Protocols and Services Technical Reference* (ISBN #0-7356-0556-4, released January 2000). This book is an excellent source of reference material for the TCP/IP networking environment and includes the many new changes to the TCP/IP suite for the Windows 2000 Server operating world.

Click the OK button to return to the Multicast Scopes tab, as shown in Figure 14.44.

FIGURE 14.44
Reviewing your newly created multicast scope.

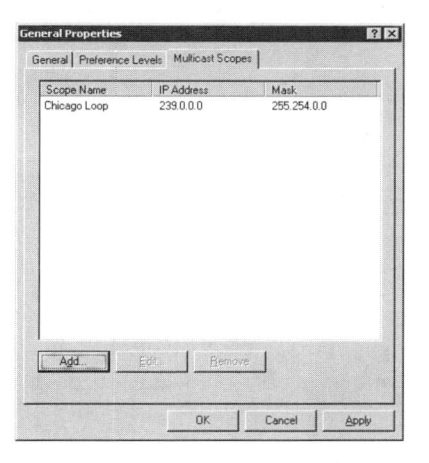

You should see the new multicast scope in this window. If you do not, then you should have encountered an error message box that explained what you did wrong (more than likely you attempted to enter an incorrect boundary address). After you have all the scopes created and the other tabs' entries selected, click the OK button to save your selections and return to the main Routing and Remote Access screen.

Adding a New Routing Protocol

The next item you might want to add to your Routing and Remote Access configuration is a new protocol for routing. To do this, click the New Routing Protocol menu selection.

In the New Routing Protocol dialog box you can add a new protocol by clicking the protocol you want to add and then clicking the OK button. You are returned to the main

Routing and Remote Access screen with your selection intact, and from there you can enter the Properties sections for each protocol and make any configuration changes needed.

Next, click the Static Routes icon, and you see the screen shown in Figure 14.45.

FIGURE 14.45
Reviewing existing static routes (if any).

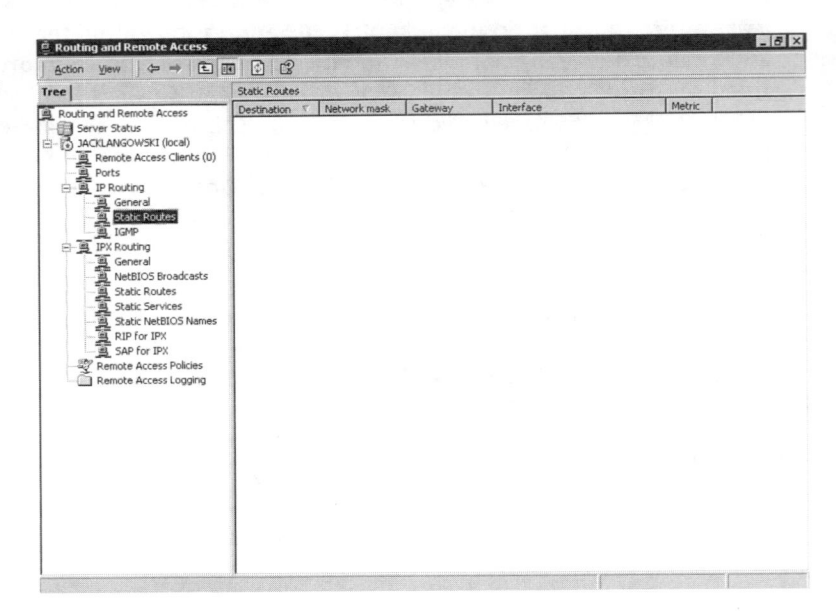

As you will probably notice, there are no static routes configured for use with your computer. You can add one quickly by right-clicking the Static Routes icon. From the popup menu that appears, click the New Static Route option, which opens the Static Route dialog box.

You use the Static Route dialog box to add a new static IP route to your server's RRAS environment. You need to enter the destination information, a network mask, the gateway's TCP/IP address, and the metric level to be used. You may or may not have the opportunity to decide whether to use this new route for demand-dial connections. If you can select or deselect the box next to the Use This New Route for Demand-Dial Connections label, then do so as your routing environment requires. The Destination is where you enter the host, IP, or subnet address, or you can use it to enter the default route information. The network mask must coincide with your destination address (that is, if you select a destination of 255.255.255.255, then the network mask will be 0.0.0.0). A Gateway IP address must be entered if this is a LAN-based routing interface, whereas for demand-dial routing, Gateway is an unused field. The Metric area is where you set the number of hops it takes to reach the destination, or it can also be set to the cost level it takes to reach that destination. The metric to determine the best route uses this setting, which is manipulated by using the up/down scrollbar next to its box. Next click the OK button to save the new route and return to the main Routing and Remote Access window.

The other static route-specific option from the small menu that appears whenever you right-click on the Static Routes icon is the Show Static Routes option, whose resulting screen is shown in Figure 14.46.

FIGURE 14.46
Reviewing your IP routing table for the JACKLANGOWSKI *server.*

Destination	Network mask	Gateway	Interface	Metric	Protocol
0.0.0.0	0.0.0.0	10.8.16.239	Local Area Connection	1	Network management
10.8.16.0	255.255.248.0	10.8.22.135	Local Area Connection	1	Local
10.8.22.135	255.255.255.255	127.0.0.1	Loopback	1	Local
10.255.255.255	255.255.255.255	10.8.22.135	Local Area Connection	1	Local
127.0.0.0	255.0.0.0	127.0.0.1	Loopback	1	Local
127.0.0.1	255.255.255.255	127.0.0.1	Loopback	1	Local
224.0.0.0	240.0.0.0	10.8.22.135	Local Area Connection	1	Local
255.255.255.255	255.255.255.255	10.8.22.135	Local Area Connection	1	Local

The information presented on this screen should look familiar to you, as it is very similar in content to the information you receive if you use the Route Print command from within a Windows 2000 command prompt.

The next IP routing protocol shown in the left pane is IGMP. The routing protocol IGMP (Internet Group Management Protocol) is used to convey group information between potential group members within Class D IP addresses (that is, multicast targets). It is used as an example here to give you an idea of where the various routing protocols appear if you add them to the IP routing tree—just under the Static Routes icon.

Sometimes when you right-click the General icon and then select the menu option New Interface, you receive an error message box like the one shown in Figure 14.47.

FIGURE 14.47
A typical IP routing error message box.

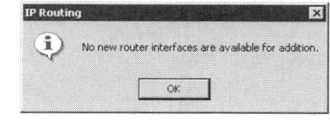

Error messages like this may occur whenever you attempt to perform a routing that exceeds the capabilities of your Windows 2000 Server computing environment. This does not mean that it will happen every time, but it may occur following a change to your computing environment. It is for this reason that you should very carefully test any alteration in a mock development environment instead of on your production systems.

> **Tip**
>
> Routing configurations form the basis of any network within an organization as well as between organizations (such as Internet connectivity). It is for this reason that you must always test any and all configuration changes within a pure test environment and not a production operating environment. Failure to do so typically results in data loss, lost productivity, and wasted resources, not to mention the possibility of business failure (for a "dot-com" type of business).

If you want to display various types of information regarding your routing interfaces, including the general loopback and local area connections and any static routes, all you need to do is right-click the applicable option that appears in the right pane; this brings up the menu shown in Figure 14.48.

FIGURE 14.48
Reviewing potential IP routing configuration information.

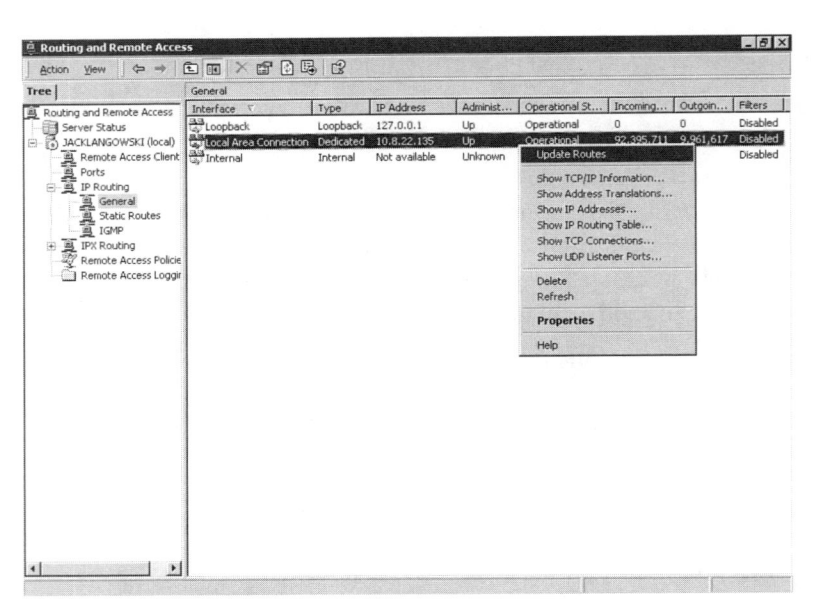

Additionally, from some of the items that appear in the right pane, you are able to update or change the various properties for those routing interfaces. The screens for configuring routing protocols are similar from one protocol to another. For example, examine the IPX Routing section shown in Figure 14.49.

FIGURE 14.49
Reviewing general IPX routing information.

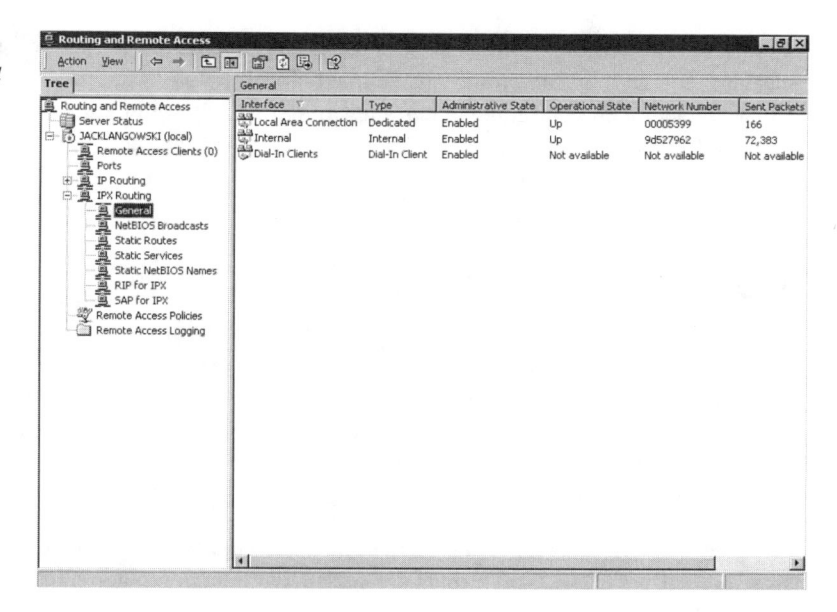

As you can see, the General icon is the first one shown in the subtree under the IPX Routing icon, with the NetBIOS broadcasts and the various static routes coming next; this is not very different from how the IP Routing section is presented. Unfortunately, there are literally thousands of different routing configurations that cannot possibly be covered within the tiny routing scope of this book, so we only touch on where and how to configure these items. If you just remember Routing and Remote Access, then you are more than halfway there.

Protocol Support

RRAS supports many protocols, including the multiprotocol routing that is handy in organizations that must deal with multiple protocols simultaneously. Using the multiprotocol support of Windows 2000 Server, you can configure servers to support a wide variety of networking protocols such as TCP/IP, NetBEUI, IPX/SPX, and AppleTalk. The RRAS servers that handle these many protocols can be installed inside the organization's demilitarized zone (DMZ). Doing this can help ensure that one networking protocol is used inside the walls of the company, while a different protocol is used outside those same walls (this was an early means of networking security, although it is not recommended for anything more than small workgroups in today's Internet-capable world).

Another facet of protocol support is known as *multihoming*. This is the process by which a Windows 2000 server can be configured to have more than a single TCP/IP address. Multihoming is supported within Windows 2000 Server in a variety of ways, the most popular of which is through the assignment of multiple IP addresses for a single network interface card (NIC). The reason this can be helpful to you as the network administrator is that you can then configure static routes to more easily join networks that are normally disjointed in nature. For example, you might have a few disparate networks that you want to connect to each other, and using the multihoming support provided within Windows 2000 Server will enable you to connect them all together.

Modem Considerations

Although Windows 2000 Server supports many different modems of both digital and analog varieties, it is critical that you obtain hardware that is fully compatible with the Windows 2000 Server operating system environment. As discussed earlier in the chapter, you should check your hardware's compatibility via the Microsoft Hardware Compatibility List (HCL). Checking your hardware before installing it helps limit RRAS problems that will most certainly appear later if you do not.

If you are planning to establish a modem pool for your remote bands of users, you should select the COM ports expansion equipment from a reputable hardware vendor such as Digi (which makes the multiple-port boards in many sizes—8, 16, 32, and up). Doing this makes it easier for you to then configure those ports through the RAS portion of the Windows 2000 Server RRAS feature. Likewise, if you are going to be using smart cards with your RAS connections, make sure that all the equipment you plan to use is fully compatible with Windows 2000 Server before purchasing it.

From the software side of things, make sure that you have properly configured any dialing rules, remote access policies, and the RAS logging options before doing any deployment, including pilots. This helps you to control your RAS implementations, especially those that will be crossing national or even international boundaries.

WAN Support

WAN support in Windows 2000 server is provided in a number of ways. Within the Windows 2000 RRAS service, there is support for multiprotocol LAN-to-LAN, LAN-to-WAN, VPN, and NAT routing services. All these services are fully configurable from either the local server's screen or from across the WAN, via the same MMC snap-in you use locally. Additionally, the routing capabilities of Windows 2000 Server include the ability to add, change, and delete the protocols in use, such as TCP/IP, IPX/SPX, and AppleTalk, without much difficulty. Additionally, a Windows 2000 server that has the RAS service enabled can partake in a Simple Network Management Protocol (SNMP) environment as an SNMP agent.

Another useful feature of the WAN support provided within Windows 2000 Server is connection sharing. Connection sharing permits a smaller network to share a single WAN connection, which typically goes to the Internet. This connection-sharing Windows 2000 server acts as a network address translator, a simplified DHCP server, and a Microsoft DNS and/or WINS server, as necessary, which thus lowers the costs of making a connection of this sort. There are two connection types to consider when using the connection-sharing feature for your LAN/WAN environment:

- Translated—The translated method is by far the best method because it provides the network with an added layer of security through its ability to shield the network from the Internet (or the other WAN) by using NAT.
- Routed—The routed method merely routes the data packets from your network out to the other WAN or the Internet, which means your network is not really very safe.

Regardless of the connection type used, keep in mind that the connection-sharing technology is really only suited for connecting a small internal network with a larger WAN such as the Internet. It does not work between two WANs.

Authentication

The authentication support provided within Windows 2000 Server RRAS has improved immensely over the older RAS authentication support provided with Windows NT Server 4. Back then, beyond the simple user ID/password authentication schemes, there was very little a network administrator could do to try to halt the plague of unauthorized users from attempting to infiltrate a network. Now, within Windows 2000 Server, you have several methods at your disposal, including CHAP and SPAP/PAP authentication methods.

Remember back during the installation and initial configuration process for the RRAS service (in the section entitled "Remote Access Policies"), we discussed how to use the properties available for a particular server and then selected the Security tab to reach the Authentication Methods area? That area is where the various authentication methods for RRAS service are set. In that same area you can set the authentication provider for your RRAS configuration: either Windows authentication or RADIUS authentication. These authentication methods are used by RRAS to determine how remote access or dial-in authentication is conducted. Windows authentication uses the built-in security features of Windows 2000 Server and/or the Windows NT SAM (Security Accounts Manager) database to control access to your network's resources. RADIUS authentication means that the RAS uses a RADIUS server to determine the method by which demand-dial routers and remote access authenticate clients to the network.

One of the most important aspects of authentication that you should keep in mind is that the more levels you impose on your users, the greater the affect on those client machines.

For instance, were you to impose the use of IPSec upon all your RAS users, you would quickly notice approximately a 40 percent increase in overhead for those remote users. Of course, there is another side to this equation. The less you impose on the user community, such as not using any method of encryption and permitting clear-text passwords, the more open your network is to perhaps otherwise unauthorized users. Somewhere in the middle of these is the balance that your organization must seek, in order to survive these rapidly changing times in an Internet economy world.

Troubleshooting RAS

The process by which you troubleshoot a RAS connection is simple in theory but very hard to duplicate in practice. Whatever methodology you decide to use, it should be one that is always repeated, regardless of the situation at hand. The reason why you will want to maintain a specific troubleshooting methodology is simple: It makes the process work better, since you will be able to figure out problems faster (because many problems have similar symptoms and causes). The troubleshooting strategy and procedural approach should be simple to follow and contain at least these steps, in the following order:

1. Document everything. Never begin a troubleshooting process without writing down everything that was tried to fix the problem, or after a while you will begin going in circles without realizing it.

2. Discuss the problem with the person who first noticed something was amiss, even if that person is a not a technically knowledgeable user, and be sure to listen very attentively. If you discovered the problem, then write it down in full detail and then re-read what you wrote. Perhaps you will notice something there that you missed when just thinking about the problem.

3. Make sure that the problem is reproducible. If it is not, then document the issue fully and place it in an Unresolved category. However, do not waste time and valuable company resources theorizing about what might have gone wrong and agonizing over it. If it cannot be reproduced, then it cannot be fixed.

4. Write down verbatim the steps it takes to reproduce the problem. Make sure that you keep screen shots of error messages (if there are any) that appear, as well as a copy of the Dr. Watson and Windows 2000 system event log files.

5. Make sure you know precisely when the problem first arose and how long it has been around, as well as what the system administrator or user does when it first appears (assuming that a human is the first to notice, and not one of the Windows 2000 logging devices).

6. After the issue has been resolved, document exactly what was done to fix the problem and perhaps what can be done in the future to prevent the problem from reoccurring. Save this documentation in an electronic format and post it in some sort of

online database or intranet site so that other network administrators with the same or higher levels of authority can learn from issues that others in the organization have encountered.

When your troubleshooting strategy is in place, it is time to actually solve the problems. The Windows 2000 Server event log is a great place to start because it logs RAS warnings, errors, and general data regarding your remote access environment that has been installed and configured via the RRAS service. Another great source of information is the PPP Tracing option, which provides a list of the programming messages and PPP control messages that are created during a PPP connection (you may also want to refer to Chapter 24, "Optimizing Performance Tuning," for further tracing and logging capabilities). Obviously, if something goes amiss, it helps to be able to get at least some understanding of the events that were occurring just before and during the problem at hand. You can find this log file in the `%systemroot%` folder of your Windows 2000 server. To enable the PPP Tracing option at the console level, though, you must make a change to your Windows 2000 Server Registry by setting the `EnableConsoleTracing` value entry in the Registry to a value of 1. Keep in mind that you must make this entry before you start the router, which means that this is really preventive troubleshooting and not real-time. Go to the `HKEY_LOCAL_MACHINE\SOFTWARE\Microsoft\Tracing` area of the Windows 2000 Server Registry to make the appropriate change (for example, `EnableConsoleTracing REG_DWORD 1`). It is that simple.

Another great way to troubleshoot RRAS issues is through the use of the Network Monitor. This tool permits you to analyze the actual RAS traffic, which means that you might be able to discover the solution or at least a workaround to your remote access problems. Keep in mind, though, that the Network Monitor can become a drain on your network's performance, so do not overuse it or permit just anyone to use it as this could raise some serious security issues for your Windows-based applications. For more assistance with this tool, refer to the Windows 2000 Resource Kit or anyone with Microsoft Systems Management Server (SMS) experience. A full-blown version of the Network Monitor is provided in the BackOffice SMS product, which is able to "see" the entire WAN and not just a single server.

Summary

The purpose of this chapter has been to introduce the reader to many of the finer points of routing and remote access within the Windows 2000 Server world. Though there is much similarity to the RRAS features offered within Windows NT Server 4.0, not many administrators were probably familiar with RRAS prior to Windows 2000, as the Windows NT 4.0 implementations came via service packs from Microsoft and not as part of the original

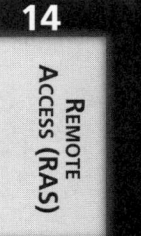

Windows NT product. Likewise, RRAS in Windows 2000 Server completely changes the face of remote access configuration that many of you probably performed in the old Windows NT environment. Hopefully, this chapter gave you the necessary tools and information that you will need to successfully deploy RRAS throughout your own organization.

Multiprotocol Environments

CHAPTER 15

IN THIS CHAPTER

- Supported Protocols in Windows 2000 *406*
- Routing and Remote Access Services *417*

As was mentioned in Chapter 8, "TCP/IP Networking," if the choice in LAN communications protocol were a war, TCP/IP has won. However, the fact is that even the losers in a war have a homeland to go back to. LAN and WAN communications protocols have strengths and weaknesses just like anything else in computing. IPX/SPX, for example, is no more dead than the Macintosh computer; however, they have both found their place in the work-a-day world to be considerably decreased.

This chapter is not meant to give the sort of coverage for each competing protocol that's nearly as complete as that contained in Chapter 8. TCP/IP goes far beyond the concept of "default" protocol and actually approaches a "required" protocol. Anyone who says that Windows 2000 can be run without TCP/IP simply needs to consider the ramifications of DNS and DHCP on the Active Directory.

This chapter presents a brief description of the communications protocols included in Windows 2000 and the technical reasons for making use of them.

Supported Protocols in Windows 2000

Windows 2000 supports the majority of industry-standard communications protocols. After more then 20 years of PC networking, the protocol list has begun to settle down a bit. This settling has left two real champions and three utility players that just won't go away.

Here's the list:

- *TCP/IP*. Transmission Control Protocol/Internet Protocol, created by the U.S. Department of Defense for LAN/WAN communications on ARPANET.
- *IPX/SPX*. Internet Packet Exchange/Sequential Packet Exchange, created by Novell for NetWare.
- *AppleTalk*. The protocol created by Apple to allow communications between Macintosh computers and Apple peripherals.
- *DLC*. Data Link Control, from Hewlett-Packard.
- *NetBEUI*. IBM and Microsoft's early attempt at a LAN protocol based on NetBIOS (Network Basic Input/Output System).

Installing New Protocol

Any of the listed protocols can be installed and configured from the Network and Dial-up Connections Control Panel (see Figure 15.1). A wonderful new feature of Windows 2000 is the ability to add and subtract new protocols while the server is still running.

This may not seem like a big deal, but when a migration or transfer requires a temporary protocol change, it can be a godsend.

FIGURE 15.1
The Network Control Panel.

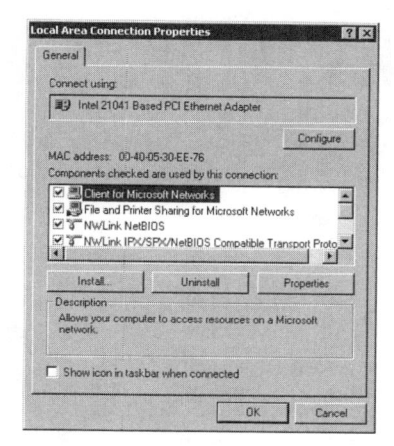

The technology of adding, subtracting, stopping, starting, or changing protocols while the server is running helps a great deal with troubleshooting (see figure 15.2). It's very difficult to chase a communications issue if you have to reboot the system every time the protocol is added or changed. If the server is running any sort of large application, it can be nearly impossible. An Exchange or SQL Server machine can take as long as half an hour to reboot.

FIGURE 15.2
The protocol selection window.

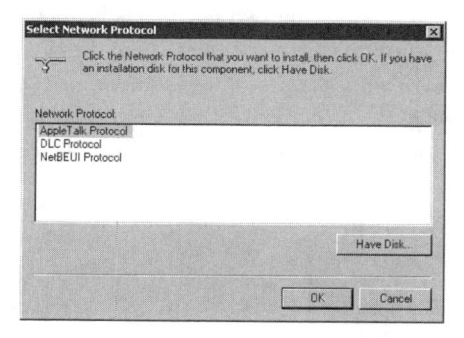

Follow these steps to add a new protocol:

1. Open the Network and Dial-up Connections Control Panel. This can be done in two ways. The first is to choose Start, Settings, Control Panel and then double-click Network and Dial-up Connections. The simplest way is to right-click My Network Places and choose Properties.

2. Click Install.
3. Click Protocol and choose Add.

> **Note**
>
> If this interface looks familiar, it is. The interface was designed to give a more uniform look and feel to Windows across the board. The new Windows 2000 interface is very much like the Windows 95/98 interface, which was thought to be easier to use.

4. The list of available protocols is presented. If a listed protocol is your choice, click that protocol and choose OK. If the protocol you want is not listed, click Have Disk and point the operating system to the source of the protocol file.
5. The protocol now appears in the general window. To finish, click Close. If further information is required to use the protocol (network number, host address, and so on), the Control Panel will prompt you for that information now.

Removing a protocol is as simple as following step 1 and clicking Uninstall at step 2. Once your choice is confirmed, it's activated.

Load Them All!

With the ease and flexibility for adding protocols, it can be tempting to simply add every protocol you can get your hands on. If speaking two languages is good, then speaking five must be great. However, you must consider that the system did not simply gain the ability to speak a new language by having the protocol installed; instead, it *agrees* to speak it almost every time it speaks. It's a bit like being a United Nations interpreter who speaks five languages and has to say everything in every language he or she can speak.

The workload in a server and on the network is effectively increased proportionally for every protocol that's added. This is not to say that every protocol generates the same amount of traffic; instead, every protocol requires consideration for every message the server wants to send out. The only relief given involves protocol-specific requirements that are not required by the other protocols.

Therefore, following the analogy, if expressing a phrase in Chinese takes 13 words and expressing it in English takes 14, the traffic is 27 words. Probably 13 more words than needed if everyone spoke English.

Just because it can be done does not mean it *has* to be done. The ideal situation is to have as few protocols as possible installed on the server. This is no different from any other process run by the server. It's not like a workstation that sometimes becomes clogged running applications. Servers are too efficient because they're shared resources.

Connection Style

Connection based and *connectionless* are ways of referring to how a protocol communicates with peers across the network wire. It's an important distinction because of the difference that's made in bandwidth and quality of communications.

In the TCP/IP world, for example, the TCP protocol is a connection-based protocol, meaning that it must first establish a connection path and then it can communicate. In these protocols, an acknowledgement of communications is also required. It's a bit like sending a certified letter. The letter is sent and before transaction is considered successful, and an acknowledgement of receipt must be received. SPX (from IPX/SPX) is also a connection-based protocol.

The opposite of this style of connection is known as *connectionless*. This is not to say that no connection can be found but rather that the protocol is not involved in the confirmation of the connection. It would be as if the communications were sent via standard U.S. mail: A letter is dropped in the mailbox; if it arrives, that's expected, but if not, the sender has no idea that it didn't arrive. A connectionless protocol simply launches the packets, and if they arrive, the protocol is unaware and frankly unconcerned. IPX and UDP (from the TCP/IP protocol suite) are examples of connectionless protocols.

TCP/IP

TCP/IP has become the standard protocol for many operating systems for many powerful reasons. In my opinion, the greatest reason is that it's a public domain product. No individual company owns the protocol because the U.S. Department of Defense (DoD) developed it. In other words, it's a free-range protocol.

During the birth of the Internet, TCP and IP were among many protocols developed by the DoD for communications between its sites. Many of these protocols today are part of what's known as the *TCP/IP suite*.

Developing a communications method within the DoD had its benefits. The protocol is very robust and is very good at working around slow or missing parts of the network. The product has also become public domain because we paid to have it developed and we own it.

This LAN Is Your LAN

This protocol, quite literally, belongs to the public. It's a public standard. The U.S. government made it so and put a group called the Internet Engineering Task Force (IETF) in charge of maintenance and upkeep of the protocol suite.

Changes made to the protocol today are made by the public through *requests for comment* (RFC). In fact, when an NOS or networking vendor brags about a change it has made to TCP/IP, it will often list the RFC number involved in the change. Microsoft has submitted many RFCs in the creation of Windows 2000.

Every submission is added to the listing for the TCP/IP standard. However not all items are deemed to required for implementation. In fact only a few submissions are made mandatory.

Time Tested, Administrator Approved

The fact is that if the NOS can speak TCP/IP, it can communicate to the world. Every major NOS uses this protocol, including those in this list:

- Microsoft Windows 2000, NT, and 95/98
- Novell NetWare 4.*x* and 5.*x* (now allowing native services through TCP/IP)
- UNIX
- Digital VMS and Pathworks
- IBM AS/400 and Mainframe System

This list of NOS players can safely cover 95 percent of all network servers in the country and pretty close to that percentage throughout the world. The TCP/IP protocol has been used for over 20 years. Much like the UNIX operating system, TCP/IP has been around long enough now that people rely on it to get things done and just won't trust other protocols.

Full Featured

TCP/IP is really the name given to many different protocols and features that make it a protocol suite. This protocol suite contains a list of protocols that control all facets of network use:

- *TCP (Transport Protocol)*. Used for reliable connection-based communications.
- *UDP (User Datagram Protocol)*. Used for simplistic communications by TCP/IP. UDP is the protocol used for connectionless communications.
- *IP (Internet Protocol)*. IP specifies the format of address, also called *datagrams*, and the addressing scheme.
- *FTP (File Transfer Protocol)*. Used to move files reliably across a network.
- *HTTP (Hypertext Transfer Protocol)*. Used for the transfer of hypertext-based documents. It allows for smooth retrievable of documents. The World Wide Web uses this protocol.
- *Telnet*. A terminal communications protocol that allows users to establish a terminal connection with a host computer.
- *NFS (Network File System)*. Used to allow users to attach network drives to their local computers and use those drives in their native environments.

> **Note**
>
> A *datagram* is the basic building block in which messages are sent across an IP network. Datagrams are called *packets* in many other protocols and can contain destination, host, and data information.

The combination of these protocols and many others make up the suite.

Strengths and Weaknesses

Here are the strengths of TCP/IP:

- Large install base and vendor support.
- Robust and time tested.
- Inherently routable.
- The Internet can provide WAN service between sites at no charge beyond Internet connectivity.

Here are the weaknesses of TCP/IP:

- Network addresses must be added to each node. Whether through DHCP or statically, the address must be added by hand.
- IP routing and segmentation can be complex if the range of registered addresses you have is small.
- IP is available to anyone who wants to use it. This can be a security loophole.

For more details on the strengths and weaknesses of TCP/IP, see Chapter 8.

IPX/SPX

In many people's eyes, IPX/SPX is considered a standard nearly as strong as TCP/IP. Although IPX/SPX was not created by the U.S. government, it has permeated a large portion of the private sector. This is because until a 1998, IPX/SPX was the only protocol that could be used for full-featured communications with the most prolific NOS over the last fifteen years—Novell NetWare.

IPX/SPX was created by Novell as part of the NetWare operating system and was initially proprietary. The protocol suite has since been released to the public domain and has become part of most every NOS. The protocol became so prevalent because the NOS it was part of possessed an estimated 70 percent of the market share at one point in it's history. This has since changed, but the protocol is so deeply entrenched in our business life that it won't go away any time soon. What's more, it probably shouldn't.

In the Microsoft Windows world, IPX/SPX is known as *NWLink IPX/SPX-compatible transport*. The *NW* most likely refers to the fact that it's a NetWare-related protocol, but it might also be an implication of when Microsoft wants this protocol used. IPX/SPX has many very nice features, though, and in small networks, it can make your life easier.

Lean and Efficient

IPX/SPX actually provides a very clean and efficient way of connecting a large number of users with very little effort. Much of the preparation needed with TCP/IP is unnecessary in the IPX/SPX world, because IPX/SPX is self-configuring in many ways.

IPX (from IPX/SPX) is the equivalent of the IP portion of the TCP/IP protocol. It's the connectionless protocol used for the majority of the communications. It has a unique addressing feature that allows administrators to set up the network address one time and then forget about it. This scheme also allows the administrator not to create host addresses.

The IPX addressing scheme involves the use of a network address that's created by the administrator during the install of the first host (often the first server) in the network segment. A new network address is created for each new network segment at the birth of that network segment and is used for that segment from that point forward. The network address must be an eight-digit number expressed in hexadecimal (for, example, 0529FA43). Any digits left blank will be expressed as zeros at the beginning of the address; therefore, 39DA3A becomes 0039DA3A.

> **Note**
>
> Hexadecimal (hex) is used for a large number of computer settings. It's a number system or way of counting that includes the digits 0, 1, 2, 3, 4, 5, 6, 7, 8, and 9 and the letters A, B, C, D, E, and F. (The old joke is that if God had intended us to use hex, he would have given us 16 fingers.) Hexadecimal allows us to use a recognizable two-digit numbers for all the binary representations of a byte (eight bits). Hex numbers are expressed starting with either an h or 0x in front of them, which indicates that the numbers are in hex. For example, 00101110 would be h2E (see Appendix B, "IP Address Decimal to Binary Table," for a binary table). The number h2E is easier to understand and write than 00101110.

> **Stupid Hex Tricks**
>
> With some ingenuity, an administrator can use a network number to be a note about where a segment is. Using phone numbers of locations, room numbers, or even wiring closet numbers can help the administrator track a problem later. Even "words" can be spelled, such as C0FFEE, FEEFEE, ABE, CA5E.

Once a network address is established at the birth of a segment, any new system added to the system communicates with the members of that segment by using that network number.

A complete network address for a host system is made up of the network address and the system's hardware address or an address known as the *MAC address* (Media Access Control address). Every Ethernet network interface card (NIC) has a unique MAC address assigned to it, and other network cards most often will have a unique hardware address. This number is most often a 12-digit hex number.

WAN Friendly

The combination of the hardware address and the network address make up the unique address of the host on the network. An example of an IPX host address would be `00400530EE76:4CA98221` (node:network).

The beauty of this system is that once the network address is established, the computers do the rest. The problem is finding any way to discover a system or its location based on the host address. In the IP world, administrators control the host address and network address so they know who has what address. IPX offers no such control. Because it has a network and host address as part of its address scheme, IPX/SPX is routable by most commercial routers, including Windows NT (Post Service Pack 3).

Noisy Neighbor

Windows networking requires name resolution in order to be able to publish resources such as printers and file shares (see Chapter 5, "Networking Brief"). In the TCP/IP world, products such as WINS and DNS help to keep the traffic used to discover these names to a minimum. IPX/SPX also uses the NetBIOS protocol for name resolution, but it does so through the broadcasting of NetBIOS names over the network on a timed basis or through the Service Advertising Protocol (SAP).

Requests are made for SAP information through the Router Information Protocol (RIP). When a request is made (RIP) for a list of available NetBIOS hosts, the IPX/SPX network provides a list of the hosts that have been participating in the SAP traffic. The request and response traffic can be called *RIP/SAP traffic*, and it can get rough during the startup of a new network or the moving of resources.

Strengths and Weaknesses

Here are the strengths of IPX/SPX:

- Requires very little network address planning
- Very fast and efficient standard communications
- Able to be routed

Here are the weakness of IPX/SPX:

- Less control over network addressing scheme
- Not as universally accepted as IP
- Not allowed on the Internet
- RIP/SAP traffic

AppleTalk

Apple Computer's Macintosh (Mac) computer is quite prevalent in the business world, no matter how much the PC world may want to deny its existence. The fact is there are many tasks that make the Mac a computer that fits a niche. With that said, an administrator of a large corporate network will most likely have to include these machines in the networking scheme at some point along the line. Windows 2000 and previous versions dating back to LAN Manager for OS/2 have always included some form of communications with the Macintosh world. (see Chapter 18, "Unix Host to Windows 2000 Server Connectivity," for complete Macintosh file and print sharing details).

The native communications protocol used by the Macintosh is an Apple Computer invention called *AppleTalk*. The AppleTalk protocol is just as verbose as the entire Macintosh line of products, which is to say that the protocol takes the approach of presenting the user with all the known resources on the network and does not leave the discovery of these resources to the user.

Another Noisy Neighbor

AppleTalk devices advertise their names across the network on a continuous basis. Macintosh clients use an interface called the *Chooser*, shown in Figure 15.3, that allows them to see a list of the available resources being advertised in the network. By selecting a resource type and a specific resource, the client is able to connect to the resource. The sheer volume of advertised resources and hosts can very quickly cause a network to become saturated.

FIGURE 15.3
The Macintosh Chooser screen.

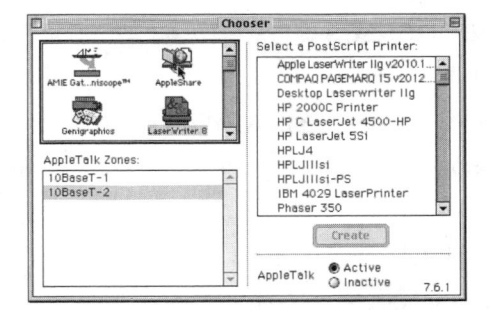

Addressing Schemes

As with IP and IPX, AppleTalk addresses consist of network and host addresses, so the protocol is routable. The protocol uses a simplified network numbering scheme when compared to IP or IPX in that each network is simply given a decimal number of between 1 and 253. Each network can contain as many hosts as needed, but if the number of hosts exceeds 253, the network number must be made a network range of contiguous numbers.

For example, if a network is created and given the network number 100 and then a 254th host is added, the network number must be made 100-101. If the network contains 584 hosts, it would have to be 100-102. However, that range is still one network.

Workstation addresses are additions to the network address just as IP addresses are, but only one decimal point separates these addresses. Like the IPX scheme, a host address is a dynamic creation, but it's nowhere near as complex as the MAC address. Each host is given a host address that's simply a number associated with its attachment to the network. Therefore, a host that attaches to the 100-102 network could have the address of 100.1 then 100.2, 100.3, and so on.

Because of the very nature of the Macintosh computer system, the user is handheld through this process by being given a name for each different network called a *zone*. The concept behind zones is to keep users in large networks from having to leaf though pages and pages of resources to see the resources in their neck of the woods. Therefore, a user in a multisegment network must first know the zone that the resource exists in and then may choose the resource host allowed by the resource.

A zone is truly just a friendly name for a network segment. Therefore, users become good at understanding that a resource on the fourth floor (for example) is located in the "fourth floor" zone. They do not need to know that it's in the 100-102 network. However, the administrator needs to be aware of the zone numbering scheme in order to maintain a consistent model.

Strengths and Weaknesses

Here are the strengths of AppleTalk:

- Allows Macintosh computers to connect to Windows servers
- Offers a great deal of help to the clients that use it
- Able to be routed

Here are the weaknesses of AppleTalk:

- Less control over network addressing scheme
- Ties up bandwidth by broadcasting the necessary information to the Macintosh clients
- Only really useful to a proprietary group of computers
- Not allowed on the Internet

NetBEUI

The NetBEUI protocol has existed in some form within the Windows networking world since the beginning. The idea behind NetBEUI is to have a protocol that simply uses NetBIOS as the complete interface. NetBEUI stands for *NetBIOS Extended User Interface*. It simply means that NetBIOS is the network.

The protocol consists of network peers making broadcasts to discover the hosts that exist on the network and calling on the those hosts when a resource is needed. The protocol was simply meant to be a way for PCs to communicate over the network.

Broadcasts by their very nature are local to the segment they're on. Because the NetBEUI protocol is broadcast based, it's not routable.

By an odd coincidence, when other protocols have trouble finding network resources on the local network, NetBEUI can often produce them. Windows NT and all other Microsoft products seem to have a cosmic connection to this protocol. The reality of the situation is that human hands do not often ruin the simple nature of the protocol. NetBEUI simply searches for NetBIOS entities and reports them, nothing more and nothing less.

This behavior makes NetBEUI a good choice for a RAS connection or a small uncomplicated network. The simplicity makes for a very fast communications method.

Strengths and Weaknesses

Here are the strengths of NetBEUI:

- Speedy and efficient in small one-segment networks
- Good choice for basic network functions when troubleshooting because of its ability to find NetBIOS entities and avoid human "help"

Here are the weakness of NetBEUI:

- Unable to be routed, which prevents networks larger than one segment
- Not supported by many other vendors

Routing and Remote Access Services

As part of the Windows 2000 update a product that has been updated is now part of the operating system. For communications through phone and serial lines, Windows NT offered a product called *Remote Access Services* (RAS). The next logical progression of this product is called *Routing and Remote Access Services* (RRAS). The addition of routing to the remote access package was done to facilitate communications to small remote installations. By making the Windows server serve a dual function as router and server it makes routing possible with less cost and complication.

RRAS is capable of the following tasks:

- LAN-to-LAN routing
- LAN-to-WAN routing
- Virtual Private Networks (see Chapter 24, "Optimizing Performance Tuning")
- Network Address Translation (NAT)
- Use of POTS (Plain Old Telephone Service) lines for dial-up network routes
- Servicing dial-up client connectivity to the network

Because the entire previous chapter was dedicated to RRAS, this chapter will simply use RRAS as a launching point for discussing the protocols involved.

PPP

Connection through POTS has been done forever in the networking world, but the ability to do so requires a special protocol that allows the PC to use modem communications to translate the LAN protocol into an analog signal. This translation allows the computer to use the phone modem as if it were a network card in the PC and allows the PC to use the POTS as a LAN cable.

Originally, this protocol was called *SLIP* (Serial Line IP) because it took the IP network and provided the serial line connection (generally a modem) to computer. Today the more commonly used protocl is know as PPP (Point-to-Point Protocol) and can be used with IP, IPX, AppleTalk, and even NetBEUI to communicate with the network over a POTS line. RRAS uses PPP to create connections.

RIP

Routers learn about the network routes available in two basic ways: One is to be told directly by humans, and the other is to find out on their own. When routers must find each other, they must participate in an information-discovery protocol. The Router Information Protocol (RIP) is just such an information protocol that's time tested. The RIP method is a basic part of the both the TCP/IP and IPX/SPX protocol suites, and the process is necessary to allow networks to learn about each other's existence.

RIP routers use a very simple process of introducing themselves to one another and then asking whether their neighbors have heard of any new routers lately. This is a very simplistic explanation of the process, but it's basically what occurs. Every router on a network must have another router available to get to a network segment it's not directly connected to. Routers that are not directly connected to a segment must also have another known router to make a connection to that segment.

Each time a router makes a connection to a new network, it records the path it took to get to that network segment. As time progresses, each router builds a more comprehensive list of routes and becomes more efficient. Many different protocols are involved in this collection and use of routing information, but all accomplish the same general goal. The Internet is a very large example of this system.

The advantage to using RIP is that it's extremely simple to configure and deploy. The disadvantage to using RIP is its inability to scale to large or very large networks. The maximum hop count used by RIP routers is 15. Networks that are 16 hops or more away are considered unreachable. As networks grow larger in size, the periodic announcements by each RIP router can cause excessive traffic. Another disadvantage of RIP is its high recovery time. When the network topology changes, it may take several minutes before the RIP routers reconfigure themselves to the new network topology. While the network reconfigures itself, routing loops may form that result in lost or undeliverable data. Obviously with all of the information exchange occuring the protocol is a bit noisy.

RIP for IP and IPX can be enabled in the RRAS, as shown in Figure 15.4, by opening the RRAS console, right-clicking the interface you want configured for RIP routing, and choosing Properties. In the General tab, choose an outgoing protocol and repeat the process for the incoming protocol.

FIGURE 15.4
The RRAS console screen.

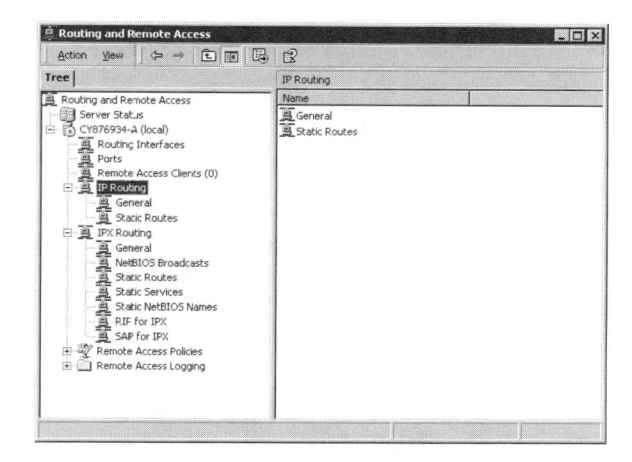

Troubleshooting

For more information on IP, see Chapter 21, "Other Internet Services for Windows 2000." For now, here are some troubleshooting methods for finding out whether you've actually set up RRAS correctly and whether route information is actually passing through:

- RAS - RIP broadcasts will *not* be sent out of serial or ISDN interfaces. RIP broadcasts will only be sent on LAN interfaces or cards, such as T1 and Frame Relay, that appear to be LAN interfaces to Windows.

- Is the default gateway correct on the NT router? Only use one default gateway configured on the appropriate NIC.

- Remember that the default gateway route is only used if there's no other valid route to the destination. Therefore, the default route will only be used for addresses outside your company or autonomous system. All routes in the company will be learned via RIP.

> **Tip**
>
> To find the IP information set for your workstation, you can use one of the following applications, depending on the OS you're running at you workstation: WINIPCFG for Windows 95, and IPCONFIG for Windows 2000 or NT. These programs are run from the DOS prompt.

- Verify the correct configuration for the client, including IP address, subnet mask, and default gateway.

Ping

Ping is a utility that's used to determine whether your machine can locate a PC on the network. It's named *ping* because it resembles the behavior of a ship that sends out a "ping" sound and listens for the echo to determine whether another ship or submarine is close. With ping, your PC sends out a signal toward an address on the IP network to determine whether it's actually connected to the same network or if the system exists at the moment. Below is a logical path to follow to find a routing problem using ping:

- Ping yourself. This will tell you whether TCP is functioning. It does *not* tell you whether your NIC is functioning.
- Ping your default gateway or next-hop router. This will show that the router is up.
- Ping beyond the next router. If a ping fails, what's the response? "Request Timed Out" can mean that the destination host is down or that there's no route back to you. "Destination Net Unreachable" will show the IP address of the router that tried to route the packet but did not have a valid route.

Summary

The TCP/IP protocol is not the only protocol Windows 2000 is capable of using, but you should realize that other protocols are simply utility players in most networks. If Windows 2000 or Windows NT is your primary NOS, TCP/IP needs to be your protocol of choice.

This chapter has given you an understanding of the strengths and weaknesses of the other protocols that are choices in the Windows 2000 operating system. Protocols such as IPX/SPX have a definite place in the networks of the corporation.

CHAPTER 16

Client Workstation Considerations

- Client Services Brief   *422*
- Specific Client Operating System Considerations   *429*

As you read this chapter, it is hoped that you will be thinking about your own organization's conglomeration of computing clients in regards to how you can shave the numbers of different operating systems and versions from the organization. The work that is required to do that first will make the actual technical connectivity work described in this chapter seem easy to do. The purpose of this chapter is to not only introduce the reader into the world of Windows 2000 Server client connectivity, but to also provide some step-by-step instruction on how to create a connected environment for the organization.

Client Services Brief

Client workstation considerations for Windows 2000 Server can be considerable if your organization does not live purely in the 32-bit Windows world. In other words, if all the client computers in your organization are running the Windows 95, Windows 98, Windows 98 second edition, Windows NT Workstation, or the Windows 2000 Professional operating system, your job becomes a cinch. Connectivity from these client computers to a Windows 2000 Server machine becomes as simple as installing one or more network protocols—TCP/IP, IPX/SPX, or NetBEUI—and the Client for Microsoft Networks software (or something similar) as well as having the proper hardware connectivity (network card, wire, hub, and so on). Voila, you're connected! Of course, the rest of us have to live in the real world, which means older Windows 3.*x*, Macintosh, UNIX, Novell, and maybe even OS/2 Warp client computers, all requiring file and print services from our Windows 2000 Server machine.

Once you've identified the various client operating systems that need to connect to the Windows 2000 Server machine, you then should determine your client access licensing (CAL) needs. Essentially, a CAL is the legal right your organization must purchase for every single client computer that will be connecting to your Windows 2000 server in any of the following ways:

- *File Services*. This is when DOS, Windows 3.*x*, Windows 9*x*, Windows NT, Windows 2000, or similar client operating systems list, retrieve, view, and/or otherwise manipulate files that presently reside on your Windows 2000 Server machine.
- *Macintosh File and Print Services*. Whenever a Macintosh computer is used for any type of file and/or printer services in conjunction with Windows 2000 Server, a CAL must be purchased for each Macintosh.
- *Print Services*. This is the use of the Windows 2000 Server machine by DOS, OS/2, Windows 3.*x*, Windows 9*x*, Windows NT, Windows 2000, and similar client operating systems for sharing, listing, managing, and/or utilizing the printer services of a Windows 2000 server.

- *Novell NetWare File and Print Connectivity*. Whenever NetWare client computers are used for any type of file and/or printer services in conjunction with the Windows 2000 Server machine, a CAL is required for each connection.
- *Remote Access Services*. Anytime the Windows 2000 Server machine is accessed via a remote connection (that is, a nondirect network connection such as Dial-Up Networking) by another computer, that computer system must possess a valid client access license (CAL) for that particular Windows 2000 server.

Licensing for most Microsoft products gets rather complicated for anything other than home use, and the determination of how many CALs you might need for your organization's Windows 2000 server(s) can quickly become complex. For example, just because you purchased a legal copy of Windows 95, Windows 98, Windows 2000 Professional, or whatever, does not mean that you have satisfied Microsoft's requirements for client access licensing connectivity. Microsoft based its licensing requirements on the number of client connections that are made to a Windows 2000 Server machine.

Therefore, to start with, each client access license will provide every client computer on your network (whether locally or via remote access services) the legal right to make the necessary connection to and from that Windows 2000 Server. Keep in mind that these CALs do not give you the right to either the client or the server operating system for that client PC, nor does it necessarily mean you'll need a single license for every user within your organization. For example, in a call center–type of operation, there are many people typically all sharing the same client computer at different times throughout the day and week (different shifts, weekend and holiday work, and so on). Even though a company may have 10 different employees during the week all using the same exact PC, it only needs to purchase a single Windows 2000 Server client access license, because there is never more than one connection at a time being made from that PC to the Windows 2000 server. However, in the case of a consultant who might be using two laptop computers to connect to the same Windows 2000 Server machine at the same time, two CALs must be purchased, even though it is the same employee making both connections. The key thing to remember is that the licensing is at the computer operating system level and that it is on a one-to-one basis, between the server and the client computer.

To actually manage the client access licenses, two methods from within Windows 2000 Server do just that:

- *Within a Windows 2000 domain*. This form of licensing is accessed through the Licensing icon from within the Start, Administrative Tools option.
- *Standalone server*. This form of licensing is done for those Windows 2000 servers that are not part of a domain. It is accessible through the Licensing icon found inside the Windows 2000 Control Panel.

The actual use of the various licensing management tools work much the same, with the difference being whether licensing is being performed at the enterprise (domain) level or at the single, standalone server level. For example, to manage client access licenses for a standalone Windows 2000 Server machine, you would need to click the Start, Settings, and Control Panel menu selections. Doing this permits you to access the Windows 2000 Server Control Panel window, from which you would need to double-click the Licensing icon to reveal the Client Licensing Mode window, shown in Figure 16.1.

FIGURE 16.1
Choosing a Licensing Mode.

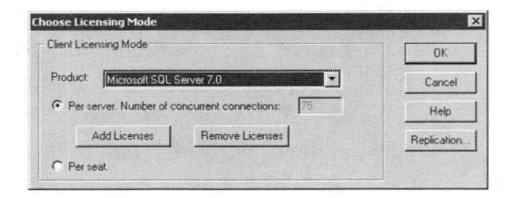

The Client Licensing Mode window that appears primarily consists of the single drop-down list box, where you select the product for which you are adding licenses. As you can see in the figure, the Microsoft SQL Server 7.0 licensing level is displayed with 75 valid licenses installed in the Per Server mode.

> **Note**
>
> There are two different types of licensing modes available within Windows 2000 Server: Per Server and Per Seat. *Per Server* means that the organization is purchasing as many CALs as there will be client computers and users connecting to that server, as would be the case for a standalone server or a server that's acting in an Internet or dial-up networking role. Of course, if the same user logs on twice from two different computers, that user has just consumed two CALs.
>
> *Per Client* means that there is a single client access license attached to each client computer (even though the license-logging service will track these licenses according to the user logon ID and really by computer name). Per Client licensing is probably the best option if your organization operates in an Active Directory/domain controller or multiserver environment.

Use the drop-down list box next to the Product label to first determine for which product you want to manage the licensing. Once you have selected your product of choice, you can then use the Add and Remove features to add/delete licenses from your Windows 2000 Server. To add additional licenses to the license manager (pretend for a moment that you really actually purchased them), click the Add Licenses button to reveal the New Client Access License window, shown in Figure 16.2.

FIGURE 16.2
Adding New Windows 2000 Server Client Access Licenses.

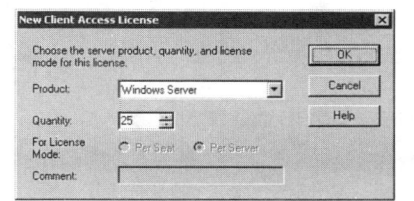

The New Client Access License window lets you select any number—from 0 through 999,999—using the up/down scrollbar. This represents the total number of licenses you want to add for a particular product. For example, if you want to 25 CALs for Windows Server (Windows 2000), you simply select the product type from the top drop-down list box and then select or type in the total number of licenses you want to add.

> **Note**
>
> You are unable to change the licensing mode from Per Server to Per Seat. This is because the changing of the master licensing mode for a particular Windows 2000 Server can only occur once. That is, if you install your Windows 2000 server using a Per Server license, it can only be switch over to Per Seat once—you cannot go back and forth.

Once you have arrived at the total number of licenses you want to add, click the OK button to proceed. A small confirmation message box will appear asking you to confirm that you have indeed purchased the client access licenses that you are now adding, as shown in Figure 16.3.

FIGURE 16.3
The Windows 2000 License Agreement Legalese Information.

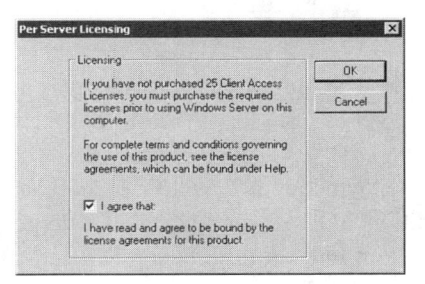

To respond affirmatively, click the check box to place a check mark in it. This will activate the OK button (until you click the check box, you will be unable to continue the transaction—you can only cancel it). Once you have place the check mark in the box (assuming that you really did already buy the licenses), click the OK button to continue the process. Once the licenses have been added, you will automatically be returned to the Choose Licensing Mode screen, shown in Figure 16.4.

FIGURE 16.4
Choosing the License Mode.

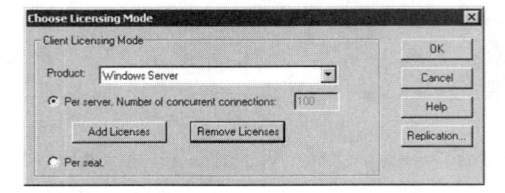

In this screen you will now be able to see the total number of CALs for the particular product, which will now also include the CALs you just added. Assuming that you made a mistake and added more licenses than you really wanted (or perhaps you just wanted to delete one or more CALs from your server), you are able to perform this function using the Remove button. Click the Remove button to reveal the Select Certificate to Remove Licenses window, shown in Figure 16.5.

FIGURE 16.5
Selecting a License Certificate for Deletion.

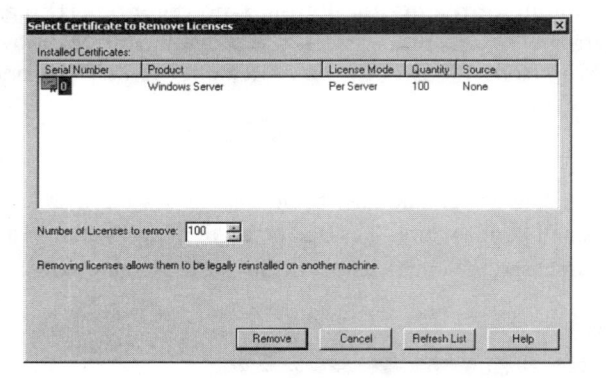

The purpose of the Select Certificate to Remove Licenses window is to permit the system administrator to selectively delete licenses from the Windows 2000 Server environment. This can include Windows 2000 Server CALs as well as those CALs for other products from the Microsoft BackOffice suite (Windows NT, Windows 2000 Server family, Site Server, Site Server Commerce Edition, SQL Server, SNA Server, Systems Management Server, Exchange Server, Proxy Server, Internet Information Server, and the full BackOffice 4.*x* product license itself). The licenses you add yourself via the licensing-management tools provided with Windows 2000 Server will have small, sequential serial numbers. However, those licenses that are installed as part of the formal product installation method (such as when you install BackOffice Server 4.5) will have more serious serial numbers.

To remove any licenses, click once on the product that you want to alter and then use the up/down scroll box to change the Number of Licenses to Remove field to the total number of license that you want to remove. Be careful here! It is a normal tendency to want to put the final number here (the total number of licenses minus those being removed) instead of just the number that you want to remove. Once you have entered the number you want to delete, click the Remove button to delete those licenses. You will be prompted with a small confirmation message box asking you to confirm your choice, along with the total number of licenses you're attempting to delete, as shown in Figure 16.6.

FIGURE 16.6
Confirming a License Certificate Deletion.

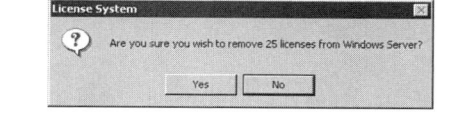

Once you click the Yes button, the licenses will be removed and you will be returned to the Select Certificate to Remove Licenses window. You will immediately notice your removal change on the screen, as shown in Figure 16.7.

FIGURE 16.7
Reviewing License Certificate Statuses.

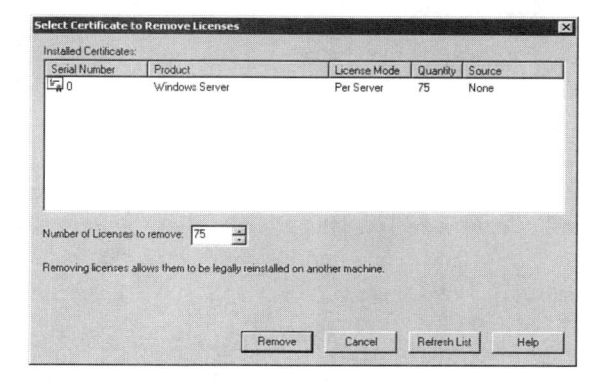

As soon as you have removed all the licenses you need to delete, you will probably want to exit this screen. However, Microsoft forgot to put a Close button on this screen, so you will need to click the Cancel button to actually close this window. There is no need to worry though; all of your changes have already been saved and you are safely returned to the Change Licensing Mode window.

Back at the Change Licensing Mode window, you will see the choice again to switch from Per Server mode to Per Seat mode. If you have ever wondered what would happen if you changed the licensing mode, you might have a chance to do that at this time. If you configured your server in a Per Seat licensing mode at the time you installed

Windows 2000 Server, you are out of luck. You cannot switch to a Per Server mode once you have installed your computer as a Per Seat licensed system. However, if you installed Windows 2000 Server in the Per Server mode, you can change over to the Per Seat licensing mode at this time. To do that, click the Per Seat radio button, which may cause a warning screen to appear, as shown in Figure 16.8.

FIGURE 16.8
Windows 2000 License Violation Warning.

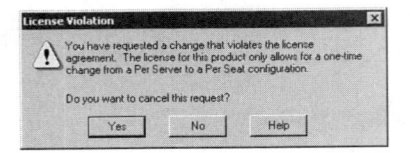

Normally, if you never altered any of the licensing for your server, this message would not appear and you would be able to switch your CALs over to the new mode. However, had you already switched once (or had been playing with the settings at some previous point in time), this licensing violation window will appear. To continue with your CAL conversion to a Per Seat licensing mode, click the No button. However, if you wish to cancel out of this conversion process, click the Yes button, and you will be returned to the Change Licensing Mode window.

The final option available to you on the Change Licensing Mode window is the Replication button. The purpose of this button is to permit the system administrator to configuration the replication of the licensing information from the organization's enterprise site license server to the other Windows 2000 and Windows NT 4.0 server domain controllers across the organization's network(s), as well as from the domain controllers back to the enterprise site license server. This process occurs automatically if all the servers involved are running some version of the Windows 2000 Server operating system (Server, Advanced Server, or DataCenter).

To configure replication, you first need to decide on the replication frequency. This frequency is based on whether you want to start the replication on a specific start time every day or you want to run the replication every x number of hours (where x equates to at least one full hour). The range on the latter option is executing the replication process between every 1 and 72 hours. To select one option or the other, click the radio button located to the left of each frequency type. Note that you can only select one or the other, as shown in Figure 16.9.

Make your selection by clicking either radio button and then using the up/down scrollbars to determine the value of the field. Keep in mind that for the Start At time fields, you must first click your pointer device inside the actual time field prior to trying to use the up/down scrollbars (it does not work as you would expect). Once you have selected your frequency and set the time or number of hours, click OK button to return to the

Choose Licensing Mode window. Once there, click the OK button to complete the use of the Windows 2000 licensing configuration manager.

FIGURE 16.9
Configuring Licensing Replication Frequencies.

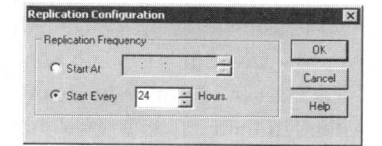

Specific Client Operating System Considerations

There are many nuances to consider when attempting to connect client computers that use non-32-bit Windows operating systems to Windows 2000 servers. These operating systems include the following:

- *Microsoft Windows 3.x*. This version of Windows dates back to 1990 and is really the first "popular" version of Windows used as a networking client (it is typically used for connectivity to Novell NetWare or IBM LAN Manager servers).

- *Microsoft Windows for Workgroups 3.1x*. First released in late 1992 as version 3.10 and then updated to version 3.11 in October 1993, Windows for Workgroups was Microsoft's first attempt at its own peer-to-peer operating system. In fact, it was this version that allegedly formed the basis of the first Windows NT (version 3.1), which was also released in October 1993.

- *IBM/Microsoft OS/2*. Microsoft originally< created the OS/2 operating at IBM's behest (versions 1.0 to 2.1) in the late 1980s, but then following their years of ideological battles, IBM wound up completing the development of OS/2 (versions 2.1 to present, including all the "Warp" versions, beginning in 1992). OS/2 is based on a networking technology known as LAN Manager (catchy name, eh?) and was supposed to be a peer-to-peer operating system that had a solid GUI design with a superior communications design. Did it live up to that? Maybe…maybe not. There are a few OS/2-based clients still in existence and even fewer OS/2-based servers running in corporate America today, but their presence is still significant enough to warrant attention by Microsoft to connect them to Windows 2000 servers.

- *Macintosh*. This technology team was originally founded in 1979 by Apple Computer's technical guru at the time, Jeff Rushkin. The team that finally produced its first version (the Lisa, named after Steve Jobs' daughter) in 1983 and the Rushkin-named project known as the Macintosh in January 1984. The Macintosh computer is mainly a client-only computer (there are not many Macintosh servers hanging around these days) that is not compatible with the majority of other *x*86 client PCs that exist just about everywhere today. Likewise, the Macintosh is also not compatible with other Apple computers.

- *UNIX*. At last count there were over 140 known flavors of UNIX (AT&T's System V, Microsoft's XENIX, IBM's AIX, HP's UX, Sun's OS and Solaris, the bazillion versions of Linux from Caldera to RedHat, and so on) and countless variants and versions of those known flavors. Although there are many ways to connect these operating systems to Windows 2000 Server, there are a few things you should keep in mind before tossing a UNIX box onto your Windows 2000 network, and vice versa.

Once you have identified all the different types of client operating systems that must be connected to your Windows 2000 Server environment, your organization might want to consider a reality check. That is, given the increased expense that will be incurred for the ongoing maintenance and support of those older client operating systems (this does not include the more up-to-date UNIX and Macintosh client workstations/computers), is it really worthwhile for the organization to maintain those older systems? That question should be asked long before you journey down that troublesome road of configuring and maintaining these older client operating systems in conjunction with your new Windows 2000 servers.

Assuming that the answer to the question is yes, the next step is to make sure you are prepared for the journey ahead. Materials that you will need (beside the obvious client access licenses) will differ according to the client computer's operating system, but each of the next four sections should help prepare you for performing these sometimes-stubborn but necessary configurations.

Novell NetWare Clients

In order for Novell NetWare client computers to use Windows 2000 Server for file and print services, the Gateway Service for NetWare (GSNW) must first be installed on the Windows 2000 server. Keep in mind that these are "pure" NetWare clients, not Windows 9*x*, Windows NT, or Windows 2000 client computers that just happen to also be connecting to your Novell NetWare servers as well as your Windows 2000 servers. To install the GSNW software, right-click the My Network Places icon found on your Windows 2000 Server desktop. This will cause a small menu to appear, as shown in Figure 16.10.

Go to the bottom of that menu and click the Properties selection. Doing this will open the Network and Dial-Up Connections window shown in Figure 16.11.

FIGURE 16.10
Accessing the Properties Area of the My Network Places icon.

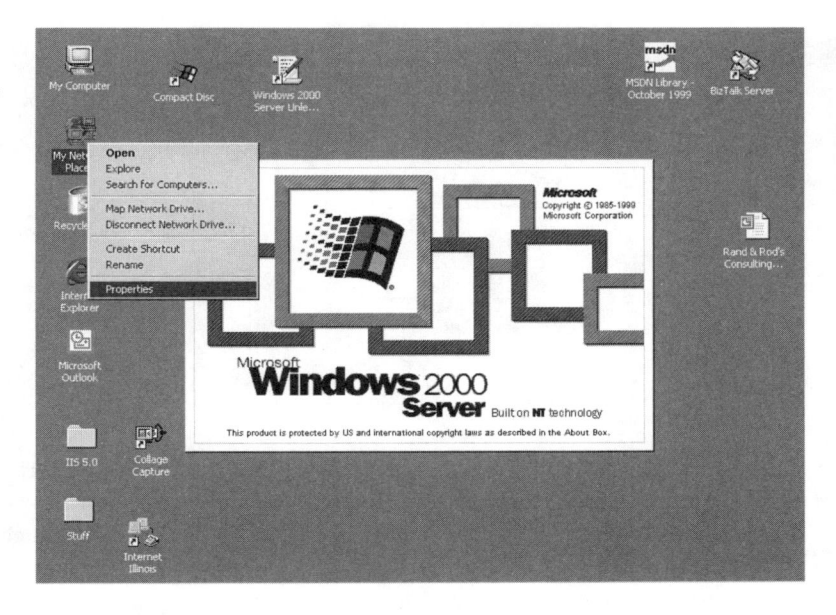

FIGURE 16.11
Reviewing Your Network and Dial-up Connections.

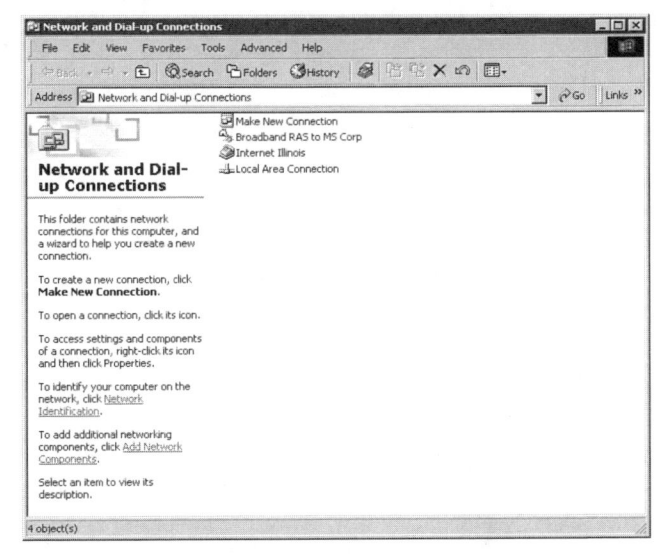

Right-click the Local Area Connection icon in the Network and Dial-Up Connections window. This opens another small menu, where once again you need to click the Properties selection. Doing this will take you into the Local Area Connection Properties window, shown in Figure 16.12.

FIGURE 16.12
Reviewing the Local Area Connection Properties.

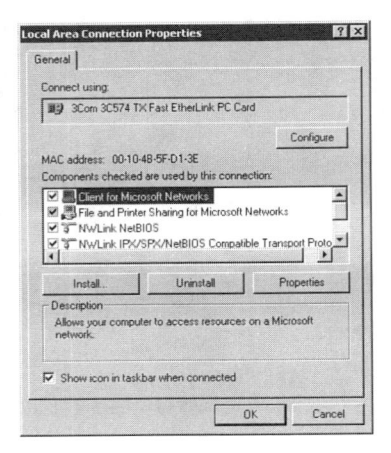

Once the Local Area Connection Properties window appears, you will want to click the Install button, which is located under the installed components listing area. The gist here is that in order to be able to use the Gateway Service for NetWare, you must first install it. However, be sure to take a quick glance at the installed components area just to be sure that you have not already installed the GSNW technology. Once you are certain that you need to install it, click the Install button to reveal the Select Network Component Type window, as shown in Figure 16.13.

FIGURE 16.13
Selecting a New Network Component.

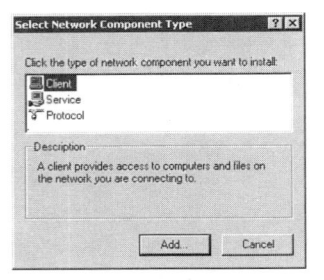

When the Select Network Component Type window appears, click the client type to highlight it (doing this selects it for further use). Next, click the Add button, which will take you into the Select Network Client window, as shown in Figure 16.14.

Chances are, when you first see the Select Network Client window, it will only contain a single component for possible installation: Gateway (and Client) Services for NetWare. Your choice at this point is simple. Just click the Gateway (and Client) Services for NetWare option to select it and then click the OK button to begin the installation process. At this point, you must either have your Windows 2000 Server CD-ROM handy to copy the new files from, or you need to have some shared network point from which to copy the few files necessary for the installation of this utility program. Once the copying process has completed, you might be presented with the Select NetWare Logon window shown in Figure 16.15.

FIGURE 16.14
Choosing the Gateway (and Client) Services for NetWare.

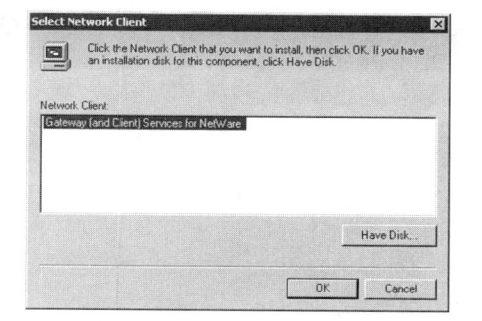

FIGURE 16.15
Assigning a Preferred NetWare Server or Default NetWare Tree and Context.

There have been times when this author followed these exact same procedures and have not been presented with the Select NetWare Logon window, while at other times, the window does appear. Anyway, if you do happen to be presented with this window, the content is not too complex. First, you need to decide to which preferred server your Windows 2000 Server administrative account should connect. This is important because this is also the Novell NetWare server that all the NetWare clients will be passing through the Windows 2000 Server to reach. Something you should be aware of, though, is that if you do happen to use a Windows 2000 Server machine as a gateway connection for the NetWare client computers, the Novell logon scripts for those NetWare clients will not be executed (users must directly connect to a Novell server in order for their logon scripts to run properly). This is not a showstopper by any means, but it is something that the system administrator should be aware of.

Along the same lines as the preferred NetWare server is the notion of a *default tree and context*. The decision to use a NetWare preferred server or a default tree and context is simple: If your organization has deployed Novell's NetWare Directory Service (NDS), you will want to use the Default Tree and Context option. Otherwise, you will want to select the Preferred Server option. To pick either one, all you need to do is click the appropriate radio button and then fill in the proper server or tree/context information. Once you have done that, decide whether you would like to have the logon script for the Windows 2000 Server's administrative account to execute (this is the script that will run on the Novell server, not one that executes on the Windows 2000 side). Once you have made your selections, click the OK button to save your entries and return to the Local Area Connection Properties window, as shown in Figure 16.16.

FIGURE 16.16

Reviewing the New Local Area Connection Installation.

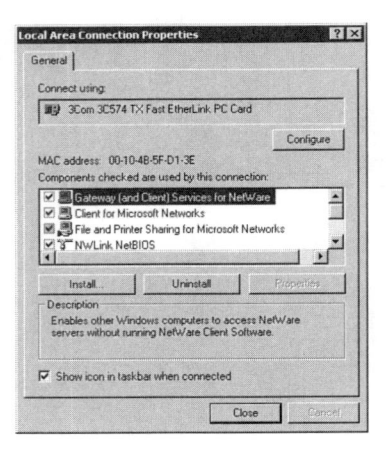

Upon returning to the Local Area Connection Properties window, you will see that the Gateway (and Client) Services for NetWare option is installed. Also, an amazing thing occurs: You are not prompted to restart your Windows 2000 Server machine in order to start using the service! This is a very welcome change from the older Windows NT 4.0 Server version of the same GSNW software. However, just to make sure that everything is configured properly, you will want to scroll down the installed components area (this is the big white box in the middle of the window with components, protocols, and services listed in it) to the NWLink IPX/SPX/NetBIOS Compatible Transport Protocol option. Select this networking protocol by clicking it once to highlight it. Then click the Properties button to reveal the screen shown in Figure 16.17.

Probably the most important option on this screen is the setting of the internal network number. By default, Windows 2000 will set this number to a series of eight zeros (00000000), but you can change this if you want. Essentially, what you need to be concerned with is that NetWare likes to have unique network numbers for each of its servers and gateways. Therefore, you may need to change this number in order for your newly installed GSNW to work properly. Likewise, there may be clashes with what Ethernet frame types are used on your local and/or wide area networks. If this is the case, change the frame type detection method from the default (top) selection of Auto Frame Type Detection to that of Manual Frame Type Detection. You do that by clicking once on the appropriate radio button and then clicking the OK button to save your changes. This will return you to the Local Area Connection Properties window, where you'll need to click the OK button there to save all your final alterations and exit that window.

FIGURE 16.17
Assigning an Internal Network Number for NetWare Connectivity.

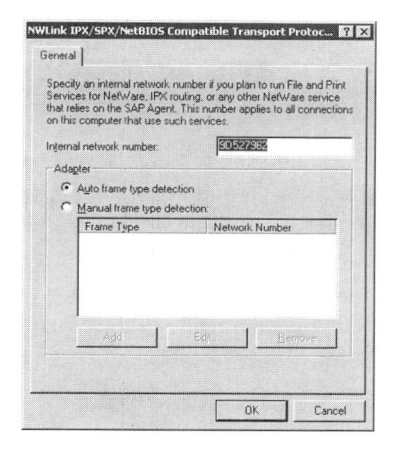

A few additional things you should keep in mind when attempting a connection to a Windows 2000 Server machine from a Novell client:

- *Environment variables.* These are the settings that are typically made in the `Config.sys`, `Autoexec.bat`, or various other batch or `*.ini` files, as well as inside the Registry files of Windows 3.*x* and Windows 9*x* client computers. Changes within these types of files can drastically alter how a NetWare client makes its connection to a Windows 2000 server, or they can even prevent such a connection—so be aware of these types of files.

- *IPX/SPX-compatible transport for printing.* Novell NetWare clients are able to send print jobs directly to a Windows 2000 server that's acting in a print server mode, by taking advantage of the IPX/SPX-compatible transport (a networking protocol available at no charge by Microsoft). All you need to do on the Windows 2000 Server side is to have the Microsoft File and Print Services installed as well as any applicable printers.

- *File and Print Services for NetWare (FPNW).* This product is available for purchase separate from the Windows 2000 Server operating system software. The way that this product differs from the more normal IPX/SPX-compatible transport for printing is that it permits a Windows 2000 server to "present" itself to NetWare clients as a NetWare server. That is, the various NetWare clients on your network will be unable to distinguish the Windows 2000 server from the Novell NetWare servers, which means you can move your File and Print Services off your Novell network and onto your Windows 2000 Server network without having to touch any of your NetWare client computers. This is a pretty amazing piece of technology for those organizations trying to migrate over to a pure Windows 2000 networking environment from a mixed Windows 2000/Novell NetWare LAN environment.

DOS, OS/2, Windows 3.x and Windows for Workgroups

Both Windows 3.x and Windows for Workgroups are nothing more than graphical user interfaces (GUIs) that sit on top of the old Disk Operating System (DOS). Because of this, their connectivity to Windows 2000 Server does not differ too much from that of purely DOS-based systems (be it Microsoft's MS-DOS or Digital Research's DR-DOS). Connectivity to a Windows 2000 server is not too difficult other than the installation of the proper client hardware and software on the client side of the equation. The hardware might actually be the more difficult task for file services, because you must find network cards with their applicable software drivers that still work under DOS, Windows 3.x, and/or Windows for Workgroups. OS/2, on the other hand, was originally co-developed by Microsoft and IBM to be the "future" of both Windows and peer-to-peer operating systems. Obviously, this did not turn out to be the case, given the development of first the Windows NT operating system and now Windows 2000 operating system.

Because Microsoft all but walked away from the 16-bit Windows world over five years ago with the release of Windows 95, coupled with the fact that Microsoft has since released a second version of Windows 95 (OSR2) and two versions of Windows 98, it may be very difficult for you to find the hardware and software drivers that permit the physical connection to your Windows 2000 network. Obviously, many organizations do have a considerable amount of older 16-bit Windows operating systems, so we will assume you could find the hardware to make the physical connection possible.

Once you have the hardware in place, you must find a suitable networking protocol to make the connection between your DOS, Windows 3.x, and/or Windows for Workgroups clients and the Windows 2000 Server machine. For the DOS clients, the IPX/SPX networking protocol is probably the way to go because that was what DOS clients used to use quite heavily for attaching to the old Novell NetWare servers. For the Windows 3.x client computers, you will probably want to also go with the IPX/SPX networking protocol. However, if this is for a small local workgroup (that is, less than 25 users and no router-based connectivity), a better selection would be Microsoft's NetBEUI networking protocol. Although TCP/IP probably sounds better to you, it is not available for the Windows 3.x GUI system. Your Windows for Workgroups client computers will benefit the most if you install the TCP/IP networking software version that Microsoft released especially for this peer-to-peer version of Windows 3.1 and 3.11 (there were two releases of Windows for Workgroups, roughly a year apart).

Once you have decided on your networking protocol configurations, you must then make sure that the protocols are installed on your Windows 2000 server. To check for the installed protocols, you need to return to the Local Area Connection Properties window that you used when configuring your Novell NetWare client computers. If you skipped that section or do not remember how to get there, you can follow these next few instructions. Otherwise, skip ahead to the discussion regarding the installation of the NetBEUI networking protocol.

To access the Local Area Connection Properties window, right-click the My Network Places icon, which is located on the Windows 2000 Server desktop. This will cause a small menu to appear. Go to the bottom of the menu and click the Properties selection. Doing this will open the Network and Dial-Up Connections window. Right-click the Local Area Connection icon in the Network and Dial-Up Connections window. This opens another small menu, where once again you need to click the Properties selection. Doing this will then take you to the Local Area Connection Properties window. Once the Local Area Connection Properties window appears, use the scrollbar to move up or down as you scan for these networking protocols:

- NetBEUI Protocol
- NWLink IPX/SPX/NetBIOS Compatible Transport
- NWLink NetBIOS (appears when you install the primary NWLink connectivity protocol)
- Internet Protocol (TCP/IP)

You will always have the Internet Protocol (TCP/IP) installed because it is the default protocol for Windows 2000 Server. If you have already installed the Gateway (and Client) Services for NetWare, you will also see both the NWLink protocols in the list. However, more than likely, you will not see the NetBEUI Protocol present; so we will perform that installation right now.

To install the NetBEUI Protocol, click the Install button (it appears in the middle of the Local Area Connection Properties window). This opens the Select Network Component Type window, shown in Figure 16.18.

When the Select Network Component Type window appears, click the Protocol selection to highlight it; then click the Add button to reveal the Select Network Protocol window, shown in Figure 16.19.

FIGURE 16.18
Selecting a New Network Protocol for installation.

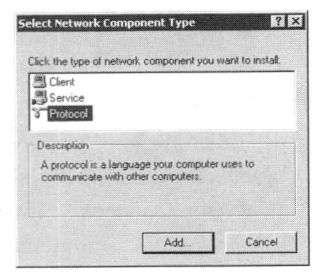

FIGURE 16.19
Installing the NetBEUI Networking Protocol.

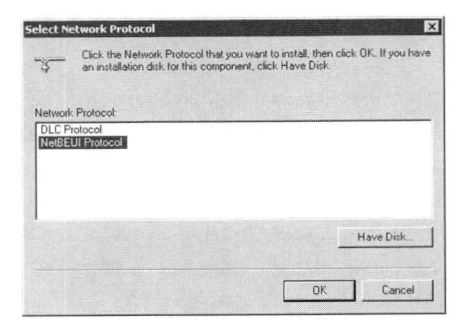

In the Select Network Protocol window, click the NetBEUI Protocol option to select it; then click the OK button to begin the installation process (you will need the Windows 2000 Server CD-ROM or a network share that contains the applicable files for this process). When the installation process completes, you will be returned to the Local Area Connection Properties window, where you will now see that the NetBEUI Protocol magically appears, as shown in Figure 16.20.

FIGURE 16.20
Confirming the Installation of the NetBEUI Networking Protocol.

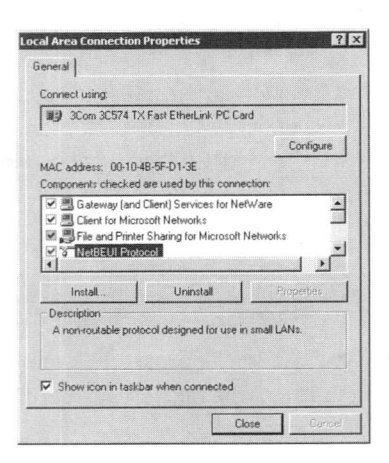

Again, once you see the Local Area Connection Properties window, you are finished with the protocol-installation process on the Windows 2000 Server side. In addition, like other networking client software and protocol installations, you will not have to reboot your Windows 2000 Server machine in order to activate this new networking protocol. Just click the Close button to exit the Local Area Connection Properties window and you're ready to have those DOS, Windows 3.*x*, and Windows for Workgroups client computers start connecting to your server.

When it comes to the use of a Windows 2000 server for Print Server Services, though, you have several additional things to remember in order to make the transition to Windows 2000 Server easier:

- *16-bit printer driver software.* You must install the appropriate 16-bit printer driver software onto the DOS client computers because they will be unable to use the capabilities of the Windows 2000 Server operating system to perform the printing process. Check the Web site of your software package to see if it still posts the DOS printer drivers for your intended printer; otherwise, you may have to write them yourself (not an easy task).

- *Print job redirection.* Printer requests from within the older DOS, Windows 3.*x*, and Windows for Workgroups client computers require the print jobs to traditionally be redirected from their serial (COM) or parallel (LPT) ports to a network destination. At the DOS level, typically the LAN Manager client redirector is used. For Windows 3.*x* clients, the Microsoft Network Client 3.0 for Windows redirector will be employed, whereas the Windows for Workgroups client computers will use the redirector that is built into the Windows for Workgroups operating system. The redirection can take place on any of the supported network protocols (NetBEUI, NWLink, or TCP/IP), and the command for the most part is simple to utilize. For example, to redirect a parallel port printer that's presently aimed at the LPT1 communications port (*1* designates the port number), the net use command is typically utilized:

    net use LPT1 \\PrintServerName\PrinterShareName

    This tells the client computer to redirect the printer traffic from the local LPT1 port to the shared network printer that is found on a particular Windows 2000 print server). Obviously, this command may vary a bit depending on the operating system that it is run on, but for the most part this is the command structure. In addition, a command such as this can be executed as part of a batch file, such as the client computer's Autoexec.bat or network logon script file.

- *OS/2 print connectivity.* In order for an OS/2 client or server operating system–based computer to connect to a Windows 2000 Server for File and Print

Services, that computer must have the LAN Manager 2.*x* client (or newer) software installed. This includes the Warp versions of OS/2 as well. Because most installations of OS/2 are TCP/IP based, the networking connectivity, itself, is not as difficult to achieve as it is on some of the other client computers. Redirection of the printer ports can be accomplished in the same manner, as you would do for a Windows for Workgroups client computer.

- *Use of Windows 2000 Server fonts and forms.* The fonts and forms that Windows 2000 print servers are able to make available to other Windows 2000 and Windows NT 4.0 computers are not accessible by any other client computer type, including UNIX, Macintosh, DOS, OS/2, Windows 3.*x*, and Windows for Workgroups.

The best thing to remember about trying to achieve file and print connectivity to your Windows 2000 servers from these older client computer types is "Why?" Why are you trying to utilize these versions with their higher maintenance and user support costs when there are many other client operating systems that have a much lower total cost of ownership (TCO)? Although it is technically possible to keep your organization's older client computers up and running within the Windows 2000 Server world, the total cost to the organization will be quite a bit higher than it needs to be otherwise. That is the most important thing to remember going forward with Windows 2000 Server—it can help to lower your TCO for its computing clients, but only if you let it.

Macintosh

The Macintosh computer community is a unique one, given its original rise to widespread growth in the late 1980s only to fall into relative obscurity as we close out the 1990s. Many aspects of the Macintosh graphical user interface that made it very popular among educational and graphic artists users are also the very same ones that greatly contributed to its problems with the corporate technical support world. The Apple Computer Company copied the graphical user interface for its Macintosh computers from Xerox, Inc. and then enhanced it to be "user friendly" for the masses. These enhancements, unfortunately, did not include any real effort at integration with either the PC or the efficient networking worlds.

In order for you to connect your Macintosh client computers to a Windows 2000 Server machine, you will need to make changes on both sides of the equation: special services must be installed and run on the Windows 2000 server, and you must ensure Ethernet networking connectivity on the Macintosh side, including support for its AppleTalk networking protocol. This includes making your Windows 2000 server look like just another AppleTalk print device.

To install these services, right-click the My Network Places icon (it is typically along the top left side of your Windows 2000 Server desktop), which will reveal a small menu. Go to the bottom of that menu and click the Properties selection to access the Network and Dial-Up Connections screen. Once there, click the Advanced menu option and then click the Optional Networking Components menu selection, as shown in Figure 16.21.

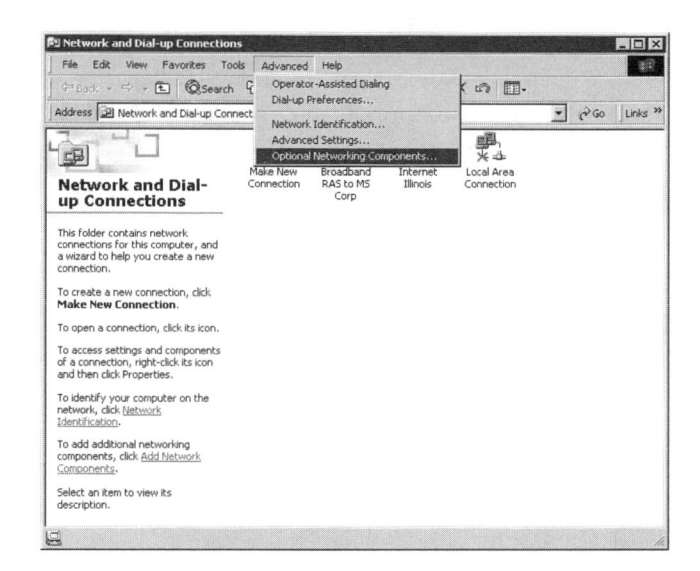

FIGURE 16.21
Installing Optional Networking Components.

Once you follow these steps, you will start the Windows Optional Networking Components Wizard, shown in Figure 16.22.

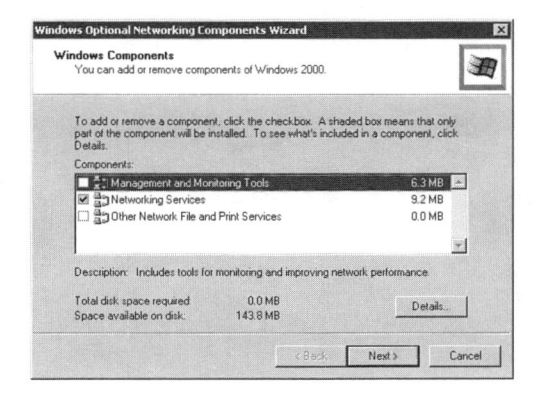

FIGURE 16.22
Beginning the Windows Optional Networking Components Wizard.

Some of the items presented to you on this screen may already have check marks in the white boxes next to them, which means that all those optional networking components have already been installed. Other check boxes may have check marks in them, but the background color of the check box is gray. This means that although at least one optional networking component has been installed, there is at least one optional networking component for that subject area that has not yet been installed. To achieve your Macintosh client computer connectivity objectives, you will want to use the optional networking components found in the bottom box (it's the one labeled Other Network File and Print Services). Click that optional networking component to select it and then click the Details button to reveal the individual components of that selection, as shown in Figure 16.23.

FIGURE 16.23
Choosing Other Network File and Print Services.

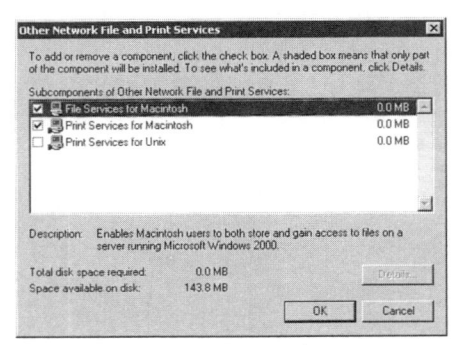

At this point, you select the top two options: File Services for Macintosh and Print Services for Macintosh. To do that, click the check box to the left of each option, which will cause a check mark to be inserted into each box. Once you have done that, click the OK button to start the software-installation process (you will need your Windows 2000 Server CD-ROM for this). This will start the software installation and configuration process, as shown in Figure 16.24.

FIGURE 16.24
Watching the Installation Process as Other Services Install.

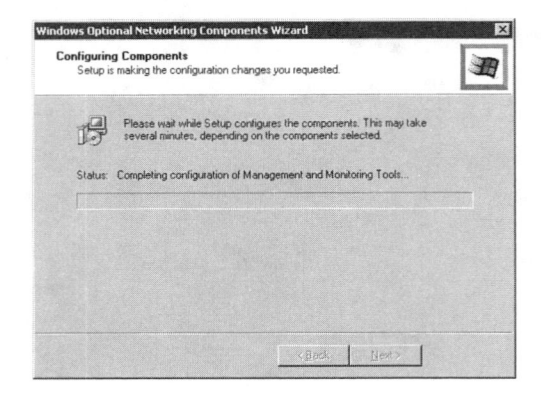

Although it says that this installation process will take several minutes, it probably will complete in less than 2 to 3 minutes. Once the installation process is complete, another window will appear, informing you of the successful installation. Once the installation process is completed, the screen will simply close without any type of message or warning.

Now that the Windows 2000 Server files have been installed, you might want to consider the security level that you will be using for your Macintosh clients. Within Windows 2000 Server, there are three levels from which to choose:

- *Guest*. This level uses the standard Windows 2000 Server Guest account.
- *User Using a Clear-Text Password Scheme*. The user will log onto the Windows 2000 server with a user ID whose password is readily viewable because it goes across the networking wire in a plain-text fashion.
- *User Using an Encrypted Password Scheme*. The user will log onto the Windows 2000 server with a user ID whose password has been encrypted so that it traverses the organization's networks in a secure manner.

Once you have made your selection, you will then need to implement it within your organization. As you can see by looking at your server's hard drive, a new folder named Microsoft UAM Volume has been created just off the root drive of your Windows 2000 Server machine. Within this folder, your Macintosh client computers will access files that exist on the server. Likewise, your other Windows 2000 Server clients may also place files in this folder, thereby making it possible for your Macintosh and PC users to effectively trade files back and forth, as needed.

At this point, your Macintosh client computers will need to have the applicable authentication files installed. To do this, you will need to perform the installation process from the Macintosh client side. Go to the Macintosh computer and open the Chooser tool. From there, click on the AppleShare and select the AppleTalk zone where your Windows 2000 server is located, then click to select that server. Continuing with the connection process, you will now choose the Microsoft UAM Volume as the item that you want to use. Once that is done, double-click the Microsoft UAM Volume icon that now appears on your Macintosh desktop area. Doing this will open that area, where you need to double-click the MS UAM Installer. The installation process will quickly finish, depending upon the speed and drive space available on your Macintosh computer.

Now that both the Windows 2000 server and the Macintosh client computers have been configured for use with Windows 2000, you now need to create user accounts for your Macintosh users. This is done in the exact same manner as you would for any other users for any other client operating system. Although many system administrators are tempted to use the standard Windows 2000 Server guest account for their Macintosh user community, you should avoid this temptation and create individual user accounts for all your

Macintosh users (for security purposes, you will always want your users to be accountable for their actions; with a general guest account, this will never be the case).

As your Macintosh computer users connect to your Windows 2000 server, they will be prompted with an authentication level, depending on which version of the Macintosh operating system they are running on their local Macintosh computers. If the Macintosh computer uses System 7.1 or later, there is no real choice: The client will use Microsoft Authentication. If the Macintosh computer uses an earlier version of the System 7 operating system, that Macintosh client computer will be given a choice: To use Microsoft Authentication or to use clear-text password protection in the form of the Apple Standard UAMs. Keep in mind that this will occur even if you have disabled both the clear-text and guest logon options for your Macintosh users from the Windows 2000 Server side.

When it comes to supporting your Macintosh users for printing via your Windows 2000 Server print server, there is just one thing you need to remember: security. Security can be a concern because AppleTalk is unable to support client user names or passwords. This means that your Macintosh clients will not be able to identify themselves on your organization's Windows 2000 network, which further means that your Windows 2000 server is going to be unable to impose user-level security on the Macintosh client computers. The implication of this is significant: If your Macintosh clients are able to send a print job to the printer, they will have implicit permissions to that printer. However, you, as the Windows 2000 Server administrator, will be able to set user-level permissions for all your Macintosh users by adding them to a group and then assigning the appropriate permissions to that print group. For more information on how to set these types of permissions, refer to Chapter 6, "Printing."

UNIX Connectivity

Much like connecting a Macintosh client computer to your organization's Windows 2000 servers, the connectivity of UNIX client computers also requires a bit of extra software to be installed on your Windows 2000 servers as well as on the UNIX client computers. Basic file services connectivity can be permitted via a technology known as the *File Transfer Protocol* (FTP). More user-friendly file services connectivity can be had through the use of a technology known as *Network File Services* (NFS). For more information on NFS, refer to Chapter 18, "UNIX Host to Windows 2000 Server Connectivity," which covers this topic in greater detail.

Printer connectivity for UNIX clients is provided by Windows 2000 through the use of the Print Services for UNIX feature, which includes support for the line printer daemon (LPD) service that UNIX clients require in order to be able to print. To install this Windows 2000 Server service, right-click the My Network Places icon (it's typically found along the top left side of your Windows 2000 Server desktop), which will reveal a small menu. Go to the bottom of that menu and click the Properties selection to access the Network and Dial-Up Connections screen. Once there, click the Advanced menu option and then click the Optional Networking Components menu selection to start the Windows Optional Networking Components Wizard, as shown in Figure 16.25.

FIGURE 16.25
Selecting Other Network File and Print Services for Installation.

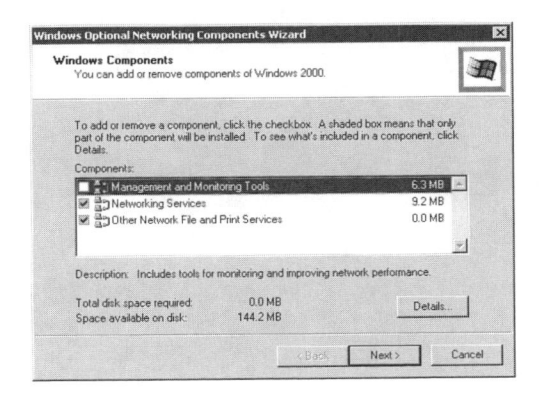

Some of the items presented to you on this screen may already have check marks in the white boxes next to them, which means that all these optional networking components have already been installed. Other check boxes may have check marks in them, but the background color of the check box is gray. This means that although at least one optional networking component has been installed, there is at least one optional networking component for that subject area that has not yet been installed. For you to enable UNIX client computer printing capabilities, you will use the optional networking components found in the bottom box (it's the one labeled Other Network File and Print Services). Click that optional networking component to select it and then click the Details button to reveal the individual components of that selection, as shown in Figure 16.26.

FIGURE 16.26
Installing Print Services for UNIX.

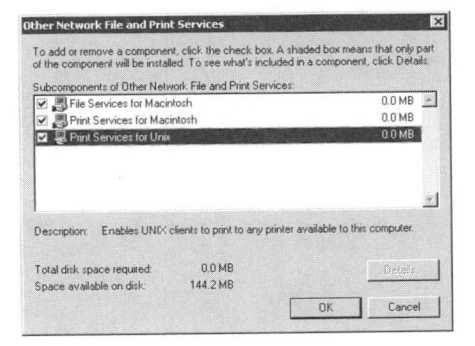

At this point, you'll select just the bottom option: Print Services for UNIX. To do that, click the check box to the left of that option, which will cause a check mark to be inserted into the box. Once you have done that, click the OK button to start the software-installation process (you will need your Windows 2000 Server CD-ROM for this). This will start the software installation and configuration process, as shown in Figure 16.27.

FIGURE 16.27
Watching the Installation Status Bar.

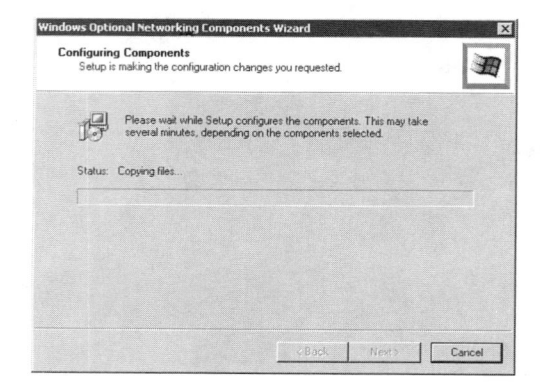

Although it says that this installation process will take several minutes, it typically completes in less than a minute. Once the installation process is completed, the screen will simply close without any type of message or warning.

You are now ready to start using your Windows 2000 Server machine as a print server for your UNIX clients. For more information on the configuration of the printer devices themselves, refer to Chapter 6. Keep in mind that you will need to install the appropriate printer software driver on the UNIX client as well as make sure that your UNIX client's operating systems support an RFC-compliant version of the line printer remote (LPR) services (this is important because some UNIX operating systems do not). Additionally, the UNIX clients will be sending their print requests to your Windows 2000 server using the standard LPR print command in this format:

```
lpr -S server_name -P queue_name file_name
```

Typically, because UNIX is case sensitive, you will want to use the exact mixed-case format presented here.

Summary

This chapter introduced a number of new terms and technologies that the reader will need to understand, to properly configure an organization's Windows 2000 Server client computer connectivity. Additionally, the occasional tidbit was provided to the reader so that they would be able to more quickly configure their client computer connectivity. The purpose has been to provide some systematic instruction on how to use mostly non-Microsoft client computers with create a connected environment for the organization. Further information regarding Windows 2000 networking can be found in Chapters 17, "NetWare Connectivity," 18, "UNIX Host to Windows 2000 Server Connectivity," and 19, "SNA Connectivity with BackOffice," of this book.

Connectivity

PART
V

IN THIS PART

17 NetWare Connectivity   *451*

18 UNIX Host to Windows 2000 Server Connectivity   *471*

19 SNA Connectivity with BackOffice   *489*

CHAPTER 17

NetWare Connectivity

IN THIS CHAPTER

- Conceptual Differences   *452*
- Connectivity to NetWare   *457*

The only real challenger that Windows has in the NOS market is the Novell operating system NetWare. NetWare, until very recently, boasted 70 percent of the NOS market share, and to this day it can be said to be in almost every Fortune 1000 company. If Microsoft only needed to be able to connect to one other NOS in the business world, it would NetWare.

NetWare also boasts a directory service (Novell Directory Service, or *NDS*) that has six years under its belt. This means a great deal in the directory services world because of the deep and complex nature of an enterprise directory. Maturity equals bugs fixed.

Conceptual Differences

The Windows path and the NetWare path have not followed the same trail, but they do have many of the same parents. Windows 2000 and NetWare both started as ways for enabling PCs to share resources. Also, both had UNIX and VMS to look to and take tools from. However, the similarities pretty much ended there.

Windows 2000 is born from a complete operating suite called Windows NT. Like UNIX, Windows NT was created with the ability to be used as a client and a server operating system. For this reason, administrators immediately gravitated to it as an application server.

NetWare was created as and is still a server operating system. Users will never sit down at a NetWare server to write their dissertations or fill out their expense reports. For that reason, many people take NetWare more seriously as an NOS.

Security

Among the differences that immediately become evident a NetWare administrator who moves to Windows 2000 is the fact that Windows 2000 is a open-to-closed system. When a shared resource is created in Windows 2000, it's automatically available to the group Everyone.

NetWare administrators are used to a closed-to-open system. When a resource is shared in a NetWare system, no one other then Admin accounts have permissions in that share.

This is an exceptional difference if the administrator is unaware of it. Imagine spending an afternoon creating resources that will be administered tomorrow. If information is stored in those resources, then that information be accessible until the next day when the permissions are changed. Neither way is right or wrong, but the difference can be a killer.

Active Directory Versus NetWare Directory Services

If this book were written two years ago, it would have been a very simple task to compare the directory services of Windows and NetWare. The difference was that what Microsoft called a directory service was not being called a directory service by anyone else in the industry. In fact, what Microsoft called a directory service was not a hierarchical directory service. NetWare's directory service (introduced in 1993) is a multilevel, hierarchical, object-oriented directory service.

Two years ago, Microsoft started playing with a directory service of its own called *Active Directory*. Its usability at that point was questionable, but Microsoft was on the hierarchical directory service map. Active Directory was an add-on product to the Windows NT operating system.

Tip

When asked for a preview of the hierarchical directory structure that Windows would use, many Microsoft personnel told you to become familiar with Exchange Server. The Exchange Server has had a hierarchical directory since its creation.

Note

Now that hierarchical directory structure has been mentioned *ad nauseam*, what is a hierarchical directory structure? The concept of a hierarchical directory structure is a structuring of directory objects (users, groups, and so on) into the same basic structure as the file system. The directory system has a root just as the file system does. The directory system also has subdirectories, but they're knows as *container objects*.

The advantage of this is that objects and object relationships become as easy to administer as the file system. Because all the objects in the directory are part of the same structure, it's not necessary to create a relationship or a path to get from one object to another, just as it's not necessary to form a relationship between subdirectories in the file system. (For more information on hierarchical directories, see Chapters 9, "Directory and Access Concepts Brief" and 10, "Active Directory Design.")

With the introduction of Windows 2000, Active Directory has become an integral part of the operating system. Any object in the operating system is in some way related to the directory.

There are three major differences in the directory structures:

- *Delegation of authority.* NetWare provides delegation of authority directly to any object over any other object in the directory. Active Directory provides delegation of authority to any user object over container objects.
- *Partitioning and replication.* NetWare partitions are separated along container lines. Active Directory partitions and replication is separated along site lines.
- *Naming convention.* The NetWare naming convention is freeform and does not conform to any search pattern. The directory is based solely on the X.500 scheme of the directory structure. Active Directory, while still based on x.500, is tightly tied to the DNS naming convention. While both systems use X.500 naming rules, only Active Directory adds the DNS layer. Both systems can be attached to the LDAP Internet standard for discovering directory objects.

Because it's not the purpose of this book to claim any grand champion in the directory services arena, let's just say that both systems have their better and worse sides.

The ability to find objects in the directory tree in Active Directory is greatly enhanced by the DNS tie. It becomes very easy to tie directory objects to the Internet when the internal network shares the same naming convention. On the other hand, you may be inadvertently sharing resources if the DNS structure is not closely monitored. That, again, just goes back to the basic philosophical differences.

The ability to divide partitions along networking lines instead of container lines does make more sense. The creation of partitions (sites) is primarily done to prevent replication traffic from occurring across areas of the network that have expensive bandwidth (WAN). Novell recommends to administrators that they create partition boundaries along container lines; for the most part, this is not difficult. However, if you're looking for the most freedom, the Microsoft solution is better.

The delegation of responsibility to an individual or group is far more flexible in the NetWare world. The ability to assign any object permissions over any other object allows for a far more granular management scheme than breaking at the container level, as is required by Active Directory. In the grand scheme of things, it's probably correct to believe that this is a problem few will encounter, but the fact is that NetWare does allow more flexibility here.

From an administrator's point of view, it's clear that both solutions have their strengths. The clear winner is the Microsoft administrator who is no longer tied to a flat-form directory that's cumbersome in the enterprise.

File Shares

The sharing of files is the most basic form of networking that exists, and it's a great difference between Windows and NetWare. The differences are in the way users access the file structure and in the way NetWare and Windows make the shares available and structure the directory.

In the Windows world, as you've learned, shares can be created at any point in the directory structure. An administrator can choose any directory on the server and choose to share it.

In the NetWare world, shares are not called *shares* but are instead called *volumes*. This is because the shares that are presented by a NetWare server are actually the drive volumes created on the servers. Every volume that's created and mounted on a NetWare server can be made available to the user base. However, directories cannot be published as separate entities.

In order to compensate for this difference, you must understand that when attached to a NetWare server, the user has the ability to create drive mappings pointing to any directory on the server. Such mappings are called *map roots*. To illustrate the difference, compare the way a user might have to gain access to the same directory on each form of server.

For example, consider how you would give users access to the folder HR without exposing the files and directories that are also listed in the rest of payroll. Allow each department to gain access to its own file and allow HR to have access to all 15 departmental directories.

- The Microsoft approach is to share all 15 payroll subdirectories and map the users in those groups to the directories they need to gain access to.
- The NetWare approach is to "map root" all users directly to the directory that they need access to.

This problem can be considered a wash if the Windows servers did not have a practical limit for the number of shares they're capable of handling. Each share being published takes a certain amount of CPU and memory resources to continue publishing. If an administrator wants to create home directories for 1,800 users and map each user to the root directory of those directories, most servers would be brought to their knees.

A feature that's very helpful to the administrator is the ability to set quotas on the amount of storage that users have on the server. Until recently, Windows servers have not been able to control this ability. A particularly nasty way of bringing a server to its knees was for a disgruntled employee to copy more files to the server than the server had the capacity to hold. A savvy administrator would not put the system files on a shared drive, but a file server with no file capacity is pretty useless. Windows 2000 and NetWare both have disk quotas today. However, there's a great difference in the way that they're enforced.

A Windows 2000 disk quota is a limit or warning placed on a user as to the amount of data that the user may place on the disk. When a quota is set, two behaviors can be made to occur. The first is that the user can be stopped from placing any more data on the disk. The second is that an event can be written to the event log. These actions are separated to allow administrators to be aware that the user has exceeded the limit while possibly avoiding interrupting an important job function for limit enforcement.

When users are given a limit, they can also be given a warning limit. This is the point when they're told they have reached a certain percentage of the maximum aloud for their accounts.

In the NetWare world, limits can be set at any point in the directory structure. Therefore, administrators can set a limit to the amount of space that a user has in his or her own home directory. The difference is that the user is then able to change directories and have a different limit. If the administrator wants to limit, for example, the amount of data the users keep in their home directories on the server but allow them to keep more data in departmental folders, this can be done.

The advantage of the Windows system is that it prevents a hacker from filling a disk from an uncontrolled location. The advantage of the NetWare system is that it allows more flexibility and control. However, it all comes back to the basic difference in the way the shares are handled.

Printing

From the user perspective, the connection to shared printers in these two operating systems is the same. Users in the Windows 95/98 world will not notice any difference between connecting to a NetWare print server and a Windows 2000 print server. By simply adding the printer and pointing to the network share, the user has access. The technical differences between the two models really make little difference in the work-a-day world.

The differences come when connecting a Windows 2000 or Windows NT client. In the Windows 2000/NT world, the drivers are delivered to a Windows 2000 or Windows NT client automatically when the client chooses the printer from the Network Neighborhood. NetWare servers are capable of delivering drivers to these and other clients, but the Windows world makes this process seamless. Windows 95/98 clients are also capable of having drivers delivered from the Windows 2000/NT server, but, as is the case with a NetWare server, this must be set up.

If the NetWare client is installed on a Windows client, then NetWare print servers will respond to the Windows `NET USE` command `NET USE LPT1 \\servername \printsharename`. However, the natural command in the NetWare environment is `CAPTURE`.

The `CAPTURE` command is very similar to the `NET USE` command in that the user will need to know the print server name and the name of the share (called a `queue` or `print object`). To execute the command, use the variables listed here:

`CAPTURE variables Common Variables List`

- `L=`. Following this variable is the number of the LPT port that is to be captured and sent to the network resource. `L=1` would be LPT1.
- `Q=`. Following this variable is the name of the print queue or print queue object to be printed to. `Q=rec_printer1` would send print jobs to the print queue rec_printer1.
- `S=`. The variable listed here is the server that contains the specific print queue desired. The server variable is not needed if the queue chosen is actually a print queue object in NDS. `S=server1` would send the print job to server1.
- `Ti=`. This variable refers to the time between the start of the print job data flow to the server and when the printer actually starts printing. This variable was far more necessary when DOS applications were prevalent because the print jobs were not released to the printer until the application was exited. `Ti=15` would start the print job 15 seconds after the print data started to arrive at the print server.
- `NB`. The NB variable tells the print server to not print a banner page after every print job. The printing of a banner page is the default in NetWare printing. A banner page indicates who printed the document to follow.
- `NFF`. This variable is used to suppress a form feed after printing to a dot-matrix or line printer.
- `SH`. Typing `CAPTURE SH` and pressing Enter will show all the LPT ports and their associated capture settings at that moment.

Connectivity to NetWare

NetWare servers are much like Windows servers in that they have many different levels of connection. The type of connection needed to make use of all the available services on the server is called a *native connection*.

To understand the difference between a native connection and other connections, it helps to employ the Internet concept of a Web connection versus a connection from a Windows client that will map to a drive share. A Web client is being given access to only a single process and is not able to map to drive or print shares. Native users in a NetWare system are able to make full use of the native NetWare utilities, such as listing available NetWare servers, sending messages to other NetWare users, and attaching to NetWare shares through local drive letters (mapping) and printer paths (capturing).

When connecting to NetWare servers, you have two basic forms of native connection:

- Bindery
- NDS

The bindery form of connection is quite comparable to the Windows NT workgroup form of connection. Users attach to each server on an individual basis, and every server has its own user and group list. NDS uses the same form of connection that's being used in Active Directory. A user attaches the directory and is then given access to the resources that the directory has to offer.

It's pointless to belabor the concepts beyond those examples, but the distinction is great when it comes to how you migrate or exchange information with a NetWare server, version 4.0 or greater. NetWare 4.x (a.k.a. intraNetWare) and NetWare 5 require that a user be attached as an NDS object before administrative information can be accessed.

Gateway Service for NetWare

The first tool used in the Windows world to integrate a Windows server into a NetWare environment was the Gateway Service for NetWare. This service allows users in a Windows domain to seamlessly interact with a NetWare server without needing to attach directly to that server. It's a bit of smoke and mirrors that doesn't make Novell happy.

The Gateway Service for NetWare is just that, a network service that runs on a Windows server and creates a gateway to NetWare servers. The process involves an administrator creating an attachment to a NetWare server shared resource (printer or drive) and then sharing the resources as if it were a shared resource on the Windows server. The advantage of this process is that users in the Windows domain do not have to install NetWare client software, and they don't have to be managed from the NetWare perspective.

> **Tip**
>
> Be aware that this is not meant to be an escape from having to purchase user licenses from Novell. The fact is that even Microsoft wants administrators to purchase license for every user that attaches to a NetWare resource in this way. The Windows server will only be using one license to make this connection to the NetWare server. The administrator's legal obligation to Novell is to purchase a license for each user connection that will be made to the gateway for this purpose.

The other great advantage to this form of integration is that the protocols necessary on the clients are reduced. Clients on the Windows domain will only need the protocols necessary to connect to that domain (most likely TCP/IP). The gateway server will make the IPX/SPX connection to the NetWare server only.

> **Tip**
>
> For more information on the NWLink IPX/SPX, see Chapter 15, "Multiprotocol Environments."

The service only supports connection to the NetWare server through NWLink IPX/SPX. Even if the NetWare server is version 5 and running in a Pure IP environment, it's necessary to install the IPX/SPX protocol to both servers. If the NWLink protocol is not installed on the Windows server, it will be added automatically when you install this service. This should make for an interesting conversation with the NetWare administrator who was finally convinced to convert to IP by his Windows brethren.

The Gateway service in Windows 2000 is capable of making connections to both NDS and Bindery resources. Legacy versions of the product were only able to access bindery resources. Any resource that a Windows 2000 client for NetWare is able to access can be captured and served through the gateway.

Preparing NetWare

The first consideration to be made is whether the NetWare server is prepared to receive the user who will attach to the Gateway service. A group called *NTGATEWAY* must exist on the NetWare server as well as a user account that's a member of the group that will be used by the Gateway service.

Be aware that any permission given to the NTGATEWAY group will be given to the service user account. Every user of the gateway will use those permissions. Therefore, if the NTGATEWAY group is given Supervisor permissions to the SYS volume on the NetWare server, any user who uses the gateway has those permissions. If that sounds particularly nasty, that's because it is. Administrators need to be very careful when creating this relationship. This is meant to be a temporary fix for the interim between migrations, not as a permanent solution.

Installing the Gateway Service

Once the NetWare server has an account and the account is part of the NTGATEWAY group, the next step is to install the Gateway service. To install this service, follow these steps:

1. Right-click My Network Places and choose Properties.
2. Right-click an existing network connection and choose Properties.

> **Note**
>
> Be aware that when this service is installed to one connection, it's installed to all connections. If you want to remove it from a particular connection, you'll have to do that on an individual basis and then you'll have to do so after the installation.

3. Choose the Install button. Click the client and then click the Add button.
4. Listed is the Gateway (and Client) Services for NetWare. Select it and choose OK (see Figure 17.1).
5. Choose Close on the Property screen.

FIGURE 17.1
The client install screen for the Gateway service.

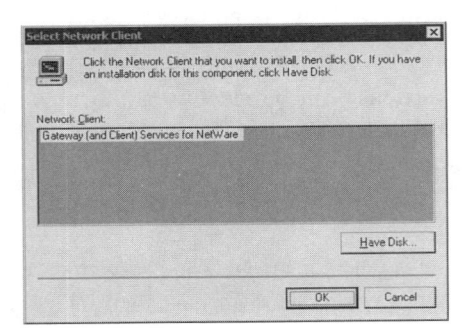

Once the service is installed, it must be configured to access the resources on the NetWare server(s). Upon installing the service, you'll be asked for the preference required for this connection (see Figure 17.2).

When selecting a preferred resource, your choice is first whether to attach to a specific bindery server or to an NDS tree. This choice is fairly simple, but it's important. If the desired result is to be able to attach to a single NetWare 3.*x* or older server, choose that server from the drop-down box in Figure 17.2. If your desire is to connect to any 4.*x* or later servers, an NDS tree should be chosen.

The other choice on this screen is to run the login script from the server or NDS tree for the user object that you're logging in as. From the perspective of a Windows server, this has little value. Keep in mind that this tool is both a client and a service, so it contains some tools for being a simple NetWare client. Running the login script is seldom a good idea for the server because it can cause confusion in the local drive mappings and it can create havoc in the way the server behaves. Unless the server is being used as a client (avoid this if you can help it), do not enable login scripts.

FIGURE 17.2
Selecting a NetWare connection.

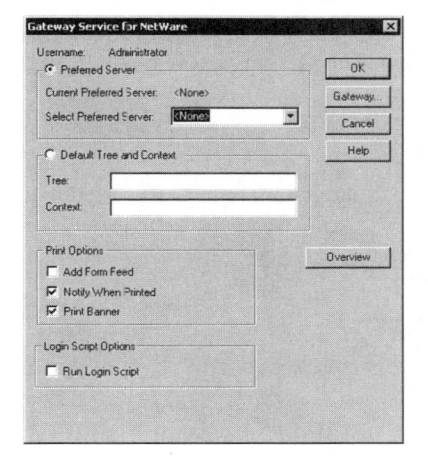

Configuring the Gateway

The Gateway service is now ready to be connected to the resources that will be shared. Just installing the service does not publish anything from the NetWare side. The administrator must individually publish each resource to be published.

The configuration of the service is done through a control panel called *GSNW* (a set of initials even the unfamiliar can deduce). The control panel once again allows for the choice of connection, as shown in Figure 17.3, but the primary purpose of the control panel in Windows 2000 Server is to configure resources. The Gateway button shown in Figure 17.3 is the opening to the mapping of resources.

FIGURE 17.3
The Gateway Service control panel.

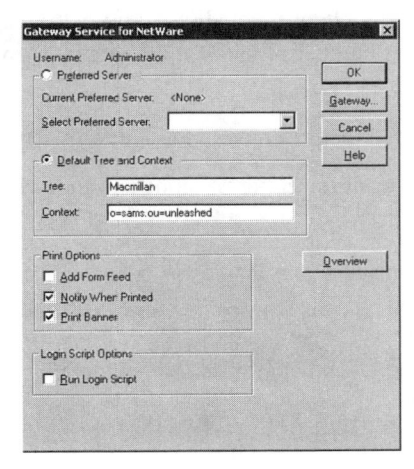

Before you create a resource, the gateway must be enabled. To enable the gateway, simply click the Enable Gateway check box on the Gateway configuration screen. Then type in the username and password (and password confirmation) created in the NetWare environment for this gateway. Keep in mind that this account will log in each time the server is started, without human intervention. The system is now ready to begin creating sharable resources.

To create a resource, follow these steps:

1. Click the Add button. The New Share window appears, as shown in Figure 17.4.

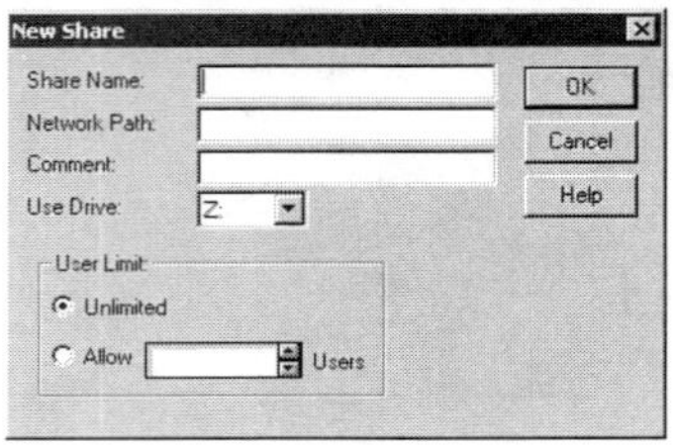

FIGURE 17.4
The New Share window for the gateway.

2. In the Share Name: field, type the name of the share as it will be presented from the Windows server. Then press the Tab key.
3. In the Network Path: field, type the UNC path to the resource on the NetWare server to be attached to (for example, \\server1\vol1). Then press Tab.
4. If a viewable comment for the Windows client is desired, type that in the Comment field and press Tab.
5. Click the down arrow beside the drive letter choice and select a drive letter for the connection on the gateway. Press Tab.
6. If you would like to limit the number of users who may use the connection (for licensing or bandwidth purposes), choose the Allow radio button and a type number in the box that indicates the number of users to allow at any given moment.
7. Click OK to finish configuring the gateway.

Once the gateway has been established, permissions to the gateway can be regulated:

1. Click the share for which you want to set permissions and then click Permissions.
2. Click Add.
3. Under Names, click the group or user and then click Add.
4. Under Type of Access, click the permission for this user or group.

File and Print Services for NetWare

File and Print Services for NetWare is not part of the Windows 2000 Server product, but it is a product that bears mentioning. It's effectively the opposite of the Gateway service just covered. This service allows NetWare users to access a Windows 2000 or NT server as if it were a NetWare 3.*x* server.

The utility of this service is basically the same as the Gateway service, but from the opposite (client) direction. It's very helpful during a transition period if the clients on an existing NetWare network are able to perceive the new server as a NetWare server. This allows the rollout team to get to each client over time, but it allows the clients to access the new server with no update until their turn comes.

NetWare clients are able to attach to the Windows server and use NetWare utilities as if connected to a NetWare server.

Directory Service Migration Tool

The conversion from a NetWare directory to a Microsoft Active Directory would be practically impossible if the administrator were to attempt it manually. If the directory is large enough, the administrator is better advised to start from scratch than to attempt the conversion. Fortunately, Microsoft has provided a tool called the *Directory Service Migration Tool*.

Much like the old NetWare migration tool provided with Windows NT, this tool is meant to pull all the users, groups, and data from NetWare servers. This tool can be used to replace NetWare servers, or it can be used to simply replicate the user and group information from the NetWare environment that exists. In either case, it saves a mountain of work.

One of the greatest features of this tool is its ability to run a model of the migration prior to actually copying a user or single piece of data. This allows the administrator to be prepared for any complications before they occur. Once a model has functioned properly, the migration can be run in real time.

The migration tool can be installed during the initial installation of Windows 2000, or it can be installed after. The installation is simply a matter of adding the service from the Add/Remove Programs control panel under Windows Components.

Migrating Directory Objects

Once the tool is installed, it's found in the Start menu under Programs/Administrative Tools. The opening screen sets you in position to create a new project (see Figure 17.5). Projects are used to create the model needed for migration.

FIGURE 17.5
The migration tool's opening screen.

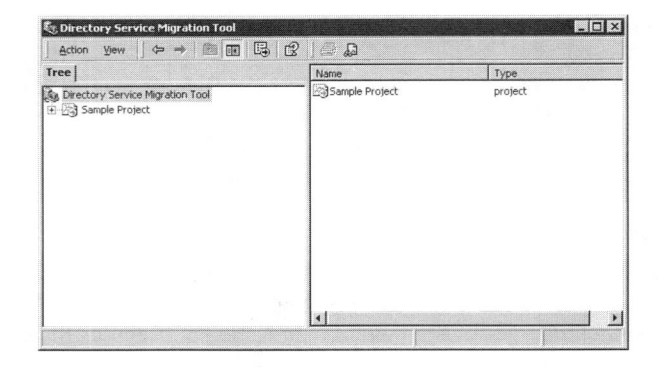

Before creating a project, you should set the options that will guide the project through the various data it will encounter. Options allow for the differences and complications that may exist in the two systems and allow the administrator to guide the way the tool will handle these differences. So you understand the options available, let's look at the options screens and cover what each of them mean.

Here are the option tabs:

- *General*. The placement of the project file is set in this tab as well as filtering of the objects that will be shown during the project. If you elect to uncheck the Display Supported Objects check box, objects that cannot be added to the Active Directory will be displayed. This can be helpful as a reality check for items that won't come along for the ride. (See Figure 17.6.)

FIGURE 17.6
The opening options window or General tab.

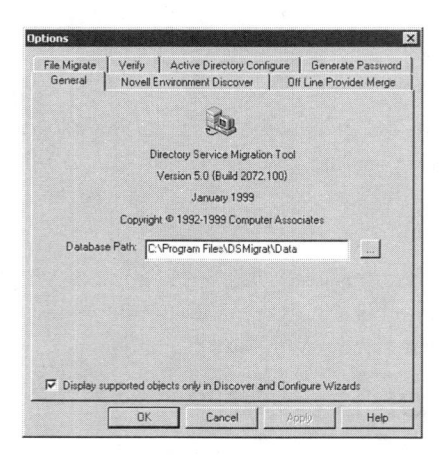

- *Novell Environment Discover*. In order to control the default Organization object created in the project, you need to type it into the Default Organization Name space. (See Figure 17.7.)

FIGURE 17.7
Novell Environment Discover.

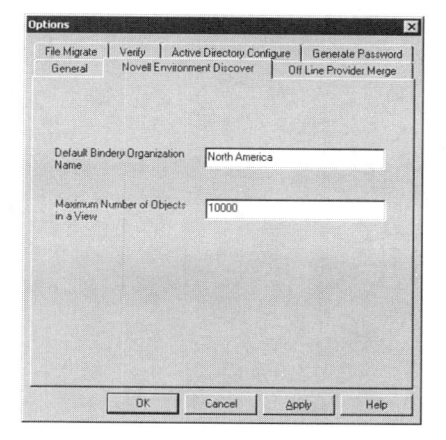

Adding a maximum number of objets in view can stop the project once it reaches an unmanageable number of objects. However, this number can also stop a project from being complete. It's best to use this option as a way of alerting you to the size of a project, not as a governor in the process.

- *File Migrate.* When you're migrating files and directories, there may be duplicate directories and files that exist on the two servers in the project. When this occurs, you can preset rules that tell the system how to behave. If these options are not set manually, directories and files may be overwritten. (See Figure 17.8.)

FIGURE 17.8
The File Migrate tab.

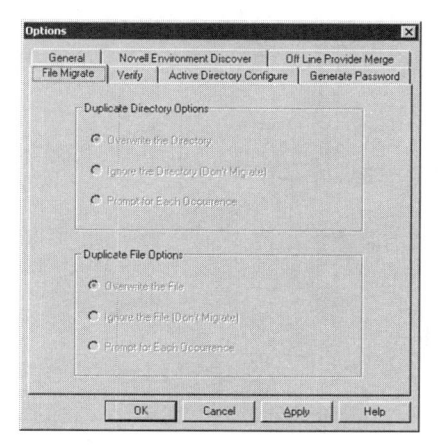

- *Verify Tree Matrix.* As the NDS tree is migrated to the Active Directory, a verification of the user and group dependencies is made. Along with this check the administrator has the ability to control the number and value of the objects that will be brought into the directory. (See Figure 17.9.)

FIGURE 17.9
The Verify Tree Matrix tab.

- *Active Directory Configure.* Some directory objects may be duplicated during migration. For those times, it's necessary to lay out rules that tell the migration tool how to handle the process. This same concept is laid out in the Offline Provider Merge tab. The difference between a single valued and multivalued object is that a multivalued object can contain several objects. Objects such as group memberships are multivalued. (See Figure 17.10.)

FIGURE 17.10
The Active Directory Configure tab.

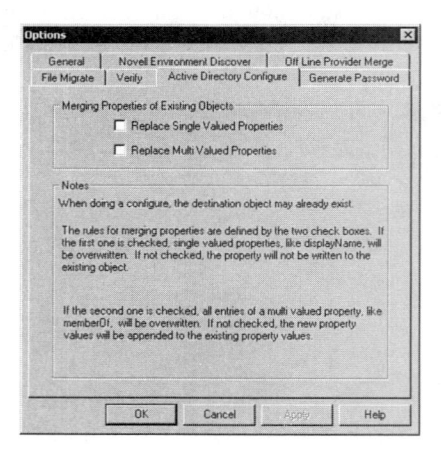

- *Generate Password.* When the migration occurs, Windows cannot read the passwords in the NetWare NDS tree even with the proper administrator permissions. Therefore, an administrator must set up a rule to control the passwords that will be given to the migrated users for their first logon. (See Figure 17.11.)

FIGURE 17.11
The Generate Password tab.

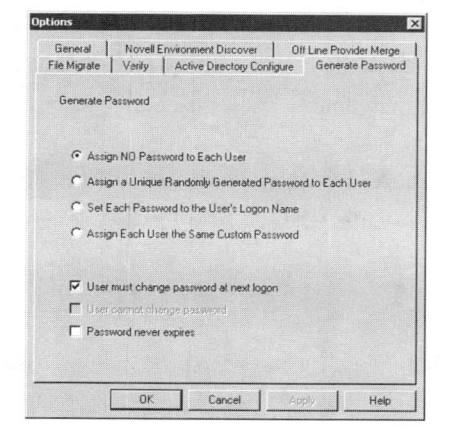

The option exists to create no password, create a random password, create a password from the user name, or assign all users the same password. Once the password is created (or not), the administrator can have users prompted to change their passwords upon first logon or stop them from changing their passwords all together. If the option is selected that generates a random password, the option to have users change their passwords upon next logon will allow the users to create passwords they can remember better. If a single password is given to all users, it's strongly advised that the Change on First option be set.

Once the options are set, the creation of the project is relatively easy. To create a new project, follow these steps:

1. Choose the Action menu and then New Project.
2. Enter the name of the project in the space provided and press Enter.

That's it. A project is created. Now the project must be populated with the resources that need to be migrated. Also, you need to specify where to migrate them to. The population of the project is called "creating views." A *view* is a graphical view/tool that can be used to gather the objects to be migrated. The extra objects or incompatible objects will not be listed and this can cause issues in large environments.

The first view to be created is the "View from NetWare." This view is the initial view of the bindery or NDS objects that will be migrated. It allows the administrator of the project to move through the bindery or NDS tree of objects.

To create the "View from NetWare," follow these steps:

1. Right-click the project, point to New, and then click View from NetWare.
2. Enter the view name, author name, and optional description and Click Next. A list of the servers available for discovery will appear.

3. Select the bindery or NDS server object and then double-click its trees.
4. Click a tree and then double-click the tree to display its Container objects.
5. Click a Container object and then double-click the container to display its child objects.
6. After selecting an object, click Add Context to set the discover context at the level of the selected object. The full name of the selected object appears in the Details pane of the dialog box.
7. Click Next, and the dialog box displays a summary of the view name and the specified context for the discover operation.
8. Click Finish, and a status dialog box displays the processing messages.

Once a view of the NetWare resource has been created, the migration tool will be populated with the objects that can be migrated. The process of migrating these objects is as simple a copying, moving, and pasting objects in Windows Explorer. If you're familiar with this process, then you're familiar with the process of moving objects. The options that were set for the migration tool or the project, itself, will guide the system though most issues.

The most important point to keep in mind while moving objects is the relationship between the object type and the object they're being moved to or from. A simple example of this is that an Organizational Unit (OU) cannot be copied to a group object. Keep in mind the directory rules from Chapter 9 regarding container and group objects and the items they can contain.

Migrating Files and Directory Structure

Migrating files from server to server or from multiple servers to a server should also be done within the migration tool. Migrating files and directories with this tool can move the attributes and permissions along with the data. This can be a difficult-to-impossible task outside of the utility.

In order to perform the migration, use the File Migration Wizard (see Figure 17.12). This wizard will walk you through the process of selecting and copying.

To start and use the wizard, follow these steps:

1. Right-click the Directory Service Migration Tool object or a volume object in the Directory Service Migration console and choose All Tasks and then File Copy.
2. When the wizard opens, choose Next.
3. Select Yes to migrate files. Then click Next.
4. To display all volumes and directories in your NetWare configuration, double-click the source view.

FIGURE 17.12
The File Migration Wizard.

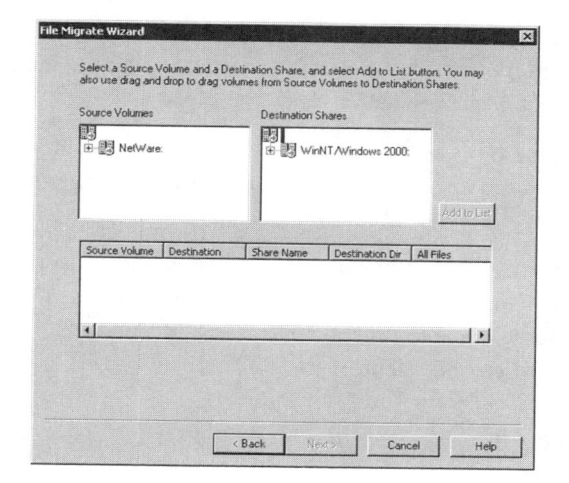

5. Click a source volume or directory and then drag it to a destination share.
6. Click Next.
7. Select a source view item and then click Delete to remove the object, or you can click Edit to display an edit dialog box.
8. Click Browse beside the destination directory. This displays a list of available directory locations. Select a destination directory.
9. Enable Create Share to create a new share location. Then click Next.
10. Click Next to migrate all files. This returns you to the edit dialog box for migrating shares and files. Click Next again. You're prompted to update volume objects. Select the individual volume objects or click Select All.
11. Click Check Disk Space to confirm that there's adequate space to complete the planned file migration. Then click Next.
12. Click Update or Don't Update. Then click Next. You're prompted to finish the migration. Click Finish to start the migration.

NDS for NT (by Novell)

Novell obviously has it opinion about all this coexistence. The NetWare product line also offers a product for the two systems coexisting, but it takes a different tactic. The product allows the administrator of a NetWare NDS structure to also manage Windows servers from the same interface. The product that is sold by Novell (separate from their NetWare line) is called *NDS for NT*.

When the product is installed, all NetWare NDS objects appear in the NetWare Administrator tool (NWADMIN) and the Windows servers also appear. The concept is that all users, groups, and objects become part of the same directory service (NDS). This allows IS teams to settle on one directory service without needing to maintain two directories. The Novell product does provide for Native IP support.

Windows domains become NDS objects and therefore become synchronized through NetWare. User passwords become the same in both environments. Permissions are now managed from one utility.

The only catch is that workstations must have the Novell client for NetWare (Client 32 or the Z.E.N.Works client). This is so that the workstation has access to the NDS services. But if the client wants to continue to function as a standard Windows NT client then they may continue to use the Microsoft client.

Summary

NetWare and Windows 2000 both contain hierarchical directory services, but they do have their differences. The basic differences in these services can be summed up in the philosophical differences of three items: partitioning/replication, the delegation of authority over objects in the directory, and the tying of the naming convention to the DNS system. Functionally, they're both used for the same purpose.

The two products are well equipped for coexistence through such products as Gateway Services for NetWare, File and Print Services for NetWare, and NDS for NT (by Novell).

The migration from one system to the other is facilitated and made possible by the Directory Service Migration Tool. Without this tool and the assorted services it provides, it would be nearly impossible to make the migration from one system to the other.

CHAPTER 18

UNIX Host to Windows 2000 Server Connectivity

IN THIS CHAPTER

- Conceptual Differences Between Windows 2000 Server and UNIX-Style Operating Systems *472*
- Different Flavors of UNIX *475*
- Simple TCP/IP Tools *476*
- Application Connectivity *484*
- Connecting to NFS *485*
- About Samba *486*
- Printing in a UNIX World *487*
- The Future: Microsoft and UNIX *488*

One of the great strengths of Windows 2000 is its ability to connect to different operating systems and environments. UNIX is and will continue to be for the foreseeable future the operating system that runs the Internet. In this chapter, we'll look at how Windows 2000 and UNIX systems can exchange information with each other. This involves concepts including security, file sharing, printer sharing, and application-level connectivity.

This chapter will discuss topics from a Windows 2000 Server role, that of providing services to SMB (Normal) clients, as well as from the opposite role, using Windows 2000 to connect to a UNIX host for file and printer sharing. These types of activities are very useful for batch processes such as database support activities, where Windows 2000 needs to send and receive files from UNIX, in addition to the capability for Windows 2000 Professional machines to be able to connect directly to UNIX for different tasks.

A quick overview of the chapter is in order, and then we'll get started:

- Conceptual differences between Windows 2000 Server and UNIX-style operating systems
- Different "flavors" of UNIX
- Using simple TCP/IP tools
- Connecting to NFS
- Samba
- Printing in a UNIX world
- The future of Microsoft and UNIX

Conceptual Differences Between Windows 2000 Server and UNIX-Style Operating Systems

Windows 2000 Server is designed to be an enterprise-scale server for providing file, print, and application services to client computers running Windows. UNIX is designed to function as both a client and a server, and it's designed to talk to other UNIX clients. As a result, different approaches are taken concerning the problems of user accounts, security, and directory services.

User Accounts

User accounts are how an operating system decides which users can perform which operations. Windows 2000 has an Administrators group that several users can be assigned to, which essentially allows those users full control over every aspect of the machine. In the UNIX world, there's one account, called *root*, that has a similar level of permissions. In Windows 2000, the user accounts are stored in the Registry, whereas in the world of UNIX, the accounts are stored in a text file just like any other piece of configuration information. Users are defined in a text file, usually called `passwd`, that has a system-dependent format that usually includes the user's name, group affiliations, an encrypted version of the user's password, the user's home directory, and which shell to run for the user when he or she logs in. In most systems, user accounts exist on each UNIX system the user has access to, and various schemes exist for copying user account information across a network.

UNIX has a similar notion to the Windows 2000 use of groups. *Groups* allow a set of users access a set of resources without having to give every user access to the resource independently. As with Windows 2000, user accounts in UNIX-style operating systems can be assigned to multiple groups.

Security

UNIX security is all based on the concept of a *file*. A file on a disk has three levels of security that can be set on it: Owner, Group, and Everyone. Every file is owned by a given user and a given group. There are three attributes that can be set at each level: read, write, and execute. These are usually shown like this:

```
-rwxr—r—   1 millcs    root       15483 Jun 26 11:57 ch6.rtf
-rw-r—r—   1 millcs    root       56320 Jun 26 13:02 final.doc
```

For the first file, `ch6.rtf`, the user is `millcs`, and the user is part of the group called `root`. The file size is 15,483 bytes, and the file date is June 26. The beginning of that line, `-rwxr—r—`, shows that the owner of the file (`millcs`) has read, write, and execute rights to the file. The owner's group (`root`) has only read access, and everyone has read access. Full access for everyone is usually shown as `-rwxrwxrwx`. The first hyphen in the list is reserved for the sticky bit. The *sticky bit*, which when set causes the first hyphen to be `s`, determines which user account is actually running the program. If a program had the sticky bit set and everyone were allowed to run it (usually this would be `srwxr-xr-x`), then that program would have the same user access as the owner of the file.

This is very useful if it's necessary to give the user the ability to read and write to a file, but only from within a given program (for example, if the program is writing output to a file with an easily corruptible format). The program would be set up with ownership assigned to a user who has access to the file, and the individual users would then not have any access to the file. Another use for this is if a program should only be run during specific hours. (For example, if games can be played only after business hours, the game programs are given to an account that can be logged into only after business hours, and then the sticky bit gets set so anyone can run them.) Because the account can only log in after business hours, the program will only be run outside of business hours.

Another interesting note in UNIX security: Everything in UNIX is a file. Therefore, if someone wants to play an audio file, the audio file gets sent to the audio device, which is attached to a file called /dev/audio in some flavors of UNIX. This also assumes that the user who's playing the file has write access to the file /dev/audio.

Windows 2000 uses the idea of *user impersonation*, but it isn't as readily available as the sticky bit system used with a UNIX-style host. Instead, it's buried deep down inside the Win32 API and inside the architecture, and this feature can only be taken advantage of by programming it that way from the beginning. Otherwise, the security models are very similar, with separate read, write, and execute security as well as the capability to set permissions to users, groups, and everyone. Windows 2000 uses a special user account, Everyone, which is given the level of access that anyone other than the specified users and groups are given. Windows 2000 also has the capability to assign security settings for multiple groups or users directly to a file, which UNIX does not. Instead, in UNIX, you have to assign all the users to a given group and then assign group ownership appropriately.

Directory Services

Directory services, such as the Active Directory and NDS, are the backbone of enterprise-wide security. These systems allow administrators central administration of all security, which is a very good thing. Security in these systems is set up one time, at one place, and it distributes itself throughout the network.

UNIX-style operating systems have a pioneering history of directory services. Sun Microsystems started the ball rolling with what was then called the *Yellow Pages* (yp). Some phone company somewhere got a little upset by this, and the name was changed to NIS, the *Network Information System*. NIS allows usernames and passwords to flow within a "domain" context so that users can get access to resources within a domain without having to have an individual user account created on each machine in the domain. NIS, however, is largely a transport system. It doesn't handle user authentication by itself; instead, it handles moving the username/password pairs (and optionally other information) around the network to allow the normal authentication mechanisms to take place.

UNIX systems also have other directory-management software that provides LDAP services, but this has only been implemented as a "people finder" application right now, providing email addresses, phone numbers, and office locations. LDAP is the Lightweight Directory Access Protocol, and it's used to access directory information. For now, this software doesn't provide the level of integration with the security model that Windows 2000 and Active Directory do.

The Samba software suite, discussed in detail later in this chapter, allow some UNIX systems (Silicon Graphic IRIX, Linux, Free-BSD, and SunOS, to name a few) to impersonate Windows NT 4.0 servers, as both domain controllers and standalone servers. It's expected that the Samba project will continue to grow and be able to emulate the Windows 2000 Active Directory. At that point, systems running the Samba suite will have the same directory services capabilities as Windows 2000 servers.

Windows 2000 directory services, in the form of the Active Directory, are much more advanced. The Active Directory is much easier to set up, maintain, and document than the NIS system. Novell has ported its NDS system to UNIX now, and it's really the only contender for providing high-quality directory services.

Different Flavors of UNIX

Windows 2000 and UNIX are very different operating systems. Windows 2000 is produced and supported by one company—Microsoft. As such, every installation of Windows 2000 is very similar to every other installation, and software that works on one machine will always work on another machine, assuming they're on the same processor architecture. In the world of Windows, there are standard directories for DLL files (`%SYSTEMROOT%\Winnt\System32`), standard directories for client programs (`\Program Files`), and a standard format for saving configuration information (the Registry). These standards, combined with a large installed user base, make programming for Windows platforms easier and more profitable than it would be without the standards. It also reduces support costs to an extent, because machines running Windows are all pretty much the same, and if one machine requires a Registry change to fix a given problem, the rest of the machines will probably require the exact same change. Windows systems also are all binary compatible within the same architecture. In other words, a program that runs in Windows 98 will most likely run in Windows 2000 (on Intel hardware) with no problems.

In the UNIX world, things aren't so easy. In the beginning, UNIX came from AT&T and was an open-source system; therefore, anyone who had UNIX could make changes to it. Later, after the breakup of AT&T, the company was allowed to start selling UNIX, which it did (and it was very expensive). So, some folks at the University of California at Berkeley created from scratch a new UNIX-style operating system called Free-BSD. The *Free* in the name referred to the fact that there was no AT&T-derived code, so it was free of the AT&T copyright. The current BSD (Berkeley System Development) versions include Free-BSD and Net-BSD.

At about the same time, a college student in Finland, Linus Torvalds, was trying to find a good, inexpensive operating system for his new workstation. His problem was that AT&T still owned UNIX, which was very expensive, and the operating systems from other vendors didn't meet his needs. Therefore, he did something that a lot of people wish they could do: He built his own operating system, called Linux. After years of development by literally thousands of people around the world, Linux has become one of the dominant operating systems on the Internet. Linux is available in several different flavors from different commercial and noncommercial companies, including Red Hat, Caldera, and SuSE.

In addition to Free-BSD and Linux, UNIX workstation vendors usually have their own flavors of UNIX, including Sun (SunOS), Data General (DG/UX), and Hewlett-Packard (HP/UX), just to name a few. Each of these takes pieces of the original AT&T System V and the BSD variants and sticks them together.

UNIX-style operating systems are all based on some underlying architectural assumptions, but the implementation of the operating systems can be widely different from one source to the next. In the mid-to-late 1980s, the UNIX vendors made a lot of noise about adhering to this standard or that one, but there are still vast differences in critical items such as operating system startup (System V Init or BSD Init), log file locations and formats, and configuration information formats, locations, and filenames. Unfortunately, most of the differences still exist to this day and are the subject for so-called "Religious Wars" on the Internet over which system is better. As a result, UNIX programs tend not to be binary compatible from one flavor to the next, even given the same architecture. That means that a piece of software usually cannot be copied from one brand of UNIX to another and run. Usually the source code has to be recompiled. What's more, the log files and configuration files are usually in different places from one machine to the next.

Simple TCP/IP Tools

The TCP/IP tools we use today, such as Telnet and FTP, have been around for a long time on various operating systems and hardware. The key to using any of these tools is finding the proper version of either the client or server side of the tool in question. Fortunately, Windows 2000 Server comes with the client-side software for FTP and Telnet; unfortunately, there's only server-side software for FTP. In the UNIX world, the Telnet and FTP programs exist both as clients and servers: The clients are called simply ftp and telnet, and their server counterparts are ftpd and telnetd (the *d* on the end stands for *daemon*, the name UNIX gives to processes that run in the background to provide services). There is also a variety of lesser-known utilities, such as TFTP and Finger, that provide some interesting uses.

Telnet

Telnet provides terminal services across a network. It's widely used in the UNIX world for remote execution and remote management. Because most UNIX workstations have a very convenient and powerful command shell, Telnet is a very powerful tool because it allows administrators to make any change to any machine's configuration, from starting and stopping services to changing configurations and IP addresses. Telnet is just like sitting in front of the console.

> **Warning**
>
> Using Telnet really is just like sitting in front of the console. Therefore, when you Telnet to a host, everything that's typed into the Telnet session is sent, character-by-character, to the host. That includes your password. If you're concerned about crackers with network packet sniffers, don't use Telnet.

Windows 2000 provides two versions of Telnet. One version is a console-mode Telnet; it's usually located in %SYSTEMROOT%\System32\telnet.exe and is a basic console-mode Telnet client (Figure 18.1). This is a standard Telnet client, so it's all command-line driven. To start it, go to Start, Run and type in **telnet** and optionally the name of the machine to connect to, as in **telnet kermit** for a machine called kermit.

FIGURE 18.1
The character-mode Telnet window, in console mode. This console is getting ready to connect to the machine kermit *using the* open *command.*

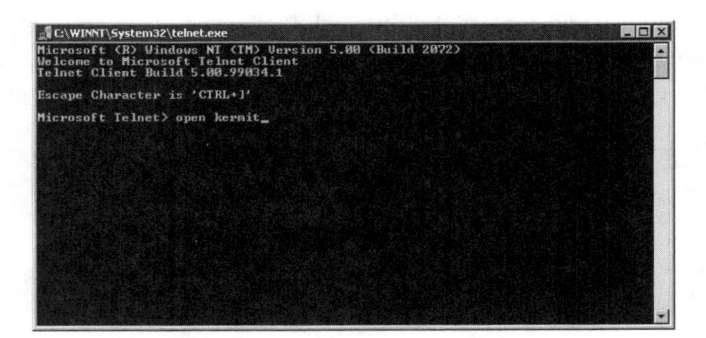

Console-based Telnet runs in two modes. The console mode has a prompt that looks like this:

Microsoft Telnet>

This prompt means that the system is in console mode. To see a list of commands to use in the console, use the help command, which will produce this output:

Microsoft Telnet> help

Commands may be abbreviated. Supported commands are:

```
close           close current connection
display         display operating parameters
open            connect to a site
quit            exit telnet
set             set options (type 'set ?' for a list)
status          print status information
unset           unset options (type 'unset ?' for a list)
?/help          print help information
Microsoft Telnet>
```

There are some basic console Telnet commands needed to use Telnet. If a computer name is not on the command line, the `open` command will open a connection. Therefore, if Telnet is started by just putting **telnet** into the Start, Run dialog box, typing **open kermit** will start a session with the machine called `kermit`. The rest of the commands are fairly self explanatory.

After the Telnet client is connected, it will automatically go into connected mode. To get back to console mode while still connected, use Ctrl+] (that's a square bracket). To return to connected mode, press Enter on a blank line. To close a Telnet console, log out of the connection and at the console type **quit**.

The other Telnet client is a nice, graphical interface to Telnet, and it's usually located in %SYSTEMROOT%\System32\TelnetC.exe. It provides two different terminal emulations: VT-100/ANSI and VT-52. Normally VT-100/ANSI is used, and it's the default. To access these configuration choices, use the Terminal, Preferences menu, shown in Figure 18.2. The configuration screen also allows the background color to be changed as well as the font and font properties.

FIGURE 18.2
The graphical-based Telnet with the Terminal Preferences window open.

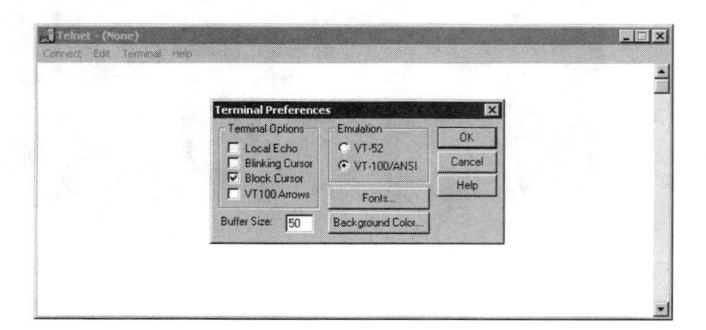

A better program that provides the same service is the shareware program NetTerm, which is available at most shareware download sites on the Internet. It provides full-color Telnet with logging, configurable key maps, and dial-up support. If the Telnet client is used a lot, it's probably a good idea to find something like NetTerm that's a little better than what comes with Windows 2000.

In addition, it's also possible to find Telnet servers for Windows 2000 systems. A company called Seattle Labs makes a Telnet server that can be used from any Telnet client. It's great for system administrators because it allows them to perform operations that require high bandwidth, such as copying large files, without having a high-bandwidth connection.

FTP

The FTP protocol allows file transfers from servers to clients. FTP relies on a series of commands to change to the correct directory and start file transfers. The file takes a user ID and password in and works within the operating system's notion of file security to determine which files can be read and whether or not an incoming file will be accepted. There's a good deal more about FTP services in Chapter 20, "Internet Information Server."

There are several different FTP clients. Windows 2000 comes with two. To access the first one, go to a Web browser and type in an FTP URL, such as ftp://ftp.microsoft.com. This will provide a familiar graphical user interface to FTP that looks just like a normal Explorer window, as shown in Figure 18.3. The other FTP client is the command-line client, and it can be started from the command prompt (or the Start menu) by typing **ftp** *address*. The address is just the name of the machine to send the FTP request to.

With either of these methods, the usernames and passwords are transmitted over the network in plain text, so anyone with a network analyzer, such as a Network General Sniffer or Microsoft's Network Monitor, will be able to see the passwords and use them.

FIGURE 18.3
This is an FTP session to the popular site ftp.cdrom.com. *It was reached by typing* **ftp://ftp.cdrom.com** *in the Start, Run dialog box.*

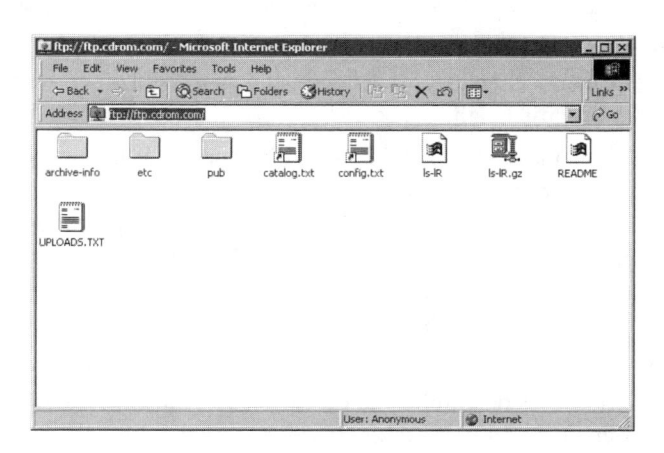

Here are the common FTP commands:

- OPEN. Used to open a connection (for example, OPEN FTP.MICROSOFT.COM would open a session with the FTP server at Microsoft).

- USER. The username to use to authenticate the session. This is either the generic user anonymous with the password (traditionally) of guest, or it's a real user ID.
- PASSWORD. Usually abbreviated as PASS, the PASSWORD command is used to transmit a password. Note that just like the Telnet protocol, FTP transmits passwords in clear text over the network and is vulnerable to crackers using network-sniffing software. An FTP server will automatically prompt for username and password upon connection, and the USER and PASS commands are usually only used in scripts.
- BINARY. Often abbreviated as BIN, this command tells FTP to use binary file transfer. Most servers use ASCII as the standard file-transfer mechanism. Because ASCII is a seven-bit standard, any binary files sent using the ASCII transfer mechanism will be corrupted. This is a mode-setting command, so after this command, all transfers will be done in binary until the ASCII command is used.
- ASCII. Often abbreviated as ASC, this command tells FTP to use ASCII to transfer files, stripping off the high-order bit. Using this with a binary file will result in a corrupt file. This is a mode-setting command, so after this command, all transfers will be done in ASCII until the BINARY command is used.
- HASH. This command tells FTP to print a hashmark (#) for every 1,024 bytes transferred. This is a good way for interactive sessions to make sure the transfer hasn't stalled.
- CD. Change Directory. This command changes from the current directory to a target directory on the server. This works the same as the CD command at the command line. For example, CD pub will change to the pub directory, whereas CD .. will move up one directory .
- LCD. Local Change Directory. This command changes the local directory on the client to the specified path.
- LS or DIR. Lists the contents of the given directory or, if no directory is specified, lists the contents of the current directory. UNIX-style ls options are supported, such as ls -l for long directory listings and ls -C for directories in columns (note that the options are case sensitive). However, the command ls -l foo.txt will create a directory list and put the list into a file called foo.txt in the current directory. This is handy because it allows the output to be redirected; therefore, commands such as ls -l ¦more can be used to paginate output.
- GET. The GET command is followed by the filename to be transferred to the client. The GET command will get one file. It won't get a directory, and it won't use wildcards. For example, the command GET *.* will try to find a file called *.* and transfer it. It won't find one, and the transfer will fail. The nice feature of GET is that it allows the specification of a destination file; therefore, GET FILE1 MYFILE will grab the file called FILE1 and write it to a file called MYFILE.

- **PUT.** The PUT command is followed by the filename to be transferred to the server. Just like the GET command, the PUT command doesn't use wildcards.
- **MGET and MPUT.** The M stands for *Multiple*. Therefore, MGET will get multiple files and accept wildcards, and MPUT will put multiple files on the server and accept wildcards. Wildcards are, of course, UNIX standard.
- **DELETE and MDELETE.** Usually abbreviated as DEL and MDEL, these are the delete commands. DEL works with single files only, whereas MDEL works with wildcards.
- **!.** This command will start a command shell within the FTP session.
- **QUIT.** This command will exit FTP.

Now the question is, why bother with all of the command-line stuff when there's a good graphical interface? Because, in many cases, the FTP program will need to be run as a batch process (for example, to get a copy of the previous day's transactions for import into a local SQL Server database). In that case, it's nice to string together a series of commands into an FTP script and then schedule the script with either the AT command or some other scheduling service. To do that, create an ordinary text file using Notepad and put in the commands that FTP needs to run. Here's an example:

```
OPEN ftp.microsoft.com
USER anonymous
guest
CD /bussys
GET README.TXT
QUIT
```

Notice that the PASS command was left out. Some servers need it, some don't. It turns out that Microsoft's server doesn't need it. To run this script, just call the ftp command from the command line with the appropriate arguments:

```
ftp -s:ftp.scr -n
```

Here, ftp.scr is the name of the script to be run. The -n option tells the FTP client not to try to log on automatically. If the -n option isn't specified, you should remove the USER command but leave the username anonymous there. Once again, some servers need this, some don't. It will take some experimentation to get this absolutely right. Another helpful hint: Always redirect the output to make it easier to debug. For example, if you run the command

```
ftp -s:ftp.scr -n > ftp.out
```

then the file ftp.out will contain the entire transcript of the FTP session:

```
ftp> Connected to ftp.microsoft.com.
OPEN ftp.microsoft.com
220 ftp Microsoft FTP Service (Version 4.0).
ftp> USER anonymous
331 Anonymous access allowed, send identity (e-mail name) as password.
```

```
230-This is FTP.MICROSOFT.COM
230-Please see the dirmap.txt file for
230-more information.
230 Anonymous user logged in.
ftp> ftp>
CD /bussys
250 CWD command successful.
ftp> GET README.TXT
200 PORT command successful.
150 Opening ASCII mode data connection for README.TXT(1715 bytes).
226 Transfer complete.
ftp: 1715 bytes received in 0.29Seconds 5.89Kbytes/sec.
ftp> QUIT
221 Thank you for using Microsoft Products!
```

Any combination of the commands listed will work inside an FTP script, so files can be sent or received. This is very useful for nightly batch processing when it's necessary to retrieve a file from any UNIX machine, but it also works with any other machine that can run FTP.

There are several third-party FTP utilities, ranging from the more-or-less standard CuteFTP, available from www.cuteftp.com, to the LeechFTP program, which is free.

The Lesser-Known Utilities

The TCP/IP protocol has bred many interesting utilities over the years, many of which have almost fallen into disuse. These include utilities such as Finger, TFTP and RSH.

TFTP

The program TFTP uses the Trivial File Transfer Protocol. Unlike the File Transfer Protocol (FTP), which uses TCP connections for data transmission, TFTP uses UDP, which doesn't have any error checking. It's not widely used for two reasons—one being the lack of error checking and the other being a number of security exploits that have been carried out using UDP against Windows NT. The program itself is quite simple, because it only has a command line:

`tftp [-i] hostname [GET ¦ PUT] source [destination]`

The -i switch specifies that TFTP is going to transfer a binary (image) file rather than an ASCII file. *hostname* is the name of the host that TFTP should connect to. GET or PUT must be specified as the direction of transfer. *source* is the name of the file to get (or put), and *destination* is the place the file will land.

Finger

The `finger` command is not used to hurl insults at people across the network. Instead, it's used to get information about a particular user at a particular host. It's another one-line utility:

finger [-l] *user* [*@host*]

The `-l` tells the Finger program to grab the long list format for the information returned. The *user* and *@host* options specify which user to get information on. If just *user* is sent, the Finger program will attach to the local machine to get the information; otherwise, the Finger program will look up the specified user at the specified host. For example, here's the author's local network:

finger millcs@kermit

```
[kermit]
Login: millcs                         Name: Chris Miller
Directory: /home/millcs               Shell: /bin/bash
On since Sun Jun 27 14:03 (CDT) on ttyp0 from 10.254.254.5
   8 seconds idle
No mail.
No Plan.
```

On a UNIX-style machine, a user can create a file in his home directory called `.plan` and another called `.project`, which will be displayed by Finger instead of "No Plan." Finger also has security problems, because it allows people outside of the network to find valid user account names and determine when the account was last used (in the example, the user `millcs` was logged in while Finger was run, so it says `On since…`.

RSH

RSH, or Remote Shell, allows a single command to be run across the network on a remote machine. It uses the following command line:

rsh hostname [-l *username*] [-n] *command*

If `username` isn't specified, RSH grabs the login name of the user running RSH. The `-n` tells RSH not to produce any output. `command` is the command to be run. The RSH utility will send passwords over the network in clear text, so the often-repeated warnings from the FTP and Telnet sections apply here as well.

That just about sums up the lesser-known UNIX tools. Next, a look at how Windows applications can connect to UNIX hosts.

Application Connectivity

TCP/IP supports a lot of different connection mechanisms between clients and servers. UNIX has a lot of different standard mechanisms it uses to connect servers to clients, including XWindows, RPC, and other proprietary protocols. Close examination of the SERVICES file, found in %SYTEMROOT%\system32\drivers\etc, shows a list of the standard ports used by UNIX systems to communicate different types of data. The file shows a list of the "well known ports" assigned by IANA, the Internet Assigned Numbers Authority. All applications that are widespread are assigned port numbers so they won't collide with each other, and the port number is attached to the IP packet, so the network services can route each packet to the correct program. It's possible to use the Telnet program to get a feel for what some of these ports do; for example, the command telnet localhost qotd will produce a Quote of the Day from the local machine, provided the local machine is running the Simple TCP/IP Services service. The qotd port is defined in the Services file.

> **Note**
>
> To change the quote of the day, edit the file %SYSTEMROOT%\system32\drivers\etc\quotes. Follow the format shown in the file. Sample quotes, also called *fortunes*, are available in the correct format on the Internet from various locations. Use your favorite search engine to find some.

XWindows and Windows 2000

Long before even Windows NT 3.1, UNIX users were using a windowing environment called XWindows (or just *X*). X is also used as a remote execution tool, and there are even unique pieces of hardware out there called *X terminals* that allow users to connect to X and run programs remotely. Terminal Server is neither a Citrix invention nor a Microsoft innovation; UNIX started using it in the late 1980s. On Windows 2000, special client software has to be obtained in order to talk to X. One provider of such software, Hummingbird Communications (www.hummingbird.com), provides a variety of Windows-to-X solutions.

> **Note**
>
> In the world of X, a client is a server and a server is a client. X looks at the definitions from a different point of view: An X server provides graphical capabilities and such to the X clients, so an X terminal will run an X server.

Connecting to NFS

NFS, the Network File System, is a set of protocols designed by Sun Microsystems that allows file sharing between workstations. It's the same concept as mounting a network drive in Windows, but it works a lot differently. For a machine acting as a server, it has a set of network shares, and the server sets up security and privileges to the shares as necessary. When the client initiates an attachment, security gets validated and the share gets mounted to a specified directory on UNIX. See the sidebar "UNIX File System Semantics" for how UNIX deals with directory structures.

> **UNIX File System Semantics**
>
> Two important notes on UNIX files and directories: UNIX uses the forward slash exclusively as the directory delimiter. Therefore, the path /home/millcs isn't a series of command-line switches; it's actually a directory.
>
> UNIX-style operating systems use a single hierarchy for their entire file system. It's very similar to how all Microsoft systems work, except that there's no concept of a drive letter. UNIX systems, instead, have different drives "mounted" to parts of the directory. The primary boot device is usually mounted to the root, called /. If there's another partition on that drive, it might be mounted to /data, and a user issuing a command such as cd /data would automatically be looking at data on another drive or partition. For some users, this system makes more sense than having to switch drive contexts all the time. In addition, as you saw in Chapter 4, "File Systems," there are features available within Windows 2000 to emulate the mount concept in UNIX.

Third-party software is required to attach a Windows 2000 workstation to a UNIX machine via NFS. One such example is a product from Intergraph, called AccessNFS Gateway. This product allows a Windows 2000 server to attach to a UNIX host and share files via NFS. The Intergraph product is very interesting because, although it gives access to NFS shares, it also allows the shares to be reshared out to Windows workstations throughout a network.

After the software is installed, which is a trivial exercise, start the Disk Administrator tool in AccessNFS Gateway by going to Start, Programs, AccessNFS Gateway, Disk Administrator. The Disk Administrator utility is very straightforward. If it's necessary to share out an NFS volume, enter a share name into the Share Name box and then choose a drive letter to map the NFS volume to. Choose which NFS volume to access by either using the Network Resources box to browse for it or by entering the name into the Network Resource field. Click the Connect button when everything is filled out, and a password entry box will ask for a username and password. Either choose a username and password or clear the boxes and the connection will be made anonymously, if the NFS volume allows anonymous connections.

At this point, the NFS volume will be shared out, if the Share Name option was filled in, and the NFS share will be available to Windows users.

About Samba

NFS is great if you have a Windows 2000 computer that needs to connect to UNIX. However, what happens if you have a UNIX machine that needs to connect to Windows 2000? How about letting a UNIX machine transparently share data with Windows computers already on the network?

To solve this problem, an open-source project called Samba (www.samba.org) was started. Samba allows many UNIX hosts to impersonate Windows, to the point where the clients cannot usually tell the difference. File permissions and security are all built in, and the newest versions can participate in domain authentication.

> **Note**
>
> For the curious, Samba was named for the Server Message Block (SMB) protocol used by Windows systems for file sharing. SMB is now called the Common Internet File System, or *CIFS*, so Samba doesn't make as much sense anymore, but many consider it to be a cool name anyway.

So, how's performance on this thing? The unenlightened assume that because Samba is an open-source project and it's free, it won't work well. The truth is, it's as fast as Windows NT 4.0 on similar hardware. What's more, because UNIX runs on bigger hardware than NT can imagine, Samba actually can serve files faster than any Windows NT machine. That benchmark, of course, was done on an SGI Oxygen server, with more RAM, network connections, and processors than most Windows 2000 server farms. This product is fast and efficient, and it works very well.

Samba runs as two daemons, or *service programs*, on UNIX machines. The first daemon, nmbd, handles browsing and the types of activities formerly handled by WINS. The second daemon, smbd, is the actual process that handles the file sharing and security services.

The Samba project is changing rapidly to meet the changing face of Windows 2000 and CIFS. Microsoft has no incentives to see the Samba project succeed, so it isn't exactly sharing information with the Samba project team. As a result, the software changes a lot, and the various configuration files also change a lot. To use and install Samba, download a copy from a local mirror. A list can be found at http://www.samba.org. Then read the documentation that comes with it, specifically a file called Samba-HOWTO. It will contain the latest installation and setup instructions as well as the locations of support newsgroups and mailing lists for questions.

Printing in a UNIX World

There are several different ways to integrate UNIX and Windows 2000 into a total network printing solution. The Samba product, mentioned in the previous section, contains all the necessary interfaces to share printers attached to UNIX workstations, making those printers accessible to all Windows clients. Samba can also be used to handle printing from UNIX to Windows.

The traditional UNIX print system is called "lp," for *line printer*. It's an archaic name—no one uses line printers anymore—but the software has been built to be flexible enough to deal with any printer imaginable, from an old dot-matrix printer up to a desk-size electrostatic plotter, through the use of specialized rendering software. The lp print system works by taking requests and spooling them to a holding area on disk, possibly somewhere in a directory called /var/spool/lpd, depending on the type of UNIX in question. The spooled file is then picked up by a process that may or may not feed it through rendering software. It then communicates with the printer, which prints the file. The rendering software may be very simple, such as tacking PostScript headers and footers on text files so a PostScript printer can print them, or it may be very complex, such as that used in the aforementioned electrostatic plotter.

To connect a Windows 2000 server to a UNIX machine, first and foremost make sure that a user logged on to the UNIX machine in question can print properly. If a local user cannot print, a network user won't be able to print either. Fix the local problems first and then set up the Windows 2000 server. After ensuring that the printer is working properly, open Control Panel, Printers and start the Add Printer item in the folder. Read the introduction and click the Next button. Believe it or not, even though the printer is a network printer, the correct choice is Local Printer. Make sure the Automatically Detect My Printer box is turned off; then click the Next button.

The next screen, Select the Printer Port, allows the network part of the print system to be set up. Choose Create a New Port at the bottom of the window; then choose LPR Port from the Type drop-down box. Enter the name of the server and the name of the printer and click OK. The rest of the setup is just like setting up a normal printer. See Chapter 6, "Printing," for a complete description.

The Future: Microsoft and UNIX

The history of Microsoft and its support for UNIX comes in two distinct periods. From its inception until it discovered it was getting creamed by Netscape, Microsoft tried to pretend UNIX didn't exist. If there are any doubts, look at the integration products that were available at the time, such as the Microsoft Mail SMTP Gateway software, which couldn't use DNS. Also, look at the Windows NT Advanced Server 3.1 system, which included one of the worst-performing, worst-featured environments ever. When Microsoft figured out that the Internet was going to be a moneymaker and that UNIX was running the entire Internet, Microsoft got a lot better at dealing with UNIX. Exchange Server, the replacement for Microsoft Mail, has an excellent SMTP component in the form of the Internet Mail Connector. Microsoft has a TCP/IP stack that performs well, even though it's constantly beset by denial-of-service attacks. Microsoft is now leading the way in some areas, with advances in Dynamic DNS, directory services, and other services that are great additions to the Internet. Almost every Internet integration feature is a UNIX integration feature, because UNIX is very much a part of the Internet. In that way, Microsoft has tied itself tightly with UNIX, and there's really no looking back now.

Summary

Windows 2000 provides many connectivity features for sharing UNIX data. This includes the ability to establish remote sessions using Telnet, to transfer files using FTP, and to share files using NFS or Samba.

CHAPTER 19

SNA Connectivity with BackOffice

IN THIS CHAPTER

- Host Computing Brief *490*
- SNA Server Concepts *491*
- SNA Connectivity Options *495*
- LU Configuration *496*

Windows 2000 Server exists in a world that contains many different servers and server types. Perhaps the oldest of these server forms that still continues is the IBM mainframe. IBM hosts systems computing, ranging from the AS400 to the giant IBM S/390 series mainframe, is still prevalent in the corporate world. LAN administrators like to think that they're replacing these "dinosaurs," but the fact is that there are some tasks for which these machines may never be replaced. With that in mind, administrators need to find the best way to integrate systems into their plans.

If an IBM mainframe has been part of your environment for any length of time, you've heard of *SNA*. SNA stands for *Systems Network Architecture* and is a protocol. IBM developed the protocol in 1971 when it saw the need to develop a protocol that would allow many different types of systems and peripherals to communicate.

The protocol has evolved but has never really taken the place in the industry that IBM had in mind. For that reason, it's not a supported protocol in the Windows Server line. However, Microsoft has seen the prevalence of the protocol in large shops and has included a product that supports SNA in the BackOffice Suite. The product is called *SNA Server* and has been added to the Windows Server to provide the ability for Windows users to make a managed connection to the hosts systems using the SNA protocol.

Host Computing Brief

Generally, the connections made to IBM hosts systems are made using what's affectionately called a *dumb terminal*. Dumb terminals are those systems that are found today in libraries and university labs and consist of just a keyboard and monitor. The traditional green screen is shown in Figure 19.1. They're called *dumb terminals* because they do not have any processing power of there own, and they're a conduit through which the user receives the results of the hosts computing "terminal."

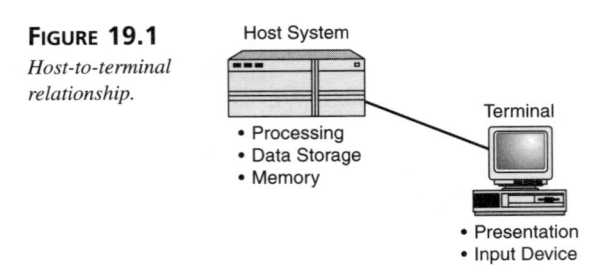

FIGURE 19.1
Host-to-terminal relationship.

Host System
- Processing
- Data Storage
- Memory

Terminal
- Presentation
- Input Device

Terminals come in many different varieties, but the two primary terminals used in SNA communications are the models 3270 and 5250. Terminal manufactures besides IBM make terminals, but most are simply emulating these terminals. The terminal connects back to the host through a connection called twinax. This cable is a thick cable that is considerably more expensive and less common than the UTP cable used by most networks today.

The problems with using terminals are many. Users feel intimidated by the interface, which only presents one session at a time. What's more, the data that it's being used from is often complex. Access to the terminal is access to the mainframe, so security can be breached fairly quickly. Finally, users cannot use individualized software because of the very nature of mainframe computing. For these reasons, the PC revolution occurred.

Now users instead use a program that allows them to open a terminal window on their PCs. This program is called a *terminal-emulation package*. Programs such as Reflections, Rumba, and IBM Client Access have for years allowed users to not leave their PCs but simply have their PCs become terminals (see Figure 19.2).

FIGURE 19.2
The terminal-emulation concept.

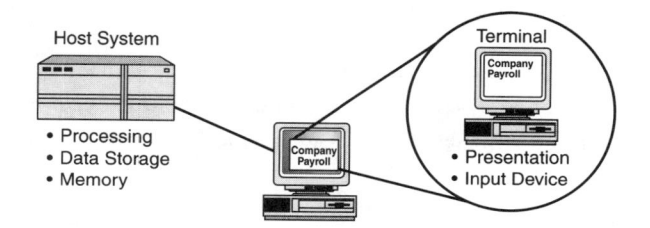

Host System
- Processing
- Data Storage
- Memory

Terminal
- Presentation
- Input Device

This solution solves many of the problems of the terminal. Users can now use several applications as well as open several host sessions at the same time. This allows a user to access items such as a spreadsheet on his or her departmental budget while referencing the mainframe data needed to form the budget. Clearly users can install their individualized (store bought) software, but there are still problems with this solution:

- Connectivity to the PC involves adding a proprietary card to connect to the SNA network.
- Terminal emulation software must be purchased.
- An extra connecting cable must be run to the PC.
- Extra host hardware must be run for each terminal added in order to control host connectivity.
- Adding a new protocol adds to the work that must be done by the PC.
- Any user in the building who has access to the user's PC often has access to the terminal-emulation package.

SNA Server Concepts

One solution to this problem is the BackOffice add-on to Windows called *SNA Server*. By adding SNA Server to a Windows domain, many of these problems are eliminated, and those that are not are reduced.

The concept of SNA Server is to connect all of the PCs using terminal emulation through a single PC host. This PC host is connected to the SNA network and provides the conduit that the client systems use to gain access to the SNA hosts.

Host connections are being initiated, managed, and distributed by a Windows Server machine running the SNA Server service. In an SNA Server installation, the host connection is made to the Windows server, and the Windows server maintains the resources that are made available. The server manages a list of users who are allowed to use those resources, and those users are given host sessions as if they were files or print services or any other domain resource.

The host computer sees the Microsoft SNA Server as what's referred to as a *cluster controller* (see Figure 19.3). The SNA Server is granted certain powers by the host to distribute host sessions to the network. The normal job of a cluster controller is to distribute terminal sessions, and terminals are usually directly connected to a controller of some sort. A controller is given a certain range of terminal sessions (*logical units*, or *LUs*) that it may distribute, and it distributes these sessions on a first-come-first-served basis.

FIGURE 19.3

The SNA Server relationship to PCs running terminal emulation.

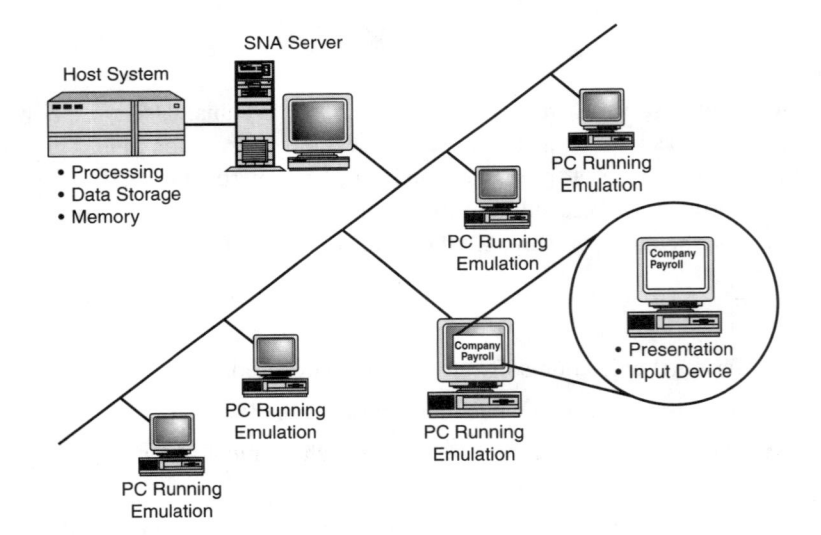

Here are the advantages of this relationship:

- No proprietary SNA card is needed for each PC.
- Domain security can be used to manage host sessions.
- Security to the host now has only one physical connection to manage.
- The hardware needed to connect to the host is reduced.
- The number of protocols is not increased because the same protocol used for domain communications is used for host communications.

- The number of connections that must be facilitated at the host can be reduced based on that fact that LU connections can be created in pools and handed out on an as-needed basis.

Manageable Secure Connectivity

The concept of using the domain security model as a way of securing host connectivity is fairly simple. With SNA Server installed, the host services become resources that can be given the following permissions:

- User access to host sessions
- Host availability based on time of day
- How many sessions one user can use
- How many sessions a group can use

Routing and Distributing Connections

The fact that SNA is a protocol that's generally only used by IBM host equipment makes the ability to use and route these connections limited to realm of a separate, mostly proprietary network. With SNA Server added to the Windows domain, the host has been given connectivity through any source that the Windows host has access to.

This connection must come in contact with the SNA network through the SNA server. In order to route this traffic, SNA network information is entered into SNA Server. Although the SNA Server package is not really routing—more accurately, it's serving as a proxy for the SNA traffic—the server has to create a connection to mediate and facilitate that traffic through.

A significant portion of the SNA network information that's needed is the VTAM (Virtual Telecommunications Access Method) information and communications information. This information must be obtained from the IS group in charge of the host. Hopefully this won't be the first communications being held about this connection. If the IS group is not the initiating party of this project, it should be involved from the beginning of the project.

If an administrator is unaware of this information, the form shown in Table 19.1 will provide a straightforward list of the information that will be needed. The administrator would give this form to the host group and ask that they fill in the VTAM portion (host parameters). In the column beside VTAM is the SNA Server variable that will be filled in with the information provided by the host administrators.

TABLE 19.1 Form Requesting SNA Network Information

VTAM parameter	Corresponding SNA Server Parameter	Description
ADDR=	Poll address (advanced SDLC setting)	A two-digit hexadecimal value that identifies the control unit that the host uses to poll.
IDBLK=	First three digits of Local Node ID (basic connection setting)	A three-digit hexadecimal value that, together with IDNUM, identifies the SNA server. The values 000 and FFF cannot be used; these values are reserved.
IDNUM=	Last five digits of Local Node ID (basic connection setting) identifies the SNA server.	A five-digit hexadecimal value that, together with IDBLK,
MAXDATA= (in the PU definition for SWPU1)	Max BTU length (advanced SDLC setting)	The maximum length of a basic transmission unit (BTU) sent or received; BTUs are also known as I-frames.
LOCADDR=	LU number	The LU local address at the PU. For independent LUs that communicate with a host, the LOCADDR parameter must be set to zero. For dependent LUs with VTAM, the LOCADDR must be at least 2. Also, for dependent LUs, the LU numbers set in SNA Server must match the LOCADDR values on the host.

A connection to the host system must be intentionally set up. It's not the same as simply creating an open NIC in a Windows server. Before a connection is granted to the system, all the preceding information must be entered, as well as many other items that are not directly exposed. For most changes made, the system must be regenerated.

Setup of the connection to the host system may take the host group weeks to complete and more time to return the information. Time on these host systems is very valuable (and is one of the reasons for the birth of the PC world). In order to imagine the issues involved in generating a connection for the SNA server, it's helpful to imagine having to reboot all the PCs in the corporation at one time. If a host system exists in a corporation, it's most likely effecting the daily computing power of everyone in the company.

SNA Connectivity Options

SNA Server can make a connection to the SNA host over any of the following forms of connection:

- *Synchronous Data Link Control (SDLC)*. Leased or switched telephone line connections.
- *X.25/QLLC*. Public or private packet-switched X.25 connections, using qualified logical link control (QLLC).
- *Distributed function terminal (DFT)*. Coaxial or twisted-pair connections using IBM 3x74 cluster controllers.
- *802.2*. Token Ring or Ethernet connections via IBM 37x5 front-end processors or 3x74 cluster controllers.
- *Ethernet TCP/IP*. Many AS/400 connections today are through standard TCP/IP over Ethernet.

The connection the SNA server makes can only be one of these types. The important point is that an emulation card will most likely be necessary in order to connect to the host. The cards supported by Microsoft can be found in a document hosted by Microsoft at the following location:

www.microsoft.com/sna

Because this document may change at any time, it's best to simply point to that location.

Here's a partial list of the adapters supported by SNA Server:

- Any Windows NT NDIS–compliant Token Ring or Ethernet device driver, using Windows NT 802.2 DLC transport protocol
- Attachmate SDLC
- Barr Systems T1-SYNC (for SDLC)
- DCA IRMA (for DFT)
- DCA ISCA (for SDLC and X.25)
- Microgate MGx, Microgate DSA, and Microgate USA (for SDLC and X.25)
- IBM SDLC
- IBM MCPA
- IBM MPA/A
- IBM DFT
- IBM 3270 Connection A,B
- IBM 3278/9 Advanced Emulation adapter
- Any driver developed through the SNADIS interface

LU Configuration

When communication is established with a terminal, printer, or other network entity that can access applications on the mainframe, this connection is made through a network unit known as an *LU*. LU simply stands for a *logical unit*, and the mainframe needs an LU to be at each end of an application in order for communications to function. When the mainframe personnel are creating available connections for the terminals to make use of, they create LUs to be available for these connections.

When an SNA host receives a request for communications, the general rule is that the host will require a specific unit address for each LU. SNA Server allows for the return of the proper unit address for several LUs from one machine. This makes it possible to take the LU connections created by the mainframe group and assign them to a single user or to pool the LUs and make them available on a dynamic basis.

The SNA protocol also allows for the use of peripheral units (PUs) to create communications points for LUs on the outside of the central SNA network. SNA Server will also impersonate a PU in order to gain access to LU connectivity. It's necessary to have the information in Table 19.1 to configure the PU (see Figure 19.4).

FIGURE 19.4
The SDLC Connection menu.

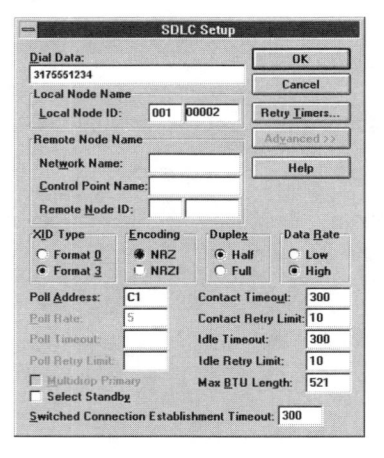

Also necessary to configure LUs at the SNA server is a mainframe that has a configured group of LUs, including LU names, that can be used by the SNA server. The following list shows the ways in which the information from the IS group is helpful in setting up these LUs and LU ranges:

- Connection type. (See Figure 19.5.)

FIGURE 19.5
LU pool properties.

- LU type: printer or display. (See Figure 19.6.)

FIGURE 19.6
LU pool range numbering.

- LU names and display type if applicable. (See Figure 19.7.)

FIGURE 19.7
LU range naming and typing.

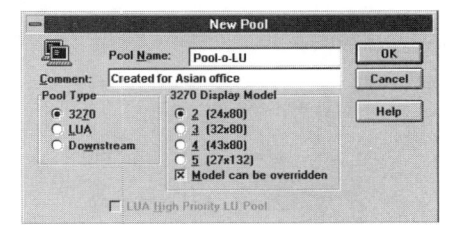

Summary

The need for better network management and the clamor for real estate in the corporate PC world has caused a need for a more creative way to access the mainframe. BackOffice SNA Server offers a way of creating that connection. The solution is part of the same family as Windows Server and allows the use of domain security to control connectivity.

By attaching SNA host connectivity to the Windows Server platform, the administrator gains the ability to deliver host connectivity in places not available before. Systems attached to WAN connections that deliver only standard PC protocols become conduits through which SNA connections can be delivered.

Through pooling resources, the ability to provide more functionality to the users with less SNA equipment becomes a reality. LUs become a commodity to be dispensed, not a resource that must be continually created for a system only occasionally used.

Internet Applications, Communications, and Tools

PART VI

IN THIS PART

20 Internet Information Server *501*

21 Other Internet Services for Windows 2000 *549*

22 Virtual Private Networks *569*

Internet Information Server (IIS)

CHAPTER 20

IN THIS CHAPTER

- Internet Information Server Concepts *502*
- Before You Begin with IIS *503*
- Installing IIS *507*
- Administering and Configuring IIS *511*

Microsoft's foray into the Internet server world arrived in the form of its IIS technology, which literally means 'Internet Information Server'. Microsoft bundled several technologies into this new item, including that of a Web server, an FTP server, and a newsgroup server. IIS now comes as a fully integrated feature of the Windows 2000 Server operating system, which is a change from its past. This first section, Internet Information Server Concepts, will walk you through the history of IIS, along with an introduction into the various technologies that comprise the IIS features.

Internet Information Server Concepts

The technology known as Internet Information Server (IIS) is a relatively newer concept to the Windows NT/Windows 2000 world. IIS originated with the release of Windows NT 3.51 as a Hypertext Transfer Protocol (HTTP) Web server and File Transfer Protocol (FTP) server service that was very limited in scope. Before the 3.51 version of Windows NT was released, Microsoft provided very little Internet support within its operating systems.

IIS version 2.0 was released with Windows NT Server 4.0 in July 1996. What many consider the essence of IIS today, its support for Active Server Pages (ASP), was not even a part of either of the first two versions of IIS. Microsoft introduced the concept of ASP in its version 3.0 release of IIS, which was included, along with an update of Internet Explorer and several multimedia utilities, as part of the third Service Pack (SP) release of Windows NT Server 4.0. Not too long after that, according to Bill Gates, Microsoft got serious about becoming "the Internet Company of the future" and released its most popular version of IIS, 4.0. IIS 4.0 was released to the computing public in the form of the Windows NT Option Pack, which was a nice way of saying it was a "free add-on" to the Windows NT 4.0 operating system. IIS 4.0 has remained fairly stable through the next three versions of the Windows NT 4.0 service pack releases (4, 5, and 6).

With Windows 2000 comes yet another version of IIS, version 5.0, which is thoroughly integrated into the operating system for security and scalability. It introduces a number of new features, including the following:

- Improvements to the Active Server Pages
- Administrative changes, including full support of the Microsoft Management Console (MMC) technology, enhanced remote administration, and better error tracking and logging
- Numerous Registry changes
- Security, including full integration with the Windows 2000 Kerberos-based encryption

- Performance, including a revised approach to socket pooling
- Greatly enhanced documentation, including an HTML-based Help utility that provides for searching of all the documentation as well as an improved index of topic

To describe the Windows 2000 version of IIS as just an update to its previous patched-together versions would be an injustice. IIS 5.0 provides so many new features as well as dozens of enhancements to the old ones that it has really become an excellent Internet services server.

Before You Begin with IIS

Before embarking on your new career as an Internet Service Provider (ISP) or virtual Webmaster, there are a few things you need to consider in using IIS:

- You must first acquire and configure the appropriate level of hardware, from the appropriate categories on the Microsoft Hardware Compatibility List (HCL) for Windows 2000 Server.
- Next, you need to make sure that you have the proper network connectivity if you are building a local area network (LAN)/wide-area network (WAN)–based intranet server. If you plan to use this IIS as a stopping point on the Internet, then you must already have the proper connectivity to the Internet.
- You might want to ensure that you have the proper backup hardware, software, and user procedures in place, along with a security plan to safeguard your IIS server after it is operational on your organization's intranet or poised for operation in conjunction with the Internet.

System Requirements

IIS 5.0 functions only on the Windows 2000 series of operating systems, including the following:

- Professional
- Server
- Advanced Server
- DataCenter

The version of IIS on the Windows 2000 Professional is slightly slimmed down from the three server versions, mostly in its inability to support a few of the transaction- and security-oriented events. However, because this is a Windows 2000 Server book, we focus on the installation, configuration, and use of IIS on just the Windows 2000 Server platform.

From a hardware perspective, you need to ensure that the IIS base platform slightly exceeds the Microsoft-recommended hardware requirements, which are as follows:

- CPU: Pentium 166MHz
- Memory: 64MB RAM
- Hard drive space available: 2GB
- Removable drive: 12-speed (12X) CD-ROM drive
- Display monitor: 16-color SVGA with at least 800×600 resolution
- Pointing device: Mouse preferred (Microsoft, of course)

An IIS server tends to consume a bit more of the CPU cycles and the system's memory resources than just the basic operating system consumes. This is not unusual or bad because all application programs you install on Windows 2000 Server require at least a bit more of the physical resources than Microsoft recommends for a Windows 2000 Server operating environment.

If your server is to be used as a Web server, then you might want to ensure that your Domain Name Service (DNS) or Microsoft's Dynamic Domain Name System (DDNS) (see Chapter 8, "TCP/IP Networking," for more details on DDNS) networking functions are operational. Although the use of DNS or DDNS is not required with a Web server, it is typically much easier for your user community to remember a computer name than a Transmission Control Protocol/Internet Protocol (TCP/IP) address when attempting to find the Web server on the intranet or Internet.

> **Note**
>
> DNS is an Internet and TCP/IP standard name resolution service that enables client computers to register and resolve computing device names. However, where Microsoft's Windows 2000 implementation of DNS varies from the past is that DNS will now dynamically update, store, and retrieve computer names and IP addresses. This new version is known as the *Dynamic Domain Name System* (DDNS).

Likewise, it would be very helpful to already have a Web site authoring tool chosen to help in the creation of your Web sites. Again, this is not a requirement because anyone can write HTML code inside the Windows 2000 Server Notepad accessory, but an authoring tool goes a long way in making things easier for both the Webmaster (the IIS administrator who focuses on the Web portion of the server) and the end users (who tend to like graphics and showy items on the Web site, which are very difficult to produce with elementary HTML).

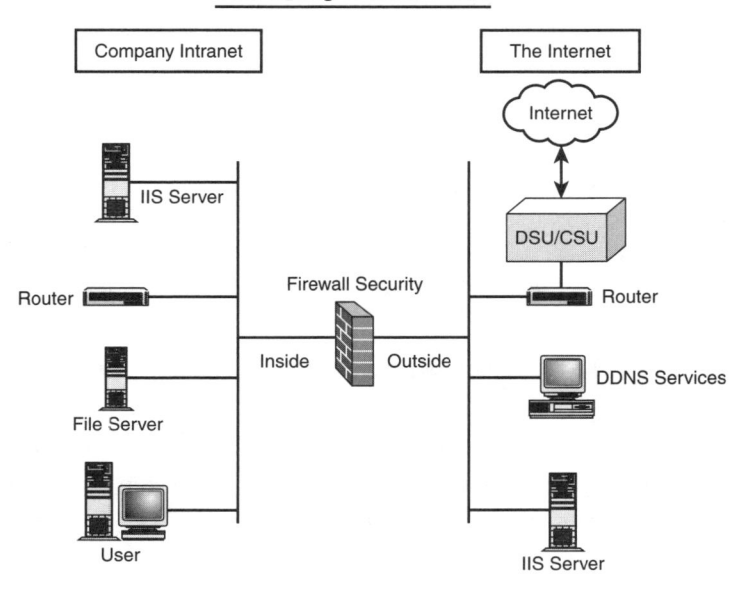

Windows 2000 Server is the only software required because IIS is integrated into Windows 2000. When you install Windows 2000 Server, IIS installs as well by default, unless you specifically cancel its installation. This is the case with system upgrades as well, provided that some version of IIS was installed with the prior version of the operating system.

Internet Connectivity

IIS can operate just fine without any connectivity to the Internet, especially in the realm of being either a Web or an FTP server for a corporate intranet. IIS can make a very nice intranet server for your organization, which you can install, configure, and operate at a relatively low cost to the organization. However, if yours is like many organizations, the reason you are embarking on this new IIS journey is to obtain an Internet-based Web server.

One of the first things you need for Internet connectivity is either a network card or a modem. Obviously, if you are really hoping that more than one or two people use your Web site at a time, you might consider using a network card that can be connected to a high-speed network access path to the Internet instead of a much slower dial-up modem connection. Your Internet access path could resemble the diagram shown in Figure 20.1.

FIGURE 20.1
Basic IIS Connectivity.

> **Note**
>
> A few quick things, of which the reader needs to be cognizant. First, while it is generally an accepted "best practice" to use a firewall, one is not required for Internet connectivity. Therefore, as you examine the diagram shown in Figure 1, you will notice that there is not a firewall included between the IIS server and the Internet connection on the right side of the picture. In addition, the DSU/CSU is a digital modem for connecting LAN-based servers to either a VAN or the Internet directly, which is why it is shown in the diagram. One can never go directly from a router to the Internet without some type of telecommunications hardware in-between the router and the Internet.

Figure 20.1 includes the IIS that services the organization's intranet sites on the left and shows Internet connectivity on the right. As you can see, all the organization's users remain on the left side of the firewall (the "inside"), and the IIS that hosts the organization's Web and FTP sites is on the right (on the "outside" of the firewall). Do not assume that just because the diagram shows the IIS server as being outside the firewall, it is left unsecure as a sacrificial lamb. It is not. There are safety mechanisms built into the router between the IIS machine and the Internet, as well as into the Internet Information Server itself. Additionally, for the sake of brevity here, we have left out some of the more detailed security techniques that any normal company would use to properly secure their IIS servers and information away from unauthorized users, such as a hardware/software-based firewall located between the IIS box and the Internet. For more details on how to properly lock-down your IIS servers, you should make a visit to the following Microsoft Web sites:

 http://www.microsoft.com/security/

 http://www.microsoft.com/technet/win2000

Alternatively, check out Network Computing's security guide location, which can be found here:

 http://www.networkcomputing.com/core/core8.html

When you are in a position to make a physical connection to the Internet, you still either require the services of an ISP or you need to build (i.e., buy the services from your local telephone provider) your own direct connection to the Internet. After this is achieved, you are able to connect your IIS server to the Internet.

Now, the final step for building a Web server (other than the IIS portion, that is) is to secure a domain name that you can use in conjunction with your Web site. To do this, you can contact Network Solutions (http://www.networksolutions.com/), which can both help you find an unused name and sell you the rights to your chosen name. (Note that this domain name is for identifying your Web or FTP server on the Internet. Do not confuse it with the Windows 2000 Server domain names that you probably have somewhere within your computing environments.) The cost of such a domain name is $70 for the first two years, and then there is a similar maintenance cost beyond that. Also, to help you find a name that has not yet been chosen by anyone else, you might want to use Network Solution's "Whois" Web page to conduct those searches. This page can be found at the following URL:

```
http://www.networksolutions.com/cgi-bin/whois/whois/
```

After you have met the basic IIS hardware and software requirements, have succeeded in developing your Internet connectivity, and acquired at least one Internet-ready domain name, you can get started installing (if needed) and configuring your IIS software on your Windows 2000 Server.

Installing IIS

As mentioned previously, IIS is automatically installed on your computer when you install Windows 2000 Server, if this is a new installation of the operating system. If you are upgrading from an existing version of Windows NT or Windows 9x and there was an existing version of IIS or the Windows 9x or Windows NT Workstation personal Web server (PWS) already installed, then Windows will automatically upgrade you to IIS 5.0.

If you are upgrading from an existing version of Windows NT or Windows 9x and you have never had IIS installed, you need to start the Windows Components Wizard by following these steps:

1. Click the Start button, the Settings option, and then the Control Panel option. The Windows 2000 Control Panel window appears.
2. Double-click the Add/Remove Programs icon, and the initial Add/Remove Programs window appears.
3. Click the Add/Remove Windows Components button option on the lower-left side of this window. The Windows Components Wizard dialog box, which is shown in Figure 20.2, appears.

FIGURE 20.2
Adding new Windows components.

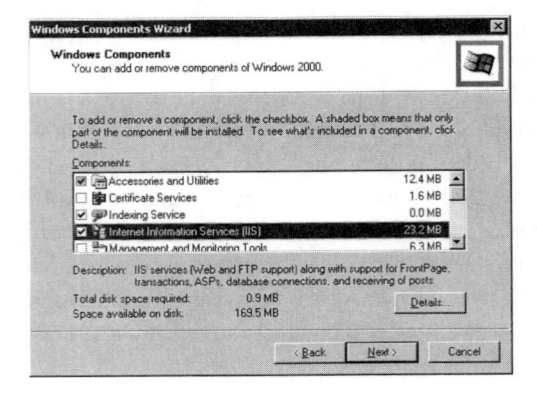

4. Select the Internet Information Services (IIS) option from the Windows Components Wizard dialog box. Of the many items that appear in the Windows Components Wizard dialog box, just a few require immediate attention:

    - Certificate Services—The Certification Server that is provided with this option gives you the ability to create basic digital signature and encryption certificates for use with your Web site, rather than purchase these types of services from a third-party provider such as Thawte or VeriSign.

    - Indexing Service—The Indexing Service not only provides indexing capabilities for your computer as a whole, but for all your Web and FTP sites as well. Do not worry—this option is very configurable and does not pose a security threat to your operating environment, if it is configured correctly.

    - Internet Information Services (IIS)—This is obviously the most important item in this dialog box at this point. It consists of the base Web, FTP, and newsgroup server services, which is required in order for any of the other Internet services to work properly.

To install these services, click the box to the left of each option's label to place a check mark in that box. If a box has a check mark in it but with a grayed-out background, that option has not been completely chosen (that is, not all of its suboptions are selected). To selectively browse through the various suboptions for any of these services, click the Details button to reveal the screen shown in Figure 20.3.

The Internet Information Services dialog box contains the following items:

- Common Files—These are the core files that make up the basic IIS system.
- Documentation—This is the general IIS, ASP, Web, and FTP information.
- File Transfer Protocol (FTP) Server—This includes the binary files required to install the FTP server services.

FIGURE 20.3
Adding an Internet Information Services (IIS) Component.

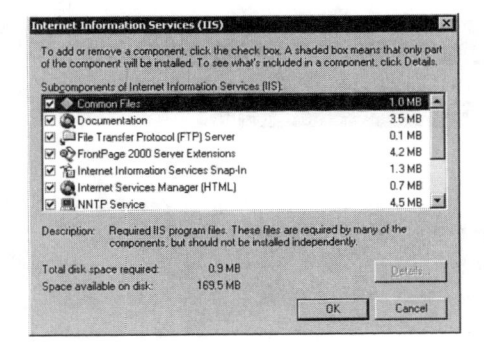

- FrontPage 2000 Server Extensions—This provides for the use of Microsoft FrontPage 2000 and Microsoft Visual InterDev 6.0 as the authoring, development, and management tools for your Internet sites.
- Internet Information Services Snap-in—This is the management console interface tool required for completely managing IIS.
- Internet Services Manager (HTML)—This is the Web-based version of the Internet Information Services Snap-in management tool.
- NNTP Service—This provides support for Network News Transfer Protocol (NNTP, which is used for newsgroups).
- SMTP Service—This provides support for Simple Mail Transfer Protocol (SMTP), which is used for email.
- Visual InterDev RAD Rapid Deployment Support—With this option you can remotely deploy various applications on your Internet server. You should use this option sparingly, and only on development servers. Never install or invoke this tool on production IIS servers, due to the many inherent security risks involved.
- World Wide Server Support—The core of the IIS server, this provides the basic Web server support. When this service is installed, it can never be turned off because if it is, you might crash the entire IIS system.

After you have selected all the components you want to install, click the OK button to save your choices and return to the Windows Components Wizard dialog box.

The next area you need to examine closely is the Certificate Services option. To selectively browse through that short list of suboptions, click the Details button, and the Certificate Services dialog box, shown in Figure 20.4, opens.

FIGURE 20.4
Adding Certificate Services Components.

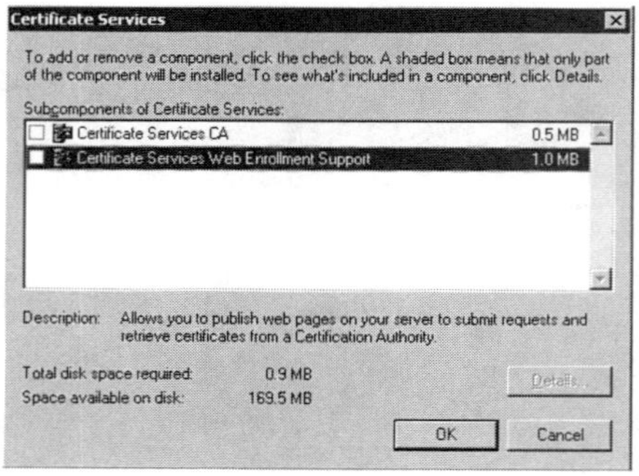

The detailed options in this dialog box are as follows:

- Certificate Services CA—These are the core files of the Certificate Services certificate authority. If you are planning to configure your Web site for use with Secure Sockets Layer (SSL) or want to use digital signatures on your site, then you need to either buy these technologies or use the Windows 2000 Server Certification Authority service that is installed via the Certificate Services options. Most organizations tend to use these options for their intranet capabilities and then request public versions for their Internet functions.

- Certificate Services Web Enrollment Support—This handy utility permits you to publish Web pages on your site from which anyone (with the correct permissions) can easily pull down copies of your certificates for use with their applications (presumably to work only with your Web server installation).

After you have made your selections by clicking the check boxes to the left of the desired options, click the OK button to save your choices and return to the Internet Information Services (IIS) dialog box. Because you have now made all the pertinent selections, you can click the OK button to start the actual installation process, as shown in Figure 20.5.

FIGURE 20.5
Reviewing the IIS Installation Status Bar.

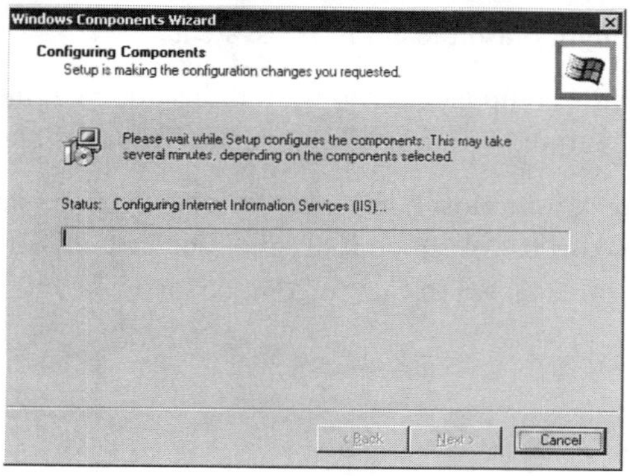

This process may take from just a minute or so up to 10 to 15 minutes, depending on many factors such as the total number of options selected, the amount of available memory, and the speed and location(s) of your hard drives. Be patient, as the process will eventually result in a successful completion, as shown in Figure 20.6.

FIGURE 20.6
Reviewing the successful installation completion screen.

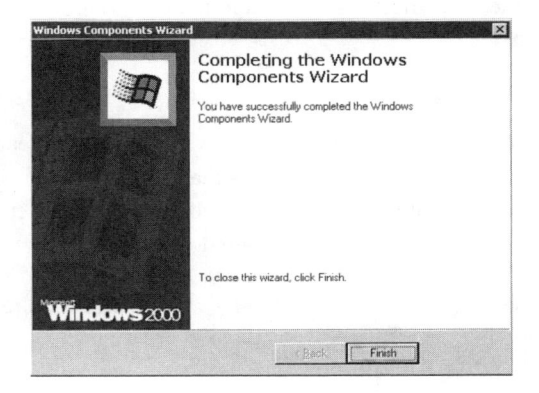

Click the Finish button to exit the Windows Components Wizard and return to the Add/Remove Programs dialog box. You might need to reboot your computer, depending on the options you selected.

Administering and Configuring IIS

Administration of IIS is easy to accomplish, but it can be difficult to understand. That is, there are graphical user interfaces (GUIs) for managing all aspects of the Web, FTP, SMTP, and NNTP sites, but the thousands of possible configurations and variations can make the overall management of these technologies difficult to completely figure out. In fact, you will probably need to play with some of the more complex functions in a trial-and-error mode in order to determine the exact configuration for your organization's Internet/intranet operating environments.

The functions of IIS are discussed in this section, to help you figure out exactly where a particular feature or function fits into the overall scheme of the IIS architecture. This should enable you to better configure and administer the various IIS functions that your organization requires.

Common IIS Controls

There are several ways to administer an IIS environment:

- Basic service control—A discussion of items such as anonymous users and the various IIS logging options

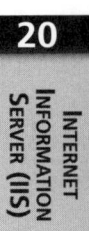

- Directory management—This contains a discussion of the directory structures of IIS, including that of virtual servers
- Advanced administration—These topics are generally beyond those discussed with beginners, including IIS performance and bandwidth tuning options and features, access control, and the concurrent user limitations of the Internet Information Server.

Basic Service Control

There are many basic service controls within the IIS, most of which are readily available from within the main administration screen. To access that screen, click the Start button, the Programs option, the Administrative Tools option, and then the Internet Services Manager option. The Internet Information Services window, shown in Figure 20.7, appears.

FIGURE 20.7
Using the Internet Information Services window.

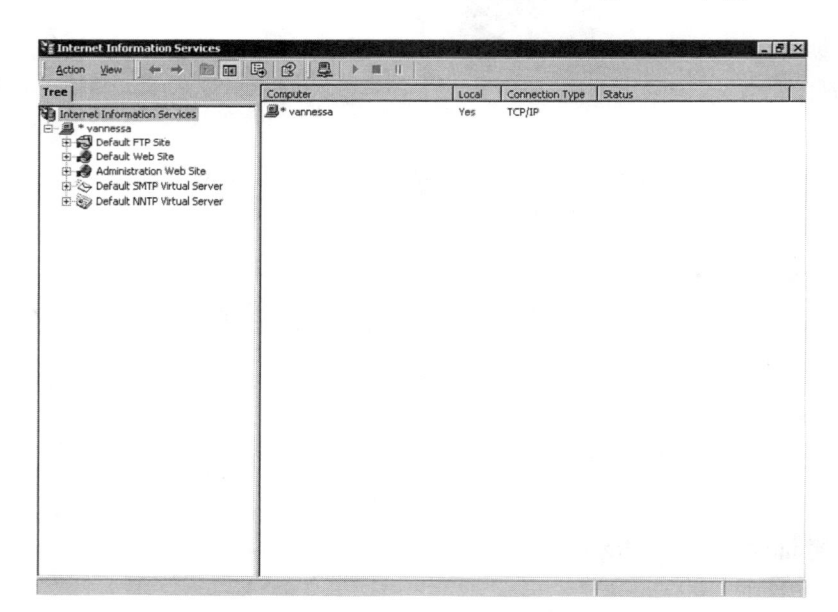

There are three main parts to this screen: the menu bar, the left pane, and the right pane.

The menu bar contains the Action and View drop-down menus, along with the Back, Forward, Up one level, Show/Hide Console Tree, Help, Add a computer to the list, Start the Server, Stop the Server, and Pause the Server buttons. From this menu bar, you can manage the general activities of your FTP, Web, and SMTP/NNTP virtual servers. If you choose View, Customize, you can modify which buttons and menu bars actually appear on the menu bar.

The left pane has at least one tab, labeled Tree, which contains most of the information we are interested in here. You can use the top-level icons in the tree to modify the following items:

- Internet Information Services—This item permits you to connect to one or more IIS servers found within your domain or global catalog (an Active Directory listing server)
- *computername*—This is the computer name of the IIS server that contains the various FTP, SMTP, NNTP, and Web sites. There will always be one or more computer names present under the Internet Information Services icon.
- FTP site(s)—This area is used to modify the attributes for the file transfer protocol site(s) that may exist within the boundaries of this IIS server's control. This may include sites that are physically located on the same computer as the Windows 2000 Server operating system, or they may be other physically separate computers located elsewhere within the Windows 2000 domain.
- Web site(s)—This area is used to modify the attributes for the Web site(s) that may exist within the boundaries of this IIS server's control. This includes sites that are physically located on the same computer as the Windows 2000 Server operating system and any virtual directories stored elsewhere.
- Administration Web Site—You can think of the Administration Web site as the place to manage the global attributes for all the Web sites controlled by this IIS installation, including the ability to define multiple identities for this Web server.
- Default SMTP Virtual Server—This is the POP3-compliant email system that is supported by IIS, which is configured through the screen choices presented here.
- Default NNTP Virtual Server—This is the network news information system that is supported by IIS, which is configured through the screen choices presented here.

The right pane of this dialog box includes all the information that is initially selected by choices made in the left pane. For example, if you click the Internet Information Services icon in the left pane, notice that information regarding that selection appears in the right pane (as shown in Figure 20.7). All the various icons in the left pane operate this way, which makes the maintenance processes of an IIS server relatively simple to perform after you figure out what you want to do (that is the hard part).

Customize the IIS Display View

Now, let us assume that you think there is just too much information displayed here for you to focus on at any one time. To change the viewing layout of this screen, click the View menu option, and then click Customize, which opens the window shown in Figure 20.8.

FIGURE 20.8
Customizing your IIS Display View Format.

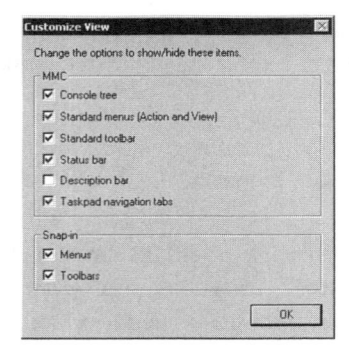

By clicking any of the available check boxes, you are able to hide or display any of the options that were just discussed.

> **Caution**
>
> It is possible to hide all the menu bars and panes that include all the management tasks, which means that you can effectively lock yourself out of your own IIS MMC. It is not a pretty scene when you do this. To recover, you need to close out of the Internet Services Manager and restart that services' management console.

Click the **computername* icon shown in the left pane to reveal the screen shown in Figure 20.9 (on your Windows 2000 Server, you may have a few different sites shown, but that is nothing to worry about).

The right pane contains a description of each of the sites installed in your Internet Information Services manager, as well as the present condition for each of those sites. The state of any site will be one of the following:

- Running—This is the most common state, and it means that your service is active on this IIS machine
- Stopped—This is another common state, which means that this particular service is no longer running on this particular Internet Information Server
- Paused—This is the least frequently used state, which means that the service has been temporarily stopped for some reason (for example, you might be performing temporary maintenance on your administrative Web site).

The remaining columns shown in the right pane—Host Header Name, IP Address, Port, and Status—are all used to provide configuration information regarding a particular installed IIS service. For example, it is helpful to know that any computer with any TCP/IP address can hit your Web site (you can narrow this area down by either TCP/IP

Internet Information Server (IIS)
CHAPTER 20

addresses or port numbers for security reasons). Likewise, it can be helpful for administrative reasons to quickly see what sites have host header names assigned to them.

FIGURE 20.9
Viewing the Installed IIS Sites.

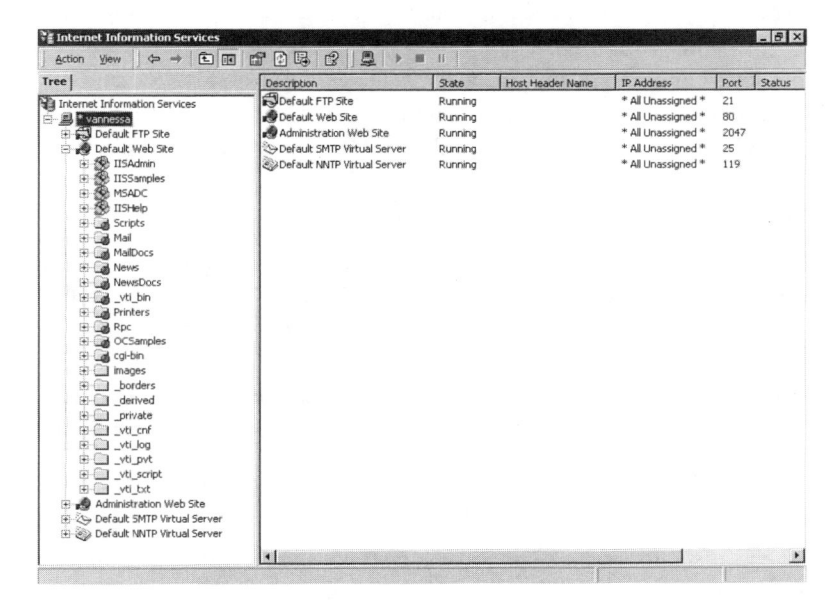

Right-click *computername* (in the example this is *vannessa). A popup menu with multiple sections appears, as shown in Figure 20.10.

FIGURE 20.10
Reviewing the Main IIS Administration Menu.

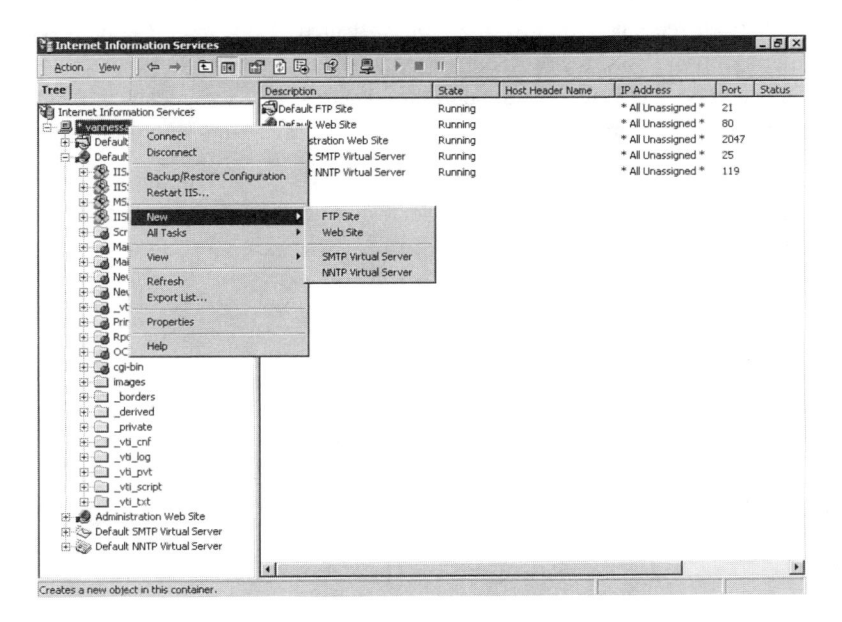

You will begin most administrative tasks for your IIS machine from this menu. Connection to, and disconnection from, an IIS server is made from the top section. The next section is used to back up and/or restore the configuration information for a particular computer's IIS information. This is a critical option to maintain your organization's business continuity plan, especially in the area of electronic commerce and other digital operations (such as the corporate intranet, extranet, and so on). Likewise, you are able to use this section to restart the Windows 2000 Server IIS services, which is also a very useful option (remember that within the older versions of IIS, such as 3.0 or 4.0, this could not be done through the Web Control Panel).

The next section, beginning with the New menu option, permits you to create new FTP and Web sites, as well as SMTP and NNTP virtual servers. This is the fastest way to get a new Web or FTP site up and running on any IIS. The All Tasks option is used to check the FrontPage Server Extensions for your IIS. Obviously, if IIS was not configured for use with the Microsoft FrontPage or Visual InterDev Web development software packages, then this option would not apply to your organization's configuration.

The next section, which contains only the View menu option, works exactly the same way as the View menu option from the menu bar.

The next section (which has just the Refresh and Export List... options shown) is used to refresh the views shown of both the right and left panes (it is possible that they might change, especially if someone else is maintaining your Internet Services Manager configuration through the use of another Windows 2000 Server elsewhere on the domain). If you click the Refresh menu option, the screen is updated with any changes that might have occurred since the last time you refreshed or opened the screen. The Export List menu option permits you to copy the list shown in the right pane into an ASCII text file. This can be useful for documentation purposes, and also means you can keep better track of the dozens, hundreds, or even thousands of Web sites stored on any particular IIS.

The next section contains a single option: Properties. Clicking this option causes the Properties window (shown in Figure 20.11), which permits you to monitor and manage your IIS server's basic layout, to appear.

The Properties window is where you set the global attributes for all the Web sites that are controlled by this IIS server. It has three primary sections:

- Master Properties
- Bandwidth Throttling
- Computer MIME Map

FIGURE 20.11
Setting the Primary Internet Information Services Properties.

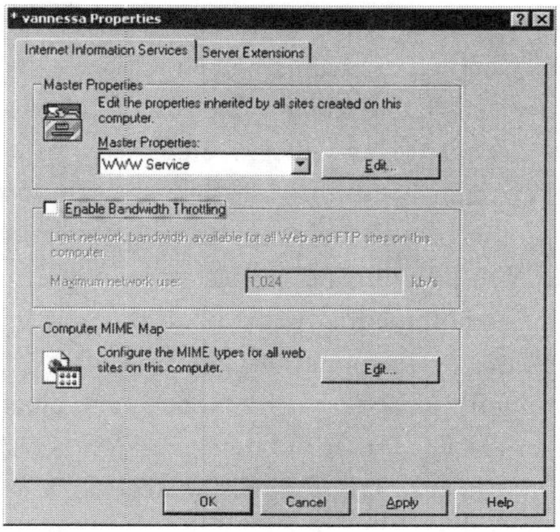

The Master Properties section is used to modify the global settings in a way that is nearly identical to how you can set the specific attributes for each of your Web sites and virtual directories. For example, by clicking the Edit button that appears to the right of the drop-down list box (for simplicity's sake, leave the default selection WWW Service in the list box), you are taken to the WWW Service Master Properties for *computername* (in this example, *vannessa) window.

> **Note**
>
> Please note that since all but one of the subsequent screens are the same as the ones used for individual Web sites, we will skip the same ones and just proceed directly to the one that differs (the others will be discussed shortly, when we modify a sample Web site). The window appears with the Web Site tab showing, so you need to click the Service tab to reveal the screen shown in Figure 20.12.

FIGURE 20.12
Accessing the Service tab for Modifying the Master Properties of a Web Site.

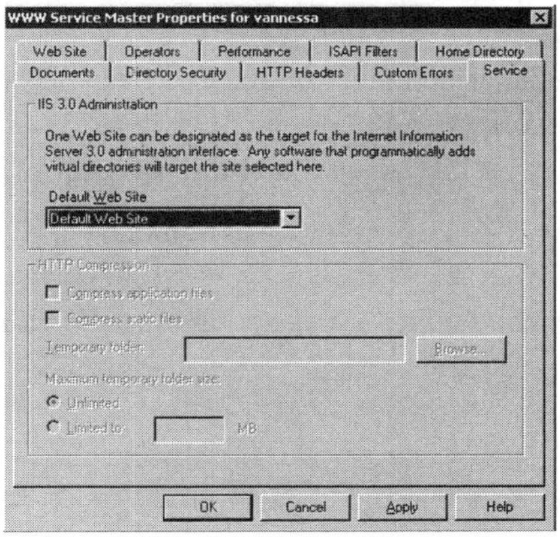

The purpose of this screen is simple: Sometimes applications programmatically attempt to create new Web virtual directories, which means you should designate a default Web site to act as the starting point for those directories. This screen permits you to do that. When you first install IIS, there are just two choices: Default Web Site or Administration Web Site. For security and perhaps manageability reasons, you should probably create a new Web site and use that site as the starting point for all new programmatically created virtual directories. For example, you might want to make a default site called Default Programmed Sites, from which you automatically install all the new virtual directories. Although you obviously do not have to do something like this, after you have more than 100 or so virtual directories, you will probably wish you had (and changing your mind after the fact is virtually impossible to do). If HTTP compression is enabled on your sites, then you are able to modify the currently grayed-out section at the bottom of this screen. After you have made your selections, click the OK button to confirm them and return to the Internet Information Services screen.

> **Note**
>
> There appears to be a flow bug in the IIS software. Instead of being returned to the Properties window, you are taken all the way back to the Internet Information Services window. This means that you need to reselect the Properties menu option from the popup window of the *computername*, just as you did at the start of this section.

So, again, start up the *computer name* Properties screen and examine the middle section's checkbox (refer back to Figure 20.11 for further details), labeled Enable Bandwidth Throttling. The purpose of bandwidth throttling is to limit the impact that IIS will impose on your physical network, which is especially useful in an intranet working environment. To enable bandwidth throttling, simply click that check box to place a check mark in it, which makes following options available. When you first enable this option, it defaults to one-megabit (1,024 kilobits per second) selection. You can change this setting, but it is a good idea to make sure you do not select a number that exceeds your total bandwidth. For example, on a 10Base-T network (10,240 kilobits per second), you would not want to put 102,400 in the box because for that you would need a 100Base-T network.

The bottom section, Computer MIME Map, allows you to modify the MIME types that are presently installed for all the Web sites installed on this IIS. To modify those MIME types, click the Edit button to reveal the File Types dialog box, shown in Figure 20.13.

FIGURE 20.13
Registered Windows 2000 Server File Types.

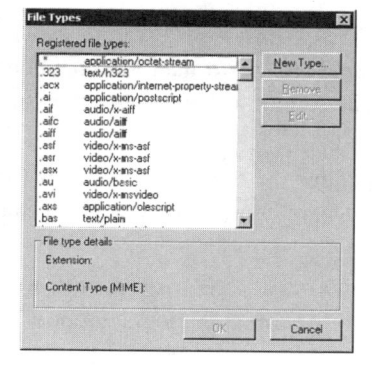

This screen should look familiar to experienced Windows 9x and Windows NT users. In this dialog box you can modify the file types for this IIS server in a manner very similar to how you would modify file types for any of the 32-bit Microsoft operating systems. To add a new file type, click the New Type button. To modify a file type, click that file type to select it, and then click the Edit button to begin the modification process. After you have completed your modifications, click the OK button to confirm them and return to the *computername* Properties dialog box.

The final option that you might want to modify in the *computername* Properties dialog box is on the Server Extensions tab, so click that tab to reveal the Server Extensions tab, as shown in Figure 20.14.

FIGURE 20.14
Configuring Server Extensions Properties.

This screen has three sections:

- General—You use this section to set basic performance tuning configuration as well as to define how the client-side scripting should be performed (that is, JavaScript versus VBScript).
- Options—You use this section to define the basic email settings for persons who will be browsing your Web sites (this, of course, you can change at each site's level as well).
- Permissions—You use this section to modify the basic permissions for publishing content to your Web sites as well as to turn on the logging options for your Web sites.

Click the Settings button on this tab, and the Email Settings dialog box appears, as shown in Figure 20.15.

FIGURE 20.15
Defining Applicable Email Address Settings.

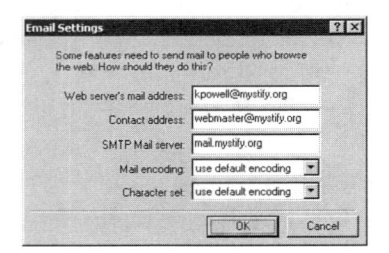

In this dialog box you define the email addresses for your Web sites, the SMTP mail server address, the mail encoding, and the character set options. Make your choices as applicable and then click the OK button to confirm them and return to the *computername* Properties window. Upon returning there, click the OK button to confirm all your choices and modifications and then return to the Internet Information Services dialog box.

Anonymous Users

Anonymous users are individuals or programs that do not need to actually present a logon ID and password in order to gain authorized access to your Web or FTP sites. To permit or deny anonymous users from accessing your Web sites, you need to use the Directory Security tab from within the Default Web Site Properties dialog box, as shown in Figure 20.16.

To perform the same feat for your FTP sites, you need to use the Security Accounts tab from within the Default FTP Site Properties dialog box, as shown in Figure 20.17.

FIGURE 20.16
Setting Directory Security for a Web Site.

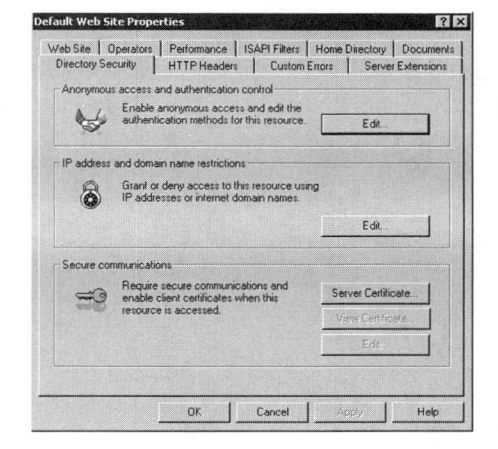

FIGURE 20.17
Configuring the FTP Security Accounts.

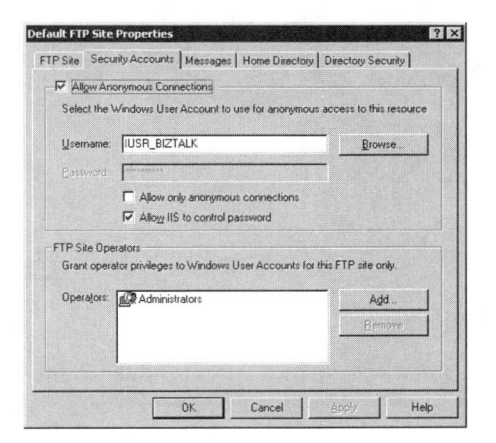

To get to either of these screens, right-click the Default Web Site or the Default FTP Site icon (depending on which one you want to modify), which brings up a popup menu. On that menu, click the Properties option to reveal the general properties window. Next, click the appropriate tab to gain access to the screen whose properties you want to modify. In the Web Site Properties dialog box you need to click the top Edit button to make the appropriate modifications, and in the FTP Site Properties dialog box you should use the top check box (Allow Anonymous Connections) to determine whether you want to enable this feature for your FTP user community. For more information on why the use of anonymous users can be important, refer to the "Access Control" section later in this chapter.

Logging Options

There is a multitude of logging options available to the typical IIS administrator, from breadth to depth. For example, when you first access either the Default FTP Site Properties dialog box or the Default Web Site Properties dialog box, you see the Web Site tab first, as shown in Figure 20.18.

FIGURE 20.18
Configuring the Default Web Site's Options.

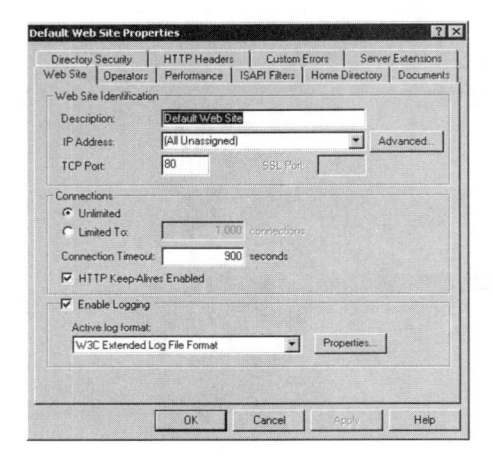

The bottom option, Enable Logging, permits you to turn on the logging capabilities of the IIS. When the option has been enabled, you should select the appropriate logging type from the drop-down list box that appears:

- Microsoft IIS Log File Format—This fixed ASCII format is the standard IIS format that Microsoft originally developed for its first incarnation of IIS, and it is still the format in use today. It contains more information than the standard NCSA (National Center for Supercomputing Applications) format, but it is not customizable in its layout.

- NCSA Common Log File Format—Like the Microsoft logging method, the NCSA format is also a noncustomizable, fixed-length formatted file, which stores just the basic information regarding the activities surrounding the IIS. The NCSA format was developed by the National Center for Supercomputing Applications at the University of Illinois at Urbana, as part of that institution's original Internet research program (which also developed Mosaic, the first Internet Web browser). Note that this log file format option is not available for your FTP sites because it is strictly limited to Web site (so this file type will not even appear in any FTP site's drop-down list box).

- ODBC Logging—This option permits you to save your IIS server logs to a database of your choice, provided that it supports the Open Database Connectivity (ODBC) standard, and is not customizable regarding what is recorded.
- W3C Extended Log File Format—This is the default format, which is arranged according to the World Wide Web Consortium's (W3C) standard, though it is a customizable ASCII format. In addition, unlike the other formats, time entries are noted as Greenwich Mean Time, not local time.

After you have made your logging type format choice from this drop-down list box, click the Properties button to reveal the Extended Logging Properties dialog box, shown in Figure 20.19.

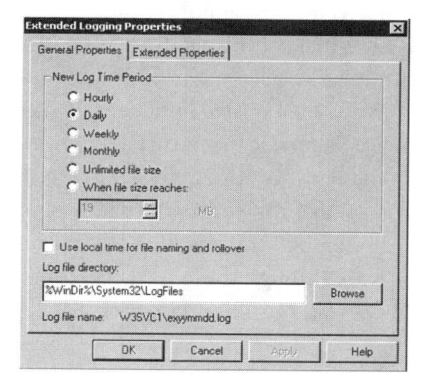

FIGURE 20.19
Setting the Advanced Properties for Log Files.

The Extended Logging Properties dialog box is where you select the log time period—by the hour, day, week, or month—as well as the maximum size and location of the logging files. You can also modify the time that a log file is stored as on your computer (the local time versus the Greenwich Mean Time). After you make your selections, click the Extended Properties tab, and you see the screen shown in Figure 20.20.

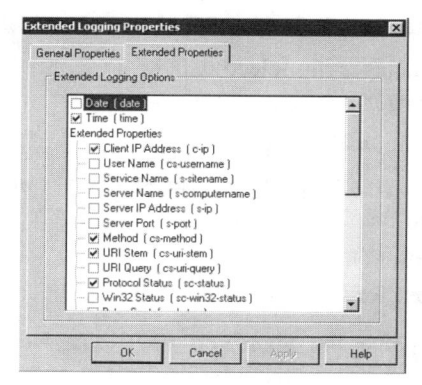

FIGURE 20.20
Configuring Extended Properties for Extended Log Files.

The options on this screen permit you to customize just the W3C Extended logging file format, as none of the other file formats support customization. Check the box next to each option that you want to include and deselect any you want to exclude: a check in the box means that the option will be recorded in the log file, while an empty check box means that that particular option will not be included in the log file. After you make all your selections, click the OK button to return to the Default FTP Site Properties dialog box or the Default Web Site Properties dialog box (depending on whether you are modifying your Web or FTP site). Next, click the OK button to close the Default Properties window completely.

Directory Management

Managing the various directories within your Web and FTP sites is probably one of the most important site management tasks. When we use the term *directory*, it connotes much more than just the physical location of your Web or FTP site; rather, it means logically how you go about finding your Web or FTP site. For example, the home directory of a Web site defines whether a Web site is physically located on the same computer that is running the IIS server services or whether it is stored via a share provided by another computer running some 32-bit Microsoft operating system, or if it is nothing more than a redirection to another URL (this last option only relates to Web sites, as FTP sites do not support the use of URLs). So as you walk through these next few topics, try to keep in mind that a directory is more than just a static location in which to keep your files.

Managing Directories

When you create a Web site through a directory structure, you create a folder on your server, probably within the \inetpub\wwwroot directory. For example, use the following steps to get a new Web site location to appear under the Default Web Site icon inside the Internet Services Manager:

1. Go to the \inetpub\wwwroot folder on your Web server and create a new folder (name it anything you want, but do not put spaces in the folder's name; for example, use GenevieveSnow instead of Genevieve Snow).
2. Start the Internet Services Manager (by selecting Start, Programs, Administrative Tools, Internet Services Manager).
3. Open the items under the Default Web Site icon.
4. You will now see that the Web site labeled GenevieveSnow has magically appeared (or whatever you named your new site).

See, that was not too difficult, was it? Of course, there are a few more things that you need to do to actually create content for the Web site, but you get the idea.

To modify some basic information regarding your Web site, use the Home Directory tab from the Default Web Site Properties dialog box, as shown in Figure 20.21.

FIGURE 20.21
Setting the Home Directory Properties for the Default Web Site.

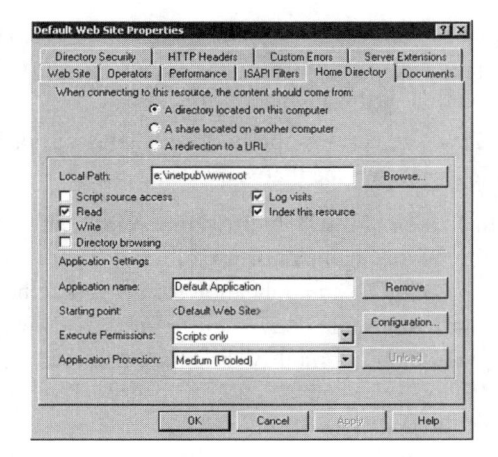

From this tab you can set the location from where the content for your default Web site will originally exist. That is, you need to select one of these three options:

- A Directory Located on This Computer
- A Share Located on Another Computer
- A Redirection to a URL

You should take the time to carefully examine how your organization should best deploy its Web site content on an ongoing basis, both manageability as well as security reasons. Keep in mind that it is generally easiest to manage and secure Web sites that physically are located in roughly the same place.

Other options you should carefully examine are the access modes:

- Script Source Access—This option permits scripts to run on your Web server.
- Read—This option allows users of the Web site to read and copy material from the Web site, but not modify anything.
- Write—This option gives users read rights in addition to the ability to modify content. (Be careful with this one!)
- Directory Browsing—This is one of the most dangerous options to permit on an open Web site, as it permits users to scroll up and down through your physical directory structure, which they might do to look for weak points from which to start a hacking attack. I cannot think of a good reason for an IIS administrator to permit this on a Web site, although there are many ways in which to start penetration efforts against a site that does indeed permit this.

- Log Visits—You use this option to make sure all visits to the Web site are logged in your IIS server's logging format (defined in the "Logging" portion of the Common IIS Controls section of this chapter).
- Index This Resource—If you select this option, the contents of this Web site will be indexed via the IIS indexing service that is available with IIS.

You use the Application Settings area of the Default Web Site Properties dialog box to define an application to help in the management or use of your default Web site (or any other Web site, for that matter). To install an application for use, click the Create button, which enables the other previously unusable options in this area. Clicking the Configuration button permits you to add or modify the Internet Server Application Programming Interface (ISAPI) tools that are available to your Web server, including the caching of ISAPI applications; the ability to set session state and timeout as well as defining the default ASP language, which is typically VBScript; and to set the various application debugging options.

The Execute Permissions drop-down list box is very important for both security and usability purposes. The security side is easy: The more flexibility you permit, the less secure your Web site is. The balance that you strike depends on the application, and usually requires a trial-and-error approach (which is why you originally configure this in a test environment and never in a production setting). The usability side is a bit trickier: You must determine the least amount of usability needed to ensure that your application runs properly.

The Application Protection drop-down list box contains three levels of protection:

- Low (IIS Process)—The application runs in the same process as do the Web services (using the `InetInfo.exe` file).
- Medium (Pooled)—The application executes in a pooled process, which means that typically all applications are running together outside any Web server services (using the `DLLHost.exe` file).
- High (Isolated)—The application executes in its own isolated space away from both the Web server services and other applications (using another instance of the `DLLHost.exe` file).

When we use the term *protection* in the IIS 5.0 sense, it means that this is the process in which that particular application is run. For example, if an application is run in the Low mode and it crashes, it could bring down part or all of the Web server's services. Of course, on the other side, if you set all the applications to run as Isolated (High), then the performance impact on your IIS server could be very significant. For this reason Microsoft recommends you do not set more than 10 applications to run in the High (Isolated) application protection level.

> **Note**
>
> Because you get the same Home Directory tab from within the Web Site Properties dialog box for any of your Web sites as you do for the Default Web Site dialog box, you can follow these same steps to modify each one of the Web sites that exist on your IIS. Likewise, all the other options that appear on this screen are also there for each of your other Web sites, so make note of those options that you think should be modified for every site available via this IIS server.

The best way to create a Web site from within the Internet Services Manager is to use the wizard Microsoft provides. To access it, right-click Default Web Site (or any other Web site, just not a virtual directory) and then click the New menu option that appears on the popup menu. From there, click the Site menu selection that appears just to the right of the New menu option, which causes the Web Site Creation Wizard to begin. Answer the questions the wizard asks, and in about two minutes you will have a new Web site.

The final thing you need to remember is the difference between a Web Site and a Web virtual directory. A Web site contains the actual content that originates from the home directory or any other directory from your Web site, whereas a virtual directory uses an alias to lead Web users to think that that particular virtual directory still originates from within that same Web site's directory structure.

Managing Virtual Servers

Virtual servers are nothing more than virtual directories, which can be created for both Web and FTP sites. To clarify exactly what a virtual directory is, we'll walk through the creation of one. To do this, follow these next few steps:

1. Right click one of the Web or FTP sites on your IIS, and then click the New menu option from the popup menu that appears.

2. Next, click the Virtual Directory menu selection that will appear just to the right of the New menu option. The Virtual Directory Creation Wizard begins, as shown in Figure 20.22.

3. Click the Next button to start the essence of the wizard process. This takes you to the screen shown in Figure 20.23.

4. At this point you need to create the alias with which your Web or FTP site's users will find your new virtual directory. For example, if you enter the alias kavpconsulting (and assuming the Windows 2000 Server computer name of Vannessa), then the end user would use the URL of http://vannessa/kavpconsulting/ to locate this new Web virtual directory.

FIGURE 20.22
Starting the Virtual Directory Creation Wizard.

FIGURE 20.23
Creating the Virtual Directory Alias.

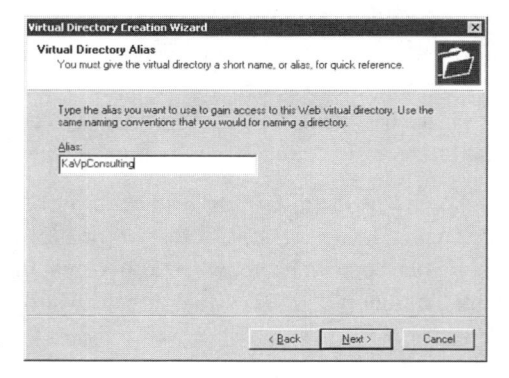

5. Once you have typed-in your new alias, click the Next button, and you see the screen shown in Figure 20.24.

FIGURE 20.24
Creating the Web Site Content Directory.

6. Now that you have the alias for this new virtual directory, it is time to determine from where the content for this new site will originate. Typically, you would probably put the physical content for your Web directory within the same folder structure as your other Web sites. After you have entered the directory path, click the Next button, and you see the screen shown in Figure 20.25.

FIGURE 20.25
Setting Directory Access Permissions.

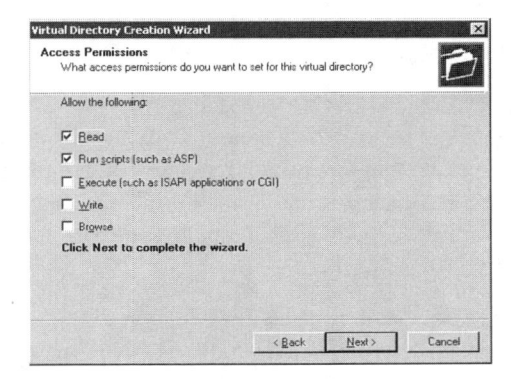

7. This step is to determine the basic permissions that will be applied to this new virtual directory Web (or FTP) site. Refer to the section "Managing Directories" for more information on the differences between all the options. Click the Next button, and you see the final wizard screen.
8. Click the Finish button, which takes you back to the Internet Information Services window, with your new virtual directory now listed, as shown in Figure 20.26.

FIGURE 20.26
Reviewing the Internet Information Services Window for the newly created directory.

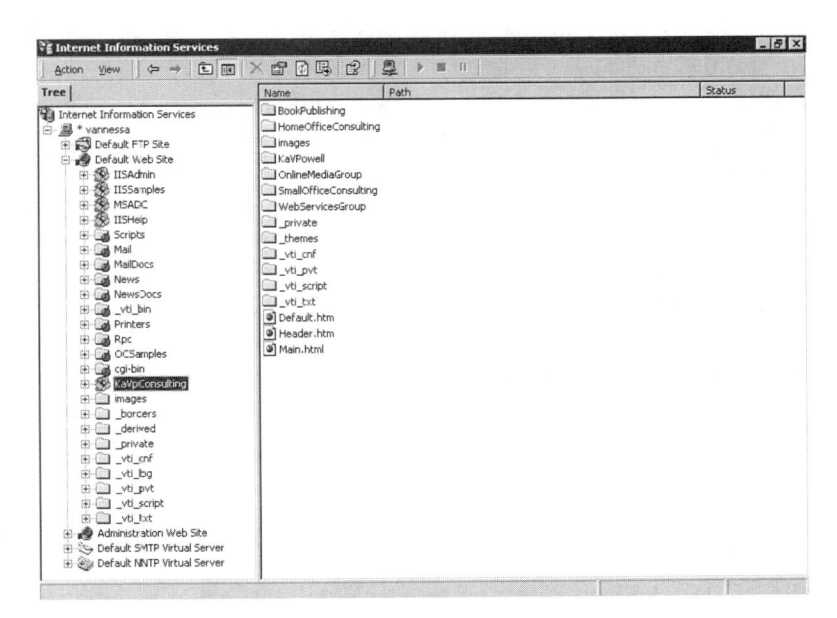

If your new directory does not appear right away, you might need to click the Refresh button (it looks like a small piece of paper with two small circular green arrows on it). This refreshes the Internet Information Services window, which then displays your newly created virtual directory. When you are looking at this main screen, the virtual directories are represented by the icons that resemble a folder with a small globe in the corner (whereas a site icon looks like a globe in the palm of an outstretched hand). You will never see a site inside of a virtual directory—only the other way around.

Advanced IIS Topics

IIS 5.0 has thousands of features, most of which cannot be explained in the detail they deserve in this chapter. However, so that you do not feel like you are missing something really important, in this section we discuss some of the more advanced IIS 5.0 features that are not really designed for use by the masses, including the Site socket pooling, access control issues, and concurrent user limitations.

For more information on the various features, see the Windows 2000 Server Resource Kit from Microsoft (although its discussions of IIS 5.0 are brief in many ways, it does offer a few very technical topics that are not covered here). Additionally, you might want to pick up a copy of the Microsoft Press book known as "Microsoft® Internet Information Services 5.0 Documentation," which really is the printed documentation guide to IIS 5.0 straight form the source (Microsoft). In the past, using Microsoft documentation has typically been downright scary, but this guide really does provide decent coverage of several topics including ASP and technical Web site management.

Site Socket Pooling

In IIS 5.0, the server administrator is able to bind more than one Web site to a single IP address socket. This is a drastic improvement from IIS 4.0, which does not permit a Web site to share an IP socket with another site. This means the server administrator saves non-paged memory because in the past each socket would consume this memory and could not share it with other sockets. In the new IIS 5.0 world, the IIS administrator can permit all his or her sites to share sockets with the others. This means that a single Web server can host a much greater number of additional Web sites than could an identically configured IIS 4.0 server. Of course, if you have a critical Web site that requires its own socket, you can disable the site socket pooling capability of IIS 5.0 on an as-needed basis (you should do this at the site level instead of at a global level). Unfortunately, this disabling of socket pooling can only be accomplished via scripting, which means there is no way to disable it via the IIS MMC GUI screens.

Access Control

Access control is the method by which end users are granted access to IIS resources. Access control permits an end user to gain access or be denied permission to access your

Web, FTP, SMTP, and NNTP sites that are proffered by the IIS 5.0 server. An access control list (ACL) is used to quickly determine which users and/or groups are permitted to access and/or make changes and deletions to an object within your IIS-controlled site.

The access control process is not too complicated. Essentially, whenever someone attempts to see or use content on your Web site, a series of access control steps are automatically carried out by the Internet Information Server:

1. The IP address is evaluated to see if it is valid for this Web site (it is possible for you to block access to specific IP addresses, domains, or DNS lookups). If the user is successful here, he or she continues on to the next step.
2. The user is evaluated for access permissions. This evaluation takes the form of a user ID and password access control method. If the user is successful here, he or she continues on to the next step.
3. The Web server confirms that its set permissions permit access to the resource(s) that are being requested. If the user is successful here, he or she continues on to the final step.
4. The NTFS 5.0 permissions are checked for verification of the access being sought. If they are valid, then the user is finally granted access to the resource(s) that he or she is seeking.

If at any point in the process access is denied, the user is presented with an error message and denied access to the resource. Additionally, that user's attempt is logged in the IIS log files (assuming that the logging options are enabled). If a user is rejected during any of the first three steps, then the 403 type error message (Access Forbidden) is sent back to the user's browser window. If the rejection occurs during the final step in the process, then a 401 type error message (Access Denied) is sent back to the user's browser window.

Another aspect of the access control mechanisms is known as the authentication process. *Authentication* is the means by which end users prove that they have valid Windows user accounts and passwords, in order to access the resources being sought. There are several types of Web authentication methods, but just two types for FTP sites. Use the following to determine the method that is best for your organization:

Web Authentication Methods

- Anonymous authentication—Users can gain access to your Web site without having to present any user ID or password to prove that they are valid users of your Web site. When someone attempts to access the Web server using this type of authentication, that user is assigned to the Windows user account `IUSR_computername`, where *computername* portion generally equates to the name of the server on which IIS 5.0 has been installed.

- Basic authentication—This is the industry standard method for browser-based authentication to a Web site, although it is also the most insecure authentication method for accessing resources from your IIS server. Essentially, the basic authentication method means that an end user types his or her Windows 2000 Server user ID and password into the logon box that appears when he or she attempts to access your Web site. That user ID is sent in clear text and the password in base-64 encoding back to the Web server for authentication. If you ever have an authentication choice, do not make it this one, for the obvious security considerations.

- Digest authentication—This Windows 2000 version of the basic authentication method ensures that the authentication credentials cannot be easily compromised, as they are through the basic method. This is accomplished through a one-way security technology known as *hashing*, which can only be used with Windows 2000 domain controllers within a Windows 2000 domain.

- Integrated Windows authentication—This old NTLM/Windows challenge/response authentication method has been updated with the Kerberos version 5.0 encryption technologies that come with Windows 2000 (NTLM literally means NT LAN Manager, which was the original form of authentication possible on a Windows NT server that originated way back in the days of Windows NT 3.1). In order to use this authentication method, though, both the browsing client and the IIS server must have a trusted connection to the Key Distribution Center and must be Directory Services compliant. This means you need to have a full deployment of Windows 2000 Servers and at least a partial deployment of Active Directory with at least one Key Distribution Center, one global catalog, and one Active Directory tree (or forest).

- Certificate authentication—This is the method by which client computers are authenticated to the Web site via the secured sockets layer (SSL) technology. Authentication takes place via an encrypted digital identification method, which comes in two basic flavors in the United States: 40 bit and 128 bit (internationally, just the 40-bit method is presently available).

FTP Authentication Methods

- Anonymous FTP authentication—Users access the FTP site without ever having to present any user ID or password to prove that they are valid users of the FTP site. When someone attempts to access the FTP server using this type of authentication, that user is assigned to the Windows user account `IUSR_computername`, where `computername` is typically the name of the server on which IIS 5.0 has been installed. Note that this works just the same way as the Web version of anonymous authentication.

- Basic FTP authentication—This is the clear-text version of authentication to the FTP site, which means that an end user uses his or her Windows 2000 Server user ID and password when he or she attempts to access the FTP site. If you ever have an authentication choice, do not make it this one as your end users will be sending their otherwise secure Windows 2000 Server user IDs and passwords in a clear and open fashion for anyone with a sniffer to read.

Concurrent User Limitations

To prevent an overload on either your organization's Web or FTP site(s), you can place a user limit on the number of concurrent connections to those FTP and/or Web sites. To do this, access the Internet Information Services screen by selecting Start, Programs, Administrative Tools, Internet Services Manager. Then right-click either the Default Web Site (or Default FTP Site) icon, and then click the Properties menu selection that appears near the bottom of the small popup menu you see. This takes you into the Default Web Site Properties dialog box, with the Web Site tab showing, as in Figure 20.27.

FIGURE 20.27
Web Site Properties for the Default Web Site.

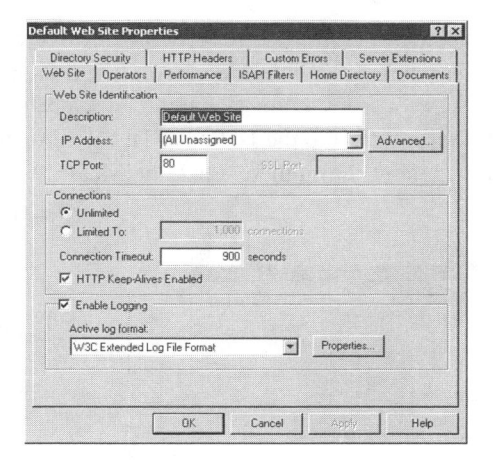

Midway down this screen is the Connections area, where you determine the limitation, if any, that is placed on the total number of concurrent user connections to your Web site (there is an identical screen in the FTP Site tab of the Default FTP Site dialog box). The default selection is Unlimited; to change it, click the Limited To radio button and enter a number that you believe is the correct limit. For example, if this is a private Web site and your company has only 200 employees, then the obvious choice is 200. Your organization needs to determine the limitations for each of its Web and FTP sites, although the information technology group will probably have a few opinions, based on the hardware that is being used to support those Web and FTP servers. After you have made your choices, click the OK button to confirm your selections and return to the primary Internet Information Services screen.

Administering the FTP Site

The File Transfer Protocol (FTP) Site is also based on the TCP/IP networking protocol, just as are the Web services and Telnet. The purpose of FTP is to copy files to and from nonlocal computer systems such as those that are Windows NT or Windows 2000 based, as well as UNIX, Macintosh, and NetWare based. Obviously, you are able to use other, more effective, means to transport files back and forth from other Windows-based computers, as well as NetWare based systems, but that is beside the point. In addition, it is possible to use FTP commands to obtain file and directory listings on those remote computers, which is very useful if you are working with UNIX-based systems in a non-NFS (Network File System) world (from the Windows client's perspective).

Most of the FTP configuration has already been touched on in this chapter because the configuration and management screens for FTP services work identically to those of most of the Web services that are also provided by IIS 5.0.

Configuring FTP Messages

To add, change, or delete a welcome or exit message for your FTP server, select Start, Programs, Administrative Tools, Internet Services Manager. Then right-click the Default FTP Site icon, and then click the Properties menu selection that appears near the bottom of the small popup menu. This takes you into the Default FTP Site Properties dialog box, with the FTP Site tab shown by default. From there, click the Messages tab, to reveal the screen shown in Figure 20.28.

FIGURE 20.28
Setting the Welcome Message for your FTP Site.

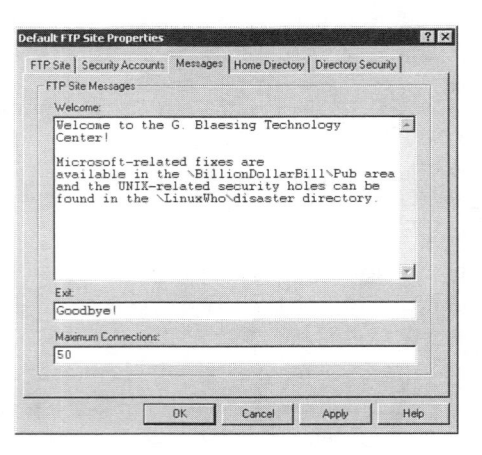

In the Messages tab you can configure both the Welcome and the Exit text-based messages that users see upon first connecting to and then departing from your FTP server site. The messages you leave can only be textual in nature (a drawback that permits backward compatibility for DOS, UNIX, NetWare, OS/2, and other non-Windows clients and servers), and should be relatively short and to the point. Making them too long just confuses users, as the messages may scroll by quickly, not giving an option to stop, pause, or back up. The other option you need to review here is the bottom one, which gives you a way to limit the total number of users that can be connected to your FTP site at any one time. Enter a number that appears reasonable to you (or leave it blank), and then click the OK button to confirm and save your changes. You return to the main Internet Information Services window.

Advanced Web Site Administration

The WWW Site service is the primary focal point of IIS that is built into the Windows 2000 Server operating system. This Web service has come a long way because the first version of IIS did not even support ASP much less the new remote administration tools and secure authentication capabilities. The Web sites, both the real and the virtual directories, are managed from within the Internet Services Manager tool that you access through the Administrative Tools option. Starting this tool takes you into the Internet Information Services window.

Something that is not commonly known is that when IIS is installed, it automatically selects a random port number from the 2,000–9,999 range to act as the default port for your organization's administration Web site. This is important for the general security of your IIS installation, because it now becomes just that much more difficult for unauthorized individuals to determine on which port your administrative Web site is located. (Yes, it is possible to detect using port scanners, though your organization's other network security tools should be tracking who is running a port scanner on your network and against what server or servers.) For example, to use the Web-based version of the administration Web site, you need to enter the full URL for your server's Web site, as in the following example:

```
http://localhost:2047/iis.asp
```

In order for you to be able to access the administration Web site via your Web browser (Internet Explorer 5.0 is obviously the preferred browser because that is the browser that comes with Windows 2000 Server), you must type the correct port number for your organization's administration Web site. If you cannot provide this number, then the IIS server assumes that you are not an authorized requester of the information and thus are blocked from administering the site remotely. The port number is the part of the Web address just to the right of the localhost or your computer's name designation; it has the colon symbol, followed by the four-digit port number. Chances are that if you attempted to remotely access your Web site without using this port designation, you would see a screen similar to the one shown in Figure 20.29.

FIGURE 20.29
Remote IIS Administration Access Error.

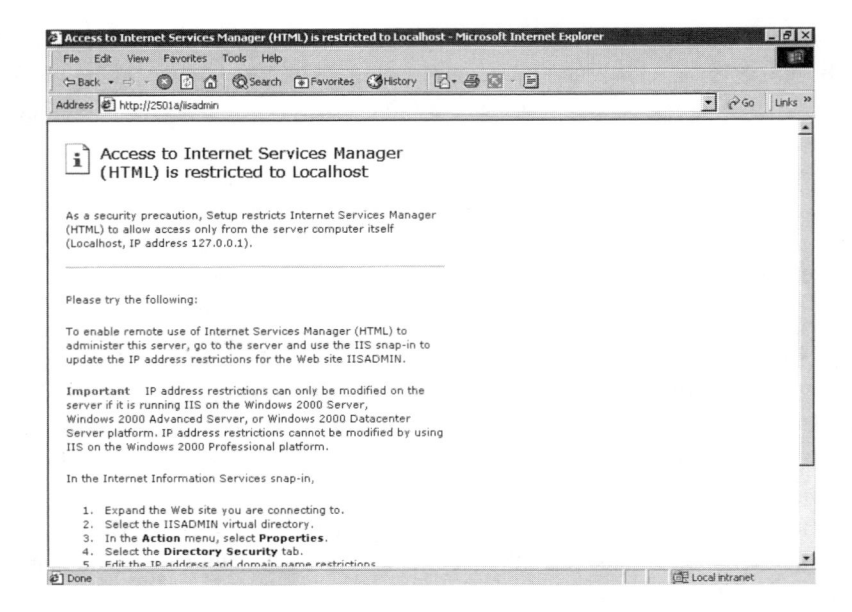

Keep in mind that only users who are actually members of the Windows 2000 Administrators group are permitted to use the administration Web site. Everyone else is denied access.

Choosing a Default First Page

When the IIS service is first installed, it does not automatically set a default home page, even for the default Web site. Therefore, if a user were to attempt to access your default Web site, that person would receive an error message such as the one shown in Figure 20.30.

To set a default home page, select Start, Programs, Administrative Tools, and Internet Services Manager. Then right-click the Default Web Site icon, and then click the Properties menu selection that appears near the bottom of the small popup menu. This takes you into the Default Web Site Properties dialog box, with the Web Site tab shown by default. From there, click the Documents tab to reveal the screen shown in Figure 20.31.

To set a default home page, click the Enable Default Document check box at the top of this screen. Note that you can alter the order of the document types present (`Default.htm`, `Default.asp`, and `iisstart.asp`) by clicking on one of them to select it and then clicking either the up or the down arrow button to move that default document toward the top or bottom of the list. After you have made your selections, click the OK button to confirm any modifications and return to the previous screen.

FIGURE 20.30
What you see when there is no Default Home Page.

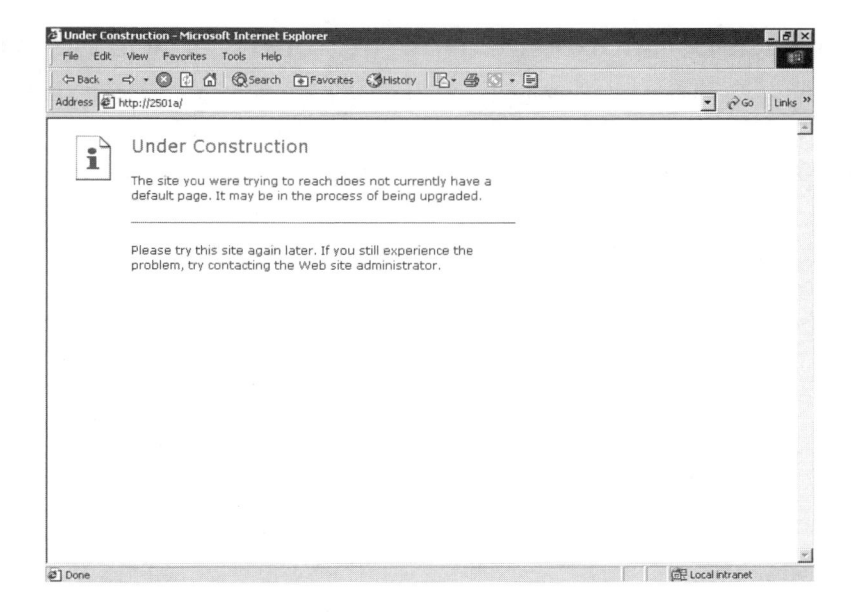

FIGURE 20.31
Enabling a Default Document Type.

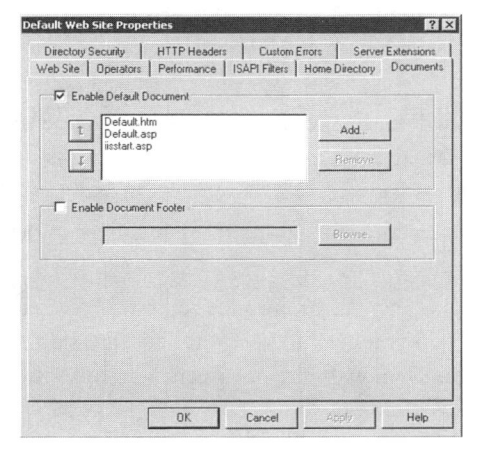

If you have already set this feature and still no default page appears when you attempt to access your default Web site, then it is possible that the physical file (Default.htm, Default.asp, or iisstart.asp) does not exist in your default Web page's file folder. To confirm this, go to that folder (probably \inetpub\wwwroot) and visually confirm the existence of one of these files. If you do not see one, then create one, and make sure that you have created the contents for that particular file correctly. Check your Web authoring tool's (such as Microsoft FrontPage 2000 or Dreamweaver) documentation for more details.

Web Distributed Authoring and Versioning (WebDAV)

WebDAV is a new technology with IIS 5.0. Essentially, WebDAV permits Web clients to perform the following tasks on the IIS 5.0 server:

- Manipulate resources—Users can copy and/or move resources around within a WebDAV directory, if they have the proper permissions.
- Modify resource properties—Web users can modify the properties of Web resources, again assuming that they have the proper permissions to do so.
- Secure resources—Multiple users are able to lock and unlock resources on-the-fly so that many people can read the file concurrently, but just a single person has write access.
- Search—Users are able to search the content and properties of their files within a WebDAV directory.

Configuring the WebDAV publishing directory is a lot easier than you might think. It simply requires the creation of a WebDAV virtual directory, which requires these simple steps:

1. Create a physical folder inside your \inetpub\wwwroot folder structure, with a name such as WebDAV (in which case the full path would be \inetpub\wwwroot\WebDAV).
2. Start the Virtual Directory Creation Wizard and enter the name WebDAV as the alias. Refer to the Managing Virtual Servers section for more details on precisely how to start this wizard if you are unsure.
3. Designate the permissions read, write, and browse by clicking the check boxes next to those options.
4. Only if you want to provide modification rights to your organization's ASP or any other script-mapped files do you need to perform this final step. Grant script source access to your newly created WebDAV virtual directory in the Virtual Directory tab of the WebDAV Properties dialog box.

That is all you need to do to configure your server for WebDAV publishing access. Obviously, though it is possible for you to configure your entire Web site to be one giant WebDAV process, it is not wise to do this because of the obvious security concerns. However, if your organization is small, perhaps a tiny educational or not-for-profit association, then you might want to consider using WebDAV throughout your organization.

Administering the Gopher Site

Unfortunately, especially for those IIS users from the great state of Minnesota, the Gopher text-based database technology, along with its VERONICA searching capabilities, is no longer a part of the Microsoft IIS technology. For many new users to the

Internet, this is probably not a big loss, but for those of us who have been surfing for the past decade or so, it is disheartening to see one of the originators of the Internet fade away so quickly.

Administering the Telnet Service

The Telnet service is not actually a part of IIS technology. From a purely technical standpoint, the WWW functions as sort of a "rider" on top of the Telnet technology, but the server service itself is not integrated into the Microsoft IIS feature. To use either the GUI or command prompt–based versions of the Telnet service with a Windows 2000 Server, you need to simply use the Run command from the Windows 2000 Server Start button. The Telnet service for Windows 2000 Server consists of just a few files:

- `telnet.chm`—Found in the `%systemroot%\Help` folder, this is the compiled GUI help file for the Telnet service.
- `telnet.hlp`—Found in the `%systemroot%\Help` folder, this file is used in conjunction with the command prompt–based Telnet services.
- `telnet.exe`—Found in the `%systemroot%\System32` folder, this is the command prompt–based Telnet client application.
- `telnetc.exe`—Found in the `%systemroot%\System32` folder, this is the GUI-based Telnet client application.

Advanced Security Concepts

Completely securing an IIS from unwanted and unauthorized users is one of the most difficult, if not downright impossible, tasks to perform. However, to make your Web and FTP server services secure from the vast majority of those out on the Internet who might be seeking to do you harm is not as difficult as you might think. Like anything else in computing, there is a fine line between ensuring that your users have enough access and making sure that unauthorized individuals and programs do not have any access.

First, a little terminology. The unauthorized folks who may wish to access your IIS server's services really fall into three main groups:

- Script kiddies—This refers to the typically under-21 crowd of users who think that they are being 3l33t (elite) by attempting to hack their way into a Web site for either the pure conquest of it or to graffiti it (that is, leave behind some crude/rude slogans and/or pornography pictures on your corporate Web site). These individuals are referred to as *script kiddies* because they have no real computing skills (networking or programming), and are just using someone else's hacking tool (typically GUI based) to gain unauthorized access to your Web site. The end result? If you had taken just a little bit of time up front when configuring your Web and FTP sites, you can prevent the vast majority of these attackers from ever being successful against your organization.

- Hackers—A hacker is someone who does possess the networking and programming skill sets to unlawfully penetrate your organization's Internet defenses. This type of individual often works alone and is doing it for the challenge. It is very rare that a hacker will actually do damage to your site, though just the posting of pornographic materials on an otherwise normal business site can be very damaging from a public relations standpoint. Never assume that your organization is too bland for anyone to try to get in, as no group is ever totally excluded by all the hackers out there.

- Crackers—A cracker is someone with all the skills of a hacker, but with an evil bent. Not only do they attempt (and often succeed) to hack Web and FTP sites at an alarming rate, but they are doing this with the intent of doing harm to your site(s). In many cases, a cracker will be satisfied with denying all your normally authorized users from obtaining access to your sites. This is done through an attack method known as a denial-of-service attack. Unfortunately, it is a relatively simple, effective, attack against a Windows NT or Windows 2000 server. Crackers are very good at what they do, and are often willing to do this work for hire (perhaps your organization has a less-than-scrupulous competitor that just might hire a few to take down your Internet-based business), so you need to take extra precautions to guard against these types of people.

For starters, there are several simple things you can do to begin protecting yourself against script kiddies and some hackers and crackers:

- Audit IIS servers—Turn on the very comprehensive auditing features of IIS, which should include the tracking of all logon attempts (both valid and failed), the tracking of all failed attempts to access unauthorized content and/or resources, and the tracking of any attempts by unauthorized individuals to run programs or execute restricted commands.

- Limit domain controller use—Never surf the Internet from a Windows 2000 Server domain controller, including global catalog or Key Distribution Center servers. This unwarrantedly exposes your most critical servers to the Internet for no good reason. Additionally, never install the IIS software onto any domain controller, Key Distribution Center, or global catalog, as this not only negatively affects the response time of your user community, but it unnecessarily exposes you to the Internet community.

- Use antivirus software—This one cannot be mentioned often enough. Always run antivirus software on all your servers, as well as on all your end users' computers. An obscene number of Fortune 500 corporations, Big 5 accounting firms, and global not-for-profit organizations do one or the other (client side or server side), but not both.

- Select the most secure authentication method possible—If your Web and FTP sites are open only to internal users, as would be the case on an intranet, do not enable anonymous login capabilities, and only use a secure authentication process. The same goes for Internet-based access. Train your end users to get used to using the highest level of authentication possible. For example, use Integrated Windows or digest authentication on your intranet side, and perhaps certificate authentication on the Internet side for those users who are known (perhaps the ones buying merchandise from your organization). All others on the Internet side would remain as anonymous users until they cross that imaginary boundary to becoming real customers, at which time you could invoke the certificate-based authentication process.
- Implement physical security—Never leave the physical IIS server exposed to the general public or even your general employee base. This would include the "storing" of the Web or FTP server under someone's desk or an unsecured data center (that is, no doors or walls for the data center, much less a lock on the door), and be sure to use BIOS-level and screen saver–level passwords on the IIS computer itself. Likewise, if this server is to be accessed via just the Internet, do not connect it to your organization's LANs or WANs. On the other side, if this is strictly an intranet-based IIS, then make sure that it cannot be accessed via the Internet.
- Implement logical security—It is a good idea to use separate administrative accounts (never let three or more people all use the same account, or you will never be able to figure out who did what and when) and to set secure Web and user permissions.
- Minimize the ISS services used—Do not run other services on this server that are not necessary to the operation of your Web, FTP, SMTP, or NNTP sites. This includes using the IIS server for file and print services, application services, and the like. In addition, you should probably disable the following Windows 2000 Server base services: Application Management; ClipBook; Computer Browser; Fax Services; File Replication; Net Logon; Infrared Monitor; Kerberos Key Distribution Center (this assumes that your IIS server is not a domain controller, key distribution center, or a global catalog); NetMeeting Remote Desktop Sharing; Print Spooler; Quality of Service (QoS) RSVP; Remote Registry Service; Routing and Remote Access; Telnet; Terminal Services; Windows Installer; and the Windows Time service.
- Use NTFS on all IIS servers—To facilitate the use of more stringent file security controls, you must change the file allocation table format from FAT or FAT32 to NTFS 5.0 format (this is new to the Windows 2000 operating system). Note that after you upgrade a FAT or FAT32 partition to NTFS, you cannot downgrade it back to FAT or FAT32 except by reformatting that partition (which means you need to back everything up and then delete it all).

- Enforce password security—Do not permit your Windows-authorized user community to get in the habit of using the same weak password repeatedly. Set the base security policy to make passwords at least eight alphanumeric characters long, and encourage users to incorporate a special character into the mix. Also, you should expire your passwords for all users and administrators on periodically: perhaps every 90–120 days for end users and every 30 days for administrators.
- Use encryption—Use SSL protection for all administrative duties on your Web site, both local and remote, including posting new content.
- Restrict site permissions—If read-only access will suffice on your Web or FTP sites, never give the user community anything more. Do not open up your security structure with the plan that you can always shrink it back down. Rather, start at the opposite extreme: Initially, make each piece of your site as restricted as possible. Then, as the organization's users require, open up the access capabilities on an as-needed basis. This would mean that you would start with only read access and eventually expand it outward to perhaps include write and script source access.

There are hundreds of other tips and tricks you can use to lock down the IIS environment, but we only have room to scratch the surface here. Continue to seek out the many tips that are available on the Internet, which will help you secure your server(s) from unauthorized access. The following is a short list of sites you might find useful:

- http://www.microsoft.com/security/
- http://www.10pht.com/
- http://www.networkcomputing.com/netdesign/
- http://windowsupdate.microsoft.com/nt5help/Enterprise/en/nt_frame.htm
- http://www.rsa.com/
- http://www.nmrc.org/files/snt/index.html

Good luck!

Directory Rights Assignment for Secure Sites

Securing a Web site is not easy. It takes a good deal of time and effort to secure a site, and even then, it will not be 100% secure from prying eyes. Nothing, regardless of how you approach it, will ever be 100% secure from the hacker/cracker community as long as your Web site is connected to the Internet. Nevertheless, there are some steps you can take to deter most people who might try to violate your security.

Permissions Settings

First, you need to set your Web permission levels. This is a relatively simple task, but how your organization determines who gets what access can take quite a bit of time to resolve. There are essentially four levels of access, which are then coupled with the ability to log visits to the site, along with indexing. The permissions levels are as follows:

- Read access—This is the default setting for any Web site, which gives the user the ability to access and copy any content that exists on the site.
- Write access—This setting permits visitors to modify Web site content and properties, including the deleting of files and setting some security boundaries.
- Script source access—This level is a bit trickier to deploy than read and write access, but it gives Web site users the ability to access the source code of your script files, such as ASP-based applications, for reading and/or modification purposes. If you have enabled read access along with script source access, then your Web users can use those scripts. However, if you have enabled write access along with the script source access, then your Web users can modify the source code of any of your scripts.
- Directory browsing access—This permission setting permits your Web users to scroll up and down through the folder levels of your IIS server. This is a dangerous setting for any Web server, but it is a normal setting for FTP sites since FTP sites are meant to be browsed for specific files and folders information. No secure data should ever be stored on an FTP site for distribution of any kind for that reason.

After you have decided what Web permissions to apply, you need to formulate the NTFS permissions for your IIS server (this part assumes that you have altered your partition structure to NTFS instead of FAT or FAT32).

Access Control Settings

After you have converted your partition table structure to NTFS, you are able to modify the permissions based on these choices:

- Full control—Users with this level can do anything they want to the files and folders that make up the sites in question.
- List folder contents—This is one of the safer levels, which permits users to read the contents of a folder but not access them.
- Modify—This permits your site users to change files and folders, as well as their associated properties.
- No access—Users with this level of permission are completely barred from accessing any of the files or folders that exist on your organization's IIS.
- Read—Users can view files and folders, as well as their associated properties, but they cannot modify any of those contents.

- Read and execute—This is an extension of the read rights, in that users can also run applications and scripts on your site.
- Write—This builds on the read and execute privileges by permitting users to not only see and run scripts, but to modify files and folders as well.

Directory Browsing

As mentioned earlier in the chapter, directory browsing is one of the most dangerous options to permit on an open Web site. On Web sites that are open to just your organization's intranet-based users, however, there is one reason for directory browsing to be enabled: for the purposes of using WebDAV as your publishing mechanism. For more information on WebDAV, refer to the section "Web Distributed Authoring and Versioning (DAV)" earlier in this chapter.

Directory browsing of FTP sites, though, is an entirely different matter. Of course, it is assumed that you would never put anything else (data, services, whatever) on the same IIS server that is running your organization's FTP site(s), as that would be a terrible security breach. The use of directory browsing is considered a typical act that most FTP sites permit. Of course, you should use and enforce some sort of password authentication for those areas of your FTP site that you consider private to your organization.

Troubleshooting Security Breaches

Troubleshooting a security breach within your Web or FTP sites is not quite as easy as one might originally think. It is not just a matter of determining that some unauthorized individual has indeed gained access to your private information, rather, you must also be able to determine precisely how that person gained that access to your organization's sites. This is because you must be able to figure-out how someone walked into your organization, otherwise after you boot them out they will come right back in.

Of course, there is also a flip side to troubleshooting security issues. You may have set the incorrect level of security for a particular IIS server-based resource, and someone has unknowingly violated your perceived wall of security. In those cases, it helps to first understand exactly what you are trying to protect, why you want to do that, and the methodology as to how your protection scheme will be deployed.

Now that you understand the two sides of security breaches, let us try to figure out how to deal with both of them. If permissions are set incorrectly, you need to carefully review your sites' Web and NTFS permissions structures, as well as review the access control patterns of your user community. For more details on the permissions structures and the access control processes, refer to the sections "Permissions Settings " and " Access Control Settings" earlier in this chapter. Next, review where you have created your WebDAV virtual directory. Does it point to a location high up in your folder hierarchy?

That is, did you initially set the WebDAV permissions to begin with your `\inetpub\www-root` folder, or did you think to push these permissions lower into your folder organization? Obviously, the higher the permissions were set, the greater the chance that someone will be able to surf your IIS server beyond just the WebDAV area that you originally wanted them to be able to manipulate. A good practice here is to put the WebDAV folder onto a computer that is physically separate from your general IIS server computer, and even then you should put it onto an NTFS partition that contains nothing but the WebDAV content.

Another potential error or unintentional security problem area is what may occur when a Web browser is sent a 404—Access Denied error message. These types of messages happen when a user has worked his or her way done the ACL, but is still unable to reach an authenticated stage. Many times, anonymous Web and FTP users receive this type of error. As discussed earlier in the chapter, overeager administrators who change the password or policies for the `IUSR_computername` account in Windows can cause this type of error. This account controls the anonymous access for both your FTP and Web service users, and changes to it may result in the IIS server refusing to establish an anonymous connection for a specific resource controlled by that IIS server.

A similar error or unintentional security problem is the 403—Access Forbidden error message. Making sure that you have not erroneously blocked the IP addresses of your user community from gaining access to the IIS server can rectify this error. Likewise, if the user who is receiving this message no longer has a valid Windows 2000 Server or domain account and password, then he or she will also be served up with this error message. All you need to do to fix it is make sure that the person's account is active and valid.

To determine if you have unauthorized users on your Windows 2000 Server, you should use the Computer Management. To start that tool, right-click the My Computer icon on the desktop, and then click the Manage option on the popup menu that appears. This causes the Computer Management tool to start, as shown in Figure 20.32.

Open the System Tools icon by clicking its plus symbol, and then click the Shared Folders icon to reveal its contents as well. From there, click on the Sessions folder to reveal all the active users on your server in the right pane (keep in mind that anonymous users would not be individually listed here). It is up to you, the system administrator, to determine which of the users listed are valid ones, which is not always easy, especially if someone has hacked into your networks via an otherwise valid user's account.

After you have identified the hacker's account, though, deleting that person from the system is relatively easy. Just right-click that user's account to reveal the small popup menu shown in Figure 20.33.

FIGURE 20.32
Viewing active Sessions.

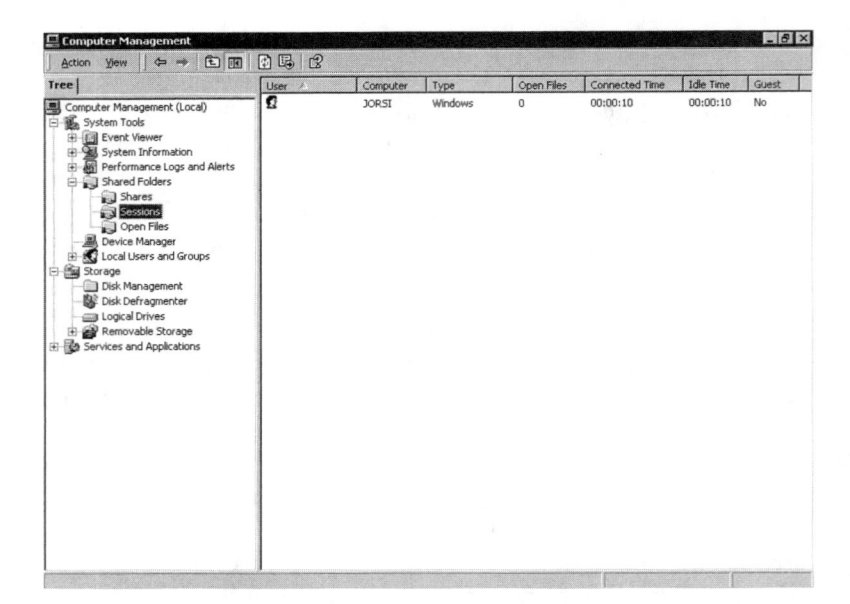

FIGURE 20.33
To forcibly close a user session choose the top Close Session option. The system prompts you with an MMC confirmation message box.

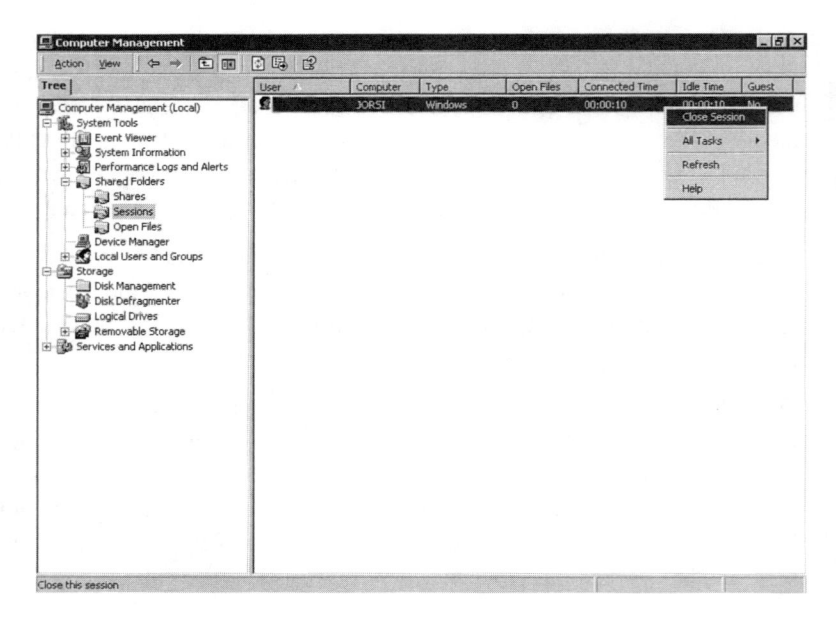

Click the OK button, and the unauthorized user's session is removed from your Windows 2000 Server. However, unless you are able to track down the path the user used to gain the original access, chances are the user will be back in no time. You need to carefully examine the various Windows 2000 Server event logs to see which users, if any, have repeatedly tried to gain access to areas that perhaps they should not have been trying to access. Another tracking method is to carefully examine your IIS logs for abnormal levels of activity. As you are probably beginning to guess, the tracking of a script kiddie, hacker, or cracker can easily begin to consume large amounts of your time and perhaps the time of others within your organization. On any given day, there are perhaps dozens of unauthorized penetration attempts against your organization's Internet and intranet-based servers. Finding them all before something terribly wrong occurs can be a full-time pursuit.

Summary

This rather lengthy chapter has been an introductory look into the inner workings of the version 5.0 release of the Internet Information Server. IIS 5.0 has been greatly modified and enhanced to correct many of the problems of its predecessors, as well as to continue to offer many of the latest technologies the Internet has to offer. IIS is well integrated into Windows 2000 Server, which you have seen through many of the more detailed administrative functions covered here. As you continue to work with IIS it would behoove you to obtain a more detailed working knowledge of TCP/IP as well as ASP, both of which have an enormous impact upon the inner workings of this Windows 2000 technology.

CHAPTER 21

Other Internet Services for Windows 2000

IN THIS CHAPTER

- Access Security and Speed with Proxy Server *550*
- Exchange Email Server *556*
- FrontPage *564*

The obvious Internet service associated with any server these days is the World Wide Web service (or *HTTP server*). In fact, some people think the World Wide Web is the Internet (okay, it is). However, the Windows 2000 platform offers many more options in Internet publishing, control, and security than those offered by Web and FTP.

Because Windows 2000 was originally designed to be an operating system as powerful as UNIX but as user friendly as the Macintosh, it's a good choice for the applications of the Internet. It could be argued that the operating system has not met either of these goals, but Windows 2000 is another step in that direction and makes a nice operating system for the Internet front end.

Windows 2000 is friendlier to use than the UNIX command line, the Cisco OS, and even Linux. For this reason, many companies have gravitated to it. The product is powerful enough to get the job done well, and it allows its users to enjoy in the warmth of the Windows 95 interface—and there's a lot to be said for the comfort factor.

Access Security and Speed with Proxy Server

Among the products that have made a large splash in the business world is one that allows companies to monitor and improve some Internet performance, control Internet access, and protect against outside attack. The product is Microsoft Proxy Server.

An administrator who is familiar with the Internet will recognize Proxy Server as a combination of firewall, content-caching server, and access controller. Proxy Server is able to perform all these tasks because it sits between the internal network and the public network. This one machine can control everything that comes and goes between the two networks (see Figure 21.1).

Acquisition and Caching

In the preceding figure, the client initiates communications with the Internet by making a request to the proxy server. The proxy then makes the request to the host system. The host system returns the requested data to the proxy, which services the request to the client. Depending on its settings, the proxy server will most likely keep a copy of the information until it's sure no other system will want the data.

The proxy server, in this case, does the job of a human proxy. It's not a system that makes a connection between systems; instead, it's a system that makes a request for the other system and delivers the request after having received it. This is an important distinction—connection by proxy.

FIGURE 21.1
A conceptual view of Proxy Server.

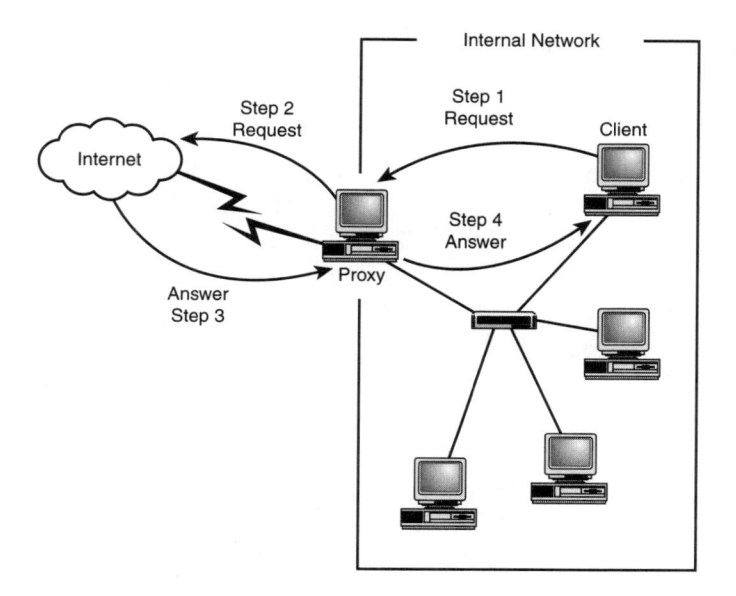

If the proxy had simply connected the two systems and monitored the connection, it would have been functioning as a *router*. Instead, it's a kind of food taster. Anything that passes to the client has been on the proxy, and no other system makes direct connection to the systems inside the proxy.

Another important distinction is the fact that the proxy will keep a copy of the data that's retrieved. The majority of the data that will come through a proxy will be Web-related data. The Web, by nature, is very graphical, but it's also very cyclical. Once users in a building find a site or sites that help them get their jobs done, they will frequent those sites. Repeatedly tying up the costly Internet connection to go to the same site can be avoided if the users only download the new information.

Access Control

Many companies find that their in-house staff spends an excessive amount of time "surfing" the Internet when the service is first introduced. As time goes on, though, most employees begin to get over the novelty of the tool and begin to use it for what it's meant for (shopping). However, some will never conform, and some have no real reason to have access to the Internet at work.

Proxy Server allows the administrator to control access to the Internet in the same way access is given to any other resource on the network. Once the proxy is in place, all access to the Internet can be directed through it. Also, access can be controlled on several levels.

Web access can be controlled through the Web Proxy applet in the Permissions tab in the Proxy Manager (see Figure 21.2). This simple screen first allows the administrator turn access control on or off and then to control the specific users or groups that have access.

FIGURE 21.2
Web access control and permissions.

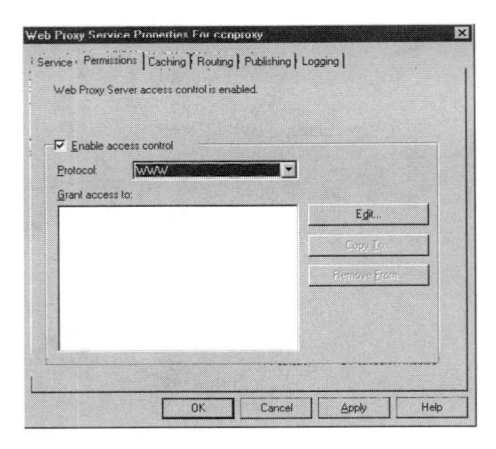

By turning on access control, the administrator must allow users to have access. As with any other Windows security scheme, it's best if a group is created that's allowed access. This way, the process of allowing a user access becomes as easy as making a user a member of the group.

All other protocols are controlled through the Winsock or Socks Proxy tabs. This is because all the other protocols come through different TCP/IP ports, and the distinction is based on this fact. Web Proxy actually can control tools other than HTTP (such as FTP and Gopher), but everything it controls must come through port 80 (the HTTP port).

Winsock and Socks Proxy control the use of each individual port including HTTP (see Figure 21.3). Each individual protocol is either listed or can be created by the administrator. The protocols are identified by the type of protocol they are (UDP or TCP, for example) and the ports they use. The groups or users allowed to use the protocol are then identified.

This makes it possible for administrators to make subtle decisions. One group may be allowed all protocols, whereas another may only be allowed Web access. Also, all users might be restricted from using the Real Audio port so that bandwidth is saved.

The idea is more granular control, but with granular control comes granular work. For every lock that's set, a disgruntled group of users may appear with a perfectly valid reason why that protocol was important to them. If the Web proxy is used for most traffic, it makes life much simpler to administer.

FIGURE 21.3
Winsock proxy access control.

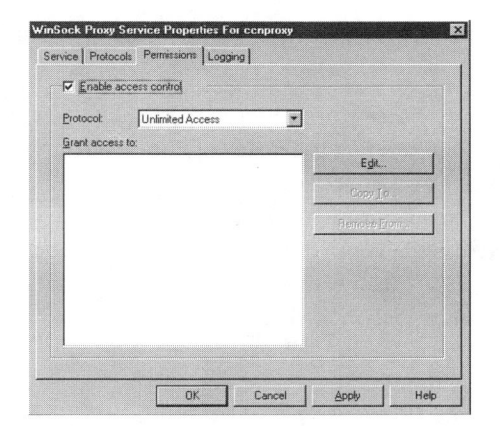

Network Security: Firewall

Proxy Server is also a fairly powerful firewall device. To get some idea what a firewall is, it helps to understand where the term comes from. Between rooms and suites in buildings, you'll always find walls, but there are many types of walls. A *firewall* is a wall that goes all the way to the roof and won't allow fire (or neighbors) to climb into the next suite.

A network firewall, as shown in the figure, 21.1 is the only connection between the internal network and the external network. Because of this, every bit of traffic must pass through the firewall. This allows the proxy server to block fire and unwanted neighbors, so to speak.

Instead of people and fire, the proxy server controls the passage of network packets. This control is handled in several different ways.

The first is that all incoming calls to Proxy Server are ignored unless it's given explicit direction to do otherwise. It's a bit like the Buckingham Palace guard who just doesn't respond. No need for response means no distraction.

Second, any traffic that wants to leave the system must be directed to the proxy explicitly. Either the traffic is made up of Web-based requests that are proxied and cached or it's any other protocol (FTP, SMTP, POP, and so on). In this case, the client machine must have a client control panel application installed that tells the proxy and client how to handle the communications.

Finally, a special relationship can be established between a proxy server and publishing devices that sit inside the firewall. Servers such as Web and email servers can be set up to alert the firewall that any call that comes in for them should be allowed on a given set of TCP/IP ports. For example, an Exchange server can inform the proxy server that any SMTP or POP traffic should come to the Exchange server. This allows the Exchange server to not suffer attack on other ports that might compromise the domain, and it allows SMTP traffic to continue.

Web servers can be placed inside of the proxy server very easily. In fact, because of Proxy Server, any server inside of the firewall that has a NetBIOS or DNS name and an HTTP service can be served to the Internet. Within the settings of Proxy Server is a page called Publishing (see Figure 21.4). The default for this setting is to ignore any request. However, it can be set to either send all HTTP traffic to one server or many servers (based on the DNS request). When an HTTP call comes in, the proxy server acts as an operator, connecting the call, and as a censor, only allowing certain types of traffic through.

FIGURE 21.4
Proxy Server's Publishing screen.

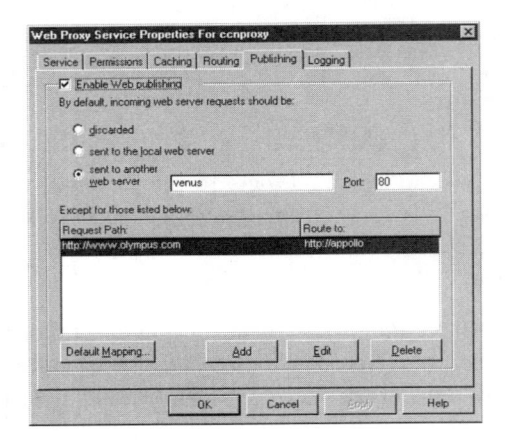

Logging of Traffic

Proxy servers have the capability to track every packet that passes through the connection to the Internet. This allows the administrator to log activity that passes that connection (see figure 21.5). Proxy Server keeps a log of the traffic both coming and going across the connection and does it in two possible formats: SQL and plain text. The recording of this information can be as powerful as a tool that stops traffic.

When an administrator looks at a log file, what is seen is the IP address of the traffic creator, the destination of the user, and the time and date the user was online. If access control has been turned on, the user's name will also appear for any traffic exiting for the Internet.

These logs will tell the administrator several things that should be reviewed regularly:

- Where users are going
- How much time users are spending on the Internet

FIGURE 21.5
Proxy Server's Winsock Proxy log.

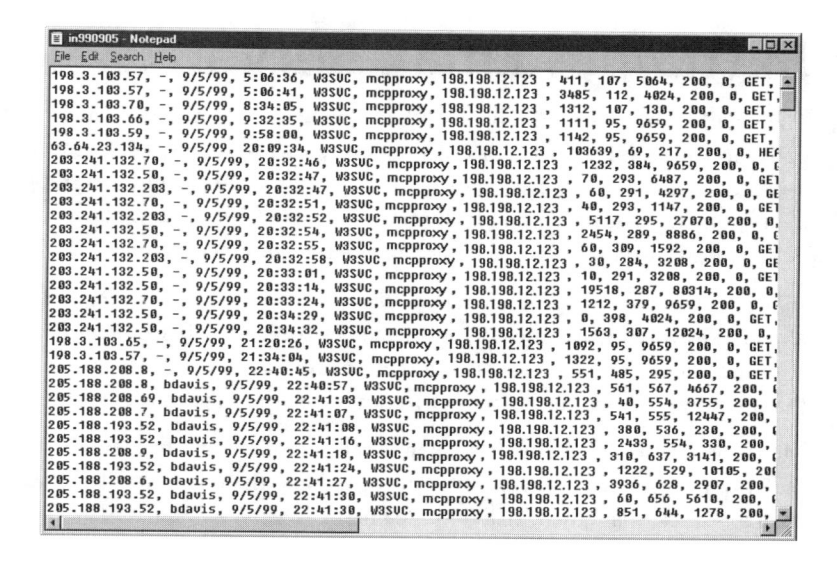

- Who is accessing the company's Web site
- How often the Web site is being hit and which pages are popular
- Whether someone is spending a great amount of time in sensitive areas of the company's data and who it is

With this information, an administrator can truly justify the existence of an Internet presence. He or she can also see whether a problem has arisen. If it's found that an important customer is spending a great deal of time at the Web site or making use of the FTP resource posted for it, then the money spent in this area begins to be justified.

In a politically charged atmosphere, it can be difficult to know how to approach the issue of inappropriate use of Internet time and bandwidth. Simply alerting the staff that logs of Internet traffic exists can be a great way to keep the honest folk honest.

> **Tip**
>
> One administrator simply laid a report with the Web usage of an employee on the employee's desk anonymously. The report showed an entire day spent at inappropriate sites from the user's login account and workstation. The problem disappeared and nothing more was said. Accurate information can put things in the right light without shouting or finger pointing.

Exchange Email Server

The email server is seldom meant to be as powerful in an organization as it turns out to be. When an email server is installed, it's often set up in a small department that needs to share a bit of data. However, shortly after it's in operation, another group is added, and then another. Soon that little email server is responsible for a majority of the in-house network traffic. Microsoft Exchange allows this trend to explode even further.

In the "enterprise" (large corporate, government, or educational installation) email is already known as a significant part of the network. They battle with finding an email system that does not require constant attention and maintenance. Many of the email systems that function for smaller business will not stand up to the traffic of enterprise users.

Microsoft Exchange Server has taken email servers to another level—someplace between the "flat file" message storage systems of old and the database GroupWare products, such as Notes, that have existed in the enterprise.

Robust General Email

Email systems just four years ago mostly consisted of what are called *flat file message systems*. The idea was that every user attached to a single file on a file server share and sent and received mail by attaching and detaching from the file for each send or receive. Even if you haven't experienced this, you can see that this is not ideal. Here are just a few reason why not:

- Every user in the system must have access to the file. This means that every user can corrupt or destroy the file.
- File maintenance must be performed, whether it's manually started or batch driven. Because it's a single file, this can only be done when users are logged out of email.
- Backup of the data is all or nothing. If one user's data must be restored, all users' data must be restored.

The digression of picking on flat file email systems is necessary in order to understand the value of a system like Exchange Server.

Exchange is a messaging system that's made from two basic building blocks: a robust relational database and a three-year-old hierarchical directory structure. The combination of these two items allows for the system to be both robust and serviceable while maintaining the agility to do the job.

By using the Jet database system, the Exchange server allows the system to maintain the email system like it maintains a database. Many sources of data are separate, but all the data can be used to provide services.

> **Note**
>
> A relational database is a gathering of databases that maintains separate collections of information (databases) that are then tied through a common string. For example, a base of accounts used for accounting and a base used for marketing can be joined by the account numbers of the clients.

An example of this advantage is the fact that a message that's sent from one user to a group of users within the Exchange system is only stored once. Every user who receives the message recovers the message from a common store. Imagine the space this saves, if a 1MB attachment is sent to 25 people (25X1MB= 25MB, but if all gather from one location it only equals 1MB).

The Jet database also helps by performing self-maintenance. Database files first create space and then fill that space. Rarely do databases give space back. A database is very difficult to size and maintaining this sizing is also hard; therefore, it's nice that the Jet database does its own sizing and checking of data consistency.

Public Folders

A very difficult part of business today is keeping people communicating in a world in which people are constantly moving. The Exchange system adds a feature to the email system that allows users to keep a sort of electronic version of the old bulletin board on the wall. It's called *public folders*.

Within Exchange and Outlook (the user interface for Exchange), the concept of a *folder* keeps appearing. A user's email comes from a personal folder or mailbox folder on the server. Task lists, calendars, journals, and archives are all stored in folders. The concept of a *public folder* is to create yet another folder that exists in a space that everyone can get to.

The administrator initially creates a folder, but from that point on, folders really belong to the users. An administrator can't even create a public folder (beyond the first folder) from the Exchange administrator's program.

A user can create a folder in the public pool of folders and even administer the users who can use the folder (see Figure 21.6). In effect, they can become little public and private conversations or idea pits. Once the folder is created, users can post text messages, place files from any application, or even begin group calendars inside the folder (see Figure 21.7).

FIGURE 21.6
Public folders in Outlook.

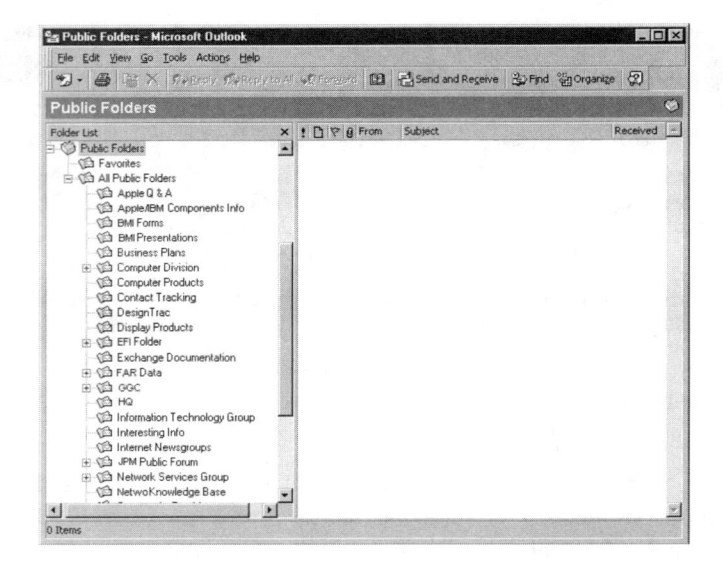

Also once the folder is created, the administrator can now control access and participate in administering the folder. These places are not free-for-alls but rather simple open areas to promote communications.

FIGURE 21.7
An open public folder with varied documents.

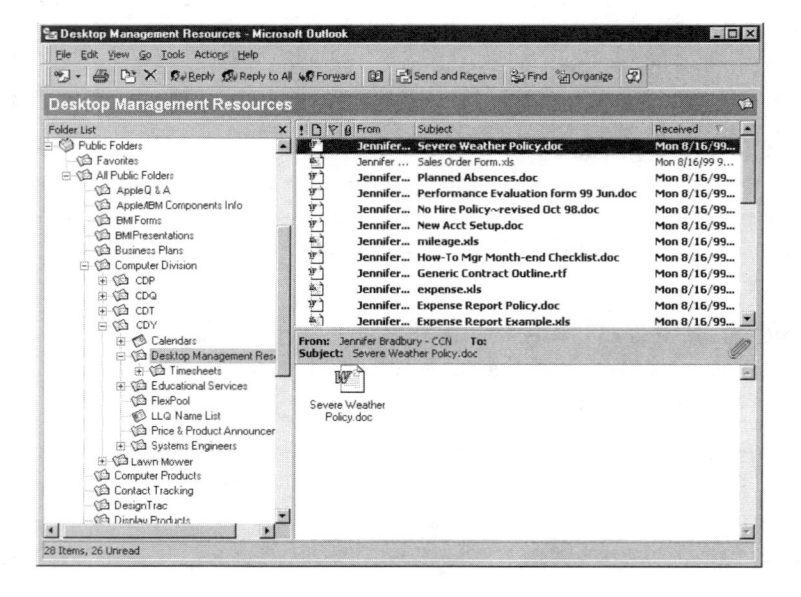

Directory Structure

The structure of the Exchange directory is quite similar to the structure of Active Directory. In fact, Microsoft might argue that it has cut its teeth on the directory structure found here (see Figure 21.8). Even the concept of a site exists in the Exchange directory. You won't find an exact match from one system to another, though.

FIGURE 21.8
The directory of the Exchange system.

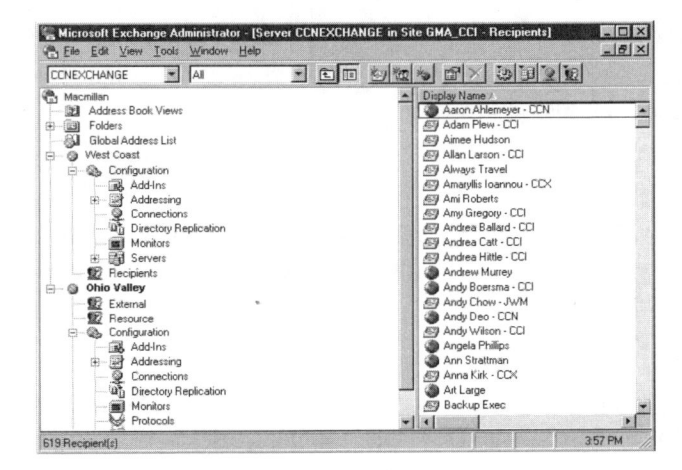

The concept of *container objects* exists in the form of sites and recipient containers. The directory is replicated throughout the organization just as it is in the domain. Finally, administrative tasks and responsibilities can be given to container objects in the system.

This granularity contributes to the strength of the system. Because of the distributed nature of the system, it can better survive problems. If the public information store is lost that does not mean that the private information stores are lost. If a single mailbox is lost that does not mean that everyone has lost there mail.

Internet Access and Reception

Internet connectivity is such an integral part of Exchange that it's necessary to make a conscious choice to completely remove it. As with the Windows Server family, Microsoft has made Internet connectivity part of the system, not just a component that's added later.

The concept of *Internet connectivity* can mean numerous things when it comes to email. Some Internet protocols are automatically installed and but many Internet services are not. So don't be fooled into believing that just because you see the SMTP and POP protocols, in the Exchange administrative interface, that you have connected your email system to the Internet. Here are some terms used when discussing email connectivity:

- **POP.** Provides a client connection to the server from across the Internet for reading mail
- **SMTP.** Provides a connection from one Internet email server to another for exchanging mail
- **LDAP.** Provides the capability for an external source to gain access to a user list on the server without having other access
- **HTTP Client.** Provides the capability to access email through the Web
- **NNTP.** Used for publishing public bulletin boards to the Internet for open discussion and exchange of ideas
- **X.400.** Provides the capability to create private connections between Exchange systems using the Internet as an inexpensive WAN

Exchange provides all these services out of the box with no additional software, which makes it a very worthy Internet mail host. However, it does all of this without compromising the internal email system.

POP Mail

From the beginning, the Internet craze has been driven by standards (*de facto* or otherwise). POP mail is the standard for email reception. The capability to connect to the server with a POP client from across the Internet to read mail is a feature that needs to be universal. One of Microsoft's initial goals for Exchange was for it to be accessible to all clients—and POP is as common keyboards.

POP email is not something that must be added or installed in Exchange; it's added as part of the default installation. If a user has an account and can access the Exchange server through the network, he or she can use POP mail. The rules are the same as they are for any other POP server:

- Know the IP address or DNS name of the server
- Know your account name
- Know your password

Web Mail

The capability to interact with email systems over the Web is a fairly recent introduction to the Internet. The idea involves the access a Web page that allows the user to see his or her inbox and to create new email from anywhere that he or she has access to the Web. Exchange takes this idea a bit further by allowing the user access to nearly any feature of the Exchange system that's accessible from the Outlook client (see Figures 21.9 and 21.10).

FIGURE 21.9
The Outlook client.

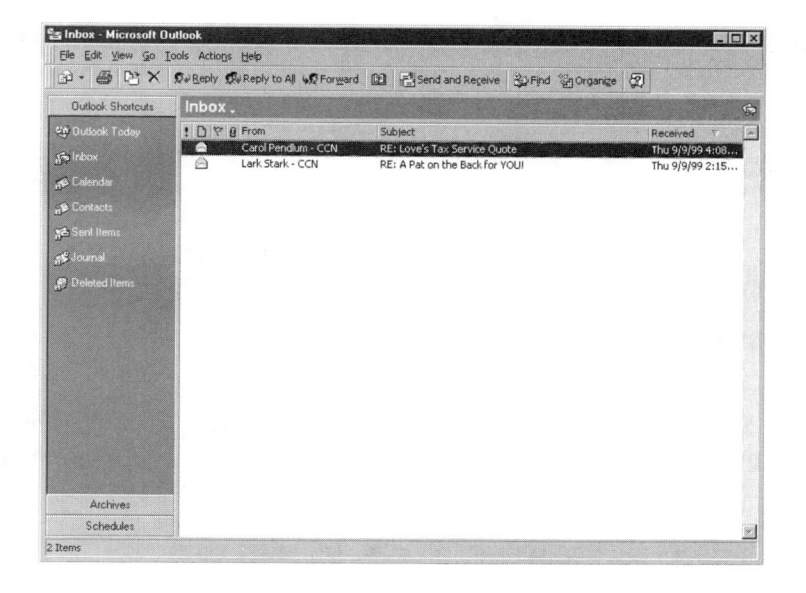

FIGURE 21.10
The Web Outlook client.

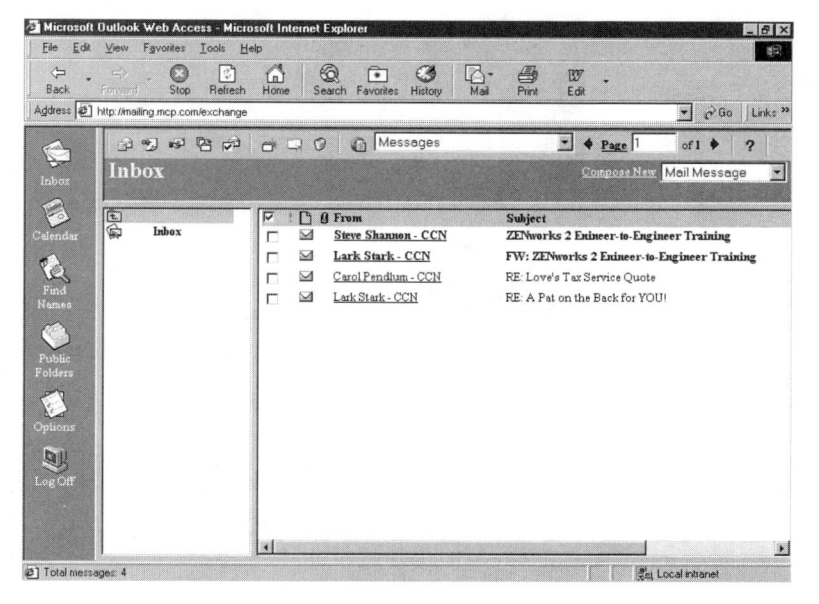

This feature is a choice that's made during the installation of Exchange, and it requires Internet Information Server be installed along with Active Server Pages. It's also best if the Exchange 5.5 service packs have been added.

Once installed, the Web Outlook client allows the user to see and update his or her calendar, read email, send email, access public folders, and create tasks. This effectively removes any barrier that might exist between the server platform and the client. This product makes a client available to any computer that can access the Internet (a Macintosh, a UNIX Workstation, a Windows 3.1 client, and so on).

SMTP Mail

When Exchange creates a connection to any server other then those within its own site, it uses something called a *connector*. The Internet connector is installed by starting a wizard for new Internet connection (see Figure 21.11). Once the wizard is started, it asks several simple questions and then the SMTP server is created.

FIGURE 21.11
The Internet Connection Wizard.

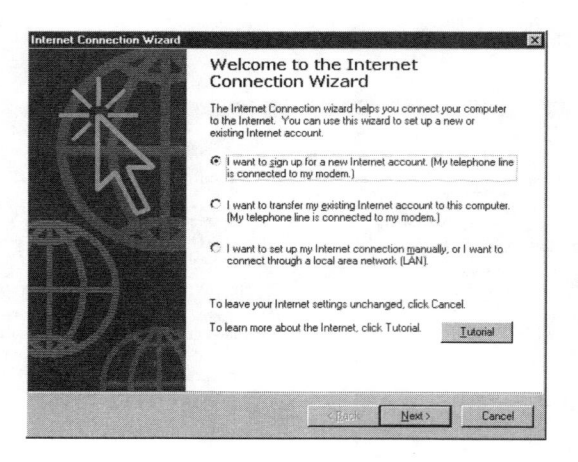

SMTP (Simple Message Transfer Protocol) makes Exchange capable of exchanging email with any Internet email server that uses this standard form of communications. It also makes any user in the system capable of sending and receiving email from the Internet. This was an important part of making the Internet basic to the system. It's not an add-on purchased at an extra cost; instead, it's a basic service.

This is not to be confused with the POP server. SMTP is the service used to receive and send email between servers. To use it in the public system of the Internet, an administrator has to register the domain name (DNS) with the InterNIC and an MX record must be part of that listing. (See Chapter 8, "TCP/IP Networking," for more on DNS and MX records.)

Exchange as an SMTP host makes for a powerful implementation of a fairly simple protocol. Exchange allows the administrator to leverage a strong administration tool to perform some elaborate tasks with relative ease.

An administrator can choose specific URLs that are allowed to send and receive mail within the company. This allows the server to be set up as a private email system that happens to use the Internet as a WAN. It also allows the system to block particularly obnoxious groups that may "spam" or "storm" the server.

By using the mail queues for monitoring and managing traffic in and out of the site, the administrator can pinpoint problems. If, for example, an email that's arriving in the queue can be seen leaving again, it's probable that something is amiss with the recipient or server protocols. Obviously, the message was sent and the server saw it. By watching the inbound and outbound queues, the administrator can see mail messages, who they are to, and where they came from.

You can choose which services are allowed to interact with the Internet, thus preventing the server from becoming a junk mail (spam) utility. Many junk email generators will first find a site that automatically replies that an email recipient doesn't exist or will allow any SMTP client package to forward email through it. If this isn't controlled, an email system can be brought to its knees pretty quickly.

Exchange will allow email for several URLs to come into the same server. This allows users to maintain several email addresses but one inbox and server. Each user in Exchange has multiple addresses that are associated with them. Addresses are associated with a particular email service. Any email that's received is checked against the list of user address space. Because each user can have several addresses, he or she can also receive for several names.

NNTP

Public folders were discussed in the opening of this section, but I didn't discuss quite how public these folders could really become. In Exchange clients, the public folders are accessed in the Folders portion of the user interface. However, this interface is really an access to a private data store. NNTP (Network News Transport Protocol) is the public form of this system.

NNTP is sometimes called Usenet news, news, and bulletin boards, but the concept is the same. Users attach to NNTP servers using a "newsreader" that's often part of a Web browser package or a POP email reader (see Figure 21.12). Once in these servers, the users see a hierarchical representation of a directory system that contains public notes and information. This system sounds a great deal like the public folders that exist in Exchange, and Exchange can serve and receive this protocol.

FIGURE 21.12
The Outlook Express news reader.

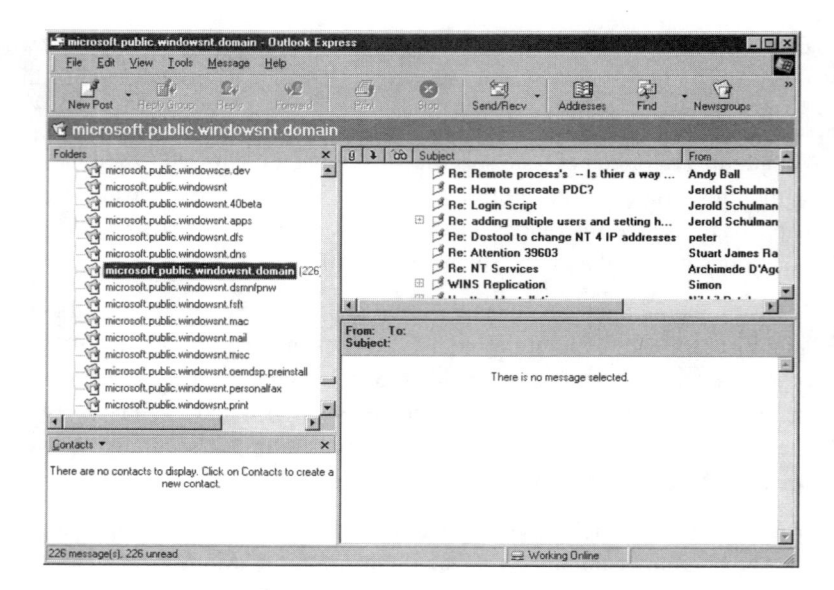

By enabling the public folders in Exchange to use NNTP, the Exchange server becomes capable of receiving public feeds of news and discussions to add to the information store kept for the user base. Exchange is not able to receive these feeds but will take the postings of the internal users and send them back to the source of the group. This allows the internal user base to participate in a public debate and gather information from within the private system.

FrontPage

When the World Wide Web was introduced, Web sites were in the realm of the computer savvy. This often lead to sights that were technically correct but left a great deal to be desired in the way of formatting and creativity. The design and marketing people who would normally work with the presentation of the company were not only unaware of how to manage a Web site, they were often downright scared. What was needed was a way to create content that catered to the creative group but that was powerful enough to make a technically sound product.

Many different Web-content editors have been introduced in the last five years, and Microsoft has introduced several of its own. The mainstream editor for Microsoft is a product called *FrontPage*. The difference between FrontPage and most of Microsoft's other Web editors is that FrontPage is the only one dedicated to Web editing.

Creating Web Sites, Not Just Web Pages

The FrontPage package was purchased by Microsoft as a flagship package for Web publishing for the mainstream. What was needed was a package that allowed editors to edit Web pages as easily as they could word-processing documents—a package that allowed the administrator to edit a single page as well as allowed the editor to see and manage the ramifications of that page on the whole Web site.

> **Note**
>
> Web editors are often simply HTML (Hypertext Markup Language) editors. The HTML language is the root of the Web page and is a type of code that's used to tell the Web browser how to present a page. Originally, Web pages were written like programs in a program language.

The majority of Web-editing packages are glorified HTML editors that simply take the page that's created in a WYSIWYG (What You See Is What You Get) front end and translate it into HTML code. FrontPage also presents a WYSIWYG way of editing single documents. However, the strength of the product is Web site management.

When Web publishing began, sites run by most publishers were literally collections of Web pages. They had no relationship to each other and they were, for most part, just "billboards" in cyberspace. FrontPage was a product that allowed administrators to see the relationship between pages (see Figure 21.13). By offering the ability to manage and see relationships between pages in a site, FrontPage becomes a site manager, not just an editor.

A FrontPage Web site begins by allowing the creator to open either a blank web or any of the numerous templates that are offered to get the site started. The templates come with a prebuilt web that requires all information to be personalized to match a company's needs. However, it requires far less creativity from the creator. Once a template is chosen from the New Web menu, you are lead through the creation of your web by wizards. You answer their questions to create the Web site.

A *blank web* is just what it sounds like. However, this doesn't mean that no help is offered. Throughout the process of adding content to the pages in the site, you are offered help. If, for example, you're working on the first page and would like to reference a page that will exist in the progression of your work, you can do this. In fact, FrontPage will allow you to create the link and then either edit the referenced page immediately or add the page to a to-do list.

FIGURE 21.13

FrontPage Hyperlink view.

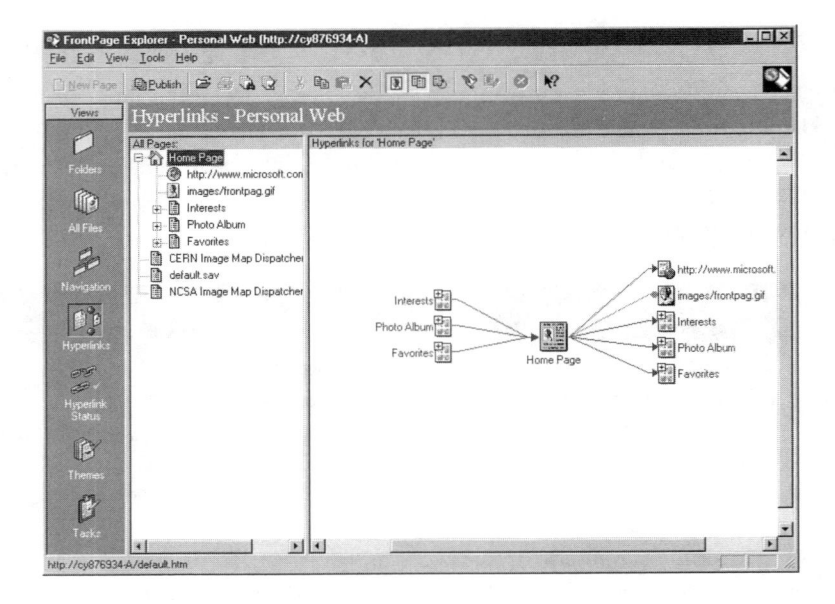

The to-do list is another helpful feature in FrontPage. A difficult part of creating any Web site is keeping track of links that have been created and where they go. At any point throughout the project, you can open the to-do list and see the items that remain unconnected or need to be created to complete the site.

Imagine that at some point during the life of a complete and mature Web site, the company's name changes or the Marketing department decides to call a product by a different name. Simple: The editor just needs to find every time the company name is mentioned or every occurrence of the product on the Web site. FrontPage, being a site-editing and management package, makes this process much easier.

The tools are present in FrontPage for editing every page in a site from one place. Here are some of the things you can do:

- Spell-check the site
- Find and/or replace a word or word combination
- Change the URL to access a page or site and have that change propagated throughout the site wherever the URL is used
- Find an image and replace all instances of it throughout the site

The fact that a Web site is created on a Windows server allows FrontPage to manage security onsite. FrontPage has a menu tool that allows the security of a Web site to be managed directly from the same tool used to manage the other facilitates of the site. This allows the administrator of the Web site to understand and manage Web sites without having to be an NOS administrator. Nuances like this help to allow the creative people to get more deeply involved in the complete management of a site.

As part of the delivery of complex content in a simplified form, FrontPage contains page wizards known as *bots*. The term *bot* is obviously an abbreviation of the term *robot*, and the bot in FrontPage behaves a bit like a robot—it performs tasks for the editor without the editor needing to write complex code.

Here are some examples of bots:

- *Forms Bot*. Helps create forms in the body of a Web page that will either save the content to a separate text file or send it to an email recipient.
- *Include Bot*. Includes content from another Web site on the current page. This is useful when a common piece of data must appear on every Web page in a site, especially if that content might change regularly.
- *Date Bot*. Includes the date of the last revision for the page it's used on.

In order for some bots to function, it's necessary for the server to contain code written for the servicing of FrontPage webs. This code is called a *FrontPage extension*.

Server Extensions

Web sites in FrontPage can be created on the local machine that the author is sitting at and copied to the server, or they can be created and edited right on the server. In order for you to get the most functionality from FrontPage, it's best if the Web site is created and edited on the server. This is necessary to allow the administrator to control security, use bots, and to see issues that may arise on the site.

In order to create and manage FrontPage Web sites on the server, you need to install FrontPage server extensions on the server. Microsoft includes extensions for several different Web site servers, including some competitors. The extensions add code that's needed to make the magic that occurs in a FrontPage Web site.

Summary

The Web is not the Internet. It's actually just a presentation tool for the resources that exist on the Internet. Windows 2000 can host many tools as part of a complete Internet presence.

Exchanging information over email can be more than a nice feature of the company network—it can consume it. The Exchange Server product from Microsoft makes it possible to host a full-featured email system in house and provide complete Internet mail services.

Security is a concern that's often overlooked in a company that's connected to the Internet. Microsoft Proxy Server creates a simple-to-use and powerful firewall between the company and the outside world. While providing security, Proxy is also maintaining a cache of the sites and information being accessed. This allows the Internet connection to be less taxed and more efficient.

Finally, having a Web site is of little value if the content on that site is no better then a billboard of tacked-up information. Marketing personnel and creative groups within the corporation can be empowered to create Web content with FrontPage. Not only can better content from a creative standpoint be created, but with bots and server extensions, sites can be technically sound as well.

CHAPTER 22

Virtual Private Networks

In This Chapter

- Making the Internet Your Own WAN   *570*
- What Is a Virtual Private Network?   *571*
- Security and Encryption   *572*
- Tunnel Servers   *573*
- VPN Tunnel Servers and Firewalls   *574*
- Filtering Traffic with a Tunnel Server   *575*
- Microsoft Windows 2000 VPN   *576*
- IPSec   *577*
- Layer 2 Tunneling Protocol   *577*
- Synchronous and Asynchronous Keys   *578*
- L2TP and IPSec   *579*
- Setting Up a Basic VPN in Windows 2000   *579*
- Setting Up a Tunnel Server VPN with Windows 2000   *582*
- RRAS Enhancements   *582*

Virtual Private Networks (VPNs) have become one of the fastest growing uses of the Internet today. As corporations become more and more connected, their telecommunication costs can skyrocket. Branch offices, the traveling sales force, and telecommuters all need access to network resources in a secure fashion that's also cost efficient. Not too long ago, your only option was a WAN (wide area network) over leased lines (private links purchased from the phone company). The advantage was that this was your private link—no other company could use it. This is very secure, and bandwidth is guaranteed. The disadvantage was cost: A single T1 line (1.54Mbps) could cost you $1,500 a month. If you needed more bandwidth, T3 lines (45Mbps) could be purchased at a cost of $15,000 to $100,000 per month, depending on location. A rather secure solution indeed, but not one that easily fits into the budget of many IT departments. This is where VPNs are able to span the gap.

But to many, the concept of VPNs is foreign, sometimes even mystical. This problem has been brought on by the network industry itself. The term *VPN* has been used rather recklessly to describe many sorts of solutions that are not necessary to a VPN. This chapter will attempt to remove some of the mystery behind VPNs and demonstrate the usefulness, cost effectiveness, and security of this technology.

Before we go any further, let's take an overview look at the chapter:

- Making the Internet your own WAN
- What is a Virtual Private Network?
- Security and encryption
- Tunnel servers
- Microsoft VPN
- Layer 2 Tunneling Protocol and IPSec
- Setting up a basic VPN in Windows 2000
- RRAS improvements

Making the Internet Your Own WAN

Most IT department budgets are not infinite, and costs need to be balanced. You need to connect your office in Los Angeles with the corporate headquarters in Kansas City. So, you make a call to your favorite telecommunications giant and order a T1 line between the two offices. As you look over the numbers you realize that you'll either have to get rid of your existing T1 connection to the Internet or fire the boss's son, who currently works as your System Administrator. Realizing that the latter option is not really an option, you look into the first option, but you cannot afford to lose your connectivity to the Internet. The Sales department uses this connection to communicate with clients, the engineering staff researches technology through the Web, and you use it to find information to keep your network running. There must be another solution. As you look at the problem some more, you realize that you're paying for a 24-hour, 7-days-a-week solution that you only truly utilize 5 percent of the time.

The truth is you already have a WAN solution. After all, you're already sending email between offices using the Internet. Why not the rest of your files? What if you have a connection that offers you a similar level of security and reliability as your private T1 without all the cost? This is where VPNs come into the picture. VPNs offer you the ability to use the Internet or other public networks as a WAN connection while still offering the security of a private link.

What Is a Virtual Private Network?

A *Virtual Private Network* is a private connection between two machines or networks that sends private data over a public or shared network, such as the Internet. The connection between the machines or networks is created in such a way as to simulate a private connection similar to the one that these machines would have over a private leased line. Applications will see the connection as a private link and not need to be aware of the connectivity issues associated with the Internet. This is accomplished through the concept of *tunneling*. Basically, two IP devices create a tunnel between them, where data from any application is wrapped up (or *encapsulated*) at one end, unwrapped at the other end, and then passed on to the application receiving the data as if a direct connection existed. The applications are not aware of any of the routing or various connections through the Internet. Data is packaged up, sent down the tunnel, unpacked at the other end, and handed off to the application.

The concept of tunneling is actually very similar to a protocol you may already be familiar with—the Point-to-Point Protocol (or PPP). This is what you already use to connect to the Internet when you dial up with a modem. Along with having some of the same concepts as PPP, tunneling also has similar benefits. The two major benefits are simplicity and transparency. Tunneling keeps VPNs from needlessly implementing the functionality of higher-level protocols; data is simply packaged up and sent to the other end to be taken care of there. You can even transport other protocols such as IPX and AppleTalk by encapsulating them in an IP packet. In a nutshell, VPNs simulate a point-to-point connection while utilizing a public network.

So where does encryption come in, or what about all those other mysterious concepts such as private keys, public keys, and authentication? These are all important concepts to VPNs and will be covered later in the chapter, but the important thing to realize here is that VPNs do not have to be that complicated. You can choose to send your private data through the Internet unencrypted, but you probably won't make this choice. The head of engineering may frown upon the fact that the designs for the latest and greatest technology are being passed through the Internet in a clear format for anyone who can capture them to read. This is where VPNs are really effective. When you combine VPN tunneling and encryption technologies, you get a connection that's as secure, if not more secure, as private leased lines. Data is not only encapsulated but also encrypted to ensure the privacy and integrity of your files.

Security and Encryption

So we've decided that it's not such a good idea to just bundle up our data packets and send them out into the Internet for anyone to see. Who knows who's out there listening? However, we have more to be concerned about than just who's listening. How do you know that the file you send out says the same thing it did when it left? How can you be sure that the people logging into your network via a VPN are who they say they are and that their passwords and credentials are not compromised? How can you keep unwanted traffic out? VPN technology covers all these issues quite well with very little complexity for the end user.

Currently, Microsoft's Point-to-Point Tunneling Protocol (PPTP) is the most widely used protocol for VPNs. This protocol was developed by Microsoft and 3Com as an open industry standard. It was included in Windows NT Server 4.0, Windows 98, and as a component of the Dial-Up Networking 1.2 Upgrade for Windows 95. In Windows 2000 there has been considerable functionality added to PPTP and VPN services, including support for certificates, the Layer 2 Tunneling Protocol (L2TP), and Internet Protocol Security (IPSec). PPTP's popularity is due in part to its ease of use. PPTP handles both data encapsulation and data stream encryption, even when transporting other non-IP-based protocols.

Microsoft's implementation of PPTP uses Microsoft Point-to-Point Encryption (MPPE) to encrypt VPN traffic. MPPE is based on the RSA RC4 encryption algorithm and can use 40-bit or 128-bit keys (use of 128-bit keys is restricted by the U.S. government to use only in North America). PPTP creates a tunnel between the client workstation and the server. The client negotiates PPP with the server, often referred to as the *tunnel terminator*, and an encryption session is initiated. MPPE encrypts PPP packets on the client side before they enter the PPTP tunnel. The tunnel terminator decrypts the packets and passes them on to their final destination.

MPPE also utilizes Microsoft Challenge-Handshake Authentication Protocol version 2 or MS-CHAP. MS-CHAP is an authentication method for validating user credentials against

Windows NT domains. When a server receives an MS-CHAP authentication request from a remote client, it sends a challenge. This challenge includes an arbitrary challenge string and the session ID. The remote client will then return the username, a hash of the challenge string, the session ID, and a hashed password.

This form of authentication is important not only to the server to validate the user but also to the client. There's a form of network intrusion known as the "man in the middle" attack. In this situation, potential intruders place themselves in the middle of a communication between a server and a client after communication is established so that they can trick a user into passing them information. Because connectivity includes Session IDs and hashed arbitrary challenge strings, the client can be relatively sure that the server it's communicating with is the server it intended to communicate with. Therefore, you can see that not only is it important to encrypt data packets before they're transmitted to a public network but that authentication, the capability on both ends of the tunnel to ensure that someone is who they say they are, is equally important.

Although all this encryption and authentication is necessary, there's also considerable overhead to go along with it. Encryption is often not for the weak of heart or of processor. With every data packet there's data overhead, which lessens the effective bandwidth. Then comes the encrypting and decrypting. There's latency to go with this, as well, which gives the impression of even less bandwidth. Sometimes it seems amazing that we get any information through this VPN tunnel at all. If you have less than the latest and greatest processor, your users' impressions of VPNs might not be so great. However, this issue can be minimized with the use of dedicated VPN tunnel servers.

Tunnel Servers

If the use of encryption is going to slow your users' late-model computers to a crawl, you have two options. You can replace everyone's computers or offload some of this encryption overhead to a dedicated machine built to handle this task, such as a tunnel server. You could set up your entire VPN without the use of VPN software on the client workstations. If you have two LANs to connect, you set up a tunnel server—otherwise known as the *tunnel initiator*—to create the tunnel to the server on the other LAN, a terminating tunnel server, and allow these machines to handle all encryption and building of the tunnel. This brings in two concepts we should probably cover before going any further: voluntary and compulsory tunnels.

There are two forms of tunnels: voluntary and compulsory. To create a voluntary tunnel, the client must be VPN enabled, meaning it must have the software and hardware to create the VPN tunnels itself or volunteer to use a VPN. Compulsory tunnels are used when the client relies on a VPN-enabled tunnel server, rather than the client workstation, to handle creating tunnels and encrypting. These clients have no control over the use of a VPN; therefore, they're compelled to use it (hence the name *compulsory tunnels*).

You may have a situation where all your traffic from Kansas City is routed to a tunnel initiator where the tunnel is created and data is encrypted. This data is passed down the tunnel to the Los Angeles office, where it's decrypted at the tunnel terminator and passed on to the network. Client workstations are not aware that this is even happening, and no overhead is taken by the workstation. This would be an example of a compulsory tunnel.

A common example of a voluntary tunnel is a single workstation that dials up to the Internet. This workstation negotiates the tunnel and encryption with a server on the LAN it wants to communicate with. This machine does take on the overhead of the VPN connection itself. Often this form of VPN is used with single remote users such as traveling salespersons and telecommuters.

We could even take this a step further and pass the overhead of VPNs onto someone else entirely. Many Internet service providers and Network service providers offer VPN services where you pass your traffic off to them and they create the VPN tunnel for you. In this situation, you connect your network with theirs and pass the traffic to be routed to them. Then, they encrypt it, send it through the Internet, and decrypt it at the other end, finally passing it off to you. This will cost more than a plain Internet connection but will be considerably less than a leased line.

VPN Tunnel Servers and Firewalls

Use of a dedicated VPN tunnel server with some form of encryption does not necessarily answer all your security worries for VPNs. The next issue you'll need to tackle is where to put your tunnel server. Because most networks connected to the Internet use some form of a firewall to protect their networks, the question of tunnel server placement is relative to the firewall. You'll have three options for placement: inside your network (behind the firewall), outside your network (outside the firewall), and actually on the firewall. All these placements have their benefits and detractions.

Your first inclination may be to put the tunnel server behind the firewall; after all, you use the firewall to protect most other servers by limiting access to them. In most cases, this is a reasonable assumption and there are benefits to doing this. The firewall would protect the tunnel server from attacks based on weaknesses in the tunnel server—either in the OS or your implementation of it. It could also minimize the likelihood of a Denial of Service (DOS) attack. This occurs when a not-so-friendly person on the Internet attacks your system, not to break in, but to deny the use of that system, either by exploiting a bug in the system or overwhelming it with traffic to the point where it will not respond. A firewall will protect you from these exploits but, by placing the tunnel server inside, you actually lose part of the main functionality of your firewall—control of the destination of traffic into your network.

When traffic destined for your tunnel server passes through the firewall, the data packets are encrypted. The firewall cannot examine them to see where they're going. Therefore, traffic can go to any server via the tunnel server, and the firewall is powerless to control it. You may have a rule on your firewall that protects your mainframe from unauthorized traffic, yet your tunnel server may inadvertently pass that traffic through. Your firewall would be unaware of the destination of the packet after it leaves the tunnel server. Actually, the safer placement of the VPN tunnel server is outside the firewall.

When the tunnel server is placed outside the firewall, all traffic destined for the inside is decrypted before it gets to the firewall. The firewall can still control the destination for traffic with its rule set. A tunnel is created with the tunnel server; data is encrypted at the far end of the tunnel and decrypted at the terminating tunnel server. The terminating tunnel server then will attempt to pass the data to the inside network but not before the firewall verifies the connection is allowed. However, this leaves your tunnel server somewhat exposed to the Internet. At this point, you would apply filtering on the tunnel server.

Filtering Traffic with a Tunnel Server

PPTP has the option of filtering the traffic it accepts. This can be done in different ways. First, you can control whether the tunneling server accepts any non-PPTP traffic. If this option is enabled, all non-PPTP traffic will be ignored. Traffic can also be filtered based on the final destination of the data. Why pass the traffic on to your firewall if it's already known that this traffic is not allowed through? Traffic can also be filtered based on the client it comes from. Conversely, outgoing traffic can also be filtered based on its destination or where it originated.

Filtering on the tunnel server is a useful tool. When you're setting up security in a network, it's very important to layer your security. What this means is that you can never count on just one aspect of your security policy to secure your network. When you utilize filtering on your VPN tunnel servers, you add additional layers to your security model. First, traffic is controlled or filtered at the tunnel server; if it's allowed by this security level, the traffic is then passed on to the firewall. The firewall examines the traffic based on its rule set; if it's permissible, it passes the traffic on to the internal network. Finally, your internal network verifies permissions to specific network resources; if the requesting party has the proper credentials, the resource is made available. Because the security policy includes many layers, you're not dependent on a single layer to protect every aspect of the network. If a layer, for whatever reason, fails to restrict access, there's a good chance that the next layer will still restrict access to the network resource.

You do have another option for tunnel server placement. On some firewalls you have a network that's often referred to as a *DMZ* (this is analogous to the military's Demilitarized Zone). A DMZ is another network connected to your firewall, with its own interface on the firewall, but it's not connected directly to your internal network or the Internet. Often, Web servers and mail servers are placed in the DMZ so that they're protected by the firewall but do not directly expose the internal network to outside traffic. You could place your tunnel server in a DMZ. This keeps the tunnel server protected by the firewall, but the firewall still controls the destination of data after the tunnel server passes it on, because the data has to go back through the firewall to reach its final destination. This gives you the best of both worlds. The only downside to this implantation is the added complexity of the network. Also, your firewall might not have an extra interface available to create a DMZ.

One final note about firewalls and tunnel server placement. Many implementations of firewalls use what is known as *Network Address Translation* (NAT). NAT translates IP addresses at the firewall so that a network can hide its true IP structure or use private networking schemes and still connect to the Internet. Often VPNs do not handle NAT very well because the data packet is encrypted. You may have some problems if you decide to put your tunnel server behind a firewall that implements NAT.

One other option that's available to you in the VPN world is the *front-end processor* (FEP). A FEP is a dial-up server that can create a PPTP tunnel on behalf of its dial-up clients. This service is really useful when provided by a third party. Someone else can handle the hassle of modem pools and providing local or toll-free access to users. Many ISPs and NSPs offer many points of presence for dialing in to FEPs, which then pass data on to a terminating tunnel server connected to your local network. Keep in mind where the ISP's points of presence are located; they should be a local call for your remote users, thus lowering the cost of communication. Also, if you like, you can purchase your own FEP equipment and create your own dial-up modem pool.

Microsoft Windows 2000 VPN

In Windows 2000, Microsoft has added many features and security enhancements to Routing and Remote Access Services Server (RRAS) and its VPN implementation. The two major enhancements are Layer 2 Tunneling Protocol (L2TP) and IP Security Protocol (IPSec). With the implementation of these protocols, Microsoft has also increased Windows 2000's capability to interconnect with other non-Microsoft devices, such as routers and firewalls.

IPSec

IPSec is a protocol designed to provide data integrity protection and authentication. It also offers privacy and replay protection options for IP traffic. Because this is an open protocol and not proprietary to Microsoft, it provides interoperability to other systems.

IPSec is broken into two packet types: IP protocol 50 and IP protocol 51. IP protocol 50—otherwise known as the Encapsulating Security Payload (ESP) format—provides privacy, authenticity, and data integrity. IP protocol 51 (or the Authentication Header (AH) format) only provides integrity and authenticity but not privacy. IPSec is used in two modes: transport mode and tunnel mode.

Transport mode provides security for IP traffic from source to destination between two systems. This mode would provide encryption from end to end of a connection but no real tunneling capability. The packet is encapsulated and encrypted and sent to the end destination. But what if you would like to route this packet through a more complex network? The packet is encrypted; therefore, some necessary routing information is encrypted also. This is what the tunneling mode provides.

IPSec tunnel mode puts an existing IP packet inside a new packet to be sent to the tunnel endpoint. Tunnel mode is designed mainly for midpoints in the network, such as routers, gateways, and firewalls. Through IPSec, these devices can decrypt part of the IP packet so that they can be aware of routing issues and pass the data packet to its final destination in a secure fashion. IPSec is not really designed for remote-user VPN access; it was designed more for point-to-point security or compulsory tunnels. Layer 2 Tunneling Protocol is better suited for use in a situation where a single user is creating a voluntary tunnel to a tunnel server over a public network.

Layer 2 Tunneling Protocol

When PPTP was first implemented and offered with Windows Dial-Up Networking version 1.2 Upgrade, some features were in need of further development. Layer 2 Forwarding was being developed by Cisco and would cover some of these features that PPTP lacked. Therefore, it was understood that eventually these two protocols would be merged. The product of this merger was Layer 2 Tunneling Protocol.

Layer 2 Tunneling Protocol is a proposed Internet Engineering Task Force (IETF) standard protocol that uses public-key technology to perform user authentication and operates over a wider variety of communication media than PPTP. L2TP does not provide encryption but is used to create tunnels over which encrypted data is passed. Data can be sent over IP, X.25, Frame Relay, and asynchronous transfer networks (ATNs). When configured to use IP, L2TP can be used over the Internet and can even transport non-Internet protocols such as IPX and AppleTalk.

L2TP encapsulates PPP frames and sends them to the terminating tunnel server using UDP port 1701. This communication includes L2TP control messages for tunnel maintenance as well as the encapsulated PPP frames. These frames can be compressed or encrypted. L2TP can utilize authentication options such as CHAP, MS-CHAP, and Extensible Authentication Protocol (EAP). L2TP was designed for both end-to-end use and client connections to access servers. L2TP is a natural evolution from PPTP because it adds security features and greater media flexibility. Combined with IPSec, it provides an open standard for creating very secure and reliable VPNs.

Synchronous and Asynchronous Keys

Both IPSec and L2TP use Internet Key Exchange (IKE), which in turn uses Public Key Infrastructure (PKI) certificates for mutual authentication. This means that you can now use asynchronous keys that are considerably more secure than synchronous keys.

Originally with PPTP, synchronous keys were utilized. This meant that in order to have a secure connection, both parties had to agree on a key. In order for them to use this key, it would have to be transported from one system to the other. Both sides used the same key. If you wanted another system to use this key, you had to provide a copy of it via email, fax, written letter, Morse code, verbal communication, or a built-in mechanism in the VPN software. This communication could be intercepted and used to decrypt your data, or the party on the other end could share this with others, without your control.

This is where you could benefit from asynchronous keys. Each party creates a set of keys: a public key and a private key. These keys are not the same but are mathematically similar. You can give out your public key to anyone you like, and you keep your private key secret. If someone wants to send you encrypted data, he or she encrypts it using your public key. This is one-way encryption, so if someone else captures your data, he or she cannot decrypt it even if he or she has your public key. Only you can decrypt this data with your private key, because only you have this key. Likewise, if you encrypt data with your private key, it can be decrypted with your public key. This does not provide data privacy, because anyone may have your public key, but it does give you a method of signing your data to prove that it only came from you. Because only you possess your private key, only you could have sent this data.

With IPSec, both ends of the connection utilize a public and a private key, thus providing the capability to encrypt and verify data integrity. When a tunnel server receives data from you, it can utilize your public key to verify that the data was encrypted by you using your private key. Likewise, when you receive data from the tunnel server, encrypted with its private key, you can verify the integrity of the data and decrypt it with the server's public key. Therefore, both sides of the connection can ensure the privacy and integrity of the data. You don't have to worry too much about implementing this with Windows 2000, but it is important to understand the concept and how much more beneficial the use of IPSec and L2TP is over PPTP as it relates to data privacy and integrity. With minimal added complication comes a much greater level of security.

L2TP and IPSec

L2TP is a well-designed protocol with greater interoperability than IPSec. It addresses the deficiencies of IPSec in relation to voluntary or client-to-gateway applications and has wide support among other vendors. Yet, it cannot handle encryption—only tunnel creation. IPSec offers excellent encryption and authenticity options but does not support voluntary tunneling very well. Why not combine the two for greater security and interoperability in your VPN?

By combining L2TP and IPSec, you can create a VPN with L2TP as the payload with an encrypted IPSec packet. This combination is often referred to as *L2TP/IPSec*. The use of L2TP in this combination also allows you to utilize some of the benefits of PPP, such as connections, support for multiple protocols (such as IPX), and multicast support.

The only real downfall of this combination is its lack of interoperability with Network Address Translation. As mentioned earlier, VPNs and NATs do not always mix. Because IPSec uses the Internet Key Exchange protocol, it cannot be used with NAT. IKE uses your IP address as part of its authentication. Your IP address is changed by NAT, and IKE cannot verify you. Therefore, if you're using NAT at your firewall, you would need to put your tunnel server outside the firewall. PPTP will handle NAT, and you also may have clients with older software, such as Windows 95, that does not support L2TP/IPSec; therefore, you still may need to implement PPTP for this reason.

Setting Up a Basic VPN in Windows 2000

Before you begin to set up your VPN, you'll need some basic information. First you'll need the IP addresses assigned to your endpoint servers. You can use the IP address to reference these, or you can use a DNS entry. DNS may be a better option here so that if you ever need to change the IP address of your endpoint servers, you'll only need to change it in DNS and not on all your clients. Once you've determined the placement of your VPN server relative to your firewall and set your rule set to allow access through the firewall, you're ready to begin. You may also want to set up Dynamic Host Configuration Protocol (DHCP) so that your clients receive valid IP addresses on your network.

First, let's start with a voluntary VPN. As discussed earlier, with a voluntary VPN, the client handles the task of creating the VPN tunnel and encryption for itself. A good example of this would be a Windows 98 client utilizing the Internet to connect to a domain on your network. Your first step would be to set up the RRAS server to allow this connection.

On the Windows 2000 server, under the Control Panel, choose Network and Dial-up Connections. Here, you'll choose Make New Connection. This will take you to your first splash screen, which explains your options. Choose Next. Your next screen is Network Connection Type. Here, you can choose to dial up to private networks, connect to the Internet, connect to private networks though the Internet, accept incoming connections, or connect directly to another computer. Choose Accept Incoming Connections and click Next (see Figure 22.1).

FIGURE 22.1
The Network Connection Type screen. Choose the Accept Incoming Connections option to set up a voluntary VPN via the Internet.

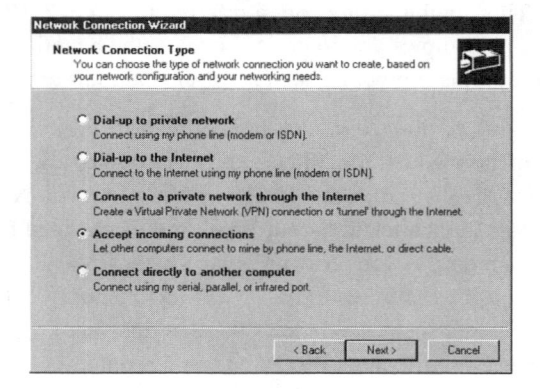

Your next screen will be the Incoming Virtual Private Connection screen. On this screen, choose the Allow Virtual Private Connections and choose Next (see Figure 22.2).

Your next screen is the Allowed Users screen. On this screen, you can choose which users will be allowed to access this machine via the VPN connection. It's important here to only allow users who will be using VPN, not just everybody. Excess user rights can lead to security breaches. This screen will also allow you to add users and change properties per user, such as callback options and passwords. Choose only the users you want to allow connect to VPN and click Next (see Figure 22.3).

FIGURE 22.2

The Incoming Virtual Private Connection screen. Choose the Allow Virtual Private Connections option.

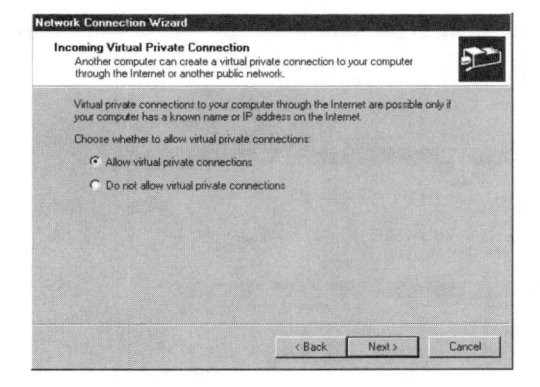

FIGURE 22.3

The Allowed Users screen. Remember to choose only the users who need VPN access.

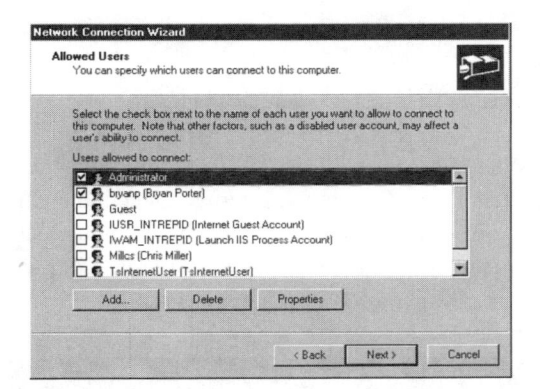

The next screen is Networking Components. This screen allows you to enable or disable network components for your VPN clients. With this screen, you can even add non-Internet standard protocols such as IPX and NetBEUI. Under the properties of each protocol, you can determine whether you'll allow users to access your network with this protocol. Under the Internet Protocol (TCP/IP), you can also determine whether your VPN clients will receive an IP address through DHCP or be directly assigned an IP address by your VPN server. You can also allow the user to choose his or her own IP address. Once again, it's very important to choose only the network components your VPN clients will need. Select these and choose Next (see Figure 22.4).

At this point, you're finished with the setup of your VPN. Choose Finish, and let's look at the setup of the Windows 98 client. Under My Computer, choose Dial-Up Networking. Under Dial-Up Networking, choose Make a New Connection. Here you'll be asked to choose a name for this connection and then choose a device. The name is of your choosing and, under the drop-down menu labeled Select a Device, you'll need to choose Microsoft VPN Adapter. Then click Next. The next screen will ask you for the hostname or IP address. Because you set up DNS to handle resolving this name, you can enter the hostname and choose Next. You're now finished setting the Windows 98 VPN connection. Choose Finish.

FIGURE 22.4

The Networking Components screen. This screen will allow you to choose which network components can be used via VPN. Only choose those that will be needed by VPN clients.

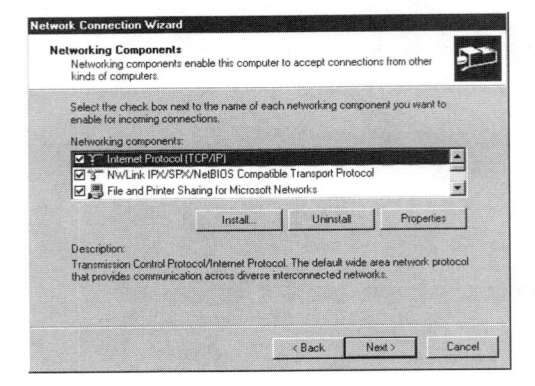

In order to use this across the Internet, the Windows 98 client will need to have an ISP connection through some dial-up medium to the Internet. Once the connection to the Internet is established, the user can choose the VPN connector you created. This connector will resolve the hostname to an IP address using your public DNS server and then connect to the machine, thus creating a VPN tunnel.

> **Note**
>
> Many national ISPs offer multiple points of presence (POPs). Larger national ISPs have a lot of POPs, so you have a better chance of having dial-up connections to the Internet locally as your clients travel. This will cut down on telecommunication expenses. Look for ISPs that offer a large number of POPs and easy-to-use software for choosing to which POP the user dials in.

Setting Up a Tunnel Server VPN with Windows 2000

For our next scenario, let's assume you have a branch office in Wahoo, Nebraska. At this branch office, you have dial-up ISDN access to the Internet and need connectivity to the head office in Omaha. You could set up every workstation as a voluntary VPN client using the ISDN connection, or you could set up a tunnel server and allow the workstations to use this server as a method of connection to the Omaha office.

Setting up a tunnel server VPN (or compulsory VPN) with Windows 2000 is done in much the same way as a voluntary server setup. Under Network and Dial-Up Connections, you choose Make a New Connection. You'll receive the Welcome to the Network Connection Wizard screen; choose Next. Then, you'll go to the Network Connection Type screen; this time choose Connect to a Private Network Through the Internet. Choose Next.

If you already have a dial-up connection established, you'll receive an alternate screen. In this screen (the Public Network screen), you'll be asked whether you want to automatically dial this initial connection. If this is not the initial connection you want to use, choose Do Not Dial the Initial Connection and then click Next (see Figure 22.5).

FIGURE 22.5
The Public Network screen will only come up if you've already established a dial-up connection.

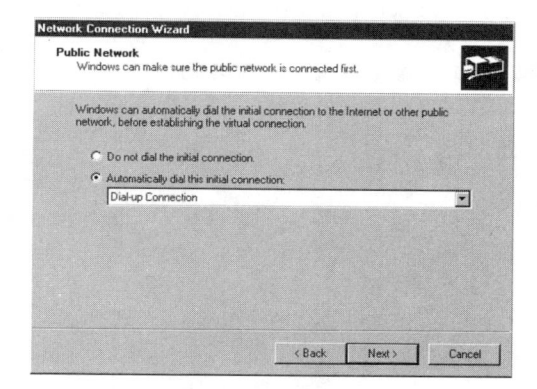

The next screen is the Destination Address screen. Enter the hostname of the terminating VPN server or an IP address and then click Next (see Figure 22.6).

FIGURE 22.6
The Destination Address screen. You can specify the terminating tunnel server by IP address or by hostname.

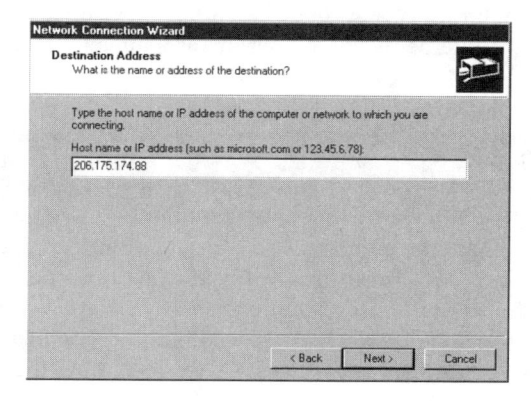

> **Note**
>
> Because you'll only have one server referencing another instead of many clients (as was the case with the Windows 98 example), it might not be necessary to use a hostname and DNS. In fact, it may be more beneficial to use the IP address. If your DNS fails for any reason, it may cause your VPN servers to be unable to connect.

The next screen is Connection Availability. Here you determine whether other clients can use this server as a tunnel server or whether access to the tunnel will be limited to the server. You should choose For All Users and then click Next (see Figure 22.7).

FIGURE 22.7
On the Connection Availability screen, you'll be asked whether to make your VPN open to all users or just this machine. If you're creating a tunnel server, you should choose the For All Users option.

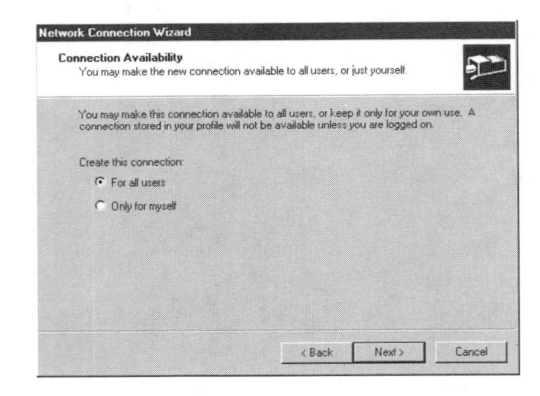

On the Internet Connection Sharing screen, you'll be asked whether you want to enable Internet connection sharing for this connection. This will allow all users to use your machine as a gateway to the Internet while it's serving as a tunnel server. For this example, don't choose this option. Click Next.

> **Warning**
>
> If you do choose to allow Internet connection sharing, you'll need to set up the server to perform network address translation for you. Because the server will be acting as a gateway to the Internet, it will need some Internet legal addresses to assign your users as they go out to the Internet. Windows 2000 will set this up automatically if you really want it to. If you do not have NAT set up, it will assign your inside interface the IP address 192.168.0.1, and you'll have to set all your workstations on this same network. It's probably best to set up NAT ahead of time if you would like to use this option.

You're finished setting up your tunnel server connection, so hit Finish. You'll be prompted to create the connection. If you would like this to log in automatically next time, you'll need to save the password. If you need to change options that you chose, you can right-click on the icon for this connection and choose Properties.

RRAS Enhancements

Microsoft first came out with Routing and Remote Access Server (RRAS) as an upgrade to the Remote Access Server (RAS) that came with Windows NT Server 4.0. This upgrade included additional features such as PPTP/VPN support and greater routing support with additional routing protocols, such as Open Shortest Path First (OSPF). In Windows 2000, further enhancements have been added that allow you to use RRAS as a more full-featured VPN solution. Let's look at these upgrades and how to implement them.

RAS and RRAS supported PPP Multilink, where multiple physical links (ISDN, X.25, or modem links) could be combined into a single logical link that results in greater bandwidth. In Windows 2000, this option is enhanced by the addition of dynamic control of dial-up connections. RRAS can add or eliminate bandwidth by dialing up additional lines or dropping them, as needed. This provides more efficient use of your communication resources by freeing up phone lines if they're not being used. This also lowers resource utilization on the RRAS server.

Windows 2000 also offers enhancements with the AutoDial feature. AutoDial tracks IP addresses and network connections so that they can be dialed only as needed. This allows you to automate the dial-up process so that when a network is referenced, it's dialed up without any user intervention.

To use this feature, open the Network and Dial-up Connections window, choose the Advanced menu, and then choose Dial-Up Preferences. Choose the AutoDial tab. You can enable AutoDial by location. You may want to remove the check mark from the Always Ask Me Before Dialing option, because this is going to be used on a tunnel server.

If you've ever transferred 90 percent of a 20MB file only to lose connectivity, you'll certainly appreciate the restartable file-copy feature of RRAS. This feature automatically resumes a file transfer after a line has been dropped. Where you were in the file-transfer process is tracked and reestablished once you reestablish your connection. There are no attributes to set for this function; just enjoy this enhancement next time you trip over the phone cable and rip it out of the wall.

Earlier in this chapter, we looked at the combination of L2TP and IPSec. Now let's look at some of the issues involved in implementing this enhancement in Windows 2000. As stated before, when you use L2TP for VPN in Windows 2000, you automatically use IPSec. Therefore, there's no real configuration for IPSec at this point. In order to use L2TP, you'll need to create certificates for both sides. This is done with the Microsoft Management Console (MMC). You'll need to create a certificate for each tunnel server and exchange them between servers. Finally, you'll need to change the properties of your connection.

First right-click the VPN connection you created and choose Properties. Under Properties, choose the Networking tab. Here, you'll have a pull-down menu labeled Type of VPN Server I Am Calling. This is set to Automatic. In order to use L2TP, you'll need to set at least one of the servers to L2TP, but you'll probably want to lock in both of them (see Figure 22.8).

FIGURE 22.8
The Properties page for the VPN connection. Here, you can change properties such as the type of VPN server being called.

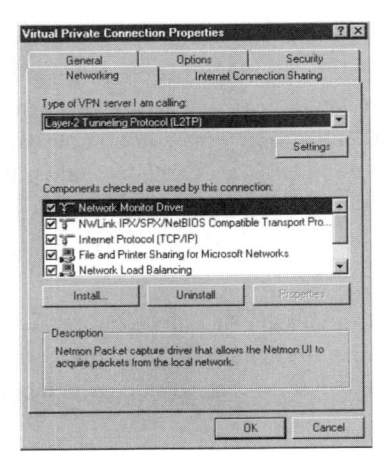

> **Note**
>
> RRAS, by default, only sets up five PPTP or L2TP ports. Therefore, you may want to increase this number. To do so, open Routing and Remote Access, right-click Ports, and choose Properties. Here, you can configure the number of ports. The maximum is 1000.

Summary

As you can see, Microsoft has greatly enhanced the VPN options of Windows 2000 to create a very powerful and versatile server. With the addition of L2TP and IPSec, the level of security offered to the VPN solutions has grown exponentially. These VPN options will allow you to use the Internet as a WAN connection and therefore use your IT budget more efficiently.

Server Administration

PART

VII

IN THIS PART

23 Server Management *589*

24 Optimizing Performance Tuning *605*

25 Server Backup Utilities *669*

26 Recovering from a Disaster *707*

Server Management

CHAPTER 23

IN THIS CHAPTER

- Microsoft Management Console (MMC) *590*
- Server Management Utilities *593*
- SNMP *603*

The administration of a server can take several forms but, for the purpose of this chapter, I refer to the ability to manage the server hardware and hardware as they exist on the server unit. In other words, I am not going to spend a great deal of time concentrating on creating user accounts, deciding on protocols, or dealing with a directory structure, because that has been discussed elsewhere.

I am going to explain how to manage the server itself and the tools you use. Server management can involve

- Server health
- Server involvement in the domain
- Application and service maintenance
- Monitoring user and group activity
- Discovery of services
- Power management

The tools to manage these issues have changed a great deal in Windows 2000, but they have opened up an incredible amount of control and information.

Microsoft Management Console (MMC)

The beginning of the server interface in Windows 2000 is a new front end called the Microsoft Management Console, or MMC. Even though you might have heard the nickname "Mickey Mouse Console," the tool is actually very useful. The console is a customizable management interface that allows the administrator to complete the tasks needed on all servers from one interface.

In its initial form, the tool is nothing more than a blank page waiting for the administrator to add a set of tools that he needs to complete his daily tasks (see Figure 23.1). In that way, the MMC is a bit like an empty tool box that the administrator can fill with tools for specific tasks.

The tools in the MMC are familiar to anyone who has been using this book up to this point because they are the same tools discussed throughout the book. You can use the console tools separately; as individual tools, they do not function any differently. Some examples are the Active Directory Users and Computers tool, Computer Management tool, and DHCP Console.

FIGURE 23.1
An empty Microsoft Management Console (MMC).

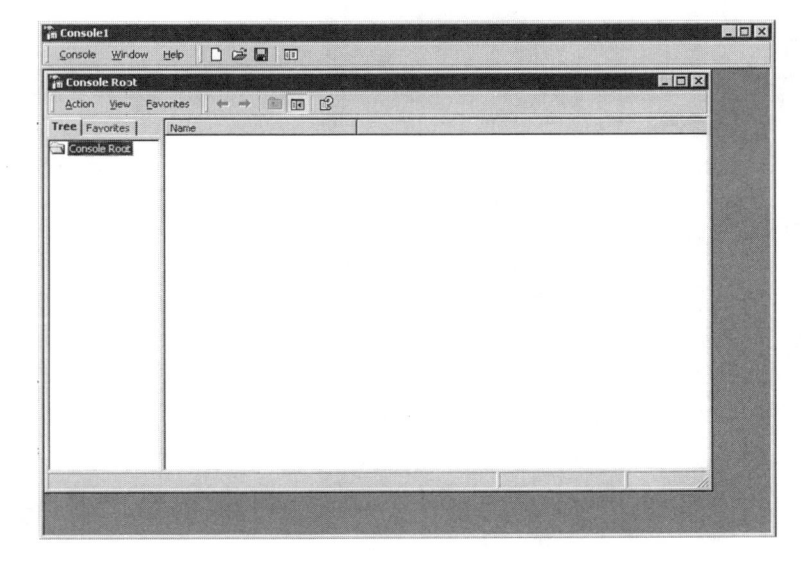

All of the tools added to the console are called "snap-ins" because they are snapped into the console and appear as if they are part of the console. The administrator can add as many or as few snap-ins to the console as he wants and even save different consoles (console settings) as separate tools to be used for different occasions. The look resembles the Windows Explorer in Windows 95/98 and NT 4.0, but you are "exploring" tools. Figure 23.2 shows a populated console with opened tools available in one console.

FIGURE 23.2
Populated MMC console.

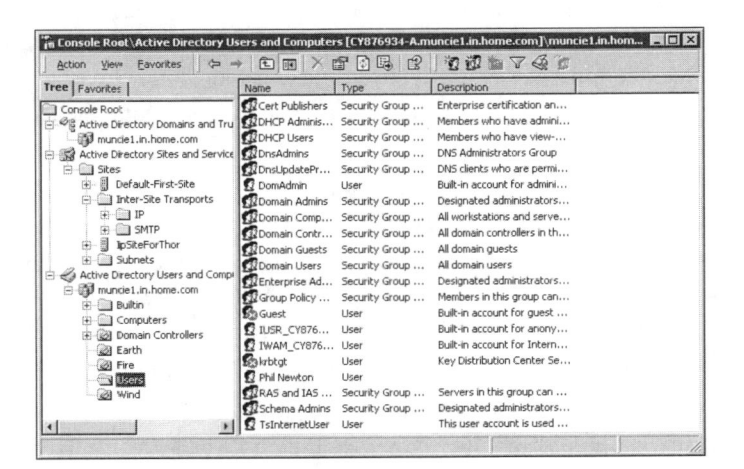

To populate a console, the administrator needs to follow these steps:

1. Open the MMC by choosing Start, Run.
2. Type **MMC** in the text box and press Enter.
3. From the menu, choose Add Standalone Snap-in (see Figure 23.3).

FIGURE 23.3
Add Standalone Snap-in screen.

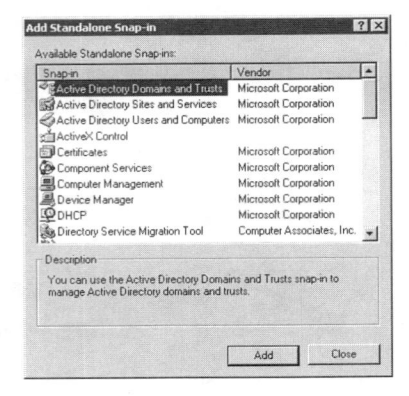

4. Click Add, choose from the list of snap-ins, and click Add again. (Some snap-ins require that you make configuration entries.)
5. When you are finished selecting snap-ins, choose Close and then OK on the next screen.

Once you set up a console the way you need it for certain tasks, consider saving the console as it is. If you do not save the console, then every time that MMC is opened, it must be repopulated in order to be useful. To save a console, simply choose Console, Save. Once a console is saved, you can use it again by double-clicking the icon. You can create all sorts of custom consoles.

You can create and send consoles to remote locations to direct administrators at their areas of responsibility. You might create a console with Active Directory for Users and Computers and Active Directory Domains and Trusts for the administrator of directory issues. A console might include the Computer Management Services and system information could be given to a local hardware administrator. A console could also include DHCP and DNS for a manager of the company domain name system.

The point is that the MMC is not a standalone tool but a tool for creating packages of tools. These tools can be mobile if you save them to a diskette. They can also be adaptive, not limiting an administrator to a single tool.

Server Management Utilities

The previous versions of Windows Server (NT) counted on a product called Server Manager for a great deal of the administrative tasks on the domain and servers. Windows 2000 still has the capability to open this tool (see Figure 23.4), but it is not meant for use in Windows 2000 domains. The Server Manager tool is still around for use in legacy systems.

FIGURE 23.4
Server Manager in Windows 2000.

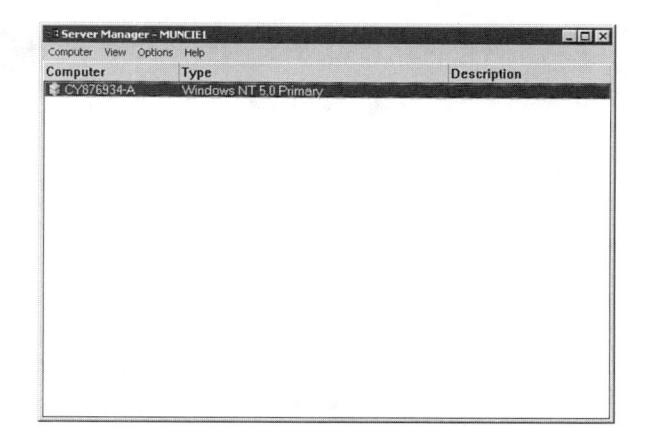

To access Server Manager, follow these steps:

1. Choose Start, Run.
2. Type **SRVMGR** in the text box and press Enter.

The Server Manager utility handled a large number of tasks. The following list shows each task with the Windows 2000 alternative:

- Determine which servers were in control of the domain:

    This can now be done from Active Directory for Users and Computers by simply opening the domain and choosing the Domain Controllers container.

- Determine the resources being shared by the server:

    Shares can be seen in the Computer Management snap-in. This snap-in can be easily reached for each computer in the Active Directory for Users and Computers snap-in by finding the computer that you would like to manage, right-clicking it, and then choosing Manage.

- Control the services being used on a given computer:

    Services can be seen in the Computer Management snap-in.

Many of the services from Server Manager are now in Computer Management. Server Manager could just as easily have been called Computer Management because the tool offers views of workstations and servers that are running Windows 2000 or Windows NT.

Computer Management Console is a tool that breaks down the individual components of the computer in question and allows the administrator to monitor or control them. Figure 23.5 shows the different components.

FIGURE 23.5
Computer Management screen viewing services.

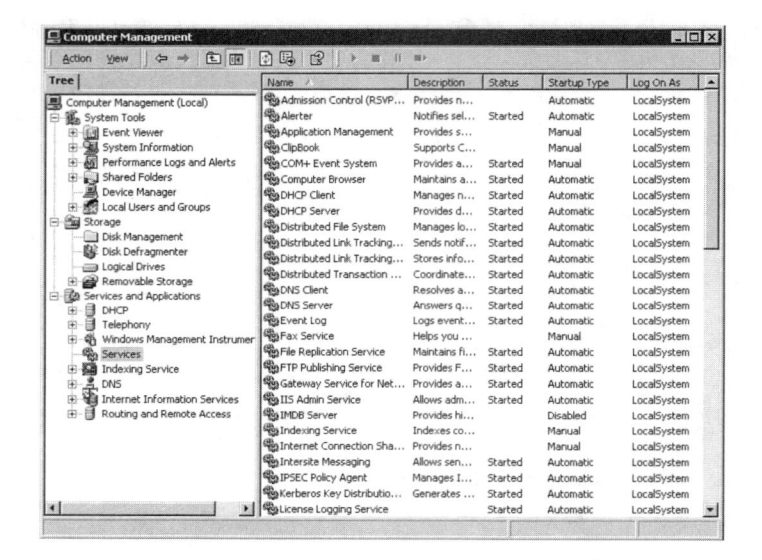

The majority of the things listed in the figure have already been covered extensively throughout the rest of the book, because almost every tool required to manage this server and its services is listed here. This list includes tools for managing the services installed on individual servers, both the disks on the server and those shared by the server, and finding information on the status of the server.

Services not found anywhere else are covered here.

Event Viewer

The majority of support calls logged with Microsoft and its partners can be avoided if the administrators check the Event Viewer tool. The Event Viewer can be run separately or as part of the Computer Management tool. Its primary purpose is to allow the administrator to track the changes that occur in the operating system and the applications that run on a server.

All too often, field engineers or phone support people answer a call about a system failing with no record of the specific error that occurred. The caller becomes aggravated when it takes a long time to resolve. These intermittent problems can most likely be solved with help from the specific information in the Event Log.

Viewing Events

To start the Event Viewer separately from Computer Management, simply run Event Viewer from the Programs, Administrative Tools menu (see Figure 23.6).

FIGURE 23.6
The Event Viewer tool.

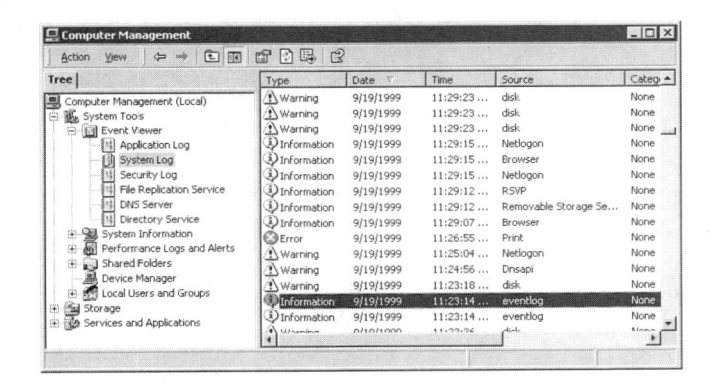

Within the Event Viewer are several logs that are kept, depending on the configuration of your system. The list will vary, but normally there is a base list of items tracked by the System Log, Application Log, and Security Log. Whether other logs exist depends on the installation of those services.

> **Note**
>
> You might notice in Figure 23.6 that the Local Users and Groups icon is Xed out. The server being observed is a Domain Controller so it does not have local users.

The System Log tracks the events that affect the performance or function of the server. When the system is started, a System Log begins, and the Event Log registers its own startup in the log (see Figure 23.7). Each event following that one is recorded and marked according to the type and urgency of the message.

FIGURE 23.7
Event Viewer opened.

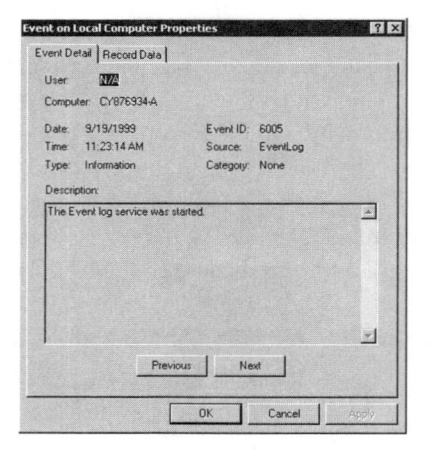

The Application Log is used solely by the applications that have been written to log items to the log. In other words, the operating system does not log all applications and write events from them to the Application Log. An example is a groupware package written by Microsoft called Exchange. Exchange writes many events to the Application Log that tell the administrator what has occurred in the application.

The Security Log does not log anything unless you turn on auditing in a specific piece of the security system in Windows 2000. The process of starting this audit trail is based on a group policy change and can include the default policy for the whole domain.

The steps for setting up auditing include the following:

1. Open Active Directory for Users and Computers.
2. In the console tree, click Domain Controller.
3. Click Action, and then click Properties.
4. On the Group Policy tab, click the policy you want to change and then click Edit.
5. In the Group Policy window, in the console tree, open this chain of settings to get to the audit policy: Computer Configuration, Windows Settings, Security Settings, Local Policies, Audit Policy.
6. In the Details pane, click the attribute or event you want to audit.
7. Click Action and then click Security.
8. In Change Configuration Setting To, click the options you want.

The event in Figure 23.7 has several properties. When you track down an issue with a server, the items in this event can lead to an answer by pointing to a specific location. The Type, Event ID, Source, and Category are the unique pieces of the puzzle. They offer information that will lead to a specific culprit.

Take the following information and search Microsoft TechNet (support.microsoft.com/search), and you will be amazed how often you find the answer without calling Support. You can be the hero if you note the following properties:

- Event ID: An ID used by the Support personnel at Microsoft or at the support.microsoft.com site to help you look up a specific incident that has occurred. If you get nothing else from the event, get this number.
- Type: The severity of the event. The types include Informational, Warning, and Error. Each type contains a symbol in the Event Viewer, as shown in Figure 23.7.
- Source: The application or service that caused the event to occur or logged the event. Because events can include good and bad items, this does not mean that the application source has failed but simply that it made note to the system.
- Category: An application-specific listing that is generally not used unless in security. In security, the category can help provide a location for audit data.
- Description: Data that lists the specific information about the error on this server. It is generally a list created by the writer of the application or service to report to the Event Log when a specific error occurs. This portion of the event is the second most important item to list and search for.

I do not mean to say the time and date can be ignored, but their meaning is rather obvious. In fact, if an event is occurring exactly at 10 p.m. on every Thursday, then any good administrator will be at the server this Thursday at 10 p.m. Knowing when an error occurs or how long it takes to recur is important.

Log Settings

The logs can be controlled and manipulated to keep the information that the administrator has in mind, at least to some degree. Among the first errors reported by a company that is having server trouble is that the Server Log is full. Although this is a good indication that there are many events to be logged at the server and something should be checked, it is also not the best way to run a server. It makes more sense to check the logs and control their size. A full log usually indicates a full hard drive.

The settings available for each log appear in the properties of each log. Right-click the log and choose Properties to see these settings (see Figure 23.8).

The first thing you see is the General tab. This area allows the administrator to decide how to store the log file and whether to empty the log.

The Maximum Log Size setting is simply that. The log file size is 512KB by default, and this should be plenty of room to log the general event of a Windows 2000 server. It is easy to increase the size to watch an event over a longer period of time. Select the text box and type the amount of disk space in kilobytes.

FIGURE 23.8
Application Log Properties.

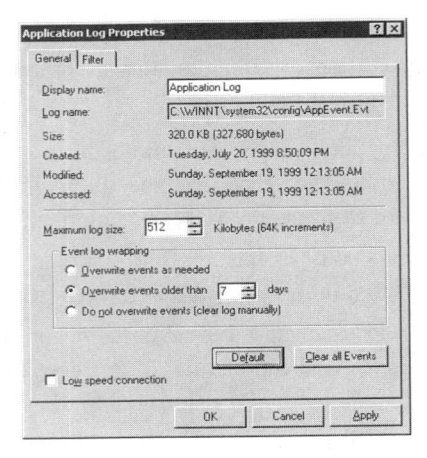

The Event Log Wrapping portion of the Properties page controls the size and age of the log; it contains the following options:

- Overwrite Events as Needed: Events are written to the log until it is full (it has reached its maximum size), and then the newest event simply replaces the oldest. This is true event wrapping.

- Overwrite Events Older Than __ Days: Events are written for as many days as are listed in the entry point, and all events older than this time are dropped from the list. This setting reports that the log is full if the log hits the maximum but has not yet reached the time limit.

- Do Not Overwrite Events (Clear Log Manually): In the event of a server issue that is hard to track, this setting prevents the log from being cleared before the administrator has a chance to see it. This setting reports that the log is full if the log hits the maximum but has not yet been cleared.

Rarely does an administrator clear a log in this way. Sometimes, the only way to see an event from its inception is to clear the slate and then start from scratch. But generally, it is best to increase the log size so that the log does not get overwritten. Once you have seen and corrected the event, you can put the settings back to normal.

The log can also be filtered to allow for less or more pointed data in the log. You choose this option in the Filter tab of the log properties.

You can set filters to control the date and time span of the logged data. If an event is occurring every night between midnight and 1 a.m., then an administrator can set up a log to catch that time. This step is usually accompanied by setting a higher logging level in the security or application being monitored. For example, suppose a hacker is logging in as an executive and you want to detail the information without logging the other events on your system for the record.

You can set the types of events that will be logged. Type filters allow the administrator to stop messages that are merely informational or success audits to allow more space for errors. In the example I just described, you might want to see only security success audits.

> **Tip**
>
> Controlling the events you want to see is not a recommended practice unless you are very sure of the events you are looking for. Even an experienced troubleshooter can be surprised by what shows up in the Event Viewer. If you set a filter but the event that is causing the problem is outside the filter range, you waste valuable time.

System Information

The information in the System Information section of the Computer Management Console is just that, information only. It is not information that can be changed or manipulated in any way, but it is a good resource for finding the answer to the kinds of questions that come up in the event of a problem (see Figure 23.9). You cannot change the information from this interface, but you can print it.

FIGURE 23.9
The System Information screens expanded.

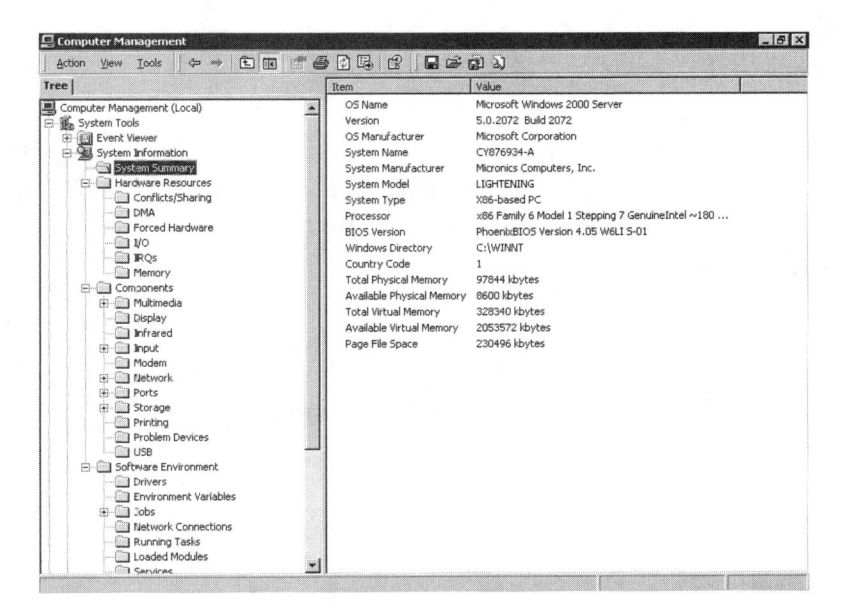

Device Manager

If the administrator seeing the Device Manager screen for the first time has managed Windows 95/98 before, then what he sees will not be new. It might be a surprise, but it won't be new. Windows 2000 has taken the Device Manager interface from Windows 95/98 and made it available even in the server platform.

The nice thing about the Device Manager is that it allows an administrator to see all of the hardware devices for the server in one clear hierarchical form. If you can speak fluently in the language of computer hardware, then you can find the hardware device here (see Figure 23.10) and get some idea about its current state.

FIGURE 23.10
Device Manager in Computer Management Console.

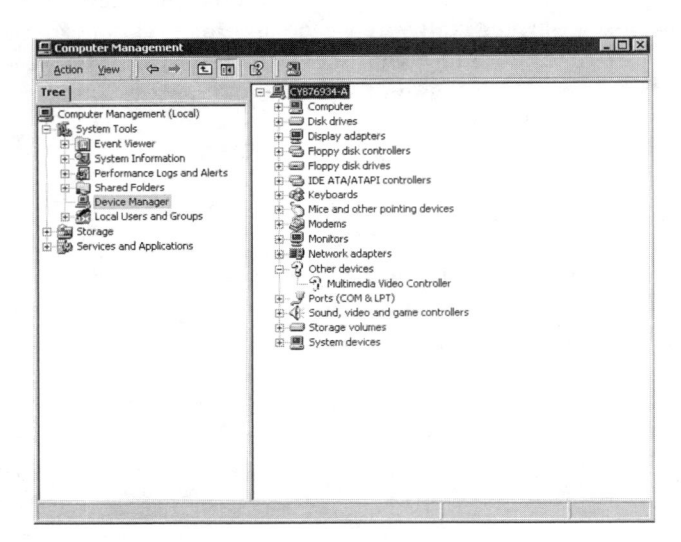

Clicking the Device Manager icon in Computer Management opens the Device Manager. The interface is like the Windows Explorer interface. All of the device types are listed in general categories (Disk Drives, Display Adapters, Network Adapters, and so on), and each category has a plus sign (+) beside it. This plus sign means there is a device listed under that category. When you click the plus sign, you see a list of the items in the category.

As shown in Figure 23.10, if an item is not identified or is misidentified by the Device Manager, then a question mark appears on top of it.

> **Note**
>
> This question mark is a hint at a new piece of Windows 2000 that again marries it to Windows 95/98—and that is the addition of Plug and Play. Plug and Play is responsible for the fact that the Windows 2000 Device Manager can find a piece of hardware that it was not formally introduced to. Windows NT did not allow for such items to be discovered because it maintained strict control over the hardware in the operating system. Unidentified items would have been manually installed or ignored.

To further explore an item in the Device Manager, click the plus sign beside the category and then double-click the time in question. Once the item is open (see Figure 23.11), you see general options and hardware-specific options. Because not all hardware has the same sets of variables, it is not possible to manage all of them from one interface, but there are some general pieces of information.

FIGURE 23.11
The Device Manager interface for a device that is not working.

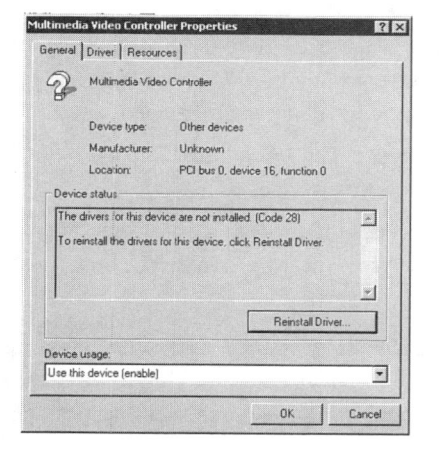

In Figure 23.11, you see a video controller that was detected by the operating system, but the system could not find a proper driver for it during installation. The system indicates that the driver couldn't be found, and it offers a chance to reinstall a driver (which in this case is installing it for the first time). This example allows you to see what the general information screen displays and how it allows for immediate resolution of the issue.

The Driver tab presents the user with a chance to change the driver but, if all is well, it serves better as an informational screen. This screen contains the pertinent information about the driver. The Version and Date information helps you know whether the driver is up to date even if it seems to be working properly. By comparing this information against the information on the vendor's Web site or support papers, you can see whether the system is up to date.

If you click the Update Driver button on this page, you open the Upgrade Device Driver Wizard. This wizard walks you through the process of finding and implementing the latest driver if it is available.

The Resources tab allows the administrator to see the hardware resources that are set for the specific hardware device and whether those resources are available. The term *hardware resource* refers to different things, depending on the piece of hardware. But the general idea is that a hardware resource is a group of unique identifiers needed to be seen as unique by the processor. Think of it as an auction where, to get the pieces purchased, the buyer must have a number and know the proper behavior. That behavior and those numbers are the resources, and they must be unique for each piece.

Here is a list of common resources:

- Interrupt Request: An interrupt or IRQ setting is the unique number used to interrupt the processor and request services.
- Memory Range: The memory range is used by the hardware device to write information that it needs in order to function. Different pieces of hardware have different memory needs and may have larger range needs.
- Input/Output Range (I/O Address): The I/O address is used by the device itself and other devices to participate with this device.
- DMA Channel: Rather than access the processor for all memory needs, some devices make Direct Memory Access (DMA). To do so, they must use a unique or available DMA channel.

If a resource is in conflict, then the device is marked with an exclamation point in the Device Manager. By double-clicking the device and moving to the Resources tab, the administrator can see a list in the Conflicting Resource section of the tab.

> **Note**
>
> Hardware resource conflicts are becoming less common in our PCI world, but they do occur. A common issue today is the PCI Plug and Play BIOS adding numerous hardware devices with the same IRQ setting. Because the PCI bus enables the sharing of IRQs, this is not always a problem. But often, a new piece of hardware will have intermittent problems or will cause the failure of an old piece of hardware when it is added. If possible, you should manually set these devices their own IRQ.

Some pieces of hardware allow the user to change the settings from within the Device Manager. This does not mean that the hardware setting is changed, but you can change the setting in Windows and then make the setting in the hardware match later. Changing the setting in Windows first allows the user to see whether a conflict is going to exist before committing the change in hardware. To make a change, follow these steps:

1. Double-click the device in Device Manager and choose the Resource tab.
2. Uncheck Use Automatic Settings.
3. Select the setting that you want to change and choose the Change Settings button.
4. Enter the value that you want and click OK. Watch the Conflicts box at the bottom of the screen for help in selecting a resource value.

After you make any resource change, you must reboot the system before the change takes effect. This is one of the areas that Microsoft cannot control when it comes to reducing the number of times you must reboot the system. Hardware settings cannot take effect with the hardware running.

Remember to make the actual hardware changes to change the resource being used. Changing a resource value in the Device Manager does not mean that the hardware change takes place.

SNMP

Managing Windows servers from a remote location has become much easier because of the improvements provided by the MMC and Computer Management. These tools allow the administrator to manage any of the Windows settings from any place in the domain. Managing a server remotely is no longer a trick. But that form of management is dependent on the health and well-being of the operating system.

No discussion of server management should neglect to mention management of the hardware health, or SNMP. SNMP, or Simple Network Management Protocol, is a protocol used by many hardware manufacturers to continually send hardware and software health information to collecting devices. By maintaining a record of the health of these systems, administrators can be alerted to many of the problems before they occur.

Companies such as Compaq, Hewlett-Packard, and IBM have created their own software services that run in Windows 2000 to track the continuing health of the server. Compaq's Insight Manager and Hewlett-Packard's Open View install SNMP agents on their servers that listen to the hardware and report trends and failures.

By tracking the hardware they have received to service over many years, these companies have learned what causes the hardware to fail. They have also learned what happens during the days before failure. This knowledge can be invaluable to the administrator when viewed from inside of a device collecting SNMP data.

The interface can be either the proprietary interface created by the vendor of the system or a third-party program that notes multiple forms of hardware. Hewlett-Packard's Open View and Computer Associates NetManageIT are such products. These products monitor not only servers but any device that produces SNMP traffic.

Each device that produces SNMP data generates data that is meant to be collected and displayed in a management information base (MIB). By collecting these MIBs and adding them to open SNMP managers, an administrator can manage the server operating system and hardware and also control routers, switches, printers, and any device that will report to SNMP.

Summary

Microsoft has made a great effort to make management utilities more accessible. It doesn't take an engineer in human behavior to see that there are too many different tools to work effectively and track. The answer to this issue has been to add the MMC and some Windows 95/98 functionality to this complex operating system.

The MMC provides the freedom to use the tools that are best for the job but keep the same interface and basic behavior among them. Keep in mind that the consoles created in the MMC are not stuck in the computer where they were created. They can be saved and shipped to the specific administrator who can use those tools. Obviously, other vendors are going to write to this tool.

By replacing most of the functionality of the Server Manager tool with the Computer Management utility, Microsoft has created a complete tool. By combining the Active Directory for Users and Computers console and accessing Computer Management, you now have a more far-reaching tool. This tool combination offers all of the functionality of Server Manager but adds directory context and deeper computer control. In a large directory environment, this tool is invaluable.

CHAPTER 24

Optimizing Performance and Tuning

IN THIS CHAPTER

- Windows 2000 Support Tools *606*
- Automatic Optimization *611*
- Stripe Sets and Virtual Memory Pagefiles *630*
- Performance-Monitoring Utility *641*

Windows 2000 Server installs with a minimal amount of effort on your part and provides a horde of tools that you can then use to precisely tune your server for its performance and overall security. However, a savvy Windows 2000 systems administrator must first be able to understand how his Windows 2000 Server is performing in order to be able to properly tune it. This is where Chapter 24 comes in. This chapter provides that person with the information to know what is happening with his server as well as how to tune the server.

Windows 2000 Support Tools

Microsoft has created an additional utility belt of tools known as the *Resource Kit*. A Windows Resource Kit has existed for every version of the Windows GUI shells and operating systems since the Windows version known as 3.0 (it was released in mid-1990). The Windows 2000 Resource Kit, like all its predecessors, contains a bevy of tools and operating system resources that no system administrator should be without. A subset of the more formal Windows 2000 Resource Kit that ships with the Windows 2000 Server operating system is known as the Windows 2000 *Support Tools*.

You can obtain a copy of the Windows 2000 Support Tools free of charge from Microsoft (look on the Windows 2000 Server CD), but the Windows 2000 Resource Kit must be purchased from Microsoft Press. However, with that purchase, you also receive a very technical, in-depth supplemental Microsoft Windows 2000 Resource Kit book, which typically contains many of those "features" that Microsoft has "forgotten" to document elsewhere.

Because the Windows 2000 Resource Kit is an add-on to the Windows 2000 operating system and just the Support Tools ship with the OS itself, we will limit our discussions here to only the Windows 2000 Support Tools. Contained within the Windows 2000 Support Tools are many utilities and Help files that are definitely useful to a system administrator who maintains a Windows 2000 server (see Table 24.1).

TABLE 24.1 Windows 2000 Support Tools

Tool Name	Description
Active Directory Administration Tool	This tool permits Windows 2000 Server administrators to customize their Active Directory implementations.
Active Directory Replication Monitor	This monitoring tool will show the replication topology of connections between servers on the same site in an organization's Active Directory structure. It can also help to optimize Active Directory queries.

Tool Name	Description
ADSI Edit	This tool aids a system administrator in performing low-level edits of the organization's Active Directory structure.
Command Prompt	A standard Windows 2000 Server command shell window.
Dependency Walker	This tool is used to build a hierarchical tree diagram of all dependent modules that were identified during the scanning of any Win32 module.
Deployment Planning Guide	This compiled Help file contains the full Windows 2000 Server Resource Kit Deployment Planning Guide, which is a document that helps to walk an organization through the many facets of planning for a Windows 2000 Server enterprise-wide deployment.
Disk Probe	This probe permits an administrator to perform hard disk drive sector edits within Windows 2000 Server.
Error and Event Messages	This Windows 2000 Error and Event Messages Help file contains an amazing amount of data that will greatly assist administrators in optimizing their Windows 2000 Server installations.
Global Flags Editor	Enables administrators to edit the NtGlobalFlag settings for a Windows 2000 Server through the use of a GUI screen.
Process Viewer	This tool can be used to show data regarding a specific active process, including a very detailed memory usage details screen.
Release Notes	Contains updated tips and notes pertaining to last-minute changes of the Windows 2000 operating system.
Security Administration Tools	System administrators can use this SID (Security ID) Walker tool to manage the various access-control policies on a Windows 2000 server.
SNMP Query Utility	Windows 2000 Server administrators can conduct SNMP queries of various other SNMP-enabled TCP/IP devices found on the organization's network(s).
Tools Help	Provides help for the Windows 2000 Support Tools, describing the required files, syntax, and other usage issues, along with examples for using these tools.
WinDiff	This is a file and directory comparison tool.
Windows Installer Cleanup Utility	This utility is used to remove some or all the applications on a Windows 2000 Server system that had used the Windows Installer technology during its installation processes.

To install the Support Tools, you will need your organization's Windows 2000 Server installation CD and probably administrative rights to the server (although this is not a requirement, per se, it's strongly recommended for obvious reasons). Once you have inserted the CD into the drive, navigate over to the Support Tools folder on the CD to reveal the five directory items shown there, including a setup executable file.

To begin the installation process, double-click the Setup.exe file. Once the process starts, you will see the first screen of the Windows 2000 Server Support Tools Setup Wizard.

This first screen is informational only and does not require any input or information from you. To continue the Support Tools installation process, you must click the Next button. This will take you to the User Information window portion of the process, as shown in Figure 24.1.

FIGURE 24.1
Entering your user information.

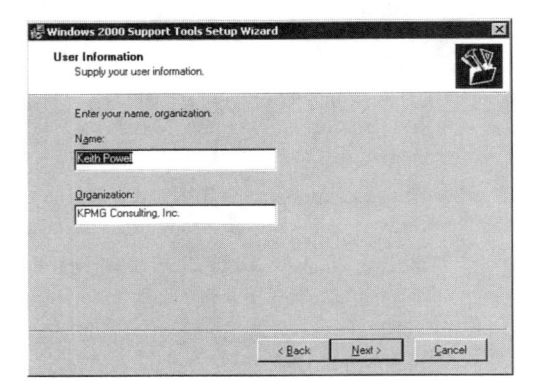

On this screen you enter the name and organization data for which this version of Windows 2000 Server is legally registered. Of course, because there is no possible way that Microsoft can conceivably check up on the information you're entering, the use of a name such as Mickey Mouse and an organization such as The Magic Kingdom can quite easily be inserted should you desire. Once you have made your entries, click the Next button to reveal the Select an Installation Type window, as shown in Figure 24.2.

The purpose of the Select an Installation Type window is to permit you to decide which of the tools you want to install onto your Windows 2000 server. It does, however, appear that the Typical selection still installs all 16 of the Windows 2000 Support Tools anyway. Of course, because the entire set of tools only consumes 16mb of hard drive space, choose the Custom option so that you can mark all the tools for installation. Once you've decided what type of installation process you want to perform, click the radio button next to the option you prefer to select it. Once that has been done, click the Next button to reveal the Custom Installation window, as shown in Figure 24.3 (obviously, had you selected the Typical option, you wouldn't be seeing the screen shown in Figure 24.3; instead, you would skip this one and jump ahead to Figure 24.4).

FIGURE 24.2
Selecting an installation type.

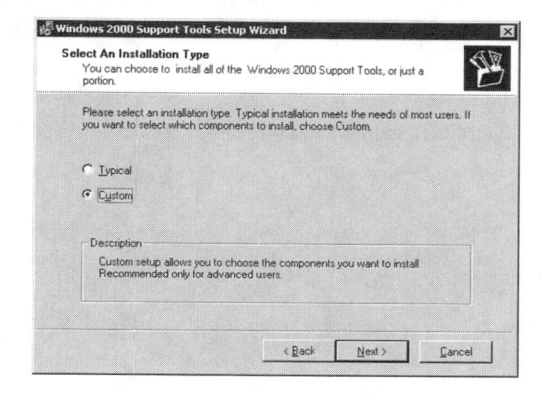

FIGURE 24.3
Choosing your installation options.

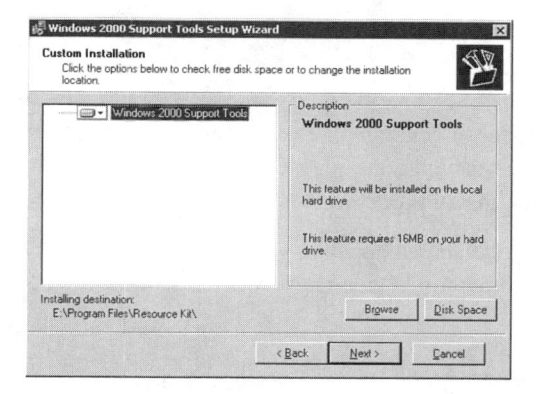

The Custom Installation window is used to help you decide which of the support tools you want to implement. If your organization wants all the tools, click the drop-down arrow box (this is the little white box that has a small hard drive picture and a down arrow icon within it) to reveal a short menu (note that this is a "left" click and not a "right" click, as is typically done). From this menu, you have three choices:

- Will Be Installed on the Local Hard Drive
- Entire Feature Will Be Installed on the Local Hard Drive
- Entire Feature Will Not Be Available

At the present time, Microsoft's implementation of this Windows 2000 feature is set to be an all-or-nothing approach, which means that the top two options will also end with the same result: the entire Windows 2000 Support Tools kit is installed. If the bottom selection (Entire Feature Will Not Be Available) is made, nothing will be installed. The two buttons near the bottom of the screen, Browse and Disk Space, are used to help you determine where you want to install the Windows 2000 Support Tools as well as whether you have enough hard disk drive space available for the installation. Once you've made your selections, click the Next button to reveal the Begin Installation window, as shown in Figure 24.4.

FIGURE 24.4
Making the decision to start the actual file installation process.

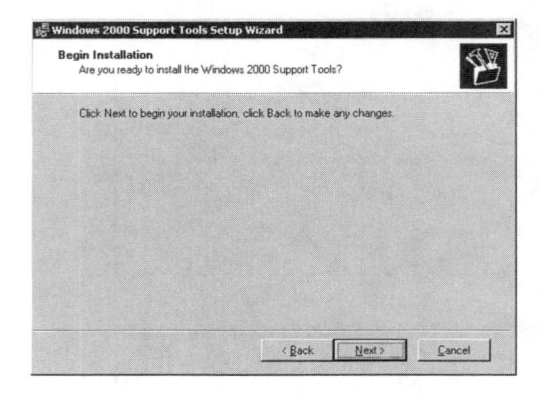

This is another informational screen, which again prompts you to make certain that you want to begin the actual file-installation process. Once you've made your decision, click the Next button to start the install process.

Once the Installation Progress screen appears, you will see a status bar that indicates where you are in the install process. Once the process finishes, the screen shown in Figure 24.5 will appear.

FIGURE 24.5
Ending a successful installation process.

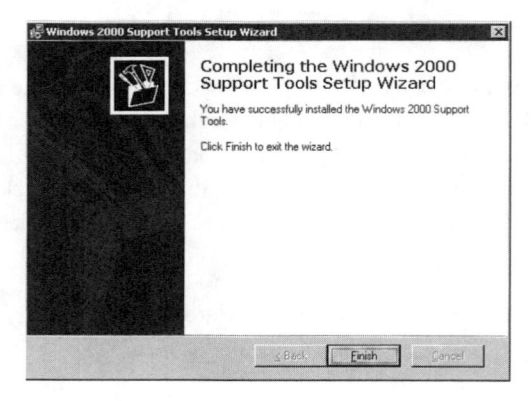

This final screen in the installation process informs you as to whether you have successfully completed the installation of the Windows 2000 Support Tools. Once you are ready to continue, click the Finish button to complete the process and exit the screen entirely.

To actually use any of the Windows 2000 Support Tools, you will need to click Start, Programs, Windows 2000 Support Tools and then select the utility tool that you want to use.

Automatic Optimization

Optimization of the Windows 2000 Server operating environment is both a simple and a complicated task. Microsoft has made it very easy to perform basic performance tuning and optimization of its newest operating system through a series of GUI-based management consoles. However, do not let these Microsoft Management Consoles (MMCs) mislead you; they are not the "end all" in Windows 2000 Server optimization—there are many steps to optimizing the many aspects of your organization's Windows 2000 operating environment. An organization's system administrators can ensure a well-tuned Windows 2000 Server operating environment by closely monitoring the optimization process as well as through the automation of some of these optimization tasks.

Avoiding Fragmentation

Trying to avoid the fragmentation of your hard disk drives can greatly enhance the performance of your systems. Fragmentation can occur on any type of hard drive (EIDE, SCSI, and so on) as well as on single-drive systems and RAID-enabled systems. The more fragmented a hard disk drive becomes, the more difficult it becomes for the operating system and applications to find the files they need for any particular operation. Obviously, if it takes more time to find a file spread across one or more disks, the overall speed or apparent speed of the operating system and/or application will diminish. Within the Windows 2000 Server operating system is a tool that can aid you in the identification of fragmented disk drive areas as well as to defrag those particular disk drives. That tool is known as the *Disk Defragmenter*.

To access the Windows 2000 Disk Defragmenter utility, click Start, Programs, Accessories, System Tools, Disk Defragmenter to start the application and reveal its first screen, as shown in Figure 24.6.

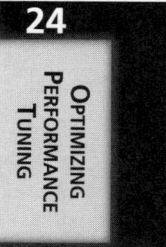

FIGURE 24.6
Viewing the main Disk Defragmenter screen.

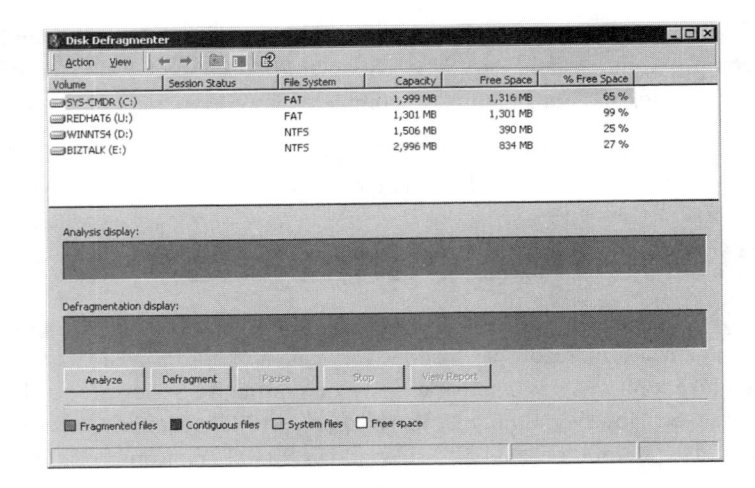

Volume	Session Status	File System	Capacity	Free Space	% Free Space
SYS-CMDR (C:)		FAT	1,999 MB	1,316 MB	65 %
REDHAT6 (U:)		FAT	1,301 MB	1,301 MB	99 %
WINNTS4 (D:)		NTFS	1,506 MB	390 MB	25 %
BIZTALK (E:)		NTFS	2,996 MB	834 MB	27 %

When you first enter the Disk Defragmenter tool, you'll see a listing of the available hard disk drive volumes on the top half of the screen. The bottom half of the screen is dedicated to the analysis and defragmentation processes, should you choose to initiate either or both of those features. There are six columns of information listed for each drive volume available:

- *Volume*. This is the logical hard disk drive that can be analyzed and/or defragmented (in case the defragmentation process is necessary).
- *Session Status*. In this column you'll see a status label for that particular drive volume. For example, when running the analysis portion, you'll see the term Analyzing... appear, and for the defragmentation process, the term Defragmenting... appears. A status of Paused or Stopped means that you either paused or halted the defragmentation process during its executing phase.
- *File System*. This is the format type of the file system installed on a particular drive. The term *FAT* means that a 16-bit Windows 9*x* file allocation table format has been installed, whereas *FAT32* implies that a Windows 98 32-bit version of the file allocation table format has been installed. *NTFS* means that the Windows NT file allocation table format has been utilized. Although there are other file system types that may appear here, these three are the most prevalent. Also, if a different format should appear, you might not want to defragment it because doing so could actually corrupt a non-Microsoft operating system (such as Red Hat Linux, OS/2, Sun Solaris, and so on).
- *Capacity*. This is the total formatted size of the disk drive volume.

- *Free Space*. This is the amount of unused disk drive space present on a particular drive.

- *% Free Space*. This is the total percentage remaining unused on a particular disk drive.

If you click View, Customize, you can modify the options for viewing the Disk Defragmenter tool, as shown in Figure 24.7.

FIGURE 24.7
Customizing your MMC view format.

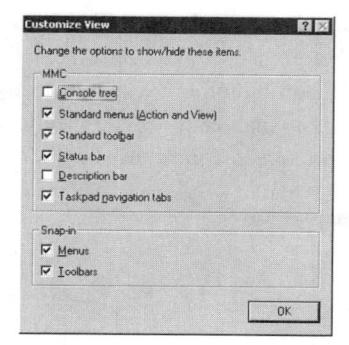

The top portion of this options screen, labeled MMC, lets you add or remove the various menu and navigational bars for the MMC (Microsoft Management Console) itself. You should note that the Disk Defragmenter tool is actually just an MMC snap-in whose navigational options are very similar to the many other MMC snap-in tools built into the Windows 2000 Server operating system. The bottom half of the Customize View window permits you to modify whether you will use the snap-in tools and menus as well. Make the selections that you desire and then click the OK button to confirm and save your selections.

Next, you should select a drive for analysis. To do this, click a particular drive to highlight it (this means that you've decided to perform these next operations on that particular drive volume; in the example shown, this is the E: drive). Once you've done that, either click the Analyze button (it's near the bottom-left side of the screen) or click the Action, Analyze menu selection (both of these do the same thing) to start the Disk Defragmenter analysis process.

As the analysis process begins, you'll see a multicolored line appear in the Analysis Display area of the screen (it's on the bottom half of the screen). Use the color-coordinated menu key to decipher exactly what's occurring on your disk drive volume. Chances are, if you've never run this utility on that particular disk drive volume, you'll see many fragmented areas on your drive. Once the analysis is complete, a small window will appear, as shown in Figure 24.8.

FIGURE 24.8
Deciding what to do once the analysis phase finishes.

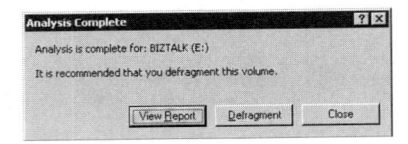

When the Analysis Complete window appears, it will contain a recommendation for that particular drive volume. It's very likely that your disk drive will require defragmentation, especially if this is a volume that exists on either a database or file server, or if you've never used the Disk Defragmenter utility before. Before you start the defragmentation process, you may want to click the View Report button to review the analysis report that's automatically generated each time you run the Analyze process. Once you click the View Report button, you'll see the Analysis Report screen appear, as shown in Figure 24.9.

FIGURE 24.9
Reviewing the Analysis Report online.

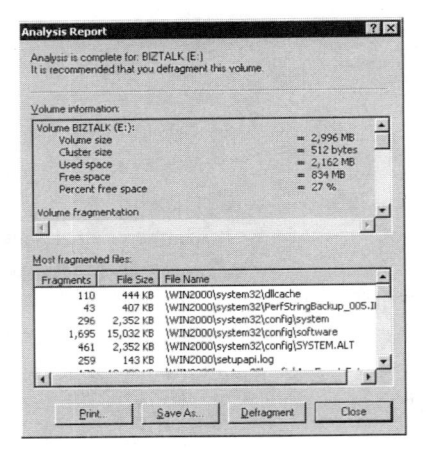

Note that as soon as the Analysis Report screen appears, the Analysis Complete window disappears. Inside the top portion of the Analysis Report screen (labeled *Volume Information*), you'll find lots of great information regarding the disk drive volumes on your Windows 2000 server machine. Use the scrollbar along the right side of the screen to move up and down inside this informational-only section of the screen. The bottom portion of this screen (labeled *Most Fragmented Files*) contains a listing of those files that contain multiple fragments beyond what's considered average for that particular drive volume (the average is given in the Volume Information section). Once you've reviewed this report, click the Close button to exit this screen. Of course, you can also start the defragmentation process from the Analysis Report window by clicking the Defragment button. The Save As button is useful for saving defragmentation reports to some spot on the server for later or more detailed analysis.

Assuming that you clicked the Close button to exit the Analysis Report window and now want to run the defragmentation process without having to restart the analysis process, you can do just that by clicking the Defragment button in the main Disk Defragmenter window. This will cause the defragmentation process to ensue.

As you will see, the Session Status column for that particular drive volume in the top portion of the screen will now read "Defragmenting," which means that the defragmentation process has indeed begun. There is also some activity within the Defragmentation Display section of the main Disk Defragmenter window, which will initially mirror the disk volume image shown in the Analysis Display portion just above it. Once the disk defragmentation process has finished for one particular volume, you can then select another drive volume to defragment or simply exit this utility. To exit the defragmentation process, click the Close button to exit from the end of the defragmentation process. Otherwise, you can also click the Report button to reveal the Defragmentation Report window, before you exit the defragmentation process.

Multiprocessing

The Windows 2000 Server operating system supports computers with one or more processors (also known as *CPUs*). Although there's no *set* limit to the theoretical number of Intel-based processors for the Windows 2000 DataCenter operating system, 32 processors is probably around the upper limit. Of course, within the Server version of the Windows 2000 operating system, two CPUs is the maximum supported. There are two types of multiprocessing computer systems: asymmetric and symmetric.

Asymmetric is where the operating system automatically assigns designated processes to a specific CPU. This means that instruction sets assigned to one CPU cannot dynamically be shifted over to the second CPU in cases where the first CPU becomes overwhelmed. Luckily, the Windows 2000 Server operating system does not follow the asymmetric path and instead is a symmetric multiprocessing system (SMP).

The symmetric processing structure of the Windows 2000 Server operating system permits the computer system to dynamically run either system processes or applications on whatever CPU is available. This feature, coupled with the multitasking capabilities of the Windows 2000 Server OS, makes this latest version of Windows NT by far the most powerful/scalable one. Of course, all this newfound power and scalability means that the management, monitoring, and performance tuning become even more complex. As you read on through the remainder of this chapter, you'll learn the basic ways in which you can better prepare your organization's computing infrastructure to handle the complex world of Windows 2000 Server optimization and performance tuning.

Prioritizing Processes and Threads

As was possible within the older Windows NT Server 4.0 operating system, Windows 2000 Server is capable of prioritizing the various system processes and threads. Of course, it helps to know what a process is and does as well as what a thread is, too. Therefore, let's delve into those two terms quickly first and then we'll chat briefly about how to manage both of them. From there, we can then discuss how and why you might want to change priorities in order to optimize the performance of a particular process or thread.

What is a process? Well, a *process* is a program that executes using a prespecified series of steps. That program will consist of its base source code and data as well as a private memory address space (within the Windows 2000 Server operating system), along with the applicable Windows 2000 Server and system resources and one or more threads.

A *thread* is nothing more than a precise arrangement of instructions within any one program. The Windows 2000 Server kernel controls the executing of all threads. For example, a thread within Microsoft's Word program might include the commands that initiate the Print Preview process. You'll hear about multithreaded processes, which means that a single process is capable of processing more than a single thread at a time. This is very helpful for programs such as the WordPad utility, which comes with the Windows 2000 Server operating system. WordPad is able to accept input from the user's keyboard and mouse concurrently, while simultaneously printing a document. In a single-threaded process, all three of these functions would have to occur in a systematic fashion (that is, step 2 could not start until step 1 has completed, and so on).

This multithreaded processing capability is better known as *multitasking*. Unfortunately, if your server only contains a single central processing unit (CPU), it's unable to truly take advantage of multitasking, because it must process a single thread at a time. However, the Windows 2000 Server operating system is able to use a multitasking process known as *context switching* that leads users of Windows 2000 Server to believe there are multiple threads executing at the same time (this is where the smoke-and-mirrors approach to computer processing occurs). Context switching works in a fairly straightforward manner: A thread will begin to execute and will work until it either stalls on its own (that is, it needs to wait for other system or OS resources) or the operating system tells it to wait (that is, it interrupts its processing). When this occurs, the operating system will save the context of the thread. As soon as that event occurs, the operating system will then load the context of another thread so that it can process. As you can see, the system just swaps (or *switches*) threads in and out of this until all the threads have been processed.

Of course, it would be excessively easy to understand threads and processes if Microsoft just left it this way (plus, a CPU would be idle way too much). That's why you have another concept to understand: preemptive multitasking. Preemptive multitasking is the process by which the Windows 2000 Server operating system controls all access to the computer system's CPU(s). This means, then, that the Windows 2000 Server OS is able to preempt (or *interrupt*) executing threads for one of two reasons:

- *Quantum.* This is a thread that executes for a prespecified period of time, at the end of which the OS will preempt that thread and then permit a different thread to access the CPU.
- *Priority.* If a thread comes along that has a higher priority than the one that's currently executing, the operating system will interrupt the executing thread in favor of this newer prioritized one.

Within Windows 2000 Server, there are 32 different priority levels, which are numbered from 0 to 31 (interesting numbering scheme, eh?). These priority levels are broken into two different levels:

- *User-mode Components.* Ranging from 0 to 15, these priority levels deal strictly with the various Windows 2000 Server subsystems (POSIX, Win32, OS/2, and the Integral Subsystem) as well as the various applications that will execute on any Windows 2000 server.
- *Kernel-mode Components.* Ranging from 16 to 31, these priority levels service the Executive components of Windows 2000 Server, including all system data and hardware devices as well as direct memory access and the process manager (which creates and terminates all system processes and threads).

Each thread that's processed by the Windows 2000 Server operating system will have a base priority set for it. The base thread priority, as a tool such as the Windows 2000 Task Manager reports it, will appear as being in one of six priority class levels (ranked from the lowest at the top to the highest at the bottom):

- *Idle.* From 1 to 6
- *Normal.* From 6 to 10
- *High.* From 10 to 15
- *Realtime.* From 16 to 31

Keep in mind that within each of these priority class levels there may be additional Dynamic Priority Level settings, which are labeled as Low, BelowNormal, Normal, AboveNormal, High, and Realtime. The Dynamic Priority Level is managed by the Windows 2000 Server kernel, which keeps system administrators from "fixing" their systems into some irreparable manner. You therefore have a ranking within each ranking that will help to drive a thread's specific priority level within Windows 2000 Server.

As you can see from the preceding list, each one of these levels has a set priority number range assigned to it (although your real concern is simply the level name itself). When you view your processes through the Windows 2000 Server Task Manager (don't worry, this utility will be discussed in just a few more short paragraphs), you'll see just these level names and not specific priority numbers.

> **Warning**
>
> Never, ever assign any application, utility, thread, or anything else to a base priority of Realtime. Should you do something this dastardly, your Windows 2000 Server system will quickly hit a "seizure" and die a quick, painful death. This is due to the simple fact that any process you give this threshold to will very quickly take over the entire operating system. A setting of Realtime must therefore only be managed by the Windows 2000 Server operating system and never by one of its administrators.

The base priority for any thread will never exceed a range greater than two levels below the base, nor will it go above two levels higher than the base. For example, the Microsoft Photo Editor application will start with a base priority of Normal, which really translates into a base priority of 8, meaning that its priority range will be between 6 on the low side and 10 on the high side.

To be able to see which processes are presently active on your Windows 2000 server, press Ctrl+Alt+Del, which will then cause the Windows Security window to appear. From that window, click the Task Manager button. Once the Task Manager utility appears, click the Processes tab to reveal the screen shown in Figure 24.10.

FIGURE 24.10

Using the Windows Task Manager.

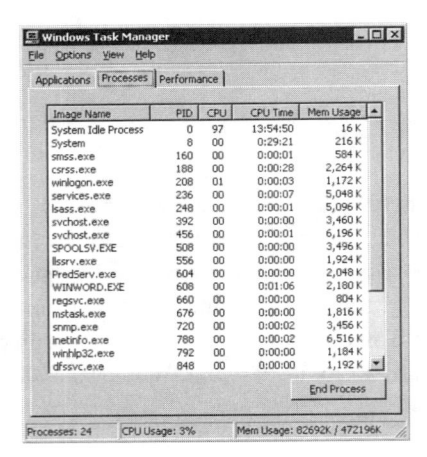

As you examine the contents of the Processes tab for the first time, you'll notice five columns:

- *Image Name*. This is the name assigned to the process.
- *PID*. This is the process identifier.
- *CPU*. This is the amount of processor time (shown as a percentage) that the threads for the process have consumed since the last update.
- *CPU Time*. This is the total processor time that has been consumed by a particular process, listed in hours:minutes:seconds format.
- *Mem Usage*. This is the amount of primary system memory used by the process, a value that's shown in kilobytes (1,024 bytes = 1KB).

If you scroll down to the bottom of the Windows Task Manager screen (while still on the Processes tab), you'll see a few items that are indented from the rest of the processes listed, as shown in Figure 24.11.

FIGURE 24.11

Analyzing a specific Windows 2000 process.

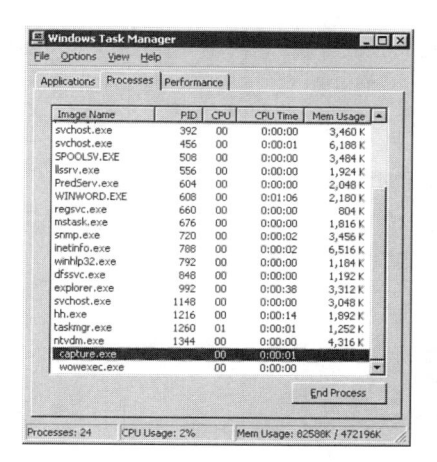

These indented items are processes that are running inside the NTVDM (Windows 2000 Virtual DOS Machine; note that it still uses the Windows NT 4.0 name of "NT" instead of some more updated "Win2k" abbreviation).

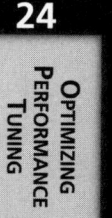

> **Note**
>
> The Windows 2000 Virtual DOS Machine is one of the various subsystems that the Windows 2000 Server operating system supports. Windows 2000 emulates a protected environment that's safe for the older MS-DOS and 16-bit Windows applications to execute in. Keep in mind, though, that just because this area is created instantly whenever you attempt to run one of these types of older programs, not all MS-DOS and 16-bit Windows applications may execute properly, if at all, under the Windows 2000 Server operating system.

To end a process from within the Processes tab (assuming that it's stoppable from here), you must first highlight a process by clicking it. Once you've highlighted a process, such as the `Capture.exe` process shown in the figure, all it takes is a single click on the End Process button to terminate that process immediately.

To modify the Processes tab view so that you can see all the possible columns of pertinent processor information, you'll need to click the View menu and then click again on the Select Columns menu selection. Performing these mouse clicks will cause the Select Columns screen to appear, as shown in Figure 24.12.

FIGURE 24.12
Selecting which process columns to view.

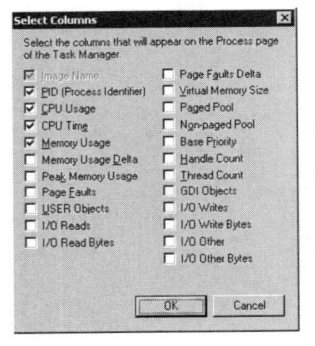

It's interesting to note that there are nine more columns of information available here (including all the I/O objects, Peak Memory Usage, the USER objects, and the GDI objects) than there were with the older Windows NT 4.0 operating systems. The purposes of these columns is as follows:

- *Image Name.* This is the name assigned to the process.
- *PID.* This is the Process Identifier number that precisely distinguishes a process in multiple other locations throughout the Windows 2000 Server operating system.

- *CPU*. This is the amount of processor time (shown as a percentage) that the threads for the process have consumed since the last update.
- *CPU Time*. This is the total processor time that has been consumed by a particular process, listed in hours:minutes:seconds format.
- *Memory Usage*. This is that amount of primary system memory used by the process, a value that's shown in kilobytes (1,024 bytes = 1KB).
- *Memory Usage Delta*. This is the difference between the memory that's presently in use for a process from what was in use the last time the Task Manager was updated.
- *Peak Memory Usage*. This is the highest amount of physical memory that has been consumed by a particular process since the start of that process.
- *Page Faults*. This is the number of times the system has had to retrieve information for a process directly from a hard disk location outside of those areas designated within either the system memory or the applicable Windows 2000 Server swap file. This value is accumulated from the very start of the process in question.
- *USER Objects*. This is the total number of USER (internal) objects that currently are being used by a particular process. These objects include windows, menus, cursors, monitors, and the like.
- *I/O Reads*. This is the number of times a process has attempted to read information from the memory address that the CPU uses to store and retrieve data.
- *I/O Read Bytes*. This is the total number of bytes that a process has attempted to read from the memory address that the CPU uses to store and retrieve data.
- *Page Faults Delta*. This is the difference between the number of page faults currently recorded for a particular process and the previous total number recorded since the last time the Task Manager was updated.
- *Virtual Memory Size*. This is the total share size of the system's paging file for a particular process.
- *Paged Pool*. This is the amount of memory that's available for paging to a disk pack, an amount that includes only USER memory (non-kernel mode memory) used by a process. This value is measured in kilobytes.
- *Non-Paged Pool*. This is the amount of non-paged memory used by a process, which means that it's system memory (that is, it's non-USER memory).
- *Base Priority*. This is the Priority Class Level range that has been established for a particular process. Keep in mind that this priority level is determined by the process's application and not the Windows 2000 Server operating system. Also, remember that the Windows 2000 OS will set and/or change the dynamic priority level within this base Priority Class Level setting.

- *Handle Count.* This is the total number of object handles available for a particular process in its object table.
- *Thread Count.* This is the total number of object threads executing for a particular process.
- *GDI Objects.* This is the total number of GDI objects that are currently in use by a particular process.
- *I/O Writes.* This is the number of times that a process has attempted to write information to the memory address that the CPU uses to store and retrieve data.
- *I/O Write Bytes.* This is the total number of bytes that a process has attempted to write to the memory address that the CPU uses to store and retrieve data.
- *I/O Other.* This is the number of times that a process has used information in the memory address area that the CPU uses to store and retrieve data.
- *I/O Other Bytes.* This is the total number of bytes that a process has used in the memory address area that the CPU uses to store and retrieve data.

To select one or more columns, simply click the check box located to the left of each item. If there's a check mark in a box, that item will appear in the Processes tab's content area. Otherwise, if there is no check mark present, that item will not appear in the listing. Once you've made all your markings, click the OK button to confirm your choices and return to the Processes tab. The contents of this tab will now display all the selections that you've made, as shown in Figure 24.13.

FIGURE 24.13

Viewing all the newly added columns of information.

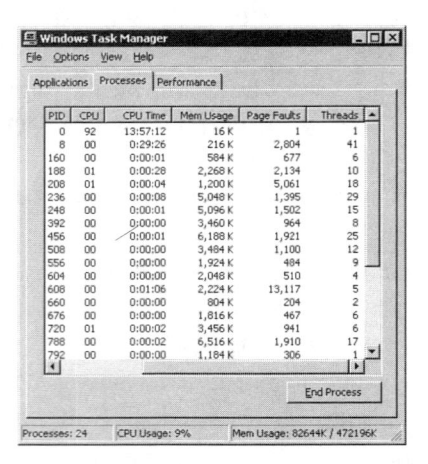

Note that you're able to resize this window so that you can see all the columns in one giant window, assuming of course that your system's monitor is capable of displaying such a large listing of items. In addition, it may help to resize the width of the columns by double-clicking the border (the thin black line) that separates the column headings, just as you would do inside a spreadsheet program such as Microsoft Excel. Another way to help you display your process data more clearly is to sort columns by clicking their header labels once. Likewise, if you click and hold the mouse pointer on a specific column heading, you can drag that column either left or right to its new location.

To reveal the contents of the Performance tab, click that tab (see Figure 24.14).

FIGURE 24.14
Reviewing system performance via the Windows Task Manager.

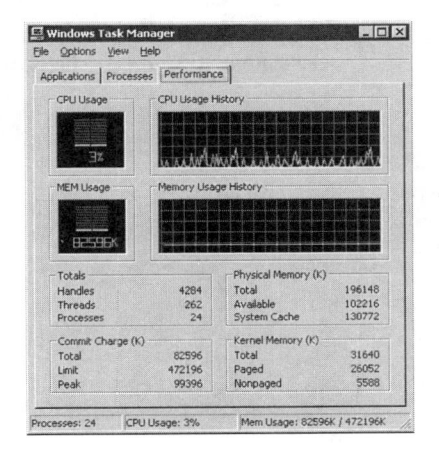

It's on this tab that you can quickly determine the basic status health of your Windows 2000 server. The four boxes arranged on the bottom half of this window contain a series of "total" and "available" statistics, which make the management of your system that much easier. For example, by taking a glance at the Totals section, you can quite readily see the total number of threads and processes that are presently active on your Windows 2000 server machine. Likewise, the Physical Memory (K) section reveals the total amount of physical memory installed and recognized by the operating system, as well as the amount of memory available for use by the system and its applications. Remember that these numbers are in kilobytes; therefore, the total shown in the example, 196148, really translates into 192mb (1mb = 1,024Kb).

In the bar and line charts on the top half of the sample screen are graphical representations of the CPU and memory components of your Windows 2000 server machine. To get just a little bit more data out of these screens, you may want to activate the showing of kernel data as well as limiting each graph to represent just a single CPU (on systems that only have a single CPU, this second option will not be available). To activate these options, first click the View menu and then click the Show Kernel Times option.

The showing of kernel times will insert a red colored line into the line chart and turn the portion of the bar chart that represents kernel time to a red color. Both of these representations are useful for those times that you're attempting to troubleshoot a poorly behaving system. For example, if a system continually pegs its kernel memory to 100 percent thresholds, you know that you're short on physical memory in your server.

To modify your charts so that they just display a single CPU in each graph, you'll need to select the View, CPU History, One Graph Per CPU menu option. Remember way back in this chapter when we discussed the use of the Windows 2000 Support Tools? Well, it's at this point that you will want to consider using at least one of those tools: the Process Viewer. To begin using this tool, click the Start, Programs, Windows 2000 Support Tools, Tools, Process Viewer menu selection. This will take you into the Process Viewer utility, as shown in Figure 24.15.

FIGURE 24.15
Reviewing the main screen of the Process Viewer utility.

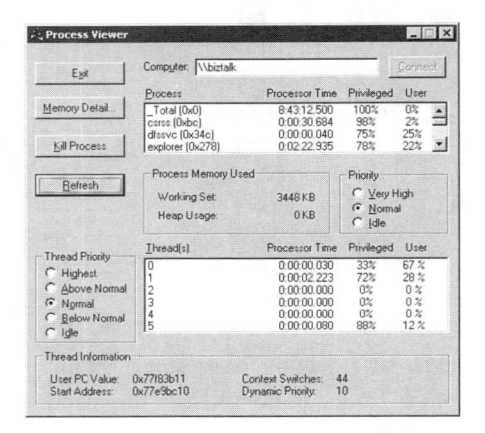

The Process Viewer tool is both a complex and confusing utility. Using this utility is akin to editing the Windows 2000 Server Registry: You become a much more powerful administrator if you can do these types of tasks successfully, but the path is fraught with peril that can cause the demise of your system if you make a mistake (which is irreversible at that moment in time). One thing that you will probably notice very quickly is that there's absolutely no help available within this utility and very little assistance provided by the general Windows 2000 Server online Help. Do not expect any of the printed manuals provided by Microsoft Press to be of much use either, because the concepts required for using the Process Viewer utility go beyond the levels of all but the most advanced system administrators.

Okay, going back to the Process Viewer tool, you can see that the main screen is split into two parts: management of processes on the top and thread management on the bottom. The very top box contains the computer that these processes run on. To manage a computer different from the one you're presently using, assuming that you have the proper administrative rights to that machine, all you need to do is type in the Universal Naming Convention (UNC) path (use the \\ServerName format) for that particular server and then click the Connect button. The second box from the top contains information about the processes that are active on your server:

- *Process.* This is the name of the process, along with its initial memory address in parentheses.
- *Processor Time.* This is the total amount of CPU time that that particular process has been active, in hours:minutes:seconds:thousandths of a second format.
- *Privileged.* Sometimes called the *Kernel mode*, this is the percentage of time that a particular process has run in the Privileged mode versus the User mode.
- *User.* This is the percentage that a particular process has run in the User mode versus the Privileged mode. Note that the Privileged plus the User percentages will always add up to 100 percent.

> **Note**
> The Privileged or Kernel mode is the level of hardware and memory operation that's beyond the reach of applications, which means that this is a protected area. Other names sometimes associated with the Privileged mode include the Protected mode, the Supervisor mode, and Ring 0. Processes running in the Privileged mode have access to all the advanced CPU features for I/O and memory management, making them more efficient.

In the third section of this screen, labeled *Process Memory Used*, you can get a quick assessment of just how much memory a specific process has consumed. To check this feature out, just click any process name listed in the top Process box, and you'll see the Working Set and Heap Usage values change accordingly.

Located just to the right of the Process Memory Used section is the Priority area, where you can determine the priority set for a specific process. Typically, the setting here will be the Normal level, but you're able to change the priority for a process simply by clicking the radio button of your choice. For example, should you want to change the sample shown to a higher priority, all you would need to do is click the radio button next to the Very High label. Again, if you're unsure as to what they will mean for your Windows 2000 server machine, it's unwise to "play around" with these settings unless you're on a test box (the wrong choice here could very easily crash a server).

The bottom half of the Process Viewer utility screen is dedicated to thread management. To the far left is the Thread Priority area, where you're able to manipulate the priority level for a particular thread for a specific process. Again, if you're unsure as to what this will mean for your Windows 2000 server machine, it's unwise to play around with this setting. Most processes will have threads with a Normal priority, although many of the system processes (that is, OS-level programs) may have a slightly higher setting, such as Above Normal. The difficulty you'll face when attempting to manipulate thread priorities is in knowing which one(s) to change. In other words, threads typically are not given good names (taking a look at the example in Figure 24.15, you can see that the threads are simply labeled in numerical order), which means that, unless you're the software developer who wrote the application in question, you may have difficulty in knowing what thread to change.

Just like processes, the thread area also contains an active thread section, which is located just to the right of the Thread Priority area. In this box you can quickly determine the longevity of any thread for a particular process. Although it may seem like it's possible to modify the priority of any thread, these radio buttons are just for show—you're unable to modify any thread's priority from within the Process Viewer utility. Just below this box is the Thread Information area. It's here that you can check the status of a thread to the degree of knowing the following information:

- *Start Address*. This is the starting virtual address for a thread.
- *User PC Value*. This is the virtual address for the value of the User mode.
- *Context Switches*. A context switch is when the microkernel switches the processor from one thread to another; therefore, this value is the number of switches that have occurred thus far on your Windows 2000 server for a specific process. Keep in mind that on a single-processor system, this number might not be as meaningful as it is for a multiprocessor server.
- *Dynamic Priority*. This is the level of a priority boost that the Windows 2000 operating system will automatically assign to a thread as it waits its turn to be processed. However, you have the ability to modify this setting for some processes, such as when you change the Performance level for Application Response by clicking the Performance Options button from within the Advanced tab of the Computer Management (Local) Properties window.

Along the left side of the Process Viewer utility window are four buttons that control several important Process Viewer activities:

- *Exit*. If you click the Exit button, the Process Viewer utility will close.
- *Memory Detail*. This button's use will reveal a more detailed screen containing specific memory usage details for a specific process.
- *Kill Process*. This button is used to cancel the execution of a specific process.
- *Refresh*. The Refresh button is used to refresh the contents of the process information window.

To help better understand how this utility might best work for you, let's take a sample application and walk through the entire process, using all the areas of the Process Viewer utility. To keep the example simple, we'll use the Windows 2000 server game Minesweeper. To start, make sure the Process Viewer utility is active (use the previous instructions to start it if it's not already started); then open this game on your Windows 2000 Server computer. To start the game, select Start, Programs, Accessories, Games, Minesweeper. If you scroll to the bottom of the process information box (it's the larger box on the top half of the Process Viewer window), you should see the process for the Minesweeper game appear, as shown in Figure 24.16.

FIGURE 24.16
Viewing the characteristics of a specific process.

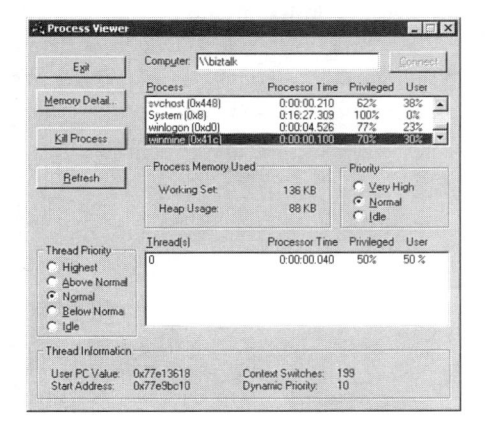

It will have the process name *winmine* (because that's the name of the executable file that actually runs the Minesweeper game). If you do not see this process in your Process Viewer utility, you may need to click the Refresh button to refresh the process information box's contents. Once you do that, you'll see the process appear, assuming that you've successfully started the Windows 2000 Minesweeper game. Take a good look at the various bits of information presented to you for this game through the Process Viewer utility. It may be interesting to note that for the only thread present for this game, its resources are evenly split between the Privileged and User modes. Also, even though this is a very simplistic game, it does use a fair amount of working set and heap process memory.

Now that you have spent time examining the resource requirements of this game, it's time to exit the game. However, instead of using the old fashioned way of doing this (through the game, itself), you will end the game by using the powers of the Process Viewer utility. To do this, click the winmine process to select it and then click the Kill Process button. You will immediately be prompted with a Terminate Process response pop-up box, which will contain the precise memory location of the process you wish to terminate.

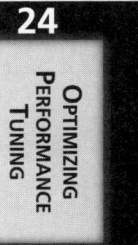

There are two buttons positioned on this pop-up window: OK and Cancel. If you click the Cancel button, nothing will happen and the process in question will continue to function (that is, the game will still be running). However, if you click the OK button, the game will end instantly, and the process will also die immediately. Now, this is the interesting part: If you re-examine your Process Viewer utility window, you will still see the winmine process showing as still being active. This is due to the fact that the Process Viewer utility window does not automatically update itself on any periodic basis. The only way to clear a terminated process is by clicking the Refresh button, which will cause the process information window's contents to be updated.

The final area of the Process Viewer tool that we should explore is the Memory Detail area. To do this, you need to click any process to select it, such as the explorer process (which is the shell process for Windows 2000 Server), and then click the Memory Detail button. This will reveal the Memory Details window, as shown in Figure 24.17.

FIGURE 24.17

Viewing the memory details for a specific process.

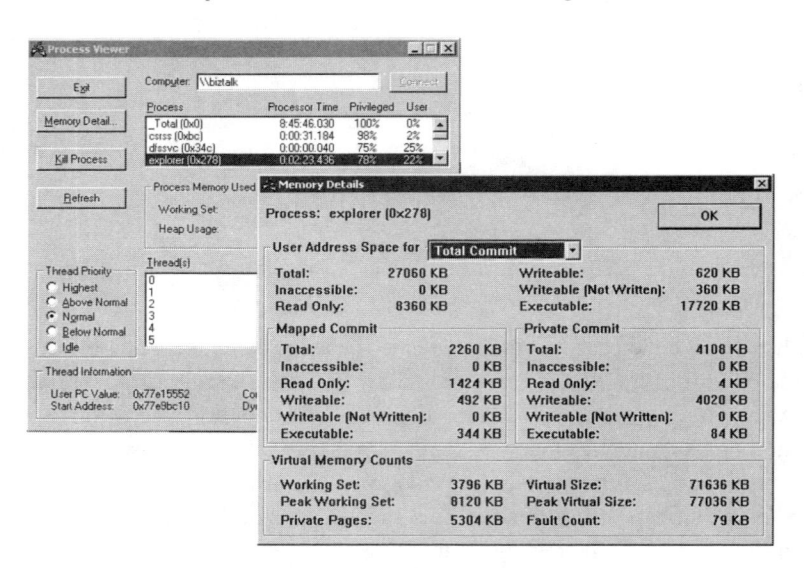

The Memory Details window displays a variety of statistics for the explorer process that was selected back on the main Process Viewer window. The memory details shown are determined by the use of the only drop-down list box shown on this screen—User Address Space For. In the example shown, the User Address Space For selection is Total Commit, which means that you will want to review the memory details for all the active DLL (dynamic link library) files in use for this specific process. If you want to look at the memory details for a specific DLL file, such as those for the document properties (`docprop2.dll`) DLL file, just click the drop-down list box to reveal that DLL file.

Once the DLL file has been clicked, its memory details information will subsequently appear within the confines of the Memory Details window. Once you have finished examining the memory details for a process, just click the OK button to close the Memory Details window and return to the main Process Viewer window. To exit the Process Viewer completely, click the Exit button found on that screen.

Caching Disk Requests

Another way to optimize and improve the performance of the organization's Windows 2000 Server environment is through a technology known as *caching*. More specifically, it's through the caching of disk requests that a Windows 2000 Server application can increase its overall performance. Unfortunately, it's very possible for the application developers to write their source code poorly, which means that even with the best-of-breed server hardware, including memory and disk drives/controllers, applications can still thrash around and perform miserably. The best way to manage this process is to confront your organization's developers with hard-core proof that their applications are not as good as required. To obtain that proof, you should turn to the Windows 2000 Performance tool. This tool is the update to the old PerfMon (or Performance Monitor) tool that shipped with the Windows NT 4.0 operating systems. Usage of this tool is thoroughly discussed later in this chapter.

However, if you already understand how to use the Performance tool, you might want to start it at this point. To start using this tool, click the Start, Programs, Administrative Tools, Performance menu selection. This will start the Performance tool, from which you'll run your diagnostics. Table 24.2 shows several key monitors that you will want to peruse with the Performance tool, all of which will help you to find that errant application (proof for the organization's development staff).

TABLE 24.2 Monitoring for Disk Cache Problems

Performance Object	Performance Counter
Memory	Cache Bytes
Memory	Cache Faults/Sec
Memory	Page Fault/Sec
Memory	Page Reads/Sec
Cache	Copy Reads/Sec
Cache	Data Flushes/Sec
Cache	Copy Read Hits%
Cache	Fast Read Not Possible/Sec
Cache	Read Aheads/Sec
Logical Disk	Disk Reads/Sec
Logical Disk	Pages Input/Sec

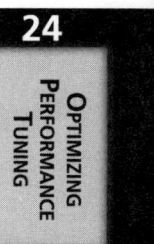

Stripe Sets and Virtual Memory Pagefiles

To increase performance on your Windows 2000 server there are two key areas: the type of hard drive space and controllers available to the system as well as the amount of memory (a.k.a. RAM) that's available to the operating system. To maximize performance of your system from a hard disk drive perspective, consider using a technology known as *RAID* (Redundant Array of Inexpensive Disks), which includes a concept known as *stripe sets*. This technology will be discussed thoroughly in the next section. Striped disk volumes will also provide your organization with the best Windows 2000 Server disk performance strategy. Of course, there are tradeoffs to consider, so you will want to closely examine this next section.

To maximize system performance from a memory perspective, you should focus on the use of a technology concept known as *virtual memory pagefiles* (also discussed in more detail in the section after next). The virtual memory technology uses a process known as *demand paging* to move data back and forth between the physical RAM of your Windows 2000 server machine and the server's paging files. If your organization fully exploits the use of its Windows 2000 virtual memory configurations, it's certain to maximize its Windows 2000 server performance. A full discussion of the virtual memory pagefiles for a Windows 2000 server is in the section immediately following the striped volumes discussion.

Striped Volumes

When running the Windows 2000 Server operating system on your organization's networks, you can increase the performance of the OS using a technology known as a *striped volume*. A striped volume improves disk reading and writing due to the multiple disks involved and improves data protection from a fault-tolerance perspective. With Windows 2000, as in the old Windows NT 4.0 world, there are two types of striped volume sets: without parity and with parity, which is now known as a RAID-5 volume. Only a RAID-5 disk volume has redundancy, whereas a striped volume without parity does not.

Before we get ahead of ourselves, though, you need to first understand the differences between the two types of storage available within the Windows 2000 operating system. Remember back in Windows NT 4.0 when you had the traditional version of hard disk drives with primary and extended partitions? These were the disk drive volumes with the extended partitions, which contained one or more logical drives. That form of disk storage in the Windows 2000 world is now known as *basic storage*. Although it's still possible to use the basic storage concept—especially because it's the default disk format—it's not the recommended path for both performance and disk data redundancy. The new disk methodology that has been introduced with the Windows 2000 operating system is known as *dynamic storage*. Dynamic storage permits you to have one of five different storage formats for your Windows 2000 server machine:

- *Simple volume*. This single hard disk drive contains a single partition that includes the complete hard drive. A simple volume can be mirrored, though, which would then provide a level of fault tolerance for your Windows 2000 system.

- *Spanned volume*. This form of hard disk storage means that more than one disk drive (up to 32 disk drives) is utilized as a single partition, which makes it very easy to create very large disk partitions without the cost of purchasing one large drive. An obvious downside to using a spanned volume, though, is that if you lose one of the drives, you'll lose all the data across all the drives.

- *Mirrored volume*. A mirrored volume is a fault-tolerant way to preserve information on your Windows 2000 server machine. This requires a minimum of two hard disk drives that have been initially set up as simple volumes. An upside to mirrored volumes is that all system information and data are protected 100 percent, with the obvious downside being that you'll always lose the functionality of 50 percent of your total disk space (due to the mirroring process).

- *Striped volume*. A striped volume is the fastest form of disk storage in the Windows 2000 world, because it optimizes the reading and writing of information across all the disks at the exact same rate. To create a striped volume, you must have at least two (but not more than 32) disk drives for use with the volume set. However, be aware that a striped volume does not provide any level of fault tolerance for your organization's computer systems.

- *RAID-5 volume*. A RAID-5 disk volume is a fault-tolerant version of the striped volume and does optimize disk reads, although it's considerably slower for the writing of data across the disks in the volume. RAID-5 requires a minimum of three disk drives (again, with a maximum of 32 drives) using a parity-striping feature to save data across the multiple drives in such a way as to provide a measure of fault tolerance for the organization's data.

The Windows 2000 disk storage feature known as *dynamic storage* provides something that system administrators in the Windows NT 4.0 world could only dream about: the ability to dynamically size or resize a disk volume without having to reboot the operating system. However, as it was in the Windows NT 4.0 world, you are not permitted to store either the boot or the system partitions on a RAID-5 volume (although it's permissible to put either of these on a striped volume).

From a fault-tolerance perspective, a RAID-5 (striped volumes with parity) volume does have a lower cost per byte of information, will have exceptional data read performance, and will require more system memory than will a RAID-1 (mirrored volume) disk volume. Furthermore, a RAID-1 volume can protect both the boot and system partitions, whereas the RAID-5 volume cannot. Even so, if all your organization desires is system performance (meaning that you can live with no fault tolerance other than your backup tapes), the path to choose here is a dynamic storage striped volume.

To make changes to your disk configurations, once you've already installed the Windows 2000 Server operating system, there's an MMC snap-in tool just for the occasion: the Storage snap-in that's already a part of the Computer Management tool (although you can use this to create your own "special" MMC format if you so desire). To access the Windows 2000 Server Computer Management tool, click the Start, Programs, Administrative Tools, Computer Management menu selection to reveal the screen shown in Figure 24.18.

FIGURE 24.18
Using the Disk Management portion of the Windows 2000 Server Computer Management MMC.

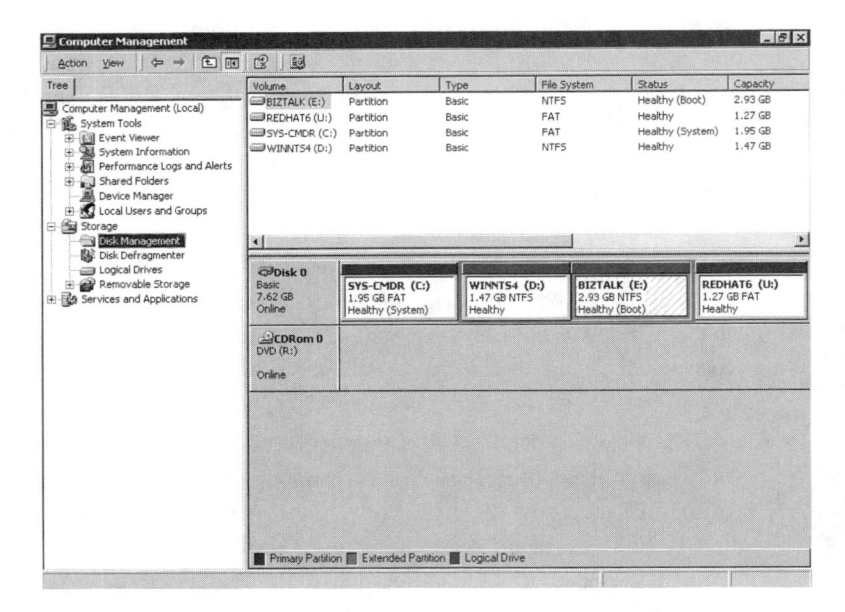

Another way that you could have gotten to this tool (much faster, as well) would have been to just right-click the My Computer icon found on the Windows 2000 desktop and then click the Manage menu selection (it's at the bottom of the small menu that appears). Nonetheless, seeing how you have already arrived at the Computer Management tool's main menu, it's time to get started. If you click the plus symbol (+) located to the left of the Storage option, that area will automatically expand. Inside the Storage area, you'll find the Disk Management folder. Click that folder to reveal a listing of all your system's disk volumes, which will appear in the frame to the right.

As you can see, the system in the example has multiple drive volumes already created and in use. If you're planning to use any kind of a multiboot system, like the one shown here (this computer also boots to Red Hat Linux, Windows NT 4.0 Server, and Windows Millennium), you must not format your system as a Windows 2000 dynamic volume using the NTFS 5.0 file allocation system. However, if you plan to use just Windows 2000 Server on your system (this is the recommended methodology, except for perhaps test systems), you can indeed use the Windows 2000 dynamic volume structure with the NTFS 5.0 file allocation system format. To change the format structure of any volume, you must first click that volume (located in the bottom half of the frame to the right) to select it and then right-click that same disk volume to reveal a small menu like the one shown in Figure 24.19.

FIGURE 24.19
Choosing a selection from the Disk Management pop-up menu.

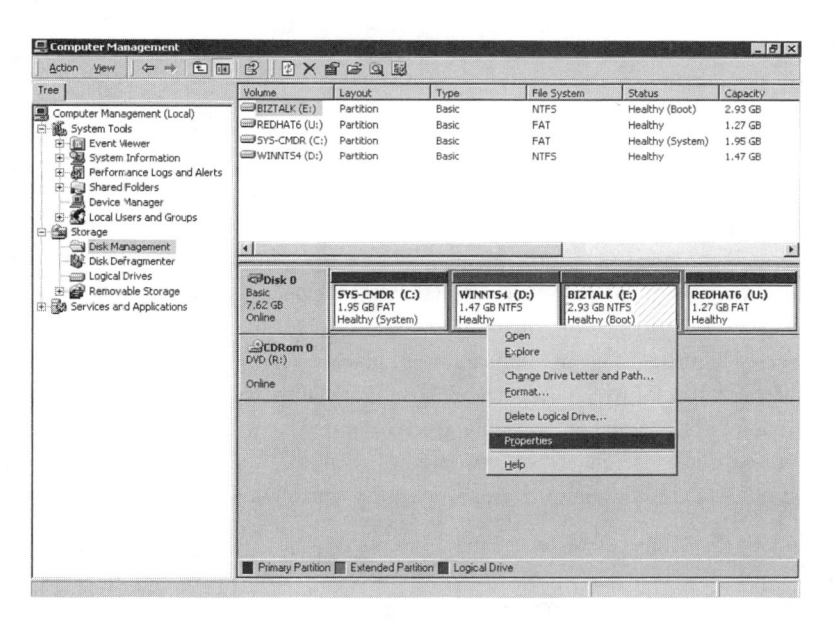

To perform simple disk management tasks, such as the changing of an assigned drive letter or the formatting of a disk volume, simply click either of those menu selections. However, to continue on your quest for better system performance through the use of the Disk Management tool, click the Properties menu selection found at the bottom of the small menu. Performing this will reveal the *ServerName* Properties window (this is the BIZTALK (E:) Properties window in the sample), shown in Figure 24.20.

FIGURE 24.20
Accessing the Properties window for a specific fixed-disk drive.

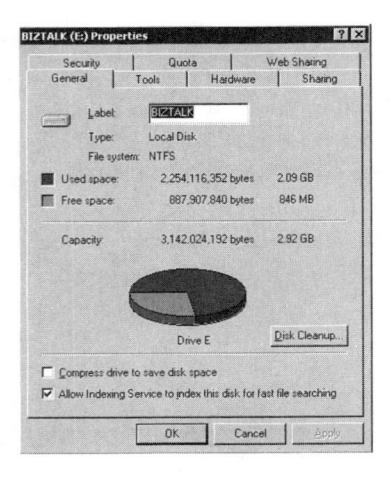

In the Properties window you'll initially be taken to the General tab, which contains a few important items. First, the use of the two check boxes at the bottom of this tab will greatly affect the performance of your Windows 2000 server machine. Using the Disk Compression feature will give you more disk space to work with, but it will definitely affect the performance of your disk volume in a negative fashion. Enabling the Indexing Service will improve the file location performance for your user community, but this will decrease the overall performance of your Windows 2000 server machine, especially if this Windows 2000 server happens to be an application or database server instead of a file server. Clicking either of these check boxes will place a check mark in the appropriate box, meaning that it's now enabled for use on that particular disk volume. Use of the Disk Cleanup button will permit you to find those unused or unwanted files on this Windows 2000 server machine, which, by itself, can aid in the improvement of the system's overall performance.

Click the Tools tab to reveal the contents of that screen, as shown in Figure 24.21.

FIGURE 24.21
Choosing a system tool to use with your Windows 2000 server.

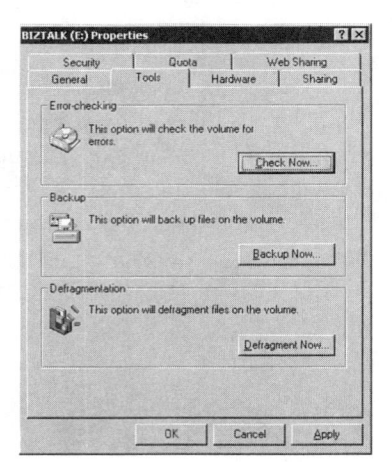

Frequent use of this screen will permit you to enhance the performance of your Windows 2000 servers, because a defragged and error-free disk volume will always perform better than a fragmented or error-induced disk volume. Click the Check Now button to run the Windows 2000 ScanDisk utility, which is used to locate and fix disk problems. Click the Defragment Now button to run the Windows 2000 Disk Defragmenter tool, which is used to defragment a fragmented Windows 2000 server. Once you've performed all the necessary disk maintenance options, click the Sharing tab to reveal that screen.

The fewer drive volumes you share, the better your overall system performance will be. Obviously, though, the fewer drive volumes you share, the less empowered your organization's computer users will be, so this is, of course, a very fine balance. The real performance-related function on this screen is the use of the Caching button, which is used by the Windows 2000 Server administrator to determine the configuration of caching for the organization's users in regard to their accessing of offline files. Click the Caching button to reveal the screen shown in Figure 24.22.

FIGURE 24.22
Confirming the cache settings for your Windows 2000 server.

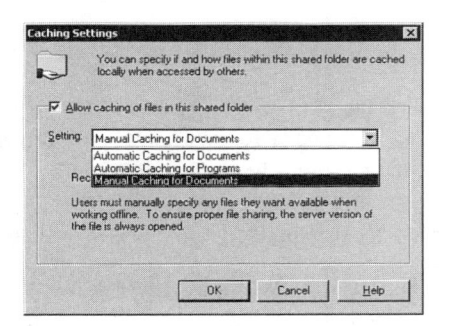

Once the Caching Settings screen appears, you have to decide whether to permit the use of cached files and folders for this local disk volume. Assuming that the answer is Yes, you'll need to make sure that the top check box (Allow Caching of Files in This Shared Folder) is marked. To do this, click that empty check box to place a check mark inside it. From there, you'll need to select a default caching setting for this disk volume. To do that, click the drop-down list box next to the Setting label. The choices are quite self-explanatory, so just click your selection and then click the OK button to save the Caching Settings screen options. Performing these steps will then return you to the main ServerName Properties screen. From there, click the OK button to save your selections and exit this screen. Once you're done examining the Computer Management/Storage folder options, click the "X" found in the upper-right corner of the MMC to exit the management console window.

Optimizing Virtual Memory Pages

The options available for the Windows 2000 Server Virtual Memory Manager (VMM) are managed from within the Virtual Memory screen. Before you go there, there are some basic concepts you need to understand first. The memory management options for Windows 2000 are varied, depending on the hardware configuration of your server, but there are a few ways in which you can maximize the performance of your Windows 2000 server machine:

- Create a paging file for each physical disk that you've installed on your Windows 2000. Doing this will permit your server to read paging file information from multiple locations simultaneously, thus reducing the time necessary to access that data. Likewise, when your system needs to write information to the paging file, it will theoretically use the least busy disk drive to write that information.

- Set the initial size of the Windows 2000 paging file to the maximum size, which will save your system the time it would normally otherwise take to enlarge the paging file at some future point (this typically is not a big performance increase, but, hey, anything helps).

- Move the Windows 2000 Server paging file off the disk drive volume that presently contains the Windows 2000 %systemroot% folder (this is probably called \WinNT or \Win2000, depending upon how you initially configured your system). Doing this will avoid the data request collisions that are sure to result from having both the paging file and the system boot partition on the same physical disk drive.

To change the various options available for the Windows 2000 Server Virtual Memory Manager (VMM), which is managed from within the Virtual Memory screen, you need to go to the Computer Management tool. To access the Windows 2000 Server Computer Management tool, click the Start, Programs, Administrative Tools, Computer Management menu selection to reveal the main Computer Management screen.

Once there, right-click the Computer Management (Local) option that appears at the top of the menu tree in the left pane. Doing this will cause a small menu to appear, with just a few options: Connect to another computer…, All Tasks, View, Export List, Properties, and Help.

Near the bottom of that menu, you'll see a menu selection labeled *Properties*. Click the Properties menu selection to reveal another screen, as shown in Figure 24.23.

FIGURE 24.23
Viewing the basic configuration for a Windows 2000 server.

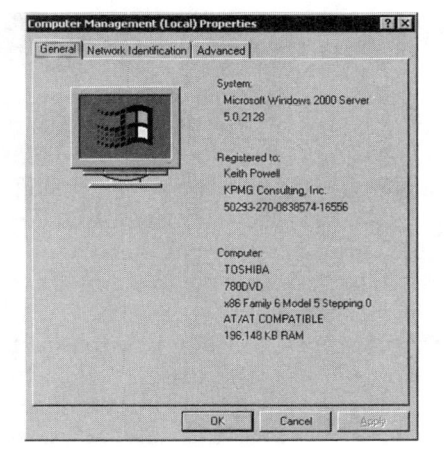

Once the Computer Management (Local) Properties screen appears, you will be located on the General tab, by default. The most useful bit of data on this screen can be found near the bottom: The total amount of RAM (memory) is listed here. In this example, the total amount of RAM is 192Mb, which translates into 196,148 kilobytes of memory. Once you have noted the total amount on your Windows 2000 server machine, click the Advanced tab to reveal the screen shown in Figure 24.24.

FIGURE 24.24
Viewing the advanced properties choices for managing your server.

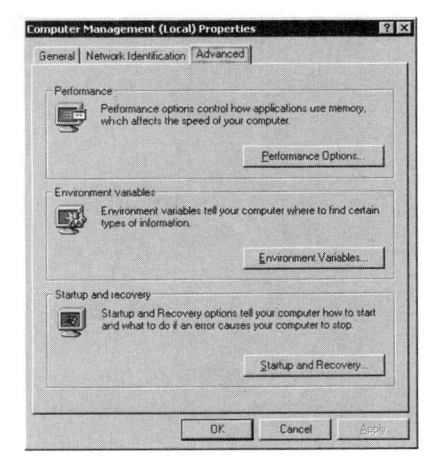

> **Note**
>
> The Windows 2000 operating system was built much in the same fashion as the Windows NT and Windows 9x operating systems: They all have a slew of undocumented features. For example, what you just did in three separate steps to reach the Computer Management (Local) Properties screen could have been achieved much faster with a single mouse click plus keyboard combination. By holding down the Alt key on the keyboard and double-clicking the My Computer icon on the Windows 2000 desktop, you would be transported directly onto the General tab of the System Properties screen. The interesting thing to note here is that for the two tabs' worth of information that we're interested in, both of them appear in the exact same format on the Computer Management (Local) Properties screen as they do on the System Properties screen. As you can test later on your own time, this quick-access method works just as well in the Windows NT and Windows 9x operating systems in many areas. Interesting "features," eh?

Of the three sections found on the Advanced tab, the top one is going to be the focus here. It's in the Performance area that you're able to access the Windows 2000 Virtual Memory Manager (VMM), in order to perform the various memory and page file management tasks. To do this, click the Performance Options button, which will then cause the Performance Options screen to be revealed, as shown in Figure 24.25.

FIGURE 24.25

Changing the performance options for a Windows 2000 server.

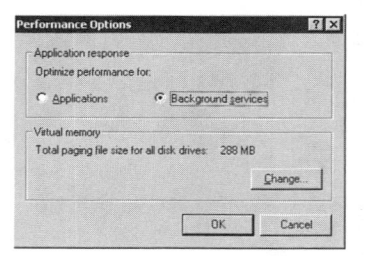

On the Performance Options screen, you're able to optimize your Windows 2000 server machine either for the applications running on it or for the background services being processed by it. If your choice is to select the Applications radio button by clicking it once, what you're doing is telling your Windows 2000 server to give more of its CPU resources to whatever application is running in the foreground (that is, the active application). This means that an active application (the application running in the foreground) is the one that's presently responding to inputs by one or more users. If your choice is to select the Background Services radio button by clicking it once, what you're doing is telling your Windows 2000 server to allocate an equal amount of system resources to all the programs installed on it, regardless of which one might actually be running in the foreground. Once you've made your performance optimization choice here, either click the OK button to close this screen and return to the Computer Management (Local) Properties screen or click the Change button found within the Virtual Memory section of the Performance Options screen to reveal the screen shown in Figure 24.26.

FIGURE 24.26
Reviewing/changing the Virtual Memory configurations.

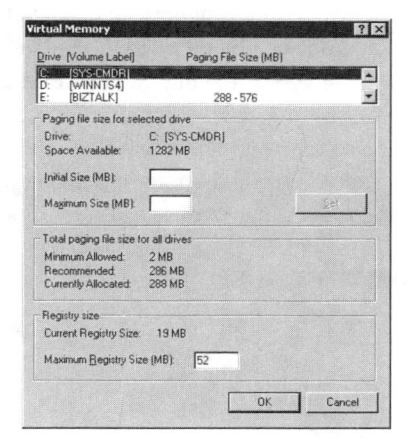

Once the Virtual Memory screen appears, you should notice the total size of your existing paging file as well as the Registry size. Remember that the Windows 2000 Server paging file is the swap file for your system that contains the memory pages that are no longer stored in the physical RAM of your server. This means that these memory pages have been "swapped out" by the operating system to this specialized hidden file on the hard drive, a process whose utilization can be tracked by the performance-monitoring utility discussed in detail in the next section of this chapter.

To change either the initial or the maximum size of your Windows 2000 server's paging file, click the drive volume that presently holds the paging file. Once there, you'll see that the Set button is grayed out. This merely means that because no changes have been made, there's no reason to "set" those changes (that is, to save them) into the Registry of your Windows 2000 server. However, once you make a change, such as by altering the initial size of the paging file, the Set button will no longer be grayed out.

From this screen you can also split your paging file across multiple hard drives by simply clicking other drive volumes, creating both minimum and maximum paging file sizes, and then clicking the Set button to confirm those entries. As you make your entries, you'll see that the third section (from the top) on this screen, labeled *Total Paging File Size for All Drives*, changes its total paging file size numbers. By watching the section, you'll be able to properly manage your paging file sizes and location(s).

The final section on this screen, *Registry Size*, is also an important one. If you do not permit your Windows 2000 Server Registry files to access enough disk space, you risk your system's capability to keep track of all the information it needs to operate properly. Likewise, if the Registry cannot grow to meet its needs, you'll see error messages whenever you attempt to install additional programs and applications on your Windows 2000 server machine.

Once you've made all your selections on the Virtual Memory screen, click the OK button to confirm your choices and exit the screen. You'll be returned to the Performance Options screen. Click the OK button on that screen to confirm your choices, exit that screen, and return to the Computer Management (Local) Properties screen. From there, there's one more option you'll want to examine: the Startup and Recovery area. To access this area, click the Startup and Recovery button found near the bottom of the Computer Management (Local) Properties screen to reveal the screen shown in Figure 24.27.

FIGURE 24.27
Reviewing your Startup and Recovery options.

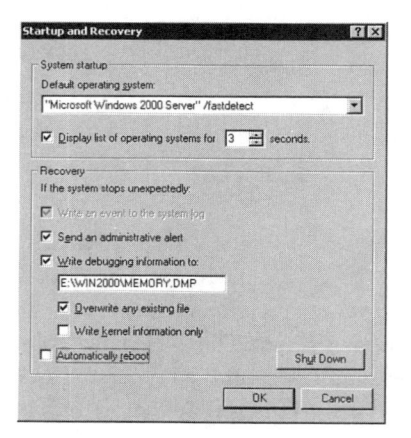

On the Startup and Recovery screen, you are able to set your system recovery options. Normally, the setting of these options might be construed as being outside the scope of performance tuning operations, but this is one area that Microsoft has yet to fix: the separation of saving system debugging information and the location/size of the system swap files.

In other words, if you choose to split your Windows 2000 system's paging file across multiple disk drives, you are foregoing the opportunity to save system debugging information in the unlikely event of a system fault, such as every Windows NT/Windows 2000 system administrator's favorite: the blue screen of death (BSOD). The problems you face here are twofold: The paging file must be on the same disk partition as the one that contains the `%systemroot%` folder, and the paging file must be at least one megabyte larger than the total amount of physical RAM that exists on your computer. What this means, for those inexperienced system administrators out there, is that Microsoft is forcing you to choose between improving the performance of your Windows 2000 Server system and its ability to provide you with the proper recovery information that may be needed for you to diagnose the reasons why your Windows 2000 server just crashed. Some choice, eh? Because the arguments for both sides are usually quite persuasive, I will leave this one up to you to decide. However, I'll toss in one parting thought: If you have a good backup/recovery plan and procedures in place as well as the forethought to purchase some of the more useful tools from Winternals Software, Inc. (such as the Administrator's Pak, which includes the Blue-Save tool), you should opt for the system performance side of the equation. Just a thought, anyway.

To exit from the Startup and Recovery screen, just click the OK button, which will cause you to be returned to the Computer Management (Local) Properties screen. However, if you made at least one change to either the Windows 2000 server's paging file configuration or on the Startup and Recovery screen, you'll be prompted to restart your Windows 2000 Server system with a small message dialog box.

Once you have read the information contained within this dialog box, click the OK button to close the box. You will then see another message box appear immediately. This one asks you whether you want to restart your system immediately.

Click the Yes button to perform the automatic restart, or you can click the No button to enable yourself to perform the system restart on your own terms. Once the system has been restarted, all your changes will take effect.

Performance-Monitoring Utility

The Windows 2000 Server Performance utility enables you to monitor the performance of your server's system hardware as well as the operating system and application-level software installed on it. This is a very useful tool, although its overuse can negatively affect server performance. This means that you should put at least a little bit of thought into how you'll perform your system monitoring efforts, especially if your Windows 2000 Server environment includes any type of Internet Web farm or e-commerce configuration.

If you have never performed any type of server or network monitoring before, you may want to check out the monitoring methodology order that Microsoft suggests as a checklist inside the Windows 2000 Server Help file:

- Read the key concepts regarding system performance monitoring. Simply put, this means that you should do your homework before turning on all the various network and server monitors within your organization's production server environment.

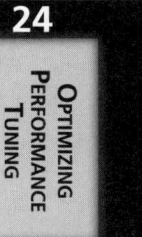

- Ensure that you have appropriate permissions on the computer you want to monitor. To perform most monitoring functions within Windows 2000 Server, you must have administrative-level rights to the various components of your Windows 2000 network.

- Install Network Monitor driver to monitor network performance counters. There's a special Windows 2000 Server network monitor driver whose installation is required first. Use the Network and Dial-Up Connections icon found within the Windows 2000 Server Control Panel to perform the installation process. You'll need to install the Network Monitor Driver networking protocol in order to perform most networking-level monitoring.

- Set up a monitoring configuration. This step is designed to ensure that you have a separate Windows 2000 member server computer from which the monitoring process will be coordinated. This is a good idea considering the negative performance impact too much monitoring may otherwise place on your production server environment.

- Evaluate monitoring results and establish a baseline. Once you have figured out what you're going to monitor and how, you need to set a base performance level against which you'll compare future results. The differences will tell you whether your system is performing better or worse than it was before. Failure to set a performance baseline simply means that you're probably wasting your time trying to monitor your Windows 2000 Server environment.

- Investigate variations in performance data and tune or upgrade components as needed. As you discover performance differences, especially the negative ones, you need to go back to your general Windows 2000 Server population and tweak the hardware and software applications as necessary. If you do not do this, you're probably wasting your time trying to monitor your Windows 2000 Server environment.

- Archive monitoring data and use archives to monitor trends. Trend analysis of the performance of your Windows 2000 Server environment is very important. You never know when you might run into a performance problem in the future, and there just might be some monitoring data in your systems' past that can help you to resolve future problems.

Once you're prepared to start your system monitoring programs, the next thing to do is to make sure the Windows 2000 Server administrators are properly prepared and trained to determine what changes should be implemented based on the results of the monitoring process. In other words, there needs to be organization-wide policies and procedures (that is, an organizational strategy) in place to ensure that the changes that the monitoring suggests should be implemented are actually implemented into your organization's Windows 2000 Server environment. Likewise, it's imperative that one system administrator does not have the ability to implement a change differently from how another system administrator would in the same production environment. A lack of consistency here would most certainly do more harm to your Windows 2000 Server environment than not monitoring at all. One final thought: As you implement changes that were suggested by your monitoring efforts, you would be wise to implement just a single change at a time so that you do not compound your problems by fixing one problem only to spawn a few new problems elsewhere within your Windows 2000 Server environment.

Okay, it is now time to get started with the monitoring process, which is accomplished by accessing the Windows 2000 Server Performance utility. To access the Windows 2000 Server Performance tool, click the Start, Programs, Administrative Tools, Performance menu selection to reveal the screen shown in Figure 24.28.

FIGURE 24.28
Viewing the main performance monitoring MMC screen.

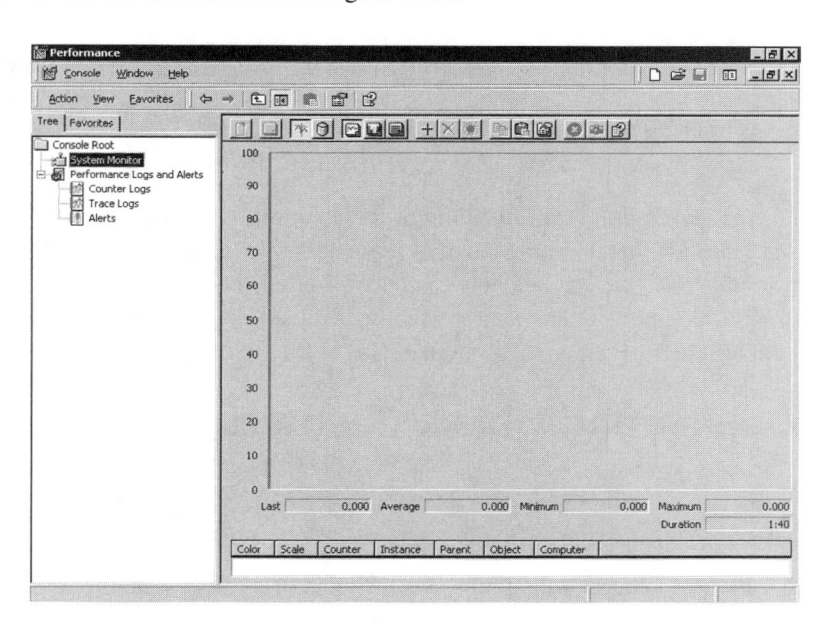

When the main Performance screen opens, you will see two panes: The one on the left contains the menu tree that includes the System Monitor itself, along with the Performance Logs and Alerts folder below it; the pane to the right has the System Monitor's display (if it looks familiar to you, you've obviously used the PerfMon tool from the Windows NT 4.0 operating system). Along the top row of the System Monitor display are the 16 buttons that control every operation of the monitor. Here they are (from left to right):

- New Counter Set
- Clear Display
- View Current Activity

- View Log File Data
- View Chart
- View Histogram
- Report
- Add
- Delete
- Highlight
- Copy Properties
- Paste Counter List
- Properties
- Freeze Display
- Update Data
- Help

For the most part, the functionality of these buttons is self-explanatory. However, we will walk through them in more detail in these next few subsections. The discussion will start with an overview of the objects and counters used. Then it will progress into the addition of a few counters to the monitor window and then cover the creation/interpretation of monitor charts, reports, logs, and the like.

Objects and Object Counters

To start any monitoring process, you'll need to add at least one counter (and probably more) to your System Monitor display area. To do this, click the Add button (it looks like a plus symbol), which will then reveal the Add Counters screen.

A very nice feature of the Performance tool is that you can monitor either your local server (that is, the one on which the Performance tool is active) or some other Windows 2000 server that exists somewhere else on your organization's networks. Select the appropriate radio button to determine whether you are going to be monitoring a local system or a remote box. To make your selection, just click the radio button of your choice. If you are going to be using a remote system, you must also enter the UNC path to that remote system. Computers that you've connected to in the past will automatically be added to the drop-down list box so that you don't always need to enter their UNC paths every single time you want to perform your monitoring.

Just below the server selection is the Performance Object drop-down list box. A *performance object* is an assortment of monitoring counters that are associated with system resources and services available for monitoring. For example, the Memory performance object contains a variety of monitoring counters such as Available Bytes, Page Faults per Second, Pages per Second, and so on. There are literally dozens of counters available within those 38 performance objects in this drop-down list box, including the following:

- *ACS/RSVP Service*. For monitoring QoS admission control activities
- *Active Server Pages*. For monitoring activities surrounding Internet Information Server–based ASP pages
- *Browser*. Web browser–related objects
- *Cache*. File system physical memory cache activities
- *Distributed Transaction Coordinator*. Transaction monitoring
- *HTTP Indexing Service*. Indexing Service monitoring
- *IAS Accounting Clients*. Monitoring of an IAS Accounting Client
- *IAS Accounting Server*. Monitoring of an IAS Accounting Server
- *IAS Authentication Clients*. Monitoring of an IAS Authentication Client
- *IAS Authentication Server*. Monitoring of an IAS Authentication Client
- *ICMP*. For monitoring TCP/IP
- *IMDB Service*. Transaction and database monitoring
- *Indexing Service*. Indexing Service monitoring
- *Indexing Service Filter*. Indexing Service monitoring
- *Internet Information Server Global*. Monitoring of the Internet Information Services server
- *IP*. For monitoring TCP/IP
- *Job Object*. For monitoring certain aspects of a Job Object
- *Job Object Details*. For monitoring certain aspects of a Job Object at a specified moment in time (such as current activities only)
- *Memory*. RAM monitoring
- *NBT Connection*. For monitoring TCP/IP
- *Network Interface*. For monitoring specific objects related to the network interface (such as an ethernet adapter or a TCP loopback interface)
- *Network Segment*. For monitoring a specific network subnet or segment
- *Objects*. Specific software application objects
- *Paging File*. Swap file monitoring
- *Print Queue*. To monitor available printer queues
- *Process*. To monitor an application process

- *Processor*. To monitor the available processor(s) (a.k.a. CPUs)
- *RAS Port*. To monitor available remote access communications ports
- *RAS Total*. To monitor various totals of activity for the RAS ports, such as total bytes received, total bytes transmitted per second, and so on
- *Redirector*. To monitor the network redirector
- *Server*. To monitor specific server activity
- *Server Work Queues*. To monitor various aspects of the work queues associated with a particular server
- *System*. To monitor system-wide objects, such as active threads, system up time, and so on
- *TCP*. For monitoring TCP/IP
- *Telephony*. To monitor telephonic activities of the Windows 2000 server
- *Thread*. To monitor the activities of one or more specific threads on a server
- *UDP*. For monitoring TCP/IP
- *Web Service*. To monitor particular aspects of the IIS Web server service, such as total current anonymous users, the rate files are transferred by the Web service, and so on. This monitoring can be done at a total or specific Web site level (such as for just the default Web site).

The vast majority of these performance objects are self-explanatory, but for those that are not there's quite a bit of Microsoft Help text available online via the Performance utility itself. It's well worth the time to examine the Help system files anyway, in case you're a beginner at the whole monitoring game. For the most part, the Help files provided with the Windows 2000 Server operating system are far more advanced than they ever were in previous versions of Windows NT. Besides, being good at system monitoring requires a solid systems development and network engineering background, along with a high degree of intelligence and troubleshooting capabilities, which means that everyone should try to always add to their repertoire of monitoring information form any source possible.

Once you've selected your performance object, you must then choose one or more counters from the listing below the performance object drop-down list box (this listing is contained inside the box just below the radio button Select Counters from List). However, if you click the radio button next to the choice of All Counters, every single counter for that performance object will subsequently be added to your chart. This is probably a bad idea in nearly every case, because you'll very quickly hit an information overload, besides the fact that you'll also overload your server with performance-monitoring tasks (a lose-lose monitoring proposition).

On several of the monitoring counters, there may be a third option: Instance. There are a few instances available for the % Processor Time counter. In the case of choosing an instance, you may want to click the top radio button (All Instances) to select all the available instances for that counter. Chances are most counters will have just a few instances. However, if you want to be meticulous, you may click the Select Instances from List radio button, which then will permit you to select one or more instances from the box listing below it. To select more than one counter or instance, you'll need to hold down the Ctrl key on your server's keyboard as you click each separate counter or instance. Doing this will enable you to pick and choose among the many options for each counter and instance.

If you become confused as to what a specific counter is used for, click the counter that you require assistance for to select it and then click the Explain button. Doing this will then cause the Explain Text window to appear just below the Add Counters window, as shown in Figure 24.29.

FIGURE 24.29
Viewing an explanation for a particular performance monitor counter.

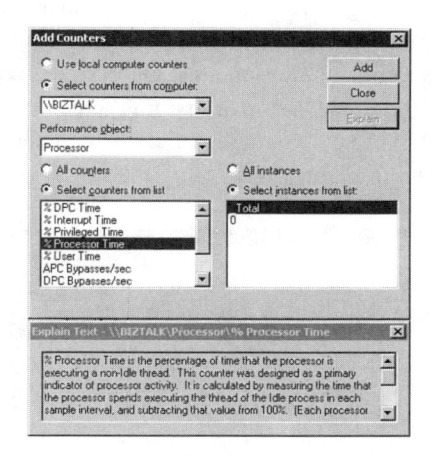

For the most part, the explanation given for any particular counter is typically very usefully. However, on a few rare occasions the explanation given might actually confuse you more. In these cases you will want to consult third-party materials, such as the guides that came with your system's hardware or application documentation. In the event that you do not possess documentation from either of these sources, you might want to consider using a different counter or contacting Microsoft's premier (that is, *paid*) technical support services.

One more thing you need to watch for is the use of counters and instances for very specific uses. For example, in the case of the example shown in Figure 24.30, you would want to make sure you pick the correct instance for the Web site that you want to monitor.

FIGURE 24.30
Choosing a specific instance of a performance monitor counter.

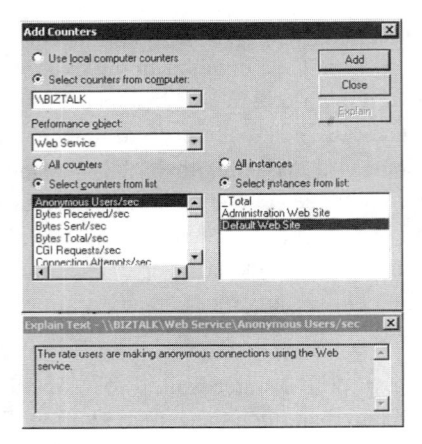

Chances are you would never want to monitor the entire Internet Information Server's Web farm but instead just focus on a single Web site on that particular Windows 2000 Web server. Once you have made your specific counter selections, click the Add button to add your counters and instances to the monitoring area. Once you have added all the counters/instances you want, click the Close button to exit this screen. You will now be back on the System Monitor screen, but now you will see all the counters and instances that you have just selected, as shown in Figure 24.31.

FIGURE 24.31
Reviewing the performance monitor counters in action.

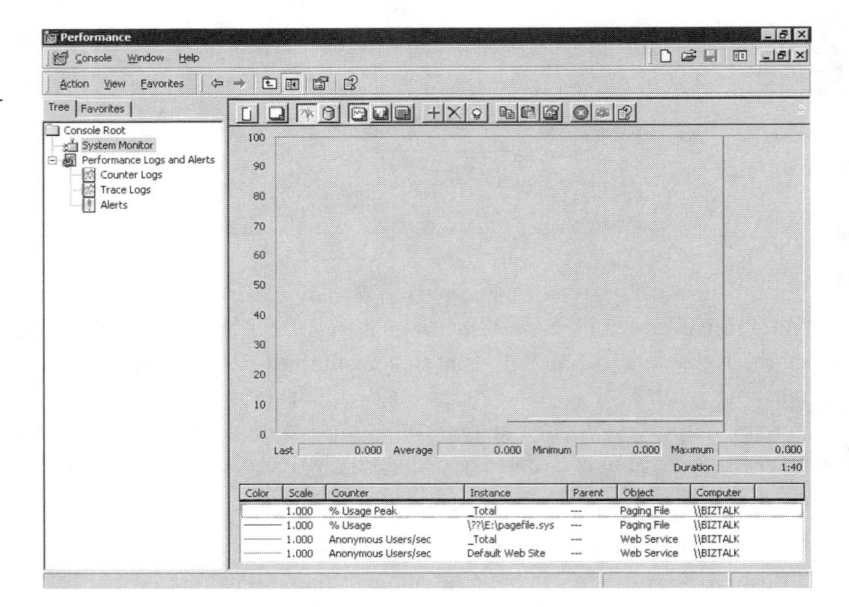

Creating a Chart

At the end of the previous section, you learned how to create a system-monitoring chart. At this point, it's time to expand on that knowledge. Let's begin by taking a closer look at the chart shown in Figure 24.32.

FIGURE 24.32
Interpreting the data shown by a performance monitor counter.

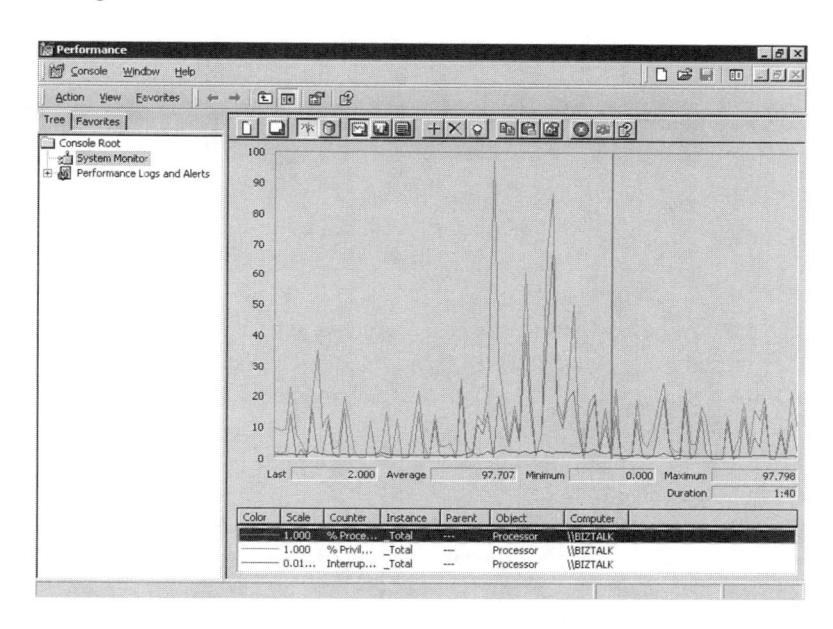

This chart contains just a few counters (%Processor, %Privileged, and Interrupts) from a single object (Processor) and similar instances (_Total). If you look at the bottom of this screen, you can find all this information readily available to you. If you had several counters all running simultaneously for multiple objects, you might want to sort the information shown. To do that, just click the header label for that piece of information. For example, if you clicked the term *Instance*, all the instances would quickly be sorted in alphabetical order. Likewise, do the same thing with the Object header; now all your objects appear as being grouped together. To expand the column for any counter, simply click and drag the boxes to the width that you desire by "grabbing" the line between the headers, just as you would when stretching columns in a Microsoft Excel spreadsheet.

To set the default properties for a Performance tool chart, as well as to set the defaults for the other types of information (histogram, reports, graphs, and so on), click the Properties button to reveal the screen shown in Figure 24.33.

FIGURE 24.33

Setting the general system monitor properties.

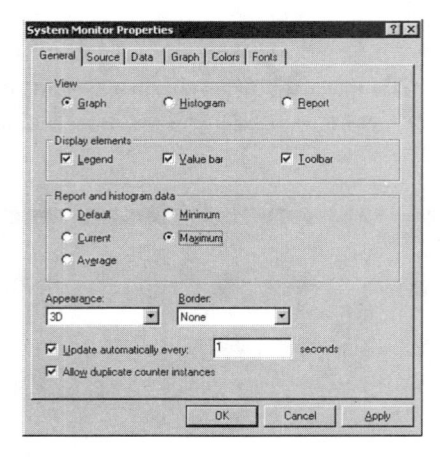

Once the System Monitor Properties window appears, you will be taken directly to the General tab (this is the default). From this screen you can set the default View type (Graph, Histogram, or Report), the display elements, the level of report and histogram data reported, as well as the default appearance and update frequencies for this tool. Once you have made all your selections and/or changes, click the Source tab to move to the screen shown in Figure 24.34.

FIGURE 24.34

Selecting a data source for the server activities monitored.

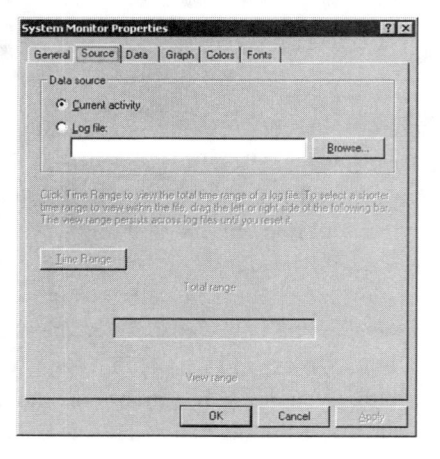

The Source tab enables you to determine whether you will be viewing data as a real-time activity (Current Activity) or from a previous monitoring session (Log File). To make your selection, click the radio button next to the option of your choosing. Only if you choose to use a log file will you be able to use the functionality of the Time Range button found on the bottom half of this screen. Once you have made all your selections and changes, click the Data tab to move to that screen.

The Data tab provides a very quick way to determine precisely which counters are active on your Windows 2000 server. Likewise, you are able to add more counters at will from this screen as well as change the appearance of the active counters. To remove any counter, simply click that counter to first select it and then click the Remove button to delete that specific counter. Once you've made your choices, click the Graph tab to move to that screen, as shown in Figure 24.35.

FIGURE 24.35
Setting the graph formatting attributes.

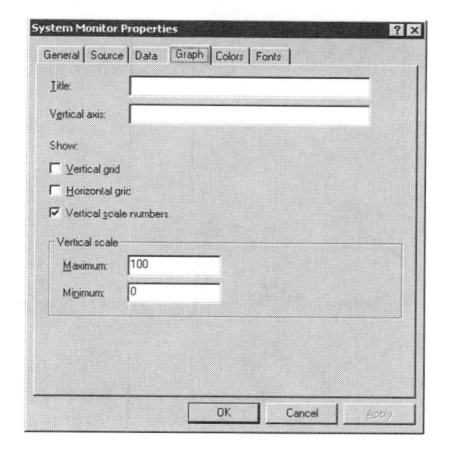

The Graph tab permits you to set the default settings for the graph view of your monitoring information. This includes the ability to add a title, change the axis values, and alter the vertical scale information. Once you have made all your selections and changes, click the Colors tab to move to that screen.

The Colors tab is the most simplistic one you will find within the monitoring tool set. With this tab, you can set the various color schemes that are in use during the visual presentation of the monitoring data. Use the drop-down list boxes to find your target area; then click the color of your choice to make the change. Once you have made your choices, click the Fonts tab to move to that screen.

The Fonts tab is the next-most simplistic one you'll find within the monitoring tool set. With it, you are able to change the display font and its characteristics for use with the system monitoring tool. It works just like most any other Windows-based application, in that you click on a drop-down list box to select a font type and then use the other list boxes to choose the font style and size. The Sample area shows you how your font will look, depending upon what choices you have made, so it is always very clear what impact your selections will have upon a particular font choice. Once you have made your choices, click the OK button to save all your changes and return to the main system monitoring screen.

Once there, you may want to make it easier to see a specific counter's information. To do that, first click that counter in the bottom legend and then click the Highlight button (it's the one that looks like a light bulb) to reveal the screen shown in Figure 24.36.

FIGURE 24.36
Highlighting a specific counter's value within the chart for easy viewing.

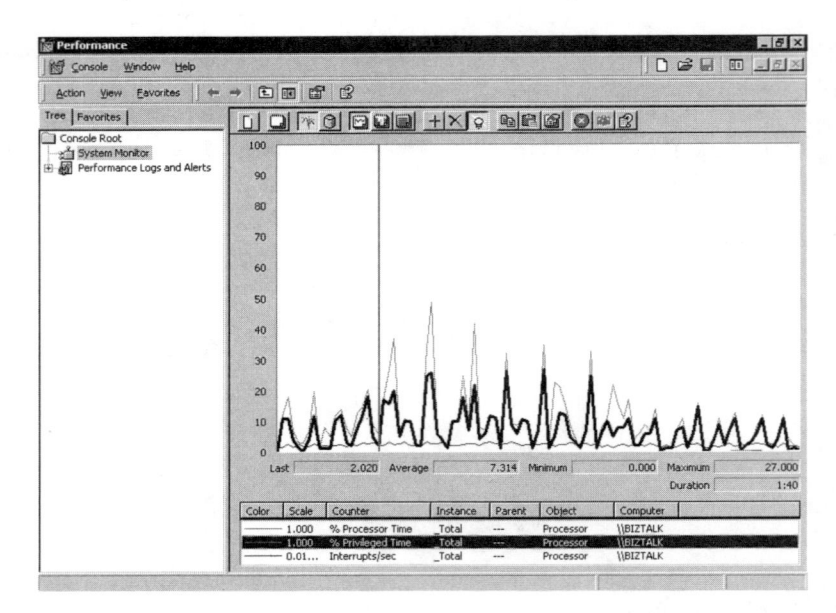

As you can see, use of the Highlight button makes it easy for you to quickly determine the charting values for the counter in question. You can change your highlighting selections as fast as you want, without needing to reset anything. Now that you know how to make a system-monitoring chart and manipulate the System Monitor tool, let's delve a bit deeper into the black magic art of chart interpretation.

Interpreting Charts

Interpreting the data displayed within the chart or histogram format of the Windows 2000 Server System Monitor is not quite as easy as it looks. You have now had quite a bit of practice at creating monitoring charts. Another quick way to look at your real-time data activity is through a format known as a *histogram*, which really is not much more than a simple bar chart. However, if you would like to view a chart in a histogram format, just go back into the System Monitor software (assuming that you closed it) and then click the Histogram button (this is the one that looks like a small bar chart icon). Doing this will cause the data from the System Monitor chart to appear in histogram form, as shown screen in Figure 24.37.

FIGURE 24.37
Reviewing a System Monitor chart in histogram format.

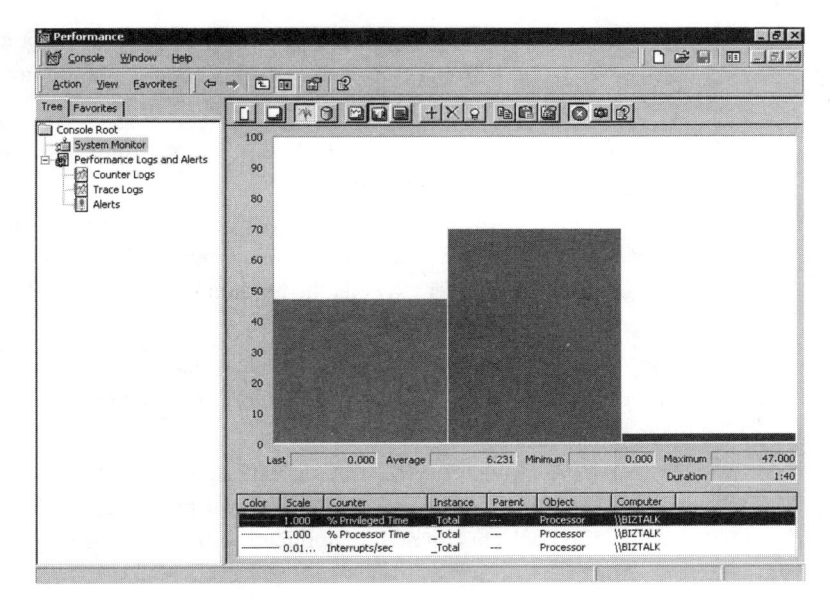

Although the histogram format does make it easier for the human eye to separate the multiple counters, it does little in the way of helping you actually analyze your data that has already been collected. For starters, you might want to try to determine a baseline analysis for your Windows 2000 server machine. This will include information such as whether any process is attempting to overwhelm the computer system with excessive memory, CPU, or disk drive utilization requests. Once you have at least a vague idea of what's considered "normal" for your computer, you can then start monitoring that computer system in such a way as to determine what is abnormal activity for that server system.

Another area that you will want to at least touch upon is the determination of what should be the monitoring standards for your organization. For example, the following is a list (in an *Object {Counter}* – Description format) of those areas that many organizations do indeed monitor, as well as a quick explanation as to what the monitoring may mean for your organization's Windows 2000 servers:

- *Memory {Pages/sec}*. If this counter continues to run higher than expected, your system does not have enough physical memory (in other words, add more RAM to the Windows 2000 server machine).

- *Logical Disk {Avg. Disk Queue Length}*. This counter will help you decipher the amount of activity on each disk volume of your server. If this counter results in high values over a long time (what constitutes a "long time period" is something that will need to be determined by comparing it to your baseline measurements), most likely you have a disk bottleneck issue.

- *Server {Bytes Total/sec}*. On an ethernet network, this counter should not exceed .83mbps, whereas on a Token Ring network, this counter should not go over .5Mbps (on a 4Mbps ring) or 2Mbps (on a 16Mbps ring).
- *Memory {Available Bytes}*. This should always exceed 16mb; otherwise, you may be coming up short in the RAM area.
- *Memory {Committed Bytes}*. This should always be a number less than the total amount of physical memory installed on this particular Windows 2000 server machine. If this monitor ever exceeds the amount of physical RAM, you need to add more memory to the server.
- *Memory {Pages/sec}*. This should always be less than 20 for Pentium-class servers. If it exceeds 20, you have a page frame memory problem (that is, a memory shortage that can cause a RAM bottleneck).
- *Memory {Pool Nonpaged Bytes}*. If this number continues to grow, one of the applications running on the Windows 2000 server machine has a memory leak. You will need to approach this one on an application-by-application basis.
- *Processor {% Processor Time}*. This should be less than 90 percent; otherwise, you may need to upgrade the performance of your processor (be careful about adding additional processors on a system that already has more than one—this is a topic that needs a lot more research).
- *Processor {Interrupts/sec}*. You might want to watch both the _Total as well as the individual processor numbers. If your system is not handling the interrupts fast enough (typically, this is a number that's less than 3,500 per processor), you may have a CPU bottleneck. Excessive interrupts are typically a hardware problem such as a defective card or a software problem such as the use of a nonstandard software driver.
- *Process {Working Set}*. Keeping a close watch on this counter will help your organization determine which applications are gobbling up the lion's share of available memory on the server. If the memory is going to a single, non-OS application, you definitely have a problem.
- *Process {Page File Bytes}*. Use this monitor with an instance setting of _Total to track the full size required for the Windows 2000 server machine's swap file. By determining the total page file size, you can then tweak your page file's location(s) and size accordingly.

The counters listed just barely scratch the surface as to what an organization can do with the system- and network-monitoring tools available as part of the Windows 2000 Server operating system. The additional questions that your organization's system administrators will want to ask themselves include: Should we be using all these counters and, if not, which ones? Should there be more? What are we hoping to gain from the usage of the

Windows 2000 Server performance-monitoring software? Once your organization has the answers to all these questions, you will be more apt to properly analyze the data that you're already receiving.

Reports and Logs

One final area that you will want to examine in regard to using the Windows 2000 Server Performance tool is that of the various reports and logging options available to you. Let's take a look once again at the main Performance utility screen (see Figure 24.38).

FIGURE 24.38
Reviewing a series of performance monitors in action.

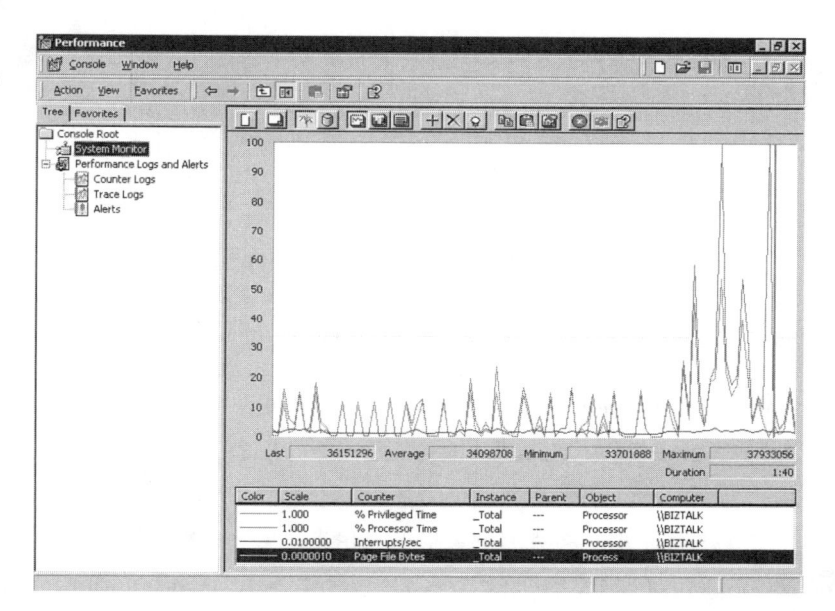

As you look along the left side of the screen, you should notice the Performance Logs and Alerts section found just under the System Monitor icon inside the menu tree. This is a section you will be spending a lot of time in, in just a few more minutes. However, before we get there, click the Report button found along the top row of the right pane (this is the one that looks like a spiral notepad) to reveal the screen shown in Figure 24.59.

One of the more interesting views, the Report view permits you to quickly see hard numbers for all the counters you presently have activated within the System Monitor toolset. The Report view will subtotal by ServerName first, then by Object. This makes it quite easy for you to grab a quick status of your various servers and their monitoring objects.

Let's now take a closer look at the Performance Logs and Alerts section by clicking that icon in the left pane.

FIGURE 24.39
Reviewing performance monitors in action with a Report view format.

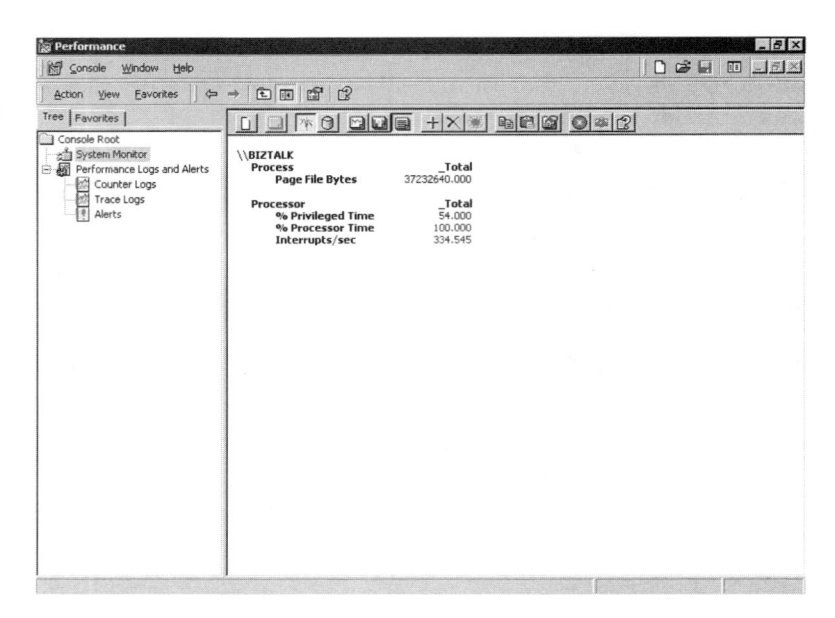

Once you click that icon, the contents of the right pane change drastically, revealing the names and descriptions of the three components that currently comprise the Windows 2000 Server Performance Logs and Alerts section:

- Counter Logs. This feature is used to configure performance data counter logs.
- Trace Logs. This area is used to configure the trace event logs.
- Alerts. This area is used to configure the various performance monitor alerts.

Moving on, click the Counter Logs icon, which is found just underneath the main Performance Logs and Alerts icon. Doing that will then cause the sample counter log to appear in the right pane.

The System Overview counter log is a sample file you can use to play with this portion of the Performance utility, which helps a new system administrator better understand the capabilities offered by Windows 2000 Server. If you right-click the System Overview counter log, you will be presented with a small pop-up menu. Move the mouse pointer down toward the bottom of that menu and then click the Properties menu selection to reveal the screen shown in Figure 24.40.

The System Overview Properties window appears, with the default tab selection of General. Examine the details of this screen's contents, keeping in mind that when you create your own version, you may want to modify some of its tasks. Once you have finished your review, click the Log Files tab to reveal that screen's contents, as shown in Figure 24.41.

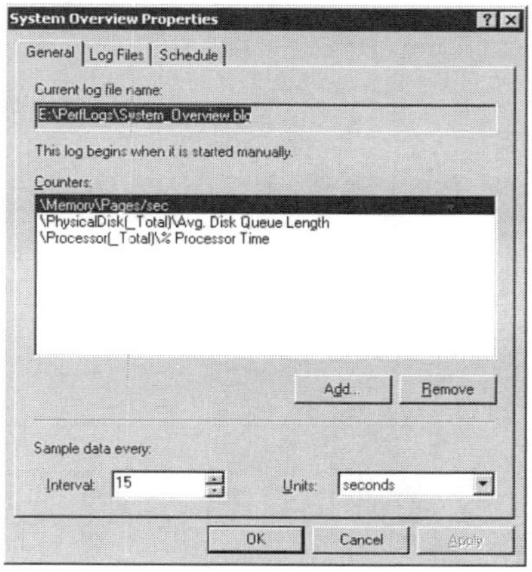

FIGURE 24.40
Reviewing the general properties of the log file counters.

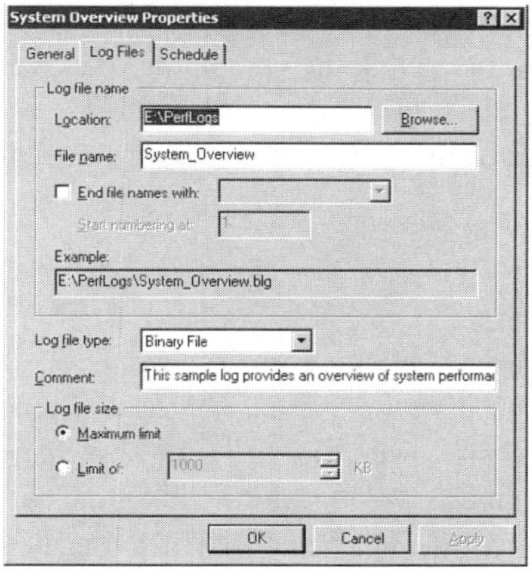

FIGURE 24.41
Configuring the name, location, size, and type of a log file.

Like the contents of the General tab, the contents of the Log Files tab include several self-explanatory items. One of the more important features of this screen is the capability to limit the total size of the log files (which, if left unchecked, could possibly grow to a size that exceeds the available hard disk drive space for your Windows 2000 server machine). Once you have finished your review of this tab's contents, click the Schedule tab to reveal that screen's contents, as shown in Figure 24.42.

FIGURE 24.42
Configuring scheduling options for the start and stop log.

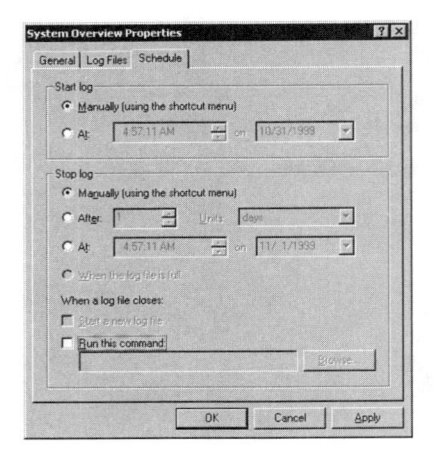

The Schedule tab is used to schedule the time, date, and possible frequency of the task at hand. Review this tab's contents and then click the OK button to exit the System Overview Properties window. If by chance you attempted to make any changes to this sample file, the System Overview error message box will prompt you to not make changes with this message:

> *Modifications are not allowed for default logs and alerts. You can start or stop the session from the context menu Start or Stop items from the associated toolbar buttons.*

Click the OK button to close the System Overview error message box and then click again on the Cancel button to properly exit the System Overview Properties window (you use the Cancel button because you do not want to try to save any changes that you may have already made). To add your own counter log, right-click the Counter Logs icon in the left pane to reveal a small menu, which has just a few meaningful options:

- New Log Settings
- New Log Settings From
- View
- New Windows From Here
- New Taskpad View
- Refresh
- Export List
- Help

From this menu, click the New Log Settings menu selection found at the very top of the menu. Performing that step will cause the New Log Settings prompt box to appear. In this box you'll select and then input the name of your new log file. Once you have typed in the name you want, click the OK button, which will then take you into the *Log File*

Name screen (this is called the Page File Monitors screen in the example shown in Figure 24.43).

FIGURE 24.43
Reviewing the general options for a specific monitor counter log.

In the General tab, you will need to add at least one counter to the Counters section. In addition, you may modify the data sample interval, should you desire. Once you have made your entries, click the Log Files tab to reveal the contents of that screen.

Make your filename entries and file type/size configurations on the Log Files tab. This screen is exactly the same as the one that you saw previously for the default log, so you should not be surprised by any of the options. Keep in mind that you can save the log files anywhere, including on other networked computers, which might make your monitoring process a little bit more manageable. Once you have made your entries, click the Schedule tab to reveal the screen shown in Figure 24.44.

FIGURE 24.44
Schedule a running time for your monitor counter log.

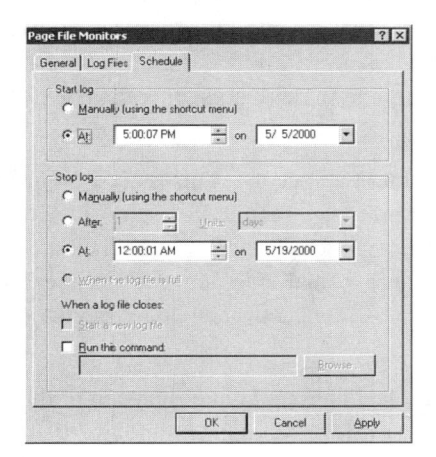

Like on the Schedule tab you saw previously, simply set the time and date you want the log to start and stop processing. These settings do assume that you will perform the starting and stopping process manually only on the local server and not across a network share. Once you have made your entries, click the OK button to return to the primary Performance screen, as shown in Figure 24.45.

FIGURE 24.45
Viewing your newly created monitor counter log on the main performance monitor screen.

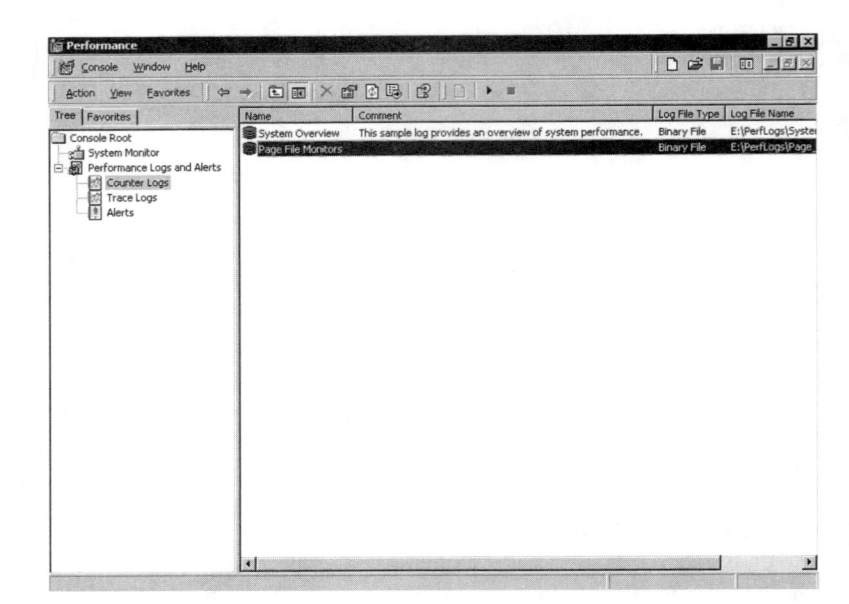

Once you arrive back at the full Performance screen, you will notice that your newly created Page File Monitors counter log has been established. To actually start the monitor right at this instant, though, without waiting for the designated start time, just right-click the name of the counter log and then select the Start menu selection from the ensuing pop-up menu. Your newly created counter log will then turn from red to green, with the contents of the line remaining exactly the same (that is, only the color of the Counter Log icon changes and nothing else).

The next topic to cover is the creation of a trace log. This time, the Windows 2000 Server Performance utility does not provide a sample file from which to learn. Therefore, this will be a trial-by-fire learning experience. To begin, right-click the Trace Log icon found in the left pane, which will cause a small pop-up menu to appear. Don't worry, this is the exact same pop-up menu that you saw back when you wanted to configure your first monitor counter log.

Click the New Log Settings menu selection found at the very top of this menu. Performing this step will cause the New Log Settings prompt box to appear. In this box, you will select and then input the name of your new log file. Once you have typed in the name you want, click the OK button, which will then take you into the *TraceLogFileName* Trace Log screen (this is called the Win2k Trace Log screen in the example shown in Figure 24.46).

FIGURE 24.46
Reviewing general property settings for your new trace log.

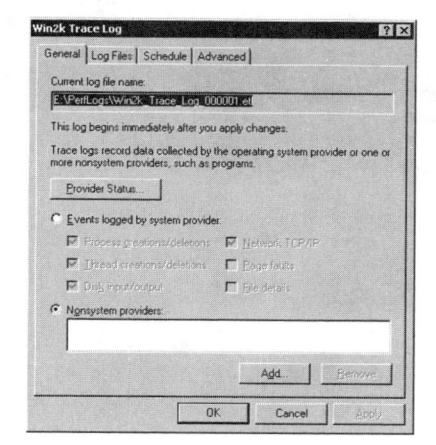

In the General tab, you will need to at least check the status of the log provider. Failure to do so will immediately result in the display of a trace log error message box should you attempt to move on to the Log Files tab. The message you will see is as follows: "You must add at least one general trace provider or enable the system trace provider."

Therefore, click the Provider Status button to reveal the screen shown in Figure 24.47.

FIGURE 24.47
Reviewing available providers.

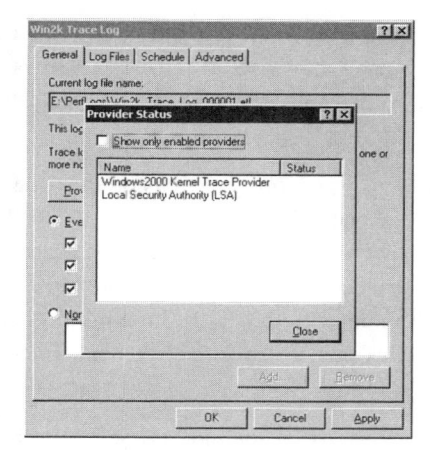

If you click the Show Only Enabled Providers check box, then it is most likely both the entries shown will disappear from use. Because of that fact, it is advised that you do not click on that check box. Once you've reviewed the options for this box, simply click the Close button to exit this screen and return to the *TraceLogFileName* Trace Log screen, as shown in Figure 24.48.

FIGURE 24.48

Using the Provider area of the General Properties screen.

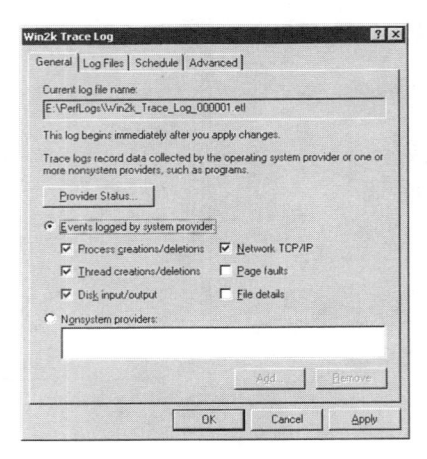

Next, click the Events Logged By System Provider radio button option to reveal the assorted check boxes available. These options can be selected without any problems, with the possible exception of one option: Page Faults. If you place a check mark in the Page Faults check box, you will immediately be prompted with a trace log message box.

Place a check inside the check box on this message box only if you are certain you'll never again want this message to appear. Otherwise, just click the OK button to exit this message box window. Once you have made all your entries, click the Log Files tab to reveal the contents of that screen.

Make your filename entries and file type/size configurations on this Log Files tab. This tab is identical to the one that you saw back when you were modifying the properties of your Counter Logs, so you should have no problem here either. Keep in mind that like the counter logs, you can save the trace log files anywhere, including on other networked computers, which might make your monitoring process a little bit more manageable. Once you have made your entries, click the Schedule tab to reveal the contents of that screen.

Like on the Schedule tab you saw previously (when modifying the properties of your counter logs), simply set the time and date you want the log to start and stop processing. These settings do assume that you will perform the starting and stopping process manually only on the local server and not across a network share. Once you have made your entries, click the Advanced tab to reveal that screen, as shown in Figure 24.49.

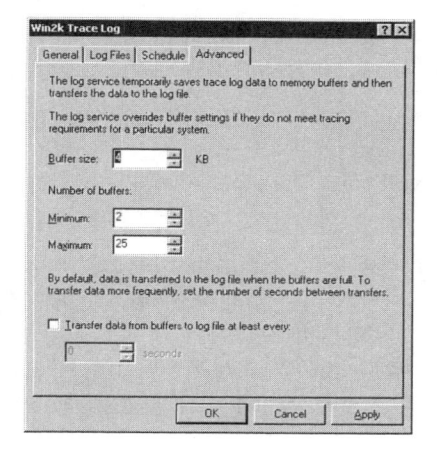

FIGURE 24.49
Setting advanced configuration options for a trace log data session.

Use the Advanced tab's contents to modify the memory buffers in an attempt to maximize the performance of your trace log. Once you have made your changes here, click the OK button to return to the primary Performance screen, as shown in Figure 24.50.

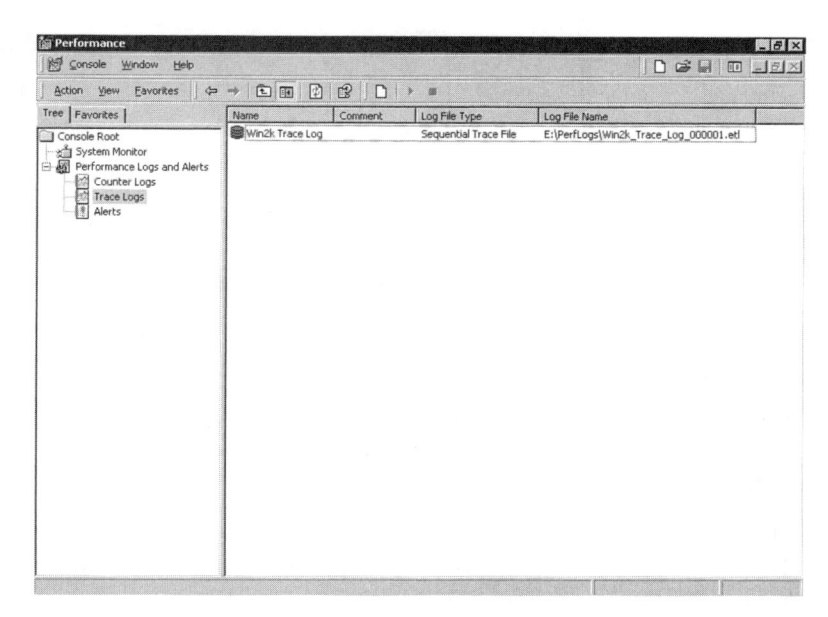

FIGURE 24.50
Reviewing your newly created trace log file from the main performance monitor screen.

Once you arrive back at the full Performance screen, you will notice that your new trace log has been created. To actually start using the log right at this instant, though, without waiting for the designated start time, just right-click the name of the trace log and then select the Start menu option from the ensuing pop-up menu. Your newly created trace log will then turn from red to green.

Last up is the creation of a Performance tool alert. When creating an alert, you again do not have a sample file from which to learn. Therefore, to begin, right-click the Alerts icon found in the left pane, which will cause the same small pop-up menu to appear, just as it did when you were working with the Counter and Trace Logs options.

Click the New Alert Settings menu selection found at the very top of this menu. Performing this step will cause the New Alert Settings prompt box to appear. In this box, you will need to select and then input the name of your new alert file. Once you have typed in the name you want, click the OK button, which will then take you into the *AlertFileName* Alert screen (this is called the Win2000 Alert screen in the example shown in Figure 24.51).

FIGURE 24.51
Configuring general alert scan options.

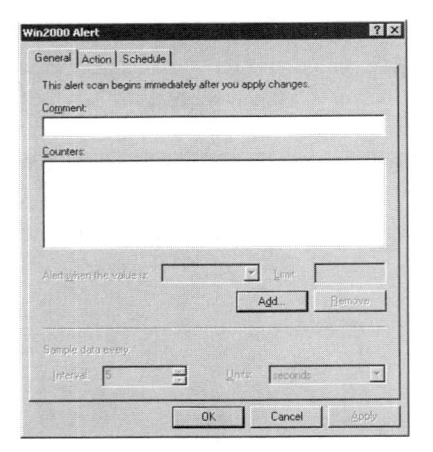

In the General tab, you will add a comment describing the new alert as well as at least a single counter. Failure to do so will immediately result in the display of an alert error message box, should you attempt to move on to the Action tab without first adding a counter. This message will say that "You must add at least one counter to monitor."

Therefore, click the OK button to return to the General tab to create the counter. You will also need to provide a limit of some sorts for the alert limit, a value that will vary, depending on the counter used. Make all your entries so that they at least cover all the variables shown in Figure 24.52.

FIGURE 24.52
Reviewing your alert entries to ensure their accuracy.

Once you have completed your changes, click the Action tab to reveal the screen shown in Figure 24.53.

FIGURE 24.53
Setting alert actions.

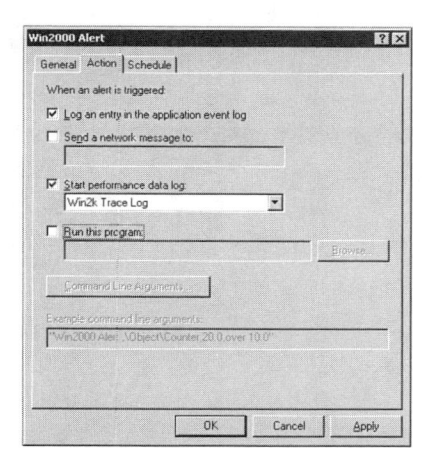

On the Action tab you're giving the system instructions on how to act in case the system fails in some manner. You may want to use the services of the Start Performance Data Log drop-down list box, which permits you to designate a specific log file for use with this alert. Once you have made your entries, click the Schedule tab to reveal the screen shown in Figure 24.54.

FIGURE 24.54
Scheduling the start and stop times for your alert scan.

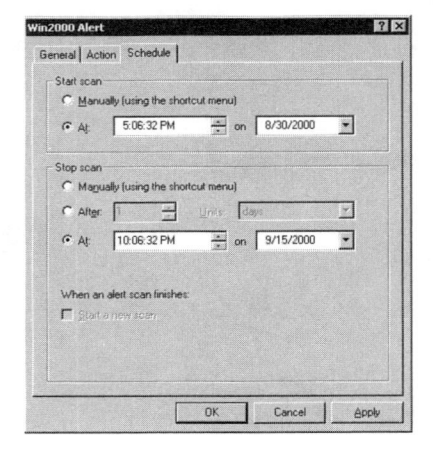

Like on the Schedule tab you saw previously, simply set the time and date you want the log to start and stop processing. These settings do assume you will perform the starting and stopping process manually only on the local server and not across a network share. Once you have made your entries, click the OK button to return to the primary Performance screen, as shown in Figure 24.55.

FIGURE 24.55
Reviewing your newly created alert on the main performance monitor screen.

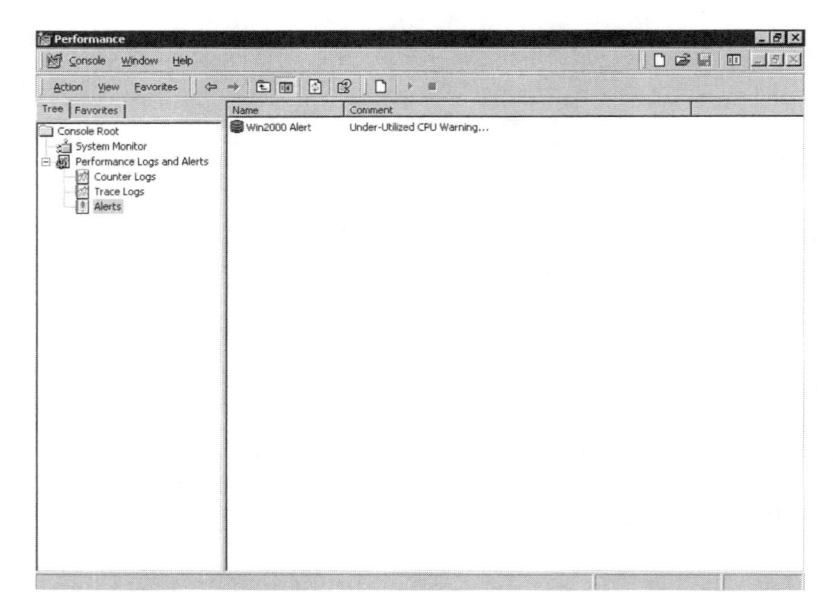

Once you arrive back at the full Performance screen, you will notice that your new Win2000 alert has been created. To actually start using the alert right away, though, without waiting for the designated start time, just right-click the name of the alert and then select the Start menu option from the ensuing pop-up menu. Your newly created counter log will then turn from red to green.

That's it. That is all you need to do to get well on your way to effective performance monitoring and tracking.

Summary

The purpose of this chapter is to introduce the practice of system tuning and performance monitoring of a Windows 2000 server, as well as to aid a system administrator in how he can perform tasks of that type. As there are literally thousands of different monitoring combinations, especially for those Windows 2000 servers that are used within a Web farm, the material contained here really was an introduction and not an all-encompassing tutorial on how to monitor every aspect of a Windows 2000 server. However, if you can understand the basics of the PerfMon tool and can maintain a standardized performance monitoring methodology, then this chapter will have prepared you to better manage your Windows 2000 servers in a proactive mode (meaning that you should be able to recognize the trouble spots before they turn into disasters).

For those systems administrators who are in need of additional Web-enabled tools, a very useful one known as Site Scope is produced by Freshwater Software, Inc. (More information is available on their Web site at http://www.freshwater.com/.) Site Scope provides you with a Web-based interface that basically acts as a more user-friendly GUI interface to the Windows 2000 Server Performance Monitor tool (there are additional scripting capabilities as well, which are very useful when monitoring a Windows 2000 server that is acting in a Web farm capacity). You might want to take a closer look at this tool as well as those offered by Keynote, Inc. (http://www.keynote.com) or WebTrends (http://www.webtrends.com), in case you happen to be using your Windows 2000 Server environment to run a Web farm.

Server Backup Utilities

CHAPTER 25

IN THIS CHAPTER

- Windows 2000 Backup Utility *670*
- Windows 2000 Server Backup Operator Permissions *672*
- Backing Up Windows 2000 *673*
- Restoring a Backup *694*
- Supported Backup Drive Devices *703*
- Recovery Console *703*
- Emergency Repair Disk *704*
- Third-Party Backup Tools *705*

Windows 2000 Backup Utility

The Windows 2000 Server backup utility has the potential to be the most important facet of the new operating system from Microsoft, should you permit it. Countless organizations do not have formal backup plans, to say nothing of formal business continuity plans in place for departmental servers and other small server-based implementations. Many organizations take the stance that servers outside of the Information Technology (IT) department's reach and control are those servers that are easily replaceable and thus do not require enterprise-level backup and restoration services that most IT groups otherwise provide. Typically, this thought process lends itself to business disaster whenever an organization's server crashes and there is no means of recovery.

In past versions of Windows NT, a backup and restore facility was built into the operating system. Although it provided a rudimentary way in which companies could easily back up and eventually recover their business data, the term "fast" never would have been associated with that process. Thanks to rapid enhancements in backup device technologies, coupled with a few upgrades to the backup utility software itself, these shortcomings of the old Windows NT Server backup utility were not always noticed until it was too late (during a multi-day recovery process or when attempting the full recovery of a server's Registry entries). Now, however, with the latest release of Windows 2000 Server, many of the previous versions' shortcomings have finally been improved through the implementation of a Recovery Console, a Safe Mode, an Emergency Repair Process, and the like.

Windows 2000 provides its suite of backup tools in the form of version 5.0 of the Microsoft Windows Backup program. This backup utility program is licensed from the Veritas Software Corporation and works similarly to the older versions found in the many versions of Windows NT. This software is accessed by clicking Start, Programs, Accessories, System Tools Backup. You see the opening screen of the Microsoft Windows Backup program. From that point, you can access the majority of this backup tool's features and options. (Obviously, the command-line functionality is not available from inside the GUI program.) Use the Microsoft Windows Backup program properly, and the risk of unrecoverable data loss will diminish greatly.

> **Note**
>
> There will always be some level of data loss risk present in any organization because not everything can always be under the control of a particular group. For example, in the event of catastrophic events that can occur in nature (floods, typhoons, earthquakes, volcanoes, tidal waves, tornadoes, and so on) or those that are manmade (riots, conventional or nuclear war, fire, and so on), there will always be risk of data loss to an organization's Windows 2000 Server environment because these types of events tend to be widespread and can overwhelm even the most prepared multinational organization at any time.

Before we jump into how to use the Microsoft Windows Backup tool, you should at least think about a few operational-level matters before implementing your backup solution. These operational concerns include all of the following:

- **Business continuity planning**—This should include a complete strategy for not only the backup and restoration of the organization's data, but also disaster recovery testing plans and schedules as well as the use of a potential hot site.

- **Backup tape/disk rotation schedule**—It is imperative that you keep more than one backup copy of the data that your organization has deemed critical to its business processes. (Refer to your business continuity planning sessions for a list of just what that data includes.) This includes the rotation of those backup tapes or disks to offsite locations. (If you are a small group, have a few of the organization's members take home a day's worth of data each day.)

- **Security**—A backup tape contains one of the most valuable resources any organization has: its data. Do not permit these backup tapes to fall into the wrong hands, especially those of your competitors. Likewise, be wary of those persons who might seek to do your organization harm by stealing or otherwise harming your backup tapes or disks.

- **Backup logs**—It is critical that you create and keep accurate logs of your backup operations. Otherwise, when it is time for a restoration procedure, you might actually do more harm than good to your organization's business data.

- **Staff training**—The organization's Information Technology (IT) staff must be properly trained in the backup process and procedures as well as the restoration of the materials created by the applicable backup processes. Obviously, a poorly trained systems operator can inflict far more damage on the data structure of your organization than most other disasters. For example, if Joe Operator mistakenly restores an older version of an e-commerce database and no one notices it for at least a few hours, then your organization's database structure might quickly become hopelessly corrupted.

- **Separation of duties**—If just a single person (such as the system administrator) has the ability to perform both data backups as well as restores, then you have deployed a single point of failure onto your organization's infrastructure. For example, should that person become disgruntled or merely incompetent, then the entire organization is at risk of a system meltdown from which there is no recovery.

- **Directory services backups**—It is imperative that you perform a complete backup of the Windows 2000 Server Active Directory from a Windows 2000 Domain Controller. Failure to back up the Directory Services database from a Domain Controller will result in the loss of user account information, as well as other pertinent security information.

- **Entire versus partial backups**—From a systems recovery standpoint, it will always be more efficient for you to back up the entire system volume at once instead of performing incremental or differential backups. Of course, from the initial backup time, this time savings is reversed. You must use a trial-and-error approach to determine the most effective means for your organization. Many organizations discover that once they grow to a certain size, there just is not enough time in the day to do full backups, so they must perform incremental/differential backups. This will have a serious impact upon the organization's ability to recover in a time of crisis, so you must treat this issue with the utmost respect and care during the planning stage.

- **Test, test, test**—A set of backup tapes that cannot be restored is completely useless to the organization. It is for this reason that you must be certain that you are able to use all those backup tapes you have been creating all this time. The only surefire way to do this is to actually perform a restore of the organization's data from the backup tapes on a periodic basis.

- **Documentation**—As unhappy a topic as this is, you must carefully and diligently document the organization's backup and recovery process in such a way that anyone can perform the server restoration process. Obviously, you need to keep the secretive information such as the backup operator/administrator IDs and passwords in a secure offsite location so that an unauthorized person cannot access the organization's data. The primary purpose for this documentation is to ensure the continuity of the business even if all the employees are wiped out during some catastrophic event.

Now that you have taken care of all the administrative and business-continuity planning processes and procedures, it is time to actually start arranging for the backup and restore process itself. To do that, you need to first ensure that your backup/recovery operators have all the correct permissions and rights to do their jobs, as well as make sure that those persons are performing the backup processes from the proper locations.

Windows 2000 Server Backup Operator Permissions

Many organizations tend to skip over this critical step—the assignment of the proper permissions to those persons who are responsible for the backup and recovery procedures of the servers and the organizational data structures that are deemed mission critical. Within the Windows 2000 Server operating environment, only those persons who are either system administrators or whose user accounts are members of either the Administrators or the Backup Operators group are capable of backing up the proper files and folders on the server.

The permissions and security levels granted administrators are pretty straightforward: Administrators are next to God in the IT world. Nothing happens on the organization's systems that they do not have the ability to notice and affect. (Of course, this does not mean that they will notice everything or actually do anything.) The rights and privileges granted to the members of the Windows 2000 Server Backup Operators group is an entirely different matter, however. For example, someone who is a member of that group can back up or restore any file or folder on the Windows 2000 server, in spite of any preset permissions or encryption that currently protects that file or folder. On the upside, members of the Backup Operators group are not permitted to change any permissions that are already in place on a particular file or folder, thereby protecting it somewhat from the members of this group.

Another relatively scary aspect of the Backup Operators group is that members of this group are not only able to log onto the Windows 2000 server, but also they can shut it down at will. This alone can be frightening in an e-commerce world where 99.99 percent uptime can mean the loss of millions of dollars worth of sales when that .01 percent of downtime occurs. It is for this last reason that it is strongly recommended that membership to the Backup Operators group be as strictly governed and limited as the Administrators group is controlled.

One final thing to note: To back up the System State data for a particular Windows 2000 server, you must be performing the backup process locally. That is, you cannot back up this important system data remotely, such as over the corporate network. When it comes time for you to perform a complete restoration of a particular Windows 2000 server (such as what you do following a disk platter crash), you will be unable to do it without the System State data for that server.

> **Note**
>
> The Windows 2000 Server expression known as *System State data* is an encompassing name that Microsoft gave to the group (for backup purposes) that contains the server's Registry, the COM+ Class Registration database, the system boot files, the Certificate Services database (should the Certification server be installed on this Windows 2000 server), the Active Directory directory service, and the SYSVOL directory. (These last two are found only on Windows 2000 servers that are acting as Domain Controllers.)

Backing Up Windows 2000

Just prior to starting the backup process, you might want to make one final decision regarding the backup that you are about to do. That is, you need to decide just what kind of backup you are about to make. The Microsoft Windows Backup tool supports five different types of backup (in alphabetic, not ranked, order):

- **Copy backup**—This is useful when you want to copy specific files from the Windows 2000 server to a backup device (tape, disk, and so on) without clearing the archive attribute from those specific files.
- **Daily backup**—This is used whenever you want to back up all of the files that have been altered somehow (modified, added, and so on) since the last time you performed the backup process. Again, this does not mark the files as having been backed up, which makes it useful for those nightly backup sessions.
- **Differential backup**—This backup scheme permits you to back up any file or folder that has been created or modified since the last incremental or normal backup session. A combination of differential, incremental, and daily or normal backups is what many companies use as their backup methodology. This is a popular backup method because the time to restore is much less than that for a combined normal and incremental backup scheme, due to the lower number of tapes or disks that you need to use. On the downside, however, a normal/differential backup scheme does take longer to perform than a normal/incremental backup process.
- **Incremental backup**—Although this backup type might seem appealing in that it greatly shortens the amount of time required to perform the backup process, keep in mind that you need the normal backup tapes along with all the incremental backup tapes in order to be able to recover your systems properly. Incremental backups set a special marker on your files to denote that they have been backed up.
- **Normal backup**—This backup process marks each file and folder with a special attribute that tells other backup types that this particular file or folder has already been backed up.

To access the Windows Backup and Recovery Tools application, click Start, Programs, Accessories, System Tools Backup.

> **Tip**
>
> If you place your mouse pointer on top of any built-in Windows 2000 Server menu option, you see a quick ToolTip about that particular option. For example, you can see a brief description of the Backup option. (The text in the box is "Archives data to prevent it from accidental loss.")

Performing this series of mouse clicks through the Windows 2000 menu structure will enable you to access the Windows Backup and Recovery Tools application. The initial screen of the Windows Backup and Recovery Tools application is shown in Figure 25.1.

FIGURE 25.1
Main Windows 2000 Backup screen.

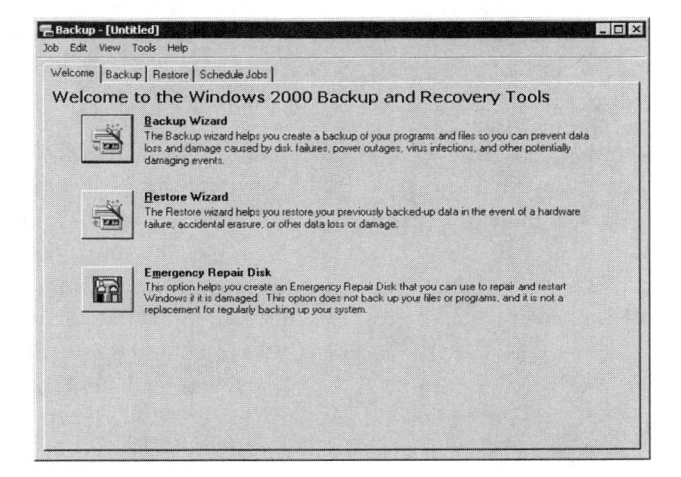

The first thing that you want to do is define the variables that delineate precisely how the backup and recovery jobs for your system are to be conducted. To do this, you need to access the backup system options area, which permits you to define all types of attributes for your backup/recovery process. To start this process, click Tools, Options to reveal the screen shown in Figure 25.2.

FIGURE 25.2
Setting backup options.

The first time you access the Options window, you see the preset options that are configured by default for you on the General tab. I do not mean to say that these options are the perfect fit for your organization, but they do represent a selection of the best choices. Of the two options not automatically chosen (the data verification and the new media import), the data verification is one that you should strongly consider using. However, choosing this option considerably slows the backup process, so use it only if you have plenty of time for conducting the full backup operation that you have planned.

All of these options are self-explanatory but, should you have any questions regarding precisely what an option will do, consult the help system that is now built into the Windows 2000 Backup utility. To take advantage of this system, click once on the option that you are curious about to select it, and then press the F1 button on your computer's keyboard. This causes a small ToolTip box to appear, which contains a brief description of the item in question and why you might want to use it. For example, if you select the second option from the top (Use the Catalogs on the Media to Speed Up Building Restore Catalogs on Disk) and then press the F1 key, you see a ToolTip appear. The tip that appears tells you that this option creates a catalog on your backup media that gives you the ability to restore a failed system from the backup media much quicker than if you do not use a catalog at all. Of course, this tip also informs you that the creation of the initial catalog system might take several hours if the backup media is large. Once you have finished reading the ToolTip, just click anywhere else on the screen, or use your mouse to perform another function and the tip will automatically disappear.

Once you have set all your General options, click once on the Restore tab to reveal the restoration options, as shown in Figure 25.3.

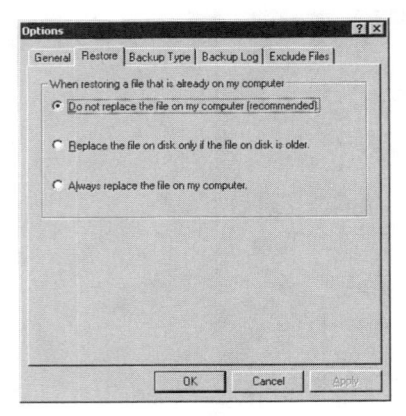

FIGURE 25.3
Setting restoration options.

The Windows Backup System will default to never replacing existing files on your computer, which is typically the recommended setting. Obviously, if the file already exists on your computer, then the one on the backup medium is probably an older version of that same file. Given that fact, you most likely will not want to replace the file. Of course, the preferred setting of this author is the middle radio button option: Replace the File on Disk only if the File on Disk Is Older. If you think about it, this choice might well make the most sense for the majority of organizations. About the only time the final option, Always Replace the File on My Computer, makes sense is for educational institutions. That is, many schools have computer labs in which they like to "reset" each computer to a default configuration, and the lab administrator typically restores that configuration from a backup source such as tapes or disk.

To set your organization's default restoration selection, click once on the radio button next to the selection that best fits your organization. Once you have done this, click once on the Backup Type tab to reveal that screen.

At this point, you need to select your default backup type, which was explained in detail earlier in this section. To refresh your memory, here are your five choices:

- Copy backup
- Daily backup
- Differential backup
- Incremental backup
- Normal backup

Windows 2000 Server defaults to a selection of Normal, although many organizations also seem to like Daily as their default selection. In any event, select the backup type according to your organization's needs by clicking once on the drop-down list box and then highlighting the selection of choice by clicking on it once. This returns that backup type value to the top of the list and thus makes it your default backup type selection. Once you have made your selection, click once on the Backup Log tab to reveal that screen, as shown in Figure 25.4.

The purpose of the Backup Log screen is to define your default logging actions for your backup jobs. The worst case for the vast majority of organizations is to use the default setting of Summary for backup jobs. A Summary setting for a backup job creates a type of an event log of your backup job. That is, you do not get a list of the various files and folders that were backed up; instead, you get a line for each backup event such as the job starting, job stopping, tape loading, and tape unloading events. If you have the extra time and media space that is required by a Detailed logging operation, then by all means do it. A Detailed list gives you the ability to see precisely which files and folders have been backed up as well as all the backup event options. The final selection of None means that you get nothing in the form of logging your backup operations. Once you have made your selection, click once on the Exclude Files tab to reveal that screen, shown in Figure 25.5.

FIGURE 25.4
Choosing a logging level.

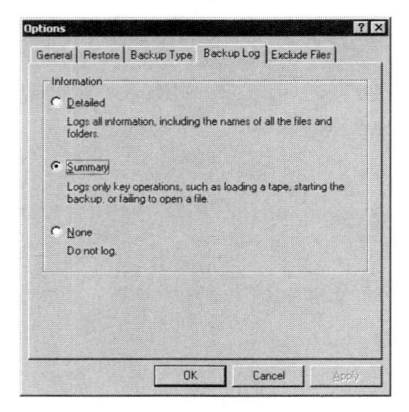

FIGURE 25.5
Deciding which files to exclude.

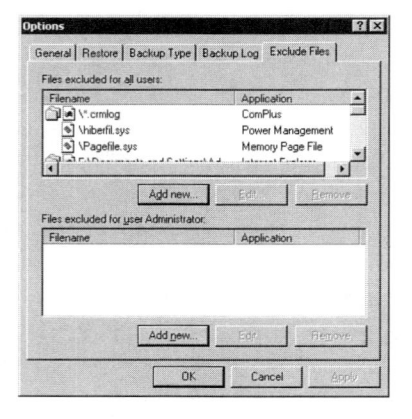

The purpose of the Exclude Files screen is to permit the backup operator to intentionally not back up certain types of files on the Windows 2000 server. For example, it is likely that you will not want to back up your power management hibernation file or the Windows 2000 memory page file because these are both typically large files that are not really germane to your computer working correctly. (That is, the Windows 2000 Server operating system will automatically re-create these files anyway, so there is no reason for you to back them up to begin with.) The top window on this screen shows all those files and file types that are excluded for all users of this particular Windows 2000 server computer. The bottom window on this screen reveals just those files that are being excluded for the administrator user on this Windows 2000 server computer. To add new files in either case, just click once on the Add New button to add a new file to your exclusion listing. (Both buttons work exactly the same way.) You are able to exclude files either by file type (such as just those file types that have already been registered within Windows 2000 Server) or at the file or folder level (that is, exclude just a single file or everything within a particular folder or subtree). Once you have made your selection, click once on the OK button to confirm all your option alterations and exit the Options screen.

Now that we have configured the base Windows 2000 server backup options, it is time to begin a backup of our Windows 2000 Server. To do this, click once on the Backup Wizard button that appears near the top of the main Backup screen. An interesting thing to notice is that you are automatically taken to the second tab of this screen's options (the Backup tab), even though it is presently hidden by the start of the Backup Wizard window, which you see on the screen in Figure 25.6.

FIGURE 25.6
Starting the Backup and Recovery Tools Wizard.

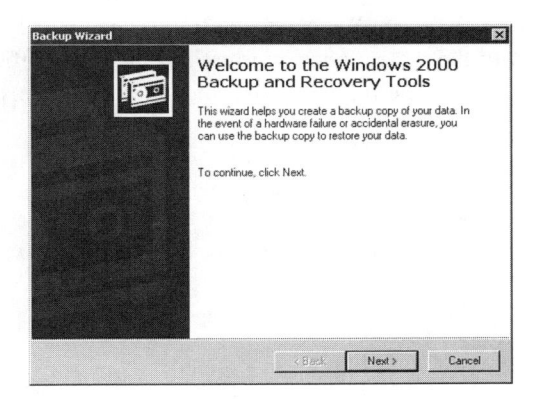

This first screen of the Windows 2000 Backup and Recovery Tools Wizard is really just informational. About all this first screen is good for is to permit you to cancel the backup operation in case you did not mean to start it. Assuming that you do, click once on the Next button, which then continues the wizard process. You see the What to Back Up portion of the wizard, as shown in Figure 25.7.

You can perform three types of backups using the Windows 2000 Backup :

- Back up everything on my computer.
- Back up selected files, drives, or network data.
- Only back up the System State data.

FIGURE 25.7
Deciding what to back up.

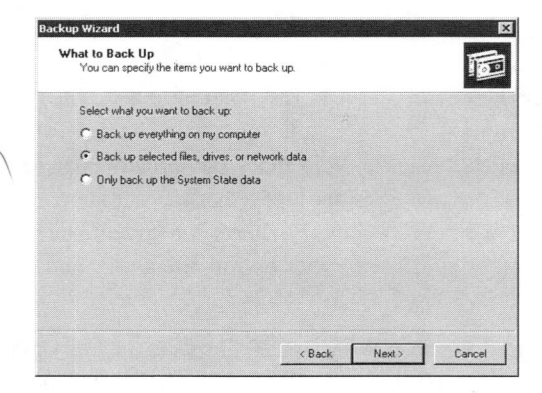

The first two are self-explanatory: Either back up everything on your Windows 2000 server or be particular in what you want to save to your backup media. The third radio button option, backing up the System State data, is a bit trickier. System State data, as you might recall from earlier in the chapter, are the special system files that you must back up to properly recover your entire Windows 2000 server, including the user and system accounts, the integrity of the system boot information, and the certificate services (if any were installed on the server). The following list contains all the items that formulate the System State data:

- The Windows 2000 Server Registry
- COM+ Class Registration database
- System boot files
- Certificate Services database
- Active Directory directory service
- SYSVOL directory

Keep in mind that the Certificate Services database exists only on those Windows 2000 servers that have the Certification Server installed. In addition, the Active Directory directory service and the SYSVOL directory are only found on Windows 2000 servers that are acting as Domain Controllers. (Member servers and standalone servers do not have these System State data files.) Once you have made your high-level decision on what you want to back up, click once on that option to select it. To continue the Backup Wizard process, click once on the Next button, which then reveals the screen shown in Figure 25.8.

FIGURE 25.8
Marking specific items for backup.

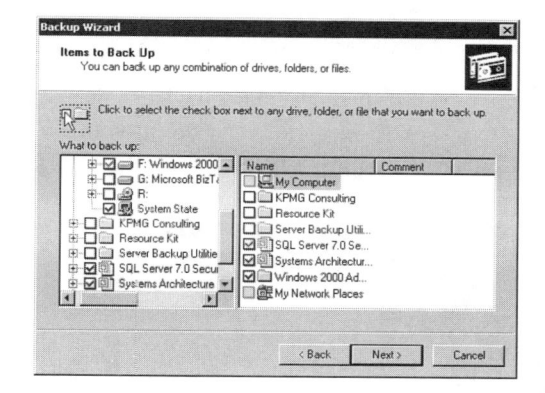

On the Items to Back Up screen that appears, you need to click once on each open box that appears to the left of the option that you want to back up. For example, in Figure 25.8, you can see that just above the folder labeled KPMG Consulting is the entry for System State. Clicking once on the box next to System State causes it to be included in this backup job. From this screen, you are able to choose any combination of files, folders, and entire drives (networked drives included) to include in your backup job. Once you have made all your selections, click once on the Next button to reveal the screen shown in Figure 25.9.

FIGURE 25.9
Selecting a backup media destination.

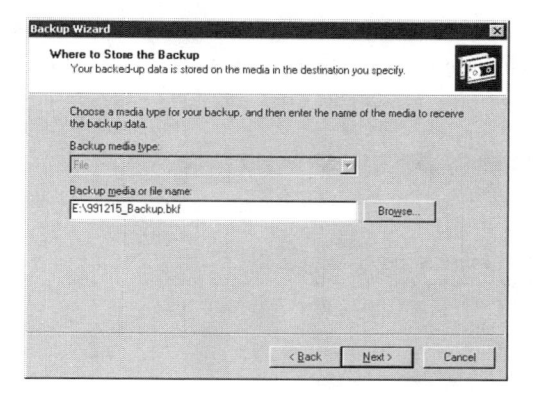

On the Where to Store the Backup screen, you need to pick a destination for your backup job's information. If you do not have a backup media device (such as a tape or disk drive) attached to your Windows 2000 server, then the default choice of File is the only backup media type option presented to you. (Look in the top drop-down list box.) If you do have a backup device attached to your Windows 2000 server, then you will be able to make the other selection of that tape device. Remember, if you are attempting to perform this backup process across the network, you will be unable to back up the System State data. In the bottom box, you are able to browse to your backup media's destination (another drive if this is a file backup or perhaps a tape device if one is available to you). Once you have made your entries, click once on the Next button to reveal one of the final Backup Wizard screens, as shown in Figure 25.10.

FIGURE 25.10
Confirming backup settings.

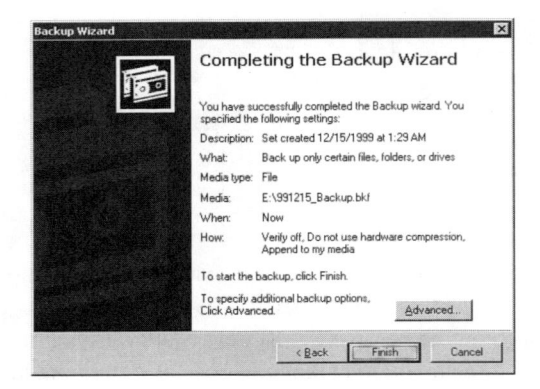

This screen is a nice touch by Microsoft: It permits you to review all your previous selections and what they mean to your backup operation. If you are done, you can click once on the Finish button to conclude the Backup Wizard process, which then initiates the actual backing up of your system's data files. Otherwise, you might want to re-check your backup options by clicking once on the Advanced button. If you do click once on the Advanced button, you see the screen shown in Figure 25.11.

FIGURE 25.11
The first advanced option: selecting a backup type.

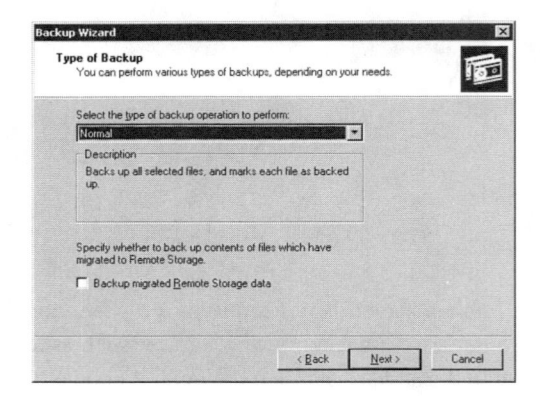

From the Type of Backup screen that appears, you have two choices to make: to change the backup type and whether you want to back up the files that have migrated to remote storage. Use the drop-down list box to change the backup type option. If you want to enable the backup to include those files that have migrated to remote storage, then click once on the bottom check box to select this option. Once you have made your selections, click once on the Next button to reveal the screen shown in Figure 25.12.

FIGURE 25.12
Setting the verification and compression options.

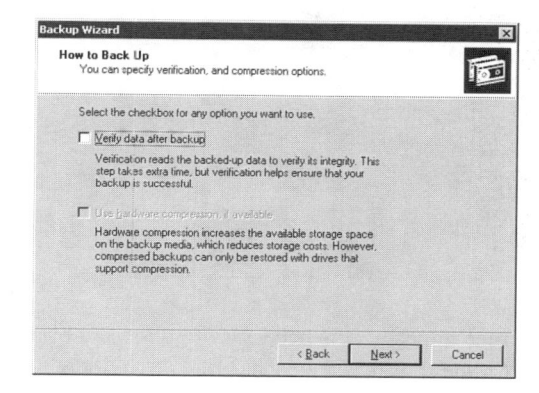

> **Note**
>
> Within the Windows 2000 Server operating system is a new data management tool that permits the operating system to automatically move those less frequently used files to a secondary storage location. Once the primary disk storage system reaches a certain threshold, the cache of the data that was moved to the remote location is then reused by the primary system for storage purposes. This remote storage location can only exist on a Windows 2000 NTFS volume and is achieved through the use of removable storage media such as tapes or discs.

The How to Back Up screen appears, where you have the option to verify the backup process as well as use hardware compression for the backup device. Make either or both of these selections by clicking once on the appropriate check box to select it. Once you have made your choices, click once on the Next button to reveal the Media Options screen.

When the Media Options screen appears, you again see two choices: to either append or overwrite data that might already exist on this backup tape. If you are using a new tape, then you do not need to make any selections on this screen. If you are choosing to overwrite the content that already exists on the backup media, then you can also choose the bottom option that then protects this backup file from accidental deletion by anyone other than the owner of the backup tape or the system administrator. Once you have made your choices, click once on the Next button to reveal the screen shown in Figure 25.13.

FIGURE 25.13
Creating the backup label.

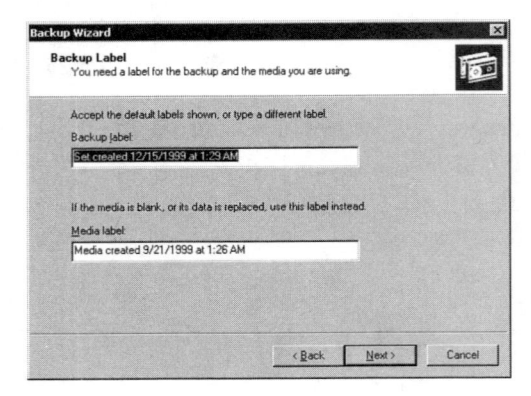

When the Backup Label screen appears, it is necessary to choose a backup and a media label for your backup job. Although it is not a requirement of Windows 2000 Server, you might want to add some logic to your backup or media label by using descriptive words regarding the data being backed up along with the time and date of the backup itself. Once you have made your entries, click once on the Next button to continue on to the screen shown in Figure 25.14.

FIGURE 25.14
Deciding when to backup.

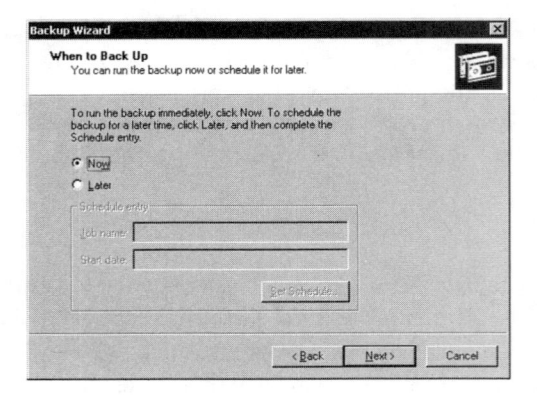

At this point, you must decide when you want the backup process to begin: now or at some later point in time. Make your selection by clicking once on the radio button next to the option that makes sense to your organization. If you choose the Later radio button, then the Schedule Entry portion of the screen becomes available to you to use. Otherwise, click once on the Next button to continue the process. Assuming that you clicked once on the Later radio button, you are immediately presented with the Set Account Information pop-up window, shown in Figure 25.15.

FIGURE 25.15
Entering the Run As account information.

It is on the Set Account Information pop-up window that you need to enter the account name and password for the administrative or backup operator account that will be used in conjunction with this backup job. It is imperative that you enter the account information for a security level that equates to either a system administrator or an account that is a member of the Windows 2000 Backup Operators group. Failure to do so will most likely result in the failure of your backup job running properly. Note that the domain name of the account in question precedes the actual account name. In the sample shown, SOCRATES is the domain name, and Administrator is the account name. Once you have made the appropriate entry, click once on the OK button to continue the process. This takes you to the next screen.

If this screen looks familiar, well, it should. It is the same screen that you saw just a few moments ago with one exception: The Schedule entry area is available for use. Type a descriptive name in the Job Name area and then click once on the Set Schedule button to access the screen shown in Figure 25.16.

FIGURE 25.16
Scheduling the backup job.

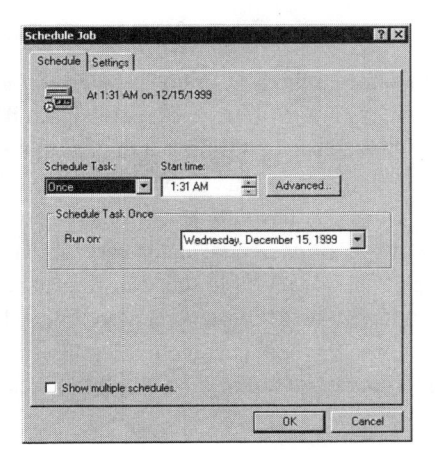

The Schedule Job screen appears, which gives you the ability to precisely set the start time of your backup job. The options on this screen are all self-explanatory and present numerous ways in which you can specifically fix the kick-off time of your backup job. The Schedule Task drop-down list box permits you to select from a variety of different scheduling methods:

- Daily
- Weekly
- Monthly
- Once
- At System Startup
- At Logon
- When Idle

Obviously, it depends upon which type of task schedule you opt for, which in turn makes the Backup Wizard prompt you for different scheduling options. (For example, you are not able to pick a specific backup month if you are scheduling a daily backup task.) To choose from some of the more advanced scheduling techniques, click once on the Advanced button to reveal the screen shown in Figure 25.17.

FIGURE 25.17

Choosing the Advanced Schedule Options.

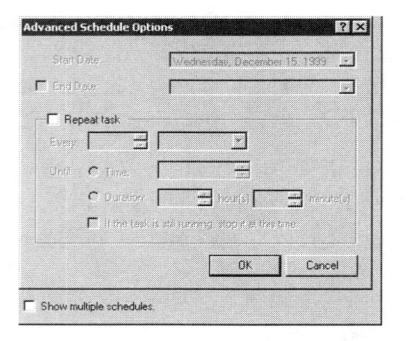

One of the nicest features of the Advanced Schedule Options screen is the ability to stop a daily backup job that perhaps is taking too much time to execute. To do that, use the Repeat Task option box (click on it once to select it) and use the Duration radio button option to set a backup length time. (Click once on the If the Task Is Still Running, Stop It at This Time to invoke the feature.) Once you have made all your selections, if any, click once on the OK button to return to the previous Schedule Job screen. One other function on this screen that is quite useful is the use of multiple schedules for the same backup job. To access this feature, click once on the Show Multiple Schedules check box near the bottom of the screen to activate this feature. As soon as you click on this check box, a new function is automatically revealed to you at the top of the Schedule Job screen.

The icon along with the backup job's scheduled time is suddenly covered up by a new drop-down list box that enables you to select a backup time from a list of several scheduled times. To delete any of the scheduling items in this list, just click once on that scheduled time to select it and then click once on the Delete button to remove it from the list. Likewise, to add a new time scheduling to the list, click once on the New button to add another entry to the list. All the items in the list are numbered, which is shown along the inside portion of the left side of the list box.

Once you have made all your selections on this portion of the Schedule Job screen, you might want to examine the various other scheduling features available to you. To do that, click once on the Settings tab to reveal the screen shown in Figure 25.18.

FIGURE 25.18
Confirming the scheduled backup job's settings.

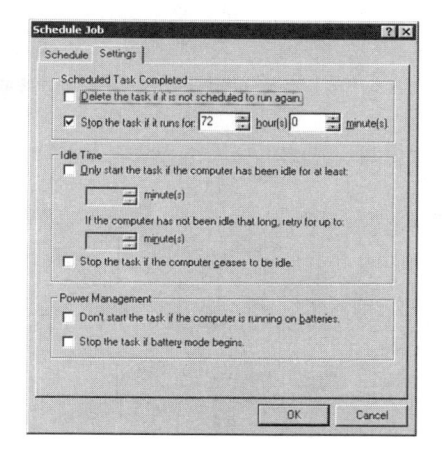

The Settings tab permits you to limit the maximum time length that a backup job can take, which should keep the system backups from spilling over into the daily operations of your organization. Another nice feature is the Power Management functions that permit you to avoid kicking off a backup job when your computer (such as a notebook PC or a server whose main power has crashed and is functioning off of an emergency battery backup system) is running solely on battery power. Once you have made all your selections, click once on the OK button to save those choices. You see the final screen in the Backup Wizard, as shown in Figure 25.19.

Like the initial Backup Wizard screen, this one also displays a summary of all the features and options that you have set for your backup job. Once you have concluded that these are the correct settings for your organization, click once on the Finish button to close the wizard screen and start the actual backup process.

FIGURE 25.19
Verifying the Backup Wizard settings.

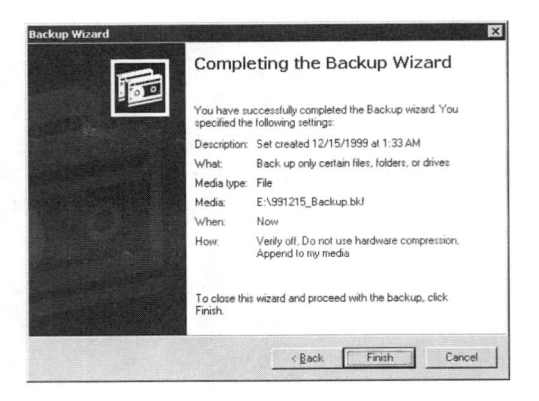

When the backup process finally starts, you will notice that you see the Backup tab of the Backup – [Untitled] screen. (It is only untitled because you have not yet saved this backup job—something that we will get to do in just a bit). In front of that screen is the much smaller Selection Information status window, as shown in Figure 25.20.

FIGURE 25.20
Reviewing the status window of an active backup job.

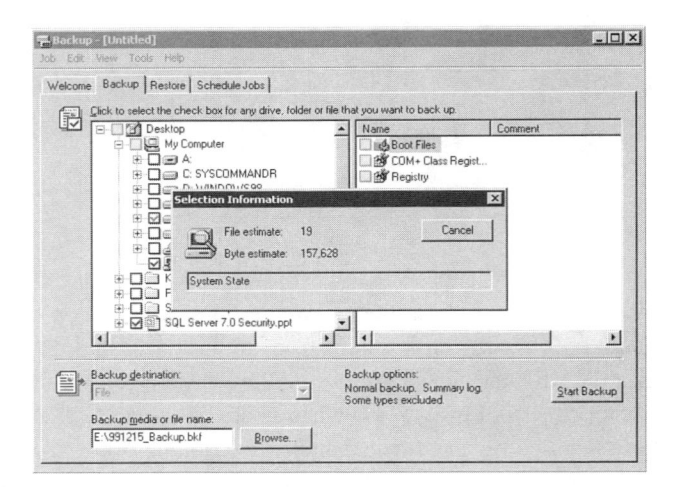

The Selection Information status window gives you a running total of the files and bytes of information that are being processed during the initial backup setup by the running backup job. If at any time you want to stop the backup process for any reason, just click once on the Cancel button on this status window. Once the backup job starts in earnest, you see the full Backup Progress screen.

Although the primary purpose of the Backup Progress screen is to give the backup operator information regarding the backup job's progress, it again presents you with the ability to stop the backup process for any reason by clicking once on the Cancel button.

Something that I have always found to be useful is the four boxes at the bottom of this screen: the ones that show the processed and estimated levels for both the byte and file counts for the backup job. Obviously, if you have 243MB of files to be backed up, and you have completed only about 1.8MB worth of files thus far, then you can conclude that this backup job is far from being complete. Once the backup job finishes, you are automatically taken to the Backup Progress screen shown in Figure 25.21.

FIGURE 25.21
Viewing the Backup Progress results screen.

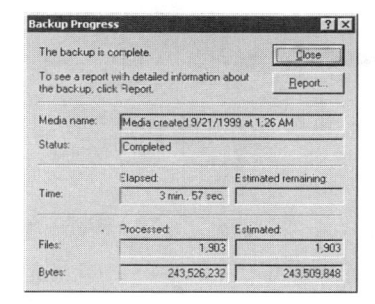

Although this is strictly an informational screen, you want to pay close attention to it because it will quickly let you know whether the backup job was successful. (The numbers at the bottom of the screen must match each other: Processed versus Estimated.) For a more detailed look at this information, click once on the Report button to initiate a Microsoft Notepad-formatted report of this information, as shown in Figure 25.22.

FIGURE 25.22
Reviewing a backup results report.

The nice thing about the ability to create these ASCII text reports is that you are able to save them to some folder, perhaps one named `Backup Reports`. By doing this, you can then search through these reports at later dates to prove out an audit trail that the various backup jobs indeed were run and did so successfully. Once you have finished examining the report, either save it or just close it. Once you do that, you are returned to the Backup Progress screen. Once there, click once on the Close button to exit that screen, which takes you back to the general Backup screen, as shown in Figure 25.23.

FIGURE 25.23
Using the main Backup window.

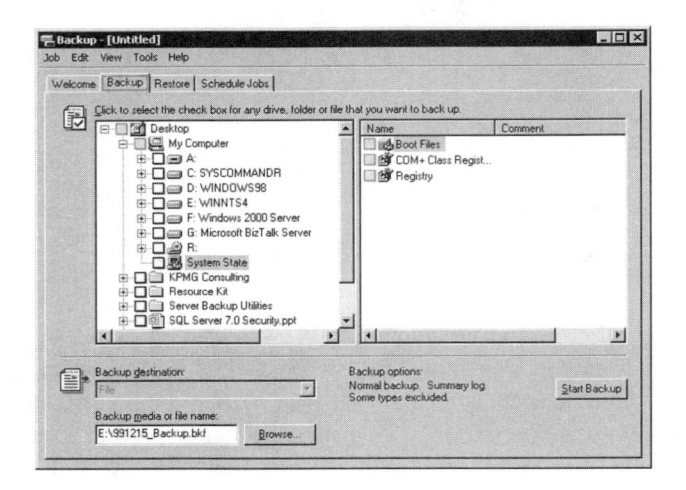

As you can see, the backup job is now complete. You can start another version of this backup job using the same settings by clicking once on the Start Backup button that appears in the lower-right corner of the screen. (Chances are that you probably do not want to do this right away.) To save the settings for this particular backup job, you need to first click on the Job menu option and then click once again on either the Save Selections or the Save Selections As menu selections. (If you have never saved this backup job before, then you want to use the Save Selections option.) Once you have made your choice, click once on the Job menu option and then on the Exit menu selection to exit the Backup utility.

Attended Operations

An "attended" backup operation is nothing more than a backup operation in which the Windows 2000 Server backup operator is controlling the entire process in an interactive mode. A scheduled backup job that runs automatically is not necessarily an attended backup. An example is when you use the Windows Backup and Recovery Tools utility application directly to run a backup job. For small- to intermediate-size organizations, an attended backup procedure is probably the norm. The process of performing an attended backup is fully detailed in the previous section of this chapter ("Backing Up Windows 2000"). However, for larger or multi-location organizations, the use of scheduled automated or unattended backups is typical. To do this, simply use the information in this next section.

Unattended Operations

Unattended backup operations are nothing more than backup jobs that have been scheduled to run at times when there is no backup operator present to interactively run the Windows 2000 Server Backup tool. To configure such an operation, you need to first start the Windows 2000 Server Backup utility. To do that, click Start, Programs, Accessories, System Tools, Backup. You see the Windows 2000 Server Backup utility start. Click once on the Schedule Jobs tab to reveal the screen shown in Figure 25.24.

FIGURE 25.24
Using the Backup jobs scheduling calendar.

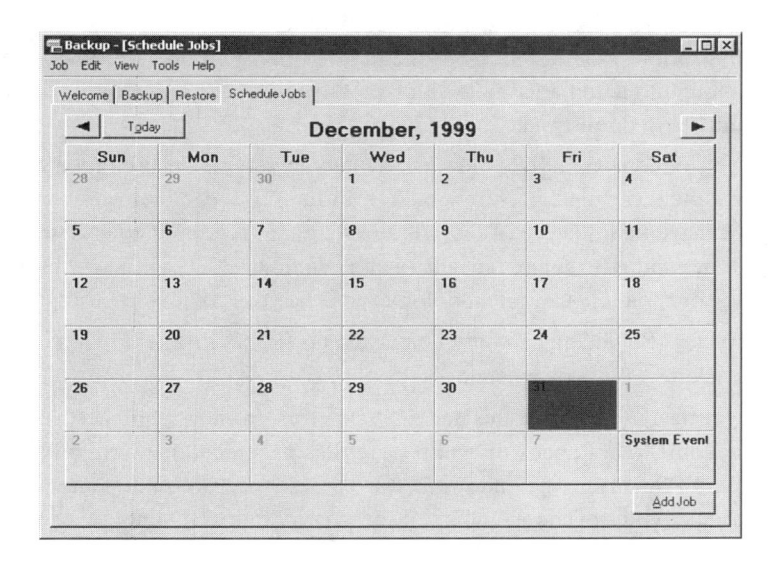

To schedule a backup job, you simply need to double-click on the date when you want that job to run (or begin if this is a job that will be repeated over time). For example, should you want to run a special backup job on New Year's Eve 1999 (right before the end of the world), then you double-click on that date, as is shown in the previous example (refer to Figure 25.24). Doing this immediately starts the Windows 2000 Backup Tool's wizard process. (Refer to the "Backing Up Windows 2000" section earlier in this chapter for more details on how to use the wizard.) It is during this wizard process that you select all the files and folders that you want to back up, along with determining the backup method, the media type, and various other settings and the specifics regarding the backup's scheduling opportunities. Once you complete the wizard, you see a tiny Backup

Utility icon appear on the date that you had originally double-clicked within the Schedule Jobs tab's calendar. That is all you need to do to schedule a backup job. However, you should keep in mind a few things as you schedule any backup job:

- Backups can be run on FAT16, FAT32, NTFS 4.0 (Windows NT), and NTFS 5.0 (Windows 2000) volumes. However, if you ever back up an NTFS 5.0 volume, you really should try to restore it to a Windows 2000 Server volume so that file permissions, encryption settings, disk quota information, and the like are not inadvertently lost. (These features are all new to the Windows 2000 operating system.)

- The backup job needs to be controlled by either an Administrator level account or an account that is a member of the Windows 2000 Server Backup Operators group. If the job does not have the proper permissions, then it will most likely fail at some point during the backup operation.

- Obviously, make sure that your organization's backup device has the proper media in it prior to the execution of the backup job. Windows 2000 Server is not "smart" enough to automatically load a tape drive yet, so do not be surprised when it is unable to do just that.

- The Windows 2000 Server Task Scheduler service must be running for you to be able to schedule a backup job. To start the service, either use the Computer Management feature of the Windows 2000 Server operating system or just type the command **net start schedule** at a Windows 2000 command prompt. (Use the \Start, \Run, \Cmd methodology to initiate the command prompt window.)

- System State data can only be backed up from a local computer; network-based backups of this data cannot be performed.

- Because members of the Backup Operators group as well as system Administrators are able to both back up and restore files or folders that have been encrypted using the EFS feature of Windows 2000, it is strongly advisable that you closely monitor the activities of the members of these two groups. (Do not worry; EFS files and folders are never decrypted during the backup or restore process.)

- If removable storage or remote storage is a part of your backup solution, then make sure that you back up all of the files in the \NtmsData folder as well as the \RemoteStorage folder. (Both of these top-level folders appear in the SystemRoot \System32 folder of Windows 2000 Server.) You must do this to ensure that it will be possible to restore the information stored on either removable or remote storage.

Command-Line Backup

Although it is possible to perform a command-line backup of a Windows 2000 Server, it really is not a great way to perform the backup process (especially given that Microsoft has finally provided a pretty decent GUI backup interface, through its licensing deal with the Veritas Software Corporation). However, should you still want to perform a command-line–based backup, use these next steps to do just that.

First, you need to open a Windows 2000 Server command prompt. To do that, click Start, Run, type the command **Cmd** in the Run box, and then either press the Enter key on your keyboard or click once on the OK button. Doing this opens a Windows 2000 Server command prompt window.

Once the window opens, you need to use the NTbackup command to initiate a command-line backup (interesting name, given that the OS is now known as Windows 2000). Keep in mind that all the limitations (IDs, permissions, local versus network backups, and so on) of the GUI-based backup exist in the command-line version, but also remember that the restoration of files cannot be performed from a command line: You must use the GUI version of the Windows 2000 Server Backup and Restore tool for all file restorations! You can invoke the 18 command-line switches (and their appropriate parameters) during the use of the NTbackup command, for which a detailed description of each switch can be obtained by simply typing the command of NTbackup /?. (This accesses the GUI version of the Windows 2000 Server Backup utility, which in turn starts the Backup utility's Help system and takes you directly to the correct screen for the Help system.)

To actually perform the backup process, the full command syntax is as follows:

```
NTbackup backup [systemstate] "bks file name" /J {"job name"}
➥[/P {"pool name"}] [/G {"guid name"}] [/T { "tape name"}]
➥[/N {"media name"}] [/F {"file name"}] [/D {"set description"}]
➥[/DS {"server name"}] [/IS {"server name"}] [/A] [/V:{yes¦no}]
➥[/R:{yes¦no}] [/L:{f¦s¦n}] [/M {backup type}] [/RS:{yes¦no}] [/HC:{on¦off}]
```

This is quite a command to be typing each time you want to perform a backup, eh? Of course, many system administrators perform this type of backup from a batch or script file, so the typing probably is not too bad after the first batch or script file is configured. For example, perhaps you might configure a command-line backup job to look like the following:

```
NTbackup backup [systemstate] \\Socrates\d$ /J "Backup Job 1"
➥/P "BackupPool" /D "Command Line Backup" /V:yes /R:yes /M daily
```

This backup job will back up the System State data from the D: drive of the server known as SOCRATES with a backup name of BACKUP JOB. The backup media will be a tape from the BACKUPPOOL media pool, which will have a tape name of COMMAND LINE BACKUP. The backup job will be verified upon completion, access to the tape will be restricted to either system administrators or the backup job's owner, and the backup type will be that of a daily backup.

The key thing to remember is that you do not have to use all 18 parameters every time, nor do you need to type the parameters in any special order. (Of course, if you do not stick to a set pattern, then reading or debugging your batch/script files is going to get a bit ugly in the future.) Also, instead of the UNC name for the path, which is probably a network drive, the actual drive letter could have been used instead (had it been a local drive). Personally, I believe that it is much easier and more efficient to stick with the Windows 2000 Server GUI version of the Backup utility, but to each his or her own.

Restoring a Backup

Obviously, at some point all organizations need to restore one of their backup media archives. Typically, this happens for testing purposes (to make sure that you have the process down cold and that it will always work) but, in some unfortunate times, it might happen due to a failure in your organization's business systems. In any event, the restoration process should be checked out thoroughly on a regular basis.

To initiate the restoration process, you need to return to the Windows 2000 Server Backup and Recovery Tools application. To do that, click Start, Programs, Accessories, System Tools, Backup. Once in the Windows 2000 Server Backup utility, click once on the Restore tab to reveal the screen shown in Figure 25.25.

FIGURE 25.25

Using the main restore screen.

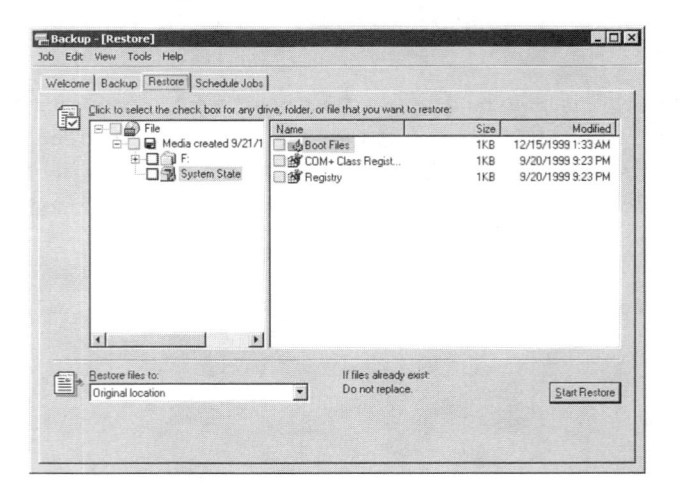

Once the Windows 2000 Backup and Recovery Tools utility is running, you want to verify a few things just prior to starting the actual restore process:

- Make sure that you are logged onto the Windows 2000 Server as either the Administrator or as a member of the Backup Operators group.
- Ensure that the backup media is properly loaded in the drive from which the recovery is to be made (that is, load the backup tape).
- Verify your network connections, should this restoration process be taking place via a network.
- Ensure that the remote storage is running, in the event that the restoration process will be occurring from a media pool.
- If the System State data is to be restored, then Windows 2000 must be started in its Safe Mode.
- Use the GUI-based Windows 2000 Backup and Recovery Tools utility to perform the restoration process either manually or automatically (via the wizard process).

To run the restore process via the wizard, you simply need to click Tools, Restore Wizard. Doing this initiates the wizard process, which is a series of GUI-based screens that automatically walks you through every step of the restoration process. Although this is a nicely constructed feature of the Windows 2000 Backup and Recovery Tools utility, I do not cover it here because it is self-explanatory in nature (plus, all of the options on these screens are covered in the manual restoration process that I am about to discuss).

To perform a manual restore of your backed up data, you still need to access the Windows 2000 Server Backup and Recovery Tools application in the exact same way you did for the wizard-based process. This takes you into that same screen that you saw in Figure 25.25. From there, the first thing you need to do is decide precisely where the restored files are to be placed. You have a few choices:

- Original location
- Alternate location
- Single folder

Although all of these choices are pretty obvious as to their meaning, you want to carefully consider your choice because you will not be able to properly restore System State data to an alternate location. Likewise, if you restore to an alternate location, it is possible for you to wind up with multiple versions of the same file on the Windows 2000 server. (This can lead to confusing conditions for the organization's endusers, so be careful about how you perform the restore process.) Should you select the Alternate Location option from the Restore Files To drop-down list box, then you need to select the full path for that alternate location. To do that, click once on the Browse button that appears along the bottom of the screen, which reveals the Restore Path window that you see in Figure 25.26.

FIGURE 25.26
Choosing a restore path.

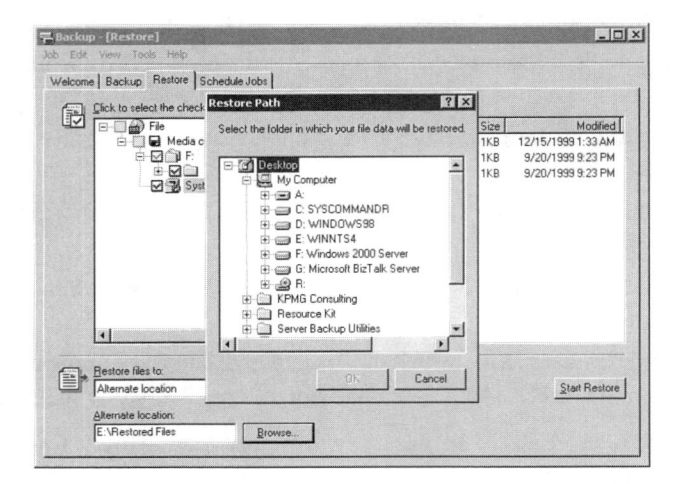

Use the Restore Path window to browse your server for the proper location to which you want to restore the backed up files. Once you have located that location, click it once to select it and then click once on the OK button to confirm your choice, which then returns you to the main Backup – [Restore] screen.

Once there, you should confirm the primary options that will be in play during the restore process. To do this, click Tools, Options, which reveals the Options screen shown in Figure 25.27.

FIGURE 25.27
Setting the restore options.

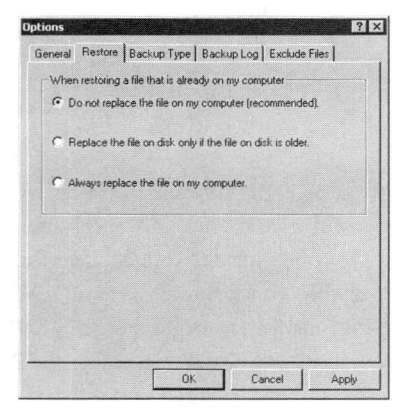

When the Options screen appears, you notice that you have to choose from one of three base options: how to react when the file that you are restoring already exists on your system. The default choice, which also happens to be the Microsoft-recommended one, is to not replace the existing file. The least favorite choice of most organizations is the last one in the list (to always overwrite the existing file). In any event, make your selection by clicking on the radio button next to that option, and then click once on the OK button to confirm your selection and exit the Options screen.

To continue the process, click once on the Start Restore button. If your backup file includes System State data, then you immediately see the Warning pop-up window shown in Figure 25.28.

FIGURE 25.28
Viewing the restore warning.

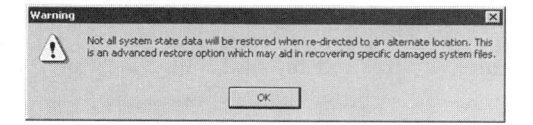

Otherwise, the process continues on to the Confirm Restore screen shown in Figure 25.29.

FIGURE 25.29
Confirming a restore action.

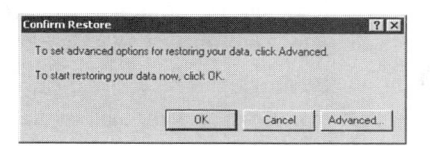

If you believe that all of your options, both the primary ones you just set and the advanced ones, are set to your organization's satisfaction, then click once on the OK button to begin the actual folder and file restoration process. If you want to stop the entire restoration process, then click once on the Cancel button to end the entire restore program completely and return to the main Backup – [Restore] window. However, if you want to continue but are unsure of the advanced options that can be configured, click once on the Advanced button to reveal the Advanced Restore Options screen shown in Figure 25.30.

FIGURE 25.30
Setting Advanced Restore Options.

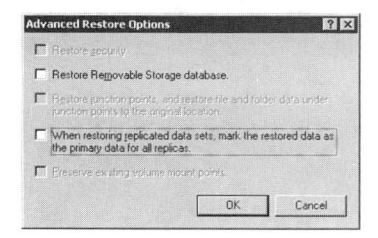

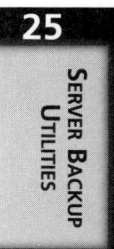

The five options on this screen are all important to a restore process, any of which can make the difference between a successful restoration of your business data and potentially corruption of that same data. Those options are as follows:

- **Restore Security**—This option will restore the exact security configuration for every single file and folder that is restored during this recovery process. Unfortunately, this option is only available for those Windows 2000 NTFS 5.0 volumes that were backed up (FAT16, FAT32, and NTFS 4.0 volumes will not work with this option) and are also being restored to an NTFS 5.0 volume.

- **Restore Removable Storage database**—This only pertains to those organizations using removable storage to manage their storage media. Keep in mind, however, that the restoration of this database will overwrite any existing removable storage database, which might be important in and of itself.

- **Restore junction points, and restore file and folder data under junction points to the original location**—This option is pretty self-explanatory. Essentially, it means that all of the data will be restored to their original junction points' pointer locations. You want to select this option if you were using junction points that were then backed up because the data that those junction points pointed to will not otherwise be accessible. Furthermore, if you are restoring the data for a mounted drive, then you must also check this option to retrieve that data properly.

- **When restoring replicated data sets, mark the restored data as the primary data for all replicas**—This restore option will ensure that any restored File Replication Service (FRS) data is automatically replicated out to the other Windows 2000 replication servers on the organization's networks. Failure to use this option might cause you to eventually lose all of your restored data because the other FRS servers will "see" the restored data as older (and thus disposable) than the data they might have.

- **Preserve existing volume mount points**—This will ensure that you do not accidentally overwrite any existing volume mount points that you might have created during the installation of a new drive (that replaced a failed drive device). However, if you are attempting a restoration to a recently reformatted drive, then you might not want to use this option because you will probably want to restore all of your original volume mount points.

Click once on the check box next to each option that you want to invoke for your restoration process. Click once on the OK button to continue the restoration process, which then reveals the Enter Backup File Name screen.

On the Enter Backup File Name screen, you must enter the exact path and name of the backup file that you are attempting to restore during this restoration process. Use the

Browse button to "surf" your computer or network in search of the proper backup file that you want to restore. Once you find it, click it once to select it, which returns you to this screen. Once back here, click once on the OK button to continue the restore process. If you are attempting to restore your data to an alternate location or trying to restore System State data across a network drive, then you see the caution pop-up window shown in Figure 25.31.

FIGURE 25.31
Viewing a restoration caution message.

Your only real choice here is to ignore the warning and continue the restore process, by clicking once on the OK button. Of course, you can always cancel out of the restore process by clicking once on the Cancel button to halt the restore procedure. Make your selection as need be. Let us assume that you clicked once on the OK button, which takes you into the Restore Progress screen shown in Figure 25.32.

FIGURE 25.32
Reviewing the Restore Progress window.

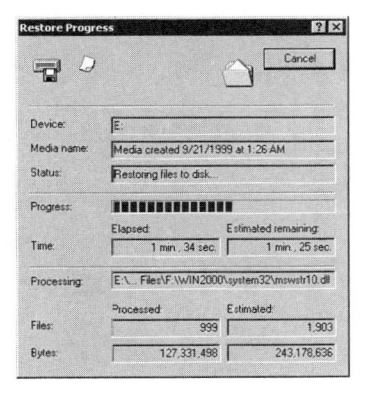

On the Restore Progress screen, you can monitor the status of the file and folder restoration process that can be halted at any point with the Cancel button. Once the restore process finishes, you see a slightly revised Restore Progress screen, as shown in Figure 25.33.

Just like the Backup Progress screen, this Restore Progress screen displays a brief explanation of the restoration process. For further details on what was done during the restore process, click once on the Report button to reveal the contents of that screen.

FIGURE 25.33
Reviewing a completed restore process.

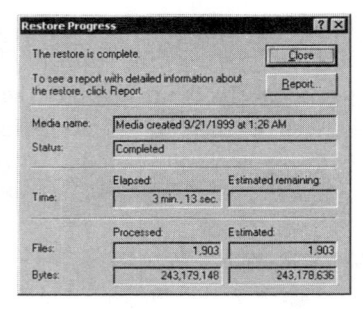

When the Microsoft Notepad application appears with the restore data information in it, you can save that ASCII text file to some audit location (where it can be retrieved at some future date should you need to explain the events of the restore process). Once you are finished looking at this report, close out of the Microsoft Notepad application to return to the Restore Progress screen. Once back there, click once on the Close button to exit that screen. To confirm the success of the restoration of your files and folders, you might want to use the Windows Explorer tool to wander over to the restored location, as was done in Figure 25.34.

FIGURE 25.34
Viewing your Restored Files.

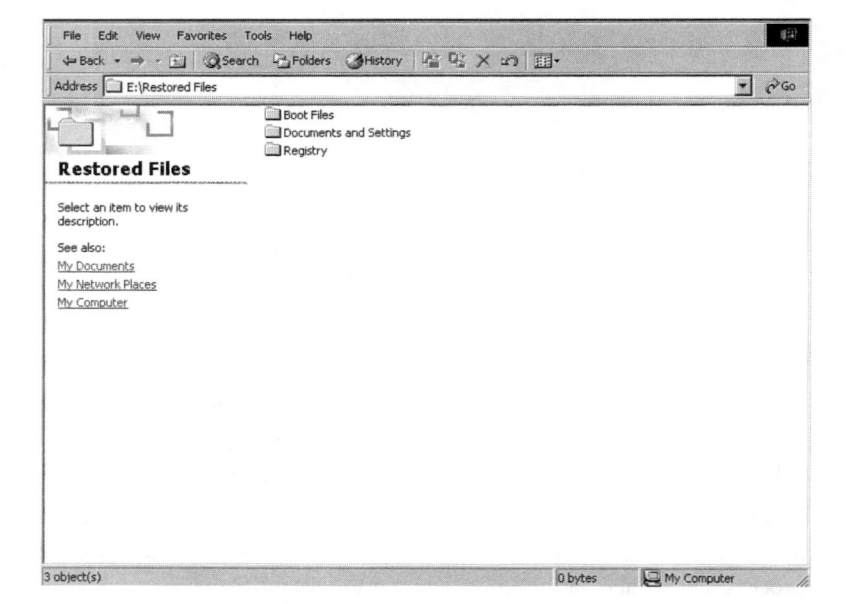

Open a few of the restored files and folders to ensure that the data that has been restored is the correct stuff, as well as to ensure the integrity of the data. (You might need to use an application to test the validity of the data that was restored.) To conclude the restore process, simply close the Windows 2000 Backup and Recovery Tools application.

Authoritative Restore

When performing a restore of mission-critical System State data that involves the use of multiple Domain Controllers within your Windows 2000 Server network, you must perform a procedure that is known as an *authoritative restore*. Essentially, when you attempt a recovery of distributed services such as the Active Directory or the SYSVOL directory and the Windows 2000 Server Registry, then you must perform an authoritative restore prior to rebooting the server, but after the actual files themselves have been restored.

Failure to do an authoritative restore will result in your restored data being viewed by the other Windows 2000 Domain Controllers as "older" data, so it will be overwritten by information that resides on the other Windows 2000 Domain Controllers within your organization's Windows 2000 forest. A normal data restore process will restore your Active Directory objects with their original sequencing number. This means that those object numbers are certain to be lower than the objects of the same name that exist in a replicated mode somewhere else out on the Windows 2000 network. Those newly restored objects will actually become targeted for replacement by the older objects, which will then corrupt your organization's Active Directory structure. To avoid this, you need to run the Authoritative Restore tool that comes with the Windows 2000 Server operating system.

To perform an authoritative restore, all you need to do is first perform the normal restore process of the System State data. Once it has finished, do not restart your Windows 2000 server. Instead, open up a Windows 2000 Server command prompt (\Start, \Run, \Cmd), and then run the NtdsUtil utility program. This utility program appears in the %systemroot%\system32 folder (you might need to install it from the Windows 2000 installation CD-ROM disc, if it is not present on your Windows 2000 server) and has the full name of NtdsUtil.exe (presently in its version 2.0 release). The NtdsUtil utility will automatically mark the restored Active Directory objects for authoritative restore. What this means is that Windows 2000 will then update the sequence number for each object that is marked for authoritative restore. This in turn means that the sequence number assigned to those Active Directory objects will be given a higher number so that any replicated versions of those objects will be of a lesser sequencing number and thus cannot overwrite your newly restored System State data files.

To actually run this utility, go to the command prompt and type the command **NtdsUtil**. The utility program executes by immediately returning with a `NtdsUtil:` prompt. (Yes, this command-line tool is a bit cryptic.) At that prompt, type the full command of **Authoritative Restore** and then press the Enter key. Next, type the command **Quit** and again press the Enter key, which causes the NtdsUtil utility to close. Now, reboot your Windows 2000 server, which finishes the authoritative restore process upon the startup of that Windows 2000 server.

Restoring Encrypted Files

The restoration of files and folders that were encrypted using the new Windows 2000 Encrypting File Service (EFS) is straightforward, provided that you are not attempting a restoration to a different computer (one that is different from the Windows 2000 server where the files and folders were originally created and encrypted). There is one caveat to this restore process: If you have a roaming user profile that permits you to log onto that non-original Windows 2000 computer where you want to restore the encrypted files, then you do not need to go through this process because the restoration process will work as if you were logged on locally to the original computer.

For the sake of argument, let us assume that you are on a different computer without a roaming user profile to use as the restoration account ID. The first thing that you need to do is export your encryption certificate and private key from the original Windows 2000 server computer. Use the `Export` command from Certificates in the Microsoft Management Console (MMC), which permits you to create a `.PFX` file onto a floppy diskette that contains this information. (Refer to the Security section of this book for more information on how to export encryption and private key data to an external device such as a floppy disk.)

Once you have the floppy diskette that contains your original Windows 2000 Server's `.PFX` file information, take that diskette over to the new computer via your local sneaker net (that is, walk it over to the new computer). Once there, insert the floppy diskette into the drive at that new computer and use the `Import` command from Certificates in the MMC, which permits you to import that `.PFX` file into the local personal store.

Once this has been done, you can restore the encrypted files to the new computer and access them as necessary. If you fail to follow this process, then you are prohibited from accessing any file or folder that had been encrypted on your old Windows 2000 server computer. Keep in mind that if you made the backup files on a Windows 2000 server that had 128-bit cipher strength for its encryption keys, then you must restore to a like machine. You will not be able to restore and subsequently access files or folders that were originally encrypted on a 128-bit encryption PC and then restored on a computer with just the basic 56-bit cipher strength encryption.

Supported Backup Drive Devices

The Windows 2000 Server operating system supports a wide variety of tape and disk backup drive devices. The best way to ensure that the device you are attempting to use will work with Windows 2000 Server is to consult the Windows 2000 Hardware Compatibility List (HCL) that is readily available on a variety of sources:

- **On the Internet**—http://www.microsoft.com/windows2000
- **Microsoft TechNet**—Microsoft's lower-end support subscription, which contains an electronic version of the Hardware Compatibility List for all of its 32-bit operating systems.
- **Microsoft Developer's Network (MSDN)**—Another Microsoft subscription service that contains an electronic version of the Hardware Compatibility List for all of Microsoft's 32-bit operating systems.

The sheer number of devices that are now supported by the Windows 2000 Server operating system is greatly enhanced from that of the older Windows NT operating systems (which did not support SCSI tape drives, a matter that has been rectified in the Windows 2000 Server OS). Your best bet is always to refer to the most recent version of the HCL before purchasing any tape or other media backup system for your Windows 2000 server.

Recovery Console

Another item that you should be aware of is the new technology known as the Windows 2000 Recovery Console. This command-line tool permits you to use a special console for starting and stopping server services, formatting hard drives, and the like. The Windows 2000 Recovery Console is started from within the Windows 2000 Server installation disks, which makes it possible to perform more in-depth recovery techniques on a failed Windows 2000 server. Keep in mind that this new technology is powerful and its misuse can easily result in the damage or total loss to your Windows 2000 server computer, so do not permit anyone other than experienced Windows 2000 system administrators to invoke the Recovery Console tool.

You have two choices for invoking the Recovery Console tool: from the Windows 2000 setup disks or the CD-ROM disc and from an installed version of the Windows 2000 Recovery Console (which is probably not something that you want to make available on your organization's production-quality servers—only the test ones). To start the Recovery Console, you need to maneuver your way to the Windows 2000 setup CD-ROM and then execute the Recovery Console command \i386\winnt32.exe /CmdCons.

Doing this starts the Recovery Console application. Follow the prompts, which includes the ability to permanently install the console onto your computer system. Keep in mind that you must be logged in as either the system administrator or as a member of the Windows 2000 Server Administrators group to be able to execute the Recovery Console application.

Emergency Repair Disk

The Windows 2000 Server Emergency Repair Disk (ERD) works just like the Windows 98 Startup Disk operates. Essentially, the ERD permits you to repair problems with your base Windows 2000 Server system files, the boot environment (this is especially handy in dual or multi-boot configurations), and your partition boot sector that is located on the boot volume. Creating this disk is a snap. Simply put, you use the Windows 2000 Backup and Recovery Tools utility to create an Emergency Repair Disk.

First, you need to return to the Windows 2000 Server Backup and Recovery Tools application. To do that, click Start, Programs, Accessories, System Tools, Backup to reveal the main backup screen.

Once there, click once on the Emergency Repair Disk button (it is the bottom option on the Welcome tab of the opening screen). Doing that takes you to the Emergency Repair Diskette screen, which is shown in Figure 25.35.

FIGURE 25.35
Creating an Emergency Repair Diskette.

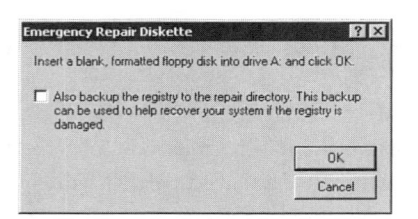

You need two things to perform the disk creation process: access to a high-density, dual-sided 1.44MB floppy drive and a blank, formatted high-density, dual-sided 1.44MB floppy diskette. Simply plop the blank disk into the floppy drive, make sure that the floppy drive is properly attached to the Windows 2000 server (this is mostly an issue for laptop-based Windows 2000 servers), and then click once on the OK button to run the ERD creation process. Once the creation process ends, remove the disk from the drive and store it in a safe, dry place. Close the Windows 2000 Server Backup and Recovery Tools application, and you are (ERD)done.

Third-Party Backup Tools

Numerous third-party backup tools work great with the older Windows NT operating systems and are expected to work just as well with the newly released Windows 2000 series of operating systems. These backup tools include the Veritas Software Corporation's suite of backup tools, along with Seagate's BackupExec software, both of which appear to work just fine with all the versions of Windows 2000. Of course, your organization must make sure that it has the latest version of backup software from its backup device vendor, should it decide not to use the fine Windows 2000 Server Backup and Recovery Tools application that is built into the Windows 2000 Server operating system.

Summary

This chapter discussed the various methods in which you can safely backup and/or restore data to and from your Windows 2000 server, using the Windows 2000 Backup utility program that is integrated into the operating system. All the facets of the various backup and recovery options were discussed, including the more advanced topics of backing-up System State data, performing authoritative and encrypted file restores, as well as how to create an Emergency Repair Disk for your Windows 2000 Server operating environment. If your organization practices solid backup and recovery processes, then the potential for data loss within your Windows 2000 operating environment will be greatly minimized.

CHAPTER 26

Recovering from a Disaster

IN THIS CHAPTER

- Have a Plan, Work the Plan *708*
- Data Recovery *712*
- Hardware Fail-Over Options *718*
- Disaster-Recovery Planning Software and Sites *727*

If you're reading this chapter after a disaster, you're reading it at the wrong time. This chapter is meant as a guide to both avoiding disaster and recovering from one gracefully when it occurs. The problem with most disasters is that no one is prepared for them. That's what I help you with here—preparation. After a hard drive has crashed is not the time to start the recovery process. It's when the process gets truly tested.

A disaster can range from a data disaster that will require a hard drive or server to be rebuilt, to a catastrophic natural disaster that requires the building and employees to be relocated. There isn't enough space here to cover all the possible scenarios, but we can cover the tools necessary to begin disaster planning. All levels of disaster need a plan and test. Don't let the first restoration of data from tape at your company be the one done after the server is destroyed.

Have a Plan, Work the Plan

The first thing you must do is the one thing that most companies do not do—create a plan. This is not a general concept or feeling that one of the guys in MIS has about how the system was all built. It must be tangible, written plan—a plan for every level of disaster, hard drive failure, server failure, and fire. Recovery plans can be made to fit general categories of failure or disaster, but a plan must exist.

When you're forming a recovery plan, the first thing that must be defined is what *recovery* means to the company. For some companies, this means that they must be up and functioning with all data resources within 24 to 48 hours. Still others may be able to function with only customer data in that same time frame. In the financial world, minutes may cost millions. Each individual company must decided for itself.

A good plan must include each of the following items:

- *Staff list*. Includes staff responsible for each item in the plan (backup media, reassembling systems, vendor relations) and vendors to be called
- *Physical plan*. Includes equipment and alternate site plan
- *Documentation*. Includes equipment list, employee phone lists, chronological event list, and meeting places

The most important thing is that you have a plan and work the plan. If a plan exists and isn't implemented, it can be more destructive than if it had never been conceived. People count on the system working once it is in place and don't cover their own tracks if a plan exists that they believe is covering them.

Documentation and Events

When beginning to formulate a disaster-recovery plan, you should include as many people as necessary to make the proper decisions. The time to find out that you have the wrong data or not enough data is not after restoring in a hotel meeting room. The best idea is to include one representative from each group who will be affected by the server or servers in questions.

Documentation needs to include the following items:

- Equipment Lists
    - Required computer systems for reconstruction.
    - Tape drives and software for restoration of backup media.
    - Phone lines and leased lines necessary to re-create WAN connections.
    - General office equipment and supply needs (paper, pens, staplers, and so on).

> **Tip**
> Your ISP may be able to offer help in reestablishing your Internet presence by allowing your company to host a presence at the ISP site. It most likely has been hosting the IP traffic already. It's best to make arrangements in advance.

- Employee Phone Lists
    - Home phone numbers of all disaster team members.
    - If possible, keep the home phone list for all employees offsite. This will all you to alert them if the disaster is catastrophic.
- Vendor Help Required
    - Listing of warranties and contracts held with each vendor.
    - Key technicians and systems engineering staff.
    - Sales staff that can help to acquire needed equipment.
- Chronological Event List
    - Event listings for each disaster scenario or range of severity must be created, including hard drive failure, data corruption, natural disaster (site loss), black out, and so on.
    - When each event must occur.
    - The events that trigger the beginning of each event.

- Meeting Places
    - Simple meeting places to begin reconstruction meetings (branch offices, restaurants, hotels, and so on).
    - Possible offices in the company that can house employees or equipment in the event of a major catastrophe.

Disaster Staff

The planning of these groups can be tough. What the planner is hoping for is to not send the invitees running away screaming "The sky is falling." Panic can infest these meetings very quickly, and once faith is lost in the information system, the situation can get ugly. Groups want their own control, their own hardware, and separate plans developed.

When explaining the meeting to department heads who must pick a representative, you should note that a computer-savvy member is needed. He or she needs to understand and be comfortable with the concept of hard drive storage, memory, backup, and servers versus workstations. This person doesn't need to be a Certified Engineer; he or she just needs to understand the concepts on an experienced home-user level. If you tell these group members that the data is stored on the most likely item to fail in the server, no one should pass out.

The group cannot just be members of the IS staff. It should be representative of the whole company. Disaster will include the entire company, and the recovery plan must include the entire company. This helps avoid animosity and misunderstanding later in the event. If in the disaster-planning meeting the accounting representative says that they can withstand 24 hours of downtime, it becomes much easier to announce that the new hard drive for the accounting server will be in tomorrow morning.

The purpose of these meetings must be to create the aforementioned documentation and to get the approval of everyone for the resulting recovery.

Tasks need to be broken down into assignment groups of responsibility. This allows each member of the disaster-recovery group to have manageable items that he or she can take care of. No matter how tempting it is, no member should be left out of having some responsibility.

Physical Considerations

The physical need to relocate is part of a catastrophic disaster that must be thought of but no one wants to ever use. If the building that the company is currently in is destroyed or becomes unusable, the company must have an alternate location quickly. For many companies, a single missed bid could alter the company's existence forever.

Alternate Site Plan

It's obviously best if the company can make use of branch office locations. This allows the use of preexisting phone connections, company documents, and the systems in place to a greater or lesser degree. However, it may be necessary to locate the company in a hotel or conference facility. A member of your disaster-recovery team should be in charge of making contact with and evaluating these facilities.

Here are some things to consider in choosing an alternate site:

- Will the power needs be met?
- Can the network WAN connectivity needs be met?
- How many phone lines will be needed and available?
- Can furniture be provided?
- Are shipping and receiving services available?

Offsite Materials Storage

As part of any recovery plan, there needs to be a contingency for the storage of company data offsite. As you'll see in the next section, a good data backup plan always includes the storage of tapes in an offsite location. The fact is that disaster planning includes the offsite location being destroyed. If this site includes all the company records and data, it may be as valuable as the company as a whole.

Many cities have companies that specialize in recovering data and documents on a scheduled basis for storage off the company grounds. Vault companies, banks, and warehousing companies will send trucks to the company with containers that have the items your company wants to store. This allows for the exchange of media or papers now wanted in house and the removal of the next shift of offsite material.

This process does not have to be so involved, though. In small one-server companies, it can be as simple as one employee taking the tapes home. However, it's important to realize the power that this invests in this person, who could make or break the company in a time of disaster.

It's also important to note that paper documents can be very important in a disaster. Licenses, certifications, agreements, and so on can all stop your company from existing if copies are not stored offsite.

Data Recovery

Backing up a server and the software to perform this backup was covered in detail in Chapter 25, "Server Backup Utilities," but the planning necessary to make sure that the data is available for recovery is covered here.

Many administrators think of server backup as a recovery method only for the total loss of a hard drive. However, it's best to think of server backup as a way to recover data at any point. Backup media can be used for many forms of data recovery:

- Recovering from hard drive failure
- Recovering from individual file corruption or loss
- Rollbacks to previous versions of file content
- Record keeping for history or audit purposes

Hard drive failure is probably the least common use of the recovery process. More commonly, disasters are related to user error. These disasters are capable of being even worse than physical failure. User errors are often not found for days, weeks, or even months. This means that recovery of the data from yesterday is not good enough. If the corruption occurred on Tuesday and isn't found until Monday, the tape from last night contains the corrupted data.

Be very aware of the fact that backup tapes and tape drives fail just like floppy disks, videotapes, and audio cassette tapes. They're magnetic media and, as such, are only good for a given amount of time. For this reason, among others, be sure to restore some piece of benign data from the tape drive from time to time. No system is perfect, and even a good system goes south.

It never ceases to amaze Network Field Engineers how often they arrive at a client site to find that the restoration that they're being asked to do is the first ever done on the system. Have faith in no man or backup system. Test your system backup and restore the system yourself.

Backup Operations

Because of these issues, you need to understand the different types of backup and the different backup plans that can be implemented. As part of that understanding, here are some basic rules of thumb that should be present in any system for data recovery:

- Avoid human intervention in the backup process whenever possible. Humans forget things. No matter how good the intention, humans will always forget at the most inopportune times. (Specific examples of how to do this will follow as part of the other rules.)

- Eliminate points of failure by reducing the number of variables to the minimum. Each new piece that can fail probably will at some point fail. (Humans count as double points.)
- Whenever possible, complete the backup to one piece of media. This may not be possible, but if it is, it keeps human intervention to a minimum. If a tape must be changed, the backup must wait for intervention, and some files may be in use once it's started again. Automated tape changers can change tapes and are preferable to manual changing them. However, each tape adds a new point of failure.
- Backing up during off-peak times preserves the server and network performance. Servers have files that are open during peak times of the day that will not be backed up because they're open. It may even be necessary to have the backup process log out users before starting the backup. It's possible to use open file utilities that will backup anyway. However, a server that's being backed up is not servicing clients as efficiently as when it's not.

  During peak hours, the network will be severely hampered if the backup server is pulling from other servers. This is because a backup of the server will maintain a constant flow of data across the network, as opposed to the occasional calls of the users. Some systems actually have a SAN (server area network) dedicated to the process of server backup for this reason.

  Many backup packages have utilities that cause the server to dedicate more resources to the process of delivering files to the backup. This causes even further reduction in what's available to the users.

> **Note**
>
> A *SAN* (Server Area Network) is a network created specifically for the purpose of server communications. These systems can be as simple as an Ethernet segment dedicated to servers only, or they can be as elaborate as proprietary gigabit switching systems.

When a backup occurs, the archive attribute of the file can be changed to show that the file was backed up. When the file is written to, the attribute is changed back. This allows the backup to differentiate which files have changed in the case of a more elaborate backup method. There are three backup methods that can be used each time a server is backed up. The choices will cause changes in the backup speed, the restoration speed, and the amount of backup media that's used. Here are the types:

- *Full backup*. A backup of all data on a given resource (drive or share). If a full backup is done for the C: drive, all files from that server are backed up to the tape without regard for how long it has been since last backup or if changes have occurred. Generally, the archive attribute is changed to indicate that a backup has occurred during a full backup.

    Here are some advantages of this type of backup:
    - All data is found in one backup set.
    - Ease of file restoration.
    - Less human intervention required.

    Here are some disadvantages of this type of backup:
    - Uses more storage media (tapes, opticals, disks) to complete.
    - Takes more time to complete.

- *Incremental backup*. Files are backed up based on the state of the archive attribute. All files that have changed since the last backup are backed up. The archive attribute is always set to indicate the file was backed up.

    Here are some advantages of this type of backup:
    - Uses the least amount of tape media to complete.
    - Takes the least amount of time to complete.
    - Single-file restoration can be faster because less tape must be searched to find a given file.

    Here are some disadvantages of this type of backup:
    - Restoring data requires a knowledge of which tape contains the data.
    - Full restoration takes more time because the last full backup is needed as well as all incremental backups since the last full backup.

- *Differential backup*. Files are backed up based on whether they have been backed since the last "full" backup (*full* is the difference between incremental and differential). Therefore, if a full backup is done on Friday and a file is changed on Monday, that file will be backed up everyday up to and including the next full backup. The distinction is to allow for faster restoration. Because the current state of the file is now on one of two tapes, you avoid having to track numerous incremental tapes.

    Here are some advantages of this type of backup:
    - Full restore is faster then incremental backup.
    - Uses the less tape media to complete than another full backup.
    - Takes less time to complete backups than another full backup.

Here are some disadvantages of this type of backup:

- Restoring data requires a knowledge of which tape contains the data.
- Full restoration takes more time since the last full backup and a differential tape is needed.

Time-tested Backup Plans

Having a backup plan means that you have a method for backing up and storing data that allows for smooth backup and restoration of data over a sufficient amount of time. The amount of time is variable. Some companies can afford to lose any data older than a week, whereas others cannot lose any data from the last 24 hours. Still other companies are responsible for being able to produce records from seven years past.

As mentioned earlier, the concept of backup should not be thought of only as a fault-tolerance measure. It must be thought of as a way of recovering data that's changed. The change may be an accounting ledger that has been closed and must now be reopened, or it could be a hard drive that has crashed. In either case, the data must be backed up and stored with a plan in order to be recovered.

Grandfather/Father/Son (GFS)

The concept of the Grandfather/Father/Son backup rotation is to maintain the ability to restore from any day up to five days back, any week up to four weeks back, and as many months back in history that company cares to keep. This system is named based on the relationship that the tapes in the full set have to each other.

The rotation scheme follows a pattern of rotations that involve daily tapes labeled (Monday, Tuesday, Wednesday, Thursday), weekly tapes labeled (Friday 1, Friday 2, Friday 3, Friday 4, Friday 5), and one tape for each new month (see Table 26.1). Here's the scheme:

- *Son*. On each day of the week (Monday, Tuesday, Wednesday, and Thursday) the appropriate day's tape is used for a full backup.
- *Father*. On Fridays, the respective Friday tape is used for that Friday of the month (Friday 1, Friday 2, Friday 3, Friday 4, Friday 5) to complete another full backup.
- *Grandfather*. On the last day of the month, that day's backup tape is removed, marked, and stored as a monthly tape. The tape is replaced and properly marked for replacement in the scheme.

The Friday and monthly tapes are kept offsite in order to avoid physical disasters at the building site. Many variations on this scheme are popular.

TABLE 26.1 A Four-Week Tape Rotation Schedule

Day of the Week (1st Month)	Tape
Monday	Monday
Tuesday	Tuesday
Wednesday	Wednesday
Thursday	Thursday
Friday	Friday 1
Monday	Monday
Tuesday	Tuesday
Wednesday	Wednesday
Thursday	Thursday
Friday	Friday 2
Monday	Monday
Tuesday	Tuesday
Wednesday	Wednesday
Thursday	Thursday
Friday	Friday 3
Monday	Monday
Tuesday	Tuesday
Wednesday	Wednesday
Thursday	Thursday
Friday	Friday 4

One variation involves using one tape for the Monday–Thursday backup (a daily tape) and making those backups differential. This allows for the saving of media but also creates a gap in the weekly recovery if the daily tape should fail, leaving the company to re-create a week's worth of data.

If the full backup is taking up more than one tape, another alternative is to do incremental or differential backups on the Monday–Thursday tapes. This allows for the stability of multiple tapes but the media savings of incremental or differential backups.

Tower of Hanoi

The Tower of Hanoi scheme uses a more complex scheme (the Tower of Hanoi Algorithm) in order to allow for recovery of older data in one rotation and a perceived safety factor. The process is very complex. It's meant to use fewer tapes but still provide a backup history. Its greatest downfall is the complexity of restoration.

The rotation scheme follows a pattern of rotations that involve tapes labeled A through E:

- The A tape is used first, and for every other backup from then on, meaning days 1, 3, 5, 7, 9, and so on (notice it's every odd number).
- The B tape is used second and again on every fourth backup after that, meaning days 2, 6, 10, 14, 18, and so on.
- The C tape is used on the fourth day and again on every eighth day after that, meaning days 4, 12, 20, 28, 36, and so on.
- The D tape is used on the eight day and again on every sixteenth day after that, meaning days 8, 24, 40, 56, 72, and so on.
- The E tape is used on the sixteenth day and again every sixteenth day after that, meaning days 16, 32, 48, 64, 80, and so on.

The algorithm is interesting to lay out on paper because no repeating will occur (see Table 26.2). This rotation keeps a certain number of tapes in rotation for varying periods of time. The A tapes, for example, will always contain fairly current data. Whereas the D and E tapes will include historical data that may be needed if corruption is found.

TABLE 26.2 A 16-Day Tape Rotation

Day of the Week (1st Month)	Tape
Monday	A
Tuesday	B
Wednesday	A
Thursday	C
Friday	A
Monday	B
Tuesday	A
Wednesday	D
Thursday	A
Friday	B
Monday	A
Tuesday	C
Wednesday	A
Thursday	B
Friday	A
Monday	E

> **Note**
>
> French mathematician Edouard Lucas created the Tower of Hanoi in 1883 as a puzzle for students. The students were given a stack of eight disks of decreasing size, top to bottom, and three pegs. These disks were stacked on one of the pegs. The object of the puzzle was to transfer the entire "tower" from one peg to the another. Movement must be one disk at a time while never stacking a larger disk on a smaller one.

This system is meant to use differing numbers of tapes based on the choice of the administrator. If, for example, the choice is made to use four B tapes, then B tapes (B1, B2, B3, B4) become much like the Friday tapes of the GFS plan. However, using odd combinations of tape quantity defeats the purpose of the tower algorithm. Also, the rotation covers 16 days before tapes begin getting reused and recovery beyond 24 days is not possible without pulling a tape aside for archival.

Many companies will use this scheme and replace tapes for archival purposes. However, at this point, you must ask why not just use the GFS approach, which contains archival as part of the scheme.

Here are some advantages of this method:

- Uses few tapes to contain a long range of time. One rotation contains sixteen days.
- The complex nature of the system makes it less accessible.

Here are some disadvantages of this method:

- Restoration can be very frustrating. A full understanding of the rotation scheme must be at hand.
- The complex nature of the system makes it less accessible.
- It's difficult to explain to the staff and to implement. If the cycle is broken, restoration can be impossible.

Hardware Fail-Over Options

In any machine, the most likely parts to fail are the moving parts. In a PC, the only part that's moving constantly is the hard drive(s). Hard drives spin like a record on a record player, and they do so from the moment they're turned on. Some hard drives stop for energy conservation, but this should not include server hard drives.

The hard drive contains all the data stored in the PC. If the entire PC should fail and the hard drive can be recovered, the data is easily recoverable. This makes the hard drive the most important piece of hardware in the server. Any hardware-recovery plan has to include the hard drive subsystem as part of that plan. There are two mainstream hardware implementations that are used in servers today to maintain use of hard drive space during hardware failure.

The most common is the use of hardware managed RAID (Redundant Array of Inexpensive Drives). This allows the operating system to continue functioning when one or more hard drives fail without allowing the operating system to know of the failure.

A solution becoming more popular and more available is the use of *server clustering*. This involves attaching two servers to a single hard drive subsystem and allowing control to alternate between the two based on failure or administrator control. Today, these system are mostly used for fault tolerance, but they'll eventually grow far beyond this use.

We will soon see multiple server controlling and/or sharing multiple hard drive subsystems. This would allow for access to data based on server availability, and not just drive availability. Beyond that we enter the world of processor and memory clustering. These are not new technologies, but as the PC world begins to infringe even more on the mainframe the technologies come along.

Hardware-Controlled RAID

RAID has already been covered in Chapter 4, "File Systems," as part of the Windows 2000 operating system. This form of RAID is known as *software RAID* because the management and control of the array is done by the operating system. Hardware-controlled RAID maintains control of the RAID array at the hard drive controller.

The advantage of this system is that the operating system does not expend time or processing power dealing with this process. In hardware solutions, the controller contains the processor and RAM to maintain the stripping and fault tolerance. This allows the system to run faster.

Management communications with the controller is maintained by the operating system, but this communication is for alert purposes. By alerting utilities in the operating system of a failure, the operating system can then alert the administrator of the failure.

Clustered Servers

Clustering of systems has numerous meanings in the computer world. For the purposes of the operating system, it involves attaching two servers to a single hard drive subsystem and allowing control to alternate between the two based on failure or administrator control.

The hardware in this configurations is most often a proprietary combination of the following items (see Figure 26.1):

- One hard drive controller (SCSI or Fibre) in each server to attach to the common hard drive subsystem.
- A hard drive subsystem consisting of the following items:
    - A subsystem internal hard drive controller
    - Hard drives
    - A cabinet or enclosure

FIGURE 26.1
Windows server cluster.

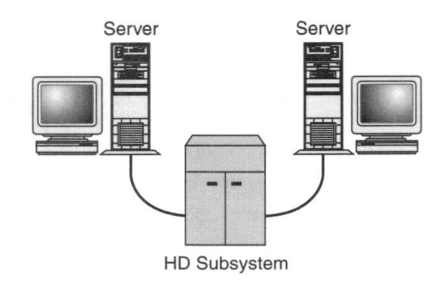

The connection is made between the servers, and the subsystem is made through either SCSI or through Fibre Channel, depending on implementation. Shared SCSI is the older of the two solutions and is more constrained by the physical limits of SCSI cables and technology. Fibre Channel is a newer technology and has the distance advantages of fiber-optic cable. It also allows for multiple servers and peripheral connections (including hard drives) to a hub.

> **Note**
>
> *Fibre Channel* is not a misspelling of the word *fiber* but is instead a separate technology that was developed to allow for the connection of mass storage to multiple computers. It has developed to allow other peripheral devices as well.

Windows clustering in this environment is often called *Shared Nothing* because the systems do not have common access to any storage at any given moment (see Figure 26.2). One server will always have control of a given drive. If, for example, a drive subsystem contains two logical drives, any of the following combinations can be used:

- Server 1 controls drives A and B.
- Server 2 controls drives A and B.
- Server 1 controls drive A, and Server 2 controls drive B.
- Server 1 controls drive B, and Server 2 controls drive A.

FIGURE 26.2
A Shared Nothing example.

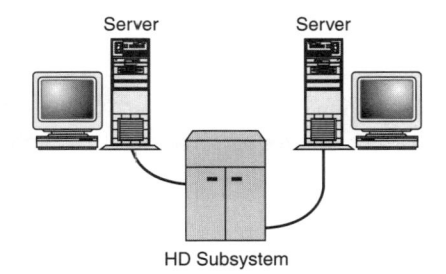

The point is that at no point can servers A and B control drive A at the same time. Nor can they control drive B at the same time. They both can take control using any of the aforementioned combinations, but they cannot share control.

Once the common storage is established, the cluster can be formed. From a user standpoint, these two servers will be presented with one common name. The cluster presents itself through that name as if it were a separate "logical" server. Just as separate hard drive spaces can be presented as one logical hard drive, the two servers and their common shares can be presented as one logical server.

In Figure 26.3, servers A and B would be seen as the server Cluster_1.

FIGURE 26.3
The Cluster presentation.

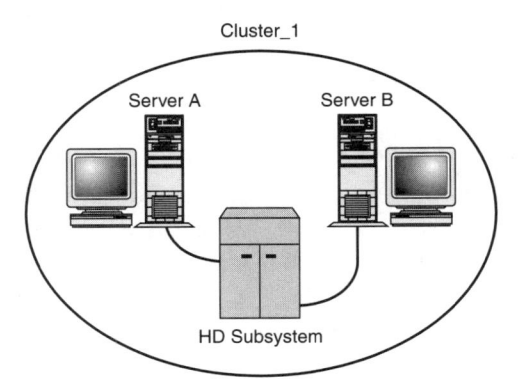

The servers communicate their current status to one another by sending a "pulse" or "heart beat" signal to their partner through a network connection. When a server in the cluster has a failure (software or hardware) that stops the processor, the pulse will stop. If a server fails to see its partner in the cluster for a given period of time, it will take control of the partner's portion of the disk subsystem.

Because all the cluster resources are being presented through a logical server name, the users should notice nothing more then a lag in service as the change occurs. Clustering can include printer shares and disk shares, but neither should stop during the switch.

Because the resources are on the drives that were assumed by the cluster partner, the logical server will continue on.

As mentioned earlier, hard drives can also fail. For this reason, it makes the most sense to have these common hard drives also be controlled by some form of hardware RAID. It makes no sense to spend the money necessary to make the servers highly available and to then have a hard dive failure cause the resource to be unavailable.

Clustering is not covered in depth in this book because it's part of the Advanced Server version of Windows 2000, but it is a important technology to be aware of.

Soon, multiple servers will be able to attach to a field of disk subsystems in a sort of "free range" clustering, but that day is not here in Windows just yet. It's available in systems such as Compaq's (Tandem's) Himalaya Non-Stop Systems. This process is believed to be arriving with the Windows 2000 Datacenter addition.

Disaster-Recovery Planning Software and Sites

The planning involved can be very tough if you have a great deal of experience. But if it is your first time then you are most likely going to miss something. It can be helpful to get a professional involved and in today's world there is piece of software for everything. Disaster recovery is no different. Here are some suggestions.

Binomial's Phoenix 3.0

The company Binomial has found a niche that few companies have taken up—disaster-planning software for systems and staff. The software package it sells, Phoenix 3.0, is a tool that guides the user through creating plans and documents. As you've seen in this chapter, the creation of disaster-planning documents can be very difficult. It can be very easy to forget an item or to be totally unaware of some aspect of the process. A program such as Phoenix can help you create a comprehensive plan.

There are two modules in the Phoenix 3.0 Disaster Recovery Planning System: Procedures and Databases.

The Procedures module contains information on risk analysis, protection, prevention, impact, teams, procedures, maintenance, testing, and training. This module contains complete information that you're able to pick up and choose, as needed, to quickly and easily build your plan. The activities for each member of 20 recovery teams are listed for the time before, during, and after a disaster.

The Databases module is made up of a series of databases that will contain information you'll need to recover your business. These include not only the normal computer assets, such as hardware, software, systems, and applications, but also other noncomputer assets, such as suppliers, people, teams, skills, and emergency telephone contact information. A unique feature is the inclusion of replacement information so that the decisions as to what to replace current equipment with are made before, not during, a disaster.

The greatest aspect of this product is that it prods you to think about the items I've listed so far in this chapter as well as many more items that couldn't be listed here. The product runs on all the Windows workstation formats (3.1, 95/98, NT, and 2000).

http://www.disasterrecovery.com

CDI Vaults Company

CDI has created a Web page to promote its services, which allow users to keep a planner. The Web site, http://www.cdivaults.com/clients/dr_plan.doc, takes you to a page that's helpful when you need ideas about what to be ready for.

Business Protections Services' Business Protector for Windows

Like the Binomial product, Business Protections Services has created software (Business Protector for Windows) that allows you to document your own system. The company offers two versions of the product: Business Protector for Windows and Business Protector Express.

The base product, Business Protector for Windows, is a Microsoft Access database, thus making the data quite portable and usable. It facilitates the production of easy-to-use and comprehensive plans in a document-like format. The product is network ready and can be shared among users.

The Express version is a pared-down version for small businesses and runs from a CD-ROM or Web browser. The user is presented with a sample business continuity plan from which to choose a section to edit. Once a plan section is selected, a form appears showing all the text and data in that part of the plan. The user then can edit the text of the plan and the data appearing in that section.

Any data that's entered (name of hardware item, IT application, employee information, and so on) is saved and becomes available for use later on. This eliminates the need for reentry of information. Once a section has been edited, the plan may be printed from the application.

http://www.businessprotection.com

Summary

Recovering from disaster can mean many things to a company—recovering the data lost on a secretary's hard drive, to relocating the entire company core because of natural phenomenon. However, in either case, the most important item in recovery is an existing recovery plan. Your company should be equally prepared for these problems.

Disaster recovery requires more then just a good tape backup each night. There needs to be a distribution of duties, equipment must be inventoried and prioritized, and documentation of key resources must be available offsite.

Backup, itself, is not just the process of storing data to tape every night. The process requires that more then one tape be involved in the total backup plan. A plan for backup should involve multiple tapes, varying ages of tape, and offsite storage. Keep in mind that data loss or the need for archive data is not just due to failure.

Appendixes

PART VIII

IN THIS PART

A Troubleshooting/Error List *727*

B IP Address Decimal to Binary Table *741*

APPENDIX A

Troubleshooting/ Error List

IN THIS APPENDIX

- Service Packs *728*
- STOP Errors *728*

Windows 2000 is hopefully more stable in many ways than previous versions of Windows, but realistically many things can go wrong with any operating system.

Service Packs

Every operating system worth having has had some sort of patch or bug fix fairly shortly after the release of a new version. A *patch* is simply a rewriting of software to fix a problem that was found. It can be a full-blown rewrite of an entire subsystem, or it can be as simple as one intervening link file.

For Microsoft's part, it has always been good about making the patches for its operating systems available fairly soon after the release of a new version. Microsoft calls these patches *Service Packs*. For example, Windows NT 4.0 is up to Service Pack 5.

Obviously Windows 2000 has no Service Pack as of the writing of this book. It's just being released. But when the operating system has been out for approximately one to two months, begin to watch the Web site http://www.microsoft.com/windows/server/.

STOP Errors

A STOP error is often referred to as a "Blue Screen of Death." When one occurs, the server comes to a complete halt, thus the name *STOP error*. STOP errors can occur at any point in the life of a server, but you'll most likely find them after the installation of some new piece of software or during the initial install of Windows 2000.

Steps for Kernel Mode STOP Screens

The following list, provided by Microsoft, details the stop errors that are most common in Windows 2000. It gives you a general idea of what to expect and provides the steps for how to deal with these errors:

1. Gather the following information from the system:
    - The top four lines of the STOP screen. Generally the information you need will look something like this:
        ```
        STOP 0x0000000A(0x0000000B, 0x00000002, 0x00000000, 0xFE34C882
        IRQL_NOT_LESS_OR_EQUAL
        ADDRESS 0xFE34C882 has base at 0xFE000000: NTOSKRNL.EXE
        ```
    - Full hardware information, including:
    - System information (BIOS, CMOS settings, and so forth)

- All controllers/adapters installed and their BIOS versions
- The version of Windows installed and any service packs, SSDs, hotfixes and third-party drivers installed.

> **Tip**
>
> The term SSD is used by many hardware manufacture for the Software Support Disk that is provided along with the hardware they provide. These disks often contain drivers, utilities, and operating system enhancements.

- When the STOP screen occurs and how frequently it occurs. If possible, get answers to the following questions:
    - What has changed since the last good start of the server?
    - Does the STOP screen always appear when you perform a certain operation?
    - If it appears to be random, how often does it occur?
2. Determine whether the problem is a known issue with a hotfix or workaround.

> **Tip**
>
> A *Hotfix* is a minor change that is published by Microsoft in between Service packs. If a client has a specific issue they can sometimes find relief from a hotfix.

The next step is to search the Microsoft Knowledge Base and other resources to see if this particular STOP screen is a known issue with a hotfix or workaround. Try the following keyword searches in the Microsoft Knowledge Base:

- Search the word "STOP," the STOP code, and the program modules named in the top four lines of the STOP screen as one string. In the preceding example, you would search on the keywords "`STOP 0x0000000A NTOSKRNL.EXE`."
- If this search doesn't turn up anything, search on just the STOP code to see whether there are any general troubleshooting articles on the subject. Be warned, for some common STOP errors this will turn up a large list.

Once you get the results of each search back, check through the list for an article where the symptoms appear to match the problem as closely as possible and apply any fixes or workarounds listed in that article.

3. Determine whether the problem is caused by hardware.

   A STOP screen can be easily caused by a hardware failure, an out-of-date BIOS, or a hardware configuration issue, even when the system and components are on the Hardware Compatibility List (HCL). The following indications frequently point to a failure or problem in hardware:

   - The system has been working fine until now and suddenly fails when a specific operation is performed. An example of this would be a daily backup that has worked until now but is suddenly failing with a kernel STOP. In these cases, any hardware systems involved are suspect and should be checked out and, if possible, swapped for different ones as a test.

   - A new piece of hardware was added and a STOP screen appeared during system restart or when the new hardware was used. This definitely points to the new hardware even if that hardware is on the HCL. Investigate the possibility of bad hardware, old BIOSes that need to be updated, conflicting settings (IRQ, I/O address, and so forth) as well as an incorrect configuration. Another possibility is that an updated driver is needed to fix the problem.

   - Be mindful of a STOP error occurs when a certain operation is carried out (such as booting the system, copying a file, or doing a backup) but doesn't happen every time. A problem in software will generally occur every time a certain operation or set of operations is carried out, whereas a hardware problem can show up at random times. Although randomness is not always a sign of hardware problems, it is suspect and you should carry out normal hardware troubleshooting in these cases, checking for outdated or problem BIOSes as well as for interrupt and I/O conflicts. Swap out any components that appear to be related to the problem.

   Even if you don't find any of the indications listed, verify that the problem is not hardware related by doing the following:

   - Check BIOS versions on the motherboard as well as the SCSI controller and any other controller.
   - Look for IRQ, I/O address, and DMA conflicts.
   - Verify that all hardware is configured correctly, especially SCSI devices.

4. Troubleshoot well-known STOP codes.

   You may not find an article with a specific workaround or solution; however, there are a number of STOP error messages that have common causes. Here are some examples:

   - `STOP 0x0000000A IRQL_NOT_LESS_OR_EQUAL`
   - `STOP 0x0000001E KMODE_EXCEPTION_NOT_HANDLED`

- STOP 0x00000024 NTFS_FILE_SYSTEM
- STOP 0x0000002E DATA_BUS_ERROR
- STOP 0x0000003E MULTIPROCESSOR_CONFIGURATION_NOT_SUPPORTED
- STOP 0x00000058 FTDISK_INTERNAL_ERROR
- STOP 0x00000077 KERNEL_STACK_INPAGE_ERROR
- STOP 0x00000079 MISMATCHED_HAL
- STOP 0x0000007A KERNEL_DATA_INPAGE_ERROR
- STOP 0x0000007B INACCESSIBLE_BOOT_DEVICE
- STOP 0x0000007F UNEXPECTED_KERNEL_MODE_TRAP
- STOP 0x0000008B MBR_CHECKSUM_MISMATCH
- STOP 0xC0000218 STATUS_CANNOT_LOAD_REGISTRY_FILE
- STOP 0xC000021A STATUS_SYSTEM_PROCESS_TERMINATED
- STOP 0xC0000221 STATUS_IMAGE_CHECKSUM_MISMATCH

A detailed description of each of these errors, along with possible solutions, has been included in the final section of this appendix, "STOP Error Solutions."

5. Determine whether the problem is caused by non-HCL hardware.

If the system is not on the HCL or if a non-HCL component such as the hard disk drive controller, network card, or video card appear to be involved in the problem, Microsoft might not be able to fully support and diagnose the problem.

STOP Error Solutions

In this section you'll find each of the errors listed in step 4 of the troubleshooting STOP errors list, complete with possible solutions.

STOP 0x0000000A IRQL_NOT_LESS_OR_EQUAL

One of the most common kernel STOP messages, STOP 0x0000000A, indicates that a kernel mode process attempted to access and address a memory address it did not have permission to access. The most common cause of this STOP is a bad pointer, which in turn is caused by a software bug, memory corruption, or bad values returned by hardware queries.

In general, the only way to determine the specific cause of a STOP 0xA is by using the debugger; however, the STOP screen itself can frequently give you clues to the cause. For more information on interpreting the STOP screen and determining the cause of a STOP 0xA error, see the following Microsoft Knowledge Base article:

- Q130802: General Information on STOP 0x0000000A

You can also search the Microsoft Knowledge Base on the STOP code; this may turn up a hotfix or workaround if this is a known issue. The Microsoft knowledge base is a very valuable tool for finding specific errors and can be found at http://support.microsoft.com/search.

STOP 0x0000001E KMODE_EXCEPTION_NOT_HANDLED

A STOP 0x000000001E error is probably the second most common STOP error message under Windows 2000. This message indicates that an error condition was detected by the kernel and Windows was unable to continue running because of this error condition. The types of problems that can cause this STOP error message are very similar to the problems that cause a STOP 0x0000000A error, including bad pointers, invalid addresses, and other types of access violations.

The top four lines of a STOP 0x1E error message will generally appear as follows:

```
STOP: 0x0000001E (0xAAAAAAAA,0xBBBBBBBB,0xCCCCCCCC,0xDDDDDDDD)
KMODE_EXCEPTION_NOT_HANDLED AAAAAAAA from BBBBBBBB (CCCCCCCC,DDDDDDDD)
Address BBBBBBBB has base at XXXXXXXX - MODULE1.SYS
Address CCCCCCCC has base at YYYYYYYY - MODULE2.SYS
```

In the top line, the four hexadecimal parameters after the STOP code have the following meanings:

- 0xAAAAAAAA is a code identifying the exception that was not handled.
- 0xBBBBBBBB is the address at which the exception occurred.
- 0xCCCCCCCC is the first parameter of the exception; sometimes this is another address in code.
- 0xDDDDDDDD is the second parameter of the exception, which can vary in meaning.

Interpreting the Parameters

The first parameter is a Windows 2000 error code; these codes are defined in the file Ntstatus.h, which can also be found in the Software Developer Kit (SDK). This parameter tells you the type of error. The second parameter is also important in that it tells you in which code module the error occurred. This can frequently point to an individual driver or piece of hardware that's at fault, which will generally be listed on the third line of the STOP screen. The last two parameters vary depending on the exception that has occurred; you'll generally find a description of the parameters included with the name of error code in Ntstatus.h. If there are no parameters associated with the error code, the last two hexadecimal numbers are 0x00000000.

> **Tip**
>
> An SDK is released by the publisher of an operating system or application. It is most often used by software developers to help them be in compliance with the standards of an operating system or application. These kits are usually purchased as part of packages, but Microsoft publishes portions of these tools at http://www.microsoft.com/technet/support/drivers.htm.

For example, in the following STOP error message

```
STOP: 0x0000001E (0xC0000005, 0xFCA733B9, 0x00000000, 0x00000000)
KMODE_EXCEPTION_NOT_HANDLED 0xC0000005 from 0xFCA733B9 (0x0, 0x0)
Address FCA733B9 has base at FCA70000 - SRV.SYS
```

an access violation (`0xC0000005`) occurred in module `Srv.sys`, which is the kernel mode server service. No parameters are associated with this error code.

Troubleshooting the STOP Error

When trying to determine the cause of this STOP error, check the following:

- Search the Microsoft Knowledge Base on the STOP code, the error code, and the module in which the violation occurred. This may turn up a hotfix or workaround if this is a known issue. For example, a search of the Microsoft Knowledge Base on the key words "STOP" and "Services for Macintosh" could turn up the following article:

    Q135667: STOP 1E When Using File Manager and Services for Macintosh (SFM)

- Look up the error code in `Ntstatus.h` and search the Microsoft Knowledge Base on the text of the error (for example, "access violation") and the module in which it occurred.

- If the module in question is a third-party driver, contact the manufacturer of the third-party driver for help.

If your Knowledge Base searches do not turn up anything or if a third-party driver or piece of hardware is not indicated by the STOP screen, a debug will be necessary in order to determine whether the problem is caused by hardware or software.

STOP 0x00000024 NTFS_FILE_SYSTEM

Although not as common as some other STOP codes, `STOP 0x00000024` is specifically tied to error conditions and traps in the Windows 2000 file system (NTFS) driver. A STOP error in the NTFS is unlikely to be caused by hardware problems, although it is a possibility.

STOP 0x0000002E DATA_BUS_ERROR

A STOP 0x0000002E error indicates that a parity error in system memory has been detected. This STOP error is almost always caused by a hardware problem, such as a configuration issue, bad hardware, or incompatible hardware. The exception to this is when a device driver has accessed an address in the 0x8XXXXXXX range that does not exist (that is, it does not have a physical address mapping).

The parameters of a STOP 0x2E error appear as follows:

STOP: 0x0000002E (0xAAAAAAAA,0xBBBBBBBB,0xCCCCCCCC,0xDDDDDDDD)

These parameters have the following meaning:

- 0xAAAAAAAA is the virtual address that caused the fault.
- 0xBBBBBBBB is the physical address that caused the fault.
- 0xCCCCCCCC is the processor status register.
- 0xDDDDDDDD is the faulting instruction register.

Troubleshooting the STOP Error

The most common cause of this STOP error is a hardware problem. However, without debugging, you'll find it difficult to be sure whether the cause is hardware or a faulty driver. The following guidelines can help:

- If the system has been up and running for some time and the STOP error suddenly occurs, bad hardware is the likely suspect.
- If the STOP error occurs after installing a new or updated device driver, the driver is suspect and should be removed or replaced. If the STOP error occurs during boot, this may require installing a separate copy of Windows 2000 in order to rename or replace the driver file.
- If a new piece of hardware is added, the hardware may be suspect and should be removed to see whether the problem still occurs.
- If the problem appears on a freshly installed system, check the following items to see whether they need to be updated:
    - Firmware on RISC systems
    - BIOS revisions on the motherboard
    - BIOS revisions on the SCSI controller or network cards

STOP 0x0000003E MULTIPROCESSOR_CONFIGURATION_NOT_SUPPORTED

A STOP 0x0000003E error indicates that a system has multiple processors that are asymmetric in relation to one another. In order to be symmetric, all processors must be of the same type and level. For example, trying to mix a Pentium-level processor with an 80486 processor causes this bugcheck. Additionally, on *x*86 systems, either all processors should have floating-point capabilities or none should.

Also, Windows NT 3.5 and greater no longer support 386 multiprocessor computers. You'll get this bugcheck if you somehow install a Windows NT 3.5 or later multiprocessor build on an multiprocessor 386 computer. This STOP error does not indicate a mismatch between the Hardware Abstraction Layer (HAL) and kernel; that mismatch results in a STOP 0x00000079 error.

This STOP is always caused by hardware incompatibilities or misconfigurations and should be dealt with accordingly.

STOP 0x00000058 FTDISK_INTERNAL_ERROR

A STOP 0x00000058 error occurs when your boot or system partition is mirrored and the image on the mirror drive is more up-to-date than the image on the primary.

This situation can occur when you've booted off the mirrored partition while the primary partition was offline and then brought back online. For more information on recovering from this error, see the following article in the Microsoft Knowledge Base:

- Q128630: How to Recover From a STOP 0x00000058 FTDISK_INTERNAL_ERROR

STOP 0x00000077 KERNEL_STACK_INPAGE_ERROR

Both a STOP 0x77 error and a 0x7A error indicate that Windows attempted to read in a page of kernel data from the paging file and was unable to do so. Both of these STOP errors are frequently caused by hardware problems, although in a few rare situations they could also be the result of software failure. For more information on troubleshooting a STOP 0x77 or 0x7A error, see the following Microsoft Knowledge Base article:

- Q130801: Common Causes of STOP Messages 0x00000077 and 0x0000007A

STOP 0x00000079 MISMATCHED_HAL

This is not a common STOP error message; a STOP 0x00000079 error has a very specific cause. It indicates that you're using a single-processor Hardware Abstraction Layer (HAL) with the multiprocessor kernel, or vice versa. It can also indicate that one of those two files is out of date (for example, the HAL is designed for Windows NT 3.5 and the kernel is from Windows NT 3.51). In any case, you need to determine which HAL and which kernel (`Ntoskrnl.exe` or `Ntkrnlmp.exe`) to use and then replace the incorrect file with the correct one.

The kernel file will always be `Ntoskrnl.exe` for single-processor systems and `Ntkrnlmp.exe` for multiprocessor systems. Keep in mind that these filenames correspond to the file on the installation media; once Windows has been installed, the file will be renamed to `Ntoskrnl.exe` regardless of which one was installed.

The HAL file will also always be renamed `Hal.dll` after installation, but there are several possible HALs on the installation media. The default HAL for single-processor $x86$ systems is `Hal.dll`, and the default HAL for multiprocessor $x86$ systems is `Halmps.dll`.

STOP 0x00000077 and 0x0000007A KERNEL_STACK_INPAGE_ERROR

Both a `STOP 0x77` error and a `0x7A` error indicate that Windows attempted to read in a page of kernel data from the paging file and was unable to do so. Both of these STOP errors are frequently caused by hardware problems, although in a few rare situations they could also be the result of software failure. For more information on troubleshooting a `STOP 0x77` or `0x7A` error, see the following Microsoft Knowledge Base article:

- Q130801: Common Causes of STOP Messages `0x00000077` and `0x0000007A`

STOP 0x0000007B INACCESSIBLE_BOOT_DEVICE

Another very common STOP error, `0x0000007B`, indicates that during the boot process Windows lost access to the boot drive for some reason. This STOP error always occurs while booting the system and cannot be debugged, because it generally occurs before the operating system has loaded the debugger.

Troubleshooting the STOP

You can almost always resolve a `STOP 0x7B` error without calling Microsoft Support by first checking for the following causes:

- *Master boot record (MBR) and boot sector viruses.* Even on an NTFS partition, it's possible to contract an MBR or boot sector virus if the system has been booted recently from an infected disk. An MBR or boot sector virus will frequently result in a `STOP 0x7B` error. To check for viruses, boot from a disk that has already been virus checked and then run an up-to-date antivirus utility. It may also be possible to boot by creating an NTFS boot disk (also called an *FT boot disk*) that's clean of all viruses. This will bypass the boot sector on the hard disk drive and prevent the virus from loading. At this point, your system will not be clean, but you will be able to run one of the antivirus programs designed for Windows.

- *Incorrect device driver installed.* Windows will generally start its boot by using INT 13 to access the hard disk drive; however, during the load of the operating system, Windows will load a device driver for the drive controller. If the device driver is incorrect, out of date, or corrupted in some way, a STOP 0x7B error will result.
- *Incompatible, incorrectly configured, or corrupted hardware.* A common cause of a STOP 0x7B error is a drive controller or drive that's incompatible with Windows, incorrectly configured, or has developed other problems. Check for the following items:
    - Verify that the drive or controller is on the Windows Hardware Compatibility List (HCL). Note that most SCSI and EIDE drives are compatible with Windows, even if they're not listed on the HCL.
    - For a SCSI controller, check the firmware revision on the controller, make sure the SCSI bus is correctly terminated, and verify that the cabling is good. It might not hurt to swap out the cable, just in case.
    - If possible, try swapping out the drive controller, the cabling, or even the drives.

STOP 0x0000007F UNEXPECTED_KERNEL_MODE_TRAP

A STOP 0x0000007F error occurs on systems with Intel *x*86-based processors, and it indicates that an unexpected failure condition has been signaled by the processor. This STOP error message indicates that a failure has occurred at the processor level; therefore, this STOP message is almost always caused by hardware problems, except in rare cases.

STOP 0x0000008B MBR_CHECKSUM_MISMATCH

A STOP 0x0000008B error message indicates that the checksum of the master boot record (MBR) found during boot did not match the checksum passed in by the loader. This almost always indicates an MBR virus. If possible, run an antivirus program to clean the system. Alternatively, booting from an MS-DOS disk and running FDISK /MBR might also clean out the MBR.

Search the Microsoft Knowledge Base on the STOP code in which the violation occurred. This may turn up a hotfix or workaround if this is a known issue.

STOP 0xC0000218 STATUS_CANNOT_LOAD_REGISTRY_FILE

This STOP error message indicates that a Registry file failed to load during startup. The most likely cause is that the Registry file is corrupt or missing. Either use the emergency repair disk or reinstall and restore from a backup; this will usually correct the problem.

Another frequent cause of this error message is physical disk corruption, generally a bad sector in one of the Registry files. In this case, a low-level format of the drive, followed by reinstalling and restoring from a backup, will probably be required. If access to the drive is required before the low-level format, a second installation of Windows on an alternate drive will generally work.

STOP 0xC000021a STATUS_SYSTEM_PROCESS_TERMINATED

This STOP error message indicates either Winlogon or CSRSS (Win32 API support) quit unexpectedly. The exit code gives further information. Usually the exit code is c0000005, meaning that an unhandled exception caused Winlogon or CSRSS to stop. There's not much you can do unless this becomes a persistent problem. For information on exit codes, see the file Ntstatus.h. Because Windows cannot run without Winlogon or CSRSS, this is one of the few situations where a user-mode service can bring down the system.

This STOP error message cannot be debugged, because the actual error occurred in a user-mode process. The first step in troubleshooting this STOP error is to gather information on when it occurred and then search the Microsoft Knowledge Base on the keywords 0xC000021A, the module that the violation occurred in, Winlogon or CSRSS, and the exit code.

If that doesn't turn up any likely hits, the system needs to be configured for a user-mode debug so that the user-mode process can be debugged when the true error occurs. If the STOP error message occurs during every startup, you'll need to get the system into a startup state. Try the following:

- Click the Last Known Good Configuration option during startup.
- Run emergency repair on the system.
- If the problem occurs after adding a driver, adding a piece of hardware, or making a change in the system, try backing out the change.
- Search the Microsoft Knowledge Base on STOP 0xC000021A. For example, a search on STOP 0x00000021A could turn up the following article:

    Q139274: Updated System Environment Variables Result in STOP 0x0000021a

STOP 0xC0000221 STATUS_IMAGE_CHECKSUM_MISMATCH

A STOP 0xC0000221 error message indicates that a driver is corrupt or that a corrupt system DLL was detected. Windows does its best to verify the integrity of drivers and important system DLLs; if they are corrupt, Windows returns a STOP error message with the name of the corrupt file. This prevents the system from stopping when corruption occurs later.

To correct this problem, do the following:

- Run emergency repair and select the option to repair system files.
- Run an in-place upgrade (that is, an upgrade on top of the existing copy of Windows). This preserves all Registry settings and configuration information but replaces all system files.
- If a specific file was identified as corrupted in the STOP screen, try replacing that individual file by hand. If the system partition is FAT, boot from an MS-DOS disk and replace the file by hand; if the system partition is NTFS, you need to install a second copy of Windows in another directory and then replace the file by hand.
- If all else fails, try reinstalling and restoring from a backup.
- Search the Microsoft Knowledge Base on `STOP 0xC0000221` and any keywords describing the circumstances under which the STOP error occurred; there are many articles on specific causes of this STOP error message.

Summary

It is important to realize that finding the solution to any problem depends on the amount of information you bring to your reference. If you write down the errors in detail and look them up in this reference or in the Microsoft Knowledge Base then you will most likely find the answer. If you start by looking for general answers then you will be frustrated.

APPENDIX B

IP Address Decimal to Binary Table

IN THIS APPENDIX

- **Subnet Mask Answer Sheet** *750*

TABLE C.1 Decimal to Binary Table

Decimal Number	Binary Equivalent
0	00000000
1	00000001
2	00000010
3	00000011
4	00000100
5	00000101
6	00000110
7	00000111
8	00001000
9	00001001
10	00001010
11	00001011
12	00001100
13	00001101
14	00001110
15	00001111
16	00010000
17	00010001
18	00010010
19	00010011
20	00010100
21	00010101
22	00010110
23	00010111
24	00011000
25	00011001
26	00011010
27	00011011
28	00011100
29	00011101
30	00011110
31	00011111

Appendix B — IP Address Decimal to Binary Table

Decimal Number	Binary Equivalent
32	00100000
33	00100001
34	00100010
35	00100011
36	00100100
37	00100101
38	00100110
39	00100111
40	00101000
41	00101001
42	00101010
43	00101011
44	00101100
45	00101101
46	00101110
47	00101111
48	00110000
49	00110001
50	00110010
51	00110011
52	00110100
53	00110101
54	00110110
55	00110111
56	00111000
57	00111001
58	00111010
59	00111011
60	00111100
61	00111101
62	00111110
63	00111111

continues

TABLE C.1 continued

Decimal Number	Binary Equivalent
64	01000000
65	01000001
66	01000010
67	01000011
68	01000100
69	01000101
70	01000110
71	01000111
72	01001000
73	01001001
74	01001010
75	01001011
76	01001100
77	01001101
78	01001110
79	01001111
80	01010000
81	01010001
82	01010010
83	01010011
84	01010100
85	01010101
86	01010110
87	01010111
88	01011000
89	01011001
90	01011010
91	01011011
92	01011100
93	01011101
94	01011110
95	01011111

Decimal Number	Binary Equivalent
96	01100000
97	01100001
98	01100010
99	01100011
100	01100100
101	01100101
102	01100110
103	01100111
104	01101000
105	01101001
106	01101010
107	01101011
108	01101100
109	01101101
110	01101110
111	01101111
112	01110000
113	01110001
114	01110010
115	01110011
116	01110100
117	01110101
118	01110110
119	01110111
120	01111000
121	01111001
122	01111010
123	01111011
124	01111100
125	01111101
126	01111110
127	01111111

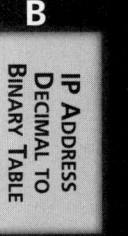

continues

TABLE C.1 continued

Decimal Number	Binary Equivalent
128	10000000
129	10000001
130	10000010
131	10000011
132	10000100
133	10000101
134	10000110
135	10000111
136	10001000
137	10001001
138	10001010
139	10001011
140	10001100
141	10001101
142	10001110
143	10001111
144	10010000
145	10010001
146	10010010
147	10010011
148	10010100
149	10010101
150	10010110
151	10010111
152	10011000
153	10011001
154	10011010
155	10011011
156	10011100
157	10011101
158	10011110
159	10011111

Decimal Number	Binary Equivalent
160	10100000
161	10100001
162	10100010
163	10100011
164	10100100
165	10100101
166	10100110
167	10100111
168	10101000
169	10101001
170	10101010
171	10101011
172	10101100
173	10101101
174	10101110
175	10101111
176	10110000
177	10110001
178	10110010
179	10110011
180	10110100
181	10110101
182	10110110
183	10110111
184	10111000
185	10111001
186	10111010
187	10111011
188	10111100
189	10111101
190	10111110
191	10111111

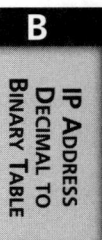

continues

TABLE C.1 continued

Decimal Number	Binary Equivalent
192	11000000
193	11000001
194	11000010
195	11000011
196	11000100
197	11000101
198	11000110
199	11000111
200	11001000
201	11001001
202	11001010
203	11001011
204	11001100
205	11001101
206	11001110
207	11001111
208	11010000
209	11010001
210	11010010
211	11010011
212	11010100
213	11010101
214	11010110
215	11010111
216	11011000
217	11011001
218	11011010
219	11011011
220	11011100
221	11011101
222	11011110
223	11011111

Decimal Number	Binary Equivalent
224	11100000
225	11100001
226	11100010
227	11100011
228	11100100
229	11100101
230	11100110
231	11100111
232	11101000
233	11101001
234	11101010
235	11101011
236	11101100
237	11101101
238	11101110
239	11101111
240	11110000
241	11110001
242	11110010
243	11110011
244	11110100
245	11110101
246	11110110
247	11110111
248	11111000
249	11111001
250	11111010
251	11111011
252	11111100
253	11111101
254	11111110
255	11111111

Subnet Mask Answer Sheet

Decimal Added by Mask	Binary Translation	Number of Networks	Possible Hosts Class A	Possible Hosts Class B	Possible Hosts Class C	Possible Host Address Ranges
0	00000000	1	16777214	65534	254	1 to 254
128	10000000	2	8388606	32766	126	1 to 126 129 to 254
192	11000000	4	4194302	16382	62	1 to 62 65 to 126 129 to 190 193 to 254
224	11100000	8	2097150	8190	30	1 to 30 33 to 62 65 to 94 97 to 126 129 to 158 161 to 190 193 to 222 225 to 254
240	11110000	16	1048574	4094	14	1 to 14 17 to 30 33 to 46 49 to 62 65 to 79 81 to 94 97 to 110 113 to 126 129 to 142 145 to 158 161 to 174 177 to 190 193 to 206 209 to 222 225 to 238 241 to 254
248	11111000	32	524286	2046	6	1 to 6 9 to 14 17 to 22 25 to 30 33 to 38 41 to 46

Decimal Added by Mask	Binary Translation	Number of Networks	Possible Hosts Class A	Possible Hosts Class B	Possible Hosts Class C	Possible Host Address Ranges
						49 to 54
						57 to 62
						65 to 70
						73 to 78
						81 to 86
						89 to 94
						97 to 102
						105 to 110
						113 to 118
						121 to 126
						129 to 134
						137 to 142
						145 to 150
						153 to 158
						161 to 166
						169 to 174
						177 to 182
						185 to 190
						193 to 198
						201 to 206
						209 to 214
						217 to 222
						225 to 230
						233 to 238
						241 to 246
						249 to 254
252	11111100	64	262142	1022	2	1 to 2
						5 to 6
						9 to 10
						13 to 14
						17 to 18
						21 to 22
						25 to 26
						29 to 30
						33 to 34
						37 to 38
						41 to 42
						45 to 46
						49 to 50

continues

Decimal Added by Mask	Binary Translation	Number of Networks	Possible Hosts Class A	Possible Hosts Class B	Possible Hosts Class C	Possible Host Address Ranges
						53 to 54
						57 to 58
						61 to 62
						65 to 66
						69 to 70
						73 to 74
						77 to 78
						81 to 82
						85 to 86
						89 to 90
						93 to 94
						97 to 98
						101 to 102
						105 to 106
						109 to 110
						113 to 114
						117 to 118
						121 to 122
						125 to 126
						129 to 130
						133 to 134
						137 to 138
						141 to 142
						145 to 146
						149 to 150
						153 to 154
						157 to 158
						161 to 162
						165 to 166
						169 to 170
						173 to 174
						177 to 178
						181 to 182
						185 to 186
						189 to 190
						193 to 194
						197 to 198
						201 to 202
						205 to 206

Decimal Added by Mask	Binary Translation	Number of Networks	Possible Hosts Class A	Possible Hosts Class B	Possible Hosts Class C	Possible Host Address Ranges
						209 to 210
						213 to 214
						217 to 218
						221 to 222
						225 to 226
						229 to 230
						233 to 234
						237 to 238
						241 to 242
						245 to 246
						249 to 250
						253 to 254
254	11111110	N/A	N/A	N/A	N/A	
255	11111111	N/A	N/A	N/A	N/A	

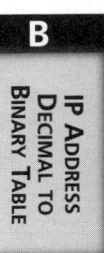

INDEX

NUMBERS

802.2 Token Ring or Ethernet connections, 495

A

Access Control Entries (ACEs), 239
Access Control Lists (ACLs), 239
access controls
    IIS (Internet Information Server), 530-531
        authentication, 531-533, 543-544
    Microsoft Proxy Server, 551-552
    user accounts, 294-298
access policies, configuring RAS (Remote Access Server), 373-375
    adding new policies, 383, 387
    dial-in constraints, 375-376
    options
        advanced, 381-382
        authentication, 378-380, 401-402
        encryption, 380-381
        IP address, 376-377
        multilink, 377-378
AccessNFS Gateway (Intergraph), 485-486
Account Operators groups, 303
ACEs (Access Control Entries), 239
ACLs (Access Control Lists), 239
Active Directory, 8, 10-11, 138-139, 264
    compared
        to NDS (Novell Directory Service), 453-454
        to UNIX, 474-475
    converting directories from Novell NetWare, 463
        files/directory structure, 468-469
        objects, 463, 466-468

DDNS (Dynamic Domain Name Server), 276
directory design
    geographic, 271-272
    mixed, 272
    political, 270-271
domains, 241-245
    DCs (Domain Controllers), 247-248, 265, 353
    forests and trees, 245-246
    native and mixed modes, 249-250
    objects, 251-252
    OUs (Organizational Units), 246-247, 253-254, 272-273
    trust relationships, 248-249
    UPNs (User Principle Names), 250-251
    user and group accounts, 252-253
GCs (global catalogs), 333, 353
integrating with RRAS (Routing and Remote Access), 356
MSIEXEC.EXE, 324-325
network browsing considerations, 352-353
no masters, 139-140
PDC emulators, 353
replication, 266
sites, 265-266, 269
structure, 139
Users and Computers console, 251
    computer accounts, 255-256
    creating object, 253
    group accounts, 255
    logon/logoff scripts, 289
    permissions, 257-260
    shared folders, 256
    shared printers, 256
    user accounts, 254-255, 284
workgroups, 239-240

Active Server Pages (ASPs), using with Exchange Server, 562
Add Remote Access Policy Wizard, 383, 387
Administrator accounts, 278-280
Administrators groups, 303
    backups, 685
    permissions, 672-673
Adobe PostScript, 151
analyzers, 234
announcements (browser), 342-343
anonymous authentication, 531
anonymous FTP authentication, 532
anonymous users, 520-521
APIs (application programming interfaces), 24, 29
Apple Computer, FireWire devices, 69
Appletalk protocol, 358, 414
    addressing schemes, 415
    Chooser, 414-415
    strengths and weaknesses, 416
Application Log, Event Viewer, 595-596
application programming interfaces (APIs), 24, 29
application services
    Win32 API, 15
    WSH (Windows Scripting Host), 15
applications
    connectivity issues with UNIX and Windows 2000 Server, 484
    installing with Windows Installer, 320-325
    Registry interaction, 185-187
AS/400 (IBM), TCP/IP (Transmission Control Protocol/Internet Protocol) protocol suite, 410
ASPs (Active Server Pages, using with Exchange Server, 562

asymmetric multiprocessing, 615
asynchronous and synchronous keys, 578-579
Asynchronous Transfer Mode (ATM) adapters, 14
AT&T version, UNIX, 475
ATM (Asynchronous Transfer Mode) adapters, 14
authentication, 8
    configuring RAS (Remote Access Server) policies/profiles, 378-380, 401-402
    IIS (Internet Information Server), 531-533
    Internet Authentication Services, 55
    Kerberos, 8, 11-12, 232-233
        communication processes, 233-236
        DC (Domain Controller) long-term keys, 236-237
    NTLM (Windows NT LAN Manager), 237
        communication process, 238
        SIDs (security identifiers), 238
    VPNs (Virtual Private Networks), 572-573
authoritative restoring of backup data, 701-702

B

BackOffice Suite, SNA (Systems Network Architecture) Server, 490-493
    connection options, 495
    LUs (logical units), 496-497
    routing connections, 493-494
    security, 493
    supported adapters, 495
backup browsers, 334-337
    browser announcements, 342
    browsing failures, 349-350
    client capability, 343
    election process, 337, 340

Backup Operators groups, 303
backups, 16, 712
    Backup and Recovery Tools utility
        Administrator and Backup Operators groups, 685
        Administrator and Backup Operators group permissions, 672-673
        attended operations, 690
        Backup and Recovery Tools Wizard, 679, 682, 685-688
        configuring, 674-677, 685
        ERD (Emergency Repair Disk), 704
        features, 670
        files excluded, 678-679
        labeling, 684
        logging levels, 678
        media, 681-682, 703
        planning before implementation, 671-672
        restoring data, 694-698, 701-704
        results reports, 689-690
        selected data, 679-681
        status window, 688-689
        time frequency, 684-687
        types, 673-674, 677, 682-683, 713-715
        unattended operations, 691-692
        verification and/or compression option, 683
        verifying settings, 688
    command-line, 693-694
    data recovery guidelines, 712-713
    plans, 715
        GFS (Grandfather/Father/Son), 715-716
        Tower of Hanoi, 716-718
    System State data, 679
        authoritative restoring, 701-702
    third-party tools, 705
    Veritas Software Corporation utility, 670

base priorities, threads and processes
    Process Viewer, 624-626, 629
    Task Manager, 617-624
basic authentication, 532
basic disks, 83, 630. *See also* **partitions (hard disks)**
    upgrading to dynamic, 85
basic FTP authentication, 533
batch files, 288
Berkeley System Development (BSD), Free BSD version, UNIX, 475-476
binary numbers, IP address equivalents for decimals, 197, 742, 747-749
bindery native connections, 458
Binomial, Phoenix 3.0 software, 722-723
"Blue Screen of Death" (BSOD), 23, 728
Boot Loader section, BOOT.INI file, 65
boot process, Windows 2000 installation, 45-47
BOOT.INI file, 65
bots, 566-567
bridging. *See* **switched segmentation**
browsing networks, 205, 332, 334
    Active Directory environment, 352-353
    browser announcements, 342-343
    browse lists, 344
    browser elections
        criteria, 336-337
        process, 337, 340
    browsing failures, 349-350
    browsing operations, 340-342
    Computer Browser service, 334
        browse lists, 344
        browser computer roles, 334-336
    domain master browsers, 344

browsing networks

master browsers, 343
multiple domains, 344-349
server configuration to never browse, 350-352
versus naming, 217
WANs (wide area networks), 344-349
WINS (Windows Internet Naming Service), 217
BSD (Berkeley System Development), Free BSD version, UNIX, 475-476
BSOD ("Blue Screen of Death"), 23, 728
bus devices
    EIDE (Extended Integrated Drive Electronics), 68
    FireWire, 69
    PCI, 69
    PCMCIA, 69
    USB (Universal Serial Bus), 69
Business Protections Services, Business Protector for Windows software, 723
Business Protector for Windows software, 723
Bypass Traverse Checking user right, 33

C

C-name (canonical) records, 221
CA (Certificate Services), Windows 2000 installation optional components, 53
caching, 629
CAL (client access licensing), 422-423
    managing, 423-429
Calculator, 52
Caldera version, Linux, 476
CAPTURE command, 457
capturing screens, VMWare for Windows NT, 49
case sensitive passwords, 280
catalogs (global), GCs, 333

CD-ROM drives
    Remote Storage Server, 123
    RSM (Removable Storage Management), 124-126
CDI Vaults Company Web site, 723
certificates
    PKI (Public Key Infrastructure), 578-579
certificate authentication, 532
Certificate Services (CA)
    installing IIS (Internet Information Server), 509-511
    Windows 2000 installation optional components, 53
Certificate Services Web Enrollment Support
    Windows 2000 installation optional components, 53
CFIS (Common Internet File System), 486
channels, ATAPI and SCSI controllers, 76
CHAP (Challenge Handshake Authentication Protocol), 359-360, 379, 401
Character Map, 52
charts (System Monitor)
    creating, 649-652
    interpreting, 652, 655
Chat program, 53
Chooser (Macintosh), 414-415
CIFS (Common Internet File System) protocol, 116
Classes hive (Registry), 181-182
client access licensing (CAL), 422-423
    managing, 423-429
clients
    backup browser capability, 343
    browser announcements, 342
    CAL (client access licensing), 422-423
        managing, 423-429

DHCP (Dynamic Host Configuration Protocol), 216
Novell NetWare, 430, 433, 436
operating system connectivity, 429-430
    DOS, 436-437, 440
    Macintosh, 440, 443-444
    OS/2, 436-437, 440
    UNIX, 444-446
    Windows 3.x, 436-437, 440
    Windows for Workgroups, 436-437, 440
per-client licensing, 59-61
RAS (Remote Access Server), 370-371
troubleshooting problems
    printing, 172, 174
Windows 2000 installation/configuration, 56-57
CLSID Registry key, 181
cluster controllers, 492
clustered servers, 719, 722
clustering services, Windows 2000 installation optional components, 53
clusters
    FAT and FAT32 file systems, 100-101
    NTFS ((NT File System) file system, 102-103
collision domain segments, 142-144
.com (commercial companies) domain identifier, 132, 241
COM objects, Internet services proxies, 54
command-line backups, 693-694
    restoring System State data with NtdsUtil utility, 701-702
commands
    CAPTURE, 457
    FTP (File Transfer Protocol), 479-482
    net, 290-291
        parameters, 291-292

NET USE, 457
net user, 284, 287
ping, troubleshooting printer problems, 171
Common Internet File System (CFIS) protocol, 116, 486
complete trust, 249
compulsory tunnels, 573
computer accounts (Active Directory), 255-256
Computer Browser service, 333-334
　browse lists, 344
　browser computer roles, 334, 336
　browsing operations, 340-342
Computer Configuration policies, 313-314
Computer Management Console, 593-594
　Device Manager, 600-603
　Event Viewer, 594-595
　　log settings, 597-599
　　viewing events, 595, 597
　System Information, 599
ComputerName Registry key, 184
Connection Manager, 54
connection-based and connectionless protocols, 409
container objects, 139, 559
　GPOs (Group Policy Objects), 312
context switching, 616
controlling domains. *See* **domains**
cooperative multitasking, 31
copy backups, 674
counters (performance objects), 644-648
　charts
　　creating, 649-652
　　interpreting, 652, 655
Create Partition Wizard, 93-94
Create Volume Wizard, 112
Creator Owner groups, 303
CSRSS.EXE. *See* **Win32 subsystem**

Current Configuration hive (Registry), 185
CurrentControlSet Registry key, 184
CurVer Registry key, 181

D

daily backups, 674
data recovery. *See* **backups**
data storage
　hard disk partitioning, 81
　　basic disks, 83-85, 630
　　dynamic disks, 84-85, 96, 630-631
　　system startup, 81-82
　Remote Storage Server, 13, 123
　RSM (Removable Storage Management), 13, 124-126
　Windows 2000 installation optional components, 55
datagrams, 410-411
DCs (domain controllers), 135-136, 243-248, 265, 353
　long-term keys, 236-237
　replication, 266
DDNS (Dynamic Domain Name Server), 215, 222, 273-276
　configuring, 223-224
　installing, 222-223
　managing, 224-225
　migrating from WINS (Windows Internet Naming Service), 226
　name resolution, 337
　network browsing, 345, 348
　security, 276
debuggers, Script Debugger, installation optional components, 55
decimal numbers, IP address binary equivalents, 742, 747-749
defragmenting hard disks, 611-615

Delegate Control Wizard, 319-320
delegation of authority, Novell Directory Service (NDS) compared to Active Directory, 454
demand paging, 630, 636-641
Desktop Wallpaper, 52
Device Manager, Computer Management Console, 600-603
DEVICEMAP Registry key, 183
DFS (Distributed File System), 13-14, 121-123
DFT (distributed function terminal), 495
DHCP (Dynamic Host Configuration Protocol), 54, 208-211
　enabling clients, 216
　installing, 211
　scope, 211-216
　superscopes, 216
　Windows 2000 installation/configuration, 57
differential backups, 674, 714-715
digest authentication, 532
Digital VMS, TCP/IP protocol suite, 410
direct file I/O printing, 153-154
directories
　AD (Active Directory), 264
　　DCs (domain controllers), 265
　　design standards, 269-272
　　replication, 266
　　sites, 265-269
　Exchange Server (Microsoft), 559
　managing, IIS (Internet Information Server), 524-527
　　virtual directories, 527, 530
　sharing, 116-119
　trees, container and leaf objects, 139

Directory Service Migration Tool, 54, 463
migrating
files/directory structure, 468-469
objects, 463, 466-468
directory services
converting directories from Novell NetWare to Active Directory, 463
files/directory structure, 468-469
objects, 463, 466-468
Novell NetWare, NDS for NT, 469-470
Windows 2000, compared to Novell NetWare, 453-454
Windows 2000 Server, compared to UNIX, 474-475
disaster recovery, Registry, Last Known Good configuration, 193
disaster-recovery planning, 708
CDI Vaults Company Web site, 723
data recovery, 712
backup guidelines, 712-713
backup plans, 715-718
backup types, 713-715
documentation, 709-710
hardware, 718-719
clustered servers, 719, 722
hardware-controlled RAID, 719
physical considerations, 710-711
software
Business Protector for Windows, 723
Phoenix 3.0, 722-723
staff, 710
Discover utility, 323-324
Disk Administrator utility. *See* **Disk Management utility**
Disk Defragmenter utility, 611-615

Disk Management utility, 86-87, 632-635
disk properties, 87-88
formatting partitions/volumes, 109
starting, 87
volume and partition management, 93-95
hard disk quotas, 96-99
volume and partition properties, 88-92
volumes
extending, 112-113
disk mirroring, 78
disk striping, 78
with parity, 80
with striped parity, 80
Distributed File System (DFS), 13-14, 121-123
distributed function terminal (DFT), 495
DMZ networks, 576
DNS (Domain Name System), 54, 217, 220, 242
browser elections, 336
domains, 221
name resolution, 337
records, 221
Windows 2000 installation/configuration, 57
domain controllers (DCs), 135-136, 243-248, 265, 353
long-term keys, 236-237
replication, 266
Domain Name System (DNS), 54, 217, 220-221
browser elections, 336
domains, 221
records, 221
name resolution, 337
Windows 2000 installation/configuration, 57
domains, 131-132, 241-245
Domain container objects, 312-314
forests and trees, 245-246
groups
accounts, types, 252-253
Domain Admins, 303
Domain Guests, 304

Domain Computer, 304
Domain Controllers, 304
Domain Local, 253, 300-304
Domain Users, 304
identifiers, 241
master browsers, 334-336, 344
browser announcements, 342-343
browsing failures, 349-350
election process, 337, 340
multiple network browsing, 344-349
names, 217
native and mixed modes, 249-250
objects, 251-252
operations masters, 134-135
OUs (organizational units), 133, 246-247
registering names, 132
trees and forests, 133, 353
trust relationships, 136
explicit, 136-138, 248-249
intransitive, 138, 249
transitive, 138, 249
UPNs (User Principle Names), 250-251
user accounts, types, 252-253
DOS
client connectivity, 436-437, 440
running under Win32 subsystem, 30-31
dot-matrix printers, 150
Drivers tab, Print Server Properties pages, 166
dumb terminals, 490-491
dynamic disks, 84, 96, 630-631. *See also* **volumes (hard disks)**
upgrading from basic, 85
Dynamic Domain Name Servers (DDNS), 215, 222, 273-276
configuring, 223-224
installing, 222-223
managing, 224-225

migrating from WINS (Windows Internet Naming Service), 226
name resolution, 337
network browsing, 345, 348
security, 276
Dynamic Host Configuration Protocol (DHCP), 54, 208-211
enabling clients, 216
installing, 211
scope, 211-216
superscopes, 216
Windows 2000 installation/configuration, 57

E

EAP (Extensible Authentication Protocol), 356, 359
.edu (educational organizations) domain identifier, 132, 241
EFS (Encrypted File System), 13
restoring data, 702
EIDE (Extended Integrated Drive Electronics) devices, 68
email, Microsoft Exchange Server, 556-557
directory structure, 559
Internet connectivity, 559-560
NNTP (Network News Transport Protocol), 563-564
POP, 560
public folders, 557-558
SMTP (Simple Message Transfer Protocol), 562-563
Web mail, 560-562
Emergency Repair Disk (ERD), 66, 704
Encapsulating Security Payload (ESP) packet format/IP protocol, 577

Encrypting File Service (EFS), 13
restoring data, 702
encryption
configuring RAS (Remote Access Server) policies/profiles, 380-381
EFS (Encrypted File System), 13
restoring data, 702
Kerberos, 233
long-term keys, 236-237
public keys, 12
VPNs (Virtual Private Networks), 572-573
Enterprise Admins groups, 304
ERD (Emergency Repair Disk), 66, 704
ErrorControl Registry key, 184
ESP (Encapsulating Security Payload) packet format/IP protocol, 577
Ethernet TCP/IP connections, 495
Event Viewer, 594-595
events
log settings, 597-599
viewing, 595-597
troubleshooting printer problems, 170-171
Everyone groups, 303
exceptions (kernel), 26
Exchange Server (Microsoft), 556-557
directory structure, 559
Internet connectivity, 559-560
NNTP (Network News Transport Protocol), 563-564
POP, 560
SMTP (Simple Message Transfer Protocol), 562-563
Web mail, 560-562
public folders, 557-558

Executive (Windows 2000), 26
I/O Manager, 28
LPCs (local procedure calls), 28
Object Manager, 27
Process Manager, 27
SRM (Security Reference Manager), 28
VMM (Virtual Memory Manager), 27
explicit permissions, 259
explicit trust relationships, 136-138
explicit trusts, 248-249
Extend Volume Wizard, 112
Extended Integrated Drive Electronics (EIDE) devices, 68
Extensible Authentication Protocol (EAP), 356, 359

F

Fast SCSI (Small Computer Standard Interface) standard, 77
Fast Wide SCSI (Small Computer Standard Interface) standard, 77
FAT and FAT32 (file allocation table) file system, 99-101
recommendations, 110
Windows 2000 installation, 47-48
fault tolerance
RAID (Redundant Array of Inexpensive Disks), 80-81
volumes
mirrored, 112-114, 631
RAID-5, 115, 631
striped, 114-115, 630-631
FEPs (front-end processors), 576
Fibre Channel controller technology, 81, 720
clustered servers, 720

File Migration Wizard, 468-469

file systems
   CIFS (Common Internet File System) protocol, 116
   DFS (Distributed File System), 13-14, 121-123
   FAT and FAT32 (file allocation table), 99-101
      recommendations, 110
      Windows 2000 installation, 47-48
   NFS (Network File System), 410, 485-486
   NTFS (NT File System), 99, 101
      formatting hard disks with Disk Management utility, 109
      security, 103-109
      transactional systems, 102-103
   recommendations, 110
   selecting, 47-48

File Transfer Protocol (FTP), 53, 410, 444
   authentication, anonymous and basic, 532
   IIS (Internet Information Server) site services, 534-535
   integrating UNIX and Windows 2000 Server, 479-482
      TFTP (Trivial File Transfer Protocol), 482

filtering
   tunnel initiator (server) traffic, 575-576

finger utility, 483

firewalls, Microsoft Proxy Server, 553-554, 574-576
   DMZ networks, 576
   NAT (Network Address Translation), 576

FireWire devices, 69

fixed-width fonts, 152

flat file (email) message systems, 556

forests (domain), 11, 245-246, 133, 353

Forms tab, Print Server Properties pages, 164-165

forward lookup records, 221

FPNW (File and Print Services for NetWare), 435

FQDNs (fully qualified domain names), 221

Free-BSD (Berkeley System Development) version, UNIX, 475-476

FreeCell game, 53

Freshwater Software, Inc., Site Scope Web site, 667

front-end processors (FEPs), 576

FrontPage
   FrontPage 2000 Server Extensions, 53
   server extensions, 567
   Web sites
      creating, 565-566
      editing pages, 566
      security, 566-567

FTP (File Transfer Protocol), 53, 410, 444
   authentication, anonymous and basic, 532
   integrating UNIX and Windows 2000 Server, 479-482
      TFTP (Trivial File Transfer Protocol), 482
   Site services, IIS (Internet Information Server), 534-535

full backups, 713-714

fully qualified domain names (FQDNs), 221

G

games, Windows 2000 installation optional components, 53

Gateway Service for NetWare (GSNW), 358, 430, 433, 436, 458-459
   configuring, 461-462
   installing, 459-461
   NTGATEWAY group, 459

gateways, 203

GCs (global catalogs), 333, 353

general protection faults, 35

geographic directory design, 271-272

GFS (Grandfather/Father/Son) backups, 715-716

global catalogs (GCs), 333, 353

global groups, 253, 300-304

Gopher Site services, IIS (Internet Information Server), 538

.gov (government agencies) domain identifier 132, 241

GPOs (Group Policy Objects), 312
   creating/assigning, 315-317
   editing, 317-319
   filtering, 318
   permissions, 318-319

Grandfather/Father/Son (GFS) backups, 715-716

group accounts
   creating, 251-252, 255, 302
   naming conventions, 280-282
   permissions
      files/folders, 257-260
      printers, 260
   predefined, 278-280, 302-304
   scope
      Domain Local, 300-302
      Global, 301
      Universal, 301
   types, 252-253

group policies, 311-313
creating/assigning, 315-317
Delegate Control Wizard, 319-320
editing, 317-319
filtering, 318
managing, 315
passwords, 281-282
permissions, 318-319
types, 313-314
Group Policy Admins group, 304
Group Policy Objects (GPOs), 312
creating/assigning, 315-317
editing, 317-319
filtering, 318
permissions, 318-319
GSNW (Gateway Service for NetWare), 358, 430, 433, 436, 458-459
configuring, 461-462
installing, 459-461
NTGATEWAY group, 459
Guest accounts, 278-280
Guests groups, 303

H

HAL (Hardware Abstraction Layer), 22-25
hard disks, 73
controllers, 78
disk mirroring, 78
disk striping, 78
disk striping with parity, 80
disk striping with striped parity, 80
Fibre Channel, 81
IDE (Integrated Drive Electronics) standard, 75
mirrored disk striping with parity, 80
parity, 79-80

RAID (Redundant Array of Inexpensive Disks), 80-81
striped volumes, 630
SCSI (Small Computer Standard Interface) standard, 77-78
defragmenting, 611, 613, 615
Disk Management utility, 86-87, 632-635
disk properties, 87-88
hard disk quotas, 96-99
starting, 87
volume and partition management, 93-95
volume and partition properties, 88-92
file systems
FAT and FAT32 (file allocation table), 47-48, 99-101, 110
NTFS (NT File System), 99-109
recommendations, 110
selecting, 47-48
formatting, 109
memory
caching, 629
virtual memory pagefiles, 630, 636-641
partitions, 81
basic disks, 83-85, 630
dynamic disks, 84-85, 96, 630-631
system startup, 81-82
Windows 2000 installation, 47-48
quota systems, 13-14
space limitations for users, 298-299
technology, 73-75
volumes, 111
mirrored, 112-114, 631
RAID-5, 115, 631
simple, 111-112, 631
spanned, 112-113, 631
striped, 114-115, 631
hard page faults, 38

hardware. *See also* **HCL (Hardware Compatibility List)**
Device Manager, 600-603
disaster-recovery planning, 718-719
clustered servers, 719, 722
hardware-controlled RAID, 719
hard disk controller standards 73-75, 78-81
IDE (Integrated Drive Electronics), 75-77
SCSI (Small Computer Standard Interface), 75-78
hard disk partitioning, 81
basic disks, 83-85, 630
dynamic disks, 84-85, 96, 630-631
system startup, 81-82
IIS (Internet Information Server) requirements, 504
installing devices
EIDE (Extended Integrated Drive Electronics), 68
FireWire, 69
IRQs (interrupt request lines), 67-68
PCI buses, 69
PCMCIA, 69
USB (Universal Serial Bus), 69
Windows Update Web site, 68
modems, RRAS (Routing and Remote Access), 400
SNMP (Simple Network Management Protocol), 603-604
Hardware Abstraction Layer (HAL), 22-25
Hardware Registry key, 183
hashing, 532
HCL (Hardware Compatibility List), 41-42. *See also* **hardware**

Hewlett-Packard Graphics
    Language (HPGL), 151
histograms, 652, 655
hivelist Registry key, 184
hives, Registry, 181
    Classes, 181-182
    Current Configuration, 185
    Local Machine, 183, 185
    Users, 182-183
HKEY_CLASSES_ROOT
    (Registry), 181-182
HKEY_CURRENT USER
    (Registry), 182-183
HKEY_CURRENT_CONFIG
    (Registry), 185
HKEY_LOCAL_MACHINE
    (Registry), 183-185
home directories for users,
    293-294
host adapters, 77
hosts systems (IBM)
    dumb terminals, 490-491
    SNA (Systems Network
        Architecture) Server,
        490-493
        connection options, 495
        LUs (logical units),
            496-497
        routing connections,
            493-494
        security, 493
        supported adapters, 495
hosts, IP addressing, 198-199
HPGL (Hewlett-Packard
    Graphics Language), 151
HTML (Hypertext Markup
    Language) editors, 565
HTTP (Hypertext Transfer
    Protocol), 410, 560
HyperTerminal, 53
Hypertext Transfer Protocol.
    See HTTP (Hypertext
    Transfer Protocol)

I

I/O Manager, 28
IBM AS/400, TCP/IP
    (Transmission Control
    Protocol/Internet Protocol)
    protocol suite, 410
IBM Client Access program,
    491
IBM hosts systems
    dumb terminals, 490-491
    SNA (Systems Network
        Architecture) Server,
        490-493
        connection options, 495
        LUs (logical units),
            496-497
        routing connections,
            493-494
        security, 493
        supported adapters, 495
IBM/Microsoft OS/2 client
    connectivity, 429, 436-437,
    440
IDE (Integrated Drive
    Electronics) standard, 75-77
IETF (Internet Engineering
    Task Force), 409
IIS (Internet Information
    Server)
    access controls, 530-531
        authentication, 531-533
    administering controls,
        511-512
        Internet Services Manager,
            512-513, 516-524
    basics, 503
    concurrent user limitations,
        533
    directory management,
        524-527
        virtual directories, 527,
            530
    hardware requirements, 504
    installing
        Certificate Services, 509-
            511
        components, 507-509

Internet connectivity, 505-507
IP address socket pooling, 530
releases, 502-503
security, 539
    access controls, 543-544
    directory browsing, 544
    permissions, 542-543
    protection against unau-
        thoritized access,
        540-542
    troubleshooting, 544, 547
    unauthoritized access,
        539-540
    Web site help, 542
services, 53-54
    FTP (File Transfer
        Protocol) Site, 534-535
    Gopher Site, 538
    IIS Snap-In, 53
    Telnet, 539
    WWW Site, 535, 538
system requirements, 503-505
using with Exchange Server,
    562
IKE (Internet Key Exchange),
    578
Implicit Groups, 302-304
incremental backups, 674,
    714
Indexing service, 53
inherited permissions, 259
inkjet printers, 151
installing
    applications, Windows
        Installer, 320-325
    DDNS (Dynamic Domain
        Name Servers), 222-223
    GSNW (Gateway Service for
        NetWare), 459-461
    hardware
        EIDE (Extended
            Integrated Drive
            Electronics) devices, 68
        FireWire devices, 69
        IRQs (interrupt request
            lines), 67-68
        PCI buses, 69

PCMCIA devices, 69
USB (Universal Serial Bus) devices, 69
Windows Update Web site, 68
IIS (Internet Information Server)
   Certificate Services, 509-511
   components, 507-509
operating systems, Remote Installation Service, 325-327
protocols, 406, 408
   DHCP (Dynamic Host Configuration Protocol), 211
   RRAS (Routing and Remote Access) tools, 361
     hardware requirements, 361-362
   TCP/IP (Transmission Control Protocol/Internet Protocol) protocol suite, 205-206
Windows 2000 Server
   automatically, 61
   boot process, 45-47
   configuration, 50-52
   disk partitioning, 47-48
   HCL (Hardware Compatibility List), 41-42
   licensing options, 58-61
   migration from preexisting systems, 66-67
   network configuration, 55-57
   optional components, 52-55
   Recovery Console, 62-65
   setup procedures, 44-45
   setup switches, 42-44
   system requirements, 40-41
   upgrading from NT, 50
Windows 2000 Support Tools, 608-611
WINS (Windows Internet Naming Service), 219

Integrated Drive Electronics (IDE) standard, 75-77
integrated Windows authentication, 532
Intellimirror, 306
Interactive groups, 303
Intergraph, AccessNFS Gateway, 485-486
International Standard Organization (ISO) standard, X.500 directory structure, 232
Internet
   using as WAN (wide area netowork), 570-571
Internet Authentication Services, 55
Internet Engineering Task Force (IETF), 409
Internet Information Server (IIS), 505-507
   access controls, 530-531
     authentication, 531-533
   administering controls, 511-512
     Internet Services Manager, 512-513, 516-524
   basics, 503
   concurrent user limitations, 533
   directory management, 524-527
     virtual directories, 527, 530
   hardware requirements, 504
   installing
     Certificate Services, 509-511
     components, 507-509
   Internet connectivity, 505-507
   IP address socket pooling, 530
   releases, 502-503
   security, 539
     access controls, 543-544
     directory browsing, 544
     permissions, 542-543
     protection against unauthoritized access, 540-542

     troubleshooting, 544, 547
     unauthoritized access, 539-540
     Web site help, 542
   services, 53-54
     FTP (File Transfer Protocol) Site, 534-535
     Gopher Site, 538
     IIS Snap-In, 53
     Telnet, 539
     WWW Site, 535, 538
   system requirements, 503-505
   using with Exchange Server, 562
Internet Key Exchange (IKE), 578
Internet Packet Exchange/Sequential Packet Exchange (IPX/SPX), 14, 411
   addressing schemes, 412-413
   strengths and weaknesses, 414, 411
Internet Protocol Security (IPSEC), 13, 227
Internet Protocol (IP), 410
Internet Services Manager, 54, 512-513
   anonymous users, 520-521
   concurrent user limitations, 533
   configuring FTP (File Transfer Protocol) messages, 534-535
   directory management, 524, 526-527
   display views, 513, 516-520
   logon options, 522, 524
   virtual directory management, 527, 530
Internetwork Packet Exchange/Sequenced Packet Exchange/NetBIOS Compatible Transport (IPX/SPX/NetBIOS), 358
InterNIC, 132
interrupt handling, 25
interrupt request lines (IRQs), 67-68

intransitive trust relationships, 138, 249
IP (Internet Protocol), 410
IP addresses
    Appletalk, 415
    binary equivalents for decimals, 742, 747-749
    configuring RAS (Remote Access Server) policies/profiles, 376-377
    IPX/SPX (Internet Packet Exchange/Sequential Packet Exchange), 412-413
    TCP/IP (Transmission Control Protocol/Internet Protocol), 196-198
        binary addresses, 197
        multiple addressees, 226-227
        network and host portions, 198-199
        ports, 204-205
        routing, 203-204
        subnet masks, 199-202
IP Multicasting, 356
IP protocol packets, 577
IP protocol (Encapsulating Security Payload) packet format, 577
IP Security Protocol (IPSec), 576-577, 579
    synchronous and asynchronous keys, 578-579
IPSEC (IP Security protocol), 13, 227, 576-577, 579
    synchronous and asynchronous keys, 578-579
IPX/SPX (Internet Packet Exchange/Sequential Packet Exchange) protocol, 14, 411
    addressing schemes, 412-413
    strengths and weaknesses, 414
IPX/SPX/NetBIOS (Internetwork Packet Exchange/Sequenced Packet Exchange/NetBIOS Compatible Transport, 358

IRQs (interrupt request lines), 67-68
ISO (International Standard Organization) standard, X.500 directory structure, 232

J-K

Jet database system, Microsoft Exchange Server email, 556-557

KDC (Key Distribution Center). *See* DCs (Domain Controllers)
Kerberos security protocol, 232-233
    authentication, 8, 11-12
    communication processes, 233-236
    DC (Domain Controller) long-term keys, 236-237
kernel, 22-23
    exceptions, 26
    interrupt handling, 25
    processes and threads, 25
Kernel mode, 23-24
    components, 617
    Windows 2000 Executive, 26
Key Distribution Center (KDC). *See* DCs (Domain Controllers)
keyboards, 52

L

L2TP (Layer 2 Tunneling Protocol), 356, 359-360, 576-579
    synchronous and asynchronous keys, 578-579
landing zone, hard disks, 75
LANs (local area networks), 141

laptop computers, PCMCIA devices, 69
laser printers, 151
Last Known Good configuration, Registry, 193
Layer 2 Tunneling Protocol (L2TP), 356, 359-360, 576-579
    synchronous and asynchronous keys, 578-579
LDAP protocol, 560
leaf objects, 139
libraries, RSM (Removable Storage Management), 124
License Manager, 59, 61
licenses
    CAL (client access licensing), 422-423
        managing, 423-429
    options, Windows 2000 installation, 58-61
line printers, 150
links, DFS (Distributed File System), 122
Linux versions, UNIX, 476
LMHOSTS file, 219-220
local area networks (LANs), 141
Local Machine hive (Registry), 183-185
local printers, 156
local procedure calls (LPCs), 28
local profiles, 308-309
logical units (LUs), 492
    configuring, 496-497
logoff scripts, 288
    directory placement, 288, 290
    net command, 290-292
logons
    configuring RAS (Remote Access Server), 387-389
    options, 522-524
    scripts, 288
        directory placement, 288-290
        net command, 290-292
logs, Performance utility, 655-657, 661, 664, 667

long-term keys, 236-237
LPCs (local procedure calls), 28
LPR ports, printers, 153-157
LUs (logical units), 492
    configuring, 496-497

M

MAC (Media Access Control) addresses, 413
Macintosh
    Appletalk protocol, 358, 414
        addressing schemes, 415
        Chooser, 414-415
        strengths and weaknesses, 416
    client connectivity, 429, 440, 443-444
    File and Print Services for Macintosh, 55, 422
managing networks. *See* network management
mandatory profiles, 310
MANs (metropolitan area networks), 141
manual tombstoning, WINS (Windows Internet Naming Service), 219
map roots, 455
masks (subnet), 199-202
master boot records (MBRs), 81
    system startup, 82
master browsers, 334-336, 343
    browser announcements, 342-343
    browsing failures, 349-350
    election process, 337-340
master devices, 68
mathematic calculations, Calculator, 52
MBRs (master boot records), 81-82

media (storage)
    backups, 681-682
        supported by Windows 2000 Server, 703
    Remote Storage Server, 123
    RSM (Removable Storage Management), 124-126
memory
    caching, 629
    printer requirements, 151
    process and task models, 34, 37
    virtual memory pagefiles, 630, 636-641
    VMM (Virtual Memory Manager), 27, 37-38
metropolitan area networks (MANs), 141
microkernel design, 25
Microsoft Challenge Handshake Authentication Protocol (MS-CHAP), 379
Microsoft Challenge Handshake Authentication Protocol, version 2 (MS-CHAP v2), 356, 379, 572
Microsoft Exchange Server, 556-557
    directory structure, 559
    Internet connectivity, 559-560
        NNTP (Network News Transport Protocol), 563-564
        POP, 560
        SMTP (Simple Message Transfer Protocol), 562-563
        Web mail, 560-562
    public folders, 557-558
Microsoft Management Console (MMC). *See* MMC
Microsoft Message Queue (MMQ), 54
Microsoft Point-to-Point Encryption (MPPE), 572

Microsoft Proxy Server, 550-551
    access controls, 551-552
    acquisition, 550-551
    caching, 550-551
    firewalls, 553-554
    traffic logs, 554-555
Microsoft/IBM OS/2, client connectivity, 429, 436-437, 440
MineSweeper game, 53
mirrored volumes (hard disk), 78, 112-114, 631
    disk striping with parity, 80
mixed mode domains, 249-250
MMC (Microsoft Management Console), 9-10, 590, 592
    Disk Management, 87
    System Performance Monitor, 9
MMQ (Microsoft Message Queue), 54
modems, RRAS (Routing and Remote Access), 400
modes, User and Kernel, 23-24
mouse pointers, 52
MPPE (Microsoft Point-to-Point Encryption), 572
MS-CHAP (Microsoft Challenge Handshake Authentication Protocol), 379
MS-CHAP v2 (Challenge-Handshake Authentication Protocol, version 2), 356, 379, 572
MS-DOS, running under Win32 subsystem, 30-31
.msi files, 320-324
MSIEXEC.EXE, 324-325
multimedia optional installation components, 53
multiprocessing, 615

multitasking
cooperative, 31
preemptive, 32
processes and threads, 616
MX (Mail Exchange) records, 221

N

name resolution
DNS (Domain Name System), 54, 337
Windows 2000 installation/configuration, 57
Novell Directory Service (NDS), 280, 282, 454
NAT (Network Address Translation), 576
native connections, 457-458
native mode domains, 249-250
NDS (Novell Directory Service)
compared to Active Directory, 453-454
converting directories to Active Directory, 463
files/directory structure, 468-469
objects, 463, 466-468
native connections, 458
NDS for NT, 469-470
net command, 290-292
NET USE command, 284, 287, 457
NetBEUI (NetBIOS Extended User Interface), 14, 359, 416-417
NetBIOS (Network Basic Input Output Service) names, 217
NetBT (NetBIOS over TCP/IP)
browser elections, 336-337
network browsing, 344, 347-349
NetWare (Novell), 430, 452
compared to Windows 2000, 452

directory services, 453-454
file sharing, 455-456
print sharing, 456-457
security, 452
directory conversion to Active Directory, 463
files/directory structure, 468-469
objects, 463, 466-468
File and Print Connectivity, 423
File and Print Services, 463
GSNW (Gateway Service for NetWare), 430, 433, 436, 458-459
configuring, 461-462
installing, 459-461
NTGATEWAY group, 459
IPX/SPX (Internet Packet Exchange/Sequential Packet Exchange) protocol, 411-414
NDS for NT, 469-470
server connectivity, 457-458
TCP/IP (Transmission Control Protocol/Internet Protocol) suite, 410
Network Address Translation (NAT), 576
Network Basic Input Output Service (NetBIOS) names, 217
Network File Services (NFS), 444
Network File System (NFS), 410, 485-486
Network groups, 303
Network Information System (NIS), 474
Network Monitor, 9, 54
Network News Transport Protocol (NNTP), 563-564
network operating systems. *See* NOSs (network operating systems)
New DFS Root Wizard, 122
NFS (Network File Services), 444

NFS (Network File System), 410, 485-486
NIS (Network Information System), 474
NNTP (Network News Transport Protocol), 54, 560, 563-564
non-browsers, 334-336
browsing failures, 349-350
election process, 337, 340
normal backups, 674
NOSs (network operating systems), 6. *See also* operating systems
features, 7
IPX/SPX (Internet Packet Exchange/Sequential Packet Exchange), 411, 413-414
Novell NetWare, compared to Windows 2000, 452-457
performance monitoring, 8-9
security, 8
TCP/IP (Transmission Control Protocol/Internet Protocol) protocol suite, 410
Novell Directory Service (NDS)
compared to Active Directory, 453-454
converting directories to Active Directory, 463
files/directory structure, 468-469
objects, 463, 466-468
native connections, 458
NDS for NT, 469-470
Novell NetWare, 452
compared to Windows 2000, 452
directory services, 453-454
file sharing, 455-456
print sharing, 456-457
security, 452
directory conversion to Active Directory, 463
files/directory structure, 468-469
objects, 463, 466-468

optimizing system performance

File and Print Connectivity, 423
File and Print Services, 463
GSNW (Gateway Service for NetWare), 430, 433, 436, 458-459
  configuring, 461-462
  installing, 459-461
  NTGATEWAY group, 459
IPX/SPX (Internet Packet Exchange/Sequential Packet Exchange) protocol, 411-414
NDS for NT, 469-470
server connectivity, 457-458
TCP/IP (Transmission Control Protocol/Internet Protocol) protocol suite, 410
NT Executive Services, 24
NT Virtual DOS Machine (NTVDM), 31
NTCONFIG.POL file, 313
NtdsUtil utility, 701-702
NTFS (NT File System) file system, 99-101
  formatting hard disks with Disk Management utility, 109
  recommendations, 110
  security, 103-109
  transactional systems, 102-103
  Windows 2000 installation, 47-48
NTGATEWAY group, 459
NTLM (Windows NT LAN Manager), 237
  communication process, 238
  SIDs (security identifiers), 238
NTVDM (NT Virtual DOS Machine), 31
NWLink IPX/SPX-compatible transport, 412

O

Object Manager, 27
Object Packager, 52
objects (Active Directory)
  computer accounts, 255-256
  group accounts, 255
  OUs (Organizational Units), 253-254
  shared folders and printers, 256
  types, 251-252
  user accounts, 254-255
objects (performance), 644-648
  charts
    creating, 649-652
    interpreting, 652, 655

Open Shortest Path First (OSPF) protocol, 585
Open Systems Interconnection Model (OSI Model), 144
operating systems. *See also* **NOSs (network operating systems)**
  architecture
    HAL (Hardware Abstraction Layer), 24-25
    kernel, 22-26
    memory, 34, 37-38
    modes, 23-24
    subsystems, 22, 28-34
    Windows 2000 Executive, 26-28
  BOOT.INI file, 65
  client connectivity, 429-430
    DOS, 436-437, 440
    Macintosh, 440, 443-444
    OS/2, 436-437, 440
    UNIX, 444-446
    Windows 3.x, 436-437, 440
    Windows for Workgroups, 436-437, 440
  controls
    access, 294-298
    home directory, 293-294

  logon scripts, 288-292
  profiles, 294
  IIS (Internet Information Server) requirements, 503-505
  installing, Remote Installation Service, 325-327
  Novell NetWare, 430, 433, 436, 452
    compared to Windows 2000, 452-457
  resource allocation, 6-7
  UNIX
    finger utility, 483
    FTP (File Transfer Protocol, 480-482
    FTP (File Transfer Protocol), 479
    RSH (Remote Shell), 483
    Telnet, 477-479
    TFTP (Trivial File Transfer Protocol), 482
    versions, 475-476
  Widows 2000 Server
    compared to UNIX, 472-475
    future of Microsoft and UNIX, 488
    Samba, 486-487
Operating Systems section, BOOT.INI file, 65
operations masters (domains), 134-135
operator requests, RSM (Removable Storage Management), 126
optical disk drives
  Remote Storage Server, 123
  Removable Storage Management, 124-126
optimizing system performance
  base priorities, threads and processes
    Process Viewer, 624-626, 629
    Task Manager, 617-624
  Disk Defragmenter, 611-615
  Disk Management utility, 632-633, 635

769

performance objects/counters, 644, 646, 648
Performance utility, 641-643
   logs, 655-657, 661, 664, 667
   memory caching, 629
   reports, 655-657, 661, 664, 667
RAID (Redundant Array of Inexpensive Disks), striped volumes, 630
System Monitor, 643-644
   charts, 649-652, 655
virtual memory pagefiles, 630, 636-637, 639, 641
.org (not-for-profit organizations) domain identifier, 132, 241
organizational units (OUs), 246-247, 312-314
   creating, 253-254
   domains, 133
   permissions, 272-273
OS/2 (IBM/Microsoft)
   client connectivity, 429, 436-437, 440
   subsystem, 33-34
OSI Model (Open Systems Interconnection Model), 144
OSPF (Open Shortest Path First) protocol, 585
OUs (Organizational Units), 246-247
   creating, 253-254
   domains, 133
   permissions, 272-273

P

package delivery, MSIEXEC.EXE, 324-325
Package Editor, 324
packets, 411
   sniffers, 54, 234
page faults, hard and soft, 38
page printers, 151
Paint program, 53

PAP (Unencrypted Authentication), 379, 401
parallel printer ports 153
   troubleshooting problems, 174
parity, 79-80
   disk striping with parity, 80
   disk striping with striped parity, 80
   mirrored disk striping with parity, 80
partitions (hard disks), 81
   basic disks, 83-85, 630
   changing, 94-95
   creating new, 93-94
   deleting, 95
   dynamic disks, 84-85, 96, 630-631
   formatting, 109
   managing, 93
   Novell Directory Service (NDS), compared to Active Directory, 454
   properties, 88-92
   quotas, 96-99
   system startup, 81-82
   Windows 2000 installation, 47-48
passwords, user/group accounts
   conventions, 280-281
   policies, 281-282
Pathworks, TCP/IP (Transmission Control Protocol/Internet Protocol) protocol suite, 410
PCI devices, 69
PCMCIA devices, 69
PDC emulators, 353
peer-to-peer networking
   Active Directory, 138-139
      no masters, 139-140
      structure, 139
   domains, 131-132
      DCs (domain controllers), 135-136
      operations masters, 134-135
      OUs (organizational units), 133

      trees and forests, 133
      trust relationships, 136-138
   network services, 140
   routed segmentation, 144-145
   RRAS (Routing and Remote Access Services)
      multiprotocol routing, 146
      remote dial-in, 145
   switched segmentation, 142-144
   types of networks, 140-142
   workgroups, 129, 131, 239-240
Per Seat client licensing mode, 59-61, 424-425, 428-429
Per Server client licensing mode, 59, 424-425, 428-429
Performance Monitor utility. *See* **Performance utility**
performance monitoring, 8-9
   base priorities, threads and processes
      Process Viewer, 624-626, 629
      Task Manager, 617-624
   Disk Defragmenter, 611-615
   Disk Management utility, 632-635
   Performance utility, 641-643
      logs, 655-657, 661, 664, 667
      memory caching, 629
      reports, 655-657, 661, 664, 667
   RAID (Redundant Array of Inexpensive Disks), striped volumes, 630
   System Monitor, 643-644
      charts, 649-652, 655
      performance objects/counters, 644-648
   virtual memory pagefiles, 630, 636-641
   Windows 2000 installation optional components, 54
Performance utility, 641-643

logs, 655-657, 661, 664, 667
memory caching, 629
reports, 655-657, 661, 664, 667
System Monitor, 643-644
　charts, 649-652, 655
　performance objects/counters, 644-648
peripheral units (PUs), 496
permissions
　GPOs (Group Policy Objects), 318-319
　Microsoft Proxy Server, 551-552
　NTFS (NT File System), 103-109
　OUs (organizational units), 272-273
　security, IIS (Internet Information Server), 542-543
　shared resources, 257
　　files/folders, 257-260
　　printers, 260
persistent connections, WINS (Windows Internet Naming Service), 218
Phoenix 3.0 software, 722-723
Phone Dialer, 53
ping utility, 420
　troubleshooting printer problems, 171
PKI (Public Key Infrastructure) certificate, 578-579
plotter printers, 151
Point-to-Point Protocol (PPP), 418, 571
Point-to-Point Tunneling Protocol (PPTP), 146, 572, 575
policies (access), 311-313
　configuring RAS (Remote Access Server), 373, 375
　　adding new policies, 383, 387
　　advanced options, 381-382
　　authentication options, 378-380, 401-402

　　dial-in constraints, 375-376
　　encryption options, 380-381
　　IP address options, 376-377
　　multilink options, 377-378
　group
　　creating/assigning, 315-317
　　Delegate Control Wizard, 319-320
　　editing, 317-319
　　filtering, 318
　　managing, 315
　　permissions, 318-319
　passwords, 281-282
　types, 313-314
political directory design, 270-271
POP protocol, 560
Portable Operating System Interface (POSIX), 32-33
ports
　configuring RAS (Remote Access Server), 371-373
　printers, 153-155
　　troubleshooting problems, 174-175
　TCP/IP (Transmission Control Protocol/Internet Protocol) protocol, 204-205
Ports tab, Print Server Properties pages, 165-166
POSIX subsystem, 32-33
POST (Power-On Self Test) routines, 82
PostScript (Adobe), 151
potential browsers, 334-336
　election process, 337, 340
Power-On Self Test (POST) routines, 82
PPP (Point-to-Point Protocol), 418
PPTP (Point-to-Point Tunneling Protocol), 146
preemptive multitasking, 32
Presentation Manager (OS/2, 33

primary partitions, 83
Print Manager, 159-164
Print Operators groups, 303
print queues, 155, 158
　Print Manager, 159-164
　Print Server Properties page tabs
　　Advanced, 167-168
　　Drivers, 166
　　Forms, 164-165
　　Ports, 165-166
　troubleshooting problems, 169
Print Services for UNIX, 55
printers
　drivers, 152-153
　fonts, 152
　languages, 151
　mechanics, 151
　memory requirements, 151
　permissions, 260
　ports/connections, 153-155
　print jobs, 155
　Print Manager, 159-164
　Print Server Properties page tabs
　queues, 157
　sharing
　　Active Directory, 256
　　Novell NetWare, 456-457
　　UNIX, 487
　troubleshooting, 168-169
　　capturing port connections, 175
　　client-side problems, 172-174
　　device drivers, 177
　　parallel port connections, 174
　　print quality, 176
　　print queues, 169
　　printer limitations, 176
　　printer specifications, 176
　　Printing Preferences Advanced Options page, 177-178
　　server-side problems, 169-172

printers

TCP/IP (Transmission Control Protocol/Internet Protocol) port connections, 174-175
types, 150-151
Process Manager, 27
Process Viewer, 624-626, 629
processes, 25, 616
model, 34, 37
priority levels, 617
Process Viewer, 624-626, 629
Task Manager, 617-624
profiles, 308
configuring RAS (Remote Access Server) policies
advanced options, 381-382
authentication options, 378-380
dial-in constraints, 375-376
encryption options, 380-381
IP address options, 376-377
multilink options, 377-378
local, 308-309
roaming, 309-310
compatibility with Windows NT profiles, 310
incompatibility with Windows 95/98 profiles, 310-311
mandatory, 310
user accounts, 182, 294
protection faults, general, 35
Proxy Server (Microsoft), 550-551
access controls, 551-552
acquisition, 550-551
caching, 550-551
firewalls, 553-554
traffic logs, 554-555
public folders, Exchange Server (Microsoft), 557-558
public key encryption, 12

Public Key Infrastructure (PKI) certificates, 578-579
PUs (peripheral units), 496

Q

QLLC (qualified logical link control), 495
QoS Admission Control Service, 55
qualified logical link control (QLLC), 495
Quality of Service features, 14
queues (print), 155-158
Print Manager, 159-164
Print Server Properties page tabs
Advanced, 167-168
Drivers, 166
Forms, 164-165
Ports, 165-166
troubleshooting problems, 169
quota systems, hard disks, 13-14, 96-99

R

RADIUS (Remote Authentication Dial-In User Service) technology, 381
RAID (Redundant Array of Inexpensive Disks), 80-81
hardware-controlled, 719
RAID-5 volumes, 115, 631
striped volumes, 630
RAS (Remote Access Server), 14, 417
configuring, 369-370
clients, 370-371
logons, 387-389
ports, 371-373
configuring policies, 373-375
adding, 383, 387
advanced options, 381-382

authentication, 378-380
dial-in constraints, 375-376
encryption, 380-381
IP addresses, 376-377
multilink options, 377-378
security, 359-360
troubleshooting, 402-403
raster fonts, 152
raw file system, 99
RBFG.EXE utility, 326
Recovery Console, 703-704
installing Windows 2000 Server, 62-65
Red Hat version, Linux, 476
Redundant Array of Inexpensive Disks (RAID), 80-81
hardware-controlled, 719
RAID-5 volumes, 115, 631
striped volumes, 630
Reflections program, 491
REGEDIT Registry editor
tools, 187-188
tracking software installation changes, 191
using, 188, 191
REGEDT32 Registry editor
tools, 187-188
using, 191-192
registering domain names, InterNIC, 132
Registry
defined, 180
disaster recovery with Last Known Good configuration, 193
hives, 181
Classes, 181-182
Current Configuration, 185
Local Machine, 183-185
Users, 182-183
interaction with applications, 185, 187
Registry Editor. *See* REGEDIT and REGEDT32

relationships (trust), 136
　explicit, 136-138
　intransitive, 138
　transitive, 138
Remote Access Server (RAS)), 14, 417, 423
　configuring, 369-370
　　clients, 370-371
　　logons, 387-389
　　ports, 371-373
　configuring policies, 373-375
　　adding, 383, 387
　　advanced options, 381-382
　　authentication, 378-380
　　dial-in constraints, 375-376
　　encryption, 380-381
　　IP addresses, 376-377
　　multilink options, 377-378
　security, 359-360
　troubleshooting, 402-403
Remote Authentication Dial-In User Service (RADIUS) technology, 381
Remote Installation Service (RIS), 55, 325-327
Remote Installation Service Setup Wizard, 326-327
Remote Shell (RSH), 483
Remote Storage Server, 13, 55, 123-124
Removable Storage Management (RSM), 13, 124-126
replication of directories, 266
　DFS (Distributed File System), 122
　Novell Directory Service (NDS), compared to Active Directory, 454
　WINS (Windows Internet Naming Service), 218
　　manual tombstoning, 219
　　partners, 219
Replicator groups, 303
reports, Performance utility, 655-657, 661, 664, 667
requests for comments (RFCs), 409
Restore Wizard, 695-698, 701

restoring backup data, 694-698, 701
　encrypted, 702
　Recovery Console, 703-704
　System State, 701-702
reverse lookup records, 221
RFCs (requests for comments), 409
RIP (Router Information Protocol), 358, 413, 418-419
RIS (Remote Installation Service), 55, 325-327
roaming profiles, 309-310
　compatibility
　　with Windows 95/98 profiles, 310-311
　　with Windows NT profiles, 310
　mandatory, 310
robotic libraries, RSM (Removable Storage Management), 124
roots, DFS (Distributed File System), 122
rotational latency, hard disks, 73
Router Information Protocol (RIP), 413, 418-419
routing
　network segmentation, 144-145
　RRAS (Routing and Remote Access Services), 207-208, 389-395, 417-419
　　adding protocols, 395-399
　　protocols supported, 399-400
　　troubleshooting, 419-420
　　WAN support, 400-401
　SNA (Systems Network Architecture) Server, 493-494
　TCP/IP (Transmission Control Protocol/Internet Protocol) protocol, 203-204
Routing and Remote Access Configuration Wizard, 364-369

Routing and Remote Access Services (RRAS), 207-208, 417-419, 576-579, 585-586
　configuring
　　authentication policies, 401-402
　　routing protocols, 389-399
　　services, 362, 365-369
　HCL (Hardware Compatibility List), 361-362
　installing tools, 361-362
　IPSec (IP Security Protocol), 577, 579
　L2TP (Layer 2 Tunneling Protocol), 577-579
　modems, 400
　multiprotocol routing, 146
　　on-demand routing, 146
　　VPN (Virtual Private Network), 146
　new features, 356, 585-586
　remote dial-in, 145
　TCP/IP (Transmission Control Protocol/Internet Protocol) protocol suite, 208
　troubleshooting, 419-420
　VPNS (Virtual Private Networks), 576
Routing Information Protocol (RIP), 358
RSH (Remote Shell), 483
RSM (Removable Storage Management), 124-126
Rumba program, 491

S

Samba, 486-487
SANs (system area networks), 141
SAP (Service Advertising Protocol), 358, 413
Schema Admins groups, 304
scope
　DHCP (Dynamic Host Configuration Protocol), 211-216
　　superscopes, 216

scope

group accounts
    Domain Local, 300-302
    Global, 301
    Universal, 301
screen savers, 53
screen shots, VMWare for Windows NT, 49
Script Debugger, 55
scripts, logon and logoff, 288
    directory placement, 288-290
    net command, 290-291
    parameters, 291-292
SCSI (Small Computer Standard Interface), 75-78
    clustered servers, 720
SCSI-1 (Small Computer Standard Interface) standard, 77
SDLC (Synchronous Data Link Control), 495
sectors, hard disks, 73
security, 8
    Active Directory objects
        computer accounts, 255-256
        creating, 253
        group accounts, 253-255
        OUs (Organizational Units), 253-254
        permissions, 257-260
        shared folders, 256
        shared printers, 256
        user accounts, 253-255
    domains, 241-245
        DCs (Domain Controllers), 247-248
        forests and trees, 245-246
        native and mixed modes, 249-250
        objects, 251-252
        OUs (Organizational Units), 246-247
        trust relationships, 248-249
        UPNs (User Principle Names), 250-251
        user and group accounts, 252

Dynamic DNS (Domain Name Server), 276
EFS (Encrypted File System), 13
firewalls, Microsoft Proxy Server, 553-554
IIS (Internet Information Server), 539
    access controls, 543-544
    directory browsing, 544
    permissions, 542-543
    protection against unauthoritized access, 540-542
    troubleshooting, 544, 547
    unauthoritized access, 539-540
    Web site help, 542
IPSEC (Internet Protocol Security), 13
Kerberos authentication, 11-12, 232-237
NTFS ((NT File System), users and permissions, 103-104, 106-109
NTLM (Windows NT LAN Manager), 237-238
public key encryption, 12
RRAS (Routing and Remote Access), 359-360
security identifiers (SIDs), 238
smart cards, 13
SNA (Systems Network Architecture) Server, 493
TCP/IP (Transmission Control Protocol/Internet Protocol), multiple addresseses, 227
VPNs (Virtual Private Networks), 572
    authentication, 572-573
    encryption, 572-573
Windows 2000, compared
    to Novell NetWare, 452
    to UNIX, 473-474
workgroups, 239-240
Security Log, Event Viewer, 595-596
Security Reference Manager (SRM), 28
    Object Manager, 27

Security Registry key, 183
seek time, hard disks, 73
segments (network), 141-142
    routed segmentation, 144-145
    switched segmentation, 142-144
Serial Line Internet Protocol (SLIP), 418
serial printer ports, 153-154
server management
    Computer Management Console, 593-594
        Device Manager, 600-603
        System Information, 599
    Event Viewer, 594-595
        log settings, 597-599
        viewing events, 595, 597
    MMC (Microsoft Management Console), 590, 592
    Server Manager, 593
    SNMP (Simple Network Management Protocol), 603-604
Server Manager, 593
Server Message Block (SMB) protocol, Samba, 486. *See also* **CIFS (Common Internet File System)**
Server Operators groups, 303
Service Advertising Protocol (SAP), 358, 413
Service Packs, 728
session keys and tickets, 237
Shared Nothing server clustering, 720-721
SIDs (security identifiers), 238
    ACL (Access Control List), 239
Simple Message Transfer Protocol (SMTP), 54, 560-563
Simple Network Management Protocol (SNMP), 54, 603-604
Simple TCP/IP (Transmission Control Protocol/Internet Protocol) Services, 55

simple volumes (hard disk), 111-112, 631
Site container objects, 312, 314
Site Scope (Freshwater Software, Inc.) Web site, 667
Site Server ILS Services, 55
slave devices, 68
SLIP (Serial Line Internet Protocol), 418
Small Computer Standard Interface (SCSI), 75-78
smart cards, 13
SMBs (Server Message Blocks) protocol, Samba, 486. *See also* CIFS (Common Internet File System)
SMP (symetric multiprocessing), 15-17
SMTP (Simple Message Transfer Protocol), 54, 560-563
SNA (Systems Network Architecture) Server, 490-493
    connection options, 495
    LUs (logical units), 496-497
    routing connections, 493-494
    security, 493
    supported adapters, 495
SNMP (Simple Network Management Protocol), 54, 603-604
socket pooling, IIS (Internet Information Server), 530
soft page faults, 38
Software Registry key, 183
Solitaire game, 53
Space Cadet Pinball game, 53
spanned volumes (hard disk), 112-113, 631
SPAP (Unencrypted Authentication), 379, 401
spoofing, 234

SRM (Security Reference Manager), 28
    Object Manager, 27
sticky bits, 473
STOP errors, troubleshooting, 728
    kernel mode, 728-731
    list with solutions, 731-739
storage area networks, 141
striped volumes (hard disk), 78, 114-115, 630-632
    with parity, 80
    with striped parity, 80
    mirrored, 80
subnet masks, 199-202
    answer sheets, 750-753
subsystems, 22, 28-30
    OS/2, 33-34
    POSIX, 32-33
    Win32, 30-32
superscopes, DHCP (Dynamic Host Configuration Protocol), 216
SuSE version, Linux, 476
switched segmentation of networks, 142-144
switches, Windows 2000 installation, 42-44
symetric multiprocessing (SMP), 15-17, 615
synchronous and asynchronous keys, 578-579
Synchronous Data Link Control (SDLC), 495
system area networks (SANs), 141
System groups, 304
System Information, Computer Management Console, 599
System Log, Event Viewer, 595
System Monitor, 9, 643-644
    charts
        creating, 649, 651-652
        interpreting, 652, 655
    performance objects/counters, 644, 646, 648

System Registry key, 184
System State data, 679
    backups, 673
    authoritative restoring, 701-702
system tuning
    base priorities, threads and processes
        Process Viewer, 624-626, 629
        Task Manager, 617-624
    Disk Defragmenter, 611-615
    Disk Management utility, 632-633, 635
    performance objects/counters, 644, 646, 648
    Performance utility, 641-643
        logs, 655-657, 661, 664, 667
        memory caching, 629
        reports, 655-657, 661, 664, 667
    RAID (Redundant Array of Inexpensive Disks), striped volumes, 630
    System Monitor, 643-644
        charts, 649-652, 655
    virtual memory pagefiles, 630, 636-637, 639, 641
Systems Network Architecture, 490-493
    connection options, 495
    LUs (logical units), 496-497
    routing connections, 493-494
    security, 493
    supported adapters, 495

T

tape drives
    Remote Storage Server, 123
    Removable Storage Management, 124-126
Task Manager, 617-624
tasks and processes memory model, 34, 37
TCP (Transport Protocol), 410

TCP/IP (Transmission Control Protocol/Internet Protocol) protocol suite, 14, 196, 357-358, 409
addressing schemes, 196-198
binary addresses, 197
network and host portions, 198-199
ports, 204-205
routing, 203-204
subnet masks, 199-202
integrating UNIX and Windows 2000 Server
finger utility, 483
FTP (File Transfer Protocol), 479-482
RSH (Remote Shell), 483
Telnet, 477-479
TFTP (Trivial File Transfer Protocol), 482
multiple IP addresses, 226-227
NOSs (network operating systems), 410
printer ports, 153, 157
troubleshooting, 174-175
protocols included, 410-411
security, 227
strengths and weaknesses, 411
Windows 2000
installation/configuration, 56
Windows 2000 version, 205
DDNS (Dynamic Domain Name Servers), 222, 225
DHCP (Dynamic Host Configuration Protocol), 208-216
installing, 205-206
migrating from WINS (Windows Internet Naming Service) to DDNS (Dynamic Domain Name Servers), 226
RRAS (Routing and Remote Access Services), 207-208
WINS (Windows Internet Naming Service), 217-220

TCP/IP NetBIOS Helper Service browsing operations, 340-342
Telnet protocol), 410
IIS (Internet Information Server), 539
integrating UNIX and Windows 2000 Server, 477-479
templates, WordPad word processing, 52
Terminal Services, 55
terminal-emulation packages, 491
TFTP (Trivial File Transfer Protocol), 482
TGTs (ticket-granting tickets), 237
third-party backup tools, 705
threads, 25, 616
priority levels
Process Viewer, 624-629
Task Manager, 617-624
thunking, 31
ticket-granting tickets (TGTs), 237
tombstoning (manual), WINS (Windows Internet Naming Service), 219
Tower of Hanoi backups, 716-718
tracks, hard disks, 73
transitive trust relationships, 138, 249
Transmission Control Protocol/Internet Protocol (TCP/IP), 357-358
trees (domain), 11, 133, 245-246, 353
Trivial File Transfer Protocol (TFTP), 482
troubleshooting
kernel mode, 728-731
list with solutions, 731-739
printers, 168-169
capturing port connections, 175
client-side problems, 172-174

device drivers, 177
limitations, 176
parallel port connections, 174
print quality, 176
print queues, 169
Printing Preferences Advanced Options page, 177-178
server-side problems, 169-172
specifications, 176
TCP/IP (Transmission Control Protocol/Internet Protocol) port connections, 174-175
RAS (Remote Access Server), 402-403
Registry, Last Known Good configuration, 193
RRAS (Routing and Remote Access Services), 419-420
security, IIS (Internet Information Server), 544, 547
Service Packs, 728
STOP errors, 728
trust relationships, 136
explicit, 136-138, 248-249
intransitive, 138, 249
transitive, 138, 249
tunnels, 571
tunnel initiators (servers), 573-574
filtering traffic, 575-576
firewalls, 574-575
setup, 582, 585
tunnel terminators, 572
twinax connections, 490
two-way trusts, 249

U

UDP (User Datagram Protocol), 410
Ultra SCSI, Ultra2 SCSI, and Ultra3 SCSI (Small Computer Standard Interface) standards, 77
UNATTEND.TXT file, 61
Unencrypted Authentication (PAP, SPAP), 379, 401
uninstalling. *See* **installing**
Universal group scope, 252, 300-304
Universal Serial Bus (USB) devices, 69
UNIX
   client connectivity, 430, 444-446
   compared to Windows 2000 Server
      directory services, 474-475
      security, 473-474
      user accounts, 472-473
      versions of UNIX, 475-476
   integrating with Windows 2000 Server
      application connectivity, 484
      finger utility, 483
      FTP (File Transfer Protocol), 479-482
      future of Microsoft and Unix, 488
      NFS (Network File System), 485-486
      printing, 487
      RSH (Remote Shell), 483
      Samba, 486-487
      Telnet, 477-479
      TFTP (Trivial File Transfer Protocol), 482
      XWindows, 484
   POSIX subsystem, 32-33
   Print Services for UNIX, 55
   TCP/IP (Transmission Control Protocol/Internet Protocol) protocol suite, 410

UPNs (User Principle Names), 250-251
USB (Universal Serial Bus) devices, 69
   printers, 153-154
user accounts, 278
   creating, 282-284
      Active Directory User and Computer console, 284
      net user command, 284, 287
   environment, 287
   hard drive space limitations, 298-299
   naming conventions, 280-282
   operating sytem environment
      access controls, 294-298
      home directory, 293-294
      logon scripts, 288-292
      profiles, 294
   policies, 311-314
   predefined, 278, 280
   types, 252-253
   Windows 2000 Server
      compared to UNIX, 472-473
      user impersonation, 474
user accounts (Active Directory)
   creating, 251-255
   permissions
      files/folders, 257-260
      printers, 260
User Configuration policies, 313-314
user controls
   Intellimirror, 306
   policies, 311-313
      creating/assigning, 315-317
      Delegate Control Wizard, 319-320
      editing, 317-319
      filtering, 318
      managing, 315
      permissions, 318-319
      types, 313-314
   principles, 307-308

profiles, 308
   local, 308-309
   roaming, 309-311
User Datagram Protocol (UDP), 410
User mode, 23-24
User Principle Names (UPNs), 250-251
Users and Computers console, Active Directory, 251
   objects
      computer accounts, 255-256
      group accounts, 255
      OUs (Organizational Units), 253-254
      shared folders and printers, 256
      user accounts, 254-255
Users groups, 303
Users hive (Registry), 182-183

V

variable-width fonts, 152
vector fonts, 152
Veritas Software Corporation, backup utility, 670
virtual directories, IIS (Internet Information Server), 527, 530
Virtual Memory Manager (VMM), 27, 36-38, 636-641
virtual memory pagefiles, 630, 636-641
Virtual Private Networks (VPNs), 14, 146
   defined, 571-572
   IPScc (IP Security Protocol), 577, 579
   L2TP (Layer 2 Tunneling Protocol), 577-579
   PPTP (Point-to-Point Tunneling Protocol), 572
   RRAS (Routing and Remote Access)
      new features, 585-586

Virtual Private Networks (VPNs)

security, 572
   authentication, 572-573
   encryption, 572-573
setup in Windows 2000, 579, 582
sychronous and asynchronous keys, 578-579
tunnel initiators (servers), 573-574
   filtering traffic, 575-576
   firewalls, 574-575
   setup, 582, 585

Virtual Telecommunications Access Method (VTAM) parameters, 493-494

Visual InterDev
   RAD Remote Development support, 54

VMM (Virtual Memory Manager), 27, 36-38, 636-641

VMWare for Windows NT, 49

volumes

volumes (hard disk), 111, 455. *See also* **dynamic disks**
   formatting, 109
   managing, 93-95
   mirrored, 112-114, 631
   properties, 88-92, 631
   quotas, 96-99
   RAID-5, 115, 631
   simple, 111-112, 631
   spanned, 112-113, 631
   striped, 114-115, 631, 630-632

voluntary tunnels, 573

VPNs (Virtual Private Networks), 14, 146
   defined, 571-572
   IPScc (IP Security Protocol), 577, 579
   L2TP (Layer 2 Tunneling Protocol), 577-579
   PPTP (Point-to-Point Tunneling Protocol), 572
   RRAS (Routing and Remote Access)
      new features, 585-586
   security, 572
      authentication, 572-573
      encryption, 572-573

setup in Windows 2000, 579, 582
sychronous and asynchronous keys, 578-579
tunnel initiators (servers), 573-574
   filtering traffic, 575-576
   firewalls, 574-575
   setup, 582, 585

VTAM (Virtual Telecommunications Access Method) parameters, 493-494

W

wallpaper, 52

WANs (wide area networks), 141
   network browsing, 344-349
   RRAS (Routing and Remote Access) support, 400-401
   using Internet, 570-571

warm spares, 116

WBEM (Web-Based Enterprise Management), 10

Web Distributed Authoring and Versioning (WebDAV), 538

Web sites (FrontPage)
   creating sites, 565-566
   editing pages, 566
   server extensions, 567
   site security, 566-567

Web-Based Enterprise Management (WBEM), 10

WebDAV (Web Distributed Authoring and Versioning), 538

wide area networks. *See* **WANs**

Wide Ultra2 SCSI (Small Computer Standard Interface) standard, 77

Win32 API (application programming interface), 15

Win32 subsystem, 30-32

Windows 2000 Server
   compared to Novell NetWare, 452
      directory services, 453-454
      file sharing, 455-456
      print sharing, 456-457
      security, 452
   compared to UNIX
      directory services, 474-475
      security, 473-474
      user accounts, 472-473
      versions of UNIX, 475-476
   Emergency Repair Disk (ERD), 704
   features, 9-16
      Advanced Server 16-17
      Datacenter, 17
      Executive, 26-28
   future of Microsoft and UNIX, 488
      NFS (Network File System), 485-486
      printing, 487
      RSH (Remote Shell), 483
      Samba, 486-487
      Telnet, 477-479
      TFTP (Trivial File Transfer Protocol), 482
      XWindows, 484
   installing
      automatically, 61
      boot process, 45-47
      configuration, 50, 52
      disk partitioning, 47-48
      HCL (Hardware Compatibility List), 41-42
      licensing options, 58-59, 61
      migration from preexisting systems, 66-67
      network configuration, 55, 57
      optional components, 52-55

Recovery Console, 62-65
setup procedures, 44-45
setup switches, 42-44
system requirements, 40-41
upgrading from NT, 50
integrating with UNIX
application connectivity, 484
finger utility, 483
FTP (File Transfer Protocol), 479-482
Recovery Console, 703-704
Resource Kit, 530, 606
Support Tools
installing, 608-611
list, 606-607
Process Viewer, 624-626, 629
Windows 3.1, running under Win32 subsystem, 30-31
Windows 3.x (Microsoft), client connectivity, 429, 436-437, 440
Windows 3x/4x Server, migrating from preexisting systems, 66-67
Windows 95/98
compatibility with Windows 2000, 16
profiles, 310-311
TCP/IP (Transmission Control Protocol/Internet Protocol) protocol suite, 410
Windows authentication, 532
Windows Backup and Recovery Tools. See Backup and Recovery Tools
Windows Components Wizard, 507
Windows for Workgroups (Microsoft), client connectivity, 429, 436-437, 440
Windows Installer, 320-321
WinInstaller, 321-324
Windows Internet Naming Service. See WINS

Windows NT
compatibility with Windows 2000, profiles, 310
migrating from preexisting systems, 66-67
TCP/IP (Transmission Control Protocol/Internet Protocol) protocol suite, 410
upgrading to Windows 2000, 50
Windows NT LAN Manager (NTLM), 237
communication process, 238
SIDs (security identifiers), 238
Windows on Windows (WOW), 31-32
Windows Optional Networking Components Wizard, 441
Windows Scripting Host (WSH), 15
Windows Terminal Services, 17
Windows Update Web site, 68
WinInstaller, 321-324
WINNT.EXE and WINNT32.EXE, switches, Windows 2000 installation, 42-44
WINS (Windows Internet Naming Service), 55, 217
architecture, 217-218
manual tombstoning, 219
persistent connections, 218
replication, 218
replication partners, 219
browser elections, 336
installing, 219
LMHOSTS file, 219-220
migrating to DDNS (Dynamic Domain Name Servers), 226
name resolution, 337
naming versus browsing, 217
network browsing, 345-349
wizards
Add Remote Access Policy, 383, 387
Backup and Recovery Tools,

679, 682, 685-687
verifying settings, 688
Create Partition, 93-94
Create Volume, 112
Delegate Control, 319-320
Extend Volume, 112
File Migration, 468-469
New DFS Root, 122
Remote Installation Service Setup Wizard, 326-327
Restore, 695-698, 701
Routing and Remote Access Configuration, 364-369
Windows Components, 507
Windows Optional Networking Components, 441
word processing, WordPad, 53
workgroups, 129-131, 239-240
World Wide Web Server, 54
WOW (Windows on Windows), 31-32
WOW Registry key, 184
WOWEXEC, 31-32
WSH (Windows Scripting Host), 15
WWW Site services, IIS (Internet Information Server), 535-536
default home page, 536-537
WebDAV (Web Distributed Authoring and Versioning), 538

X-Z

X terminals, 484
X.25/QLLC (qualified logical link control), 495
X.400 protocol, 560
X.500 directory structure, 232
XWindows, UNIX and Windows 2000 Server, 484
ZAW (Zero Admin Windows), 306